English-German Medical Dictionary and Phrasebook

German-English

first edition 2013

ISBN is 1482794764

EAN-13 is 978-1482794762

by A.H. Zemback

Special thanks to Schwester M. Ingeborg, F.S.G.M

Cover photo is three young boys with mumps in January 1967;
the first mumps vaccine in the US was in 1967.

Contents

	english	german
Introduction	How are you?	Wie geht es dir?
	Good morning, good afternoon, good evening.	Guten Morgen! Guten Tag! Guten Abend!
	My name is ...	Ich heiße...
Demographics	What is your name?	Wie heißben Sie?
	Pleased to meet you.	Angenehm.
	Do you speak English?	Sprechen Sie Englisch?
	Speak more slowly, please.	Sprechen Sie bitte etwas langsamer.
	Say that one more time, please.	Bitte, sagen Sie es noch einmal.
	Come in, please.	Bitte treten Sie ein.
	Sit down, please.	Bitte nehmen Sie Platz.
	What province do you live in ?	Aus welcher Stadt sind sie?
	What is your address?	Wo wohnen Sie?
	What is your telephone number?	Wie ist ihr Telefonnummer?
	Can you give us the name and telephone number or address of someone to be contacted?	Könnten Sie uns bitte den Namen und die Telefonnummer oder die Anschrift von jemandem geben, den wir benachrichtigen können?
	Are you married?	Sind sie verheiratet?
	What is your age?	Wie alt sind Sie?
Chief complaint	What is your health concern? (What can we do for you today?)	Was fehlt Ihnen? (Was können wir heute für Sie tun? Was für Gesundheitsprobleme haben Sie?)
	When did you become ill?	Wann wurden Sie krank?
	Have you had an accident?	Hatten Sie einen Unfall?
	Do you feel pain... At night? Before meals? After eating?	Haben Sie Schmerzen... In der nacht? Von der Mahlzeiten? Nach dem Essen?
	When did it start? (show on the calendar and clock)	Wann fingen die Schmerzen an? (auf dem Kalender und er Uhr zeigen)
	What is your level of pain? 1 (no pain) 2 3 4 5 6 7 8 9 10 (severe pain)	Bitte geben Sie den Grad Ihrer Schmerzen an? 1 (schmerzfrei) 2 3 4 5 6 7 8 9 10 (chronische Schmerzen)
	The pain, is it constant or does it come and go?	Halten die Schmerzen an? Oder kommen und gehen sie?
	Sharp or dull?	Scharf oder leicht?
	Where does it hurt?	Wo haben Sie Schmerzen?
	Use one finger to point exactly where the pain is.	Zeigen Sie mit einem Finger ganz genau auf die Stelle, wo Sie die Schmerzen vespüren.
	Is there anything that makes it better or worse?	Wird es besser oder schlimmer?
	Have you been seriously ill before?	Sind Sie schon früher schwer krank gewesen?

4

	english	german
	What were you treated for?	Was für Krankheiten?
Common complaints	My lower back hurts.	Ich habe Rückenschmerzen.
	My neck is stiff.	Ich habe einen steifen Nacken.
	I have a sore throat.	Ich habe Halsschermerzen.
	It hurts when I swallow.	Ich habe Schluckbeschwerden.
	I have an earache.	Ich habe Ohrenschmerzen.
	I have a toothache.	Ich habe Zahnschmerzen.
	I have shoulder pain.	Ich habe Schulterschmerzen.
	I have elbow pain.	Ich habe Ellenbogenschmerzen.
	I have wrist pain.	Ich habe Handgelenkschmerzen
	I have knee pain.	Ich habe Knieschmerzen.
	I have ankle pain.	Ich habe Schmerzen im Fussgelenk.
	I am dizzy.	Mir ist schwindlig.
	I am very nervous.	Ich bin sehr nervös.
	I can't sleep.	Ich kann nicht schlafen.
	I am always tired.	Ich fühle mich immer müde.
	I have chest pain.	Ich habe Halsschermerzen.
	My heart beats very fast.	Mein Herz schlägt sehr schnell.
	I have a headache.	Ich habe Kopfschmerzen.
	I have trouble breathing.	Ich bin kurzatmig.
	I have a cough.	Ich habe Husten.
	It hurts when I take a deep breath.	Es tut weh, wenn ich tief einatme.
	I am pregnant.	Ich bin schwanger.
	I have a stomach ache.	Ich habe Bauchschmerzen.
	I am nauseated.	Mir ist übel.
	I vomited several times.	Ich habe mich mehrere Male übergeben.
	I have indigestion.	Meine Verdauung ist schlecht.
	I have no appetite.	Ich habe keinen Appetit.
	I have diarrhea	Ich habe Durchfall.
	I have constipation.	Ich habe Verstopfung.
	I feel sick.	Mir ist schlecht.
	I sprained my ankle.	Ich habe mir den Knöchel verstaucht.
	I think I broke my arm (leg).	Ich glaube, mein Arm (Bein) ist gerbrochen.
Past medical history	Do you have a past history of the following:	Hatten Sie eine der folgenden Krankheiten:
	anemia	Anämie; Blutarmut
	asthma	Asthma
	cancer	Krebs
	cirrhosis	Zirrhose

	english	german
	diabetes	Diabetes; Zuckerharnruhr
	epilepsy	Epilepsie
	hypertension	Bluthochdruck
	thyroid disease	Schilddrüsenerkrankung
	heart problems	Herzinfarkt oder Herzklappenfehler
	hepatitis	Leberentzündung
	tuberculosis	Lungentuberkulose
	HIV/AIDS	HIV oder AIDS
	What date did you start taking HIV medicine?	Wann (an welchem Datum) haben Sie angefangen, HIV Medikament zu nehmen?
	What was the date of your last CD4?	Wann (an welchem Datum) hatten Sie ihr letzte CD4?
	What was the result of your last CD4?	Was war das Ergebnis ihrer letzte CD4?
	Have you had pneumonia or meningitis?	Hatten Sie eine der folgenden Krankheiten: Lungenentzündung oder Hirnhautentzündung?
Past surgical history	Have you ever had an operation?	Hatten Sie jermals eine Operation?
	What type of surgery was done?	Was für eine Operation war es?
	What year was the surgery done?	Welches Jahr war die Operation?
Medications	Do you take medication at home?	Nehmen Sie Medikamente zu Hause?
	What is the name of the medication?	Wie heißt das Medikamente, das Sie nehmen?
	Can you show me the medication bottle?	Können Sie mir die Flasche Medikamente zeigen?
	Do you take illegal drugs?	Nehmen Sie illegale Drogen?
	Are you taking bactrim?	Nehmen Sie Bactrim?
Allergies	Have you had reactions to medications?	Sind Sie allergisch gegen irgendwelche Medikamente?
	Which medicines?	Welche Medikamente?
Family history	Is your mother living?	Lebt ihre Mutter noch?
	Is your father living?	Lebt ihr Vater noch?
	Do your brothers/sisters have health problems?	Haben ihre Geschwister Gesundheitsprobleme?
Social history	Do you drink alcohol?	Trinken Sie Alkohol?
	How many drinks per day?	Wie viele alkoholische Getränke trinken Sie am Tag?
	Do you drink alcohol every day?	Trinken Sie jeden Tag Alkohol?
	Do you smoke?	Rauchen Sie?
	How many cigarettes, cigars, pipes per day?	Wie viele Zigaretten, Zigarren, Pfeifen am Tag?

	english	german
	What is your job?	Was arbeiten Sie?
Review of systems	Do you have a skin rash?	Haben Sie Hautausschlag?
Skin	Do you have any blisters or sores?	Haben Sie Blasen oder Geschwüre?
	Have you had lice?	Haben Sie Läuse gehabt?
	Have you been bitten by ticks?	Sind Sie von Zecken gebissen worden?
	Have you seen rats, sand flies, mosquitos or bugs in your quarters?	Haben Sie in Ihrem Quartier Ratten, Sandflöhe, Mücken, Ungeziefer gesehen?
	Were you bitten by a dog or another animal?	Sind Sie von einem Hund oder anderen Tier gebissen worden?
Lymphatic	Do you have lymph node enlargement?	Haben Sie Lymphknotenvergrößerung?
Bone	Do you have bone pain?	Haben Sie Knochenschmerzen?
	Do you have joint pain?	Haben Sie Gelenkschmerzen?
	Do you have joint swelling?	Haben Sie Gelenkschwellung?
	Do you have pain in the back or neck?	Haben Sie Halsschermerzen oder Wirbelsäuleschmerzen?
Blood	Do you have bleeding problems?	Haben Sie Blutungsstörung?
Endocrine	Do you urinate frequently?	Müssen Sie oft Wasser lassen?
	Are you frequently thirsty?	Haben Sie viel Durst?
	Have you lost weight?	Haben Sie Gewicht verloren?
Head	Have you suffered from a head trauma in the past?	Haben Sie Gehirnerschütterung?
	Do you have dizziness?	Haben Sie Schwindel?
	Have you blacked-out?	Sind Sie in Ohnmacht gefallen?
Eyes	Can you see well?	Sehen Sie gut?
	Do you have double vision?	Haben Sie Doppelsehen?
	Do you have vision loss?	Haben Sie Sehstörungen?
	Do you have blurred vision?	Ist Ihr Sehen verschwommen?
	Do you have pain in bright light?	Haben Sie Schmerzen beim hellen Licht?
Ears	Can you hear well?	Hören Sie gut?
	Do you have an earache?	Haben Sie Ohrenschmerzen?
	Do you have drainage from the ears?	Haben Sie Ohrenfluss?
	Have you had gradual hearing loss in only one ear?	Haben Sie allmählichen Gehörverlust nur in einem Ohr gehabt?
Nose	Do you have nosebleeds?	Haben Sie Nasenbluten?
Mouth	Do you have a toothache?	Haben Sie Zahnschmerzen?
	Do you have a broken tooth?	Haben Sie einen gebrochenen Zahn?

	english	german
	Does hot or cold make it worse?	Werden die Schmerzen durch Heißes und Kaltes schlimmer?
	Do you have lumps or swelling in your mouth?	Haben Sie einen Knoten oder eine Geschwulst im Mund?
Throat	Do you have hoarseness? (Have you had a change in your voice?)	Haben Sie Heiserkeit?
	Do you have a sore throat?	Haben Sie Halsschmerzen?
Neck	Do you have neck stiffness?	Haben Sie Nackensteifigkeit?
Breast	Have you noticed breast lumps?	Haben Sie einen Knoten in der Brust bemerkt?
	Do you have nipple discharge?	Haben Sie Ausfluß von einer Brustwarze?
	Do you have swelling around or below your nipples?	Haben Sie eine Schwellung um oder unter den Brustwarzen?
Respiratory	Do you have difficulty breathing?	Haben Sie Atemnot?
	Do you sit up at night to breathe?	Müssen Sie sich aufrecht setzen, um in der Nacht zu atmen?
	Do you have pain when you take a deep breath?	Tut es weh tief einatmen?
	Do you have wheezing?	Haben Sie Geräusche beim Atmen?
	Do you have a cough?	Haben Sie Husten?
	How long have you had the cough?	Seit wann?
	Do you cough anything up?	Haben Sie Auswurf beim Husten?
	What color is your sputum... white? yellow-green? bloody? brown?	Welche Farbe... Weib? Gelblich-grün? Blutig? Braun?
Cardiovascular	Do you have chest pain?	Haben Sie Brustschmerzen?
	Do you have palpitations?	Haben Sie Herzklopfen?
	Do you have leg edema?	Schwellen Ihre Beine an?
	Do you have weakness?	Haben Sie Schwäche Gefühle?
Gastrointestinal	Do you have abdominal pain? (Do you have pain in your belly?)	Haben Sie Bauchschmerzn?
	...after you eat?	nachdem Sie essen?
	When did this problem start?	Wann hat das Problem angefangen?
	Has it been weeks, months, years?	Haben Sie das Problem seit Wochen, Monaten, Jahren?
	Are you in pain now?	Haben Sie jetzt sofort Schmerzen?
	Touch the spot where you have pain with one finger.	Zeigen Sie mit einem Finger ganz genau auf die Stelle, wo Sie die Schmerzen vespüren.
	Is the pain better than yesterday?	Ist sie besser als gestern?
	Do you have ...fever?	Haben Sie Fieber?
	...chills?	Haben Sie Schüttelfrost?
	Do you sweat much?	Schwitzen Sie sehr?

	english	german
	How is your appetite?	Haben Sie Appetit?
	Have you vomited?	Haben Sie erbrochen?
	What did the vomit look like?	Wie hat das Erbrochene ausgesehen?
	Have you vomited blood?	Haben Sie Blut erbrochen?
	Do you have nausea?	Haben Sie Übelkeit?
	How often do you have bowel movements?	Wie häufig haben Sie Stuhlgang?
	Are you constipated?	Leiden Sie unter Verstopfung?
	Do you have diarrhea?	Haben Sie Durchfall?
	How many times today?	Wie viele Heute?
	What do the stools look like?	Wie sieht der Stuhl aus?
	Have you passed black stools?	Haben Sie schwarzen Stuhlgang?
	Do you pass blood in your stools?	Ist in Ihrem Stuhl Blut?
	Have you recently traveled outside the country?	Sind Sie neulich ins Ausland verreist? Waren Sie neulich im Ausland?
	What color was the stool?	Was ist die Farbe Ihres Stuhles?
	Do you have anal itching?	Haben Sie Afterjucken?
	Do you have pain with swallowing?	Tut es weh, wenn Sie schlucken?
	Do you have difficulty swallowing?	Haben Sie Schwierigkeiten beim Schlucken?
	Do you often suffer from a bloated feeling?	Leiden Sie oft unter Völlegefühl?
	Do fatty foods agree with you?	Vertragen Sie fette Speisen?
	Have you had a gastroscopy in the past? (A camera that passes through your mouth to see your stomach)	Hatten Sie schonmal eine Gastroskopie? (Das ist wenn eine Kamera durch den Mund geht, so dass den Magen untersucht werden kann.)
Genitourinary	Do you have burning on urination?	Haben Sie Schmerzen beim Wasserlassen?
	Have you had penile discharge?	Haben Sie Ausfluß aus der Harnröhre?
	Do you have a sore (chancre) on the penis?	Haben Sie penil Schanker?
	Is your urine cloudy?	Haben Sie trüber Harn?
	Do you have sharp pains in your back or groin?	Haben Sie scharfe Schmerzen im Rücken oder im Unterleib?
	Do you have an aching pain under your scrotum?	Haben Sie Schmerzen unter den Hoden?
	Do you have difficulty starting to urinate?	Haben Sie Schwierigkeiten, wenn Sie anfangen wasserzulassen (zu urinieren)?
	How often do you void at night?	Wie oft müssen Sie in der Nacht wasserlassen (urinieren)?

9

	english	german
	Do you have the urge to void after just urinating and are you urinating only small amounts?	Haben Sie das Gefühl, dass Sie schon wieder wasserlassen müssen, sofort nachdem Sie schonmal nur ein bisschen wassergelassen haben?
	Is the urine stream slow?	Ist der Urinstrom langsam beim Wasserlassen?
	Do you leak urine when you cough or sneeze?	Kommt Urin aus, wenn Sie husten oder niessen?
	Do you have blood in the urine?	Haben Sie Blut im Urin?
	Have you ever passed a kidney stone?	Haben Sie schonmal beim Urinieren einen Nierenstein gelassen?
Women's health	Are you pregnant?	Sind Sie schwanger
	How many months pregnant are you?	Im wievielten Monat?
	Could you possibly be pregnant?	Wäre es möglich, dass Sie schwanger sind?
	Can we do a pregnancy test?	Können wir einen Schwangerschaftstest durchführen?
	Are your periods regular?	Ist Ihre Menstruation regelmäßig?
	Are your periods painful?	Haben Sie Schmerzen während der Menstruation?
	Is the flow heavy or light?	Is die Menstruation stärker oder schwächer?
	When did your last period start?	Wann hatten Sie Ihre letzte Menstruation?
	How many days do your periods last?	Wieviele Tage dauert sie?
	Do you bleed between periods?	Haben Sie Blutungen außerhalb der Menstruation?
	Do you take birth control pills?	Hehmen Sie die Anti-Baby-Pille?
	Do you have pain during intercourse?	Haben Sie Schmerzen beim Verkehr?
	Do you have vaginal itching?	Haben Sie Scheidenjuckend?
	Do you vaginal pain?	Haben Sie Scheidenschmerz?
	Do you have unusual discharge from the vagina?	Haben Sie Ausfluß aus der Scheide?
	...a lot or a little?	sehr oder ein wenig?
	How many times have you been pregnant?	Wieviel Schwangerschaften hatten Sie?
	How many children do you have?	Wieviele Kinder haben Sie?
	Were your deliveries normal?	Waren die Entbindungen normal?
	Have you had any miscarriages?	Hatten Sie Fehlgeburten?
	Did you have problems in your previous pregnancies?	Ist es während Iher früheren Schwangerschaften zu Komplikationen gekommen?

	english	german
	Did you have any severe bleeding after any of your deliveries?	Hatten Sie nach Ihren Entbindungen starke Blugungen?
	Do you know your blood type?	Könnten Sie mir wohl Ihre Blutgruppe sagen?
	During your pregnancy did have you had any of the following: bleeding or swelling of the ankles?	Litten Sie während Ihrer Schwangerschaft unter: Schmerzen oder gerschwollenen Beine.
	If you are in labor, please answer the following questions:	Wenn Sie in den Wehen liegen, antworten Sie bitte auf die folgenden Fragen:
	When did your contractions start?	Wann haben Ihre Wehen angefangen?
	Are they (contractions) regular or irregular?	Sind sie regelmäßib oder unregelmäßig?
	How many minutes between contractions?	Wieviele Minuten liegen zwischen den Wehen?
	Did your water break?	Haben Sie schon Fruchtwasser verloren?
Peripartum/ neonatal	How old is the baby?	Wie alt ist das Kind?
	What was the baby's birth weight?	Was hat das Kind gerade nach dem Geburt gewogen?
	How are you feeding the baby, with breast or bottle?	Stillen Sie das Kind mit der Brust, oder geben Sie ihm eine Flasche?
	Is the baby nursing well?	Trinkt das Kind gut beim Stillen?
	Has the baby had any convulsions?	Hat das Kind schonmal einen Schüttelkramp gehabt?
	Apgar at 1 minute.	Apgar Index im 1 Minuten
	Apgar at 5 minutes.	Apgar Index im 5 Minuten
	Moro reflex.	Schreckreflex
	Fontanelle.	Fontanelle
Amniotic fluid	What color was the amniotic fluid? Clear, cloudy, green (meconium)?	Welche Farbe hatte das Fruchtwasser? War es klar, trub, grün? (Mekonium)
Pediatrics	How old is the child?	Wie alt ist das Kind?
	Does the child cry often?	Schreit das Kind viel?
	Is the child gaining weight?	Nimmt das Kind zu?
	Does the child have a good appetite?	Hat das Kind einen guten Appetit?
	What kinds of pain does the child complain of?	Uber welche Schmerzen klagt das Kind?
	Is he (she) drinking ok?	Trinkt er (sie) gut?
	Is he (she) eating ok?	Isst er (sie) gut?
	Have you seen worms in the vomit or the stool?	Haben sie Würmer im Erbrochenes (in der Kotze) oder im Stuhlgang gesehen?

	english	german
Neurologic	Do you have: facial weakness?	Haben Sie Gesichtsschwäche
	facial numbness?	Gesichtstaubheit?
	leg weakness?	Beinschwäche?
	leg numbness?	Beintaubheit?
	arm weakness?	Armschwäche?
	arm numbness?	Armtaubheit?
	Have you ever been unconscious?	Waren Sie schonmal bewußtlos?
	Do you have tremors? (Do your hands shake or other parts of your body?)	Haben Sie Zittern?
	Have you had recent vision loss in one eye?	Hatten Sie neulich Sichtverlust in einem Auge?
	Have you had problems with your balance?	Haben Sie schonmal Probleme mit Gleichgewicht gehabt?
	Do you walk without problems?	Können Sie ohne Probleme gehen oder laufen?
	Do you have pain in your back that travels to your buttock and down the back of your leg?	Haben Sie Rückenschmerzen, die zum Hintern gehen und die, die Wade hinunter geht?
Psychiatric	Do you have anxiety?	Haben Sie Sorge?
	Do you have depression?	Haben Sie Krise?
	Do you feel nervous or tense?	Fühlen Sie sich nervös oder abgespannt?
	How are your spirits?	Wie fühlen Sie sich stimmungmäßig?
	Do you hear voices?	Hören Sie Stimmen?
Extremities	Is the ankle pain so severe you cannot walk on it?	Ist der Schmerz im Knöchel so schlimm, dass Sie nicht damit laufen können?
	Do your have a grinding pain in your knee? Do you have the knee lock up occasionally?	Haben Sie knirschenden Schmerz im Knie? Wird Ihnen das Knie manchmal unbeweglich?
	Do you have pain in your calf when walking that is better with rest?	Haben Sie Schmerzen in der Wade beim Gehen, die besser werden, wenn Sie sich ausgeruht haben?
	Do you feel pain when you move your shoulder?	Tut es weh, wenn Sie die Schulter bewegen?
	Do you have pain or numbness in your hand, wrist or fingers, especially when flexing your wrist?	Wenn Sie das Handgelenk bewegen, tut Ihnen die Hand, das Handgelenk, oder die Finger weh, oder ist die Hand, das Handgelenk, oder die Finger taub?
	Do you have pain when gripping a doorknob and does the pain go from the outside of the elbow to your wrist?	Haben Sie Schmerzen, wenn sie die Türklinke greifen und gehen die Schmerzen vom außerhalb des Ellenbogen bis zum Handgelenk?

	english	german
Physical exam	appearance, height	Auftreten; Körpergröße
General	pulse bp resp temp weight (in pounds/ kilograms)	Puls Blutdruk Atmung Temperatur Gewicht (Pfund/ Kilogramm)
	skin	Haut
HEENT	visual acuity	Sehschärfe
	conjunctiva, sclera	Augenbindehaut, Sklera
	pupils	Pupille
	optic disc	Sehnervenpapille
	ear canal, tympanic membrane	Außenohr; Trommelfell
	nasal mucosa	Nasenschleimhaut
	sinuses	Sinus
	teeth	Zähne
	mouth, gums, teeth, uvula "Open your mouth, please."	Mund, Zahnfleisch, Zähne, Zäpfchen "Machen Sie bitte den Mund auf."
	"Stick out your tongue, please."	"Strecken Sie bitte die Zunge heraus."
	"Say ahh."	"Sagen sie a"!
Pulmonary	auscultation "Breathe deep."	Auskultation "Atmen Sie tief ein."
	percussion	Perkutieren
Back	"Lie down on your back, please."	"Legen Sie sich bitte hin."
	"Lie on your left side."	"Drehen Sie sich bitte nach links."
	"Lie on your right side."	"Drehen Sie sich bitte nach rechts."
	tenderness "Does it hurt here?"	Empfindlichkeit "Tut es weh, wenn ich hier drücke?
	cva tenderness	Zwerchfellrippenwinkelschmerz
Cardiovascular	heart rate, rhythm "Breathe normally."	Herzfrequenz, Rhythmus "Atem Sie normal."
	heart murmur?	Herzgeräusch?
	carotid "Hold your breath."	Arteria carotis "Atem anhalten."
	jugular venous pressure	Jugularisdruck
Breasts	nipple discharge?	Brustwarzedränage?
	tenderness "Does it hurt here?"	Empfindlichkeit "Tut es weh, wenn ich hier drücke?
	breast exam	Brustuntersuchung
Vascular	carotid, radial, aortic pulsation	Karotis, Radial, Aorten Pulsation
	femoral, dorsalis pedis, posterior tibial	Femoral, Dorsalis Pedis, Tibialis-posterior
	leg edema	Knöchelödern
Abdomen	"Lie down, please."	"Legen Sie sich bitte hin."
	"Show me where it hurts, please."	"Zeigen Sie mir, wo es Ihnen wehtut."
	"Does it hurt here?"	Empfindlichkeit "Tut es weh, wenn ich hier drücke?

	english	german
	umbilicus	Umbilicus
	hernia, inguinal	Leistenhernie
	palpation	Palpation
	auscultation	Auskultation
	fluid wave, superficial abdominal veins?	Flüssigkeitwelle, Bauchdeckenvena?
Maternal/gyn	uterine height (cm)	Fundusstand
	Fetal heart sounds	kindliche Herztöne
	urine sample	Urinuntersuchung
	presentation	geburtsh Einstellung
	head presentation	Schädellage
	breech presentation	Beckenendlage
	transverse presentation	Querstand
	speculum exam	Scheidenspekulumuntersuchung
	vaginal exam	Vaginaluntersuchung
	gestational age	Gestationsalter
	amniotic fluid	Fruchtwasser
Genitourinary; male	circumcision?	Beschneidung?
	genital herpes?	Bläschenausschlag?
	testicular exam	Testikuläruntersuchung
Rectal exam	hemorrhoids, nodules, prostate?	Hämorrhoide, Knötchen, Vorsteherdrüse?
	"I want to check your rectum (for hemorrhoids), bend over please."	"Ich will ihren Mastdarm (für Hämorrhide) untersuchen. Bitte beugen Sie sich nach vorne."
	guaiac; positive or negative	Guajaktest: positiv oder negativ
Neurologic	N1 olfactory: coffee, peppermint? "Close your eyes and tell me what you smell."	N1 Nervus olfactorius: Kaffee, Pfefferminze? "Machen Sie sich die Augen zu, und sagen Sie mir, was Sie riechen."
Cranial nerves	N2 optic: snellen, confrontation "Follow my finger with your eyes, without moving your head."	N2 Nervus opticus: Snellen Tafel, Konfrontation "Folgen Sie meinem Finger mit ihren Augen, ohne sich den Kopf zu bewegen."
	N3,4, 6, oculomotor, trochlear, abducens: EOM's "Follow my finger"	N3,4,6 Nervus oculomotorius, Nervus trochlearis, Nervus abducens: "Folgen Sie meinem Finger."
	N5 trigeminal	N5 Nervus trigeminus
	"Clench your jaw."	"Machen Sie sich den Kiefer fest zu."
	"Move your jaw back and forth."	"Bewegen Sie sich den Kiefer hin und her."

	english	german
	forehead (ophthalmic), cheek(maxillary), chin (mandibular) "Do you feel this?"	Stirn (Ophthalmikus), Wange (maxillär), Kinn (mandibulär): "Spüren Sie das?"
	N7 facial: "Raise your eye brows." ("Do like this.")	N7 Nervus facialis: "Machen Sie sich die Augenbrauen hoch. (Machen Sie so)."
	"Close your eyes tightly, smile big."	"Machen Sie sich die Augen fest zu. Lächeln Sie groß."
	N8 acoustic: whisper, Rinne	N8 Nervus acusticus, Flüstern, Rinne Versuch
	"Can you hear this?"	"Können Sie das hören?"
	"Tell me when you can't feel vibration"	"Sagen Sie mir, wenn Sie das Vibrieren nicht spüren."
	N9 glossopharyngeal: swallow, (hoarseness), "Swallow now."	N9 Nervus glossopharyngeus: Schluck, (Heiserkeit): Schlucken Sie jetzt."
	N10 vagus: swallow, soft palate, gag reflex	N10 Nervus vagus; Schluck, weicher Gaumen, Würgreflex
	"Stick out your tongue, please."	"Strecken Sie bitte die Zunge heraus."
	N11 spinal acessory nerve: "Turn your head, shrug your shoulders."	N11 Nervus accessorius: "Drehen Sie sich den Kopf, ziehen Sie sich die Schulter hoch."
	N12 hypoglossal: tongue midline	N12 Nervus hypoglossus
Glasgow coma score	opens eyes to: spontaneous (4),to speech (3), to pain (2), none (1)	Augen öffnen: spontan (4 Punkte), auf Afforderung (3 Punkte), auf Schmerzreiz (2 Punkte), keine Reaktion (1 Punkt)
	best motor "Hold up 2 fingers." obeys commands (6), localizes (5), withdraws (4), abnormal flexion (3), abnormal extension (2), none (1)	Motorische Reaktion: befolgt Aufforderungen (6 Punkte), gezielte Schmerzabwehr (5 Punkte), ungezielte Schmerzabwehr (4 Punkte), auf Schmerzreiz Beugesynergismen (abnormale Beugung) (3 Punkte), auf Schmerzreiz Streckssynergismen (2 Punkte), keine Reaktion auf Schmerzreiz (1 Punkt)
	best verbal: clear (5), confused (4), inappropriate (3), garbled (2), none (1)	konversationsfähig, oreintiert (5 Punkte), konversationsfähig, desorientiert (4 Punkte), unzusammenhängende Worte (3 Punkte), unverständliche Laute (2 Punkte), keine verbale Reaktion (1 Punkte)
Motor	Motor function	motorische Funktion
	biceps brachii, elbow flexion	Bizeps; Ellenbogen Flexion
	"Pull your arm up."	"Ziehen Sie den Arm nach oben."

english	german
wrist extensors	Handwurzel Extensor
"Bend your wrist up."	"Beugen Sie das Handgelenk nach oben."
triceps brachii, elbow extension	Trizeps, Ellenbogen Extensor
"Straighten your arm out."	"Machen Sie den Arm gerade."
finger flexors, distal phalanx middle finger	Finger Flexor, Endphalanx Mittelfinger
"Bend the tip of this finger."	"Beugen Sie diese Fingerspitze."
finger abduction, little finger	Finger Abduktion, kleiner Finger
"Hold the small finger tightly" (don't let me squeeze your fingers together.)	"Spreizen Sie die Finger breit. Jetzt lassen Sie mich die Finger nicht zusammen drucken."
iliopsoas, hip flexors	Musculus iliopsoas, Hüfte Flexor
"Move your knee to your chest."	"Bringen Sie das Knie an die Brust."
quadriceps, knee extensors	Quadrizeps, Knie Extensor
"Straighten your leg out."	"Machen Sie das Bein gerade."
tibialis anterior, ankle dorsiflexors	Musculus tibialis anterior, Knöchel Dorsalflexion
"Pull your foot up." (point your foot up)	"Ziehen Sie den Fuß nach oben hoch."
extensor hallucis longus, long toe extension	Extensor hallucis longus, Großzehe Streckung
"Raise your toe up."	"Erheben Sie die Zehe hoch."
gastrocnemius, ankle plantar flexors	Gastrocnemius, Knöchel Plantarflexion
"Push your foot down."	"Drucken Sie den Fuß nach unten."

	english	german
Sensory	Sensation "Say 'yes' if you can feel this"	"Sagen Sie "Ja", wenn Sie das spüren."
	C-4 (top of acromioclavicular joint)	C-4 (Oberteil vom Gelenk zwischen dem Schulterblatt und dem Schlüsselbein
	C-5 (lateral side of antecubital fossa)	C-5 (seitliche Stelle vom Ellbogenhöhle)
	C-6 (thumb)	C-6 (Daumen)
	C-7 (middle finger)	C-7 (Mittelfinger)
	C-8 (little finger)	C-8 (kleiner Finger)
	T-4 (nipple line)	T-4 (Brustwarzelinie)
	T-10 (umbilicus)	T-10 (Umbilicus)
	L-2 (mid-anterior thigh)	L-2 (medioanterior Oberschenkel)
	L-3 (medial femoral condyle)	L-3 (medial femoral Kondylus)
	L-4 (medial malleolus)	L-4 (medial Fußknöchel)
	L-5 (dorsum of the foot, at third MTP joint)	L-5 (Fußrücken, dritte metatarsalphalangeal Gelenk)
	S-1 (Lateral heel)	S-1 lateral Ferse)

	english	german
	S-2 (popliteal fossa of the knee, in the midline)	S-2 (mittellinie Kniekehle)
	S-3 (ischial tuberosity)	S-3 (Sitzbeinhöcker)
	S4-5 (perianal area)	S-4-5 (perianal Gebiet)
reflex	Reflexes	Reflexe
	triceps right and left	Trizepsreflex, dexter und links
	biceps, right and left	Bizepsreflex, dexter und links
	brachialradial, right and left	Radiusperiostreflex, dexter und links
	patella, right and left	Patellarsehnenreflex, dexter und links
	ankle, right and left	Achillessehnenreflex dexter und links
	Babinski, right and left (great toe extension= positive)	Baninskireflex, dexter und links
Screening	Tandem walk	Hintereinandergehen.
	"Walk like this, one foot in front of other." (Or, say walk like this and demonstrate.)	"Gehen Sie so mit einem Fuß vor den anderen Fuß. Gehen Sie so."
	heel walk, toe walk	Fersegang, Zehengang
	"Walk on your heels."	"Gehen Sie auf den Fersen."
	"Walk on your toes."	"Gehen Sie auf den Zehen".
	Romberg "Stand up, hold your arms out, close your eyes."	Romberg Versuch: "Stehen Sie auf, strecken Sie die Arme aus, und machen Sie die Augen zu."
Coordination	rapid alternating movement (2nd finger, thumb) "Do this, fast".	Schnellserietechnik: "Machen Sie so aber sehr schnell."
	heel-shin "Move your right heel from your left knee to the ankle with your eyes shut."	Knie-Hacken-Versuch: "Bewegen Sie die rechte Ferse vom linken Knie bis zum Knöchel mit den Augen zu."
	finger nose finger "Touch my finger with your finger then touch your nose."	Finger-Nase-Versuch: "Berühren Sie meinen Finger mit Ihrem Finger, und dann berühren Sie ihre Nase."
Discriminative	stereognosis (key, pencil, cup) "Close your eyes; what is this in your hand?"	Stereognosie (Schlüssel, Bleistift, Tasse): Machen Sie die Augen zu. Was ist das in ihrer Hand?"
	graphesthesia (draw #3 in hand) "Close your eyes, what is the number written in your hand?"	Graphesthesie: "Machen Sie die Augen zu. Welche Nummer habe ich eben in ihrer Hand geschrieben?"
	point localization: "Close your eyes, tell me what part of your body is being touched."	Punkt Lokalisierung: "Machen Sie die Augen zu, und sagen Sie mir, welchen Körperteil angefaßt wird."
	two point discrimination "Do you feel one or two points of contact?"	Zweipunktdiskrimination: "Spüren Sie einen Kontaktpunkt oder zwei Kontaktpunkte?"
Memory	SLUMS Examination	SLUMS Examination

	english	german
	Saint Louis University Mental Status Examination	St. Louis University Mental Status Examination
SLUMS	What day of the week is it? (1)	Welcher *Wochentag* ist heute?
SLUMS	What is the year? (1)	Welches *Jahr* haben wir?
SLUMS	What state are we in? (1)	In welchem *Land* befinden wir uns?
SLUMS	Please remember these five objects. I will ask you what they are later. Apple Pen Tie House Car	Bitte versuchen Sie sich die folgenden 5 Objekte gut einzuprägen. Ich werde Sie später abfragen. *Apfel Stift Krawatte Haus Auto*
SLUMS	You have $100 and you go to the store and buy a dozen apples for $3 and a tricycle for $20. How much did you spend? (1) How much do you have left? (2)	Sie haben €100 und kaufen damit im Lebensmittelgeschäft ein *Dutzend Äpfel für €3 und ein Dreirand für €20.* (1) Wie viel Geld haben Sie ausgegeben? (2) Wie viel Geld haben Sie noch übrig?
SLUMS	Please name as many animals as you can in one minute. (0) 0-4 animals, (1) 5-9 animals, (2) 10-14 animals, (3) 15+ animals	Bitte nennen Sie innerhalb einer Minute so viele Tiere wie möglich. 0-4 Tiere (0 Pkt.), 5-9 Tiere (1 Pkt.), 10-14 Tiere (2 Pkt.), 15+ Tiere (3 Pkt.)
SLUMS	What were the five objects I asked you to remember? Apple Pen Tie House Car. One point for each correct answer.	Bitte zählen Sie die zuvor 5 genannten Objekte auf. (1 Punkt für jede korrekte Antwort).
SLUMS	I am going to give you a series of numbers and I would like yoiu to give them to me backwards. For example, if I say 42, you say 24. (0) 87, (1) 649, (2) 8537	Ich zähle Ihnen jetzt eine Reihe von Zahlen auf, und ich würde Sie bitten, diese rückwärts zu wiederholen. Zum Beispiel, wenn ich 42 sage, dann sagen Sie 24. a) 87 (0 Pkt.) b) 649 (1 Pkt.) c) 8537 (1 Pkt.)
SLUMS	This is a clock face. Please put in the hour markers and the time at ten minutes to elevel o'clock. (2) Hour markers correct? (2) Time correct?	Uhrentest: (Bitte Blatt wenden!) Dies soll eine Uhr darstellen. Ich möchte Sie bitten, in diese Uhr ein Ziffernblatt einzuzeichnen. Die Uhr soll zehn Minuten vor Elf anzeigen. a) Ziffernblatt okay (2 Pkt.), b) Korrekte Zeitangabe (2 Pkt.)
SLUMS	Place an X in the triangle. ☐△◇, (1) Which of the figures is the largest? (1)	Geometrische Figuren (Bitte Blatt wenden!) a) Bitte zeichnen Sie ein X in das Dreieck (1 Pkt.) b) Welche der abgebildeten Figuren ist die größte? (1 Pkt.)

	english	**german**
SLUMS	I am going to read you a story. Please listen carefully because afterwards, I'm going to ask you some questions about it. Jill was a very successful stockbroker. She made a lot of money on the stock market. She then met Jack, a devastatingly handsome man. She married him and had three children. They lived in Chicago. She then stopped work and stayed at home to bring up her children. When they were teenagers, she went back to work. She and Jack lived happily ever after.	Ich werde Ihnen jetzt eine Geschichte erzählen. Bitte hören Sie gut zu, da ich Ihnen im Anschluss ein paar Fragen stellen werden: Anna war eine sehr erfolgreiche Börsenmaklerin. Sie hat an der Börse sehr viel Geld verdient. Eines Tages lernte sie den umwerfend gut aussehenden Peter kennen. Sie hat ihn geheiratet und hatte drei Kinder. Sie wohnten in Berlin. Sie hat dann mit ihrer Arbeit aufgehört und blieb zu Hause, um für ihre Kinder zu sorgen. Als diese Teenager waren, fing sie wieder an, zu arbeiten. Sie und Peter lebten glücklich miteinander, bis ans Ende ihrer Tage.
SLUMS	What was the female's name? (2)	a) Wie hat der Frauenname gelautet? (2Pkt.)
SLUMS	What work did she do? (2)	b) Was für eine Arbeit hat sie ausgebt? (2Pkt.)
SLUMS	When did she go back to work? (2)	c) Wann hat sie wieder mit ihrer Arbeit angefangen? (2Pkt.)
SLUMS	What state did she live in? (2)	d) In welchem Land lebte sie? (2Pkt.)
SLUMS	Add total score, with high school education: 27-30 normal, 21-26 mild cognitive disorder, 1-20 dementia. Without high school education: 25-30 normal, 20-24 mild cognitive disorder, 1-19 dementia.	Höherer Schulabschluss (Matura): 27-30 Normal, 21-26 leicht neurokognitiv Krankheit, 1-20 Demenz. Niedrigerer Schulabschluss 25-30 Normal, 20-24 leicht neurokognitiv Krankheit, 1-19 Demenz
Counseling	Do you understand?	Verstehen Sie?
Laboratory/ imaging	I need to send you for an x ray.	Ich muss Sie zu einer Röntgenuntersuchung schicken.
	I need to take a sample of your blood.	Ich muss eine Blutprobe entnehmen.
	I need a sputum sample.	Ich brauche eine Auswurfprobe.
	Please pass water in this container.	Bitte geben Sie mir eine Urinprobe in diesem Behälter.
	We need to do an EKG (electrocardiogram).	"Wir müssen ein EKG machen."
Pulmonary	I have the result of your sputum.	Ich habe das Ergebnis von ihrer Auswurfprobe.
	You have...	Sie haben
	tuberculosis	Tuberkulose
	pneumonia	Pneumonie

	english	german
	Your lungs are...	Ihre Lungen sind...
	one is affected, the other is healthy.	Eine Lunge ist angegriffen worden. Die andere ist gesund.
	You must stop smoking.	Sie dürfen nicht mehr rauchen.
	You are suffering from...	Sie haben eine...
	Your illness can be healed.	Ihre Krankheit kann geheilt werden.
Gastroenterology	There is an ulcer in your stomach.	Es gibt ein Magengeschwür in ihrem Magen.
	You need to quit drinking beer completely.	Sie müssen ganz aufhören zu trinken.
Surgery	You need to have an operation today.	Wir müssen Sie Heute operieren.
	We need to sew up (suture) this wound.	Ich muss Sie nähen.
	When did you last eat and drink?	Wann haben Sie zuletzt gegessen und getrunken?
	You need to stay in the hospital.	Sie müssen im Krankenhaus bleiben.
Pharmacy	I will give you a prescription.	Ich gebe Ihnen ein Rezept.
	You can get the medication at any pharmacy.	Sie bekommen das Medikament in jeder Apotheke.
	You take this medicine two (one, three, four)times per day.	Nehmen Sie dieses Medikament zweimal (einmal, dreimal, viermal) am Tag.
	Do not stop this medication!	Hören Sie nicht auf, dieses Medikament zu nehmen!
	Take this medication only if you want to.	Nehmen Sie dieses Medikament, nur wenn Sie wollen.
	Take this medication before meals.	Nehmen Sie dieses Medikament vor den Mahlzeiten.
	Take this medication at bedtime.	Nehmen Sie dieses Medikament vor dem Schlafengehen.
	Take this medication after meals.	Nehmen Sie dieses Medikament nach den Mahlzeiten.
Maternity/Ob	Congratulations! You are pregnant.	Herzlichen Glückwunsch! Sie sind schwanger.
	The delivery date will probably be...	Der Geburtstermin wird voraussichtlich am...sein.
	The nurse is on her way.	Die Krankenschwester kommt gleich.
	She will help with the delivery.	Sie wird mit dem Geburt helfen.
Procedures	I need to pass this tube.	Ich muss diesen Schlauch einführen.
	I need to treat you with medication in an IV.	Ich muss Sie behandeln mit Medikamenten in die Vene.
	I need to give you an injection.	Ich muss Ihnen eine Spritze geben.
Orthopedics	You have a broken leg.	Sie haben Ihr Bein gebrochen.

	english	german
	You have a broken arm.	Sie haben Ihren Arm gebrochen.
	You have tendinitis.	Sie haben Sehnenscheidenen tzündung.
	You have fluid in your joint.	Sie haben einen Erguß im Gelenk.
	We have to put a cast on your arm/leg.	Wir müssen einen Gipsverband machen für Ihr Arm/Ihren Bein.
General	What you have is not serious.	Was Sie haben, ist nicht schlimm.
	Your condition is grave.	Die Situation ist ganz schlimm.
	Please come back if you have more problems.	Falls Sie weitere Probleme haben sollten, kommen Sie bitte zurück.
	Please return within a couple weeks.	Kommen Sie in zwei Wochen wieder.

English	German
abasia *Inability to walk due to impaired coordination.*	Abasie
abdomen *The portion of the body bordered by the diaphragm and the pelvis.*	Abdomen, Bausch
abdomen, lower	Unterleib
abdominal girth *Waist circumference.*	Bauchumfang
abdominal reflex *Elicited by stroking the abdomen lightly from mid-axillary line to umbilicus. A normal response is contraction of the umbilicus toward the stimulated side.*	Bauchhautreflex
abdominocentesis *Puncturing of the abdominal wall for drainage purposes.*	Bauchpunktion
abducens nerve *A motor nerve (6th cranial nerve) that controls the lateral rectus muscle of the eye.)*	Augenabziehnerv
abducent *Abducting or to separate.*	abduzierend
abductor pollicis brevis *Abducts the thumb.*	Abductor pollicis brevis
abductor pollicis longus *Abducts and flexes the thumb.*	Abductor pollicis longus
aberrant *Different than normal.*	aberrierend
ablation *Surgical removal or amputation.*	Ablatio
abnormal	abnorm
ABO system *The system using human blood antigens to determine blood type.*	ABO-blutgruppensystem
abortion *Premature expulsion of the fetus from the uterus.*	Abortus
above	oben, über
abrupt *Suddenly or hastily.*	hastig
abruptio placentae *The premature detachment of a normally implanted placenta resulting in maternal decompensation.*	Plazentalösung
abscess *A localized collection of pus.*	Abszess
absence of	absesenheit von
absolute	unbedingt
absorption (intestinal absorption)	Aufsaugen
abuse (sexual abuse)	Missbrauch (sexueller Missbrauch)
acalculia *The inability to perform mathematical calculations.*	Akalkulie
acanthoma *An adult cornyfying squamous carcinoma.*	Akanthom
acanthosis *Hypertrophy of the prickle cell layer of the skin.*	Akanthose
acanthosis nigricans *A skin disorder characterized by dark, thick, velvety skin in the body folds and creases.*	acanthosis nigricans
acapnia *A condition of lower than normal carbon dioxide level in the blood.*	Akapnie
acariasis *Mite infestation.*	Acaridose
acaricide *A treatment for mite infestation.*	Akarizid
acarus *A mite.*	Milbe
acatalasia *A condition characterized by the congenital absence of the enzyme catalase.*	Akatalasie
acathisia *The inability to sit quietly or to have motor restlessness.*	Unvermögen ruhig zu sitzen
accelerate *(To accelerate the healing process).*	beschleunigen
access *Means of entry.*	Zugang

English	German
accessory *Complimentary or concomitant.*	zusätzlich
accessory nerve (XI) *Supplies motor innervation to the sternocleidomastoid and trapezius.*	Nervus accessorius
accident	Unfall
acclimatization *The process of becoming adapted to a new environment.*	Akklimatisierng
accommodation *A term used to describe the ability of the eye to adjust to various distances.*	Akkommodation
accomplish, to *Achieve.*	schaffen
according to	entsprechend
accretion *The expected growth of tissue from the intake of nutrients.*	accretio
acephalous *A absence of a head.*	azephalisch
acetabular *Referring to the acetabulum.*	azetäbular
acetabulum *The cup-shaped cavity with which the head of the femur articulates.*	Acetabulum, Hüftpfanne
acetaminophen *Mild analgesic drug used for pain relief.*	Paracetamol
acetonemia *The presence of acetone in the blood.*	Acetonämie
acetonuria *The presence of acetone in the urine.*	Acetonurie
acetylcholine *A reversible acetic acid ester of choline.*	Acetylcholin
acetylsalicylic acid *The chemical name for common aspirin.*	Acetylsalicylsäure
achalasia *Inability to relax the smooth muscle fibers of the gastrointestinal tract. In the case of esophageal achalasia one has dilatation and hypertrophy of the esophagus.*	Achalasie
achieve, to *To complete something one was striving for.*	erreichen
Achilles tendon reflex *The normal response to tapping the achilles tendon with a reflex hammer is the plantar flexion of the foot.*	Achillessehnen-reflex
achilliodynia *Pain around the calcaneal tendon.*	Achilliodynie
achillobursitis *Inflammation around the calcaneal tendon.*	Achillobursitis
achlorhydria *The absence of hydrochloric acid in gastric secretions.*	Achlorhydrie
acholia *The lack of bile.*	Acholie
achondroplasia *A congenital inadequacy of enchondral bone formation resulting in a type of dwarfism.*	Achondrodysplasie
achromatic spindle *The threads between the poles of the spindle in karyokinesis.*	achromatischspindel
achromatopsia *Inability to differentiate yellow, blue, red or their intermediates.*	Achromatopsie
achylia *The absence of chyle.*	Achylie
acid phosphatase *A phosphate derived chemical that is optimally active in an acidic environment.*	saure Phosphatase
acid *Substance with a pH less than 7.*	Säuer
acid-base balance *The equilibrium of the electrolytes in the body.*	Säure-Basen-Gleichgewicht
acidemia *A lower than normal pH in the blood.*	Azidämie
acidity *Referring to an acid state.*	Azidität
acinous gland *The exocrine part of the pancreas.*	azinös Drüse
acinus *A very small grape shaped portion of an acinous gland.*	Azinus
acne *Inflamed or infected sebaceous glands.*	Akne
acne rosacea *A chronic disease characterized by the presence of flushing of the skin of the nose, forehead and cheeks.*	acne rosacea

English	German
acne vulgaris *Chronic acne occurring on the face, chest and back of youth.*	acne vulgaris
acorea *The absence of the pupil of the eye.*	Akorie
acoustic crest *A prominence on ampulla of the semicircular ducts.*	ampullaris Leiste
acoustic neuroma *A nonmalignant tumor that can cause deafness, tinnitus and vertigo.*	Akustikusneurinom
acoustic *Referring to the auditory system.*	akustisch
Acquired Immunodeficiency Syndrome (AIDS) *Presence of an AIDS defining illness or having a CD4 of less than 200/mm3.*	erworbenes Immunmangelsyndrom (AIDS)
acrocephaly *A condition characterized by a pointed head.*	Akrozephalie
acrocyanosis, Raynaud's disease *A benign condition in which the feet and hands are cyanotic, cold and sweating.*	Akrozyanose
acrodermatitis *Inflammation of the skin of the hands and/or feet.*	Akrodermatitis
acrodynia *An infantile condition exhibited by swollen bluish-red extremities and later polyarthritis..*	Akrodynie
acromegaly *Hyperplasia of the nose, jaw, fingers and toes.*	Akromegalie
acromioclavicular joint *Referring to the junction of the acromion and clavicle.*	Akromioklavikulargelek
acromion *The flattened process extending laterally from the spine of the scapula which forms the most prominent point of the shoulder.*	Akromion
acrophobia *The morbid fear of heights.*	Höhenangst
acrotic *Referring to great weakness or absence of a pulse.*	schwachpulsig
actin *A protein in the muscle that, along with myosin, facilitates muscle contraction and relaxation.*	Actin, Aktin
actinic dermatosis *A skin disease caused by exposure to radiation from the sun, ultraviolet waves or gamma radiation.*	aktinisch Dermatose
actinomycosis *A chronic bacterial infection that effects the face and neck and is caused by Actinomyces israelii. In rare cases it can cause a pulmonary infection.*	Akinomykose
actinon *A radioactive element, radon-219; short lived isotope of radon.*	Aktinon
action potential *The alteration in electrical potential associated with the movement along a nerve cell.*	Aktionpotential
activity	Aktivitär
actomyosin *Myosin and actin complex present in muscles.*	Aktomyosin
acuity *1. Relating to accuracy of hearing, as in hearing acuity. 2. Severity of illness as in, "What is the patient's acuity?"*	Gehörschärfe 2. Schärfe
acupuncture *Traditionally an aspect of Chinese medicine involving insertion of needles into the skin.*	Akupunktur
acute *Abrupt onset.*	akut
acutely ill person *Patient who has a sudden and severe illness.*	akutkranke Person
adactylia *A congenital condition exhibited by the absence of toes and fingers.*	Adaktylie
Adam's apple *A prominence on the anterior neck caused by the thyroid cartilage of the larynx.*	Adamsapfel
Adams-Stokes Syndrome *Characterized by bradycardia, syncope and convulsions.*	Adams-Stokes Syndrom
add, to *To count.*	hinzufügen
addiction *An abnormal dependency.*	Süchtigkeit

24

English	German
Addison's disease *A disease of the adrenal gland exhibited by anemia, hypotension and a bronze tone to the skin.*	Addison Krankheit
adduction *To bring toward the midline.*	Adduktion
adductor *A muscle that brings a part to the midline.*	Adduktor
adenectomy *The removal of a gland.*	Adenektomie
adenitis *The inflammation of a gland.*	Adenitis
adenocanthoma *Malignant tumor comprised of glandular tissue.*	Adenokanthom
adenocarcinoma *Cancer from glandular tissue.*	Adenokarzinom
adenofibroma *Connective tissue with glands that form a tumor.*	Adenofibrom
adenohypophysis *The anterior portion of the pituitary gland.*	Adenohypophyse
adenoid *Referring to a gland.*	adenoid
adenoidectomy *Removal of the adenoids.*	Adenoidektomie
adenoiditis *Inflammation of the adenoids.*	Rachenmandelentzündung
adenoids *Pharyngeal tonsils.*	Rachenmandelwucherungen
adenolymphoma *A salivary gland tumor, also called Warthin's tumor.*	Adenolymphom
adenomyoma *A tumor characterized by the overgrowth of endometrial and uterine muscle tissue.*	Adenomyom
adenomyosis *A condition characterized by the overgrowth of endometrial and uterine muscle tissue.*	Adenomyose
adenopathy *Generally referring to a condition of the lymphatic glands.*	Adenopathie
adenosine triphosphate (ATP) *A chemical that represents the energy reserve of the muscle.*	Adenosintriphosphat
adenosine diphosphate *A product of hydrolysis of ATP.*	Adenosindiphosphorsäure
adenosine monophosphate *A nucleotide, it is produced when ATP is converted to ADP.*	Adenosinmonophosphat
adenovirus *A type of a virus that can cause upper respiratory tract infections.*	Adenovirus
adephagia *Insatiable hunger.*	Ess-Sucht
adequate *Sufficient.*	angemessen
adherence *To stick to something figuratively or literally.*	festhalten
adhesion *The abnormal adherence of tissue exposed to inflammation or after surgery.*	Adhäsion
adhesive capsulitis *Also known as frozen shoulder.*	adhäsive Kapselentzündung
adhesive tape *Tape used to secure dressings or intravenous lines to the body.*	Klebestreifen
adiadochokinesia *The inability to perform rapid alternating movements.*	Adiadochokinese
Adie's pupil *Characterized by a weak light reaction and a strong but slow near response.*	Adie Pupille
adipose *Referring to fat. (adipose tissue)*	adipös (Fettgewebe)
adipsia *Absence of thirst which can be caused by SIADH, hydrocephalus or injury/tumor to/of the hypothalamus.*	Adipsie
aditus *The entrance to an organ or part.*	Aditus
adjust, to *To modify a plan.*	verstellen
adjustment *A modification of a plan.*	Anpassung
adjuvant *Term used to describe the medical treatment after initial therapy, as in adjuvant radiation therapy after initial chemotherapy.*	Adjuvans
admission (to hospital)	Einlieferung

English	German
adnexa *The appendages, for example, of the uterus are the ovaries, fallopian tubes and the ligaments of the uterus.*	Adnexa
adolescence	Jugend
adrenal *Referring to being near the kidney.*	adenal
adrenal cortex *The outer layer of the adrenal gland.*	Nebennierenrinde
adrenal gland *A gland located on the superior aspect of both kidneys.*	Nebenniere
adrenal medulla *The innermost part of the adrenal gland.*	Nebennierenmark
adrenalectomy *Excision of the adrenal gland.*	Nebennierenextrirpation
adrenaline (epinephrine) *A hormone secreted by the adrenal glands and a synthetic medication used for treatment of allergic reactions and cardiac arrest.*	Adrenalin
adrenergic *That which is activated or transmitted by epinephrine.*	adrenergisch
adrenocorticotrophic hormone (ACTH) *A hormone that influences the cortex of the adrenal glands.*	adrenokortikotropes Hormon
Adson maneuver *A test used to screen for thoracic outlet syndrome.*	Adson Handgriff
advanced stage *A late period of a disease.*	fortgeschrittenem Stadium
adventitia *Outermost.*	Adventitia
adverse effect *In reference to medication use, it is an undesirable consequence of the drug.*	Nebenwirkung
advise, to *To give counsel.*	raten
aerobe *An organism that grows in the presence of oxygen.*	Aerobier
aerodontalgia *The dental pain that occurs with low atmospheric pressure, like during airflight.*	Aerodontalgie, Höhenzahnschmerzen
aerophagy or aerophagia *A condition associated with hysteria in which one swallow repeatedly swallows air and then belches.*	Aerophagie, Luftschlucken
afebrile *Absence of fever.*	afebril
affect *The expression of emotions or feelings.*	Affekt
affected	affiziert
affective disorders *Manic-depressive psychosis.*	Gemütskrankheit
afferent loop syndrome *The obstruction of the duodenum or jejunum after gastrojejunostomy, resulting in duodenal distention.*	zuführende Schlinge Syndrom
afferent *Moving toward the center.*	Zuführend, Afferent
affinity *To have a natural liking for.*	Affinität
afibrinogenemia *Marked deficiency of fibrinogen in the blood.*	Afibrinogenämie
aflatoxin *A toxin produced by Aspergillus flavus.*	Aflatoxin
after-load *Referring to the amount of pressure the heart needs to pump against. If one has left heart failure it is beneficial to reduce after-load.*	Nachlast
after-pains *The pain experienced after childbirth caused by uterine contractions.*	Nachwehen
after-taste *The sensation of a prolonged savor following eating/drinking.*	Nachgeschmack
afterbirth *The tissue expelled after the birth of a child that includes the placenta and allied membranes.*	Nachgeburt; Plazenta
agar *Media used for bacterial cultures.*	Agar
age *Length of life.*	Alter
agenesis *The absence of an organ. (cerebellar agenesis)*	Agenesis (Kleinhirnagenesie)
agglutination *The process of adherence of a mass.*	Agglutination
aggression *Violent or hostile behavior.*	Aggression

English	German
aging *Becoming older.*	alternd
agitation *A state of extreme emotional disturbance.*	Agitiertheit
aglutition *The inability to swallow.*	Schluckähmung
agnathia *Congenital abnormality characterized by the absence of the mandible.*	Agnathie
agnosia *A condition exhibited by the loss of sensory stimuli.*	Agnosie
agonist *A synthetic compound that activates cells normally activated by natural chemicals.*	Agonist
agony *Anguish or torment.*	Agonie
agoraphobia *The fear of being in a large open space.*	Agoraphobie; Platzangst
agranulocytosis *A condition characterized by leukopenia and neutropenia.*	Agranulozytose
agraphia *The inability to express one's thoughts in writing.*	Agraphie
agreement *Accordance in opinion or feeling.*	Abmachung
ague *A term used to describe recurrent fever and shivering typically associated with malaria.*	Schüttelfrost
Aicardi syndrome *A rare genetic anomily in which the corpus collosum is absent or insufficient. It is characterized by seizures, microphthalmos, coloboma and developmental delays.*	Aicardi Syndrom
AIDS *Acquired Immunodeficiency Syndrome*	erworbenes Immunmangelsyndrom (AIDS)
air	Luft
air embolism *The blockage of an artery or vein by an air bubble.*	Luftembolie
air flow *The rate of air movement.*	Luftstrom
air hunger *The sensation of shortness of breath.*	Lufthunger
akathisia *A condition exhibited by motor restlessness and inability to sit quietly.*	Aktathisie
akinesia *An absence of movement or sparsity of movement.*	Akinesie
akinesthesia *Lack of perception of movement.*	Akinästhesie
albinism *Congenital absence of pigment in the eyes, skin and hair.*	Albinismus
albino *A person who lacks pigment in the eyes, skin and hair.*	Albino
albumin *A protein that is soluble in water and coagulates if heated.*	Albumin
albuminuria *The presence of albumin in the urine.*	Albuminurie
alcohol *Ethanol or ethyl alcohol.*	Alkohol
alcoholic *A person with alcohol dependence.*	Alkoholisch
alcoholism *An addiction to alcohol.*	Alkoholabhängigkeit
aldehyde *A substance derived by oxidizing and containing a CHO group from alcohol.*	Aldehyd
aldosterone *A steroid secreted by the adrenal cortex that regulates electrolytes.*	Aldosteron
aldosteronism *A condition characterized by the excessive secretion of aldosterone.*	Aldosteronismus
alert *Being in a watchful, ready state.*	aufmerksham
alexia *Inability to read due to a central brain lesion.*	Alexie; Buchstabenblindheit
algae *Nonflowering plants containing chlorophyll but without stems, roots, or leaves.*	Algen
algid *cold*	kalt

English	German
algophilia *Sexual perversion; getting pleasure in giving or receiving pain.*	Algolagnie
algorhithm *Any procedure designed to solve a problem in a step-by-step or mechanical fashion.*	Verfahren
alimentary *Referring to the gastrointestinal tract.*	alimentär
alkali *A class of compounds that form soluble carbonates.*	Alkali
alkaline *Referring to something with properties of an alkali.*	alkalisch; basisch
alkalinuria *The urine in an alkaline state.*	Alkaliruie
alkaloid *Plant derived nitrogenous organic compound.*	Alkaloid
alkalosis *A condition in which the pH is increased.*	Alkalose
alkaptonuria *A condition exhibited by the urine turning dark upon standing because of the presence of alkapton bodies in it.*	Alkaptonurie
all over the body	am ganzen Körper
allantois *A posterior portion of the hind-gut of an embryo.*	Allantois
allele *A type of a gene; in humans there are two alleles per chromosome pair.*	Allel
allergens *Compounds that cause an allergic reaction.*	Allergene
allergy *An immune response by the body to a compound it is hypersensitive to.*	Allergie
alleviate a problem, to	ein Problem entschärfen
allograft *A tissue transplant of from someone of the same species but different genotype.*	Allotransplantat
allopathy *Treatment of disease with minute amounts of natural substances.*	Allopathie
alopecia *The absence of hair in areas where it normally exists.*	Alopezie; Haarausfall
alpha wave *Electroencephalographic waves with a frequency of 8-13 per second.*	Alphawelle
alpha-fetoprotein *A glycoprotein that has a high serum level in hepatocellular and nonseminomatous germ cell tumors.*	Alphafetoprotein
alteration *The process of change or modification.*	Änderung
altitude sickness *A general term used for an illness that occurs at high altitude.*	Höhenkrankheit
alveolar *Referring to the alveolus.*	alveolär
alveolus *A small sac like structure commonly used for the pulmonary alveolus.*	Alveolus
Alzheimer's disease *A dementia of unknown cause or pathogenesis.*	Alzheimer krankheit
amalgam *An alloy that includes mercury as one ingredient.*	Amalgam
amalgamate,to *To make an amalgam by dissolving a metal in mercury.*	fusionieren
amastia *A development condition exhibited by the absence of breasts.*	Amastie
amaurosis *Blindness that occurs without an ocular lesion but may include the optic nerve.*	Amaurose
amaurosis fugax *This transient monocular blindness is considered a sign of an impending stroke.*	Amaurosis-fugax-Attacke
amaurotic pupil *A pupil that will not respond to light when directly exposed but will respond when the other eye is exposed to light.*	amaurotisch Pupille
ambidextrous *Ability to use both hands equal ability.*	Beidhändig
ambisexual *Referring to both sexes.*	bisexuell
amblyopia *Decreased vision without an ocular lesion.*	Amblyopsie; Schwachsichtigkeit
ambulation *A walk.*	Gehen

English	German
ambulatory electrocardiographic monitoring *A continuous recording of the electrocardiogram used to detect occult dysrhythmias.*	ambulante Messung elektrokardiografisch
ambulatory *Referring to one's ability to walk.*	ambulante
ameba *A one-celled protozoan.*	Amöbe
amebiasis *A condition in which one is infected with amebae, mostly commonly Entamoeba histolytica.*	Amöbiasis
amebic liver abscess *A pus filled fluid collection within the liver caused by amoebe.*	Amöbenabszess der Leber
amebicide *A compound used to treat amebiasis.*	amöbizid
ameboma *A mass caused by inflammation as seen in amebiasis.*	Amöbom
amelia *A congenital anomaly exhibited by the absence of limbs.*	Amelie
ameliorate *To make better or improve.*	verbessern
amenorrhea *The absence of menses.*	Amenorrhö
amentia *The absence of mental ability.*	Amentia
ametria *Obsolete term for congenital uterine agenesis.*	uterinagenesie
ametropia *Abnormal refractive ability of the eyes resulting in hypermetropia, myopia or astigmatism.*	Ametropie; Fehlsichtigkeit
amino acid *A compound containing a carboxyl and an amino group.*	Aminosäure
ammonia *A colorless alkaline gas.*	Ammoniak
amnesia *The inability to remember past events.*	Amnesie
amnesia, antegrade *The inability to remember events which occurred after the insult that caused the condition.*	anterograde Amnesie
amnesic stroke *Cerebral infarct exhibited by loss of memory.*	amnestische Schlaganfall
amniocentesis *Transabdominal aspiration of amniotic fluid.*	Amniozentese
amniography *X-ray of the gravid uterus after insertion of opaque dye.*	Amniographie
amnion *The membrane lining the placenta which produces the amniotic fluid.*	Amnion
amniotic fluid *The fluid surrounding the fetus.*	Fruchtwasser
amorphous *A fetus with no heart and no definitive shape.*	amorph
amount *The total or the aggregate.*	Menge
ampulla *The dilated end of a duct.*	Ampulla
ampulla chyli *Also called cisterna chyli; it is a dilated area of the thoracic duct that collects lymph from several areas.*	Cisterna chyli
amygdala *Any almond shaped structure such as the tonsil*	Amagdala
amylase *An enzyme involved in the hydrolysis of starch.*	Amylase
amyloidosis *The accumulation of amyloid in body tissues.*	Amyloidose
amyotonia *A condition associated with the lack of muscle tone.*	Amyotonie
amyotrophic lateral sclerosis *A progressive neurodegenerative disorder.*	amytrophische Lateralsklerose
amyotrophy *Atrophy of muscle tissue.*	Amytrophie
anabolism *The formation of molecules in organisms from simpler molecules.*	Anabolismus
anacrotic *Referring to a prominent bulge on the ascending portion of a pulse recording.*	anakrot
anaerobe *An organism that lives in the absence of oxygen.*	Anaerobier
anal *Near or referring to the anus.*	anal
anal fistula *An opening in the skin that tracts to the anal canal thus causing some fecal material to leak from the opening in the skin.*	Analfistel

English	German
analeptic *A medication used as a stimulant to the central nervous system.*	Analeptikum
analgesia *The absence of pain.*	Analgesie
analgesic *A medication used to remove pain.*	Analgetikum; Schmerzmittel
analogous *To resemble or be similar to.*	analog
anaphase *A stage in mitosis following metaphase.*	Anaphase
anaphoresis *Reduced activity of the sweat glands.*	Anaphorese
anaphylaxis *An exaggerated response to a foreign substance.*	Anaphylaxie
anaplasia *The loss of normal differentiation of tumor cells.*	Anaplasie
anastomosis *Surgical formation of a connection between two previously separate parts.*	Anastomose
anatomical chart *A pictorial diagram of part of the anatomy.*	anatomische Tabelle
anatomical dead space *The area between the mouth and pulmonary alveoli.*	anatomicum Totraum
anatomical *Referring to the anatomy.*	anatomicum
anatomical snuff-box *The area on the back of the hand near the base of the thumb that is between the extensor pollicus longus and extensor pollicus brevis.*	Tabatière Anatomique
anatomy *The study of body structure.*	Anatomie
ancylostomiasis *A type of nematode parasite, also called hookworm.*	Ancylostomiasis
androgen *A compound that produces masculinizing characteristics.*	Androgen
androgynous *Referring to a female pseudohermaphroditism (a genetic female with masculine characteristics).*	androgyn
android pelvis *A pelvis shaped like a man's.*	androides Becken
androsterone *A hormone excreted in the urine of men and women.*	Androsteron
anemia *Lower than normal red blood cell count.*	Anämie; Blutarmut
anencephaly *The congenital absence of the cranial vault and cerebral hemispheres.*	Anencephalie
aneroid *The absence of liquid.*	Aneroid
anesthesia *Loss of sensation.*	Anästhesie
anesthetic *A chemical that produces anesthesia.*	Anästhetikum
anesthetist *A person who administers anesthesia.*	Anästhesist
aneurysm *A condition exhibited by the dilatation of the walls of an artery or vein to form a blood-filled sac.*	Aneurysma
angiectasia *Dilation of a blood or lymph vessel.*	Angiektasie
angina pectoris *Exercise induced myocardial ischemia.*	Angina pectoris
angioedema *Also called angioneurotic edema, it is caused by a histamine reaction. It can produce welts in mild cases but in severe cases can cause swelling of the lips and tongue.*	angioneurotisches Ödem
angiogram *Radiologic imaging of blood vessels.*	Angiogramm
angiography *Roentgenographic imaging of blood vessels.*	Angiographie
angioma *A tumor comprised of blood or lymph vessels.*	Angiom
angioneurotic *Caused by a neurosis affecting the blood vessels, like vasospasm.*	angioneurotisch
angioneurotic edema *A condition exhibited by sudden edema of skin and mucous membranes.*	angioneurotisches Ödem
angioplasty *Surgical alteration of blood vessels.*	Angioplastie
angiosarcoma *A sarcoma comprised of blood vessels.*	Angiosarkom

30

English	German
angiospasm *A spasm of a blood vessel.*	Angiospasmus; Gefäßkrampf
angiotensin *A blood protein that increases aldosterone secretion.*	Angiotensin
angiotensin converting enzyme inhibitors (ACEI) *A class of medicines that prevent conversion of angiotension I to angiotensin II, a potent vasoconstrictor.*	Angiotensin Konversionsenzym Hemmer
angitis or angiitis *The inflammation of a lymph or blood vessel.*	Angiitis
anguish *Significant mental or physical pain.*	Qual
anhidrosis *A condition exhibited by reduced quantity of sweat.*	Anhidrose
anhidrotic *Something the reduces the quantity of sweat.*	schweißhemmend
anhydrous *Lacking water.*	wasserfrei
aniseikonia *A condition in which the ocular image of an object is viewed differently by each eye.*	Aniseikonie
anisocoria *Pupillary diameter inequality.*	Anisokorie
anisocytosis *Variation in size of erythrocytes.*	Anisozytose
anisomelia *Unequal size of arms or legs.*	Anisomelie
anisometropia *Refractive power inequality between the two eyes.*	Anisometropie
ankle *The area of the ankle joint.*	Knöchel
ankle clonus *An abnormal response exhibited by alternating plantar- and dorsiflexion noted after the examiner rapidly dorsiflexes the foot.*	Fußklonus
ankle edema or dependent edema *Extracellular fluid volume noted by swelling or pitting.*	Knöchelödem
ankle joint *The articulation of the tibia/fibula and talus.*	Sprunggelenk
ankle support *A mechanical device or banding to support the ankle.*	Knöchelstütze
ankle swelling *Enlargement of the ankle region with or without pitting.*	Knöchelschwellung
ankyloglossia *Limitation of tongue motion because of a short frenulum.*	Ankyloglossie
ankylosing spondylitis *A type of arthritis found in the spine that is exhibited by bony fusion.*	Spondylarthritis ankylopoetica
ankylosis *Abnormal immobility of a joint.*	Ankylose; Gelenksteife
annular *Referring to a ring.*	anular
anomia *Inability to name or recognize familiar objects.*	Wortfindungsstörung
anonychia *Congenital absence of fingernails or toenails.*	Anonychie
anoperineal *Referring to the anus and perineum.*	anoperineal
anorchous *The absence of testicles.*	Anorchie
anorectal *Referring to the anus and rectum.*	anorektal
anorexia nervosa *A mental disorder characterized by the desire to avoid eating and to lose weight.*	Anorexie nervosa
anorexia *The loss of appetite.*	Anorexie
anorrectal abscess *A localized collection of pus in the anorrectal region.*	anorektalabszess
anosmia *Lack of the sense of smell.*	Anosmie
anovulatory *Lack of ovulation.*	anovulatorisch
anovulatory cycle *A menstrual cycle in which no ovum is released.*	anovulatorischzyklus
anoxemia *Reduction in blood oxygen concentration.*	Anoxämie
anoxia *Reduced oxygen levels in body tissues.*	Anoxie
antacid *A medication, usually with a calcium or magnesium base that binds with acid in the stomach.*	Antacidum

31

English	German
antagonist *A muscle or agent that acts in counteract to effects of another muscle or agent.*	Antagonist
antiemetic *A medication used to control nausea.*	Antiemetikum
antemortem *Refers to: before death.*	vor dem Tod
antenatal *Refers to events before birth.*	pränatal
anterior root *A motor nerve root that is in the anterior part of the spinal cord between the anterior and lateral funiculi.*	Vorderwurzel
anterior *Toward the front.*	Vorder-
anterograde *Moving forward.*	anterograd
anteroinferior *Toward the front and lower part.*	anteroinferior
anterolateral *Toward the front and away from the midline.*	anterolateral
anteromedian *Toward the front and toward the midline.*	anteromedian
anteroposterior *From front to the back. (An AP x-ray has the beam directed from the front to the back.)*	anteroposterior
anterosuperior *Toward the front and the upper part.*	anterosuperior
anteversion *The forward leaning of an organ.*	Anteversio
anthelmintic *An agent used to destroy worms.*	Anthelmintikum
anthracosis *Pneumoconiosis caused by coal dust.*	Anthracosis
anthrax *An infectious disease caused by Bacillus anthracis; there are cutaneous, inhalation and gastrointestinal syndromes.*	Anthrax; Milzbrand
anti-inflammatory agents *Medications used to reduce inflammation.*	Entzündungshemmer
antibiotic *A medication that inhibits or kills microorganisms.*	Antibiotikum
antibody *A protein that combines with and counteracts foreign substances.*	Antikörper
anticholinergic *Parasympathetic blocker.*	Anticholinergikum
anticholinesterase *Cholinesterase blocker.*	Anticholinesterase
anticoagulant *Medication used to inhibit coagulation.*	Antikoagulans
anticodon *A series of three nucleotides that form a unit of genetic code for transfer RNA.*	AntiKodon
anticonvulsant *Medication used to treat seizures.*	Antikonvulsivum
antidepressant *Medication used to treat depression.*	Antidepressivum
antidiuretic hormone *Vasopressin.*	Adiuretin
antidote *A medication that neutralizes a toxin.*	Antidot; Gegengift
antigen *A foreign substance, like bacteria, that induces an immune response.*	Antigen
antiglobulin test (Coombs' test) *Test used to detect erythroblastosis fetalis.*	Antiglobulin Konsumptionstest
antihemophilic factor *Also called factor VIII. A deficiency of the factor causes hemophilia.*	antihemolitisch Faktor
antihistamine *Medication used to treat conditions exhibited by a histamine response*	Antihist-aminikum
antilymphocyte *A serum globulin that has antibodies to lymphocytes.*	Antilymphozyten
antilymphocyte globulin *The gamma globulin portion of antilymphocyte serum.*	antilymogizytär Globulin
antimalarial *Medication used to treat malaria.*	Malariamittel
antimetabolite *A substance that impedes metabolism.*	Antimetabolit
antimigraine *Medication used to treat headaches.*	medikamentöse Behandlung der Migräne

English	German
antimitotic *Impeding mitosis.*	Antimitotikum
antimycotic *Inhibition of fungal growth.*	Antimykotikum
antinuclear factor *Also called antinucleic antibody (ANA); it is found in conditions such as lupus and rheumatoid arthritis.*	antinukleärer Antikörper (ANA)
antiperistaltic *An agent that impedes normal peristalsis.*	antiperistaltisch
antipruritic *Medication used to treat pruritus.*	Antipruriginosum
antipyretic *Medication used to treat fever.*	Antipyretikum; Fiebermittel
antiseptic *A substance that inhibits microorganism growth.*	Antiseptikum
antiserum *A substance that contains antibodies to specific antigens.*	Antiserum
antispasmodic *Medication used to treat muscle spasm.*	Antispasmodikum; krampflösend
antithrombin *A substance that inhibits thrombin, thus decreasing the body's ability to coagulate.*	Antithrombin
antithyroid *A substance inhibiting the effect of the thyroid.*	Thyreostatikum
antitoxin *A substance that inhibits the effect of a toxin.*	Antitoxin
antitussive *Medication used to diminish a cough.*	Antitussivum; Hustenmittel
antivenin *An antitoxin formulated for various types of snake bites.*	Antivenin; Schlangenserum
antrotomy *To cut open the antrum.*	Antrotomie
antrum *Referring to a cavity or chamber.*	Antrum
anuria *The lack of urine excretion.*	Anurie
anus *The body opening distal to the rectum.*	Anus; After
anxiety *Nervousness or unease.*	Angst
anxiety neurosis *Abnormal presence of anxiety.*	Angstneurose
anxious *Experiencing nervousness or unease.*	besorgt
aorta *The large artery originating at the left ventricle and going to the pelvis where it bifurcates.*	Aorta
aortic insufficiency *A dysfunction of the aortic valve allowing backflow of blood into the heart.*	Aortenklappeninsuffizienz
aortic *Referring to the aorta.*	aortal
aortic stenosis *Narrowing of the aortic orifice.*	Aortenklappenstenose
aortic valve *The valve situated between the left ventricle and the aorta.*	Aortenklappen
apart *Separated by a distance.*	auseinander
apathy *Lack of interest in one's environment or indifference.*	Apathie
aperistalsis *Lack of intestinal peristalsis.*	Aperistaltik
aperture *An opening or hole, as in the hole the light passes through in a camera.*	Offnung
apex *The highest point of something.*	Apex
apex of heart *Normally found 8cm to the left of the midsternal line in the 5th intercostal space.*	Herzspitze
Apgar score *A scoring system for newborns that utilizes heart rate, respiratory effort, muscle tone, responsiveness and skin color.*	Apgar-Score
aphagia *The lack of eating.*	Aphagie
aphakia *The congenital absence of the lens of the eye.*	Aphakie
aphasia *Diminished ability to communicate via speech or writing.*	Aphasie
aphid *A minute insect that feeds on plants.*	Blattlaus
aphonia *The loss of voice.*	Aphonie
aphthous stomatitis *Grouped small lesions that occur on the tongue or in the mouth.*	Aphthen

33

English	German
apicectomy *Removal of the apex of the petrous portion of the temporal bone.*	Apektomie
aplastic anemia *Bone marrow failure causing a decrease in all types of blood cells.*	Amyelhämie
apnea *Absence of respiration.*	Apnoe
apocrine gland *A gland that releases some of its cytoplasm in secretions; an example is axillary sweat glands.*	Schweißdrüse
aponeurosis *A tendinous expansion that connects with muscle to move a part.*	Aponeurose
apophysis *Generally a bony outgrowth that forms a process or tubercle.*	Apophyse
apoplexy *Extravasation of blood within an organ.*	Apoplexie
appearance *The way someone looks or presents.*	Auftreten; Erscheinungsbild
appendectomy *Surgical excision of the appendix.*	Appendektomie
appendicitis *Inflammation of the appendix.*	Appendizitis
appendix *An appendage of the cecum.*	Appendix; Blinddarm
apperception *The ability to interpret sensory impressions.*	Apperzeption
application *The forms one fills out to obtain a grant.*	Auftragen
applicator *A device used to apply a topical medication.*	Applikator
appointment *A previously scheduled time to see a person.*	Termin
apprehension *A fear that something unpleasant will happen.*	Besorgnis
approval *Accepting something as satisfactory.*	Zustimmung
approximate *Nearly but not totally accurate.*	ungefähr
approximate, to *To bring together, as in wound margins.*	zusammenzählen
approximately *Nearly but not completely.*	ungefähr
apraxia *The inability to carry out intentional movements when paralysis is not present.*	Apraxie
apt *Suitable in the circumstances.*	passend
aptitude *A natural talent for something.*	Begabund
aptyalism *Diminished or absence of saliva.*	Aptyalismus
acquaint, to *To make someone familiar with something.*	heranführen
aqueous humor *The fluid between the cornea and lens, anterior to the globe.*	Kammerwasser
aqueous *Use of water as a solvent or medium.*	wässerig
arachnodactyly *A condition exhibited by abnormally long and slender fingers.*	Arachnodaktylie
arachnoid *Refers to that which resembles a spider web.*	Arachnoid
arbovirus *Virus that is transmitted by arthropods; responsible for diseases such as Yellow fever and dengue fever.*	Arboviren
arcuate nucleus *Small masses of gray matter found on the medulla oblongata.*	Arcuatusnukleus
arcus *Narrow opaque band.*	Arcus
areola *The pigmented skin surrounding a nipple.*	Brustwarzenhof
argininosuccinicaciduria *Presence of arginosuccinic acid in the urine; associated with mental retardation.*	Argininosukzinurie
argue, to *To debate or reason. (quarrel)*	streiten (sich streiten)
Argyll Robertson symptom *Presence of small pupils that do not react to light but will constrict when the person focuses on a near object.*	Argyll Robertson Phänomen

34

English	German
argyria *The greyish discoloration of the skin and conjunctiva.*	Argyrie
arm *One of two upper extremities.*	Arm
around *On every side of.*	herum
arousal reaction *The change in brain wave patterns upone awakening.*	Vigilitätsreaktion
arrhenoblastoma *An ovarian tumor that results in masculine secondary sex characteristics.*	Arrhenoblastom
arrhythmia *An abnormal heart rhythm.*	Arrhythmie
arterial blood gas *Measurement of the arterial concentration of carbon dioxide and oxygen.*	Blutgasanalyse (BGA)
arterial *Referring to an artery.*	arteriell
arteriectomy *Surgical excision of an artery.*	Arteriectomie
arteriography *Roentgenography of an artery after infusion of contrast media.*	Arteriographie
arterioplasty *Surgical repair of an artery.*	Arterioplastie
arteriosclerosis *Hardening and thickening of arterial walls.*	Arteriosklerose
arteriotomy *Creation of an opening in an artery.*	Arteriotomie
arteriovenous malformation *A sac like structure created by the abnormal communication of an adjacent artery and vein.*	arteriovenöse Missbildung
arteritis *Inflammation of an artery.*	Arteriitis
artery *Vessel that carries oxygenated blood from the heart to the periphery.*	Arterie
arthralgia *Joint pain.*	Gelenkschmerz
arthritis *Joint inflammation.*	Arthritis; Gelenkentzündung
arthrodesis *Surgical fusion of a joint.*	Arthrodese
arthrodynia *Joint pain.*	Arthrodynie
arthrography *Joint roentgenography.*	Arthrographie
arthroplasty *Plastic surgery involving a joint.*	Gelenplastik
arthroscopy *Viewing of the inside of a joint with a specially designed scope.*	Arthroskopie
arthrotomy *Surgical opening of a joint.*	Arthrotomie
articular *Referring to a joint.*	articularis
artifact *An aberration from the normal.*	Artefakt
artificial *Not natural produced.*	artifiziell; künstlich
arytenoid *Referring to the cartilage in the posterior larynx.*	arytenoideus
asbestos *A heat resistant silicate material.*	Asbest
asbestosis *Lung disease caused by the inhalation of asbestos.*	Asbestosis pulmonum
ascaricide *Agent that destroys ascaris.*	Medikament gegen Ascaris
ascaris *A nematode from genus intestinal lumbricoid parasite, also called round worm.*	Ascaris lumbricoides
ascending colon *The portion of the colon between the cecum and the right colic flexure.*	Colon ascendens
ascertain, to *Synonym of "to determine".*	feststellen
ascites *Serous fluid in the abdominal cavity.*	Aszites
ascorbic acid *Commonly known as vitamin C; a deficiency of this vitamin causes scurvy.*	Askorbinsäure
asepsis *Lack of infection.*	Asepsis
aseptic *Being free of septic matter.*	aseptisch
asexual *Without sex or sex organs.*	asexuell; geschlechtslos

35

English	German
asleep *To be in a dormant or inactive state.*	schlafen
Asperger's syndrome *A condition characterized by disturbed social interaction; if was named after the Austrian scientist who first described it.*	Asperger-Syndrom
aspermia *Absence of sperm.*	Aspermie
asphyxia *A condition exhibited by a lack of oxygen and subsequent loss of consciousness or death.*	Asphyxie
aspiration biopsy *Removal of fluid from a cavity for pathologic analysis.*	Aspirationsbiopsie
aspiration pneumonia *Taking air or matter into the lungs.*	Aspirationspneumonie.
aspirator *A device used to remove fluid from a cavity.*	Aspirator
aspirin *Common name for acetylsalicylic acid.*	Schmerztablette
assay *A procedure for measuring the activity of a biological sample.*	Assay
assessment *An medical evaluation.*	Beurteilung
assistance *The act of helping.*	Hilfe
assisted ventilation *The act of helping one breathe through artificial means.*	Beatmung
asteatosis *A condition exhibited by diminished sebaceous secretion.*	Asteatosis
astereognosis *Lack of ability to recognize objects by touching them.*	Astereognosie
asterixis *Commonly known as a flapping tremor, it is characterized by involuntary jerking movements of the hands and is seen commonly in hepatic encephalopathy.*	Asterixis; Flattertremor
asthenia *Diminished strength and energy.*	Asthenie
asthenopia *Visual fatigue accompanied by ocular pain.*	Asthenopie
astragalus *Synonym of talus.*	Talus
astringent *An agent causing contraction of the skin.*	zusammenziehend
astrocytoma *A tumor comprised of astrocytes.*	Astrozytom
astroglia *The neurologic tissue which is composed of astrocytes.*	Astroglia
asymmetry *Lack of symmetry.*	Asymmetrie
asymptomatic *The absence of symptoms.*	Asymptomatisch
asynclitism *Oblique presentation of the head during delivery.*	Asynklitismus; Scheitelbeineinstellung
at random *Occurring by chance alone.*	auf Geratewohl
atavism *The inheritance of characteristics from remote rather than immediate ancestors.*	Atavismus
ataxia *Lack of muscular coordination.*	Ataxie
atelectasis *Incomplete expansion or collapse of a lung.*	Atelektase
atherogenic *Something that causes atheromatous lesions in arterial walls.*	atherogen
atheroma *Degenerative arteriosclerosis.*	Atherom
athetosis *An involuntary symptom exhibited by continuous slow, writhing movements, mostly in the hands.*	Athetose
athlete's foot *Common term for tinea pedis.*	Fußpilz
atlas *The first cervical vertebra.*	Atlas; erster Halswirbel
atomizer *A device for propelling a fine mist.*	Vernebler
atony *Absence of normal muscle tone.*	Atonie
atresia *Closure of a body orifice as in atresia ani in which there is a congenital imperforate anus.*	Atresie

English	German
atrial flutter *Sawtooth waves on an electrocardiogram with atrial rate of 250-330 per minute.*	Vorhofflattern
atrial natriuretic factor *A chemical secreted by the right atrium that promotes sodium excretion in the urine.*	atriales natriuretisches Hormon
atrial *Referring to the atrium.*	atrial
atrial septal defect *An abnormal communication between the atria of the heart.*	Vorhofseptumdefekt (VSD)
atrio-ventricular block *An interruption of the electrical conduction at the atrio-ventricular node.*	Atrioventrikularblock
atrioventricular bundle *Also called bundle of His.*	His-bündle
atrioventricular *Referring to the atrium and ventricle.*	atrioventrikulär
atrium *Referring to a chamber used as an entrance, as in the entrance to the heart.*	Vorhof; Atrium
atrophic *Referring to atrophy.*	atrophisch
atrophy *A diminution in the size of a part.*	Atrophie
atropine *A parasympathetic agent derived from Atropa belladonna.*	Atropin
attack *A fit or paroxysm.*	Anfall
atypical *Not usual.*	atypisch
audiogram *The recording of a one's hearing in decibels.*	Audiogramm; Hörkurve
audiologist *A specialist in the field of hearing.*	Audiologe
audiometer *A device used to measure hearing.*	Audiometer
auditory *Referring to hearing.*	auditorisch
auditory agnosia *Caused by a temporal lobe lesion, it is characterized by inability to recognize sounds as words.*	auditorische agnosie; Seelentaubheit
aural *Referring to the ear.*	Ohrsignal
auricle *The external portion of the ear.*	Auricula;Ohrmuschel
auricular *Referring to the auricle.*	Aurikular
auriculotemporal *The area of the ear and temple.*	aurikulotemporal
auscultation *The act of listening to sounds emanating from the body.*	Auskultation
autism *A mental condition exhibited by difficulty in forming relationships, communicating and uses abstract thought.*	Autismus
autistic *Referring to autism.*	autistisch
autoantibody *An antibody that acts against the organism's own tissue.*	Autoantikörper
autoantigen *A normal tissue constituent that prompts a cell-mediated response.*	Autoantigen
autoclave *A device used for sterilization with the use of steam under pressure.*	Autoklav; Hochdrucksterilisator
autogenous *Self-generated.*	autogen
autograft *Grafting tissue from one part of person to another part of the same person.*	Autoplastik
autohypnosis *Self-hypnosis.*	Autohypnose
autoimmunization *The body's ability to promote an immune response without external resources.*	Autoimmunisierung
autolysis *A state of self destruction of cells within a body.*	Autolyse
autonomic nervous system *Responsible for regulation of cardiac muscle, smooth muscle and glandular activity.*	autonomes Nervensystem
autopsy *Examination of a body post-mortem in an attempt to determine cause of death.*	Autopsie; Leichenschau

English	German
autosomal *Referring to an autosome.*	autosomal
autotransfusion *The reinfusion of one's own blood.*	Autotransfusion
availability *A person or thing that is available.*	Erhältlichkeit
available *Attainable, obtainable.*	erhältlich
avascular *An area with no blood supply.*	avaskulär
avascular necrosis *Bone death caused by poor blood supply.*	avaskulär Nekrose
avian flu *A viral disease found in birds and fowl that can be transmitted to humans; it is exhibited by respiratory and gastrointestinal symptoms but can lead to encephalitis.*	Vogelgrippe
avian *Referring to birds.*	aviär
avitaminosis *A state of vitamin deficiency.*	Avitaminose
avoidable *That which can be stopped or inhibited.*	vermeidbar
awakening *The state of being conscious.*	Erwachen
away from *Separated from.*	fernab von
axilla *The hollow beneath the arm.*	Axilla
axillary *Referring to the axilla.*	axillar
axis *The second cervical vertebra.*	Axis; zweiter Halswirbel
axon *The structure along which nerve impulses are transmitted from the cell body to other cells.*	Axon
azo itch *A pruritis noted in people who use azo dyes.*	azobezogen Jucken
azoospermia *The absence of spermatozoa in the semen.*	Azoospermie
Azorean disease *A form of hereditary ataxia found in peoples of Azorean descent. Also called Machado-Joseph disease or Portuguese-Azorean disease.*	Azorean Krankheit
azotemia *Prerenal disease.*	Azotämie
azoturia *An excess of urea in the urine.*	Azoturie
Babinski's sign *A reflex that occurs when the plantar surface of the foot is stimulated. The great toe turns upward- normal in infancy but when it turns upward in an adult it means there is central nervous system injury.*	Babinski-Zeichen
baby *A newborn.*	Baby
baby-scale *A device used to weigh an infant.*	Baby-Waage
bacillary *Referring to bacilli.*	bazillär
bacillus *A rod-shaped bacterium.*	Bazillus
back pain *Discomfort on the dorsal surface of the torso.*	Kreuzschmerzen
bacteremia *The presence of bacteria in the blood.*	Bakteriämie
bacteria *Plural for any organism of the order Eubacteriales.*	Bakterien
bacterial *Referring to bacteria.*	bakteriell
bactericidal *An agent that destroys bacteria.*	bakterizid
bacteriostatic *An agent that impedes bacterial growth.*	bakteriostatisch
bacteriuria *The presence of bacteria in the urine.*	Bakteriurie
bagassosis *A pulmonary disorder contracted from inhalation of the waste of sugar cane (bagasse dust).*	Bagassose
Bainbridge reflex *Increase in heart rate due to increased pressure in teh right atrium.*	Bainbridgereflex
Baker cyst *A synovial fluid collection in the popliteal fossa.*	Baker-Zyste; Poplitealzyste
balanitis *Inflammation of the glans of the penis.*	Balanitis
ballottement *Presence of movement of a floating object by palpation.*	Ballottement

38

English	German
balm *A topical medical preparation.*	Balsum
bandage *A strip of gauze used to immobilize or support.*	Verband
banding *The process of encircling with a thin piece of material.*	Bändelung
barber's itch *Ringworm that is transmitted by contaminated shaving equipment.*	Bartfinne; Bartflechte
barium enema *Administration of barium into the rectum followed by roentgenography to check for rectal or colon abnormalities.*	Kontrasteinlauf
Barretts's esophagus *A condition characterized by varying degrees of esophageal injury from gastric acid.*	Endobrachyöso-phagus
Bartholin's cyst or abscess *This is a purulent fluid collection in the Bartholin cysts which are located in the perivaginal area.*	Bartholinitis
Bartter's syndrome *An autosomal recessive renal disorder with a defect in chloride reabsorption and secondary hyperaldosteronism.*	Bartter-Syndrom
basal ganglia *Structures adjacent to the thalamus that are involved with coordination of movement.*	Basalganglien
basal *Referring to the base.*	basal
basilar *Referring to the base or lower segment.*	basilär
basilic vein *A vein in the hand that joins the brachial veins to form the axillary vein.*	vena basilica
basin *A small bowl used for washing.*	Waschbecken
basophil *A polymorphonuclear granulocyte.*	Basophil
bear, to *To endure or resist.*	erleiden; ertragen
bear, to *To give birth to a child.*	gebären
bearing down *As in during labor.*	pressen
beat *As in heart beat.*	Schalg
Bechterew-Mendel reflex *Plantar flexion of the toes when the examiner percusses the dorsum of the foot; seen with pyramidal lesion.*	Bechterewreflex
bed *A mattress resting on a frame.*	Bett
bed rest *A medical order requiring one to stay in bed.*	Bettruhe
bedbug Cimex lectularius. *A small insect that is parasitic and hides in clothing or bedding.*	Hauswanze
bedpan *A metal or plastic vestibule one sits on while in bed to defecate.*	Bettpfanne
bedridden *Term used to indicate one is so ill they cannot get out of bed.*	bettlägerig
bee sting *A piercing from a bee.*	Bienenstich
beforehand *In advance or previously.*	im Voraus
behavior disorder *An abnormal mental state.*	Verhaltensstörung
Behçet syndrome *Characterized by recurrent oral and genital ulcers, uveitis, iridocyclitis and frequently arthritis.*	Behçet-Syndrom
Bell's palsy *Unilateral facial paralysis related to dysfunction of the seventh cranial nerve.*	Gesichtslähmung
below *Under.*	unter
belt *A strap used to hold clothing up.*	Gürtel
benign *Not harmful.*	benigne
bereavement *The sorrow one feels with the loss of a loved one.*	Trauerfall
berylliosis *A lung exhibited by granulomas and caused by inhalation of beryllium.*	Berylliosis
best *Optimal or ideal.*	bester; beste

English	German
betablocker *A substance that inhibits adrenergic stimulation. It is used to reduce pulse, blood pressure and to treat angina.*	Betablocker
beyond *On the farther side.*	janseits
bezoar *A concretion composed of either hair, vegetable/fruit fibers or hair and vegetable/fruit fibers that is found in the stomach.*	Bezoar
Bezold-Jarisch reflex *A reflex in the vagus, originating in the heart, resulting in sinus bradycardia, hypotension and periperal vasodilation.*	Bezold-Jarisch-Reflex
biased *Prejudiced.*	voreingenommen
biceps *A muscle with two heads usually referring to the biceps brachii which is used for forearm flexion.*	Bizeps
biceps reflex *The biceps brachii tendon is hit with a reflex hammer and results in flexion of the forearm as a normal response. This assesses the C5-C6 region.*	Bizeps(sehnen)reflex (BSR); Bizeps-femoris-Reflex
bicuspid *Having two points as in bicuspid valve or a premolar tooth.*	bikuspid
bifid *Presence of two branches.*	zweitleilig
bifurcate ligament *A ligament on the dorsum of the foot that includes the calcaneonavicular and calcaneocuboid ligaments.*	ligamentum bifurcatum
bifurcate *When one branch divides into two branches.*	zweizackig
bilateral *Referring to both sides.*	doppelseitig; bilateral
bile *An alkaline fluid secreted by the liver to aid digestion.*	Galle
bile ducts *The structures that are conduits for passage of bile from the liver and gallbladder to the duodenum.*	Gallenwege
bile pigments *The golden brown or green-yellow color associated with bile.*	Gallenfarbstoff
bile salts *Normally occurring salts of bile acids.*	Gallensäuren
Bilharzia *Historical name of a genus of flukes or nematodes now known as Schistosoma.*	Bilharzia
biliary *Referring to bile, bile ducts or gallbladder.*	billiär
bilious *Something that contains bile.*	gallig; biliös
bilirubin *A pigment found in bile that is responsible for the yellow color seen in patients with elevated serum levels of bilirubin.*	Bilirubin
biliuria *The presence of bile in the urine.*	Bilirubinurie
biliverdin *A green pigment formed by oxidation of bilirubin.*	Biliverdin
bill *A financial statement that indicates how much one owes.*	Rechnung
Bill maneuver *During childbirth, use of forceps at midpelvis to help extract the head.*	Bill Handgriff
bimanual *Use of two hands, as in bimanual pelvic examination in which the right hand touches the cervix uteri and the left hand presses above the mons pubis.*	bimanuell; zweihändig
binaural *Referring to both ears.*	binaural
binocular *Referring to both eyes.*	binokular; beidäugig
binovular *Derived from two different ova.*	zweieiig
bioassay *A laboratory test determination as compared to normal.*	Bioassay
bioavailability *The portion of a drug that is able to be utilized by the body after it is introduced to the body.*	Bioverfügbarkeit
biochemistry *The study of chemistry and physiochemical processes in living organisms.*	Biochemie
biology *The study of living organisms.*	Biologie
biopsy *The removal and examination of bodily tissues or fluids.*	Biopsie

English	German
biotin *A vitamin involved in the synthesis of fatty acids and glucose.*	Biotin
birth *The process of bearing offspring from the uterus.*	Geburt
birth control *Any method of limiting contraception.*	Geburtenkontrolle; Schwangerschaftsverhütung
birth defect *A congenital anomaly.*	Geburtsfehler
birth rate *The number of live births per 1000 of a given population per year.*	Geburtenhäufigkeit
bistoury; scalpel *A surgical knife.*	Skalpell; Seziermesser
bitemporal hemianopsia *A visual defect seen commonly in pituitary tumors in which the visual defect is in the temporal portion of each eye.*	bitemporale Hemianopsie
bitter (taste) *Having a harsh, unpleasant taste.*	bitterer Geschmack
black *Referring to the color, as in the color of coal.*	schwarz
black fly *From the family Simuliidae, a gnat that can cause disease in humans; also called buffalo fly.*	Kriebelmücken
black stools *Common term for melena.*	Melaena
blackout *Common term for loss of consciousness.*	Ohnmacht; kurze Gedächtnisstörung
blackwater fever *A term used to describe the fever associated with malaria when the urine is reddish-black.*	Schwarzwasserfieber
bladder, urinary *Vestibule for urine prior to being expelled via the urethra.*	Harnblase
blast injury *Trauma from a wave of air pressure.*	blast Verletzung
blastomycosis Infection caused by organisms of genus Blastomyces.	Blastomykose
bleach *A solution that includes sodium hypochlorite.*	Bleichmittel
bleeding *Loss of blood.*	Blutung
bleeding time *The time of bleeding after a controlled standardized puncture of the earlobe.*	Blutungszeit
blemish *A small mark on one's skin.*	Makel
blennorrhea *Discharge from the mucous membranes, usually referring to gonorrhea.*	Blennorrhö
blepharitis *Inflammation of the eyelids.*	Blepharitis; Lidrandentzündung
blepharospasm *A spasm of the orbicularis oculi muscle that causes closure of the eyelid.*	Blepharospasmus
blind *Absence of sight.*	blind
blind loop syndrome *A condition in which there is a non-functional section of the bowel that is thought to be responsible for malabsorption and Vitamin B12 deficiency.*	Blindsack-Syndrom
blind spot *An area of insensitivity to light located at the point of entry of the optic nerve on the retina.*	blinder Fleck
blindness *Absence of visual perception.*	Blindheit
blinking *The rapid opening and closing of the eyelid.*	blinzelnd
blister *Common term for bulla.*	Blase
bloated *Sensation of having an abnormally large amount of air in the viscera.*	aufgedunsen
Boerhaave Syndrome *Rupture of the esophagus from vigorous vomiting, with resultant mediastinitis.*	Boerhaave-Syndrom
blood *Plasma containing erythrocytes, leukocytes and platelets.*	Blut
blood alcohol level *A quantitative measurement of the amount of alcohol in the blood.*	Blutalkoholkonzentration

41

English	German
blood bank *An area where blood products are stored for later use.*	Blutbank
blood brain barrier *A matrix of capillaries that move blood between the blood and brain, as well as, limiting some substances from passing.*	Blut-Hirn-Schranke
blood cells *A common term that does not differentiate between erythrocyte or leukocyte.*	Blutzellen
blood clot *A mass of coagulated blood.*	Blutgerinnsel
blood grouping *Testing blood to determine which type should be used for transfusion.*	Blutgruppenserologie
blood pressure *Written as the measurement in mmHg at the time of systole of the left ventricle over the time of diastole.*	Blutdruck
blood sedimentation rate (ESR) *The settling time of erythrocytes in a prepared sample. This is a measure of the abnormal concentration of substances that are associated with pathological states.*	Blutsenkunsgeschwindigkeit
blood stream *Common term or the arterial or venous systems.*	Blutstrom
blood tubing *(used for infusion of blood)*	blut Schlauch
blood type *Determined and listed in the ABO system.*	Blutgruppen
blood volume *The amount of blood cells/plasma in the circulatory system.*	Blutvolumen
blue *A color between green and violet.*	blau
blue diaper syndrome *A disorder of tryptophan absorption. Excess tryptophan is metabolized to indicans in the bowel, excreted in the urine and oxidized in the diaper to indigo, thus the blue diaper.*	Tryptophanmalabsorptions Syndrom
blunt *Having a flat or rounded end.*	stumpf
blurred vision *Low visual acuity.*	Seheintrübung
blurt out, to *To speak without considering the repercussions.*	herausplatzen mit
blush, to *To have an increased volume of blood flow to one's face causing a red tint to the skin.*	rot werden
body surface area *Dubois formula is: (weight in kilograms)to the 0.425th power x (height in centimeters) to the 0.725th power x 0.007184.*	Körperoberfläche
body weight *Relative mass as measured in kilograms or pounds.*	Körpergewicht
bolus *A fluid bolus is a phrase used for rapid infusion of fluid.*	Nahrungsbrei
bone *Skeletal tissue formed by osteoblasts.*	Knochen
bone graft *The transfer of bone to aid in the healing of a complex fracture.*	Knochenspan
bone marrow *The soft material filling the cavity of bones.*	Knochenmark
bone marrow puncture *The aspiration of marrow to look for pressure of disease.*	Knochenmarkpunktion
bone scan *Bone imaging using technetium 99m (99mTc) diphosphate.*	Knochenscan
bonesetter *A person who sets bones without being a physician.*	Einrichter
border *Margin.*	Rand
born *Being present as a result of birth.*	geboren werden
bottle *A container used for the storage of liquids.*	Flasche
bougienage *Passage of a bougie through a body orifice with the goal of increasing the diameter of the orifice.*	Bougierung
brace, to *Application of a splint.*	stützen
brace *A splint.*	Stützapparat
brachial artery *A continuation of the axillary artery and branches into the radial and ulnar among others.*	Oberarmterie

English	German
brachial plexus *A cluster of nerves coming off the last four cervical and first thoracic spinal nerves form the nerve supply the the chest and arms.*	Plexus brachialis
brachial plexus neuropathy *Characterized by acute arm or shoulder pain followed by focal muscle weakness.*	Armplexuslähmung
brachial *Referring to the arm.*	brachial
brachium cerebelli *Synonym of pedunculus cerebellaris superior (upper portion the cerebellum).*	Kleinhirnbindearm
Bracht maneuver *Delivery of a fetus in a breech position.*	Bracht Handgriff
brachycephaly *The presence of a short broad skull.*	Brachyzephalie
bradycardia *Lower than normal cardiac rate measured in beats per minute.*	Bradykardie
bradykinin *A peptide that causes contraction of smooth muscle and dilation of blood vessels.*	Bradykinin
brain *A common term for cerebrum.*	Gehirn; Hirn
brain death *Cessation of cerebral functioning.*	Hirntod
brain stem *An organ that consists of the medulla oblongata, pons and midbrain.*	Hirnstamm
brainstem herniation *Movement of the brainstem into the incisura because of increased intracranial pressure.*	Gehirnprolaps
branchial *Referring to or resembling the gills of a fish.*	branchialis; kiemenförmig
break *A common term for a fracture in a bone.*	Bruch
breast *Mammary tissue including the areola.*	Brust
breast feeding *The process of giving milk to a baby via the nipple.*	Stillen
breath *One respiration.*	Atem
breath sounds *The noise heard upon auscultation with a stethoscope.*	Atemgeräusche
breath test (for alcohol) *A check of alcohol level by testing exhaled air.*	Atemalkoholtest
breech birth *Delivery with the feet or buttocks coming first.*	Steißgeburt
breech presentation *Position of the feet or buttocks near the cervix.*	Beckenendlage
bregma *Located at the convergence of the coronal and sagittal sutures.*	Bregma
bright *Giving out a lot of light.*	leuchtend
bring, to *To carry or transport something.*	bringen
brisk *Rapid or fast.*	flott
broad ligament of uterus *Supports the uterus on both sides.*	ligamentum latum uteri
Brodie's knee *Also referred to as chronic hypertrophic synovitis of the knee.*	hypertrophisch Synovitis
broken (arm) *Fracture of the arm.*	Armbruch
bromidrosis *Foul smelling perspiration.*	Bromidrosis
bromism *Poisoning caused by excessive intake of bromine.*	Bromismus
bronchial carcinoma *A general term for a malignancy of the bronchi.*	Bronchialkarzinom
bronchial *Referring to the bronchus.*	bronchial
bronchiectasis *The presence of abnormally wide bronchi or branches.*	Bronchiektasie
bronchiole *A small branch that a bronchus divides into.*	Bronchiolus
bronchiolitis *Inflammation of the pulmonary bronchioles.*	Bronchiolitis
bronchitis *Inflammation of the mucous membranes of the bronchioles that causes bronchospasm and cough.*	Bronchitis
bronchogenic *Referring to the bronchi.*	bronchogen

English	German
bronchography *Roentgenography of the bronchi after administration of contrast media.*	Bronchographie
bronchopneumonia *Pneumonia that starts in the distal bronchioles.*	Bronchopneumonie
bronchoscopy *Use of a scope to visualize the bronchi.*	Bronchoskopie
bronchospasm *Bronchial smooth muscle spasm.*	Bronchospasmus
bronchus *The major air channels that bifurcate from the distal trachea.*	Bronchus
brow presentation *The term used to describe which part of the body (forehead) is being delivered first in childbirth.*	Stirnlage
brown *Coffee-colored.*	braun
Brown-Séquard syndrome *Unilateral spinal cord lesions, proprioception loss and weakness occur ipsilateral to the lesion, while pain and temperature loss occur contralateral.*	Brown-Séquard-Syndrom
brucellosis *A gram-negative bacteria in cattle that causes persistent fever in humans.*	Brucellose
Brudzinski sign *Involuntary flexion of the knees and hips after flexion of the neck while supine; seen in meningitis.*	Brudzinskireflex
bruise *Common term for ecchymosis.*	Quetschung
bruit *An abnormal sound heard through a stethoscope indicating turbulent blood flow.*	Gerücht
brush *Implement used for cleaning or for taking a tissue sample.*	Bürste; Pinsel
brush biopsy *The process of tissue sampling using a brush.*	Bürstenabstrich
bubo *An inflamed, swollen lymph node in the axilla or inguinal region.*	Bubo
bubonic plague *A form of plague exhibited by the formation of buboes.*	Beulenpest
buccal *Referring to the cheek.*	bukkal; buccalis
buccinator *A thin, flat muscle in the cheek wall.*	Buccinator
buccinator muscle *Pulls the mouth posteriorly.*	Backenmuskel
Budd-Chiari syndrome *Hepatomegaly, severe portal hypertension and ascites related to thrombosis of the hepatic vein.*	Budd-Chiari-Syndrom
bug *Insect.*	Wanze
bulbar palsy *Paralysis due to changes in the motor center of the medulla oblongata.*	Bulbär-paralyse
bulbocavernosus reflex *Brisk contraction of the ischiocavernosus and bulbocavernosus muscles when the glans penis is compressed.*	Bulbokavernosus-Reflex
bulge *A proturberance on a flat surface.*	Wölbung
bulimia *Pathologic increase in hunger.*	Bulimie
bulky *Voluminous or substantial.*	sperrig
bulla *A large cutaneous serous filled vesicle.*	Spannungsblase
bullous pemphigoid *A benign disease of the aged characterized by large bullae forming on the torso and extremities.*	Pemphigoid bullöses
Bumke's pupil *Dilation of the pupil in response to anxiety.*	Bumke Pupillenzeichen
bundle branch block *A cardiac dysrhythmia produced by a blockage of a branch of the bundle of His.*	Schenkelblock
bundle of His *The atrial contraction rhythm is facilitated by this bundle to the ventricles.*	His-bündel
bunion *Swelling of the bursa of the metatarsal head of the first metatarsal.*	Ballenzeh
burn *An injury caused by exposure to heat.*	Brandwunde
burr or bur *A rotary cutting instrument.*	Klette

English	German
burr hole *A treatment of subdural hematoma that involves drilling a hole into the cranium to release the hematoma.*	Trepanationsloch
bursitis *Inflammation of the bursa.*	Bursitis
burst, to *To rupture.*	aufplatzen
buttocks *The bilateral region covering the gluteal muscles.*	Gesäß
Buzzard maneuver *Testing of the patellar reflex while the client firmly touches the floor with their toes in a sitting position.*	Buzzard Handgriff
bypass *An alternate route, typically referring to an arterial bypass.*	Bypass; Umweg
byssinosis *A disease caused by inhalation of cotton dust; a type of pneumoconiosis.*	Byssinose; Baumwollfieber
cachexia *Generalized weakness and severe wasting.*	Kachexie
cadaver *A dead body.*	Kadaver
caduceus *An ancient herald's wand with two serpents twined around that is a symbol of the medical arts.*	Hermesstab
caisson disease *Decompression sickness.*	Caissonkrankheit
calcaneal spur *A bony protrusion on the calcaneus.*	Fersensporn
calcaneus *Commonly called the heel bone.*	Calcaneus; Kalkaneus
calcareous *Referring to something containing lime or calcium.*	kalkig
calciferol *It is formed when egesterol is exposed to ultraviolet light; a D vitamin.*	Calciferol
calcification *Deposition of calcium salts causing hardening of an organic tissue.*	Kalzifikation; Verkalkung
calcitonin *A thyroid hormone that lowers serum calcium levels.*	Calcitonin
calcium *A chemical element that is an essential component in teeth and bone.*	Calcium; Kalzium
calcium channel blocker *A medication used to treat angina, supraventricular arrhythmias and hypertension; it works by blocking calcium influx into myocytes and vascular smooth muscle cells.*	Kalzium-antagonisten
calculus *A stone of minerals that can lead to the blockage of the bile duct or ureters.*	Calculus; Stein
calf *Muscles of the posterior portion of the lower leg.*	Wade
calibrate, to *To adjust an instrument using a standard.*	eichen
calibration *The process of calibrating an instrument.*	Eichung
callosity *Callus; thickened hardened skin.*	Verschwartung; Callositas
callus *Thickened hardened skin.*	Kallus; Hornschwiele
calorie *A unit of heat.*	Kalorie
calvaria *The portion of the skull that is composed of the superior aspects of the occipital, parietal and frontal bones.*	Calvaria
calyx *A cup shaped organ or cavity.*	Nierenkelch (renalis)
canaliculus *A term for various small channels.*	Canaliculus; Kanälchen
cancel, to *To stop or revoke.*	absagen
cancellous *A bony mesh-like structure with many pores.*	porös
cancellous bone *Describing the cancellous interior of bone.*	spongiöser Konchen
cancer; carcinoma *A disease of uncontrolled abnormal cell growth.*	Krebs; Karzinom
cancroid *A tumor occurring in the stomach, small or large bowel.*	Kankroid
cancrum oris *Gangrenous stomatitis.*	gangränöse Stomatitis
candle *A cylindrical piece of wax with a central wick.*	Kerze
canine teeth *Located between the incisors and premolars.*	Eckzähne

45

English	German
canker sore *An ulceration, usually of the mouth or lips.*	Aphthe
cannabis *A plant from the Cannibidaceae family that is known for its psychotropic effects.*	Kannabis
cannula *A tube inserted into the body.*	Kanüle
cantering rhythm *Gallop rhythm.*	Galopprhythmus
capillary *A vessel that connects arterioles to venules.*	Kapillare
capillary fragility test *Application of a blood pressure cuff high enough to restrict venous return and after five minutes count the number or petechiae produced.*	Kapillarfragilitätsprobe
capillary nevus *A growth of skin that involves the capillaries.*	kapilläres Hämangiom
capitate bone *The bone at the base of the palm that articulates with the third metacarpal.*	Kapitatum
Caplan nodules *These are pulmonary nodules noted in people with rheumatoid arthritis who were exposed to coal dust.*	Caplan-Syndrom
capsule *A membranous sheath that covers an organ or structure.*	Kapsel
capsulitis *Inflammation of a capsule.*	Kapselentzündung
capsulotomy *Incision of a capsule as in with eye surgery.*	Kapseleröffnung
caput *The head.*	Caput; Kopf
caput succedaneum *Edema that occurs in the scalp of an infant during child-birth.*	Caput succedaneum
carbohydrate *A group of organic compounds including sugar and starch.*	Kohlenhydrat
carbon dioxide gas *A gas expelled during exhalation.*	Kohlendioxid
carbon monoxide poisoning *This tasteless, odorless gas causes constitutional symptoms but can lead to death upon inhalation.*	Kohlenmonoxidvergiftung
carboxyhemoglobin *A compound formed from hemoglobin when it is exposed to carbon monoxide.*	Kohlenmonoxidhämoglobin
carcinogenic *That which causes cancer.*	karzinogen
carcinoid *A tumor occurring in the stomach, intestine and colon.*	Karzinoid
carcinoma *A malignant growth.*	Karzinom
carcinomatosis *Dissemination of cancer throughout the body.*	Karzinomatose
cardia *The superior aspect of the stomach at the opening of the esophagus.*	Kardia
cardiac *Referring to the heart.*	Herzmittel
cardiac arrest *Cessation of function of the heart.*	Herzstillstand
cardiac failure *Decreased cardiac output of the heart.*	Herzversagen
cardiac output *Amount of blood pumped by the heart in liters per minute.*	Herzminutenvolumen
cardiac pacing *Electromechanical stimulation of the heart.*	Herzfrequenzsteuerung
cardiology *A specialty of medical practice involve treatment and prevention of heart disease.*	Kardiologie
cardiomyopathy *Chronic cardiac muscle disease.*	Kardiomyopathie
cardiorespiratory assistance *Use of artificial means to support respiration and circulation.*	kardiopulmonale Reanimation
cardiovascular *Referring to the heart or circulatory system.*	kardiovaskulär
carditis *Inflammation of the heart.*	Karditis
caregiver *A person who provides care to another.*	Pflegekraft
caries *Referring to decay or death of a tooth.*	Karies

English	German
carina *The protrusion of the lowest tracheal cartilage.*	Karina
carneous *Synonym of fleshy.*	fleischig
carotene *A hydrocarbon that can be converted to vitamin A.*	Carotin
carotid body *Carotid artery receptors that are sensitive to blood chemistry changes.*	Karotiskörper
carotid bruit *An abnormal noise heard over the carotid artery that may be a sign of stenosis or aortic valvular disease.*	Geräusch carotis
carotid sinus reflex *Bradycardia as a result of pressure on the carotid sinus.*	Karotissinusreflex
carotid sinus syncope *Dizziness and syncope that results from hyperactivity of the carotid sinus reflex.*	Karotissinussyndrom
carotid *Referring to the large artery on each side of the neck.*	Karotis
carpal tunnel syndrome *Paresthesia that results from compression of the median nerve.*	Karpaltunnelsyndrom
carpometacarpal *Referring to the carpus and metacarpus.*	karpometakarpal
carpopedal spasm *A spasm of the carpus and the foot.*	Karpopedalspasmus
carpus *The joint between the hand and wrist.*	Handwurzel; Karpus
caruncle *A small fleshy protuberance.*	Karunkel
casein *The principal protein in milk, a phospholipid.*	Kasein
Casoni's test *Hydatid fluid is injected intradermally; subsequent formation of a larger papule indicates hydatid disease.*	Casoni Intrakutantest
cast; plaster cast *Use of plaster of paris to immobilize an extremity.*	Gips; Abdruck
castor bean *A bean that can yield the poisonous compound ricin.*	Ricinus communis Bohne
castration *Excision of the gonads.*	Kastration
casualty *A person who is killed or seriously injured.*	Verletzter
cat cry syndrome *A hereditary congenital disorder exhibited by microcephaly, hypertelorism, and cognitive deficits.*	Katzenschrei-Syndrom
cat scratch fever *An infectious disease characterized by local inflammation a the site of the scratch, local lymph adenopathy and fever.*	Katzenkratzkrankheit
catabolism *The reduction of complex molecules to more simple ones in living organisms.*	Katabolismus
catalepsy *A condition exhibited by rigidity and the person maintains the same position if he is moved by another.*	Katalepsie
cataphoresis *The use of an electric field to move charged particles in fluid.*	Kataphorese
cataplexy *A condition exhibited by rigidity and immobility.*	Kataplexie
cataract *An opacity of an eye lens or the capsule.*	Kararakt
catarrh *Inflammation of a mucous membrane.*	Katrrah
catatonia *Seen in schizophrenia, it is a state of stupor or excitability and abnormal movements.*	Katatonie
catch a cold *To come down with a viral upper respiratory tract infection.*	sich erkälten
catharsis *The act of cleansing or purging, usually referring to thought.*	Katharsis
cathartic *To be cleansed or evacuated, referring to thought or the cleansing of the bowels.*	Abführmittel; Kathartikum
catheter *A flexible tube inserted into the body.*	Katheter
cat's eye pupil *A pupil in the shape of an oval.*	Katzenauge

English	German
cauda equina syndrome *Neurologic condition manifested by pain, paresthesia and weakness but no bowel/bladder dysfunction.*	Kauda syndrom
caudal *Referring to a cauda.*	kaudal
caudate *Referring to the caudate nucleus.*	caudatus
causative *Something that induces an effect.*	ursächlich
caustic *Abrasive or corrosive.*	Kaustikum
cautery *Application of an electric current to cut something.*	Kauterisation
cavernous hemangioma *A tumor composed of connective tissue with blood filled areas.*	kavernöses Hämagiom
cavernous sinus *Large venous sinus located adjacent to the sphenoid bone and posterior to the petrosal sinuses.*	kavernöse Blutleiter
cavernous sinus thrombosis *A blood clot in the base of the brain.*	kavernöse Sinusthrombose
cavity *Pouch or chamber.*	Höhle
cecum *The portion of the bowel between the ileum and and the ascending colon.*	Zäkum
celiac *Referring to the abdominal cavity.*	zöliakal
cell body *The portion of the cell containing the nucleus.*	Zellkörper
cell membrane *The semipermeable structure surrounding the cytoplasm of a cell.*	Zellmembran
cell *The smallest functional unit of an organism.*	Zelle
cell wall *The peripheral border of the cell.*	Zellwand
cellulitis *Infection characterized by diffuse, subcutaneous inflammation.*	Zellulitis
cellulose *A polysaccharide that occurs naturally in fibrous products.*	Zellstoff
center *A point equidistant from all sides.*	Zentrum
centigrade *A scale with 100 gradations, usually referring to a temperature scale.*	Celsius-Skala
centimeter *One hundredth of a meter.*	Zentimeter
central nervous system (CNS) *The brain and spinal cord.*	Zentralnervensystem
centrifuge *Machine used to separate substances of different weights.*	Zentrifuge
centripetal *The movement toward the center.*	zentripetal
cephalic *Towards the head.*	kephalisch
cercaria *Larval trematode worm that live in a molluscan.*	Zerkarie
cerebellum *The part of the brain in the posterior portion of the skull that controls muscle coordination and movement.*	Kleinhirn
cerebral malaria *A severe form of malaria manifested by seizures and a decreased level of consciousness.*	falciparum Malaria
cerebral palsy *A condition exhibited by motor incoordination and speech changes that is the result of brain injury occurring ante-, intra- or post- partum.*	zerebrale Lähmung
cerebral *Referring to the cerebrum.*	zerebral
cerebration *Operating activity of the cerebrum.*	Hirntätigkeit
cerebrospinal fluid (CSF) *The fluid between the pia mater and arachnoid membrane.*	Liquor cerebrospinalis
cerebrovascular accident (stroke) *A decrease in level of consciousness and paralysis caused by a cerebrovascular thrombosis, hemorrhage or vasospasm.*	Schlaganfall
cerumen *Waxy substance found normally in the external ear canals.*	Zerumen

48

English	German
cerumen impaction *External ear canal full of wax resulting in hearing loss until the impaction is removed.*	Zeruminalpfropf
Cervical insufficiency (formerly incompetent cervix) *Painless changes in the cervix that result in recurrent second semester pregnancy loss.*	Zervixinsuffizienz
cervical pleura *The dome-like cap of the pleura.*	Pleurakuppel
cervical *Referring to the neck or the cervix.*	zervikal
cervicectomy *Excision of the cervix uteri.*	Zervixresektion
cervicitis *Inflammation of the cervix.*	Zervizitis
cervix uteri *The narrow end of the uterus.*	Gebärmutterhals
cesarian section *Incision of the abdominal and uterine walls in order to deliver a fetus when natural delivery is not possible.*	Kaiserschnitt
cestode *A class of parasitic flatworms.*	Cestoda; Bandwurm
chancre *The initial ulcer that is the source of entry for a pathogen.*	Schanker
chancroid *A sexually transmitted disease caused by Haemophilus ducreyi that is exhibited by ulcers without indurated margins.*	Schankroid
check for, to	überprüfen
cheek *Lateral facial tissue.*	Wange; Backe
chelating agent *A compound used to bind with metal typically used in the treatment of poisoning.*	Chelatbildner
cheilitis *Inflammation of the lip.*	Cheilitis; Lippenentzüdung
chemoreceptor *A sense organ that responds to stimuli.*	Chemorezeptor
chemosis *Swelling of conjunctival tissue adjacent to the cornea.*	Chemosis
chemotaxis *The response of an organism to chemical agents.*	Chemotaxis
chemotherapy *Use of medication (chemical agents) in the treatment of disease. This term is commonly used to refer to the treatment of cancer patients with medication.*	Chemotherapie
chest *Thorax.*	Thorax; Brustkorb
chest leads *Leads going from the skin to an electrocardiographic device.*	Brustwandableitung
chest wall *Thoracic wall.*	Brustwand
chest x-ray *Roentography of the thorax.*	Röntgenthoraxaufnahme
chew, to *Masticate.*	kauen
Cheyne-Stokes respirations *A breathing pattern characterized by alternating apnea with hyperpnea.*	Cheyne-Stokes-Atmung
chiasma *The optic chiasma is the area inferior to the hypothalamus where the optic nerves cross.*	Chiasma
chicken pox, varicella *A viral disease characterized by extremely pruritis blisters over the entire body.*	Windpocken; Varizellen
chigger *A parasitic mite of the genus Trombicula.*	Trombiculalarve
child *A person aged 1 to 8 years old.*	Kind
childbirth *Parturition; the process of labor and delivery of an infant.*	Geburt
childhood *The time between infancy and puberty.*	Kindheit
chill *Sensation of coldness.*	Kältegefühl
chimera *A mixture of genetically distinct tissues.*	Chimäre
chin *Mentum; the anterior projection of the lower jaw.*	Kinn
chiropodist *A doctor trained in the treatment of feet.*	Fußpfleger

49

English	German
chiropractic *Referring to the medical practice of adjusting malaligned joints.*	Chiropraktik
chiropractor *A medical practitioner who is involved with the treatment of disease by manipulating malaligned joints.*	Chiropraktiker
chlamydiosis *A disease caused by the species Chlamydia.*	Chlamydieninfektion
chloasma *Brown or black macula that occur on the face during pregnancy or when there is ovarian dysfunction.*	Chloasma
chloroform *A colorless, sweet smelling liquid formerly used as a general anesthetic.*	Chloroform
chloroma *A malignant tumor associated with myelogenous leukemia.*	Chlorom
choanae *The two openings between the nasal cavity and the nasopharynx.*	Choane
choanal atresia *A congenital condition characterized by blockage of the nasal passages by tissue.*	Choanalatresie
choice *Selection or decision.*	Whal
choke, to *To retch, cough or fight for breath.*	ersticken
cholagogue *A compound used to stimulate flow of bile from the liver.*	Cholagogum
cholangiogram *Radiologic imaging of the gallbladder and bile ducts.*	Cholangiogramm
cholangitis *Inflammation of the bile ducts.*	Cholangitis
cholecystectomy *Surgical excision of the gallbladder.*	Cholezystektomie
cholecystenterostomy *Creation of a surgical anastomosis between the intestine and the gallbladder.*	Cholezystenterostomie
cholecystitis *Inflammation of the gallbladder.*	Cholezystitis
cholecystolithiasis *The presence of gallstones in the gallbladder.*	Cholezystolithiasis
choledocholithotomy *Creation of an incision in the bile duct for the purpose of removing a stone.*	Choledocholithotomie
cholelithiasis *Presence or creation of gallstones.*	Cholelithiasis
cholemia *Bile or bile products in the blood.*	Cholämie
cholera *An infectious disease exhibited by vomiting and diarrhea and caused by Vibrio cholerae.*	Cholera
cholestatis hepatitis *Liver inflammation caused by obstruction of bile flow from the liver to the duodenum.*	cholestatische Hepatitis
cholesteatoma *A cystic mass that has a lining made of keratinizing material and cholesterol.*	Cholesteatom
cholesterol *A compound or its derivatives are found in cell membranes and precursors to hormones but high levels can cause atherosclerosis.*	Cholesterin
cholinergic *Referring to the stimulation, activation or transmission of acetylcholine.*	cholinerg
cholinesterase *An esterase used to cleave acetylcholine into choline and acetic acid.*	Cholinesterase
choluria *Term indicating the presence of bile in the urine.*	Cholurie
chondralgia *Cartilaginous pain.*	Chondralgie
chondritis *Cartilaginous inflammation.*	Chondritis
chondroma *Cartilaginous hyperplastic growth.*	Chondrom
chondromalacia *Excessive softening of the cartilages.*	Chondromalazie
chondromalacia of the patella *Softening of the articular cartilage of the patella.*	Kniescheibenknorpelerweichung
chondrosarcoma *Cartilaginous tumor which exhibits rapid growth.*	Chondrosarkom
chorda *A cord or sinew.*	Chorda

English	German
chordee *Downward bending of the penis.*	Gryposis pensi
chorditis *Inflammation of a vocal or spermatic cord.*	Chorditis
chorea *Involuntary, continuous rapid, jerking movements.*	Chorea
chorionic villus *Cord-like projections of a fertilized ovum.*	Chorionzotte
choroid *Similar to the chorion (fertilized ovum or zygote)*	Aderhaut
choroiditis *Inflammation of the choroid.*	Chorditis; Stimmbandentzündung
choroidocyclitis *Inflammation of the ciliary processes and choroid.*	choroidozyklitis
chromatin *A desocyribose nucleic acid that carries the genes of inheritance.*	Chromatin
chromosome *A structure in the nucleus of living cells that carries genetic information.*	Chromosom
chronic *When referring to an illness, it means recurring or persistent.*	chronisch
chyle *A combination of lymph fluid and fat that enters the blood via the thoracic duct.*	Chylus; Milchsaft
chylomicron *A one micron particle of emulsified fat.*	Chylomikron
chylous *Referring to chyle.*	chylos
chyme *The gruel produced by gastric digestion.*	Chymus
cicatricial *Referring to cicatrix.*	narbig
cicatrix (scar) *New tissue in a healed wound.*	Narbe
cilia *The hairs growing on the eyelid or a motile extension of a cell surface.*	Cilia; Zilien
ciliary body *The connection between the iris and the choroid.*	Ziliarkörper
cinchonism *The toxic effects induced by ingestion of cinchona bark; it is exhibited by tinnitus, deafness and cognitive changes.*	Chininvergiftung
circadian *Referring to a 24 hour period.*	zirkadian
circadian rhythm *Naturally recurring fluctuations in a 24 hour period.*	zirkadianer Rhythmus
circumcision *Surgical excision of the foreskin.*	Zirkumzision; Beschneidung
circumference *The distance around an object or part.*	Umfang
circumflex nerve *The axillary nerve that has an origin in the posterior branch of the brachial plexus.*	Achselnerv
circumscribed *To have well defined borders.*	unschrieben; zirkumskript
cirrhosis *A liver disease characterized by destruction of liver cells and increased connective tissue.*	Zirrhose
cirsoid *Similar to a tortuous vein, artery or lymph vessel.*	traubenartig
cisternal puncture *A trans-occipitoatlantoid ligament puncture of the cisterna magna so CSF can be obtained.*	Zisternenpunktion
clasp *Holding onto something with one's hand.*	Griff
clasp knife reflex *The lengthening of the extensor muscles resulting in flexion.*	Taschenmessersphänomen
claudication *Intermittent claudication is a phrase used to describe pain experienced in the leg from arterial insufficiency.*	Claudicatio; Hinken
claustrophobia *An unreasonable fear of being in an enclosed environment.*	Klaustrophobie
clavicle *A bone that articulates with the sternum and scapula.*	Klavikula; Schlüsselbein
clavus *A corn or horny protrusion.*	Klavus; Hühnerauge
clawhand *A hand deformity caused by ulnar nerve palsy exhibited by the hyperextension of the metacarpophalangeal joints and flexion of the interphalangeal articulations.*	Klauehand; Krallenhand

51

English	German
clean catch urine specimen *A urine specimen obtained by having a patient cleanse the perineal area prior to voiding in a collection device.*	Mittelstrahlurin
clear *Lucid.*	klar
clear *Transparent.*	durchsichtig
clear one's throat, to *To cough lightly in attempt to speak more clearly.*	sich räuspern
clearance *The process of removing something.*	Klärung
cleavage *A sharp division or demarcation.*	Spaltung; Furchung
cleft lip *A congenital abnormal opening of the lip.*	Lippenspalte
cleft palate *A congenital abnormal opening in the palate.*	Keifer-Gaumen-Spalte
cleidocranial dysostosis *A congenital condition exhibited by abnormal ossification of the cranial bones and absence of clavicles.*	kleidokraniale Dysostose
cleidotomy *A procedure used in difficult deliveries in which the clavicle is broken to facilitate childbirth.*	Kleidotomie
click *A sound heard by the sudden closure of a heart valve.*	Click
clinic *A building where patients are evaluated.*	Klinik
clinical record *The ongoing medical summary.*	Krankenakte
clinical examination *Physical assessment data.*	klinische Untersuchung
clitoris *A small erectile body in the anterosuperior aspect of the vulva.*	Klitoris
clockwise *Movement in the same direction as a normal clock.*	Uhrzeigersinn
clonic *Referring to a spasm that alternates in rigidity and relaxation.*	klonisch
closed	geschlossene
closed reduction *The realignment of a fracture without use of surgery.*	geschlossene Reposition
clot *A thrombus or embolus.*	Thrombus
clubbing *Increase in the mass of the soft tissue of the terminal phalanges.*	Trommelschlägelfinger
cluster headache *A unilateral, severe, recurrent headache.*	Clusterkopfschmerz
cnemial *Referring to the shin.*	tibial
coagulation *The formation of a clot.*	Koagulation; Gerinnung
coarctation of the aorta *A stricture, as in narrowing of the aorta.*	Aortenisthmusstenose
coated tablet *A pill covered with a substance to slow absorption or reduce gastric irritation.*	Manteltablette
cobalt *A metal that with causes polycythemia with increased ingestion.*	Kobalt
cocaine *A highly addictive opiate derivative.*	Kokain
cocaine addiction *Physical habituation to cocaine.*	Kokainabhängigkeit
coccus *A spherical shaped bacterium.*	Coccus; Kokke
coccydynia *Coccygeal pain.*	Kokzygodynie
coccyx *The small bone formed by the natural fusion of rudimentary vertebrae.*	Steißbein
cochlea *The essential organ of hearing which is in a spiral form.*	Cochlea; Schnecke
cock-up splint *A splint used to maintain the wrist in dorsiflexion; used for carpal tunnel syndrome.*	Handgelenkschoner
cockroach *A bettlelike insect with long legs and antennae.*	Küchenschabe
cod *A large marine fish, also called codfish.*	Kabeljau
codeine *A morphine derived analgesic.*	Codein
codon *A series of three nucleotides that form a unit of genetic code.*	Kodon
coffee-ground emesis *Black vomitus with appearance of ground coffee.*	Kaffeesatzartiges Erbrechen

English	German
cog wheel *As in cogwheel rigidity which is a jerky passive movement after there was increased tone.*	Zahnradphänomen
cognition *The process of acquiring thought or understanding.*	Kognition
cognitive disorders *Any disease process that involves altered cognition.*	Kognitionsdefizite
coitus *Sexual intercourse between members of the opposite sex.*	Koitus
cold *Having a sense of being cold.*	kalt
cold sore *A perioral blister caused by herpes simplex.*	Herpes-simplex-Virus
cold *Viral upper respiratory tract infection.*	Erkältung
colectomy *Surgical removal of part of the colon.*	Kolektomie
colic *Acute abdominal pain.*	Kolik
colitis *Inflammation of the colon.*	Kolitis
collagen *The principal supportive protein bone, skin, tendon and cartilage.*	Kollagen
collapse *A physical or mental breakdown.*	Kollaps
collarbone *Common term for the clavicle.*	Schlüsselbein
collodion *A product of the breakdown of colloid.*	Kollodium
colloid *A solution used for infusion, such as albumin or hetastarch, that are more likely to remain in the intravascular space than crystalloids.*	Kolloid
coloboma *A congenital defect that involves a fissure of the eye.*	Kolobom
colon *The portion of the large intestine that goes from the cecum to the rectum.*	Kolon; Colon
colonoscopy *Inspection the color, ideally to the cecum, with a lighted scope.*	Kolonoskopie; Dickdarmspiegelung
color blindness *The inability to distinguish colors.*	Farbenblindheit
color chart *A card used to check for color blindness.*	Färbeindex
color of conjunctiva *A point of assessment to check for pallor.*	Bindehautfarbe
colostomy bag *A pouch attached to the skin with a mild adhesive that collects stool emitted from a colostomy.*	Kolostomiebeutel
colostomy *Surgically creating an opening in the colon that is extended to outside the abdominal wall.*	Dickdarmafter; Kolostomie
colostrum *The fluid secreted by the mammary glands a few days around parturition.*	Kolostrum
colpitis; *vaginitis Inflammation of the vagina.*	Kolpitis; Scheidenentzündung
colpocele *A hernia into the vagina.*	Kolpozele
colporrhaphy *A surgical procedure that involves suturing the vagina.*	Kolporrhaphie
colposcope *A scope used to visualize the vagina.*	Kolposkop
colposcopy *Use of a scope to visualize the vagina and cervix.*	Kolposkopie
coma *A state of unconsciousness.*	Koma
comatose *Referring to a coma.*	komatös
comb	Kamm
comedones *The medical term for blackheads.*	Mitesser
commensal *Living in or on another organism without being a detriment.*	kommensal
comment *A remark providing an opinion.*	Bemerkung
common *That which is usual.*	gemeinsam
compatible *To coexist without problems.*	verträglich
compendium *A concise summary about a subject.*	Handbuch

English	German
complaint *Grievance.*	Klage
complement fixation test *A laboratory test for the presence of an antibody in the serum that involves inactivation of the complement in the serum.*	Komplementbindungsreaktion
complete blood count *An assay that includes white blood cell, red blood cell, platelet count, hemoglobin, hematocrit and white blood cell differential.*	Blutstatus
compliance *The act of going along with a plan.*	Volumendehnbarkeit
comply, to *Adhere to.*	einwilligen
compound *A substance formed by covalent union of two or more atoms.*	zusammengesetzt
compound fracture *Open fracture.*	offener Fraktur
comprehension *Understanding.*	Verständnis
compression *Squeezing together.*	Kompression
concavity *The state of being concave.*	Wölbung
concentration *The quantity of a substance per unit volume.*	Konzentration
concentric *Referring to circles or arcs that share the same center.*	konzentrisch
conception *The act of an egg being fertilized by sperm.*	Konzeption; Empfängnis
concha *A part of the body that is spiral shaped. Nasal concha are the small bones in the sides of the nasal cavity.*	Muschel
concretion *A hard solid mass.*	Konkrement
concussion *Head trauma resulting in temporary loss of consciousness.*	Konkussion; Erschütterung
condom *A covering for the penis or the vagina (female condom) used during sexual intercourse that is meant to reduce the chance of pregnancy or infection.*	Kondom
condyle *A rounded protrusion of a bone.*	Kondylus
condyloma *A warty papule near the anus or vulva.*	Kondylom
cone *A light sensitive cell in the retina.*	Konus
confabulation *The fabrication of experiences to compensate for memory loss.*	Konfabulation
confidence *Self-assurance.*	Vertrauen
confinement *Confined to bed.*	Bettlägerigkeit
conflict *Dispute or disagreement.*	Konflikt
confusion *Disorientation.*	Verwechslung
congenital *A disease or anomaly present from birth.*	kongenital
congenital heart disease *A cardiac disorder present prior to birth.*	angeborener Herzfehler
congenital syphilis *Passed to the child in utero, the child may have failure to thrive, fever and a flattened bridge of the nose.*	angeborene Syphilis
congestive	kongestive
congestive heart failure *A diminished cardiac output leading to passive engorgement.*	Stauungsinsuffizienz
conjugate diameter *A pelvic inlet measurement used to determine whether a woman is capable of delivering a fetus vaginally.*	Beckenausgangsdurchmesser
conjunctiva *The membrane that lines the eyelid.*	Konjunktiva; Bindehaut
conjunctival reflex *Closure of the eyes in response to irritation of the conjunctiva.*	Konjunktivaireflex
conjunctivitis *Inflammation of the conjunctiva.*	Bindehautenzündung
consanguinity *The relationship by blood.*	Blutsverwandtschaft

English	German
conscious *Being award and being able to respond to one's surroundings.*	bewusst
consensual light reflex *Constriction of the pupil of one eye in sync with the other pupil upon exposure to light.*	konsensueller Lichtreflex
conservative *Control rather than elimination of a disease.*	konservativ
consistent *Compatible with something or congruous with.*	konsistent
consolidation *An area of fixed secretions in the lung.*	Konsolidierung
constipation *A condition exhibited by difficulty in having a bowel movement due to hard stools.*	Obstipation; Darmträgheit; Verstopfung
constriction *Circumferential tightening*	Abschnürung; Konstriktion; Einschnürung
contact *The touching of two bodies or a person who has been exposed to a contagious disease.*	Kontakt; Berührung
contact lens *A lens that fits over the cornea to correct refractive errors.*	Kontaktlinse
contagious *Description of a disease that can be spread by direct or indirect contact.*	ansteckend; kontagiös
contaminate, to *To make impure by exposing to an polluted agent.*	verunreinigen
content *What something is made up of.*	Inhalt; Gehalt
contraceptive *A device or medication used to prevent pregnancy.*	Kontrazeptivum
contradictory *Two elements that are inconsistent.*	gegensätlich
contraindication *A situation in which two elements are inconsistent.*	Gegenanzeige
contusion *An area of broken capillaries in the skin causing discoloration; commonly called a bruise.*	Kontusion
convenient *Opportune or well-timed.*	geeignet
conversion reaction *When referring to a psychiatric condition it is the exhibition of physical symptoms as a manifestation of mental disease.*	Konversionsneurose
convex *Having an exterior curved the outside of a sphere.*	konvex
convulsion *An involuntary series of tonic and clonic movements.*	Konvulsion
cool *Chilly or cold.*	kalt; kühlen
cope with a situation, to	einer Lage gewachsen sein
copper *A chemical element with atomic number of 29.*	Kupfer
copra itch *A pruritis noted in people working with copra (dried kernel from a coconut).*	Krämerkrätze
copulation *Sexual relations.*	Kopulation
cor pulmonale *Heart disease that is secondary to lung disease.*	Rechtherzhypertrophie (bezogen auf Lungenkrankheit)
coracoid *A prominence on the scapula to which the biceps is attached.*	Korakoidfortsatz
cord compression *Pressure being applied to the spinal cord.*	Rückenmarkkompression
cord presentation *The presence of the umbilical cord at the cervix during active labor.*	Nabelschnurvorfall
core *Central part of a structure.*	Kern
cornea *The transparent segment located at the anterior part of the eye.*	Kornea
corneal *Referring to the cornea.*	korneal
corneal reflex *Closure of the eyelids when the cornea is touched lightly with a soft material. Also called the lid reflex.*	Hornhautreflex
corneal transplant *Surgical replacement of a cornea with a donor cornea.*	Hornhauttransplantation
coronal suture *The line of intersection of the frontal bone and the two parietal bones.*	Koronar

55

English	German
coronary angiography *Roentgenographic visualization of the coronary vessels after injection of dye.*	Koronarangiographie
coronary occlusion *A blockage in a coronary artery.*	Koronarverschluss
coronary vessel *Referring to a coronary artery.*	Herzkranzgefäß
coroner *A person who investigates sudden or suspicious deaths.*	Leichenbeschauer
coronoid *Crown-shaped.*	koronoid
corpulence *Fatness.*	Beleibtheit
corpus callosum *A point of connection between the two cerebral hemispheres.*	Großhirnbalken
corpus luteum *A structure that is discharged from an ovary; it degenerates if it is not impregnated.*	Gelbkörper des Eierstocks
corpuscle *A red or white blood cell.*	Korpuskel
cortex *An external layer.*	Kortex; Rinde
cortical *Referring to the cortex.*	kortikal
corticosteroid *A hormone developed in the adrenal cortex.*	Kortikosteroid
corticotropin *A hormone of the adrenal cortex.*	Kortikotropin
cortisol *An adrenal cortical hormone, also called hydrocortisone.*	Kortisol
cortisone *An adrenal cortical hormone responsible for carbohydrate regulation.*	Kortison
coryza *An acute condition exhibited by copious nasal discharge.*	Schnupfen
cost *The fee or penalty.*	Rippe; Kosten
costochondritis *Inflammation of the rib and or its cartilage.*	Rippenknorpelentzündung
cotton wool *Raw cotton.*	Watte
cotton wool spots *Condition characterized by blue or white discoloration on the retina related to nerve ischemia.*	Cotton-Wool-Herde
cough *Forceful expulsion of air from the lungs.*	Husten
coughing fit *An episode of prolonged, forceful coughing.*	Hustenanfall
count, to *To determine a number.*	zählen
cowpox; vaccinia *A viral disease of cows that was used for an original smallpox vaccine.*	Kuhpocken
cow's milk	Kuhmilch
coxalgia *Pain in the hip.*	Koxalgie
crab louse *Phthirus pubis is formal name for a louse that infests pubic hair and causes intense itching.*	Filzlaus
crack one's knuckles *Moving the fingers side to side or with flexion in such a manner to cause a popping or crackling sound.*	Fingerknacken
crackles or rales *A crackling noised noted while auscultating the lungs.*	Entfaltungsknisterm
cradle *A bed for an infant.*	Wiege
cramp *A painful contraction of muscles.*	Krampf
cranial mononeuropathy III *Dysfunction of the third cranial nerve causes double vision and eyelid drooping.*	Kranial Mononeuropathie III
cranial mononeuropathy VI *A disorder of the sixth cranial nerve causes double vision.*	Kranial Mononeuropathie VI
cranial *Referring to the skull.*	Kranial
cranioclast *An instrument used to crush a fetal skull.*	Kranioklast
craniopharyngioma *A tumor that originates in the hypophyseal stalk.*	Kraniopharyngiom; Erdheim-Tumor

English	German
craniosynostosis *Closure of the sutures of the skull that occurs prematurely.*	Kraniosynostose
craniotabes *Softening of the skull bones causing widened sutures; this occurs in rickets.*	Kraniotabes
craniotomy *Surgical creation of a hole in the skull.*	Kraniotomie
cranium *The skeleton of the head.*	Schädel
craving *An unusually strong urge for something.*	Verlangen
craw-craw *A pruritic papular skin eruption sometimes caused by Onchocerca.*	Onchozerkose
creatine *A compound involved with muscle contraction.*	Kreatin
creatinine *A compound excreted in the urine that is produced by the metabolism of creatine.*	Kreatinin
Credé's maneuver *Manual pressure over the bladder to assist in expression of urine in an atonic bladder.*	Credé Handgriff
cremasteric reflex *Retraction of the testicle and scrotum upon stroking of the ipsilateral inner thigh.*	Kremasterreflex
crenotherapy *A form of treatment from mineral springs.*	Krenotherapie
crepitus *A noise heard when one auscultates the lungs that is similar to the sound of rubbing hair between one's fingers. It is also considered the sound of two broken bones rubbing together.*	Krepitation; Knochenreiben
cretinism *A chronic condition caused by diminished thyroid hormone secretion.*	Kretinismus
crevice *A narrow opening.*	kleiner Riss
cribriform *Like a sieve; the olfactory nerves pass through the cribriform plate of the ethmoid bone.*	kribrifrom
cricoid cartilage *The ring-shaped cartilage of the larynx.*	Ringknorpel; Ringförmig
cripple *A person with a physical disability; not used in polite society.*	Krüppel
crisis *A turning point in the treatment of a disease.*	Krise
Crohn's disease *An inflammatory bowel disease.*	Crohn Krankheit
cross-infection *Transfer of infection between individuals, each with a different organism.*	Mischinfektion
cross-matching (blood) *Evaluation of blood to determine compatibility between the donor and recipient prior to transfusion.*	Blutprobenauskreuzung
cross-section *A transverse section through a specimen or structure.*	Querschnitt
croup *An acute laryngeal condition that is accompanied by a hoarse, barking cough.*	Krupp
cruciform *Shaped like a cross.*	kreuzförmig
crural; femoral *Referring to the femur or leg.*	krural
crush syndrome *Rhabdomyolysis occurring as a result of muscle injury from mechanical stress.*	Crush-Syndrom
crust *Dried serous exudate covering a wound.*	Kruste; Borke
crutch *Long metal or wooden stick used for support while walking.*	Krücke
cryesthesia *Abnormal sensitivity to cold.*	Kälteempfindung; Kryäasthesia
cryosurgery *The application of extreme cold to destroy tissue.*	Kryochirurgie
cryotherapy *The use of cold for therapeutic purposes.*	Kryotherapie
cryptococcal meningitis *A meningeal infection associated with AIDS.*	Kryptokokkenmeningitis
cryptorchism *A condition characterized by the failure of the testes to descend into the scrotum.*	Kryptorchismus
cryptosporidiosis *A parasitic related diarrhea seen in AIDS.*	Kryptosporidose

English	German
crystalloid *A substance that can pass through a semipermeable membrane; not a colloid.*	Kristalloid
crystalluria *The presence of crystals in the urine.*	Kristallurie
CSF *Abbreviation for cerebrospinal fluid.*	Liquor cerebrospinalis
CT scan *Computerized axial tomography.*	Computertomographie
cubital fossa *The bend at the elbow.*	Ellenbogengrube
cuffed endotracheal tube *A cannula that has an balloon on the tip that can be inflated with air and placed into the trachea.*	Manschettentubus
culdoscopy *Examination of the female pelvic viscera with a scope inserted through the posterior vaginal fornix.*	Kuldoskopie
culture *The growth of bacteria in artificial medium.*	Kultur
culture broth *A medium used to grow bacteria.*	Kulturmedium; Nährboden
cumulative effect *A consequence of successive additions.*	kumulative Wirkung
cuneiform *The three bones between the navicular bone and the metatarsals.*	keilförmig
curare *A toxic botanical substance used at one time in poison darts in South America. Curare derivatives have been used in general anesthesia.*	Curare
curative *A remedy capable of healing completely.*	Heilmittel
cure *A remedy for a medical illness.*	Heilung; Kur
curettage *Removal of tissues from a cavity.*	Kürettage
curette *The instrument used during a curettage.*	Kürette
current *Flow or stream.*	Strom; Fluss
currently *Presently.*	zur Zeit
Cushing's syndrome *Characterized by trunkal obesity, moon face, acne, abdominal striae, hypertension, decreased carbohydrate tolerance, protein catabolism, psychiatric disturbances, and osteoporosis.*	Cushing-Syndrom
cushion *A pillow or stuffed pad used to sit on.*	Kissen
cut *An incision.*	Schnitt
cutaneous *Referring to the skin.*	kutan
cuticle *The dead skin at the base of the toenail or fingernail, also called the eponychium.*	Oberhaut
cyanocobalamin *Also called B12; used to treat pernicious and other macrocytic anemias.*	Cyanocobalamin
cyanosis *Bluish discoloration of the skin and mucous membranes.*	Zyanose
cyclical vomiting *Periods of recurrent vomiting with no apparent pathologic cause and the person has a normal state of health between the episodes.*	zyklisch Erbrechen
cyclitis *Inflammation of the ciliary body.*	Zyklitis; Ziliarkörperentzndung
cyclodialysis *The surgical creation of a communication between the anterior chamber of the eye and the suprachorodial space for the purpose of treating glaucoma.*	Zyklodialyse
cycloplegia *Paralysis of the ciliary muscle.*	Zykloplegie
cyclothymia *Manic-depressive tendencies.*	Zyklothymie
cyclotomy *Surgically creating an opening in the ciliary body.*	Zyklotomie
cystadenoma *Adenoma associated with cysts of neoplastic origin.*	Kystadenom
cystectomy *Surgical removal of a cyst or the bladder.*	Zystecktomie
cystic *Referring to a cyst.*	zystisch

English	German
cystic duct *The duct connecting the gallbladder to the common bile duct.*	Ductus cysticus
cystic fibrosis *A congenital disorder exhibited by abnormal thick mucous which leads to problems in the intestines, pancreas and lungs.*	zystische Fibrose; Mukoviszidose
cysticercosis *The state of being infected with a type of tapeworm.*	Zystirzerkose
cystinosis *A congenital disorder of increased cystine that leads to renal insufficiency, rickets and dwarfism.*	Cystinose
cystinuria *The presence of cystine in the urine.*	Zystinurie
cystitis *Inflammation of the urinary bladder.*	Zystitis; Blasenentzündung
cystocele *Protrusion of the urinary bladder through the vaginal wall.*	Zystolzele; Blasenhernie
cystography *Roentgenographic visualization of the urinary bladder after insertion of contrast media.*	Zystographie
cystolithiasis *Presence of a calculus in the urinary bladder.*	Zystolithiasis
cystoscope *A device used to visualized the urinary bladder.*	Zystoskop
cystoscopy *Direct visualization of the urinary bladder with a cystoscope.*	Zystoskopie
cytology *The study of cells, their function and structure.*	Zytologie
cytoplasm *The protoplasm of the cell except for the nucleus.*	Zytoplasma
cytotoxic *Referring to being harmful to cells.*	zytotoxisch
cytotoxin *That which is harmful to cells.*	Zellgift
dacryoadenitis *Inflammation of the lacrimal gland.*	Dakryoadenitis
dacryocystitis *Inflammation of a lacrimal sac.*	Dakryozystitis
dacryocystorhinostomy *Surgical reaction of a communication between the lacrimal sac and nasal cavity.*	Dakryozystorhinostomie
dacryolith *A stone in the lacrimal sac or duct.*	Dakryolith
dandruff *Dead skin found in the hair.*	Kopfgrind; Kopfschuppen
dark adaptation *Adjustment to low light by reflex dilation of the pupil.*	Dunkeladaptation
date of admission *Beginning date of hospitalization.*	Zullasungdatum
date of birth	Geburtsdatum
daughter	Tochter
De Quervain tenosynovitis *Inflammation of the tendons of the wrist including the abductor pollicis longus and extensor pollicis brevis.*	Tendovaginitis de Quervain
dead *Deceased.*	tot
dead space *The area in the respiratory tract where air is not exchanged.*	Totraum
deadline *Cutoff date.*	Termin
deaf *Absence of the sense of hearing.*	taub
deaf-mute *Inability to hear or speak.*	taubstumm
deafness *Having impaired hearing.*	Taubheit
death *The action of dying.*	Tod
debility *Physical weakness.*	Debilität
debridement *Trimming the dead tissue adjacent to a wound.*	Wundausschneidung
decade *Ten years.*	Jahrzehnt
decapitate, to *The physical separation of the head from the body.*	dekapitieren
decerebrate rigidity *Rigid extension of the arms which is an abnormal posture associated with increased intracranial pressure.*	Dezerebrationsstarre; Enthirnungsstarre
decerebrate *The removal of the brain.*	Gerhirn entfernen
decibel *A unit used in the measurement of sound.*	Dezibel

English	German
decidua *The mucous membrane lining the uterus during pregnancy.*	decidua
deciduous teeth *The first teeth.*	Milchgebiß
decline *A decrease in status or health.*	Verfall
decompensation *The inability of an organ to respond to functional overload.*	Dekompensation
decompression *The surgical procedure relieving pressure on a part.*	Dekompression
decrease *Becoming smaller or fewer.*	Abnahme
decubitus ulcer *A wound caused by laying in one position for too long; also referred to as a pressure ulcer.*	Kekubitus
decussation *An area of intersection.*	Kreuzung
deep *Having significant depth.*	tief
deep tendon reflex *Reflexes exhibited by the stretching of a tendon.*	Tiefenreflex
deep vein thrombosis (DVT) *A blood clot that forms within a vein, typically in the lower extremities.*	tief Venenthrombose
deer tick *Ixodes scapularis.*	Hirschzecke
defecation *The discharge of feces from the rectum.*	Defäkation
defect *A shortcoming or imperfection.*	Defekt
defibrillator *A device used to convert an abnormal cardiac rhythm (ventricular fibrillation) into a normal rhythm with use of electrical stimulation.*	Defibrillator
deficiency *Insufficiency or deficit.*	Defizienz
deformity *A malformation or imperfection.*	Deformität
deglutition *The process of swallowing.*	Deglutition; Schluckakt
dehydration *The status of having a decrease in total body water.*	Dehydratation
delirium *An acute mental state exhibited by altered thought processes and restlessness.*	Delirium
delirium tremens *A condition seen when alcohol is withdrawn which is exhibited by restlessness, hallucinations and tremors.*	delirium tremens
deliver, to *To give birth.*	entbinden
deltoid *A term referring to "three". The deltoid muscle has its origin at three areas: clavicle, acromion, and spine of the scapula.*	Deltoideus
delusion *A belief that is contradictory to rational thought.*	Wahn; Täuschung
delusional *Referring to a delusion.*	wahnhaft
demanding *Requiring a lot of skill or requiring a lot of others.*	anspruchsvoll
demarcation *Having a fixed boundary.*	Demarkation
dementia *A chronic brain disorder exhibited by memory loss, personality changes and faulty reasoning.*	Demenz
demography *The study of the structure of human populations.*	Demographie
demulcent *Something that relieves irritation or inflammation.*	Linderungsmittel
demyelinating disease *A condition characterized by the loss of myelin.*	Entmakungskrankheit
dendrite *Impulses are transmitted along a dendrite to a nerve cell body.*	Dendrit
denervate, to *To remove nerve supply.*	entnerven
dengue *A mosquito-borne viral disease exhibited by fever and joint pain.*	Denguefieber
density *The denseness of an object.*	Dichte
dental *Referring to teeth.*	dental
dental calculus *Calcium phosphate and carbonate adhered to the teeth.*	Zahnstein

60

English	German
dental caries *Decay of teeth.*	Zahnkaries
dentatum *Also referred to as dentate nucleus of cerebellem.*	Dentatusnukleus
dentist *A professional capable of treating diseases of the teeth and gums.*	Zahnarst
dentition *The natural teeth.*	Zahnen
denture *A frame that holds artificial teeth.*	künstliches Gebiß
deny, to *To reject or repudiate.*	verweigern
deoxyribonucleic acid (DNA) *The carrier of genetic information.*	Desoxyribonukleinsäure
depilatory *An agent used to remove hair.*	Enthaarungsmittel
depressed *Melancholy.*	deprimiert
depressed skull fracture *Concave fracture deformity of the skull.*	Schädelmpressionsfraktur
depression *A medical condition exhibited by profound despondency.*	Depression
deprivation *The lack of a necessity.*	Deprivation
dermatitis *Non-specific inflammation of the skin.*	Dermatitis
dermatography *A description of the skin.*	Dermographie
dermatologist *A physician specializing in dermatology.*	Dermatologe
dermatology *The medical profession involving the treatment of skin conditions.*	Dermatologie
dermatome *The area of sensation of the skin supplied by a single posterior spinal root.*	Dermatom
dermatomycosis *An infection of the skin by Trichophyton, Microsporum or Epidermophyton fungi.*	Dermatomykose
dermatomyositis *Inflammation of the skin, subcutaneous tissue and adjacent muscle.*	Dermatomyositis
dermatophyte *A fungal parasite living on the skin.*	Dermatophyt; Haupilz
dermatosis *Any skin disease.*	Dermatose
dermis *The "true skin" that lies beneath the epidermis.*	Dermis; Haut
dermographia *A raised, pale line with hyperemic borders is elicited upon scratching the skin with a dull instrument, in this condition.*	Dermographie
dermoid cyst *An abnormal growth containing hair follicles, skin and sebaceous glands.*	Dermoidzyste
descending *Moving toward the inferior portion.*	absteigend
desensitize, to *To gradually expose a person to an offending agent to prevent an abnormal response upon a secondary exposure.*	desensibilisieren
desiccation *The act of drying up.*	Austrocknung
desmoid *A tumor typically found in the abdomen which contains. muscle and connective tissue.*	Desmoid; Fibromatose
despite *Notwithstanding.*	trotz
desquamation *The shedding of skin in flakes or sheets.*	Abschuppung; Desquamation
deterioration *Worsening in one's medical condition.*	Verschlechterung
detoxification *The process of removing toxins from the body.*	Entgiftung
detrimental *Harmful.*	nachteilig
detritus *Particulate matter produced by the decomposition of an organic substance.*	Detritus
detrusor urinae *Smooth muscle fibers that extend from the urinary bladder to the pubis.*	Detrusor urinae
deuteranomaly *Abnormal color vision sometimes called "green weakness".*	Deuteranomalie

English	German
deviated septum *Characterized by deviation of the nasal septum.*	Nasenscheidewandverkrümmung
deviation *Away from the norm.*	Deviation; Abweichung
dexter; *right; straight; erect*	rechts; dexter
dextran *A high glucose polymer used as a plasma substitute.*	Dextran
dextrocardia *Location of the heart in the right hemithorax.*	Dextrokardie
dhobie itch *So called because the contact dermatitis is caused by the soap used by laundry workers in India who are called "dhobie".*	Wäscherkrätz
diabetes insipidus *Caused by a deficiency in vasopressin, it is exhibited by great thirst and large volume urine output (and normal blood sugar).*	Diabetes insipidus
diabetes mellitus *A disease exhibited by a deficiency of the pancreatic hormone insulin.*	Diabetes mellitus
diabetic *A person who has diabetes mellitus.*	Diabetiker
diabetic neuropathy *Pain and burning initially in the feet, associated with diabetes mellitus.*	diabetische Neuropathie
diagnostic *A specific symptom or characteristic.*	diagnostisch
diapedesis *The outward passage of blood elements through an intact vessel wall.*	Diapedese
diaper *Undergarment worn to absorb urine in incontinent persons.*	Windel
diaper rash *Macular rash in the inguinal/perineal region related to exposure to urine.*	Windelerythem
diaphoretic *Exhibited by profuse perspiration.*	Diaphoretikum
diaphragm *The muscular separation between the thoracic and abdominal cavities.*	Diaphragma; Zwerchfell
diaphragmatic hernia *Protrusion of visceral contents through the diaphragm.*	Zwerchfellhernie
diaphysis *The central part of a long bone.*	Diaphyse
diarrhea *Increase in frequency and a loose consistency of the stools.*	Diarrhö; Durchfall
diarthrosis *An articulation allowing free movement.*	Diarthrose
diastase *Amylase.*	Diastase
diastole *The period of dilatation of the heart; between the first and second heart sounds.*	Diastole
diathermy *The use of heat produced from high-frequency electric currents to medically or surgically treat someone.*	Diathermie
diathesis *A medical tendency to develop a specific condition.*	Diathese
die, to *To stop living, to expire.*	sterben
diet *The kinds of food a person eats.*	Diät
dietitian *A professional who works with diet and nutrition.*	Diätetiker
differential *A term used to refer to the various options for diagnoses.*	Differential
differential diagnosis *A list of possible alternative diagnoses for a patient who is ill.*	Differentialdiagnose
differential leukocyte count *The percentage of different types of leukocytes.*	differentiell Leukozytenzählung
digestion *The process of enzymatic breakdown of food in the alimentary canal.*	Verdauung
digit *Finger.*	Finger; Zahl
digitalis *Cardiac medication derived from the leaf of Digitalis purpurea.*	Digitalis
dilatation *The process of becoming wider or larger.*	Erweiterung

62

English	German
dilator *An instrument that dilates.*	Dilatator; Dehner
dilution *The process of making a weaker solution.*	Verdünnung
dimercaprol *A medication used as a binding agent for heavy metal poisoning.*	Dimercaprol
dioptre *Referring to refraction or transmitted and refracted light.*	Dioptrie
dioxide *A compound containing two oxygen atoms.*	Dioxid
diphtheria *A contagious bacterial disease characterized by a grey membrane on the pharynx along with respiratory or cutaneous symptoms; caused by Corynebacterium diphtheriae.*	Diphtherie
diplegia *The paralysis of both arms or both legs.*	Diplegie
diplococcus *A bacterium that occurs in pairs including pneumococcus and Neisseria gonorrhoeae and Neisseria meningitidis.*	Diplokokkus
diploid *A nucleus containing two complete sets of chromosomes.*	diploid
diplopia *Double vision.*	Diplopie
dipsomania *Twins that are joined at some part of their bodies.*	Dipsomanie
dirty *Unclean.*	schmutzig
disability *Decreased or impaired mental or physical ability.*	Unfähigkeit
disaccharide *A type of sugar that yields two monosaccharides upon hydrolysis.*	Disaccahrid
disappearance *An instance of something/someone gone missing.*	Verschwinden
disarticulation *The separation or amputation of a joint.*	Exartikulation
discharge, ear *Otic secretions.*	Ohrenfluß
discharge, nasal *Nasal secretions.*	Nasensekret
discharge, postpartum vaginal *The secretions noted after delivery.*	Lochien
discharge, vaginal *Vaginal secretions.*	Scheidenausfluß
discharge date *The day a patient is released from the hospital.*	Entasslungdatum
discomfort *A feeling of physical or mental unease.*	Unwohlsein
discrete *Separate and distinct.*	einzeln
disease *Malady or disorder.*	Krankheit; Morbus; Erkrankung
disease outcome *The response obtained from treatment.*	Ergebniskrankheit
disequilibrium *The absence of stability.*	Gleichgewichtsstörung
disinfectant *A substance that kills bacteria.*	Desinfektion
dislocation *The displacement of a bone when referring to an articulation.*	Dislokation
disorder *Impairment.*	Unordnung; Störung
disorientation *Mental confusion.*	Desorientierung
displacement *Movement from normal position.*	Verlagerung
disrobe, to *To remove clothing.*	ausziehen
dissecting aneurysm *A condition in which blood is present between the layers of an artery.*	dissezierendes Aneurysma
dissection *Autopsy or postmortem exam.*	Leichensektion
dissemination *To be spread or dispersed widely.*	Dissemination
dissolution *Disintegration.*	Auflösung
distal *Situated away from the center of the body.*	distal
distended bladder *Urinary bladder filled beyond the normal capacity.*	gebläht Harnblase
distension *Swollen.*	Aufblähung

English	German
distichiasis *Presence of two rows of eyelashes on one eyelid which are turned inward toward the globe.*	Distichiasis
distribution *The manner in which something is shared or spread out.*	Verteilung
diuresis *Increased excretion of urine.*	Diurese
diuretic *Medication which causes an increased excretion of urine.*	Diuretikum
diurnal *Occurring during the day.*	am Tage vorkommend; diurnus
diverticulitis *Inflammation of the diverticulum.*	Divertikulitis
diverticulosis *Presence of diverticulum.*	Divertikulose
diverticulum *A sac or pouch created by herniation of a mucous membrane in the alimentary canal.*	Divertikel
diver *A person who swims in deep water.*	Taucher
dizygotic twins *Twins from two separate zygotes (non-identicle twins).*	zweieiige Zwillinge
dizziness *Sensation of losing one's balance.*	Benommenheit; Schwindel
DNA Deoxyribonucleic acid. *The hereditary material in humans and almost all other organisms.*	Desoxyribonukleinsäure
DNR Do not resuscitate. *The term used to indicate a person should not have life sustaining measures taken if they were to have cardiopulmonary arrest.*	Anordnung zum Verzicht auf Wiederbelebung
donor *Referring to a person who donates tissue or an organ.*	Spender
dopa reaction *A dopa-oxidase reaction, changing dopa into melanin.*	Dopareaktion
dopamine *An intermediate product in the creation of norepinephrine.*	Dopamin
dorsal *Referring to the back or back surface.*	dorsal
dorsal root *A description of the site of ganglion found on the dorsal root of each spinal nerve.*	Hinterwurzel
dorsiflexion *Backward bending of the foot or hand.*	Dorsalflexion
dorsum *The back part.*	Rücken
dosage *The amount and frequency a medication is given.*	Dosierung
dose *The quantity of a medication.*	Dosis
dose, maintenance *The chronic dose given after the initial bolus.*	Erhaltungsdosis
dosing interval *The number of times per unit a medication is given.*	Dosisintervall
double *Twice the size, quantity or strength.*	doppelt
douche *Cleansing of a canal; unless otherwise specified it refers to cleansing of the vaginal canal.*	Dusche
Douglas' pouch *A recess in the peritoneum between the rectum and the uterus. Also called the rectouterine pouch.*	Douglasscher Raum
down *In a lower position.*	hinunter
Down's syndrome *A congenital chromosomal defect (trisomy 21) that causes diminished intellectual function, short stature and a broad face.*	Trisomie-21-Syndrom; Down Syndrom
drainage tube *A cannula used to allow outflow of fluids.*	Schlauchdrainage
drape *The fabric used as a sterile covering in the OR.*	Operationsabdecktuch
drastic *Having significant effect.*	drastisch
dream *The thoughts or images occurring during sleep.*	Traum
dressing *The gauze applied to a wound.*	Verband
dribbling of urine *Slow, drip-by-drip urine flow.*	Nachträufeln des Urins
drill *Cylindrical metal tool uses for creating a hole in bone in surgery.*	Bohrer
drink, to *To imbibe.*	trinken
drinking water *Water clean enough to ingest orally.*	Trinkwasser
drop *A single bit of fluid as in a drop seen while giving IV fluids.*	Tropfen

English	German
drop by drop *Expression meaning little by little.*	tropfenweise
drop foot gait *A gait characterized by dragging the foot, as there is no ankle dorsiflexion; usually associated with steppage gait.*	Steppergang
drop foot *The symptom in a person with a nerve injury causing impaired ankle dorsiflexion.*	Fallfuß
dropper *A device used to administer medicines one drop at a time.*	Pipette
drops per minute *Refers to iv fluid rate.*	Tropfen je Minute
drowning *The process of dying from submerging in and inhaling water.*	Ertrinken
drowsiness *Sleepiness.*	Schläfrigkeit
drug *A medication, sometimes with negative connotation.*	Medicakment; Droge
drug dependence *Addiction to a substance.*	Drogenabhängigkeit
drug eruption *A diffuse rash caused by a medication.*	Arzneimittelexanthem
drug reaction *Typically refers to an adverse effect of medication.*	Arzneimittelreaktion
drunk *Inebriated.*	Trunkenheit
dry *Absence of moisture.*	trocken
dry cough *A cough without sputum production.*	Reizhusten
dual diagnosis *Term used to describe the presence of alcohol/drug addicition associated with a psychiatric diagnosis such as depression.*	Dualdiagnose
duct *Hollow tubular tissue used to carry fluid from a secretory organ.*	Gang; Durchgang
ductus arteriosus *A fetal artery that communicates between the pulmonary artery and the descending aorta.*	Ductus arteriosus
dumping syndrome *Characterized by rapid bowel evacuation after eating in patients with prior gastric surgery.*	Dumpingsyndrom
duodenal *Referring to the duodenum.*	duodenal
duodenal ulcer *A defect in the lining of the first portion of the small bowel, typically caused by H. pylori.*	Ulcus duodeni
duodenectomy *Excision of the duodenum.*	Duodenektomie
duodenitis *Inflammation of the duodenum.*	Duodenitis
duodenum *The portion of the small bowel between the stomach and jejunum.*	Zwölffingerdarm
duplication *The process of duplicating something.*	Duplikation
Dupuytren's contracture *A disease of the palmar fascia causing a flexion contracture of the fourth and fifth fingers.*	Dupuytrensche Kontraktur
dura mater *The outermost covering of the brain and spinal cord.*	Dura mater
dust *Dry earthen particles found on the ground and surfaces.*	Stuab
dwarf *Abnormally small person.*	Zwerg
dysaphia *Altered sense of touch.*	Dysaphie
dysarthria *Difficulty in articulation of speech.*	Dysarthie
dysbarism *Condition caused by a change in pressure, noted most commonly among scuba divers.*	Dysbarismus
dyschezia *Pain experienced during defecation.*	Dyschezie
dyschondroplasia *The formation of cartilaginous and bony tumors near the epiphyses.*	Dyschondroplasie
dyscoria *A discordance in pupillary reaction.*	Dyskorie
dyscrasia *An abnormal condition, mostly referring to the blood.*	Dyskrasie
dysdiadocokinesia *The inability to arrest one motor response and substitute its opposite.*	Dysdiadochokinesie

English	German
dysentery *A severe form of diarrhea with blood and mucous in the stool.*	Dysenterie; Ruhr
dysesthesia *1. Impairment of the sense of touch. 2. The presence of persistent pain upon receiving a light touch.*	Dysästhesie; Mißempfindung
dysfunction *Abnormal function in a gland or body organ.*	Dysfunktion
dyshidrosis *Disregulation of sweating*	Dyshidrose
dyshidrotic eczema *A dermatitis characterized by vescicobullous lesions.*	Pompholyx
dyskinesia *Abnormal movement.*	Dyskinesie
dyslalia *The absence of comprehensible speech articulation.*	Dyslalie
dyslexia *Difficulty in learning or reading written language with no effect on intelligence.*	Dyslexie
dysmenorrhea *Pain during menstruation.*	Dysmenorrhöe
dyspareunia *Pain during sexual intercourse.*	Dyspareunie
dyspepsia *Indigestion.*	Dyspepsie
dysphagia *Difficulty in swallowing.*	Dysphagie; Schluckstörung
dysphasia *Difficulty in speaking caused by cerebral dysfunction.*	Dysphagie; Sprachstörung
dysplasia *The increase in organ size due to an increase in the number of abnormal cell types.*	Dysplasie
dyspnea *Difficult breathing.*	Dyspnöe
dystocia *Difficult birth caused by fetal position, narrow pelvis or lack of opening of the cervix.*	Dystokie
dysuria *Difficulty or pain upon urination.*	Dysurie
ear *The organ of hearing and balance.*	Ohr
ear infection *General term referring to otitis media or otitis externa.*	Otitis; Ohrenentzündung
ear, external *Auris externa.*	Ohr äußeres; Außenohr
ear, inner *Auris interna.*	Ohr inneres
ear, middle *Auris media.*	Mittelohr
ear-drum *Common term for tympanic membrane.*	Trommelfell
earache *Pain associated with the ear.*	Ohrenschmerz
earlobe *The soft, fleshy inferior portion of the pinna.*	Ohrläppchen
eat, to *To consume food.*	essen
eating disorder *General term for pathologic eating habits.*	Eßstörung
ecchondroma *Hyperplastic growth of cartilage on the surface of other cartilage.*	Ekchondrom
ecchymosis *Skin discoloration caused by bleeding beneath the epidermis.*	Ekchymose
Echinococcus *A tapeworm of the family Taeniidae that can cause hydatid cysts.*	Echinokokkus
echocardiography *The use of ultrasound waves to visualize the heart and its structures.*	Echokardiographie
echolalia *The meaningless repetition of the words spoken by another person.*	Echolalie
eclampsia *A maternal condition characterized by convulsions and hypertension that can lead to maternal and fetal death.*	Eklampsie
ecmnesia *Memory loss for recent events but retained memory of remote events.*	Ekmnesie
ectasia *Expansion or distension.*	Ektasie

English	German
ectoderm *The outermost layer of the three layers of the embryo.*	Ektoderm
ectopic *Abnormal position.*	ektopisch
ectopic pregnancy *A pregnancy that is not intrauterine.*	Gravidität extrauterine
ectrodactylia *A congenital anomaly exhibited by absence of one digit or part of a digit.*	Ektrodaktylie
ectropion *Eversion of the eyelid, usually the lower lid.*	Ektropion
eczema *A medical condition exhibited by pruritic, red, scaly patches on the scalp, cheeks and extensor surfaces.*	Ekzem
edema *Extravascular fluid accumulation.*	Ödem
edematous *Referring to the presence of edema.*	ödematös
education *Instruction or guidance.*	Erziehung
effector *An organ that responds to a stimulus.*	Effektor
efficacious *Effective.*	wirkungsvoll
effort *Attempt or endeavor.*	Anstrengung
effusion *The accumulation of fluid in a body cavity.*	Erguss
egg	Ei
egocentric *Thinking of self without considering the feelings or thoughts of others.*	egozentrisch
ehrlichiosis *A tickborne infectious disease.*	Ehrlichiose
ejaculation *The emission of semen at the moment of sexual climax in a male.*	Ejakulation
elastic bandage *A stretch gauze used for compression of an extremity.*	elastische Binde
elastin *A connective tissue-based glycoprotein.*	Elastin
elbow *The joint between the humerus and radius/ulna.*	Ellenbogen
elderly *Advanced in years.*	älter
elective *Non-urgent and not life-saving.*	elektiv
electrocardiogram *Display of a person's heart beat that can be used in the diagnosis of cardiac disorders.*	Elektrokardiogramm
electroconvulsive therapy (ECT) *The electrical stimulation of the brain to treat mental disorders.*	Elektrokrampftherapie
electrode *A device used to facilitate conduction of electricity to or from a body.*	Elektrode
electroencephalogram (EEG) *A display of brain waves used in the diagnosis of brain disorders, especially epilepsy.*	Elektroenzephalogramm
electrolyte *The ionized constituents including potassium, sodium, chloride and others.*	Elektrolyt
electromyography *The display of the electrical activity of muscle.*	Elektromyographie
electron microscope *A device that uses electron beams and lenses to give high magnification.*	Elektronenmikroskop
electrophoresis *The movement of charged particles in a fluid that is under the influence of an electric field. This is used in testing for various maladies in the form of serum protein electrophoresis.*	Elektrophorese
elephantiasis *A condition caused by nematode parasites leading to lymphatic obstruction and limb or scrotal swelling.*	Elephantiasis
elixir *A medical solution.*	Elixir
emaciation *Abnormally thin and weak.*	Auszehrung
embolectomy *The removal of an embolus.*	Embolektomie
embolus *A blood clot, air bubble or fatty deposit that cause obstruction of a vessel.*	Embolus

English	German
embryo *The term used to describe a fertilized ovum in the first 8 weeks of development.*	Embryo
embryology *The study of the embryo.*	Embryologie
emergence *Coming into prominence.*	Auftreten
emergency *An urgent, life-threatening situation.*	Notfall
emergency room *A ward used for initial treatment of critical patients.*	Notfallstation
emesis *Vomiting.*	Erbrechen
emesis basin *A small bowl used to catch vomitus.*	Brechschale
emetic *An agent that induces vomiting.*	Brechmittel
emmetropia *The normal correlation between eye refraction and the axial length of the eyeball.*	Emmetropie
emollient *Having softening or soothing qualities.*	Emolliens
emotion *An intense feeling.*	Gemütsbewegung
empathy *To be concerned for and share the feelings of another.*	Einfühlungsvermögen
emphysema *Abnormal enlargement of the airspaces distal to the terminal bronchioles.*	Emphysem
empty *Containing nothing.*	leer
empty sella syndrome *Compressed or flattened pituitary related to herniating arachnoid, surgery or radiotherapy.*	Syndrom der leeren Sella
empyema *A collection of purulent material in a body cavity, usually referring to a thoracic empyema.*	Empyem
emulsion *The dispersion of one liquid into another, but it is not dissolved.*	Emulsion
enarthrosis *The type of joint in which a spherical bone is set into the socket of another bone.*	Enarthrose
encephalic *Referring to the brain.*	Enzephalon
encephalitis *Inflammation of the brain.*	Enzephalitis
encephalocele *The protrusion of the brain through a defect in the skull.*	Enzephalocele
encephalography *Roentgenography of the brain.*	Enzephalographie
encephalomacia *Abnormal softness of the brain.*	Enzephalomazie
encephalomyelitis *Inflammation of the brain and spinal cord.*	Enzephalomylitis
encephalopathy *Degeneration of cerebral function.*	Enzephalopathie
enchondroma *An abnormal increase in cartilage growth on the inside of bone or of other cartilage.*	Enchondrom
encopresis *Involuntary defecation.*	Stuhlinkontinenz; Enkopresis
end organ *The encapsulated end of a sensory nerve.*	Endorgan
end point *The last stage of a process.*	Endzeitpuntk
end stage *Terminal stage. End stage cancer means there is no cure possible and death is imminent.*	Spätphase; terminale
endarteritis *Tunica intima inflammation.*	Endarteriitis
endemic *When a disease is commonly found in a location or in a people group.*	Endemie; endemisch
endocarditis *Inflammation of the endocardium.*	Endokarditis
endocervicitis *Inflammation of the mucosal lining of the cervix.*	Endometritis cervicis
endocrine gland *A gland that secrete hormones and other substances into the blood.*	endokrine Drüse
endocrine *Referring to glands that secrete hormones and other chemicals into the blood.*	endokrin

68

English	German
endocrinology *The study of endocrine glands and hormones.*	Endokrinologie
endoderm *The innermost layer of the embryonic germ cell layers.*	Endoderm
endogenous *Originating from within.*	endogen
endolymph *The fluid collection the labyrinth of the ear.*	Endolymphe
endometrioma *An isolated benign mass containing endometrial tissue.*	Endomitriom
endometriosis *Presence of uterine mucosal tissue in the pelvis in abnormal locations.*	Endomitriose
endometritis *Inflammation of the endometrium.*	Endometritis
endometrium *The mucous membrane lining of the uterus.*	Endometrium
endoneurium *The tissue in a peripheral nerve that separates the individual nerve fibers.*	Endoneurium
endoplasmic reticulum *A framework of tubules within the cytoplasm of eukaryotic cells.*	endoplasmatisches Retikulum
endorphin *Hormone secreted that activates the body's opiate receptors and acts as an analgesic.*	Endorphin
endoscope *A device used to view the interior of a hollow organ (sigmoidoscope, gastroscope)*	Endoskop
endothelioma *A mass that propagates from the endothelium of blood vessels, lymphatics or serous cavities.*	Endotheliom
endotracheal *Within the trachea.*	endotracheal
endow, to *To supply or provide for.*	ausstatten
enema *A procedure involving insertion of fluid into the rectum.*	Klistier
enkephalin *Peptide found in the brain that has similar effects as the endorphins.*	Enkephalin
enlargement *Becoming bigger.*	Vergrößerung; Erweiterung
enophthalmos *Posterior displacement of the eyeball in the orbit.*	Enophthalmus
enormous *Very large.*	riesig
enostosis *The abnormal bony growth inside a bone or on the cortex.*	Enostose
ensure, to *To make certain of.*	gewährleisten
ENT *Abbreviation for ears, nose and throat.*	Hals-, Nasen-, Ohren- (HNO)
enteral feeding *Nutrition supplied via the alimentary canal.*	enterale Ernährung
enterectomy *Surgical resection of part of the intestine.*	Enterektomie
enteric *Referring to the intestines.*	enteral
enteritis *Inflammation of the intestines.*	Enteritis
enterobiasis *An infection caused by worms from the genus Enterobius.*	Enterobiasis
enterococcus *A gram positive cocci that occurs naturally in the intestine but is pathogenic elsewhere in the body.*	Enterokokke
enterolith *A calculus of the intestine.*	Darmstein
enteroptosis *Inferior displacement of the intestines in the abdomen.*	Enteroptose
enterotomy *A surgical opening of the intestines.*	Enterotomie
entrapment neuropathy *Weakness or numbness caused by compression of a peripheral nerve.*	Nervenkompressionssyndrom
enucleation *Surgical removal of a globe.*	Enukleation
enuresis *Involuntary urination.*	Enurese; Einnässen
enzyme *A compound that acts as a catalyst for reactions within cells as assists with digestion outside of cells.*	Enzym; Ferment
eosinophil *A cell with eosin stain used to designate a type of leukocyte that is elevated during allergic reactions.*	Eosinophiler

69

English	German
eosinophilia *An increased number of eosinophils in the blood.*	Eosinophilie
ependyma *The glial lined covering of the cerebral ventricles and the central portion of the spinal cord.*	Ependym
ependymoma *A tumor composed of cells that line the ventricles of the brain.*	Ependymom
ephedrine *A chemical used to treat asthma because it expands bronchial passages and used to control spinal anesthesia associated shock because it constricts blood vessels.*	Ephedrin
ephemeral fever *A fever lasting no more than 24-48 hours.*	Eintagsfieber
epiblepharon *A condition exhibited by the eyelashes pressing against the eyeball.*	Epiblepharon
epicardium *The serous membranous, innermost lining of the pericardium.*	Epikard
epicondyle *A protrusion at the distal end of the humerus.*	Epikondylus
epicondylitis *Inflammation of the epicondyle.*	Epikondylitis
epicranium *The skin, fibrous layer (aponeurosis), and muscles lining the scalp.*	Epikranium
epidemic *Ubiquitous development of an infectious disease.*	Epidemie
epidemiology *The study of the incidence, development and control of disease.*	Epidemiologie
epidermis *The skin cells overlying the dermis.*	Epidermis
epidermophytosis *A fungal skin infection caused by an organism from the genus Epidermophyton.*	Epidermophytie
epididymitis *Inflammation of the duct that moves sperm from the testis to the vas deferens.*	Epididymitis
epididymo-orchitis *Inflammation of the epididymis and the testis.*	Epididymoorchitis
epidural *The space around the dura of the spinal cord.*	epidural
epidural anesthesia *Medication into this space produces analgesia for surgical procedures.*	Epiduralanästhesie
epidural hematoma *Formation of a collection of blood outside the dural layer of the brain; usually caused by trauma.*	Epiduralhämatom
epigastrium *The section of the abdomen that overlies the stomach.*	Epigastrium
epiglottis *Tissue at the base of the tongue that covers the trachea when one swallows.*	Epiglottis; Kehldeckel
epilation *Removal of hair and the roots.*	Epilation
epilepsy *A condition associated with abnormal brain activity and exhibited by sudden, recurrent convulsions, sensory disturbances and loss of consciousness.*	Epilepsie
epileptic seizure *A convulsion related to abnormal brain activity (as opposed to being precipitated by hypoglycemia.)*	Epileptischer Anfall
epileptiform *Being similar to epilepsy.*	epileptiform
epileptogenic *That which induces seizures.*	epileptogen
epinephrine *A hormone secreted by the adrenal gland.*	Epinephrin
epiphysis cerebri *A small structure situated on the mesencephalon between the two sections of the thalamus.*	Epiphyse cerebri
epiphysitis *Inflammation of the end of a long bone that is separated from the shaft by a cartilaginous disc.*	Epiphysitis
episcleritis *Inflammation of the tissue lying above the sclera.*	Episkleritis
episiotomy *A surgical incision of the vagina used to aid childbirth.*	Episiotomie; Dammschnitt

70

English	German
epispadias *A congenital condition characterized by the urethral meatus being at the superior aspect of the penis*	Epispadie
epistaxis *Bleeding emanating from the nose.*	Epistaxis; Nasenbluten
epithelial *Referring to the epithelium.*	epithelial
epithelial cast *Debris found in the urine composed of columnar renal epithelium.*	Epithelzylinder
epithelioma *A malignant tumor composed of epithelial cells.*	Epitheliom
epithelium *The tissue lining the skin and the gastrointestinal tract that is derived from the embryonic ectoderm and endoderm..*	Epithel
epitrochlea *The medial condyle of the humerus.*	Epitrochlea
equal *The same or uniform.*	gleich
equilibrium *When opposing forces are in balance.*	Aquilibrium; Gleichgewicht
equipment *Apparatus or instrument.*	Gerät; Ausstattung
ergometer *A device that measures energy expenditure.*	Ergometer
ergonomics *The study of workplace design that focuses on reducing work-related injuries.*	Ergonomie
ergosterol *A compound converted to vitamin D2 upon exposure to ultraviolet light.*	Ergosterin
erosion *The gradual destruction of surface tissue.*	Erosion
error *Mistake or inaccuracy.*	Fehler
eructation *Belch or burp.*	Eruktation
erysipelas *An acute infection caused by Streptococcus pyogenes that causes fever along with swelling and inflammation. The infection frequently effects the face or one leg.*	Erysipel
erythema mutliforme *A skin condition exhibited by purpuric lesions and bullae usually on the distal parts of extremities but can affect the face and trunk.*	Erythema exsudativum multiforme
erythema nodosum *The presence of red or purple nodules on the pretibial area.*	Erythema nodosum
erythroblast *A nucleus containing immature erythrocyte.*	Erythroblast
erythroblastosis fetalis *A hemolytic disease of the newborn.*	Erythroblastose fetalis
erythrocyanosis *A condition exhibited by purple patches with asymmetric swelling, pruritis and burning.*	Erythrozyanose
erythrocyte *Called a red blood cell, it transports oxygen and carbon dioxide to and from the tissues.*	Erythrozyt
erythrocytopenia *Low level of erythrocytes in the blood stream.*	Erythrozytopenie
erythrocytosis *A higher than normal level of erythrocytes in the blood stream.*	Erythrozytose
erythropoiesis *The production of red blood cells.*	Erythropoese
eschar *Dry, hard, dead tissue commonly seen with a chronic pressure ulcer or anthrax.*	Schorf
eserine *Physostigmine.*	Eserin; Physostigmin
esophageal *Referring to the esophagus.*	ösophageal
esophagectomy *Surgical removal of the esophagus.*	Ösophagektomie
esophagitis *Inflammation of the esophagus.*	Ösophagitis
esophagoscopy *Visual inspection the esophagus utilizing a scope.*	Ösophagoskopie
esophagus *The muscular tube that connects the throat to the stomach.*	Ösophagus; Speiseröhre
esotropia *Medial deviation of the eyes at primary gaze.*	Esotropie; Strabismus convergens; Einwärtsschielen

71

English	German
essential *Crucial or necessary.*	wesentlich
estrogen *A hormone involved with developing and maintaining female sexual characteristics.*	Estrogen; Östrogen
ethanol *Synonym for ethyl alcohol.*	ethanol
ethmoid bone *A bone at the root of the nose which has perforations for the olfactory nerves to transit.*	Siebbein
etiology *The underlying cause of a problem.*	Ätiolgie
eunuch *A man who has been castrated.*	Eunuch
euthanasia *Killing someone painlessly who is thought to have a terminal condition.*	Euthanasie
evacuation *The emptying of an organ of fluids or gas.*	Evakuierung
evaluation *Assessment or evaluation.*	Auswertung
eventration *Protrusion of the intestines from the abdomen.*	Eventration
eversion *To turn outward.*	Eversion
every *Each or all possible.*	jede
every day *Each day.*	jeden Tag
every other day *On alternate days.*	jeden zweiten Tag
evident *Obvious.*	offensichtlich
evisceration *The removal of bowels from the body.*	Eviszeration
evoked potential *Electrical impulses that can be noted after stimulation of sensory organs.*	evoziertes Potential
evulsion *Forcible extraction.*	Evulsion
exacerbation *Worsening of an existing problem.*	Exazerbation
examination *Assessment or evaluation.*	Untersuchung
exanthema *A rash that accompanies a disease or fever.*	Exanthem
excess *Surplus or overabundance.*	Exzeß
exchange transfusion *Treatment of hyperbilirubinemia in neonates.*	Austauschtransfusion
excipient *An inactive substance used to deliver an active substance.*	Arzneimittelträgersubstanz
excisional biopsy *Surgical removal of tissue for pathologic examination.*	Exstirpationsbiopsie
excoriation *Superficial loss of skin.*	Exkoriation; Abschürfung
excrement *Feces.*	Exkrement
excreta *Fecal material.*	Exkrete
exenteration *Complete surgical removal of an organ.*	Exenteration
exercise-induced dyspnea	Belastungsdyspnöe
exercised induce angina *Chest pain noted during exertion related to coronary artery disease.*	Belastungsangina
exfoliation *The shedding of scales.*	Abschuppung; Exfoliation
exhumation *The process of removing a dead body from a grave.*	Exhumierung
exogenous *Referring to external factors.*	exogen
exomphalos *Umbilical hernia.*	Exomphalos; Nabelschnurvorfall
exostosis *A bony prominence growing from the surface of a bone.*	Exostose
exotoxin *A toxin released from a living cell.*	Exotoxin
exotropia *A type of strabismus that is characterized by the eyes turned outward.*	Exotropie Strabismus externus; Auswärtsschielen
expansion *Enlargement or increase in size.*	Expansion
expect, to *To suppose or presume.*	abwarten

English	German
expectorant *A substance that promotes the secretion of sputum.*	Expektorans
expectoration *The presence of sputum that has been coughed out.*	Expektoration
expiration date *The date when a medication should no longer be used.*	Ablaufdatum
expiratory *Referring to exhalation of air from the lungs.*	expiratorische
expiratory reserve volume *Amount of air left in the lung after a maximal exhalation, in liters.*	expiratorisches Reservevolumen
exploratory laparotomy *Abdominal surgery with the intent of examining the abdominal contents.*	Probelaparotomie
expulsion *Evacuation or elimination.*	Expulsion; Austreibung
expulsion of placenta *Passage of the placenta out the cervix after childbirth.*	Plazentaaustreibung
extend, to *To expand or stretch out.*	dehnen
extension *Going from a bent to straight position.*	Streckung
extensor plantar response *Great toe extension indicating a positive Babinski sign.*	Babinskisches Zeichen
extensor *Referring to the extension of an extremity or part of an extremity.*	Extensor; Streckmuskel
external ear canal *Auditory canal.*	äußerer Gehörgang
external *Outside of the body.*	äußerlich
extirpate, to *To totally destroy.*	ausrotten
extracapsular *Situated outside a capsule.*	extrakapsulär
extracellular *Outside the cell.*	extrazellulär
extract *A substance in a concentrated form.*	Extrakt
extrapyramidal tract *Motor nerves that are not part of the pyramidal tract.*	extrapyramidales System
extrasystole *Either a premature atrial or ventricular contraction.*	Extrasystole
extravasation *Referring to a situation in which blood or fluid goes out of a vessel it is normally flowing into.*	Blutaustritt
extremity *Refers to one arm or one leg.*	Extremität
extrinsic *Coming from outside or external sources.*	extrinsisch
extubation *The removal of a tube that was in a body orifice.*	Extubation; Extubieren
exudate *The fluid, cells, and debris found in the tissues or a cavity (like pleural space) during inflammation.*	Exudat
eye drops *Liquid applied to eyes for various medical problems.*	Augentropfen
eyebrow *Supercilium.*	Augenbrau
eyeglasses *Eye wear used for cosmetic or prescription purposes.*	Augengläser
eyeground *The fundus that is visualized with an ophthalmoscope.*	Augenhintergrund
eyelash *Each of the short hairs on the eyelid.*	Augenwimper.
eyelid *Palpebra.*	Augenlid.
eyesight *A person's ability to see.*	Sehkraft
face *Anterior aspect of the head from the forehead to the chin.*	Gesicht
face presentation *Referring to the part of the body coming out of the cervix first during childbirth.*	Gesichtslage
facet *A small flat surface of a bone.*	Facette
facial nerve *Cranial nerve VII that supplies the face and tongue.*	Nervus facialis
facial paralysis *Lack of movement or sensation in the distribution of the facial nerve.*	Fazialislähmung

73

English	German
facial reflex or bulbomimic reflex *Pressure on the eyeballs causes contraction of facial muscles on the side contralateral to the side of the lesion in the patient in a coma. In coma from a metabolic problem the reflex is present bilaterally.*	bulbomimischer Reflex; Mondonesi-Reflex
facies *A facial expression that is typical for a particular disease.*	Facies
faint *Weak and dizzy.*	schwach
fair *Equitable.*	unparteiisch
falciform *Referring to something that is curved. The falciform ligament attaches the liver to the diaphragm.*	falciform
fallopian tubes *Either of a pair of long narrow ducts located in a female's abdominal cavity that transport the male sperm cells to the egg.*	Eileiter; Tuba uterina
Fallot, tetrology of *Congenital cardiac defects including ventricular septal defect, pulmonic valve stenosis or infundibular stenosis, and dextroposition of the aorta.*	Fallotsche Tetralogie
falx cerebri *A fold in the dura that separates the two cerebral hemispheres.*	Hirnsichel
familial *Referring to the family*	familiär
family	Familie
family history *A review of past medical history of related persons.*	Familienanamnese
family planning *Birth control.*	Familienplanung
Fanconi's syndrome *An idiopathic refractory anemia exhibited by pancytopenia, bone marrow hypoplasia and congenital anomalies.*	Fanconi-Syndrom
faradism *The gradual increasing and decreasing of the amplitude of electricity.*	Farardisation
farmer's lung *Coined because farmers are susceptible to this disease by inhaling fungi from hay; also called Aspergillosis.*	Farmerlunge
fart, to *Slang term for releasing flatus.*	furzen
fascia *The fibrous sheath enclosing a muscle or organ.*	Faszie
fascicle *A bundle of nerve or muscle fibers.*	Faszikel
fasciculation *Involuntary contraction of muscle fibers.*	Faszikulation; faszikuläre Zuckung
fasciitis *Inflammation of a fascia.*	Fasciitis
fasciotomy *Incision into a fascia.*	Fasziotomie
fasting *Absence of caloric intake for a specified period.*	nüchtern; Fasten
fat *A greasy or oiling substance naturally occurring in the body.*	Fett
fat embolism *A deposit of fat that obstructs a vessel.*	Fettembolie
fatal *Lethal.*	verhängnisvoll
fatigue *Tiredness and exhaustion.*	Ermüdung
fatty *Greasy or oily.*	fettig
fatty acid *A carboxylic acid occurring as a an ester in fats and oils.*	Fettsäure
favus *Tinea capitis caused by Trichopyton schoenleini.*	Favus
fear *Fright or trepidation.*	Furcht
febrile *Presence of an supraphysiologic temperature.*	febril
fecal impaction *The presence of hard excrement in the rectum that requires manual removal.*	Kotstein
feces *Excrement.*	Fäzes
fecundity *The capability of producing offspring quickly and frequently.*	Fruchtbarkeit

English	German
feeble-minded *Antiquated term used to describe a person unable to make seemingly simple decisions because of a cognitive impairment.*	schwachsinnig
feeding behavior *How a child is tolerating breast or cup feeding.*	Ernährungverhalten
feel better, to *To have improved health symptomatically.*	bessergehen
feel, to *To perceive or discern.*	sich fühlen
Felty syndrome *Rheumatoid arthritis with leukopenia and splenomegaly.*	Felty-Syndrom
female *Feminine.*	weiblich
feminine pad *Gauze specially designed to absorb menstrual flow.*	Menstruationsbinde
femoral artery *Continuation of the external iliac to the popliteal artery.*	Oberschenkelarterie
femoral nerve *Supplies the motor function of the quadriceps and the sensation over the anterior and medial thigh.*	Oberschenkelnerv
femoral triangle *An area that is bordered by the sartorius muscle, the adductor longus muscle and the inguinal ligament.*	femoral Dreieck
femur *The long bone in the thigh.*	Oberschenkelknochen
fenestration *Usually referring to a surgical window.*	Fensterung
fertility *The ability of a person to contribute to contraception.*	Fruchtbarkeit
fertilization *The melding of male and female gametes to form a zygote.*	Befruchtung
fester, to *To become infected.*	eitern
festinating gait *Walking with increased speed involuntarily; often seen in Parkinson's disease.*	schlurfender Gang; Trippelgang
fetal alcohol syndrome *A condition caused by acohol use by the mother during pregnancy and exhibited by poor intrauterine growth, decreased muscle tone, delayed development and widened palpebral fissures.*	Alkoholembryopathie
fetal distress *Term used to describe an abnormal heart rate or rhythm in a fetus indicating the need for urgent childbirth.*	Fetal distress
fetal heart tone *Refers to the cardiac rate and pattern of the fetus.*	kindliche Herztöne
fetal monitor *Device used to monitor fetal heart rate and rhythm.*	Wehenschreiber
fetal movements *Sensations by the mother of fetal activity.*	Kindsbewegungen
fetal position *Refers to how the fetus lies within the uterus.*	Kinds-Lage
fetal *Referring to the fetus.*	fetal
fetichism *The glorification of an inanimate object.*	Fetischismus
fetor *A foul odor.*	Foetor
fetus *Medical term for the infant prior to birth.*	Fötus
fever *A temperature above the normal range.*	Fieber
fibrillation *Uncoordinated, ineffective contraction as in atrial fibrillation.*	Flimmern
fibrin *An insoluble protein formed when fibrinogen is acted upon by thrombin.*	Fibrin
fibroadenoma *A benign breast mass composed of fibrous and glandular tissue.*	Fibroadenom
fibroblast *A collagen producing cell in connective tissue.*	Fibroblast
fibrochondritis *The inflammation of a structure composed of cartilage and fibrous tissue.*	Faserknorpelentzündung
fibroelastosis *The abnormal increase in growth of fibrous and elastic tissue.*	Fibroelastose

English	German
fibroid *A benign mass, typically uterine, composed of fibrous and muscle tissue.*	Fibroid
fibromyoma *A mass containing fibrous and muscle tissue.*	Fibromyom
fibrosarcoma *A sarcoma composed primarily of malignant fibroblasts.*	Fibrosarkom
fibrosis *Connective tissue that is scarred and thickened after injury.*	Fibrose
fibrositis *Fibrous connective tissue that is inflammed.*	Fibrositis
fibula *The smaller of two bones in the lower leg.*	Fibula; Wadenbein
Fifth disease *Erythema infectiosum is a viral disease caused by parovirus B19.*	Fünfte Krankheit; Ringelrötein
filaria *A parasitic nematode worm that is transmitted by flies and mosquitos causing filariasis.*	Filarie
file *Patient record or folder.*	Akte
filiform *Threadlike.*	filiform; fadenförmig
filum terminale *The thin structure at the end of the conus medullaris which connects the spinal cord with the coccyx.*	Filum terminale
fimbria *A slender projection at the end of the fallopian tube near the ovary.*	Fimbrie
finger *Any of the five digits on the hand.*	Finger
finger agnosia *The inability to distinguish which finger is being touched.*	fingeragnosie
finger nose test *A test for dysmetria in which a person reaches out to touch their own nose with an extended finger with their eyes closed.*	Finger-Nasenversuch
fingerstick device *A device used to project a lancet into the skin so a drop of blood can be obtained for analysis.*	Fingerstichverrichtung
fingertip *Distal aspect of a finger.*	Fingerspitze
fingernail *Thin horny plate over the dorsal aspect of the end of finger.*	Fingernagel
finger-thumb reflex *Opposition and adduction of the thumb with flexion at the MCP joint and extension at the interphalangeal joint when there is flexion of the 3rd, 4th, and 5th finger. This is present normally and absent with with pyramidal lesions.*	Mayerscher Grundreflex
Finkelstein test *Pain elicited with thumb flexion and wrist flexion is indicitive of De Quervain tenosynovitis.*	Finkelstein-Reaktion
firm *Hard or unyielding.*	fest
first aid *The intial treatment after an injury.*	Erste Hilfe
fish *A cold-blooded vertebrate with gills and fins.*	Fisch
fissure *A general term for a cleft or deep groove. An anal fissure, for example, is a small ulcer adjacent to the anus.*	Fissur; Spalt
fist *When a person has their fingers clenched tightly to the palm.*	Faust
fistula *An abnormal communication between two organs or an organ and the skin, as in rectovaginal fistula.*	Fistel
fixation *1. An obsessive interest. 2. The securing of a body part.*	Fixierung; Bindung
flaccid *Limp. A term applied to an extremity one cannot move actively.*	schlaff
flagellation *1. The protrusion found on flagella. 2. Massage administered by tapping a body part with fingers.*	Flagellation
flagellum *A slender appendage that allows protozoa to swim.*	Geißel; Flimmer
flail chest *The term used when one has multiple rib fractures causing a segment of the chest wall to move incongruently with the rest of the chest wall.*	Flatterbrust
flame photometer *A device used to measure the intensity of light.*	Flammenphotometer

76

English	German
flap *A term used to describe a piece of tissue partially excised and placed over an adjacent surface.*	Lappen
flare-up *A sudden worsening one's condition.*	Aufflackern
flask *A narrow-necked container.*	Kolben; Flasche
flat *Level or even; without bulges.*	flache; eben
flatfoot *Common term for pes planus.*	Plattfuß; Senkfuß
flatten, to *To make even.*	abflachen
flatulence *The gas expulsed from the anus.*	Flatulenz; Blähung
flatus *Term for air that is expelled from the anus.*	Flatulenz; Blähung
flatworm *A class of worms that includes parasitic flukes and tapeworms.*	Plathelminthe; Plattwurm
flea *A small wingless insect that feeds on blood of mammals.*	Floh
flesh *The tissue between the skin and bones.*	Fleisch
flexor *A muscle that bends an extremity or part of an extremity.*	Flexor; Beuger
flexure *The action of bending.*	Flexur; Biegung
flight of ideas *Streams of unrelated ideas noted in a manic phase.*	Gedankenflucht
floating *Bouyant or suspended.*	fluktuierend
flow *Movment in a continuous stream.*	Fluß; Strom
fluid intake *The amount of oral consumption plus the amount of intravenous fluids administered.*	Flüssigkeitslunge
fluke *Parasitic nematode worm; an example is Schistosoma.*	Trematode
fluoresceine *A fluorane dye used to check for corneal ulcers.*	Fluoreszein
fluorescent antibody test (FTA test)	Fluoreszenztest
fluorescent screen *A screen used to view x-rays.*	Röntgenschirm
fluoridation *The addition of fluorine to something.*	Fluorierung
fluorine *A chemical that causes severe burns if exposed to the skin.*	Fluor
fluoroscopy *The continuous viewing of roentgenographic images with a fluorescent screen.*	Durchleuchtung
flush, to *Term used to describe an irrigation procedure, as in flushing an NG tube.*	reizen
flushing *Transient erythema due to heat, stress or disease.*	Gesichtsrötung
flutter *Used to describe a cardiac rhythm disturbance, as in atrial flutter.*	Flattern
foam *A mass of small bubbles in a liquid.*	Schaum
Foley catheter *A drainage tube placed in the urinary bladder via the urethra.*	Foley Urethralsonde
folic acid *Also called pteroylglutamic acid; a deficiency can cause megaloblastic anemia.*	Folat; Folsäure
follicle stimulating hormone (FSH) *An anterior pituitary gland hormone responsible for production of sperm or ova.*	Follikelreifungshormon
follicular *Referring to a small secretory gland.*	follikulär
fontanelle or fontanel *The space between the bones in the skull that are separate at birth.*	Fontanelle
food *Nutrition.*	Nahrung
food intake *Quantitative record of nutritional intake.*	Nahrungsmittelaufnahme
food poisoning *Poisoning where the active agent is in the food.*	Lebensmittelvergiftung
foot *The lower extremity distal to the ankle.*	Fuß

77

English	German
foot and mouth disease *A contagious viral disease exhibited by oral and digital vesicles.*	Maul- und Klauenseuche
foot drop *Caused by palsy of the nerve controlling foot dorsiflexion.*	Fallfuß
foramen *An opening in a bone.*	Foramen; Loch
foramen magnum *The hole in the skull that the spinal cord passes through.*	Foramen magnum
foramen ovale *A hole in the atrial septal wall in a fetus.*	Foramen ovale
forced vital capacity *Vital capacity measured as the patient is exhaling as rapidly as possible.*	forciertes Vitalkapazität
forced expiratory volume per second (FEV1) *The amount of air exhaled with maximal effort, measured in liters, over one second.*	Sekundenkapazität
forceps *A surgical instrument, commonly called tweezers.*	Zange; Pinzette
forearm *Segment of the arm from the elbow to wrist.*	Unterarm
forearm crutch *A long stick with a place for a hand-grip to aid in ambulation when there is lower extremity weakness.*	Unterarmkrücke
forebrain *The part of the brain that includes the thalamus, hypothalamus and cerebral hemispheres.*	Vorderhirn
forehead *Section of the face from the hairline to the eyebrows.*	Vorderhaupt; Stirn
foreign bodies *Term used to describe objects found in a body orifice that are not part of the body.*	Fremkörper
forensic *Referring to the scientific method of studying crime.*	forensisch
foreskin *Also called prepuce, the skin that naturally covers the glans but can be rolled back.*	Vorhaut
former *Prior.*	ehernalig
formulary *A list of medicines that are permissible to prescribe.*	Medikamentenverzeichnis
fornix *A vaulted structure.*	Gewölbe
forwards *Towards the front.*	vorwärts
fossa *A shallow depression.*	Grube
fourchette *The fork shaped fold of skin where the labia minora meet superior to the perineum.*	kleine schamlippe Frenulum
fovea *The area on the retina where the visual acuity is optimal.*	Fovea
Foville's syndrome *Caused by a lesion within the pons, there is ipsilateral facial and abducens nerve paralysis and contralateral hemiplegia.*	Foville-Syndrom
fracture *A broken bone.*	Kraktur; Bruch
fracture, avulsion *A broken bone associated with a ligament or tendon pulling a piece of the bone away.*	Abrißfraktur
fracture, closed *A broken bone where there is no break in the skin.*	geschlossene Fraktur
fracture, comminuted *A broken bone where one segment overrides the other.*	Splitterfraktur
fracture, depressed *The presence of concavity associated with a fracture as in a depressed skull fracture.*	Impressionsfraktur
fracture, greenstick *A spiral fracture.*	Grünholzfraktur
fracture, open *A fracture in which there is a break in the skin and bone is exposed.*	offene Fraktur
fracture, pathologic *A fracture due at least in part to another condition, such as a fracture at a location where there is bone cancer.*	Spontanfraktur
fracture, stress *A fracture associated with overuse.*	Streßfraktur

English	German
fragilitas ossium *A condition exhibited by excessively brittle bones. Also called osteogenesis imperfecta.*	Osteogenesis imperfecta
framboesia; yaws *An endemic tropical disease caused by Treponema pertenue.*	Frambösie
free *Lacking or absent.*	frei
free from *Without or clear of.*	frei von
freezing (as in ambient temperature) *Below 0 Celsius.*	unter Null
fremitus *A vibration that is appreciated with palpation.*	Fremitus
frenulum *The tissue that connects the inferior portion of the tongue to the base of the mouth.*	Zungenbändchen
frequency *Rate of occurrence.*	Frequenz; Häufigkeit
fress reflex *Chewing and sucking movements elicted by stimulation of the face and lips.*	Freßreflex
friction *Grating or rasping.*	Reibung
friction rub *A noise heard during cardiac auscultation in patients with pericarditis, for example.*	Reibegeräusch
frog *A tailless amphibian that is short with long hind legs for jumping.*	Strahl
frog in the throat, to have *An expression describing hoarseness.*	Heiserkeit
frontal *Referring to the anterior aspect, as in frontal lobe.*	frontal
frontal sinus *A paranasal sinus on both sides of the lower part of the frontal bone.*	Sinus frontalis; Stirnhöhle
frost itch *A pruritis noted when exposed to cold weather.*	Hiemalisdermatitis
frostbite *Local tissue destruction after exposure to cold.*	Erfrierung; Frostbeule
froth *Covered with a mass of small bubbles.*	schäumend
froth at the mouth, to *To have a mass of saliva with small bubbles in it coming out of the mouth.*	Schaum vor dem Mund haben
frozen *Past participle of to freeze. Freeze: turn a liquid into a solid.*	gefroren
frozen shoulder *Common term for adhesive capsulitis.*	Schulteersteife
fructosuria *Presence of fructose in the urine.*	Fruktosurie
FTA test *Fluorescent treponemal antibody test for syphilis.*	Fluoreszenz-Treponema-pallidum-Antikörper-Absorptions-Test
full-term *A normal length pregnancy.*	Reifgeborenes
fulminant *Sudden and severe.*	fulminante
function *An activity natural to a person or thing.*	Funktion
fundus oculi *Portion of the interior eyeball in the posterior aspect which can be viewed by an ophthalmoscope.*	Augenhintergrund
fundus of the stomach *Referring to the part of the stomach above the cardiac notch.*	Fundus gastrikus
fungicide *An agent that destroys fungus.*	Fungizid
fungus *A spore-producing organism that feeds on organic matter.*	Pilz
funiculus of the spinal cord *The white matter of the spinal cord that is further defined by location.*	Funiculus; kleiner Strang
funiculus, lateral *The lateral white colum of the spinal cord between the anterior and posterior nerve roots.*	Seitenstrang
funiculitis *Inflammation of the funiculi.*	Funikulitis
funnel chest *Anterior thorax funnel shaped depression, also called pectus excavatum.*	Trichterbrust
furuncle *A painful erythematous nodule with a central core.*	Furunkel

English	German
furunculosis *The presence of multiple furuncles.*	Furunkulose
fusiform *Spindle-shaped.*	spindelförmig
gag reflex *Contraction of the pharynx muscles when the back of the pharynx is stimulated by touch.*	Rachenreflex; Würgreflex
gait *The way one walks.*	Gewinn; Zunahme
galactocele *A milk-filled cyst in the mammary gland.*	Galaktozele
galactorrhea *Excessive production of milk.*	Galaktorrhö
galactose *A sugar that is a constituent of lactose.*	Galaktose
galactosemie *1. Galactose in the blood. 2. A congenital condition exhibited by impaired carbohydrate metabolism.*	Galaktosämie
gallbladder *The organ adjacent to the liver that stores bile and secretes it into the duodenum.*	Gallenblase
gallop *An abnormal heart sound.*	Galopprhythmus
gallstone *Calculus produced in the bile duct or gallbladder.*	Gallenstein
galvanism *The use of electric currents for medical treatment.*	Galvanismus
galvanometer *A device used to measure small electric currents.*	Galvanmeter
gamete *A germ cell that is able to unite with another germ cell of the opposite gender to form a zygote.*	Gamet
gamma globulin *A blood serum protein with little electrophoretic mobility.*	Gammaglobulin
gamma ray *A type of electromagnetic radiation.*	Gamma-Strahl
ganglionectomy *The removal of a benign swelling on a tendon sheath.*	Ganglionektomie
gangrene *Tissue death from either impaired blood flow or an infection.*	Gangrän
gaping *Wide open.*	klaffend
gargle, to *To rinse one's mouth out and exhale through the liquid.*	gurgeln
gargoylism *A congenital defect, also known as Hurler syndrome, it is characterized by skeletal anomalies, mental retardation and gargoylelike facial features.*	Pfaundler-Hurlersche Krankheit
gas gangrene *A life and limb threatening disorder caused associated with tissue death and caused by an anaerobic bacterium in the genus of Clostridium.*	Gasbrand
gastrectomy *Complete or partial surgical resection of the stomach.*	Gastrektomie
gastric lavage *Instillation and removal of large quantities of saline into the stomach in order to treat poisoning.*	Magenspülung
gastric *Referring to the stomach.*	gastrisch
gastric secretions *Fluids secreted from gastric mucosa.*	Magensaft
gastrin *Hormones that stimulates gastric secretions.*	Gastrin
gastritis *Inflammation of the stomach.*	Magenschleimhautentzündung
gastrocele *Protrusion of part of the stomach in the form of a hernia.*	Magenhernie
gastrocnemius *A large muscle in the lower leg, responsible for ankle plantar flexion, that is attached to the distal femur and achilles tendon.*	zweiköpfiger Wadenmuskel
gastrocolic reflex *Peristalsis of the colon produced by food entering the stomach.*	Gastrokolischreflex
gastroduodenal ulcer *A lesion in the mucosal lining of the stomach or duodenum.*	gastroduodenales Ulkus
gastroenteritis *A bacterial or viral infection that leads to vomiting and diarrhea.*	Gastroenteritis
gastroenterostomy *A surgical opening in the stomach or intestine.*	Gastroenterostomie

English	German
gastrointestinal tract *The alimentary canal from the distal esophagus to the cecum.*	Gastrointestinaltrakt
gastrojejunostomy *A surgical procedure that directly connects the stomach to the jejunum.*	Gastrojejunostomie
gastropexy *Securing the stomach to the abdominal wall.*	Gastropexie
gastroscopy *Use of an endoscope to directly visualize the stomach.*	Gastroskopie; Magenspiegelung
gastrostomy *A surgical creation of an opening in the stomach.*	Gastrostomie
gauge *The size or thickness of something. An 18gauge needle.*	Maß
gauze *A fabric used for dressing changes.*	Gaze; Verbandmull
gavage syringe *A syringe used for irrigation.*	Sondenernährungspritze
gavage *The instillation of food into the stomach with use of a tube.*	Sondenernährung
gavage tube *A tube used for instillation of liquids into the stomach.*	Sondenernährungsonde
gaze *Steady, intent look.*	Blick
gel *A jellylike substance.*	Gel
gene *A unit of heredity that is passed on from parent to child.*	Gen
general *Common or expected.*	generell; allgemein
general appearance *The overall look of a patient.*	Allgemeinbefinden
genetic counseling *A discussion of the concerns related to genetic testing.*	genetische Beratend
genetic *Referring to genes or heredity.*	genetische
geniculate *Bent at a sharp angle.*	knieförmig
geniculate body *Protrusions on the thalamus that relay visual and auditory signals to the brain.*	Kneihöcker
geniculate ganglion *The sensory ganglion of the facial nerve.*	intumescentia Ganglioformis
geniculate neuralgia *Severe intermittent pain in the external ear and deep in the ear.*	Genikulatumneuralgie
genital ambiguity *A disorder of sexual development in which the genitalia are not sufficiently developed to tell clearly if the person is male or female.*	genital Unklarheit
genital herpes *A sexually transmitted infection caused by herpes simplex.*	Herpes genitalis
genital wart *The common term for Condylomata acuminata.*	Feigwarze
genitalia *Genitals.*	Geschlechtsorgane; Genitalien
genitourinary *Referring to the urinary system through the organs or urine excretion.*	urogenital
genome *A full set of genetic information for an organism.*	Genom
gentian violet *An antiseptic derived from rosaniline.*	Gentianaviolett
genu valgum *A condition exhibited by the knees turning inward, commonly referred to as knock-knee.*	Genu valgum; X-Bein
genu varum *A condition exhibited by the knees turning outward, commonly referred to as bowleg.*	Genu varum; O-Bein
GERD gastroesophageal reflux disease *A condition characterized by gastric contents being regurgitated into the esophagus or mouth.*	gastroösophagealer Reflux
geriatrics *The study of the health of old people.*	Geriatrie
germ *Microorganism.*	Keim
German measles *(rubella) A contagious viral infection.*	Röteln; Rubella
gerontology *The study of old persons.*	Gerontologie

English	German
Gerstmann syndrome *Finger agnosia, agraphia and acalculia caused by a lesion between the occipital region and angular gyrus.*	Gerstmannsyndrom
gestation *The development of a fetus from conception until birth.*	Schwangerschaft
giant *Huge or massive.*	riesig
giardiasis *A flagellate protozoa, Giardia lamblia, that causes diarrhea.*	Giardiasis
giddiness *A tendency to fall or dizziness.*	Schwindel
gingival *Referring to the gums.*	gingival
gingivitis *Inflammation of the gums.*	Gingivitis; Zahnfleischentzündung
ginglymus *A joint that allows movement in one direction only.*	Ginglymus;Scharniergelenk
glabella *The area of the forehead above and between the eyebrows.*	Glatze; Glabella
glance *A brief look at something.*	Blick
glans penis *The distal aspect of the penis.*	Eichel
glare *An angry stare.*	Blendung
Glasgow coma scale *A scale used to grade one's level of consciousness with a score of 3 being totally unresponsive and a score of 15 being normal.*	Glasgow-Komaskala
glaucoma *A condition characterized by increased intraocular pressure.*	Glaukom; grüner Star
glenoid *Referring to the fossa that is a shallow depression, such as the hollow of the scapula where the humeral head sets.*	glenoidal
glioma *A neural malignant tumor of glial cells.*	Gliom
gliomyoma *A mass with gliomatous and myomatous characteristics.*	Gliomyom
globus pallidus *A portion of the lentiform nucleus in the brain.*	Pallidum
glomerulonephritis *Inflammation of the renal glomeruli, usually from hemolytic streptococcus.*	Glomerulonephritis
glomerulus *A grouping of capillaries where waste is filtered from the blood.*	Glomerulum
glomus tumor *A reddish-blue painful papule that occurs on the distal aspects of the digits.*	Glomustumor
glossal *Referring to the tongue.*	Zungen
glossectomy *Surgical resection of the whole or part of the tongue.*	Glossektomie
glossitis *Inflammation of the tongue.*	Glossitis; Zungenentzündung
glossodynia *Tongue pain.*	Glossodynie
glossopharyngeal *The name for cranial nerve IX that supplies the tongue and pharynx.*	glossopharyngeal
glottis *Essentially the vocal structure, including the true vocal cords and the opening between them.*	Stimmritz
glove *A covering for hand protection.*	Handschuh
glove anesthesia *Absence of sensation of the hand and wrist.*	Handschuhanästhesie
glucagon *A pancreatic enzyme responsible for breakdown of glycogen to glucose.*	Glukagon
glucose tolerance test *The oral administration of a carbohydrate load and then evaluation of the blood sugar at timed intervals.*	Glukosetoleranztest
glue *Plastic cements*	Leim
glue sniffing addiction *Habituation of plastic cement fumes inhalation which includes toluene, xylene and benzene.*	Schnüffelsucht
gluteal *Referring to the gluteus.*	gluteal; glutäal
gluteal fold *The horizontal crease between the buttock and upper thigh.*	Afterfurche

82

English	German
gluteal or gluteus muscle *A paired set of three muscles, the gluteus maximus, medius and minimus, that all have origins in the ilium and insertions in the femur. (buttocks)*	Gesäßmuskel; Glutealmuskel
gluteal reflex *After the skin of the buttocks are stimulated the gluteal muscles contract.*	Glutealreflex
glycemia *The amount of glucose in the blood.*	Glykämie
glycerin *A byproduct in the manufacture of soap that is used as a laxative.*	Glycerin
glycogen *A compound that stores glucose and when it undergoes hydrolysis forms glucose.*	Glykogen
glycogenesis *The production of glycogen from glucose.*	Glykogenese
glycolysis *The production of energy and pyruvic acid when glucose is broken down by enzymes.*	Glykolyse
glycoprotein *A protein that has a carbohydrate attached to its polypeptide chain.*	Glykoprotein
glycosuria *Presence of glucose in the urine.*	Glykosurie
gnathic *Referring to the jaws.*	Kiefer
gnosia *Ability to recognize things and people.*	Gnosie
goblet cell *Aids in the secretion of respiratory and intestinal mucous.*	Becherzelle
goggles *Close fitting, protective eyeglasses.*	Brille
goiter *Swelling of the thyroid gland.*	Kropf; Struma
gold *Precious metal with atomic number of 79.*	Gold
gonad *A testis or an ovary.*	Keimdrüse; Gonade
gonadal dysgenesis *The lack of complete development of the gonads.*	Gonadendysgenesie
gonadotrophin *Pituitary hormone that promotes gonadal activity.*	Gonadotropin
gonococcus *A diploccocal bacteria that is the causative agent in gonorrhea, formally Neisseria gonorrhoeae.*	Gonokokke
gonorrhea *A sexually transmitted disease that is exhibited by purulent discharge from the vagina or penis.*	Gonorrhö; Tripper
gonorrheal arthritis *A type of arthritis caused by the gram negative diplococcus Neisseria gonorrhoeae.*	Arthritis gonorrhoica
gonorrheal ophthalmia *An acute purulent conjunctivitis that can occur in neonates within 2-5 days of birth.*	Gonoblennorhö
Goodpasture' syndrome *Glomerulonephritis, preceded by hemoptysis. The nephritis can quickly progress to death from renal failure.*	Goodpasture-Syndrom
goose bumps *Cutis anserina.*	Gänsehaut
gouge *A chisel with a concave blade used in surgery.*	Hohlmeißel
gout *Monosodium urate crystal deposition disease.*	Gicht
gown *A sterile gown used during surgical procedures.*	Operationskittel
grade *A level of rank or quality.*	Neugrad
Graefe's sign *Also called lid lag, a sign characterized by the upper eyelid not closing over the globe. This is seen commonly in exophthalmic goiter.*	Graefesches Zeichen
graft *A piece of tissue surgically transplanted.*	Transplantat; Implantat
gram *A unit of mass, 1/1000th of a kilogram.*	Gramm
granular layer *A deep layer of the cerebellum.*	Stratum granulosum
granulation tissue *Vascular connective tissue forming granular protrustions on the surface of a healing wound.*	Granulationsgewebe
granulocyte *A white blood cell with cytoplasmic secretory granules.*	Granulozyt

83

English	German
granuloma *A mass of granulation tissue.*	Granulom
grasp reflex *Flexion of the fingers or toes when stimulated.*	Greifreflex
Graves' disease *A form of hyperthyroidism exhibited by a goiter and exophthalmos.*	Basedowsche Krankheit
gravida *Pregnant.*	Schwangere
gray matter *The section of the brain and spinal cord composed of branching dendrites and nerve cell bodies.*	graue Substanz
greater than normal *Above normal.*	besser als die Norm
grief *Deep sorrow.*	Kummer
grip strength *Quantitative measurement of the force of a hand grip.*	Greifkraft
groan *A deep inarticulate sound made due to pain or despair.*	Stöhnen
groggy *Drowsy.*	wackelig
groin pull *A muscle strain in the inguinal region.*	Leistenverletzung
groin *The genital region.*	Leistengegend
gross *Distended; not well defined.*	aufgetrieben
ground itch *Marked pruritis caused by a hookworm larvae, known otherwise as cutaneous larva migrans.*	Bodenkrätze
growth *The increase in physical size.*	Wachstum
growth hormone-releasing factor *Released by the hypothalamus, it induces the release of somatotropin.*	wachstumshormon Releasing-Faktor
grunting *A low guttural sound used to describe a person with profound respiratory difficulty.*	Gegrunze
guaiac *A substance derived from guaiacum trees used to test for trace amounts of blood, in stool for instance.*	Guajak-Harz
guarding *A symptom used to describe a patient resisting an examination because of severe pain; often seen in patients with peritonitis.*	muskuläre Abwehrspannung
Guillain-Barré syndrome *An acute autoimmune disorder that causes nerve inflammation subsequently muscle weakness.*	Guillain-Barré-Syndrom
guinea worm infection *Caused by a parasitic nematode worm that lives under the skin, formally called Dracunculus medinensis.*	Drakunkulose
gum *Gingiva.*	Zahnfleisch
gum (chewing gum)	Kaugummi
gumboil *Swelling noted on the gingiva over a dental abscess.*	Parulis
gumma *A soft granulomatous tumor of the skin or cardiovascular system seen in tertiary syphilis.*	Gumma
gunshot wound *An penetrating injury sustained from a bullet.*	Schußwunde
gustatory agnosia *The loss of the sense of taste.*	geschmacklich Agnosie
gustatory *Referring to sense of taste.*	geschmacklich
guttural *Having a harsh quality; coming from the back of the throat.*	gutteral
gynecology *The branch of medicine associated with the reproductive system of women.*	Gynäklogie
gynecomastia *Enlargement of the breasts.*	Gynäkomastie
gyrus *Convolutions of the brain where there is infolding.*	Gyrus; Windung
habit *A custom or inclination.*	Gewohnheit; Angewohnheit
hair (of body)	Körperhaar
hair (of head)	Kopfhaar
hair cell *Epithelial cells with hairlike projections.*	Haarzelle

English	German
hair follicle *Tubelike invagination of the epidermis that the hair shaft develops from.*	Haarfollikel
hairy *A profuse amount of hair.*	Haarig
hairy tongue *Lingua villosa, a benign condition associated with antibiotic used caused by candida albicans infection.*	Glossotrichie; Haarzunge
half *Divided in two.*	halb
half-life *The time a drug decreases its effect in half over time.*	Halbwertszeit
halitosis *Foul odor eminating from the mouth.*	Mundgeruch
hallucination *A perception that is not based on reality.*	Halluzination
hallucinogen *A substance that elicits hallucinations.*	Halluzinogen
hallux valgus *Also called bunion, it is the lateral deviation of the great toe.*	Hallux valgus
hallux varus *Medial deviation of the great toe.*	Hallux varus
hamartoma *A nodule of superfluous tissue.*	Hamarton
hamate bone; uncinate bone *The medial bone in the distal row of carpal bones adjacent to the fifth metacarpal.*	Hamatum
Hamman-Rich syndrome *Idiopathic pulmonary fibrosis.*	Hamman-Rich-Syndrom
hammer toe *A condition characterized by extension of the proximal phalanx and flexion of the second and distal phalanges.*	Hammerzehe
Hampton maneuver *Rolling a patient during gastrointestinal fluoroscopy in order to obtain an air contrast of the antrum and duodenum.*	Hampton Handgriff
hamstrings *Tendons of the posterior thigh.*	Kniesehne
hand *The upper extremity distal to the wrist.*	Hand
hangnail *A loose piece of skin attached near the medial or lateral nail fold.*	Niednagel
Hanhart's syndrome *Also referred to as micrognathia with peromelia. There is hypoplasia of the mandible, malformed or missing teeth, birdlike face and severe upper extremity deformities.*	Hanhart-Syndrom
Hansen's disease *Leprosy*	Aussatz
haploid *Either a single set of chromosomes or a set of nonhomologous chromosomes.*	Haploid
hapten *The molecular component that determines immunologic specificity.*	Hapten
hard *Rigid or very firm.*	schwer
hard of hearing *Decreased sense of hearing.*	schwerhörig
harmless *Safe or benign.*	unbedenklich
hay fever *An allergy exhibited by pruritis of the eyes and nose, rhinorrhea and excessive lacrimal secretion.*	Heufieber
hazy *Cloudy.*	benebelt
head	Kopf; Haupt
head trauma *Any injury to the brain.*	Kopfverletzung
headache *Cephalgia.*	Kopfschmerzen
healing *The process of becoming healthy again.*	Heilung
health *The state of being free of illness.*	Gesundheit
health center *A physical location where patients are treated.*	Ärztezentrum
healthy *In good health.*	gesund
hearing *Auditory perception.*	Gehör; Hören

English	German
hearing aid *A device that fits in the ear used to amplify sound.*	Hörgerät
heart *Muscular organ that pumps blood thru the circulatory system.*	Herz
heart beat *A single contraction of the heart.*	Herzschlagen
heart block *An alteration in the cardiac electrical conduction system.*	Herzblock
heartburn *Synonym of pyrosis.*	Sodbrennen
heart lung machine *Device used during cardiac surgery to replace the function of the heart and lungs while surgery is performed.*	Herz-Lungemaschine
heart murmur *An abnormal heart sound usually related to valvular disease.*	Herzgeräusch
heart rate *Number or cardiac contactions per minute.*	Herzfrequenz
heat *The quality of being hot.*	Wärme; Hitze
heat exhaustion *A condition that occurs secondary to prolonged exposure to high ambient temperature; it is exhibited by subnormal temperature, dizziness and nausea.*	Hitzekollaps; Wärmeschaden
heat stroke *A condition caused by excessive exposure to high ambient temperature; it is exhibited by dry skin, thirst, vertigo, muscle cramps and nausea. The three forms are heat exhaustion, heat cramps and sunstroke.*	Hitzschlag
heavy *Possessing great weight.*	schwer
hebephrenia *A type of schizophrenia exhibited by hallucinations and inappropriate laughter.*	Hebephrenie
Heberden's node *Hard nodules formed at the distal interphalangeal joints in osteoarthritis.*	Heberden-Knötchen
hedonism *Devoting oneself to being happy.*	Hedonismus
heel *Proximal portion of the plantar aspect of the foot.*	Absatz; Ferse
heel-shin test (heel to knee to toe test) *A test of position sense and coordination; one moves the heel of one foot from the knee on the other foot down to the foot.*	Knie-Hacken-Versuch
height *Distance between the bottom of the foot and top of the head.*	Höhe
Heimlich maneuver *A forceful upward thrust to the diaphragm to dislodge an airway obstruction.*	Heimlich Handgriff
heliotherapy *Treatment of disease with sunlight.*	Heliotherapie
helium *An inert gas that is the lightest of the noble gases.*	Helium
helminth *A fluke, tapeworm or nematode.*	Eingeweidewurm; Helminthe
helminthiasis *Being infected by a helminth.*	Helminthiasis
hemagglutinin *An antibody that facilitates the agglutination of blood.*	Hämagglutinin
hemangioma *A benign tumor composed of blood vessels.*	Hämangiom; Blutschwamm
hemarthrosis *Presence of intra-articular blood.*	Hämarthrose
hematemesis *Vomiting blood.*	Hämatemesis
hematin *The insoluble iron protoporphyrin component of hemoglobin.*	Hämatin
hematocele *A mass or area of swelling caused by the accumulation of blood.*	Hämatozele
hematochezia *Presence of blood in the excrement.*	Hämatochezie
hematocrit *The measurement of the volume of red blood cells compared to the total volume of blood; recorded in percent.*	Hämatokrit
hematoma *A mass containing blood.*	Hämatom
hematometra *The accretion of blood in the uterus.*	Hämatometra
hematomyelia *Accumulation of blood in the spinal cord.*	Hämatomyelie
hematoporphyrin *A derivative of heme that does not contain iron.*	Hämatoporphyrin

English	German
hematosalpinx *Presence of blood in the fallopian tube.*	Hämatosalpinx
hematuria *The presence of blood in the urine.*	Hämaturie
heme *A constituent of hemoglobin that is an insoluble iron protoporphyrin.*	Häm
hemeralopia *Night blindness.*	Hermeralopie
hemianopsia *Blindness over half the field of vision.*	Hemianopsie
hemiballismus *Severe motor restlessness unilaterally, usually from a subthalamic lesion.*	Hemiballismus
hemicolectomy *Surgical removal of part of the colon.*	Hemikolektomie
hemicrania *1. Pain on one side of the head. 2. Incomplete anencephaly.*	Hemikranie
hemiparesis *Unilateral muscle weakness (half the body).*	Hemiparese
hemiplegia *Paralysis of one side of the body.*	Hemiplegie; Halbseitenlähmung
hemisphere *Referring to either the right or left portion of the cerebrum.*	Hemisphäre
hemizygote *A cell with only one set of genes.*	hemizygot
hemochromatosis *A hereditary condition exhibited by iron deposition in the tissue and leading to liver disease, bronze discoloration of the skin and diabetes.*	Hämochromatose
hemoconcentration *Decrease in the total fluid content of the blood, leading at times to a falsely elevated hematocrit.*	Hämokonzentration
hemocytometer *A device used for counting cells from a blood sample.*	Hämozytometer
hemodialysis *The process of filtering blood outside the body to remove toxins normally excreted by functioning kidneys.*	Hämodialyse
hemoglobin *An iron containing protein used for the transport of oxygen in blood.*	Hämoglobin
hemoglobinuria *Presence of free hemoglobin in the urine.*	Hämoglobinurie
hemolysis *Breakdown of hemoglobin.*	Hämolyse
hemolytic *Something that causes hemolysis.*	hämolytisch
hemolytic anemia *Reduced number of erythrocytes due to shortened survival and inability of the bone marrow to compensate.*	hämolytisch Anämie
hemopericardium *Abnormal presence of blood in the pericardium.*	Hämoperikard
hemoperitoneum *Abnormal presence of blood in the peritoneum.*	Hämatoperitoneum
hemophilia *A hereditary bleeding disorder characterized by hemarthroses and deep tissue bleeding as a result of absence of a coagulation factor such as factor VIII.*	Hämophilie
hemophiliac *A person with hemophilia.*	Bluter; Hämophilier
hemophilic arthropathy *The permanent joint disease caused by recurrent bleeding into the joint.*	hämophilie Arthropathie
hemophthalmia *Bleeding within the eye.*	Hämophthalmus
hemopneumothorax *Accumulation of blood and air in the pleural space.*	Hämotopneumothorax
hemopoiesis *The production of blood cells from stem cells.*	Hämopoese
hemopoietic *Referring to a hormone secreted by the kidneys that stimulates the bone marrow to produce erythrocytes.*	hämopoetisch
hemoptysis *Expectoration of blood.*	Hämoptyse
hemorrhage *Bleeding from a damaged blood vessel.*	Hämorrhagie; Blutung
hemorrhoidectomy *Surgical excision of a hemorrhoid.*	Hämorrhoidektomie
hemorrhoids *Engorgement of the veins in the anus or rectum.*	Hämorrhoiden

English	German
hemostasis *The control of bleeding.*	Hämostase
hemothrorax *The abnormal presence of blood in the pleural cavity.*	Hämothorax
hence *Thus.*	daher
Henoch purpura *Exhibited by vomiting, diarrhea, abdominal pain and hematuria; a non-thrombocytopenic purpura.*	anaphylaktoide Purpura
Henri, syndrome of *Congenital anomaly exhibited by different sized external orifices of the nostrils.*	Henri Syndrom
heparin *A polysaccharide that occurs naturally in the liver and is used as a medication to induce a hypocoagulable state.*	Heparin
hepatectomy *Partial or complete surgical resection of the liver.*	Hepatektomie; Leberresktion
hepatic duct *The right and left hepatic ducts join the cystic duct to form the common bile duct.*	Leberwege
hepatic flexure of the colon *The junction of the ascending and transverse portion of the colon.*	Rechtskolon Flexur
hepatic *Referring to the liver.*	hepatisch
hepatitis *Inflammation of the liver.*	Hepatitis
hepatocyte *A liver cell.*	Hepatozyt
hepatojugular reflex *The presence of jugular venous distension with compression of the abdomen for at least 10 seconds.*	hepatojugulärer Reflux
hepatoma *A tumor of the liver.*	Hepatom
hepatomegaly *Enlargement of the liver.*	Hepatomegalie; Lebervergrößerung
hepatosplenomegaly *Enlargement of the spleen and the liver.*	Hepatosplenomegalie
hereditary spherocytosis *A familial hemolytic disease exhibited by abnormally thick erythrocytes.*	vererbung Sphärozytose
hereditary *That which is transmitted genetically*	vererbung; Erblichkeit
hermaphrodite *A person possessing gonadal characteristics of both sexes.*	Zwitter
hernia, femoral *A bulge in the upper thigh/groin region because of bowel protruding through the muscle.Also called crural hernia.*	Schenkelhernie
hernia, incarcerated *An irreducible hernia.*	inkarzerierte Hernie
hernia, inguinal *Protrusion of abdominal-cavity contents through the inguinal canal.*	Leistenhernie
hernia, lumbar *Defect in the lumbar muscles or the posterior fascia, below the 12th rib and above the iliac crest.*	Lendenbruch
hernia, umbilical *Protrusion of abdominal contents at the umbilicus.*	Nabelhernie
herniated disc *Prolapse of the nucleus pulposus into the spinal cord.*	Bandscheibenvorfall
herniorrhaphy *The surgical repair of a hernia.*	Herniorrhaphie
heroin *A morphine derivative that is highly addictive.*	Heroin
herpangina *An infectious disease caused by Coxsackie virus exhibited by vesicular lesion on the soft palate.*	Herpangina
herpes *A skin condition exhibited by formation of clustered vesicular lesions; herpes simplex is at times referred to, albeit incompletely, as herpes.*	Herpes
herpes zoster; shingles *A unilateral vesicular rash along one dermatome and caused by inflammation of a posterior nerve root by "the chicken pox virus".*	Gürtelrose
herpetic *Referring to herpes.*	herpetisch
herpetiform *Something that is characteristic of herpes.*	herpetiform

English	German
heterochromia iridis or syndrome of Eric *Congenital anomaly in which the iris of each eye is of a different color.*	heterochromie Iridis
heterogenous *That which originates outside the organism.*	heterogen
heterotropia *Synonym of strabismus.*	Heterotropie; Strabismus
heterozygous *Having different alleles concerning a certain trait.*	heterozygot
hiatus hernia *Protrusion of part of the stomach through the esophageal hiatus of the diaphragm.*	Hiatushernie
hiccup *Involuntary spasm of the diaphragm with sudden closure of the glottis; this causes a characteristic cough.*	Schluckauf
hidradenitis *Inflammation of a sweat gland. When there is purulent discharge it is called hidradenitis suppurativa.*	Hidradenitis; Schweißdrüsenentzündung
hidrosis *The production and secretion of sweat.*	Schweißsekretion
high *Elevated.*	hoch; hohe
high blood pressure *Elevated arterial blood pressure.*	Bluthochdruck
high cholesterol *Elevated serum cholesterol.*	Bluthochcholesterinspiegel
hilar *Referring to a hilus.*	hilär
Hillis-Müller maneuver *A procedure to determine the descent of the head during active labor.*	Hillis-Müller Handgriff
hilum or hilus *A depression where blood vessels and nerve fibers enter an organ.*	Hilus
hindbrain *The brainstem which includes the pons, medulla oblongata and cerebellum.*	Rautenhirn
hip *The lateral eminence of the pelvis from the waist to the thigh; it is formed by the iliac crest and greater trochanter.*	Hüfte; Haggebutte
hip joint *The lateral eminence of the pelvis from the waist to the thigh; it is formed by the iliac crest and greater trochanter.*	Hüftgelenk
hip replacement *Both joint surfaces are replaced by high density material such as plastic or metal.*	Hüftendoprothese
hippocampus *The area at the base of the cerebral ventricles thought to be the center of memory and emotion.*	Ammonshorn
Hippocratic oath *An vow taken by doctors, indicating they will treat people properly.*	hippkratischer Eid
hirsutism *Abnormal growth on hair on a person's face and body.*	Hirsutismus
histamine *A chemical responsible for the reaction exhibited when a person has an allergic reaction.*	Histimin
histidine *An amino acid precursor to histamine.*	Histidin
histiocyte *A phagocytic cell found in connective tissue.*	Histiozyt
histochemistry *Study of intracellular distribution of chemicals, reaction sites and enzymes.*	Histochemie
histology *The study of the structure and composition of minute structures.*	Histologie; Gewebelehre
histoplasmosis *A fungal pulmonary infection from bat and bird excrement.*	Histoplasmose
HIV *Abbreviation for human immunodeficiency virus.*	humanes Immundefektvirus
hoarse *A rough, harsh sounding voice.*	heiser
Hodgkin's disease *Also called Hodgkin's lymphoma, it is a cancer that begins in the lymphocytes.*	Lymphogranulomatose
hollow *An indendation.*	Mulde
homeless *Having nowhere to live.*	obdachlos

English	German
homeopathy *A treatment of disease by use of minute doses of toxic substances that would normally be harmful.*	Homöopathie
homeostasis *The tendency of an organism to maintain a stable and uniform state.*	Homöostase
homicide *When one person kills another.*	Mord
homograft *A graft of tissue from the same species as the recipient.*	Homöotransplantat
homolateral *Ipsilateral.*	homolateral
homologous *Referring to something derived from the same species but different genotype.*	homolog
homosexual *A person sexually attracted to someone of the same gender.*	homosexuelle Person
homozygous *Having identical alleles for a particular trait.*	Homozygot
hookworm *A parasitic infection of the family Strongylidae that can cause anemia.*	Hakenwurm
hordeolum *Inflammation of the sebaceous gland of the eye.*	Gerstenkorn
hormone *A substance produced in the body that effects a specific organ.*	Hormon
horn *A keratinized outgrowth.*	Horn
Horner syndrome *A lesion of the cervical sympathetic chain causes ipsilateral myosis, ptosis and facial anhydrosis.*	Horner-Syndrom
horseshoe kidney *Anomalous renal development.*	Hufeisenniere
hospital *Acute care medical/surgical facility.*	Krankenhaus
hospital discharge *To leave the hospital.*	das Krankenhaus verlassen
hot *Very warm.*	heiß
hot flash *A symptom of menopause manifested as a sudden sensation of fever.*	Hitzewallung
housemaid's knee *Also referred to as prepatellar bursitis.*	Putzfrauenknie
HPV human papillomavirus *The virus that causes genital warts.*	Papilloma-Virus
Hueter's maneuver *The application of downward and forward pressure on the tongue while passing an gastric tube.*	Hueter Handgriff
human *Homo sapien.*	menschlich
humerus *The long bone in the upper arm.*	Humerus; Oberarm
humor, aqueous *The gelatinous fluid circulating between the cornea and lens.*	Kammerwasser
humor, vitreous *The fluid circulating between the lens and retina.*	Glaskörper
hunchback *Synonym of kyphosis.*	Gibbus
hunger *A sense of discomfort caused by a lack of food.*	Hunger
Huntington's chorea *A neurodegenerative disease characterized initially by behavioral changes and later by a movement disorder. Called Huntington's disease now.*	Huntingtonische Chorea
Hutchington's mask *The sensation the face is covered in cobwebs, associated with tabes dorsalis.*	Hutchinson Maske
Hutchinson's pupil *Dilation of a pupil related to third nerve palsy on the side of the lesion as seen in herniation.*	Hutchinson Pupille
hyaline *Having a glassy, transparent appearance.*	hyalin
hyaloid *Transparent.*	Hyalin
hybrid *An animal or plant produced from two different species.*	Hybride
hydatid cyst *A cyst produced by and containing tapeworm larvae.*	Hydatidzyst; Echinokokkuszyste
hydatiform *Referring to a hydatid cyst.*	hydatidiform

English	German
hydrarthrosis *An accumulation of water-like fluid in a joint cavity.*	Hydarthrose
hydration *Used to describe fluid balance.*	Hydratation
hydrocele *The accumulation of fluid in a body sac.*	Hydrozele
hydrocephalus *The excessive accumulation of cerebral spinal fluid in the brain causing enlargement of the head.*	Hydrozephalus; Wasserkopf
hydrochloric acid *A solution with a low pH formed by dissolving hydrogen chloride in water.*	Salzsäure
hydrochloride	Hydrochlorid
hydrocortisone *A natural steroid hormone secreted by the adrenal cortex and used in a synthetic formulation for treatment of various medical conditions.*	Hydrocortison
hydrolysis *A reaction with water causing a compound to breakdown.*	Hydrolyse
hydronephrosis *Enlargement of a kidney due to interruption of outflow of urine from that kidney.*	Hydronephrose; Wassersackniere
hydrophobia *Abnormal fear of water.*	Hydrophobie
hydropneumothorax *Abnormal accumulation of fluid and air in the pleural space.*	Hydropneumothorax
hydrops *The abnormal collection of fluid in a cavity.*	Hydrops
hydrops fetalis *The total body accumulation of fluid in a fetus; the result of a hemolytic reaction in a Rh neg mother.*	Hydrops fetalis
hydrosalpinx *Collection of fluid in a fallopian tube.*	Hydrosalpinx
hydrothorax *Accumulation of fluid within the thoracic cavity.*	Hydrothorax
hygroma *A cyst or bursa filled with fluid.*	Hygrom
hygroscopic *The tendency to absorb moisture from the air.*	hygroskopisch
hymen *A membrane in the vagina.*	Hymen
hymenotomy *Surgically creating an opening in the hymen.*	Hymenektomie
hyoid bone *A horseshoe shaped bone located between the chin and thyroid cartilage.*	Zungenbein
hyperacidity *An abnormally high acid level.*	Hyperazidität; Übersäuerung
hyperactivity *Abnormal increase in activity.*	Hyperaktivität
hyperalgesia *Greater than normal sensitivity to pain.*	Hyperalgesie
hyperbaric *Use of gas at a higher than normal pressure.*	hyperbare
hyperbaric chamber *A device used to treat decompression illness.*	Überdruckkammer
hyperbilirubinemia *Higher than normal level of bilirubin in the blood.*	Hyperbilirubinämie
hypercalcemia *Higher than normal level of calcium in the blood.*	Hyperkalzämie
hypercapnia *Higher than normal level of carbon dioxide in the blood stream.*	Hyperkapnie
hypercholesterolemia *Higher than normal level of cholesterol in the blood.*	Hypercholesterinämie
hyperchromia *An excessive level of hemoglobin in erythrocytes.*	Hyperchromasie
hyperemia *An increase in blood for the area of concern.*	Hyperämie
hyperesthesia *Higher than normal skin sensitivity.*	Hyperästhesie
hyperextension *Extension of an articulation beyond the normal range.*	Hyperextension
hyperflexion *Flexion of an articulation beyond the normal range.*	Hyperflexion
hyperglycemia *Higher than normal level of glucose in the blood.*	Hyperglykämie
hypergonadism *A condition of excessive gonadal activity and subsequently precocious sexual development.*	Hypergonadismus
hyperhidrosis *Excessive perspiration.*	Hyperhidrose

English	German
hyperkalemia *Higher than normal level of potassium in the blood stream.*	Hyperkaliämie
hyperkeratosis *Excessive thickening of the outer layer of skin.*	Hyperkeratose
hyperkinesis *Excessive activity and inability to concentrate.*	Hyperkinese
hyperlipidemia *Higher than normal level of lipids in the blood stream.*	Hyperlipidämie
hypermetropia *Farsightedness.*	Hypermetropie; Übersichtigkeit
hypermnesia *Unusually good memory.*	Hypermnesie
hypermyotonia *Excessive muscle tone.*	Muskelhypertonie
hypernatremia *Elevated level of sodium in the blood.*	Hypernatriämie
hypernephroma *A renal tumor that mimic adrenal cortical tissue.*	Hypernephrom
hyperonychia *Hypertrophic nails.*	Hyperonychie
hyperopia *Farsightedness.*	Hyperopie; Übersichtigkeit
hyperosmia *Increased sense of smell.*	Hyperosmie
hyperparathyroidism *Excessive level of parathyroid hormones in the blood stream causing weak bones and hypocalcemia.*	Hyperparathyreoidismus
hyperphagia *Excessive food ingestion.*	Bulimie
hyperphoria *Upward deviation of the visual axis of the eye.*	Hyperphorie
hyperpituitarism *Excessive eosinophilic hormone resulting in acromegaly or excessive basophilic hormone resulting in pituitary compression and ultimately hypopituitarism.*	Hyperpituitarismus
hyperplasia *Excessive growth of normal cells.*	Hyperplasie
hyperpnea *Abnormal increase in rate and depth of respiration.*	Hyperpnoe
hyperpyrexia *Fever.*	Hyperpyrexie
hyperreflexia *Abnormally brisk and vigorous reflex.*	Hyperreflexie
hypersensitivity *Abnormal increase in sensitivity.*	Hypersensitivität; Überempfindlichkeit
hypersplenism *Excessive splenic activity resulting in decreased peripheral blood elements and sometimes splenomegaly.*	Hypersplenie
hypertension *Higher than normal blood pressure.*	Hypertension; Bluthochdruck
hyperthermia *Fever.*	Hyperthermie
hyperthyroidism *Increased thyroid activity resulting in exophthalmos and increased metabolic rate.*	Hyperthyreose
hypertonia *Excessive tone or tension.*	Hypertonie
hypertonic *Increased osmotic pressure.*	hypertonie
hypertrichosis *Excessive hair growth.*	Hypertrichose
hypertrophy *Pathologic organ enlargement.*	Hypertrophie
hyperuricemia *Elevated level of uric acid in the blood.*	Hyperurikämie
hyperventilation *Rapid and deep respirations.*	Hyperventilation
hypervolemia *Abnormally large amount of fluid in the blood stream.*	Hypervolämie
hyphema *A blood collection in the front of the eye.*	Hyphäma
hypnotic *Sleep inducing agent.*	hypnotisch
hypocalcemia *Lower than normal level of calcium in the blood.*	Hypokalzämie
hypocapnia *A decreased level of carbon dioxide in the blood.*	Hypokapnie
hypochlorhydria *A state of decreased secretion of hydrochloric acid in the stomach.*	Hypochlorhydrie
hypochondriac *A person suffering from hypochondriasis.*	Hypochonder
hypochondriasis *Abnormal increase in concern about one's own health.*	Hypochondrie

English	German
hypochondrium *The upper abdomen lateral to the epigastrium.*	Hypochondrium
hypochromic *Referring to the abnormal decrease in hemoglobin content of erythrocytes.*	hypochrom
hypodermic injection *Subcutaneous injection.*	subkutane injektion
hypoesthesia *Abnormally decreased skin sensitivity.*	Hypästhesie
hypofibrinogenemia *Diminished blood fibrinogen level.*	Hypofibrinogenämie
hypogastric *Referring to the hypogastrium.*	hypogastrisch
hypogastrium *The area of the central abdomen located below the stomach.*	Hypogastrium
hypoglossal nerve *Twelfth cranial nerve pair.*	Hypoglossus
hypoglycemia *Abnormally low blood sugar.*	Hypoglykämie
hypogonadism *Abnormal decrease in gonadal function with associated diminished growth and sexual development.*	Hypogonadismus
hypokalemia *Diminished level of potassium in the blood stream.*	Hypokaliämie
hypokalemic periodic paralysis *An inherited disorder that leads to muscle weakness related to a low serum potassium level.*	Gamstorp Syndrom
hypomania *A moderate form of mania.*	Hypomanie
hyponatremia *Diminished level of sodium in the blood stream.*	Hyponatriämie
hypoparathyroidism *Abnormal decrease in parathyroid function.*	Hypoparathyreoidismus
hypophoria *Downward deviation of the visual axis of the eye.*	Hypophorie
hypophosphatasia *A genetic defect of diminished alkaline phosphatase in the cells leading to bone demineralization.*	Hypophosphatasie
hypophysectomy *Surgical removal of the pituitary gland.*	Hypophysektomie
hypophysis *Pituitary gland.*	Hypophyse; Hirnanhangdrüse
hypopituitarism *Diminished pituitary activity exhibited by obesity and persistence of adolescent characteristics.*	Hypopituitarismus
hypoplasia *Incomplete development.*	Hypoplasie; Unterentwicklung
hypopyon *The presence of purulent fluid in the anterior chamber of the eye.*	Hypopyon
hyposalivation *Secretion of saliva below the normal rate.*	Hyposalivation
hypospadias *Congenital condition exhibited by development of the urethral meatus on the inferior aspect of the penis.*	Hypospadie
hypostasis *The formation of a deposit.*	Hypostase
hypotension *Abnormally low blood pressure.*	Hypotension
hypothalamus *Located inferior to the thalamus it controls visceral activities, water balance, temperature and sleep.*	Hypothalamus
hypothenar eminence *The prominence on the palm at the base of the fingers adjacent to the ulna.*	Kleinfingerballen
hypothermia *Lower than normal temperature.*	Hypothermie
hypothyroidism *Reduced functioning of the thyroid.*	Hypothyreose
hypotonia *Reduced tone or activity.*	Tonuserniedrigung; Hypotonus
hypoxia *Diminished oxygen content.*	Hypoxie; Sauerstoffmangel
hysterectomy *Surgical removal of the uterus.*	Hysterektomie
hysteria *A psychological condition exhibited by uncontrolled emotion or exaggerated manifestations.*	Hysterie
hysterography *1. Recording of uterine contractions. 2. Roentgenography of the uterus after administration of contrast media.*	Hysterographie
hysteromyomectomy *Surgical removal of a uterine myoma.*	Hysteromyomektomie

English	German
hysteropexy *Surgical fixation of the uterus by shortening of the round ligaments or by other means.*	Hysteropexie
hysterosalpingography *Roentgenography of the uterus and fallopian tubes after instillation of contrast media.*	Hysterosalpingographie
hysterotomy *Surgical opening of the uterus.*	Hysterotomie
i.e. *A latin derived abbreviation for "that is to say"(In latin: id est)*	das heißt
iatrogenic *A problem caused by medical treatment.*	iatrogen
ichthyosis *A congenital anomaly exhibited by excessively dry, thick skin.*	Ichthyose
icterus *Yellowing of the skin and sclerae because of excess bilirubin.*	Ikterus; Gelbsucht
identical twins *Twins from the same zygote.*	eineiige Zwillinge
idiopathic *Relating to a disease with an unknown cause.*	idiopathisch
ileitis *Inflammation of the ileum.*	Ileitis
ileocecal valve *The membranous folds between the ileum and cecum.*	Ileozäkalklappe
ileocolitis *Inflammation of the ileum and cecum.*	Ileokolitis
ileocolostomy *Creating a surgical opening between the ileum and colon.*	Ileokolotomie
ileoproctostomy *Creating a surgical opening between the ileum and the rectum.*	Ileoproktostomie
ileostomy *Surgical creation of an opening in the ileum that is placed at the skin surface.*	Ileostomie
ileum *The portion of the small bowel from the jejunum to the cecum.*	Ileum
ileus *A temporary obstruction in the intestine.*	Ileus; Darmverschluss
iliac crest *The upper border of the ilium.*	Darmbeinkamm
iliococcygeal *Referring to the ilium and coccyx.*	iliokokzygeal
ilium *The large bone at the superior aspect of the pelvis which is present bilaterally.*	Ilium
illiterate *Unable to read or write.*	ungebildet
immune *Being resistant to an infection.*	immun
immune response *The body's reaction to what is perceived as a foreign substance.*	Immunreaktion
immunization *A medication given to provide immunity.*	Immunisierung
immunochemistry *The study of immune response and biochemistry.*	Immunchemie
immunodeficiency *An inadequate immune response.*	Immundefizienz
immunoelectrophoresis *A means of differentiating proteins and other compounds by comparing their mobility and antigenic specificities.*	Immunelektrophorese
immunoglobulin *Serum and cellular proteins of the immune system.*	Immunglobulin
immunosuppression *The inhibition of the immune response.*	Immunsuppression
impacted tooth *A tooth that does not erupt because adjacent teeth prevent it.*	impaktierter Zahn
impaired *Having a disability.*	beeinträchtigt
impairment *A specific disability.*	Beeinträchtigung
imperforate *Lack of an opening. An infant with an imperforate anus has a congenital defect with no anal opening.*	nicht perforiert
impervious *Not affected by.*	undurchdringlich
implant *A device or prosthesis implanted in a person.*	Implantat
implementation *The process of putting a plan into effect.*	Nidation
impotence *Inability to act or inability to achieve a penile erection.*	Impotenz; Zeugungsunfähigkeit

English	German
inanition *Generalized weakness from lack of nutrition.*	Inanition
inarticulate *Indistinct speech.*	unartikuliert
incest *Sexual relations between related people.*	Inzest
incipient *Starting to happen.*	beginnend
incision *An intentional surgical cut in the skin.*	Inzision; Schnitt
incisor *Sharp-edged tooth; humans have four incisors.*	Schneidezahn
incisura *A notch or indentation usually on the edge of a bone.*	Incisura
incisure *A notch or incision.*	Inzisur; Einschnitt
inclusion body *Variably shaped bodies in the nuclei of cells found in infections such as rabies and herpes.*	Einschlußkörperchen
incoherent *Absence of intelligible speech.*	inkohärent
incontinence *Inability to control urination.*	Inkontinenz
incoordination *Absence of smooth, efficient body movement.*	Inkoordination
increment *An increase on a fixed scale.*	Inkrement
incubator *A warming device for infants.*	Brutkasten; Inkubator
incus *The middle ear bone between the stapes and malleus.*	Amboß
indeed *As a matter of fact.*	ja sogar
indigenous *Naturally occurring.*	nativ
indigestion *Inadequate digestion for various reasons.*	Verdauungsstörungen
indolent *1. Causing little pain. 2. Slow healing ulcer.*	Indolent
induce, to *Facilitated. When referring to labor, it means medication was given to assist in delivery of the fetus.*	induzieren
induced abortion *Surgical or medical evacuation of the fetus.*	Abortus artificialis
induration *An area that is abnormally hard.*	Induration
indwelling catheter *Continuous use tube usually referring to a tube in the urinary bladder.*	Verweilkatheter
indwelling foley *A catheter inserted into the urinary bladder with an inflatable ballon on the tip.*	Dauerkatheter
inebriation *Intoxication with drugs or alcohol.*	Trunkenheit; Rausch
ineffective *Unsuccessful or inefficient.*	wirkungslos
inertia *The tendency to remain unchanged.*	Inertie
inevitable *Not preventable.*	unvermeidlich
infancy *Early childhood.*	Säuglingsalter
infant *Newborn.*	Säugling; Kleinkind
infant, post-term *A neonate born after the normal gestation.*	Spätgeburt
infant, pre-term *A neonate born prior to normal gestation.*	Frühgeborenes
infant, term *A neonate born at expected date.*	Kind mit Normal Schwangerschaftsdauer
infantile *Referring to babies or young children.*	infantil
infarct *Referring to dead tissue.*	Infarkt
infarction *Dead tissue, for example, myocardial infarction.*	Infarzierung
infectious *Contagious.*	infektiös
inferior *The lower aspect.*	unterer; inferior
inferior pelvis strait *The pelvic outlet.*	Beckenausgang
infestation *The presence of large numbers, as in lice infestation.*	Parasitenbefall
inflammation *Localized redness, excessive warmth and swelling.*	Entzündung
influenza *Viral infection causing fever, muscle aches and catarrh.*	Grippe; Influenza

95

English	German
infraspinous *Below the scapular spine.*	infraspinal
infundibulum *The connection between the hypothalamus and the posterior pituitary gland.*	Infundibulum
infusion *The injection of fluid into tissue or a vein.*	Aufguß; Infusion
ingestion *The intake of food or liquid orally.*	Ingestion; Aufnahme
ingrown nail *Also referred to as onychocryptosis.*	eingewachsener Nagel
inguinal *Referring to the groin.*	inguinal
inguinal ring (deep) *Indirect inguinal hernias exit the abdominal cavity via the deep inguinal ring.*	Leistenring
inhalation *The act of breathing in.*	Inhalation
injection *The act of a needle being inserted into a body.*	Injektion
injure, to *To hurt or to wound.*	schädigen
injury *A wound, abrasion or contusion.*	Schädigung; Verletzung
injury, closed head *Brain trauma not associated with damage to the dura or skull.*	Kopfverletzung
injury, contrecoup of brain *An injury to the brain on the side opposite of that which was struck.*	contre-coup Kopfverletzung
injury, degloving *Trauma that involves the ripping of skin and subcutaneous tissue from the underlying tissue.*	hautablederung Verletzung
injury, hyperextension-hyperflexion *An injury, usually to the cervical spine, that involves rapid deceleration, causing pronounced extension and flexion.*	hyperextension-hyperflexion Verletzung
inner ear *Made up of the cochlea and semicircular canals.*	Innenohr
innervation *The presence of a nerve supply.*	Innervation
innominate artery *The first branch off the aortic arch that branches into the right common carotid and right subclavian arteries.*	Namelosarterie
innominate *Referring to the innominate artery.*	namelos
inoculation *Injection with a vaccine to provide immunity.*	Inokulation
inorganic *Not coming from natural growth.*	anorganisch
insane *A term not used in formal medical evaluations that when used by a layperson means a serious mental illness.*	geisteskrank
insanity *Referring to a serious mental illness.*	Geisteskrankheit
insensible *Unable to perceive a stimulus.*	gefühllos
insertion *The act of inserting something.*	Einführung
inside *Inner part, center.*	innen
insidious *A slow, gradual and harmful advancement.*	heimtückisch
insomnia *Sleeplessness.*	Schlaflosigkeit
inspiration *Drawing in a breath.*	Inspiration; Atemzug
inspiratory reserve volume *The amount of air that can be inhaled after a normal inhalation.*	inspiratorisches Reservevolumen
inspissate, to *To thicken or congeal.*	verdicken
instep *The medial aspect of the foot between the ankle and the ball of the foot.*	Rist
insulin *A hormone produced by the pancreas and synthetically to control blood glucose levels.*	Insulin
insulinoma *An islet cell tumor that causes abnormally high insulin secretion and thus hypoglycemia.*	Insulinom
intake *An amount of food taken into the body.*	Aufnahme

English	German
integument *Outer protective layer.*	Haut
intelligence quotient (IQ) *A number representing a person's ability to problem solve compared to a matched-control.*	Ingelligenzquotient
intensive *Very thorough or vigorous.*	intensiv
intensive care *Vigorous treatment of the acutely ill.*	Intensivpflege
intention tremor *The tremulous movement noted when a person is beginning to perform a task but not seen at rest.*	Intensionstremor
interarticular *Between the articular surfaces of a joint.*	interartikulär
intercellular *Between cells.*	interzellular
intermittent *Occurring at irregular intervals.*	intermittierend
internal *Situated on the inside.*	innerlich
interosseous *Referring to something between bones, like the interosseous muscles of the hand.*	interossär
interstitial *Referring to the interstices of tissue.*	interstitiell
intertrigo *Irritation present because adjacent surfaces rub together.*	Intertrigo
intertrochanteric *Referring to the space within the trochanter.*	intertrochantär
interval *An intervening time.*	Intervall
interventricular *Between the ventricles.*	interventrikulär
intestinal obstruction *Blockage of the intestine by mass or volvulus.*	Darmverschluß
intestinal *Referring to the intestines.*	intestinal
intestine *A general term used for the section of bowel from the stomach to the anus.*	Darm
intraabdominal abscess *A collection of pus in the abdomen.*	intra-abdominal Abszeß
intraabdominal *Within the abdominal cavity.*	intra-abdominal
intraarticular *Within a joint space.*	intraartikulär
intracellular *Within a cell.*	intrazellulär
intracerebral *Within the cerebrum.*	intrazerebral
intracranial *Within the cranial vault.*	intrakraniell
intradermal *Within the dermis.*	intradermal
intradural *Within the dural space.*	intradural
intramedullary *1. Within the medulla oblongata. 2. Within the bone marrow.*	intramedullär
intramuscular *Within a muscle.*	intramuskulär
intraocular fluid *Fluid within the globe.*	intraokular Flüssigkeit
intraosseous *Within a bone.*	intraossär
intraperitoneal *Within the peritoneal cavity.*	intraperitoneal
intrathecal *Technically means within a sheath but this term is used when medication is instilled in the dura mater spinalis.*	intrathekal
intrauterine contraceptive device (IUD) *A device used to physically prevent the implantation of a fertilized ovum.*	Intrauterinspiral
intrauterine *Within the uterus.*	intrauterin
intravenous infusion *Administration of fluid into a vein.*	intravenöse Anwendung
intravenous tubing *The tubing used to administer fluids.*	Intravenöseschlauch
intravenous *Within a vein.*	intravenöse
intubation *Placement of a tube; commonly used to refer to endotracheal intubation.*	Intubation
intussusception *The inversion of one portion of the bowel into another.*	Intussuszeption; Invagination

English	German
inulin *A polysaccharide used in the testing of renal function.*	Insulin
inunction *The application of lotion with friction.*	Einrebung
involucrum *A wrap or covering (referring to a sequestrum).*	Involucrum
involutional *The shrinkage of an organ when it is not in use, as in the uterus after childbirth.*	involutiv
involved *Difficult to comprehend.*	beteiligt
iodine *A chemical used as an antiseptic and a deficiency of it can lead to goiter.*	Iod
iodism *A condition caused by excessive iodine intake resulting in diarrhea , weakness, and convulsions.*	Jodismus
ion channel *A selectively permeable cell membrane to certain ions.*	Ionenkanal
ionizing radiation *High energy radiation that produces ion pairs in matter.*	ionisierende Strahlung
ipsilateral *On the same side.*	ipsilateral
iridectomy *Surgical removal of part of the iris.*	iridektomie
iridocyclitis *Inflammation of the ciliary body and the iris.*	Iridozyklitis
iridoplegia *Paralysis of part of the iris with subsequent lack of contraction or dilation of the pupil.*	Iridoplegie
iridotomy *A surgical opening of the iris.*	Iridotomie
iris *The colored membrane posterior to the cornea.*	Iris; Regenbogenhaut
iron *An element found in hemoglobin.*	Eisen; Fe
iron-deficiency anemia *A microcytic anemia.*	Eisenmangelanämie
irradiation *The process of being irradiated.*	Bestrahlung; Irradiation
irrelevant *Not pertinent.*	belanglos
irritable bowel syndrome *A condition exhibited by chronic diarrhea or constipation and abdominal pain; it is sometimes associated with a labile emotional state.*	Reizkolon
ischemia *Inadequate blood supply to a part of the body.*	Ischämie
ischemic contracture *A muscle's resistance to passive stretch that is related to a decrease in arterial flow from any reason.*	ischämisch Kontraktur
ischemic heart disease *Inadequate blood supply to the heart.*	ischämisch Herzkrankheit
ischemic optic neuropathy *A general category of a cause of blindness with several subcategories.*	ischämisch Optikoneuropathie
ischium *The inferoposterior portion of the pelvis.*	Ischium
islet *Tissue that is structurally separate from adjacent tissues.*	Insel
isoantibody *A situation in which an antibody of person A reacts with an antigen of person B.*	Isoantikörper
isolation *To be kept separate or apart.*	Isolation; Absonderung; Isolierung
isolation ward *A ward where patients with infectious disease are housed.*	Isolierstation
isthmus *A narrow piece of tissue connecting two larger body parts.*	Isthmus
itch *A sensation that makes one want to scratch.*	Jucken; Krätze;
jaundice *Yellowing of the sclerae and skin because of excessive bilirubin in the blood.*	Ikterus; Gelbsucht
jaundice of the newborn *A form of jaundice seen in newborns in the first two weeks of life; also called icterus neonatorum.*	Neugeborenenikterus
jaw *Mandible.*	Kiefer

English	German
jaw reflex *Contraction of the temporal muscles when a relaxed mandible is given a downward tap. Also, masseter reflex or jaw jerk.*	Unterkieferreflex
jejunectomy *Surgical removal of the jejunum.*	Jejunektomie
jejunostomy *Surgical creation of an opening in the jejunum.*	Jejunostomie
Jendrassik's maneuver *A method of distracting a patient while checking the patellar reflex.*	Jendrassikscher Handgriff
Job syndrome *Also known as hyperimmunoglobulin E syndrome, there are high levels if IgE, a leukocyte chemotactic defect, recurrent staph infections and cold abscess formation in the skin.*	Hiobsyndrom
jock itch *Pruritis caused by tinea cruris.*	Eczema marginatum
joint *Articulation of two adjacent bones.*	Gelenk; Articulatio
jugular notch *The notch on the upper border of the sternum.*	Drosselgrube
jugular *Referring to the neck, as in jugular vein.*	jugulär
jugular vein (s) *Includes the internal, external and anterior jugular veins.*	Drosselvene
juvenile angiofibroma *A noncancerous growth in the nose or pharyngeal region.*	jugendlich Angiofibrom
juxta-articular *Positioned near a joint.*	juxtaartikulär
juxtaglomerular apparatus *Cells located in the tunica media of the afferent glomerular arterioles.*	juxtaglomerulärer Apparat
kala-azar *A disease caused by Leishmania donovani that is exhibited by weight loss, fever, anemia and hepatosplenomegaly.*	Kala-Azar; viszerale Leishmaniase
Kaposi sarcoma *Typically seen in AIDS patients, it is characterized by cutaneous reddish-purple macules and plaques.Also called multiple idiopathic hemorrhagic sarcoma.*	Kaposi Sarkom; Sarcoma idiopathicum mutiplex haemorrhagicum
karyokinesis *A part of mitosis involving the cell nucleus division.*	Karyokinese
karyotype *The arrangement of chromosomes in a single cell.*	Karyotyp
Kawasaki syndrome *Begins with fever for 5 days, skin rashes, strawberry tongue, lymphadenopathy and swollen hands and feet. It is known to cause coronary artery aneurysms. Also called mucocutaneous lymph node syndrome.*	Kawasaki-Syndrom
keloid *Hypertrophic scar tissue that forms after a minor cut or surgical procedure.*	Keloid
keratectasia *Obtrusion of the cornea.*	Keratektasie
keratectomy *Excision of a portion of the cornea.*	Keratektomie
keratic *Referring to the cornea.*	keratisch
keratin *A protein found in the skin, hair, nails and enamel of the teeth.*	Keratin
keratoma *A protuberance of horny tissue.*	Keratom
keratomalacia *Softening of the cornea.*	Keratomalazia
keratosis *A growth of keratin such as a wart or callosity.*	Keratose
kernicterus *A condition associated with high bilirubin levels that causes yellow staining of cerebral tissues and subsequent neurologic dysfunction.*	Kernikterus
ketoacidosis *Usually referring to diabetic ketoacidosis in which ketones are broken down, causing a decrease in blood pH.*	Ketoazidose
ketone body *One ketone with a decarboxylation product of acetone.*	Ketonkörper
ketonemia *Presence of ketone in the blood.*	Ketonämie
ketonuria *Presence of ketone in the urine.*	Ketonurie

English	German
ketosis *The presence of an abnormally high level of ketones in the blood and body tissues.*	Ketose
kick, to *To strike an object with one's foot.*	treten
kidney *One of two glandular organs that form urine.*	Niere
kinase *An enzyme that facilitates movement of phosphate from ATP to another molecule.*	Kinase
kineplasty *An amputation done in a fashion to facilitate ambulation.*	Kineplastie
kinesis *Movement of a part in response to a stimulus.*	Kinesis
kinky-hair syndrome *Inborn error of copper metabolism, noted in the first few weeks of life. Exhibited by sparse kinky hair, failure to thrive and seizures. Also called Menke's syndrome or trichopoliodystrophy.*	Menkes-Syndrom; Trichopoliodystrophie
Klinefelter's syndrome *Presence of an extra X chromosome, it is exhibited by longer legs, narrow shoulders, small testicles and gynecomastia.*	Klinefelter-Syndrom
knee *The joint at the distal femur and proximal tibia.*	Knie; Genu
knee elbow position *Knees and elbows are on the table and the chest is in the air.*	Knie-Ellenbogen Lage
knee jerk reflex *Contraction of the quadriceps, yielding leg extension when the quadriceps tendon is tapped.*	Patellarsehnenreflex
kneecap *Common term for patella.*	Kniescheibe
kneeling *Being on one's knees as in the prayer position.*	kniend
knock knees *Common term for genu valgum.*	Genu valgum
knot *A fastening made by tying a suture, for instance.*	Knoten
known *Recognized or familiar.*	bekannt
knuckle *A metacarpophalagngeal joint or a finger joint when the fist is closed.*	Fingerknöchel
koilonychia *Thin and concave fingernails.*	Koilonychie
Koplik's spots *Red buccal macules with a blue center; seen in measles.*	Koplik-Flecken
kopophobia *A morbid fear of fatigue.*	Kopophobie
Köhler's disease *A genetic disease characterized by osteonecrosis and subsequent collapse of the tarsal navicular bone.*	Köhler Krankheit
kraurosis vulvae *Dryness and shrinkage of the vulva.*	Kraurosis Vulvae
Krebs cycle *The process of aerobic respiration by which living cells generate energy.*	Zitrat-zyklus; Krebs-Zyklus
kubisagari *Vestibular neuronitis.*	vestibulär Neuronitis
Kussmaul respiration *The slow, deep breathing noted in patients with acidosis.*	Kussmaul Atmung
Kyasanur Forest disease *A viral fever noted in Mysore, India transmitted by Haemaphysalis spinigera. It is characterized by fever, headach, generalized pains, diarrhea, and intestinal bleeding.*	Kyasnur-Wald-Krankheit
kwashiorkor *A form of malnutrition from inadequate protein intake.*	Kwashiorkor
kyphoscoliosis *An abnormal outward and lateral curvature of the spine.*	Kyphoskoliose
kyphosis *Abnormal outward curvature of the spine.*	Kyphose
lab result *The data obtained from a laboratory test.*	Laborergebnis; Laborbefunde
labial *Referring to the lip.*	labial
labile *Easily altered; emotionally unstable.*	labil
labium majus (plural= labia majora) *The folds of skin forming the lateral borders of the pudendal cleft.*	Labium majus

English	German
labium minus (plural=labia minora) *The folds of skin posterior to the labia majora.*	Labium minus
labium *Referring to any lip shaped structure.*	Labium
labor onset *The time when a pregnant woman begins uterine contractions in the process of childbirth.*	Wehenbeginn
labor pains *The intermittent pain associated with uterine contractions.*	Geburtswehen
labor room *The hospital room used while a woman is in labor.*	Kreißsaal
laboratory *A room equiped to run blood, tissue and fluid samples.*	Labor
labyrinthitis *Inflammation of the labyrinth.*	Labyrinthitis
labrum *An edge or lip. The labrum acetabular is the fibrocartilagous rim attached to the acetabulum.*	Labrum
labyrinth *Inner ear structure concerned with balance.*	Labyrinth
laceration *An injury that produced a cut in the skin or tissue such as a tear during childbirth.*	Zerreißung; Rißwunde; Einriss
lacrimal *Referring to the secretion of tears.*	Lakrimal
lacrimal fluid *Fluid secreted by the lacrimal gland.*	Tränenflüssigkeit
lacrimation *The secretion of tears.*	Tränen
lactalbumin *Proteins found in milk.*	Laktalbumin
lactase *An enzyme that facilitates the breakdown of lactose to glucose and galactose.*	Laktase
lactation *The secretion of milk from mammary glands.*	Laktation
lactic *Referring to milk.*	Milch
lactiferous duct *A canal that carries milk.*	Milchführendgang
lactose *A disaccharide present in milk.*	Laktose
lactose intolerance *The inability of the small bowel to digest lactose.*	Laktoseintoleranz
lacuna *A small cavity or depression.*	Lakune
lacunar infarction *Small non-cortical cerebral infarcts.*	lakunärer Infarkt
lagophthalmos *Characterized by the inability to close the eyelid completely over the eye.*	Lagophthalmus
laliophobia *Abnormal fear of speaking or stuttering.*	Lalophobie
lalochezia *Relief of stress by uttering obsenities.*	Lalochezie
lambdoid *The suture connecting the parietal bones with the occipital bone.*	lambdaförmig
lamella *A thin layer of bone.*	Lamelle
laminectomy *The surgical removal of part of a vertebrae.*	Laminektomie
lancet *A small sharp instrument used to obtain a drop of blood for testing.*	Lanzette
laparoscope *A fiber-optic instrument used to visualize the peritoneal contents.*	Laparoskop
laparoscopy *A procedure utilizing a laparoscope.*	Laparoskopie
laparotomy *A surgical incision of the abdomen.*	Laparotomie
laryngeal *Referring to the larynx.*	laryngeal
laryngectomy *Surgical removal of the larynx.*	Laryngektomie
laryngismus stridulus *Sudden, severe laryngeal spasm.*	Stridor laryngealis
laryngitis *Inflammation of the larynx.*	Laryngitis
laryngology *The study of the larynx and related diseases.*	Laryngologie
laryngopharynx *The pharyngeal space between the superior aspect of the glottis and the opening of the larynx.*	Laryngopharynx

English	German
laryngospasm *Sudden, involuntary muscle contraction of the larynx.*	Laryngospasmus
laryngostenosis *Abnormal narrowing of the larynx.*	Kehlkopfstenose
laryngotomy *Surgical creation of an opening in the larynx.*	Laryngotomie
larynx *A hollow muscular structure that contains the vocal cords.*	Larynx
last *Final.*	letzte
late *A time later than expected.*	spät
lateral *Referring to the side of the body.*	lateral
laterodeviation *Pushed to the lateral aspect.*	Seitverbiegung
lathyrism *A disease characterized by tremors, spastic paralysis and paresthesias caused by Lathyrus sativus.*	Lathyrismus
laugh, to	lachen
laxity *A description of a joint that is loose.*	Schlaffheit
layer *A stratum or thickness.*	Schicht; Lage
lazy feeder *An infant slow to take to the breast or to the bottle.*	trinkfauler Säugling
lead *An element with an atomic number of 82.*	Blei
lead poisoning *The ingestion of lead, exhibited in severe cases by paralysis, encephalopathy, purple gingiva, and colic.*	Bleivergiftung
leaflet *Cusp.*	Klappensegel
leakage *Unintentional escape of gas or fluid.*	Leckage
learning *The intentional aquisition of knowledge.*	Lernen
lecithin *A compound widely used by tissues, derived from egg yolks and it consists of phospholipids linked to choline.*	Lezithin
leech *An annelid used in some tropical regions for drawing out blood; they have an anticoagulant effect locally and have been attached to digits of persons with acute peripheral ischemia.*	Blutegel
left	links
left-handed *The preference of using the left hand for common tasks.*	linkshändig
leg *One of two lower extremities.*	Bein
legionnaires' disease *The name was derived after an outbreak at a convention of the American Legion; it is manifested by fever, chills, dyspnea, and cough.*	Legionärskrankheit
leishmaniasis *A condition caused by a flagellate protozoan parasite that is exhibited by visceral or dermatologic manifestations.*	Leishmaniase
length *The end to end measurement.*	Länge
lengthening *Becoming longer.*	Verlängerung
lens *The transparent chamber between the posterior chamber and the vitreous body.*	Linse
lenticular *Referring to the lens of the eye.*	lentikulär; linsenförmig
lentigo *A benign condition exhibited by flat brown patches on the skin.*	Lentigo
leontiasis ossea *Bilateral hypertrophy of the bones of the face and cranium.*	Leontiasis
Leopold's maneuver *Used to determine fetal position.*	Leopold Handgriff
leproma *A superficial granulatomous papule that is seen in leprosy.*	Leprom
leprosy *A contagious disease caused by Mycobacterium leprae that causes insensate papules and disfiguration.*	Lepra
leptomeningitis *A general term used to describe meningitis of the pia and arachnoid of the brain.*	Leptomeningitis

English	German
leptospirosis *A zoonosis caused by the spirochete Leptospira interrogans transmitted by rats and contaminated water.*	Leptospirose
lesbian *A woman with same gender preference.*	Lesbe
less *A smaller amount.*	weniger
lethal *Deadly.*	letal
lethal dose *The amount of a drug required to cause death.*	letale Dosis
lethargy *Absence of energy.*	Letalität
leucinosis; maple syrup urine disease *A condition characterized by an enzyme defect causing an increase in leucine in the urine.*	Leuzinose; Ahornsirupkrankheit
leukemia *A malignant disease causing an increase in the number of abnormal and immature leukocytes.*	Leukämie
leukine (or leucine) *An amino acid obtained from hydrolysis of some proteins.*	Leukin
leukocyte *A white blood cell.*	Leukozyt
leukocythemia *Synonym of leukemia.*	Leukozythemie
leukocytolysis *Destruction of white blood cells.*	Leukozytolysis
leukocytosis *An increase in the number of leukocytes.*	Leukozytose
leukodermia *A localized loss of skin pigment.*	Leukoderm
leukonychia *A whitish discoloration of the fingernails and toenails.*	Leukonychie
leukopenia *A decreased number of leukocytes in the blood.*	Leukopenie
leukopoiesis *Production of white blood cells.*	Leukopoese
leukorrhea *Thick white vaginal discharge.*	Leukorrhö
levator *A muscle that raises part of the body; the levator labii superioris raised the upper lip.*	Levator
levulose *Synonym for fructose.*	Lävulose; Fruktose
libido *Sexual desire.*	Libido
Libman-Sachs syndrome *A verrucous endocarditis associated with disseminated lupus erythematosus; also called nonbacterial verrucous endocarditis.*	Libman-Sachs-Syndrom
library	Bibliothek
lice *Plural for louse, a small parasite that lives on the skin. Pediculus humanus capitis is a head louse.*	Läuse
lichen *A term used to describe a variety of papular skin diseases. Lichen planus is a shiny, flat, violaceous eruption of the mucous membranes, skin and genitalia.*	Lichen
life expectancy *The length of time a person is anticipated to live.*	Lebenserwartung
life-threatening *Potentially fatal.*	lebensbedrohlich
lifetime *Duration of a person's life.*	Lebenszeit
lift, to *Raise to a higher level.*	heben
ligament *A band of fibrous connective tissue that connects two bones or cartilage.*	Ligament; Band
ligature *A thread used to tie a vessel.*	Ligatur; Unterbindung
light *Illumination, bright.*	hell
light Not heavy.	leicht
light adaptation *The pupillary adjustment after going from a dark environment to one of bright light.*	Lichtanpassung
likelihood *The probability or feasibility.*	Wahrscheinlichkeit
limb *An extremity or branch.*	Extremität

English	German
limbus *The margin of a structure, for example, of the cornea and sclera.*	Limbus
liminal stimulus *Referring to a stimulus of threshold strength.*	Schwellenreiz
lincture *A medicine mixed with a sweet substance.*	Latwerge; Electuarium
linea alba *The tendinous portion of the anterior abdomen between the two rectus muscles.*	Linea alba
lingua nigra *A condition characterized by a dark fur-like covering on the dorsum of the tongue.*	Lingua pilosa nigra
lip, lower *Labium inferius oris.*	Unterlippe
lip, upper *Labium superius oris.*	Oberlippe
lipase *A pancreatic enzyme that facilitates the breakdown of fats.*	Lipase
lipemia *Abnormally high fat content in the blood.*	Lipämie
lipid *A compound that is a fatty acid which is insoluble in water but soluble in organic solvents.*	Lipid
lipid-lowering agent *A medication used to treat hyperlipidemia.*	lipidsenkend Medikation
lipoatrophy *Fatty tissue atrophy.*	Lipoatrophie
lipochondrodystrophy *A congenital condition exhibited by short stature, kyphosis, mental deficiency and short fingers.*	Lipochondrodystrophie; Pfaundler-Hurler-Syndrom
lipocyte *A fat cell.*	Lipozyt
lipodystrophy *Abnormal fat metabolism.*	Lipodystrophie
lipoid *Referring to fat.*	Lipoid; fettähnlich
lipoidosis *Abnormal lipid metabolism.*	Lipoidose
lipoma *A benign tumor consisting of fat cells.*	Lipom
lipoprotein *A soluble protein used to transport fat or lipids.*	Lipoprotein
lipotrophic substance *A compound which causes an increase in body fat.*	lipotrop Substanz
lisping *A speech problem in which "s" and "z" are pronounced "th".*	Lispeln; Sigmatismus
listeriosis *A disease caused by Listeria monocytogenes that occurs in the pregnant and immunocompromised.*	Listeriose
lithagogue *A treatment of a calculus.*	Lithagogum
litholapaxy *The crushing and then removal of a calculus.*	Litholapaxie
lithotomy *Surgical removal of a calculus.*	Lithotomie; Steinschnitt
lithotomy position *Buttocks positioned at the end of the OR table, the hips and knees flexed and the feet strapped in. Dorsosacral position.*	Steinschnittlage
lithotriptor *An instrument used to crush a calculus.*	Lithotriptor
litmus *A dye that turns red with low pH and blue with high pH.*	Lackmus
liver *A large glandular organ in the right upper quadrant that functions in digestive processes, as well as, neutralizing toxins.*	Leber
liver abscess *A localized collection of pus in the liver.*	Leberabszeß
lobar *Referring to a lobe.*	lobär
lobe *A body part divided by a fissure.*	Lappen
lobectomy *Surgical removal of a lobe (generally lung or liver).*	Lobektomie
lobotomy *Surgical incision into the prefrontal lobe; historically a treatment of mental illness.*	Lobotomie
Lobo's disease *A condition exhibited by small, red, hard papules in the sacral region caused by Lacazia loboi.*	Lobo Krankheit; Blasttomycosis queloidana
lobule *A small lobe.*	Läppchen
localization *Establishment of a site of a disease process.*	Lokalisierung

English	German
localized *Toward one point or area.*	lokaliseirt
lochia *Vaginal secretions noted within two weeks of childbirth.*	Lochien; Wochenfluss
locked-in syndrome *A neurologic condition characterized by a person being conscious of their surroundings but being unable to verbally communicate that understanding.*	Locked-in-Syndrom; Eingeschlossensein-Syndrom
loculated *Divided into small cavities.*	Einkapselung
loiasis *A disease caused by the filarial nematode Loa loa.*	Loiasis; Loa-loa-Filariose
long-acting *Referring to a drug with long lasting effects.*	lang wirkend
long-term care *Generally referring to nursing home care.*	Langzeitbetreuung
long-standing *Having existed for a long time.*	jahrelang
longevitiy *Long life.*	Lebensdauer
longsighted *Synonym of hyperopia.*	Weitsichtigkeit; Hyperopie
loose *Not tight.*	locker; frei
looseness *Possessing a quality of not being tight.*	Schlaffheit; Lockerung
lordosis *An abnormal depth of the inward curvature of the spine.*	Lordose
loss of consciousness *Unresponsive to verbal and tactile stimuli.*	Bewusstseinsverlust
loss of function *Inability to complete routine activities.*	Funktionsverlust
lost to follow-up *This describes a situation in which a patient has a chronic medical problem but has not been seen regularly.*	abwesend Verlaufsuntersuchung
lots of *An abundance of.*	viel
low back pain *Pain in the lumbar region.*	Kreuzschmerz
low nasal bridge *A flattening of the top part of the nose.*	flach Nasenrücken
low-fat foods *Nutrients with lower than normal fat content.*	fettreduzierte Lebensmittel
lower extremity edema *Interstitial edema of the legs.*	ödematös Beine
lubricant *Emollient.*	Schmiermittel
lumbago *Pain in the region of the lumbar spine.*	Lumbago
lumbar puncture *Insertion of a needle into the spinal canal in the region of L3-4 to obtain a sample of CSF.*	Lumbalpunktion
lumbar *Referring to the spinal region inferior to the thoracic spine.*	lumbal
lumen *A hollow cavity.*	Lumen
lump *A protuberance.*	Knoten
lunate bone *A carpal bone that articulates with the wrist.*	Mondbein; Os lunatum
lung *One of a pair of respiratory organs.*	Lunge
lung capacity *The amount of air in the lungs after a maximal inhalation.*	Lungenkapazität
lunula *The pale area at the base of a fingernail.*	Lunula
lupus erythematosous *An autoimmune inflammatory disease exhibited by a butterfly shaped rash on the face along with visceral and connective tissue abnormalities.*	Lupus erythrematodes
luteinizing hormone (LH) *A pituitary hormone that stimulates ovulation in females and androgen in males.*	luteinisierendes Hormon
luteotropic *Synonym of prolactin.*	luteotrop
Lyell's syndrome *Also called toxic epidermal necrolysis, there are large portions of the skin that become erythematous with epidermal necrosis as seen with 2nd degree burns. This reaction can be seen with use of nevirapine or Bactrim.*	Lyell-Syndrom
lymph *A transparent and sometimes opalescent fluid that flows in the lymph channels.*	Lymphe

English	German
lymph node *An area of organized lymphatic tissue.*	Lymphknoten
lymphadenitis *Inflammation of a lymph node.*	Lymphadenitis
lymphangiectasis *Distention of the lymph channels.*	Lymphangiektasie
lymphangioma *A mass composed of newly formed lymph tissue.*	Lymphangiom
lymphangitis *Inflammation of the lymph vessels.*	Lymphangitis
lymphatic *Referring to the lymph system.*	lymphatisch
lymphocyte *A white blood cell produced by the lymph tissue.*	Lymphozyt
lymphocythemia *Abnormally high number of lymphocytes in the blood.*	Lymphozytose
lymphocytic leukemia *Chronic accumulation of functionally incompetent lymphocytes.*	lymphatische Leukämie
lymphocytopenia *Decrease in the usual number of lymphocytes in the blood.*	Lymphozytopenie
lymphocytosis *The organization of cysts containing lymph.*	Lymphozytose
lymphoid *Similar to lymph.*	lymphoid
lymphoma *A malignant disease of the lymph system, Hodgkin's lymphoma for example.*	Lymphom
lymphosarcoma *A malignant disease of the lymph system that does not include Hodgkin's lymphoma.*	Lymphosarkom
lysine *An amino acid found in most proteins.*	Lysin
lysis *The rupture of a cell wall or membrane.*	Lyse
lysosome *An organelle contained in the cytoplasm of eukaryotic cells.*	Lysosom
lysozyme *An enzyme in tears that facilitates destruction of certain bacterial cell walls.*	Lysozym
lytic *Referring to lysis.*	lytisch
macrocheilia *Abnormally large lips.*	Makrocheilie
macrocyte *A large red blood cell.*	Makrozyt
macrocytosis *Referring to the status of an increased number of large erythrocytes as seen in Vitamin B12 deficiency.*	Makrozytose
macrodactyly *Abnormally large digits.*	Makrodaktylie
macroencephaly *Having an abnormally large head.*	Makroencephalie
macroglobulinemia *A condition exhibited by an increase number of macroglobulins in the blood.*	Makroglobulinämie
macroglossia *Abnormally large tongue.*	Makroglossie
macromastia *Abnormally large breasts.*	Makromastie
macromelia *Abnormally large head or extremity.*	Makromelie
macrophage *A phagocytic cell that originates in the tissues.*	Makrophage
macrostomia *Abnormal increase in the width of the mouth.*	Großwuchs
macula *1. The area of the eye of greatest visual acuity that surrounds the fovea. 2. A small flat discoloration of the skin (synonym for macule).*	Fleck
macula solaris *Formal medical term describing a freckle.*	Macula solaris
maculopapular *A skin lesion that is similar to both a macule and a papule.*	makuopapulös
mad cow disease *Bovine spongiform encephalopathy, a disease that cause cerebral degeneration exhibited by ataxia.*	bovine spongiforme Enzephalopathie
madness *Common term for insanity.*	Geisteskrankheit; Wahnsinn
magnet *A piece of iron with atoms ordered to make it magnetic.*	Magnet
magnetic *Having the properties of a magnet.*	magnetisch

English	German
magnetic resonance imaging (MRI) *Images are produced by evaluating the response of body tissue. nuclei to radio waves in a magnetic field.*	Magnetresonanztomographie (MRT)
maiden name *The surname a woman uses prior to being married.*	Geburtsname
maintenance therapy *Continuing a form of treatment long-term.*	Erhaltungtherapie
Malabar itch. *Pruritis associated with tinea imbricata which is characterized by overlapping rings of papulosquamous patches. It is also known as oriental ringworm.*	Tropenringwurm
malacia *The abnormal softening of a body part or tissue.*	Malazie
maladjustment *Having the trait of being unable to cope normally.*	schlechte Anpassung
malaise *A vague feeling of discomfort or unease.*	Unpässlichkeit
malalignment (dental) *Displacement of the teeth from their normal position.*	Frakturfehlstellung
malaria *A condition caused by a protozoan of the genus Plasmodium. It is transmitted by mosquitos and is exhibited by fever, chills, headache. In the severe form it can lead to convulsions, increased ICP and death.*	Malaria
malignant *Tendency of a tumor to invade normal tissue.*	maligne
malignant hypertension *Sudden, severe hypertension associated with neuroretinitis.*	maligner Hypotonus
malingerer *A person who feigns illness.*	Simulant
malleolus *A bony protrusion on medial and lateral aspect of each ankle.*	Malleolus; Fußnöchel
malleolus, lateral *The lateral aspect of the distal fibula.*	Malleolus lateralis
malleolus, medial *The medial aspect of the distal portion of the tibia.*	Malleolus medialis
mallet finger *Flexion contracture of the distal phalanx.*	Hammerfinger
malleus *Small bone in the inner ear that articulates with the incus.*	Malleus
Mallory-Weiss syndrome *Upper GI bleeding related to a laceration at the gastroesophageal junction caused by vigorous vomiting.*	Mallory-Weiss-Syndrom
malnutrition *Lack of appropriate nutrition.*	Fehlernährung; Mangelernährung; Malnutrition
malpractice *Negligent professional activity.*	Fehlbehandlung
maltose *A disaccharide hydrolyzed by amylase.*	Maltose; Malzzucker
malunion *The union of a fracture in a faulty position.*	Fehlstellung
mammaplasty *Plastic surgery of the breast.*	Mammaplastik
mammary *Referring to the breast.*	mammär
mammary gland *The mass of tissue posterior to the nipples which has the essential task of milk production.*	Brustdrüse
mammillary *Referring to a nipple.*	mamillär
mammography *Roentgenography of the breasts, used as a screening test for cancer.*	Mammographie
man *Male human.*	Mann
management *The process of dealing with things or people.*	Versogung
mandatory *Obligatory.*	obligatorisch
mandible *The lower jaw.*	Unterkiefer
mania *A mental disorder exhibited by hyperexcitability, delusions and euphoria.*	Manie; Tobsucht
manic-depressive psychosis *A mental disorder exhibited by alternating periods of depression and mania.*	bipolare affektive Psychose

English	German
manometer *Device used for pressure monitoring.*	Manometer
manubrium sterni *The superior segment of the sternum which articulates with the clavicle and first rib.*	Manubrium sterni
maple syrup urine disease *A condition characterized by an enzyme defect causing an increase in leucine in the urine.*	Ahornsirupkrankheit
mapping *A collection of data points showing spatial distribution.*	Mapping; Kartierung
marasmus *Progressive weight loss and emaciation.*	Marasmus
Marfan syndrome *A connective tissue disease exhibited by long limbs, joint laxity and cardiovascular defects.*	Marfan Syndrom
marijuana *Cannabis.*	Marihuana
marital counseling *Therapy aimed at marriage reconciliation.*	Ehelichberatung
marital status *Single verus married status.*	Ehestand
marsupialization *Creation of a surgical pouch.*	Marsupialisation
mass *Tumor.*	Masse
mast cell *A cell containing basophilic granules that releases histamine and other substances during allergic reactions.*	Mastzelle
mastectomy *Surgical resection of one or both breasts.*	Mastektomie
mastication *Chewing.*	Mastikation; Kaubewegung
mastitis *Inflammation of the breast.*	Mastitis
mastodynia *Breast pain.*	Mastodynie
mastoid *Referring to the mastoid process.*	Warzenfortsatz
mastoid process *The posterior part of the temporal bone bordered by the parietal bone superiorly and the occipital bone posteriorly.*	Warzenfortsatz
mastoidectomy *Surgical removal of the mastoid.*	Mastoidektomie
mastoiditis *Inflammation of the mastoid process.*	Mastoiditis
matching *Corresponding in pattern or style.*	Abgleichung;Zuordnung
mattress *A fabric case filled with material, used for sleeping.*	Matratze
mattress suture *A double stitch that forms a loop and there is eversion of the edges when tied.*	Matratzennaht
maxilla *The upper jaw that also forms the inferior portion of the orbit and part of the nose.*	Oberkiefer
maxillofacial *Referring to the maxilla and the face.*	maxillofazial
mazamorra *Dermatitis caused by hookworm larvae indigenous to Peurto Rico.*	Mazamorra
Mcdonald's maneuver *A measurement of the uterus in centimeters that corresponds to gestational age in weeks.*	Mcdonald Manöver
meaningless *Having no significance.*	bedeutungslos
measles *A childhood viral, infectious disease exhibited by rash and fever.*	Masern
meatus *Opening to the body, such as urethral meatus.*	Gang
meconium *The first newborn feces which are green.*	Mekonium; Kindspech
meconium aspiration *Presence of meconium on the newborn indicating there was fetal distress in-utero.*	Mekoniumaspirationssyndrom
medial *Situated toward the midline.*	medial
medianstinoscopy *Visual inspection of the mediastinum with a scope.*	Mediastinoskopie
mediastinum *The thoracic area between the lungs.*	Mediastinum
medical record *The electronic or paper report on a patient.*	Krankenbericht
medication *A substance used for medical treatment.*	Medikation

English	German
medicine *A substance used for medical treatment or the art and science of healing patients.*	Medizin; Heilkunde
medicosurgical *Referring to medicine and surgery.*	medikochirurgisch
medulla oblongata *The inferior portion of the brainstem.*	Medulla oblongata
medullary *1. The inner part of an organ. 2. Referring to the medulla oblongata.*	medullär
medulloblastoma *A malignant tumor of the cerebellum found mostly in children.*	Medulloblastom
megacephaly *Having a larger than normal cranial capacity.*	Makrozephalie
megacolon *Abnormal enlargement and dilatation of the colon.*	Megakolon
megakaryocyte *A cell found in the bone marrow that is a source of platelet production.*	Megakaryozyt
megaloblast *A large red blood cell noted primarily in pernicious anemia.*	Megaloblast
megalomania *A mental disorder characterized by abnormal feelings of self-importance.*	Megalomanie; Größenwahn
meibomian cyst *An enclosed fluid collection along a sebaceous gland of the eyelid.*	Meibom-Zyste
meiosis *Cell division creating two daughter cells each with half the number of cells as the parent cell.*	Meiose
melancholia *Profound sadness.*	Melancholie
melanin *A dark pigment found on the skin, hair or iris.*	Menlanin
melanoma *Malignant cancer, typically found in the skin.*	Melanom
melena *The passage of black, tarry stools indicative of upper gastrointestinal bleeding.*	Melaena
melissophobia *Also called apiphobia, a fear of bees.*	Apiphobie
melitis *Inflammation of the cheek.*	Melitis
member *Referring to an extremity (arm or leg).*	Glied
memory *Ability to remember.*	Gedächtnis
menarche *The time of the initial menstrual period.*	Menarche
meningeal *Referring to the dura mater, arachnoid and the pia mater.*	meningeal
meningioma *A tumor of the meningeal tissue; generally benign.*	Meningeom
meningism *Signs and symptoms of meningitis without infection of the meninges.*	Meningismus
meningitis *Inflammation of the meninges exhibited by fever, photophobia, nuchal rigidity and in severe cases coma and convulsions.*	Meningitis
meningocele *A congenital defect exhibited by protrusion of the meninges through a defect in the spinal column.*	Meningozele
meningococcemia *Presence of N. meningitidis in the blood.*	Meningokokkemie
meniscectomy *Surgical excision of a meniscus.*	Meniskektomie
meniscus *A thin cartilage between joint surfaces.*	Meniskus
menopause *The time when menstruation ceases.*	Menopause
menorrhagia *Abnormally large amount of menstrual blood.*	Menorrhagie
menses *The blood and other material expelled from the uterus during menstruation.*	Monatsblutung
menstruation *Synonym of menses.*	Menstruation
mental *Cognitive or psychological.*	mental; geistig
mention, to *Refer to or allude to.*	erwähnen

English	German
mesarteritis *Inflammation of the middle layer of an artery.*	Mesarteriitis
mesencephalon *Midbrain.*	Mittelhirn
mesenchyme *Organized mesodermal cells that produce connective tissue, lymphatics and bone.*	Mesenchym
mesentery *The fold of peritoneum that connects the small bowel, pancrease and spleen to the posterior portion of the abdominal wall.*	Mesenterium
mesoappendix *The portion of the mesentery vermiform appendix.*	Mesoappendix
mesocolon *The mesentery connecting the colon to the posterior abdominal wall.*	Mesokolon
mesoderm *The middle germ layer in an embryo that is the source of bone, muscle and skin.*	Mesoderm
mesonephroma *Usually a tumor of the female genital tract that is thought to stem from the mesonephros.*	Mesonephrom
mesosalpinx *A portion of the broad ligament supporting the fallopian tubes.*	Mesosalpinx
mesothelioma *A tumor that stems from mesothelial tissue; a known cause is asbestos exposure.*	Mesotheliom
mesovarium *The portion of the mesentery connecting the ovary with the abdominal wall.*	Mesovarium
metabolic *Referring to the physical and chemical reactions involved with keeping an organism functioning.*	metabolisch
metacarpal *The name for any of the five hand bones.*	metakarpal
metacarpophalangeal *Referring to the metacarpus and the phalanges.*	metakarophalangeal
metaphysis *The region between the diaphysis and the epiphysis.*	Metaphyse
metaplasia *Abnormal change in the nature or character of tissue.*	Metaplasie
metatarsal *Any of the bones of the foot.*	metatarsal
metatarsalgia *Foot pain.*	Metatarsalgie
meter *Unit if measurement. (instrument for measurement)*	Meter (Meßgerät)
methemoglobin *A substance formed with the oxidation of hemoglobin.*	Methämoglobin
methionine *A sulfur-containing amino acid used in the biosynthesis of cysteine.*	Methionin
metric system	metrisches Maßsystem
metrorrhagia *Uterine bleeding in normal amounts but at irregular intervals.*	Metorrhagie
microbe *A microorganism.*	Mikrobe
microbiology *The study of microorganisms.*	Mikrobiologie
microcephalic *A congenital deformity exhibited by an abnormally small head.*	mikrozephal
microcyte *An unusually small erythrocyte associated with anemias, such as iron deficiency anemia.*	Mikrozyt
micrognathia *Abnormally small maxilla or mandible.*	Mikrognathie
microgram *One millionth of one gram.*	Mikrogramm
micrometer *One millionth of one meter.*	Mikrometer
microorganism *An organism only seen with a microscope.*	Mikroorganismus
microphthalmos *A congenital condition characterized by smallness of the eyes.*	Mikroophthalmus
microscope *A instrument used to magnify and view small objects.*	Mikroskop
micturition *Synonym of urination.*	Miktion
midbrain *The portion of the brainstem superior to the pons.*	Mittelhirn

English	German
middle ear *The portion of the ear containing the stapes, incus and malleus.*	Mittelohr
midline *A median line of bilateral separation.*	Mittellinie
midstream urine *A specimen of urine that is collected after the initial stream of urine is initiated and before one finishes urinating.*	Mittelstrahlurin
midwife *A person trained to assist in childbirth.*	Hebamme; Entbindungspfeger
midwifery *The occupation of assisting in childbirth.*	Geburtshilfe
migraine *An episodic, unilateral headache accompanied by nausea.*	Migräne
mild *Slight, nominal.*	mild, leicht
milestone *An event indicative of a certain stage of development.*	Meilenstein
miliary *Referring to a disease that is exhibited by small seed-like lesions (millet), such as miliary tuberculosis.*	miliar
Milkman syndrome *Osteomalacia with multiple pseudofractures.*	Milkmansyndrom
milligram *A unit of weight, 1/1000 of a gram.*	Milligramm
milliliter *A unit of volume, 1/1000 of a liter.*	Milliliter
millimeter *A unit of measurement, 1/1000 of a meter.*	Millimeter
Milroy's disease *Hereditary disease exhibited by leg edema.*	Nonne-Milroy-Krankheit; Lymphödem
minute *A unit of time.*	Minute
minute *Something very small.*	winzig
mirror *A device used for reflecting an image.*	Speigel
miryachit *A disease of Siberia characterized by an exaggerated startle response; also referred to as jumping disease.*	Choreomanie; Springend Krankheit
misanthropy *A severe dislike of homo sapiens.*	Misanthropie
miscarriage *Spontaneous abortion.*	Fehlgebrut; Spontanabort
misspelling *Incorrect spelling of a word.*	Rechtschreibfehler
mite fever *Synonym of typhus fever.*	Fleckfieber
mitochondria *Organelle found in cells responsible for energy production.*	Mitochondrien
mitosis *Cell division in which two daughter cells are formed that have the same number of chromosomes as the parent cell.*	Mitose
mitral *Referring to the mitral valve.*	mitral
mitral regurgitation *Backflow of blood from the left ventricle to the left atrium because of dysfunctional valve.*	Mitralinsuffizienz
mitral stenosis *Narrowing of the left atrioventricular orifice.*	Mitralstenose
mitral valve *The valve with two cusps between the left atrium and ventricle.*	Mitralklappe
modiolus *A column located in the cochlea.*	Modiolus
moist *Damp or humid.*	feucht
molality *The number of moles of a solution per kilogram of pure solvent.*	Molalität
molar tooth *Any of the most posterior teeth bilaterally which includes 8 deciduous and usually 12 permanent teeth.*	Backenzahn
molecule *A combination of at least two atoms.*	Molokül
monitoring *A person that observes a process or a monitoring device.*	Beobachten
monkey-paw *An appearance due to median nerve palsy causing atrophy of the thenar eminence with adduction and elevation of the thumb, resembling that of a simian.*	Affenhand

English	German
monkeypox *A viral disease that is similar to smallpox which occurs primarily in monkeys and rarely in humans.*	Affenpocken
monoamine oxidase inhibitor (MAOI) *A drug used to treat depression that allows accumulation of serotonin and norepinephrine.*	Monoaminoxidasehemmer
monoclonal *Asexual formation of a clone from a single cell.*	monoklonal
monocyte *A leukocyte with an oval nucleus and grey cytoplasm.*	Monozyt
monocytosis *An abnormal increase in the number of monocytes in the blood.*	Monozytose
monodiplopia *Double vision in only one eye.*	Monodiplopie
monomania *A psychotic obsession about a single subject.*	Monomanie
mononeuritis *Inflammation of a single nerve.*	Mononeuritis
mononuclear *A cell having only one nucleus.*	mononukleär
mononucleosis *An infectious disease exhibited by malaise and lymphadenopathy.*	Mononukleose; Pfeiffer-Drüsenfieber
monoplegia *Paralysis of a single limb.*	Monoplegie
mons pubis *The fleshy protuberance over the symphysis pubis.*	Schamhügel; Mons pubis
mood *A temporarty state of mind or feeling.*	Stimmung; Laune
morbid *Indicative of disease.*	morbid
morbidity *The state of disease.*	Morbidität
Morgagni's syndrome *Also called metabolic craniopathy and Stewart-Morel syndrome, it is exhibited by hyperostosis frontalis interna, obesity and neuropsychiatric disorders.*	Morgagnisyndrom
morgue *A room where deceased patients are housed until sent to a funeral home.*	Leichenschauhaus
moribund *Near death.*	moribund
morning sickness *Nausea associated with pregnancy.*	Schwangerschaftserbrechen
morphea *A condition exhibited by an elevated or depressed patch of pink skin with a purple border.*	umschriebene Sklerodermie
morphine *An opioid analgesic.*	Morphin
morphology *The study of living organisms and the correlation between their structure.*	Morphologie
morula *A solid mass created by the splitting of an ovum.*	Morula
mosquito net *A fine mesh fabric hung over a bed as a mosquito repellent.*	Moskitonetz
mossy fiber *Nerve fibers that surround the nerve cells of the cerebellar cortex.*	moosfasern
motion sickness *Nausea associated with travel.*	Reisekrankheit
motor *Referring to muscles.*	motorisch
motor end plate *The expansions on a motor nerve where the branches terminate on muscle fiber.*	motorisch Endplatte
motor unit *The complex of one motor cell and its attached muscle fibers.*	motorisch Einheit
mottled *An irregular arrangement of patches of color.*	gesprenkelt
mourning *A period of grieving.*	Trauer
mouth *The orifice on the lower part of the face.*	Mund
mouth to mouth *A manner of artificial respiration.*	Mund-zu-Mund
mouth to mouth resuscitation *A form of emergency management of respiratory failure.*	Mund-zu-Mund Beatmung
mouthful *A large quantity of something in one's mouth.*	Mundvol

112

English	German
mucilage *1. A viscous bodily fluid. 2. A polysaccharide used in medicines and glue.*	Schleim
mucin *A glycoprotein that is the primary constituent in mucous.*	Muzin
mucocele *An accumulation of mucous in a dilated cavity.*	Mukozele
mucoid *Referring to mucous.*	mukoid
mucolytic *A substance that breaks down mucous.*	mukolytisch
mucopolysaccharidosis type I *Also referred to as Hurler syndrome, persons cannot make lysosomal alpha-L-iduronidase which breaks down glycosaminoglycans.*	Mukopolysacchaaridose Typ 1
mucopolysaccharidosis type II *Also referred to as Hunter syndrome, persons with this inherited condition cannot produce iduronate sulfatase. There are mild to severe forms but all forms have deafness, coarse facial features, hypertrichosis and macrocephaly.*	Mukopolysacchaaridose Typ 2
mucopolysaccharidosis type III *Also referred to as Sanfilippo syndrome, persons cannot catabolize the heparan sulfate sugar chain. Symptoms include stiff joints, thick eyebrows, coarse facial features and developmental delays.*	Mukopolysacchaaridose Typ 3
mucopolysaccharidosis type Is *Also referred to as Scheie syndrome, persons cannot produce lysosomal alpha-L-iduronidase. Symptoms include cloudy cornea, hirsutism, prognathism and stiff joints.*	Mukopolysacchaaridose Typ 1s
mucopolysaccharidosis type IV *Also referred to as Morquio syndrome, persons do not produce galactosamine-6-sulfatase or in some cases beta-galactosidase. Symptoms include hypermobile joints, macrocephaly, short stature and wide spaced teeth.*	Mukopolysacchaaridose Typ 1V
mucopolysaccharidosis type VI *Also referred to as Maroteaux-Lamy syndrome. It is characterized by hydrocephalus, macroglossia and coarse facial features but normal intelligence.*	Mukopolysacchaaridose Typ V1
mucopurulent *That which contains both mucous and pus.*	mukopurulent; schleimig-eitrig
mucosa *A mucous membrane like the buccal mucosa.*	Mucosa; Schleimhaut
Mucune-Albright syndrome *Polyostotic fibrous dysplasia with cutaneous brown patches, endocrine dysfunction that exhibits in females as precocious puberty.*	Albright-McCune-Sternberg Syndrom
mucus *A substance secreted by mucous membranes.*	Mukus; Schleim
multigravida *A woman who has been pregnant more than once.*	Multigravida
multilocular *The presence of more than one cell within a cavity.*	mehrkammerig
multipara *A woman with more than one live births.*	Multipara; Mehrgebärende
multiple sclerosis *A chronic neurologic disease exhibited by numbness, vision and speech problems, and motor incoordination.*	multiple Sklerose
mumble, to *To speak quietly and indistinctly.*	mussitierend
mumps *A contagious viral disease that is exhibited by parotid swelling and puts males at risk for sterility. Also called epidemic parotitis.*	Mumps; Parotitis epidemica
mural thrombus *A thrombus attached to a diseased portion of endocardium.*	Wandthrombus
murmur *An abnormal heart sound heard with a stethoscope.*	Geräusch
muscle *A band if fibrous tissue that can contract.*	Muskel
muscle weakness *Decreased muscular function.*	Muskelschwäche
muscular *Refering to muscles.*	muskulär
muscular dystrophy *A hereditary condition exhibited by progressive muscular weakness and muscle atrophy.*	Muskeldystrophie; Dystrophie musculorum
mutation *A gene alteration that can be passed to the next generation.*	Mutation

113

English	German
mute *Refraining from or being speechless.*	stumm
mutism *Inability to speak.*	Mutismus
myalgia *Muscle pain.*	Myalgie
myasthenia gravis *An autoimmune disease characterized by fluctuating weakness of the ocular, limb and respiratory muscles.*	Myasthenie gravis pseudoparalytica; Hoppe-Goldflam Syndrom
mycetoma *Persistent inflammation of the tissues caused by an infection.*	Madurafuß
mycosis *A disease caused by a fungal infection.*	Mykose
mycotoxin *A substance toxic to fungus.*	Mykotoxin
mydriasis *Pupillary dilation.*	Mydriasis
myelin *The substance that forms a sheath around some nerve fibers.*	Myelin
myelitis *Inflammation of the spinal cord.*	Myelitis
myelocele *Protrusion of the spinal cord through a defect in the bony structure.*	Myelozele
myelogram *CT scan or roentgenography of the spinal canal after injection of contrast media.*	Myelogramm
myeloid *Referring to the bone marrow or spinal cord.*	myeloid
myeloma *Malignant tumor of the bone marrow.*	Myelom; Plasmozytom
myelomatosis *A leukemic disease in which there is an abnormally high amount of myeloblasts in the blood.*	Myelomatose
myelomeningocele *A protrusion of the spinal cord and its meninges through a defect in the vertebral canal.*	Myelomeningozele
myelopathy *A condition of the spinal cord.*	Myelopathie
myocardial *Referring to the muscular tissue of the heart.*	myokardial
myocardial infarction *The death of myocardial tissue as a result of an interruption in flow to the region supplied by a coronary vessel.*	Myokardinfarkt; Herzinfarkt
myocarditis *An inflammation of the heart.*	Herzmuskelentzündung
myocardium *The middle layer of the heart wall.*	Myokard
myoclonus *Contraction or spasm of a group of muscles.*	Myoklonus
myoglobin *A protein within muscle that carries and stores oxygen.*	Myoglobin
myoma *A benign neoplasm of muscular tissue.*	Myom
myomectomy *Surgical resection of a myoma.*	Myomektomie
myometrium *The smooth muscle layer of the uterus.*	Myometrium
myopathy *Muscle disease.*	Myopathie
myope *A person who is nearsighted.*	myope Person
myopia *Nearsightedness.*	Myopie
myosarcoma *A mass with myoma and sarcoma characteristics.*	Myosarkom
myosin *A protein that when coupled with actin form the contractile complex of a muscle cells.*	Myosin
myositis *Inflammation of muscle tissue.*	Myositis; Muskelentzündung
myositis ossificans *Inflammation of muscle tissue with presence of bony deposits.*	Myositis ossificans
myotomy *The surgical removal of muscle tissue.*	Myotomie
myotonia dystrophica; Steinert's disease *A condition exhibited initially by hypertonic muscles followed by atrophy of the facial and neck muscles.*	Myotonie dystrophica

English	German
myringitis *Inflammation of the tympanic membrane.*	Myringitis; Trommelfellentzündung
myringoplasty *Surgical repair of tympanic membrane defects.*	Myringoplastik
myringotomy *Surgical opening of the tympanic membrane.*	Myringotomie
mysophobia *Severe fear of dirt or contamination from common objects.*	Mysophobie
myxedema *Diffuse edema with a wax-like appearance of the skin; this condition is associated with hypothyroidism.*	Myxödem
myxoma *A tumor composed of mucous tissue.*	Myxom
myxosarcoma *A sarcoma that also has mucous tissue.*	Myxosarkom
nail *The hard surface on the dorsal surface of the toes or fingers.*	Nagel
nailbed *The area just beneath a finger or toenail.*	Nagelbett
nail biting *A habit of chewing on one's fingernails.*	Fingernägelbeißen; Nägelkauen; Onychophagie
nailing *Referring to placement of an intramedullary rod in a long bone in order to treat a fracture.*	Nagelung
name *A word by which a person is known.*	Name; Bezeichnung
nap *A brief sleep or catnap.*	Nickerchen
narcissism *Abnormally excessive self-interest.*	Narzissmus
narcolepsy *A condition exhibited by a strong desire to sleep and by sudden onset of sleep at increased intervals.*	Narkolepsie; Gélineau Syndrom
narcosis *A reversible medication-induced condition of excessive drowsiness or unconsciousness.*	Narkose; Betäubung
narcotic *A medication that produces narcosis.*	Opiat; Betäubungsmittel
nasal *Referring to the nose.*	nasal
nasogastric tube *A tube that is inserted into the nose with the distal tip in the stomach; it is used for irrigation or drainage of gastric contents.*	Nasomagensonde
nasogastric tube placement *Insertion of a tube that is placed in the stomach via the nostril; it is used for administration of fluid or to suction gastric contents.*	Nasomagensonde einbringen
nasolacrimal *Referring to the nose and tear apparatus.*	nasolakrimal
nasopharyngeal *Referring to the nose and pharynx.*	nasopharyngeal
nasopharynx *The part of the pharynx which lies superior to the soft palate.*	Nasopharynx; Nasenrachenraum
nausea *A feeling that one wants to vomit.*	Nausea; Übelkeit; Brechreiz
navel *Umbilicus.*	Nabel
navicular *1. boat shaped 2. Referring to the navicular bone of the hand or foot.*	navikulär
navicular bone *The most lateral bone in the proximal row of carpal bones.*	Kahnbein; Navikulare
near *In close proximity.*	nah
nebula *An opaque spot on the cornea causing impaired vision.*	Nebelfleck
nebulizer *A device used for transforming a liquid into a fine mist for inhalation as in nebulized albuterol for an acute exacerbation of asthma.*	Vernebler
nebulizer treatment *Administration of medication such as albuterol via a fine mist using a nebulizer.*	vernebler Verfahren
neck *The part of the body that connects the body to the head.*	Hals; Nacken

English	German
neck of the femur *The portion of the femur between the shaft and head.*	Oberschenkelhals
necropsy *Synonym of autopsy.*	Autopsie; Leichenschau
necrosis *The death of most of the cells of the affected part.*	Nekrose
necrotic *Referring to necrosis.*	nekrotisch
need *A want or obligation.*	Bedarf
needle *The slender cylindrical device attached to a syringe.*	Nadel
needle biopsy *Use of a needle to aspirate body contents for microscopic or pathologic examination.*	Nadelbiopsie
needle for lumbar puncture	Lumbalpunktionsnadel
needle holder *A surgical instrument used to grasp a needle during suturing.*	Nadelhalter
needle-stick injury *The inadvertent self-puncture with a needle that had been used previously to inject a patient.*	Nadelstichverletzung
negative *Contrary or opposing.*	negativ
nematode *An endoparasite belonging to the class of the Nemathelminthes including roundworms and threadworms.*	Nematode
neonatal *Referring to the first four weeks after birth.*	neonatal
neonate *The term for a newborn infant for the first four weeks.*	Neugeborenes
neoplasm *A new and abnormal growth.*	Neoplasma
nephrectomy *Surgical removal of a kidney.*	Nephrektomie
nephritis *A general term meaning inflammation of a kidney that is further categorized depending on the associated pathology.*	Nephritis; Nierenentzündung
nephroblastoma *Congenital tumor of the kidney, also called Wilms' tumor.*	Nephroblastom; Wilms-Tumor
nephrocalcinosis *A condition exhibited by calcium phosphate deposition in the renal tubules; a cause of renal insufficiency.*	Nephrokalzinose
nephrolithiasis *A calculus in the kidney.*	Nephrolithiasis
nephrolithotomy *Surgical removal of a renal calculus.*	Nephrolithotomie
nephroma *A renal tumor.*	Nephrom; Nierentumor
nephron *A functional unit of the kidney that consists of the glomerulus, the proximal and distal convoluted tubules, the loop of Henle and the collecting tubule.*	Nephron
nephropathy *Renal disease.*	Nephropathie
nephropexy *The surgical fixation of a kidney that was previously floating.*	Nephropexie
nephroptosis *Inferior displacement of the kidney.*	Nephroptose
nephrosclerosis *Hardening of the kidney.*	Nephrosklerose
nephrosis *A kidney disease exhibited by edema and proteinuria; also called nephrotic syndrome.*	Nephrose
nephrostomy *Surgical creation of an opening between the renal pelvis and an opening in the skin.*	Nephrostomie
nephrotic *Referring to nephrosis.*	nephrotisch
nephrotomy *Surgical incision of the kidney.*	Nephrotomie
nerve *A fibrous band made up of axons and dendrites that connects the nervous systems with other organs.*	Nerv
nerve impulse *A signal transmitted along a nerve fiber.*	Nervenimpuls
nerve block anesthesia *Locally administered anesthesia.*	Leitungsanästhesie
neural *Referring to a nerve or nerve impulse.*	neural

English	German
neuralgia *Severe pain along the course of a nerve.*	Neuralgie
neurapraxia *Paralysis from nerve injury but no degeneration of the nerve.*	Neurapraxie
neurasthenia *A psychoneurosis exhibited by severe fatigue.*	Neurasthenie
neurectomy *Excision of a section of a nerve.*	Neurektomie
neurilemma *The membrane covering a myelinated nerve fiber or the axon of an unmyelinated nerve fiber.*	Neurilemm
neuritis *Inflammation of a nerve.*	Neuritis; Nervenentzündung
neuroblastoma *A nervous system malignant tumor composed of neuroblasts.*	Neuroblastom
neurodermatitis *A pruritic, thickened eruption in the axillary and inguinal thought to be exacerbated by emotions.*	Neurodermatitis; atopisches Ekzem
neuroepithelium *Cells specialized to serve as sensory cells such as cells of the cochlea and tongue.*	Neuroepithel
neurofibroma *A tumor formed by excessive growth of perineurium and endoneurium.*	Neurofibrom
neurofibromatosis *A hereditary condition exhibited by formation of multiple soft tumors scattered throughout the skin surface. Also known as von Recklinghausen disease.*	Neurofibromatose; Reckinghausen-Krankheit
neuroglia *A type of connective tissue of the nervous system.*	Neuroglia
neuroleptic *A drug that causes neurologic symptoms.*	Neuroleptikum
neuroleptic malignant syndrome *A severe reaction to neuroleptic medications characterized by hyperthermia with autonomic and extrapyramidal symptoms.*	Neuroleptikasyndrom
neurologist *A physician who specializes in the study of the nervous system.*	Neurologe
neurology *The study of the nervous system.*	Neurologie
neuroma *A mass composed of nerve cells and fibers.*	Neurom
neuron *A nerve cell.*	Neuron
neuropathic *Referring to neuropathy.*	neuropathisch
neuropathy *Structural of pathologic changes of the peripheral nervous system.*	Neuropathie
neurosis *A mental disorder.*	Neurose
neurosurgery *Surgery of the brain or spinal cord.*	Neurochirurgie
neurosyphilis *Infection of the central nervous system with Treponema pallidum.*	Neurosyphilis
neurotmesis *The severing of a nerve.*	Neurotmesis
neurotomy *Surgical incision into a nerve.*	Neurotomie
neurotransmitter *A substance released at the end of a nerve fiber that facilitates transmission of an impulse.*	Neurotransmitter
neutropenia *Diminished number of neutrophils in the blood.*	Neurtropenie
neutrophil *A polymorphonuclear leukocyte.*	Neutrophile
nevus *A benign, well-circumscribed growth of tissue of congenital origin.*	Naevus
next *The following or upcoming.*	nächste
nick *A small groove or notch.*	Kerbe
nicotinic acid *A deficiency of this substance results in pellagra.*	Nicotinsäure
night blindness *Common term for nyctalopia, it refers to low vision with reduced illumination, often seen with Vitamin A deficiency.*	Nachtblindheit

English	German
night shift *The late shift, typically beginning at 19:00 or 23:00 hours.*	Nachtarbeit
night sweats *Profuse sweating at night occurring with tuberculosis among other conditions.*	Nachtschweiß
night terror *Sensation of profound fear upon wakening.*	Pavor nocturnus; Nachtangst
nightmare *An unpleasant or frightening dream.*	Alptraum
nipple *The small projection on the breast thru which milk is secreted.*	Mamille; Brustwarze
nitrogen *A colorless, odorless gas used as a coolant in the liquid form.*	Stickstoff
nitrous oxide *An inhalant gas used as an anesthetic agent.*	Stickoxidul
nocturia *Urination at night.*	Nykturie; nächtliches Wasserlassen
nocturnal emission *Involuntary emission of semen at night.*	Pollutio
nocturnal *Referring to events that happen at night.*	nächtlich
node *A swelling or prominence.*	Knoten
nodule *A small node in the skin of up to 1cm and in the lung up to 3cm.*	Knötchen
nonpitting edema *Subcutaneous swelling that cannot be indented with compression.*	wegdrückbares Ödem
non-rebreather mask *A type of oxygen mask used to deliver a higher oxygen concentration.*	Nichtrückatmungsmaske
non-resorbable suture (nylon) *Suture used to be permanent as it is not removed by normal body processes.*	Nylon-Sutur
noon *The 12 o'clock mid-day hour.*	zwölf Uhr mittags
norepinephrine *A hormone secreted by the adrenal medulla and a synthetic drug used as a pressor agent.*	Noradrenalin
normoblast *A precursor cell for erythrocytes.*	Normoblast
normocyte *A normal erythrocyte.*	Normozyt
Norway itch *A severe pruritis caused by scabies and is associated with immune disorders such as AIDS.*	Scabies norvegica; Boeck-Skabies
nose *The midface protuberance used for smelling and breathing.*	Nase
nosebleed *Common term for epistaxis.*	Nasenbluten; Epistaxis
nosocomial infection *An infection occurring after admission to a hospital.*	nsokomiale infektion
nosology *The medical science of disease classification.*	Nosologie
nosophobia *Unwarranted, excessive fear of any disease.*	Nosophobie
nostril *One of two openings in the nose used for air passage.*	Nasenloch
noxious *Harmful or poisonous.*	schädlich
nuclear magnetic resonance (NMR) *A type a diagnostic body imaging utilizing electromagnetic radiation in a magnetic field.*	Kernspinresonanz (NMR)
nuclear medicine *The branch of medicine associated with the use of radioactive material in the evaluation and treatment of disease.*	Nuklearmedizin
nuclear *Referring to a nucleus.*	nukleär
nucleic acid *An organic compound found in living cells; its molecules contain nucleotides linked in long chains.*	Nukleinsäure
nucleoprotein *A substance composed of a nucleic acid and a protein.*	Nukleoprotein
nulligravida *A woman who has never been pregnant.*	Nulligravida
nullipara *A woman who has never given birth.*	Nullipara
numb chin syndrome. *Generally associated with metastatic breast or prostate cancer, it is characterized by unilateral sensory loss of the chin and lower lip.*	Gefühlloskinn-Syndrom

118

English	German
numbness *Decreased sensation to tactile stimuli.*	Taubheit
nummulation *Formed as round, flat discs.*	Geldrollenbildung
nurse *A person trained to care for the sick.*	Krankenschwester; Pflegeperson
nurse practitioner *A person with advanced training capable of acting as a patient's primary care provider.*	Gemeindeschwester
nursing care *The assessment and treatment provided by nurses.*	Krankenpflege
nutation *Referring to nodding of the head.*	Nickbewegung
nutrient *A substance that provides essential nourishment.*	Nährstoff; Nahrungsstoff
nutrient foramen *A conduit for passage of nutrient vessels in the marrow of bone.*	Foramen nutricium
nutrition *The process of supplying food needed for growth.*	Ernährung
nutritional status *The relative state of one's nutrition.*	Ernährungszustand
nystagmus *Rapid involuntary movement of the eyes; it can be horizontal, vertical or rotary.*	Nystagmus
nyxis *Paracentesis or a puncture.*	Parazentese
obesity *Having a body mass index over 30kilograms/meters squared.*	Fettleibigkeit
obsession *A pathologic preoccupation.*	Zwangsvorstelung
obsolete *No longer in use; antiquated.*	obsolet
obstetric *Referring to The management of pregnancy, labor and the peuperium.*	geburtshilflich
obstetrician *A physician who specializes in the management of pregnancy, labor and the peuperium.*	Geburtshelfer
obstructed *To be blocked or halted.*	gehemmt
obturator *A device used to close an artificial or natural opening.*	Obturator
obtuse *Rather insensitive or hard to understand.*	stumpf
occipital *Referring to the back part of the head.*	okzipital
occipitofrontal muscle *Raises the eyebrows.*	okzipitofrontal Muskel
occlusion *A pathway that is blocked or obstructed.*	Okklusion; Verschluß
occlusive dressing *A synthetic covering for a wound that has a semipermeable membrane.*	Okklusivverband
occult blood *Presence of blood from an unknown source.*	okkultes Blut
occupational therapy *Rehabilitation focusing on activities of daily living.*	Beschäftigungstherapie
ocular paralysis. *Paralysis of intraocular and extraocular muscles.*	Augenmuskellähmung
ocular *Referring to the eye.*	Okular; okulär
oculogyric *Referring to movement of the eye around the anteroposterior axis.*	okulogyre
oculomotor nerve *Referring to cranial nerve III which is one of the nerves responsible for extraocular movements.*	Nervus okulomotorisch
odiferous *Having an unpleasant or distinctive smell.*	riechend
odontalgia *Tooth pain.*	Odontalgie; Zahnschmerz
odontoid *A prominence on the second cervical vertebra on which the first cervical vertebra pivots.*	odontoid
odontology *Synonym of dentistry.*	Odontologie
odor *A smell that is given off someone or something.*	Geruch; Duft
odynophagia *Pain associated with swallowing.*	Schluckschmerz
odynophonia *Pain associated with speaking.*	Sprechschmerz
offspring *One's children.*	Nachkommenschaft

English	German
ointment *A petroleum jelly based topical medication.*	Salbe; Unguentum
old age *A relative term for the period of advanced years.*	hohes Alter
older *Being around more than compared with another.*	älter
olecranon *The bony protrusion at the proximal ulna at the elbow.*	Olekranon
olfactory *Referring to the sense of smell.*	olfaktorisch
oligodactyly *Presence of fewer than 5 digits on a hand or foot.*	Oligodaktylie
oligodendroglia *The ectodermal cells forming part of the central nervous system.*	Oligodendroglia
oligohydramnios *Inadequate amount of amniotic fluid.*	Oligohydramnie
oligomenorrhea *Infrequent menstruation or low volume menstrual flow.*	Oligomenorrhö
oligoptyalism *Insufficient secretion of saliva; also oligosialia.*	Oligosialie
oligospermia *Abnormally low sperm count.*	Oligospermie
oligotrophia or hypotrichosis *Less than normal amount of head/body hair.*	Oligotrichie
oliguria *Abnormally low urine output.*	Oligurie
ombrophobia *An abnormal fear of rain.*	Ombrophobie
omentocele *A herniated protrusion of omentum.*	Omentozele
omentopexy *Surgically fastening the omentum to an adjacent tissue it was not previously attached to.*	Omentopexie
omentum *A fold of peritoneum fastening the stomach to other organs in the viscera.*	Omentum; Netz
omphalitis *Inflammation of the umbilicus.*	Nabelentzündung
omphalocele *A large congenital, umbilical hernia with only a thin membranous covering.*	Omphalozele
on going *Continuing,*	weitergehend
oncologist *A phyisician specializing in the treatment of cancer.*	Onkologe
oncology *The study of cancer.*	Onkologie
onion bulb neuropathy *Also known as hypertrophic interstitial neuropathy which is a sensorimotor polyneuropathy.*	sensorimotorisch Polyneuropathie
onset *The beginning of an event.*	Anfall; Einsetzen
onychia *Inflammation of the toenail or fingernail matrix.*	Nagelbettentzündung
onychia sicca *Brittle fingernails or toenails.*	zerbrechlich Nagelbettentzündung
onychocryptosis *Ingrown toenail.*	Onychocryptose
onychogryphosis *A deformed nail that is incurved or hooked.*	Onychogryphose
onychomycosis *Fungal disease of the toenails or fingernails.*	Onychomykose
onychophagia *Habitually chewing on one's fingernails.*	Onychophagie
oocyte *An ovarian cell that needs to undergo meiotic division to become an ovum.*	Oozyt
oogenesis *The initiation and development of an ovum.*	Oogenese
oophorectomy *Surgical removal of an ovary.*	Oophorektomie
oophoritis *Inflammation of an ovary.*	Oophoritis; Eierstockentzündung
oophoron *Synonym for ovary.*	Eierstock
oophorosalpingectomy *Surgical removal of an ovary and fallopian tube.*	Oophorosalpingektomie
ooze, to *To slowly leak.*	sickern

English	German
open reduction (of fractures) *The realignment of a fractured bone using a surgical approach.*	offene Reposition
operation *A surgical procedure.*	Betrieb; Bedienung
operative note *A detailed description of a surgical procedure performed on a specific patient.*	Operationsbericht
ophthalmia *Profound inflammation of the eye or its structures.*	Ophthalmie
ophthalmic *Referring to the eye.*	ophthalmisch
ophthalmologist *A physician specializing in diseases of the eye.*	Ophthalmologe
ophthalmology *The study of diseases of the eye.*	Augenheilkunde
ophthalmoplegia *Paralysis of the eye muscles.*	Ophthalmoplegie
ophthalmoscope *A device used to visually inspect the interior eye.*	Ophthalmoskop; Augenspiegel
opiate *Referring to opium.*	Opiat
opioid *A substance similar to opium that binds to at least one of the opium receptors in the body.*	opioid
opisthotonos *A profound spasm in which the head/neck is hyperextended, the feet are touching the bed and with the patient supine the body arched upward.*	Opisthotonus
opium *An addictive drug derived from opium poppy; synthetic versions are used as analgesics.*	Opium
Oppenheim reflex *Extension of the toes elicited by scratching of the medial leg; present when the patient has cerebral irritation.*	Oppenheimreflex
opponens *Synonym for opponent muscle.*	Opponens
opsonin *An antibody used to facilitate phagocytosis of a bacterium.*	Opsonin
optic *Referring to the eye.*	optisch
optic disk *The area of the retina where the optic nerve enters.*	Sehnervpapille
optician *A person who makes eyeglasses.*	Optiker
optometrist *A person who pratices optometry.*	Optometrist
optometry *The profession of examination of the eyes for disease (not a medical doctor).*	Optometrie
oral *Relating to the mouth.*	oral
oral contraceptive *Tablet taken by mouth to prevent pregnancy.*	orales Kontrazeptivum
oral hygiene *Cleansing of the mouth and associated structures.*	Mundhygiene
orally *By mouth.*	mündlich
orbicular *Rounded or circular.*	orbikulär
orbit *The bony structure enclosing the eyeball.*	Orbita
orbital *Referring to the orbit.*	ortibal
orchialgia *Testicular pain.*	Orchialgie
orchidectomy *Synonym of orchiectomy; removal of one or both testes.*	Orchiektomie; Hodenentfernung
orchidopexy *Surgical repair of an undescended testis.*	Orchidopexie
orchiepididymitis *Inflammation of the testis and epididymis.*	Orchiepididymitis
orchitis *Inflammation of one or both testes.*	Orchitis
organ *A part of the body that is self contained and serves a vital function.*	Organ
organomegaly *Enlargement of an organ,typically referring to an intraabdominal organ.*	Organomegalie
oriental sore *A stigmata of cutaneous leishmaniasis caused by a bite from a sand fly.*	Orientbeule; Nilbeule
orifice *Synonym of foramen.*	Öffnung; Mündung

121

English	German
ornithosis *A viral infection transmitted by birds that is manifested by chills, headache, photophobia, fever, nausea and vomiting.*	Ornithose
oropharynx *The portion of the pharynx between the soft palate and the superior aspect of the epiglottis.*	Orohypopharynx
orthodontics *A subspecialty of dentistry concerned with treatment of dental irregularities and malocclusion, including the use of braces.*	Orthodontie
orthopedics *A surgical specialty concerned with treatment of skeletal problems.*	Orthopädie
orthopnea *The inability to breath comfortably except in the upright position.*	Orthopnoe
orthosis *Straightening of a malaligned part with the use of braces and other supportive devices.*	Orthese
orthostatic *Referring to the standing position. Orthostatic hypotension is low blood pressure in the standing position.*	orthostatisch
oscillating nystagmus *Abnormal movement of the eyes in a wave-like pattern.*	Pendelnystagmus
osmolality *The concentration expressed in total number of solute particles per kilogram.*	Osmolalität
osmole *The recognized unit of osmotic pressure.*	Osmol
osmosis *The movement of a solvent from a solution of greater concentration to one of lower concentration through a semi-permeable membrane until the two solutions have equal concentration.*	Osmose
osmotic *Referring to osmosis.*	osmotisch
osseous *Possessing the quality of bone.*	knöchern
ossicle *A small bone. (auditory ossicle)*	Knöchelchen (Gehörknöchelchen)
ossification *The formation of bone.*	Ossifikation
osteitis *Inflammation of the bone.*	Ostitis
ostensibly *Synonym of apparently and seemingly.*	angeblich
osteoarthritis *A long term, progressive degenerative joint disease.*	Osteoarthritis
osteoarthrosis *Arthritis without inflammation.*	Arthrosis deformans
osteoblast *A cell that matures from a fibroblast and produces bone.*	Osteoblast
osteochondral *Referring to bone and cartilage.*	osteochondral
osteochondritis *Inflammation of bone and cartilage.*	Osteochondritis
osteochondroma *A tumor with bony and cartilaginous characteristics.*	Osteochondrom
osteoclasis *The surgical fracture of a bone usually in order to restore proper alignment.*	Osteoklasie
osteoclast *A large bone cell that is associated with bone reabsorption and removal.*	Osteoklast
osteoclastoma *A tumor composed of giant cells or osteoclasts.*	Osteoklastom
osteocyte *An osteoblast within the bone matrix.*	Osteozyt
osteodystrophy *Abnormal bone formation.*	Osteodystrophie
osteogenesis *Development of new bones.*	Osteogenese
osteolytic *Referring to the removal or loss of calcium from the bone.*	osteolytisch
osteomalacia *Softening of the bones because of a deficiency of vitamin D, calcium or phosphorus.*	Osteomalazie
osteomyelitis *Inflammation of the bone or bone marrow because of a microorganism.*	Ostomyelitis

English	German
osteopathy *1. Any disease of the bone. 2. Medical practice concerning treatment of disease by manipulation and massage of bones, joints, and muscles.*	Osteopathie
osteopetrosis *Increased bone density with no change in modeling.*	Osteopetrose
osteophony *The sound conduction of bone.*	Osteophonie
osteophyte *Abnormal growth of a bone protuberance.*	Osteophyt
osteoporosis *Loss of bone substance because the osteoblasts fail to produce bone matrix.*	Osteoporose
osteosarcoma *A tumor composed of a sarcoma and osseous material.*	Osteosarkom
osteosclerosis *Abnormal hardening of bone.*	Osteosklerose
osteotomy *Creation of a surgical opening in bone.*	Osteotomie
ostium *A vessel or body cavity opening.*	Ostium; Mündung
ostogenesis imperfecta *A connective tissue disorder characterized by bone fragility, skeletal deformity, blue sclerae, ligament laxity, and hearing loss.*	Osteogenesis imperfecta
otalgia *Ear pain.*	Otalgie
otitis *Inflammation of the ear. (otitis media or otitis externa)*	Otitis; Ohrenentzündung
otolaryngologist *Surgical specialist concerned with organs of the ears, nose and throat.*	Hals-Nasen-Ohrenarzt
otolith *A calcium based calculus in the inner ear.*	Otolith
otology *Study of conditions and anatomy of the ear.*	Otologie
otomycosis *Fungal infection of the ear.*	Otomykose
otosclerosis *A hereditary condition exhibited by progressive hearing loss because of bone overgrowth in the inner ear.*	Otosklerose
otoscope *A device used for inspection of the tympanic membrane.*	Otoskop
ototoxic *A substance harmful to the ear or its nerve supply.*	ototoxisch
outbreak (of a disease) *A sudden start of a disease in a population.*	Ausbruch
ouch-ouch disease *Common term for Itai-Itai disease that is derived from "it hurts, it hurts" said by patients suffering from cadmium poisoning.*	Itai-Itai Krankheit.
outdated *Something that has passed the expiration date.*	überholt
ovarian cysts *Generally used to describe benign tumors.*	Ovarialzyst
ovaritis *Synonym for oophoritis.*	Eierstockentzündung
overdose *An above normal dose of a medication.*	Überdosis
overriding suture *The overlapping of cranial sutures noted on vaginal exam when the head is descended.*	reitende Sutur
overt *Not hidden.*	manifest
overweight *Defined as BMI over 25kilograms per meters squared.*	Übergewicht
oviduct *The channel which an ovum passes from the ovary.*	Eifeiter
ovulation *The release of an ova from the ovary.*	Ovulation
ovule *An immature ovum.*	Ei
owing to *On account of.*	aufgrund
oxaluria *Existence of oxalates in the urine.*	Oxalurie
oxidation *The process of a chemical combining with oxygen.*	Oxidation
oximeter *A medical device used to measure the percent of oxygen that is saturated in the blood (oxygen saturation).*	Oximeter
oxycephaly *The deformation of the skull so that it appears pointed.*	Spitzschädel
oxygen *A colorless, odorless gas with atomic number 8.*	Sauerstoff

123

English	German
oxygen consumption *The body's utilization of oxygen per unit of time.*	Sauerstoffverbrauch
oxygen tent *A manner of giving supplement oxygen to a neonate.*	Sauerstoffzelt
oxygen therapy *Utilization of supplemental oxygen.*	Sauerstoffbehandlung
oxygenation *Saturated with oxygen.*	Sauerstoffsättigung
oxyhemoglobin *The combination of oxygen and hemoglobin using a covalent bond.*	Oxyhämoglobin
oxytocic *Referring to rapid parturition.*	Oxytocicum
oxytocin *A natural hormone released by the pituitary or a synthetic hormone that facilitates uterine contraction.*	Oxytocin
ozena *Various nasal conditions, all of which include fetid discharge.*	Ozäna
ozone *A toxic chemical that has profound oxidizing properties. It has three atoms in its molecule compared with oxygen which has two.*	Ozon
pace *Consistent and continuous movement.*	Schritt; Gang
pacemaker *An electrical device used to stimulate the heart used for bradyarrhythmias.*	Schrittmacher
pachydermia *An abnormally thick skin.*	Pachydermie
pachymeningitis *Inflammation of the dura mater.*	Pachymeningitis
pad *A thick piece of soft clothing.*	Polster; Kissen
pagophagia *Compulsive need to eat ice which is usually associated with iron deficiency anemia.*	Pagophagie
pain *Physical suffering or discomfort.*	Schmerz
painful *Affected with pain.*	schmerzhaft
palatal myoclonus *An involuntary, persistent, rapid regular tremor of the soft palate and face.*	palatinal Myoklonus
palate *The roof of the mouth.*	Gaumen
palatoplegia *Paralysis of the palate.*	Palatoplegie
palliative *A treatment used to reduce pain when cure is not possible.*	palliativ
pallidectomy *Surgical resection of all or part of the palate.*	Pallidektomie
pallor *Unusually pale appearance.*	Blässe
palm *The anterior aspect of the hand.*	Handteller; Handfläche; Palma
palmar *Referring to the palm.*	palmar
palpation *The assessment of the body with the use of one's hands.*	Palpation
palpebra, palpebrae *Eyelid, eyelids.*	Augenlid, Augenlider
palpitation *Sensation of a forceful, rapid, irregular heartbeat present after exercise or with anxiety.*	Palpitation; Herzklopfen
palsy *Paralysis that is usually associated with tremors.*	Lähmung
paludism *Synonym of malaria.*	Sumpffieber
pamper, to *Indulge with comfort and kindness.*	verhätscheln
panarthritis *Inflammation of the joints.*	Panarthritis
pancarditis *Inflammation of pericardium, myocardium and endocardium.*	Pankarditis
pancreas *A gland that secretes digestive enzymes into the duodenum and insulin and glucagon into the blood.*	Pankreas; Bauchspeicheldrüse
pancreatectomy *Surgical excision of part or all of the pancreas.*	Pankreatektomie
pancreatitis *Inflammation of the pancreas.*	Pankreatitis
pancreozymin *A duodenal mucosal enzyme that facilitates the secretion of amylase and other enzymes from the pancreas.*	Pankreozymin
pandemic *When a disease is present over an entire region.*	Pandemie

English	German
panhypopituitarism *Insufficiency of the anterior pituitary.*	Panhypopituitarismus
panic attack *Sudden, profound anxiety.*	Panikattacke
panniculitis *Inflammation of a section of subcutaneous tissue containing large amounts of fat.*	Pannikulitis
panophthalmia *Inflammation of the eye and all its structures.*	Panophthalmitis
panotitis *Inflammation of each part of a bone.*	Panotitis
papilledema *Swelling of the optic disc.*	Papillenödem
papillitits *Swelling of a papilla.*	Papillitis
papilloma *A benign, lobulated tumor coming from epithelium.*	Papillom
papule *A small, well-circumscribed elevation of the skin.*	Papel
para-aminobenzoic acid *A natural product (not FDA approved) reportedly beneficial for Peyronie's disease and scleroderma. It is a component of folic acid.*	Para-Aminobenzoesäure
para-aminohippuric acid (PAH) *A chemical used for calculation of renal plasma flow.*	Para-Aminohippusäure
paracentesis *A procedure involving aspiration of fluid from the abdominal cavity.*	Parazentese
paracusia *Any abnormality in the sense of hearing.*	Parakusis
paradoxical pupil *Constriction of the pupil when exposed to darkness.*	paradoxe Pupillenreaktion
paralysis agitans *Synonym of Parkinson's disease.*	Paralyse agitans
paralytic *1. Referring to paralysis. 2. A person who is paralyzed.*	paralytisch ; Gelähmter
paramedian *Situated toward the middle of the body.*	paramedian
paramedical *Hospital support staff excluding physicians.*	Angehöriger
parametritis *Inflammation of the parametrium.*	Parametritis
parametrium *The connective tissue and smooth muscle between the broad ligament serous layers.*	Parametrium
paramnesia *A condition exhibited by a person's belief they have memory for an event that never happened.*	Paramnesie
paranasal sinuses *Any of the sinuses (ethmoidal, frontal, maxillary or sphenoidal) that communicate with the nasal cavity.*	Nasennebenhöhle
paranasal *Situated adjacent to the nose.*	nasenneben
paranoia *A mental condition exhibited by delusions of persecution.*	Paranoia
paranoid *Having the symptom of paranoia.*	paranoid
paraphimosis *A condition in which the foreskin is retracted but cannot be replace because of a restricted foreskin.*	Paraphimose
paraplegia *Paralysis of the lower extremities.*	Paraplegie
parapraxis *1. Unable to perform purposeful movements. 1. Irrational behavior.*	Fehleistung
pararectal *Adjacent to the rectum.*	pararektal
parasite *An organism that lives on or within another organism without benefit to the latter.*	Parasit
parasympathetic *Part of the autonomic nervous system that opposes sympathetic stimulation.*	parasympathisch
parathormone *Synonym for parathyroid hormone.*	Parathormon
parathyroid *Positioned adjacent to the thyroid.*	Parathyreoidea; Nebenschilddrüse
paravertebral *Positioned adjacent to the vertebra.*	paravertebral
parenchyma *The functional elements of an organ.*	parenchymatös

English	German
parenteral *Other than the alimentary canal.*	parenteral
paresis *Incomplete paralysis.*	Parese
paresthesia *An abnormal sensation usually described as pins and needles.*	Paräthesie; Missempfindung
parietal *Referring to the wall of a part or cavity.*	parietal
parietal cell *Acid secreting cells of the stomach.*	Parietalzelle
Parkinson's disease *A progressive neuromuscular disease exhibited by masklike facial expression, resting tremor, cogwheel rigidity and abnormal gait.*	Parkinson-Syndrom; Parkinsonismus
paronychia *Inflammation of the tissue bordering a fingernail*	Paronychie; Nagelgeschwür; Umlauf
parosmia *An alteration in the sense of smell.*	Parasomie; Riechstörung
parotid *A gland near the ear.*	Parotis; Ohrspeicheldrüse
parotiditis *Inflammation of the parotid gland.*	Parotitis
paroxysmal *Occurring in sudden attacks.*	paroxysmal; anfallsweise
parrot-beak nail *A curved fingernail.*	gebogen Fingernagel
parthenogenesis *Reproduction that occurs without an egg being fertilized by sperm.*	Pathogenese
parting *Separating.*	scheidend
parturition *The process of giving birth.*	Geburt; Partus
passive *Not achieved through active effort.*	passiv
past history *Prior medical problems experienced by a patient.*	Vorgeschichte
paste *A thick, soft moist substance usually with medicine mixed in.*	Paste; Salbe
patch test *A test used to determine which substances provoke an allergic response in a patient.*	Läppchenprobe; Epikutantest
patella *The bone situated in the anterior portion of the knee.*	Patella; Kniescheibe
patellectomy *Surgical excision of the patella.*	Patellektomie; Patellaentfernung
patellofemoral stress syndrome *Overuse syndrome causing anterior knee pain from excessive lateral motion.*	Patellofemoral Syndrom
patent ductus arteriosus *A condition exhibited by failure of the ductus arteriosus (communication between the aorta the the pulmonary artery normally noted in a fetus) to close.*	persistierender Ductus arteriosus
patent foramen ovale *A congenital anomaly in which there is a defect in the wall between the right and left atria; this can be a benign condition or result in cryptogenic strokes.*	persistierendes Foramen ovale
pathogenesis *The course of a disease.*	Pathogenese
pathogenic *Referring to an organism that can cause disease.*	pathogen
pathognomonic *Characteristic of something.*	pathognomonisch
pathological *Referring to pathology.*	pathologisch
pathology *1. The branch of medicine dealing with the study of tissues and the forensic application. 2. Referring to a condition that is abnormal.*	Pathologie
patient *The client being treated for a medical or surgical condition.*	Patient; Patientin
patient chart *The file containing the client's medical record.*	Patientenkartei
peak flow *A measurement of lung function used in asthma.*	Atemflussrate
pectineal ligament *A continuation of the lacunar ligament along the pectineal line in the pubis.*	Pecten ossis pubis
pectoral *Referring to the pectoral muscle.*	pektoral

English	German
pectoriloquy *The examiner's voice is clearly audible when the patient speaks as when the examiner listens to an area of consolidation in the lungs of the speaker.*	Pektoriloquie
pediatrician *Physician who is a specialist in pediatrics.*	Pädiater
pediatrics *Medical specialty concerned with the treatment and prevention of childhood disease.*	Pädiatrie
pedicle *Part of a skin/tissue graft temporarily left connected to the original site.*	Stiel
pediculate *Referring to pedicle.*	gestielt
pediculosis *Lice infestation.*	Pediculose
peduncle *1. A stalk-like protrusion. 2. A bundle of nerve fibers connecting two parts of the brain.*	Stiel
pellagra *A deficiency in nicotinic acid exhibited by diarrhea and dermatitis.*	Pellagra
pelvic inflammatory disease *Generally a bacterial infection affecting a woman with potential invovlement of the uterus, fallopian tubes, ovaries and cervix.*	Adnexitis
pelvic *Referring to the pelvis.*	pelvin
pelvimetry *Measurement of the dimensions of the pelvis to determine whether a patient is capable of natural childbirth.*	Pelvimetrie; Beckenmessung
pelvis *The bony structure at the base of the spine.*	Becken
pemphigus *A skin disorder with large bullous lesions.*	Pemphigus
penetration *The process of making a way through something.*	Eindringen
penicillin *A synthetic antibiotic originally produced from blue mold.*	Penicillin
penis *Male genital organ used for the transfer of sperm and elimination of urine.*	Penis
pentosuria *The presence of pentose in the urine (a monosaccharide with five carbon atoms in the molecule).*	Pentosurie
pepsin *A proteolytic gastric enzyme.*	Pepsin
peptic *Referring to pepsin or concerning digestion.*	peptisch
peptide *A compound with low molecular weight and containing two or more amino acids.*	Peptid
percussion *A manual procedure involving tapping a body part to determine the size or density (liquid or air) of a part.*	Perkussion
perforation *Presence of a hole.*	Perforation
periaqueductal gray matter *Refers to the brain gray matter adjacent to the periaqueductal.*	periaquäduktial graue Substanz
periarthritis *Inflammation of the tissues around a joint.*	Periarthritis
pericardial *Referring to around the heart.*	Perikardial
pericarditis *Inflammation of the pericardium.*	Perikarditis
pericardium *The structure enclosing the heart which contains a fibrous outer layer and serous inner layer.*	Perikard
perichondritis *Inflammation of the perichondrium.*	Perichondritis
perichondrium *The membrane that encloses a cartilage.*	Perichondrium
pericolitis *Inflammation of the membrane covering the colon.*	Perikolitis
pericorneal ring *Also known as Kayser-Fleischer rings exhibited by presence of brown or grey-green rings on the cornea. This is from the deposition of copper and seen in Wilson's disease.*	perikorneal Anulus

127

English	German
perilymph *The fluid separating the membranous and osseous labyrinth.*	Perilymphe
perinatology *The study of disease in the period just before and right after birth.*	Perinatologie
perineal *Referring to the perineum.*	perineal
perineal laceration *Tearing of the tissue adjacent to the vaginal that can occur during childbirth.*	Perinealriß; Dammriß
perineorrhaphy *Surgical repair of the perineum.*	Perineorrhaphie
perinephric *Around the kidney.*	perinephritisch; perirenal
perineum *The area between the anus and scrotum or anus and vulva.*	Perineum; Damm
periodic paralysis *A familial muscle disorder exhibited by recurrent episodes flaccid paralysis without change in level of consciousness.*	periodische Atmung; Adynamia episodica hereditaria
periodontal disease *Present around to a tooth.*	parodontal Krankheit
periosteal *Referring to the periosteum.*	perisotal
periosteum *A layer of connective tissue covering the bones.*	Periost
periostitis *Inflammation of the periosteum.*	Periositis
peripheral *Referring to an outward part or surface.*	peripher
periproctitis *Inflammation of the tissue encircling the anus and rectum.*	Periproktitis
peristalsis *The contraction of the longitudinal and circular muscle fibers of the alimentary canal so food is propelled.*	Peristaltik
peritomy *Surgically creating an opening of the periosteum.*	Pannusoperation
peritoneal *Referring to the peritoneum.*	peritoneal
peritoneum *The serous membrane covering the abdominal organs and lining the abdominal walls.*	Bauchfell
peritonitis *Inflammation of the peritoneum.*	Peritonitis
peritonsillar abscess	peritonsillär Abszeß
peritonsillar *Surrounding the tonsils.*	peritonsillär
periurethral *Surrounding the urethra.*	periurethral
permanent teeth *Dentition that comes in after the primary teeth.*	bleibende Zähne
pernicious *1. Having a detrimental effect. 2. Pernicious anemia is a reduced red blood cell count due to Vitamin B12 deficiency.*	perniziös
peroneal *Referring to the fibula or the outer part of the leg.*	peroneal; fibular
peroneal atrophy *Progressive muscle atrophy in the peroneal region.*	peroneal Atrophie
personality *Qualities that form a person's unique character.*	Persönlichkeit; Charakter
perspiration *The process of sweating.*	Perspiration; Schwitzen
pertussis *Synonym for whooping cough.*	Keuchhusten; Pertussis
pes cavus *Excessive height of the longitudinal arch of the foot.*	Hohlfuß
pes planus *Medical term for flat foot.*	Senkfuß
pes valgus *Abnormal longitudinal arch- it is flat.*	Knickfuß
pessary *A supportive device placed in the rectum or vagina.*	Pessar
pet *An animal kept for companionship.*	Haustier
PET scan Positron emission tomography. *Production of tomographic images revealing biochemical tissue properties by analyzing positrons emitted when radioactively tagged substances are taken in tissues.*	Positronenemissionstomographie
petechia *A small red or purple macule on the skin caused by bleeding.*	Petechie
petrissage *Massage using a kneading action.*	Pétrissage; Knetmassage
petrous *Possessing a density of a stone.*	steinartig

128

English	German
Peyronie's disease *Curvature of the penis during an erection to to plaque.*	Induratio penis plastica
phagocyte *A cell capable of surrounding and digesting microorganisms.*	Phagozyt
phagocytosis *The action of a phagocyte.*	Phagozytose
phalanx *One of the long bones of the fingers or toes.*	Phalanx
phantom limb pain *Pain sensed in an area where one has had an amputation as though the limb is still present.*	Phantomgliedschmerz
pharmacist *A professional who prepares and sells medicine through various systems, including governmental organizations like the Veterans Administration.*	Pharmazeut; Apotheker
pharmacokinetics *The study of the distribution, absorption and excretion of drugs within the body.*	Pharmakokinetik
pharmacology *The study of all aspects of medicines.*	Pharmakologie
pharmacy *A business that sells prescription medication.*	Pharmazie; Apotheke
pharyngeal pouch *A lateral diverticulum of the pharynx.*	Schlundtasche
pharyngeal *Referring to the pharynx.*	pharyngeal
pharyngectomy *Surgical excision of part of the pharynx.*	Pharyngektomie
pharyngitis *Inflammation of the pharynx.*	Pharyngitis
pharyngolaryngectomy *Surgical removal of part of the pharynx and larynx.*	Pharyngolaryngektomie
pharyngotympanic tube *Synonym for eustachian tube.*	Eustachio Röhre
pharynx *The membranous cavity from the mouth to esophagus.*	Rachen; Pharynx
phenotype *The visual expression exhibited by a person from the association of the genotype with the environment.*	Phänotyp
phenylketonuria *A hereditary condition in which a person cannot excrete phenylalanine; untreated it causes brain and spinal cord dysfunction.*	Phenylketonurie
phimosis *Stricture of the prepuce preventing it from being pulled back over the glans penis.*	Phimose
phlebectomy *Surgical excision of a vein.*	Phlebektomie
phlebitis *Inflammation of a vein.*	Phlebitis
phlebothrombosis *Presence of a clot in a vein, without associated inflammation.*	Phlebothrombose
phlegmasia alba dolens *Phlebitis of the femoral vein that can occur after pregnancy or typhoid fever.*	Phlegmasia alba dolens
phlegmasia *Inflammation or fever.*	Phegmasie
phlyctenular *Related to the formation of small vesicles on the cornea or conjunctiva.*	Phlykänulär
phobia *An profound fear of something.*	Phobie
phonation *The vocalization of sounds.*	Phonation
phoniatrics *The treatment of speech abnormalities.*	Phoniatrie
phosphaturia *Presence of phosphates in the urine.*	Phosphaturie
phospholipid *A substance, such as lecithin, that when hydrolyzed produces fatty acids, glycerin, and a nitrogen compound.*	Phospholipid
phosphonecrosis *The breakdown of the mandible caused by excessive exposure to phosphorus.*	Phophornekrose
photophobia *Abnormal sensitivity to light.*	Photophobie

English	German
photosensitization *The process of reacting to sunlight by developing edema and dermatitis.*	Photosensibilisierung
phrenic *Referring to the diaphragm.*	phrenisch
phrenicectomy *Surgical excision of the phrenic nerve.*	Phrenikektomie
phrenoplegia *Paralysis of the diaphragm.*	Phrenoplegie
physical exam *Examination of a client to assess their medical status.*	körperlisch Untersuchung
physical therapy *Treatment of disease by heat, massage and exercise as opposed to medications.*	physikalische Therapie
physician *Medical practitioner.*	Artz
physiologic dead space *The combination of anatomic and alveolar dead space.*	physiologisch Totraum
physiological saline *0.9% normal saline.*	physiologische Kochsalzlösung
physiology *A subspecialty of biology that studies the normal functioning of the body.*	Physiologie
physiotherapy *Physical therapy.*	physikalische Therapie
pia mater *The first layer of three covering the brain and spinal cord.*	Pia mater
pica *A desire for unusual substances as occurs in pregnancy and some psychological conditions.*	Pica
pill *A medicated tablet or capsule.*	Pille
pillow *An encased fabric covering soft material used for a cushion.*	Kissen
pilonidal cyst *A small cone-shaped cluster of tissue situated posterior to the third ventricle of the brain.*	Pilonidalsinus
pin *Hardware used in surgery.*	Stift
pin, intramedullary *Hardware used for fracture management or during joing replacement.*	Knochenmarkstift
pineal gland *A small body posterior to the third ventricle of the brain.*	Zirbeldrüse
pinguecula *The yellow tissue on the bulbar conjunctiva adjacent to the sclerocorneal junction.*	Pinguecula
pink eye *Common term for acute contagious conjunctivitis.*	akute Konjunktivitis
pinocytosis *The absorption of fluid into a cell by the formation of vesicles on the cell membrane.*	Pinozytose
pinworm *Common term for Enterobius verminicularis; a nematode worm that is a parasite.*	Madenwurm; Enterobius vermicularia
pipet *A slender tube with a bulb used for transferring liquids.*	Pipette
pitting edema *Edema of the lower extremities characterized by an indentation being left when the examiner applies pressure with their thumb.*	dellenbildendes Ödem
pituitary gland *A gland at the base of the hypothalamus.*	Hirnanhangdrüse
pityriasis rosea *A skin disease characterized by dry pink oval papulosquamous eruptions.*	Pityriasis rosea
placebo controlled study *When a study is placebo controlled it means part of the group received an inactive treatment while the other group received active therapy.*	placebo-kontrollierte Studie
placenta *The vascular tissue that nourishes a fetus through an umbilical cord.*	Placenta; Mutterkuchen
placenta praevia *A condition in which the placenta covers the cervical os.*	Placenta praevia
placental *Referring to the placenta.*	plazentar

English	German
plagiocephaly *A condition characterized by an asymmetric skull because the cranial sutures do not close normally.*	Plaziozephalie
plantar *Referring to the bottom of the foot.*	plantar
plantar fibromatosis *Deep fascia nodules on the plantar aspect of the feet.*	Plantarfibromatose
plantar wart *A viral epidermal growth on the bottom of the foot.*	Dornwarze
plasma cell *A cell that produces only one type of antibody.*	Zellplasma
plasmacytosis *The existence of plasma cells in the blood.*	Plasmazellenvermehrung
plasmapheresis *A method of removing blood and reinfusing it after the elimination of antibodies.*	Plasmapherese
plaster cast *Use of gypsum impregnated gauze to immobilize fractured extremities.*	Gipsabdruck; Gispverband
plaster *Dehydrated gypsum that has water added to it in order to immobilize fractured extremities.*	Pflaster
platelet *An oval cell without a nucleus used in coagulation; also called a thrombocyte.*	Plättchen
pledget *A small plug of cotton or other synthetic material inserted into a wound.*	kleine Kompresse
pleomorphism *The ability of an organism or substance to attain distinct forms.*	Pleomorphie
plethora *An excess of something.*	Plethora
plethysmograph *A device used to measure the amount of blood flowing through a body part; impedance plethysmography is used to check for deep venous thrombosis.*	Plethysmograph
pleura *The serous membrane lining each lung.*	Brustfell; Pleura
pleural effusion *An abnormal collection of fluid between the internal chest wall and the pleura.*	Pleuraerguss; Pleuraerguß
pleurisy *Inflammation of the pleura.*	Pleurareizung
plica *A fold, as in a fold in the peritoneum.*	Falte; Plica
Plummer-Vinson syndrome *Also called sideropenic dysphagia. Exhibited by iron deficiency anemia, dysphagia, esophageal stenosis and atrophic glossitis. The cause is not known.*	Plummer-Vinson-Syndrom
pneumatocele *1. A hernia-like protrusion of lung tissue. 2. A collection of gas in a sac such as the scrotum.*	Pneumatozele
pneumaturia *Presence of air or gas in the urine.*	Pneumaturie
pneumococcus *A bacterium causing pneumonia and meningitis. A common type is Streptococcus pneumoniae.*	Pneumokokkus
pneumoconiosis *Fibrosis of the lung due to dust inhalation.*	Pneumokoniose
pneumocystis jiroveci pneumonia. *A pulmonary infection associated with AIDS. Formerly called pneumocystis carinii pneumonia*	Pneumocystis-jirovecii Pneumonie
pneumonectomy *Surgical excision of all or part of a lung.*	Pneumonektomie
pneumonia *Inflammation of the lung due to an infection caused by a virus or bacterium.*	Pneumonie
pneumoperitoneum *Abnormal or induced presence of air or gas in the peritoneum.*	Pneumoperitoneum
pneumothorax *Abnormal presence of air between the lung and chest wall.*	Pneumothorax
poikilocytosis *The presence of abnormally shaped erythrocytes.*	Poikilozytose
poikilothermy *A condition of cold-blooded animals in which their temperature varies based on the ambient temperature.*	Poikilothermie

131

English	German
poison *A substance that causes illness or death.*	Gift
polioencephalitis *Polio infection of the brain.*	Polioenzephalitis
poliomyelitis *An infectious viral disease exhibited by constitutional symptoms that can lead to quadriplegia.*	Poliomyelitis
polyarteritis nodosa *A systemic necrotizing vasculitis that effects medium sized arteries.*	Periarteriitis nodosa
polychondritis *Inflammation of the cartilage at more than one site.*	Polychondritis
polycystic *Possessing more than one cyst.*	polyzystisch
polycythemia *Excess in the number of erythrocytes in the blood.*	Polyzythämie
polycythemia vera *Condition characterized by increase in erythrocytes, thrombocytes and leukocytes, as well as, splenomegaly.*	Polyzythämie vera
polydactyly *Congenital anomaly exhibited by more than 5 digits on the hands and/or feet.*	Polydaktylie
polydipsia *Profound thirst.*	Polydipsie
polymenorrhea *Increase in the frequency of menstruation.*	Polymenorrhöe
polymyositis *Inflammation of several muscle groups at once.*	Polymyositis
polyneuritis *Inflammation of more than one nerve.*	polyneuritis
polyneuropathy *A condition involving more than one nerve.*	Polyneuropathie
polyopia *A condition in which one object is seen abnormally as two or more.*	Polyopsie
polyposis *The formation of multiple polyps.*	Polypose
polypus *Synonym of polyp (a prominent growth from a mucous membrane).*	Polyp
polysaccharide *A carbohydrate that upon hydrolysis forms more than ten monosaccharides.*	Polysaccharid
polysialia *Abnormal increase in saliva.*	Hypersalivation
polytrauma *A condition exhibited by multiple injuries from blunt or penetrating trauma.*	Mehrfachverletzung
polyuria *Abnormal increase in volume of urine excreted.*	Polyurie
pompholyx *A condition exhibited by interdigital vesicles of the hands and feet.*	Pompholyx
pons *The part of the brainstem that connects the medulla oblongata with the thalamus.*	Brücke
pontine *Referring to the pons.*	pontin
popliteal *Referring to the posterior aspect of the knee.*	popliteal
popliteal fossa *The hollow in the posterior aspect of the knee joint.*	Kniekehle
porphyria *A hereditary condition currently classified based on the specific enzyme deficiency. The most common form is porphyria cutanea tarda that causes blistering lesions.*	Porphyrie
porphyrin *A class of pigments that contain a flat ring of four heterocyclic groups.*	Porphyrin
port-wine mark *Also called nevus flammeus, it is a vascular anomaly characterized by purplish skin discoloration.*	Feuermal
portal *Referring to an entrance such as porta hepatis.*	portal
portal hypertension *Hypertension in the portal system of the liver as seen in conditions causing obstruction to the portal vein.*	Pfortaderhochdruck
positive *Indicating the presence of something.*	positiv
post-mortem lividity *The purplish discoloration occurring 30-120 minutes after death in dependent body parts.*	Leichenfleck

English	German
post-nasal drip *The descent of sinus drainage.*	Postnasensekret
post-term birth *An infant born after the normal length of pregnancy.*	Spätgeburt
posterior *Further back in position; opposite of anterior.*	hinterer; posterior
posterior chamber of the eye *An aqueous filled space between the cornea and the lens.*	hintere Augenkammer
posterior columns *The dorsal portion of the gray matter of the spinal cord.*	Hinterstrang
postictal *The period of time after a seizure.*	postiktal
postmaturity *Generally referring to a pregnancy that goes beyond the due date.*	Überreife
postpartum psychosis *A episode of abnormal thought or hallucinations following delivery.*	Wochenbettpsychose
postpone, to *To delay.*	verschieben
postural hypotension *A significant drop in blood pressure when going from the supine or sitting position to standing.*	Lagehypotonie
postural *Referring to position or posture.*	haltungsmäßig
potassium *A chemical of the alkali metal group.*	Kalium
potency *Strength or power.*	Potenz; Leistungsfähigkeit
Pott's disease *Also referred to as tuberculous spnodylitis it is caused by a spinal deformity caused by a tuberculosis infection of the spine.*	Wirbeltuberkulose
Potter's syndrome *A group of findings associated with oligohydramnios. Renal failure is the primary problem but the infant has abnormal limbs, broad nasal bridge, low set ears and receding chin. Death usually ensues due to renal and respiratory failure.*	Potter-Syndrom
poultryman's itch *Pruritis associated with the mite Dermanyssus gallinae.*	Taubenmilbekrätze
powder *Fine dry particles.*	Puder
pox *A general term for fluid filled papules that upon rupturing leave pockmarks.*	Hautausschlag
preauricular *Anterior to the ear.*	präaurikulär
precancerous *Referring to an early stage in cancer development.*	präkanzerös
precipitin *An antibody-antigen reaction producing a precipitate.*	Präzipitin
precordialgia *Pain in the precordium.*	Präkordialschmerz
precordium *The area occupying the epigastrum and lower sternum.*	Praecordium
preeclampsia *Hypertension with proteinuria and/or edema in the setting of pregnancy.*	Präeklampsie
pregnancy *The period of being pregnant.*	Schwangerschaft; Gravidität
premature *Occurring earlier than expected.*	frühreif; vorzeitig
premenstrual *Occurring prior to the onset of menstruation.*	prämenstruell
premenstrual syndrome *A cluster of emotional, behavioral, and physical symptoms that occur in the premenstrual phase of the menstrual cycle and resolve with the onset of menstruation.*	prämenstruelles Syndrom
premolar *The teeth anterior to the molars.*	Prämolar
prenatal care *Medical care received while one is pregnant.*	Schwangerenbetreuung
prenatal *Referring to the time prior to birth.*	pränatal
presbyacusia *An age related, progressive hearing loss.*	Presbyakusis
presbyopia *Farsightedness associated with aging.*	Presbyopie; Alterssichtigkeit
prescription *The action of prescribing a medication or treatment.*	Vorschrift

English	German
presenting symptom *The initial subjective complaint that initiated a visit.*	subjektives Hauptsymptom
pressure dressing *A dressing used for compression to reduce bleeding.*	Druckverband
pressure ulcer *Loss in skin integrity due to a portion of the body being in the same position for too long and possibly other factors.*	Druckgeschwür; Dekubitus
presystolic *The time just before systole.*	präsystolisch
prevent, to *To stave off or hinder.*	vorbeugen
priapism *A painful and abnormally prolonged erection.*	Priapismus
prickly heat *A rash with small vesicles that is pruritic and associated with a warm moist environment.*	Friesel
primipara *A woman giving birth for the first time.*	Primipara
prior status *Referring to a person's previous state of health.*	Vorherigzustand
probe *A device used for exploration.*	Sonde
problem *Difficulty or complaint.*	Problem
proctalgia *A chronic high, dull rectal pain worse with sitting position.*	Proktalgie
proctectomy *Surgical excision of the rectum.*	Proktektomie
proctitis *Inflammation of the rectum.*	Proktitis
proctocele *A hernia-type protrusion of the rectum into the vagina.*	Proktozele
proctoscopy *Inspection of the rectum with a scope.*	Procktoskopie
progeria *A childhood disorder exhibited by signs of aging including gray hair, wrinkled skin and short height.*	Progerie
progesterone *A steroid hormone that prepares the uterus for pregnancy.*	Gelbkörperphase; Progesteron
proglottis *Any segment of a tapeworm.*	Bandwurmglied
prognathism *Protrusion of the mandible which can cause malocclusion.*	Prognathie
prognosis *The likely course of a disease.*	Prognose
progressive *Developing gradually.*	fortschreitend
prolactin *A pituitary hormone that facilitates milk production.*	Prolaktin
prolapse of the uterus *Eversion of the uterus through the vagina.*	Gebärmuttersenkung
prolapse of the umbilical cord *Refers to the umbilical cord protruding from the cervix during active labor.*	Nabelschnurvorfall
prolapse *The slipping downward of a body part, such as rectal prolapse.*	Prolaps; Vorfall
prolonged rupture of the membranes *Rupture of the membranes more than 24 hours before delivery.*	verspäteter Blasensprung
promonocyte *An intermediate cell stage between monocyte and monoblast.*	Promonozyt
promontory *A protruding eminence.*	Promontorium
pronation *Turning posteriorly. When the hand is pronated, it is turned medially until the palm is facing posteriorly (when the body was initially in the anatomic position).*	Pronation
prone *Lying with the abdomen and face downward.*	in Bauchlage
prophylaxis *That which is done to prevent disease.*	Prophylaxe
proprioceptor *A receptor that responds to sensory input including position sense.*	Propriorezeptor
proptosis oculi *Synonym of exophthalmos; bulging of the eye.*	Vorwärtsverlagerung
prostacyclin *A prostaglandin that functions as an anticoagulant and vasodilator.*	Prostazyklin

134

English	German
prostaglandin *A compound first found in semen (thus "prosta" in the name from prostate) with many effects including uterine contraction.*	Prostaglandin
prostate *A gland found in men that surrounds the neck of the urethra and bladder.*	Vorsteherdrüse; Prostate
prostatectomy *Surgical excision of the prostate.*	Prostatektomie
prosthesis *An artificial body part. (above the knee) [below the knee]*	Ersatz; Prothese (Oberschenkelprothese) [Unterschenkelprothese]
prostration *Profound exhaustion.*	Prostration
protein *A class of nitrogenous organic compound.*	Protein; Eiweiß
proteinuria *The presence of protein in the urine.*	Proteinurie
proteolysis *Enzyme action on proteins to form amino acids.*	Proteolyse
prothrombin *A compound converted to thrombin during coagulation of blood.*	Prothromin
protoplasm *The cytoplasm, organelles and nucleus of a living cell.*	Protoplasma
protozoa *A single celled microscopic organism including amoebas among others.*	Protozoon
provoke, to *To evoke or elicit.*	provozieren
proximal *Situated closer to the center of the body (opposed to that which is farther away, as in distal).*	proximal
prurigo *A chronic, pruritic papular skin eruption.*	Prurigo
pruritis *A general term for conditions exhibited by itching.*	Pruritis; Hautjucken
pseudarthrosis *Deossification of weight bearing long bones.*	Pseudoarthrose
pseudobulbar palsy *Sudden outbursts of laughter or tearfulness sometimes seen in amyotrophic lateral sclerosis.*	Pseudobulbärparalyse
pseudomnesia *Sensing the memory of an event that has never happened.*	Pseudomnsesie
psittacosis *A chlamydial pneumonia that is transmitted by birds.*	Psittakose
psoriasis *A chronic papulosquamous dermatosis characterized by silver plaques.*	Psoriasis
psychasthenia *Essentially any non-hysterical neuroses.*	Psychasthenie
psychiatry *A branch of medicine specializing in the treatment of mental disorders.*	Psychiatrie
psychologist *A professional specializing in psychology.*	Psychologe
psychology *The study of the human mind and emotions.*	Psychologie
psychoneurosis *A mental disorder that could include depression or anxiety but does not include hallucinations.*	Psychoneurose
psychopathology *Scientific examination of mental disease.*	Psychopathologie
psychosis *A profound mental disorder that can include delusions and hallucinations.*	Psychose
psychosomatic *Physical ailments arising from mental disease.*	psychosomatisch
psychotherapy *Treatment of mental disease with cognitive-behavioral approaches.*	Psychotherapie
pterygium *A membrane in the interpalpebral fissure present from the conjunctiva to the cornea.*	Pterygium; Flügelfell
ptosis *Drooping of the upper eyelid usually due to paralysis of the third cranial nerve.*	Ptose
ptyalin *An enzyme found in saliva.*	Pytalin

English	German
puberty *The time when adolescents become capable of sexual reproduction.*	Pubertät
pubic hair *Hair present in the perineal area.*	Byssus
pubis *The anterior inferior part of the hip bone on each side that articulates at the pubic symphysis.*	pubisch
pudendal *Referring to the female genitalia*	pudendal
pudendum *The mons, pubis, labia majora, labia minora and the vagina.*	Pudendum femininum; Vulva
puerpera *A woman who just gave birth.*	Puerpera
puerperium *The six week period after childbirth.*	Kindbett; Wochenbett
puffiness *Having a soft, swollen area.*	Aufgedunsensein
pull, to *To exert force on something.*	ziehst
pulmonary edema *Characterized by abnormal fluid buildup in the lungs.*	Lungenödem
pulmonary embolism *A sudden blockage of a lung artery frequently eminating from a blood clot in one's leg.*	Lungenembolie
pulmonary *Referring to the lungs.*	pulmonal
pulmonary stenosis *A stricture between the pulmonary artery and the right ventricle.*	Pulmonalstenose
pulp *The tissue filling the root canals of a tooth.*	Pulpa
pulpitis *Dental pulp inflammation.*	Pulpitis
pulsatile *Relating to pulsation.*	pulsieren
pulsation *The action of expanding and contracting.*	Pulsation
pulse *The rhythmic throbbing of arteries felt at major vessels.*	Puls
pulsus alternans *A regular alternation of weak and strong beats of the pulse.*	Pulsus alternans
pupil *The opening at the center of the iris.*	Pupille
purpura *The presence of patches of ecchymosis or petechiae.*	Purpura
purulent *Referring to pus.*	eiterig
pus *Thick yellow or green opaque liquid as seen with infection.*	Eiter
putrefaction *The rotting or decaying of organic matter.*	Verwesung; Fäulnis
pyelitis *Renal pelvis inflammation.*	Pyelitis
pyelography *Use of a contrast agent to radiologically study the kidney, ureters and bladder.*	Pyelographie
pyelolithotomy *Surgical excision of a calculus from the renal pelvis.*	Pyelolithotomie
pyelonephritis *Inflammation of the renal parenchyma usually due to bacterial infection.*	Pyelonephritis
pyelonephrosis *Term, rarely used anymore,used to describe disease of the renal pelvis.*	Pyelonephrose
pyemia *Sepsis characterized by the presence of secondary abscesses.*	Pyämie
pyknic *Possessing a short, stocky physique.*	pyknisch
pyknosis *The degeneration of a cell with the nucleus shrinking.*	Pyknose
pyloric *Referring to the pylorus.*	pylorisch
pyloroplasty *Surgical enlargement of a pylorus that previously was stenotic.*	Pylorusplastik
pylorus *The opening at the distal stomach that opens into the duodenum.*	Pylorus
pyoderma *A purulent skin infection.*	Pyodermie

136

English	German
pyogenic liver abscess *A pus filled fluid collection in the liver.*	eiterbildend Leberabszeß
pyogenic *Referring to the formation of pus.*	eiterbildend
pyonephrosis *Injury to the renal parenchyma due to pus.*	Pyonephrose
pyorrhea *Emission of pus.*	Pyorrhöe
pyosalpinx *Purulent material in the oviduct.*	Pyosalpinx
pyramidal *A term that is used to describe various spinal tracts that originate in the cerebral cortex.*	pyramidal
pyrexia *Fever.*	Fieber
pyridoxine *Synonym for vitamin B6.*	Pyridoxin
pyrogen *A fever producing substance released by bacteria.*	Pyrogen
pyrosis *Synonym for heartburn.*	Sodbrennen
pyuria *Presence of purulent material in the urine.*	Pyurie
Q fever *A disease caused by rickettsiae from the ingestion of unpasteurized milk.*	Q-Fieber
quadranic hemianopia *Loss of a quarter of the visual field in one or both eyes. If bilateral, it may be further described as homonymous, heteronymous, binasal, bitemporal, or crossed.*	Quadrantenanopsie
quadriceps jerk (reflex) *Also referred to as the patellar reflex.*	Quadrizepssehnenreflex; Patellarsehnenreflex
quadriceps *The anterior thigh muscle composed of four muscles.*	Quadrizeps
quadrigeminal bodies *The cranial and caudal colliculi.*	Vierhügel
quadriplegia *Paralysis of all four extremities.*	Quadriplegie
qualify *To become eligible by fullfilling a necessary standard.*	berechtigen
quarantine *A place of isolation for infectious persons until it can be certain it is safe to let them mingle.*	Quarantäne
quickening *Signs of life noted by a mother as the fetus moves.*	fühlbare Kindsbewegung
querulousness *Whining or complaining.*	querulatorisch
quiescent *A time of inactivity.*	ruhend
quiet *Making little or no noise.*	ruhig
quinsy *Peritonsillar inflammation or abscess.*	Halsentzündung
quintan fever *Also known as trench fever as it was first noted during trench warfare in WW I. It is a rickettsial fever caused by Bartonella quintana and transmitted by a louse; signs and symptoms are myalgia, headache, malaise, fever and chills.*	Wolhynisches Fieber; Quintana; Fünftagefieber
rabies *An infectious viral disease transmitted through the bite of a mammal. Symptoms include hydrophobia, pharyngeal spasms and hyperactivity.*	Tollwut
racemose *A gland having the form of a cluster.*	razemös
radial *Referring to the radius.*	radial
radiation *1. The emission of energy in the form of electromagnetic waves. 2. Divergence from a common point.*	Stahlung; Bestrahlung
radiculitis *Inflammation of a spinal nerve root.*	Radikulitis
radioactive *Referring to the emission of ionizing particles or radiation.*	radioaktiv
radioactive isotope *An isotope with an unstable nucleus that is used in diagnostic imaging.*	Radioisotop
radiobiology *The study of the effects of radiation on organisms.*	Radiobiologie
radioepithelitis *The injury to epithelial cells due to effects of radiation.*	Strahlenhautschaden

English	German
radiography *The department where images are produced on sensitive film by x-rays.*	Radiographie; Röentgenograpie
radiologist *A physician specializing in radiology.*	Radiologe
radiology *The branch of medicine concerned with roentgenography and other high-energy radiation.*	Radiologie
radionuclide *A radioactive nuclide.*	Radionuklid
radiosensitivity *The susceptibility of the skin to radiation.*	Strahlenempfindlichkeit
radiotherapy *Treatment of cancer with radiation.*	Strahlentherapie
rage *Uncontrollable anger.*	Raserei
raise, to *To lift or bring up.*	erhöhen
rale *An abnormal lung sound noted during auscultation.*	Rasselgeräusch
ramus *A branch; a term used to describe a smaller vessel branching off from a larger one.*	Ramus; Zweig
ranula *A retention cyst formed because of obstruction of a salivary gland in the floor of the mouth.*	Ranula; Froschgeschwulst
rape *Forced sexual relations.*	Vergewaltigung
Rapid Eye Movement *The movement of a person's eyes during this period of sleep.*	schnelle Augenbewegung
rash *Exanthema or urticaria.*	Hautausschlag
rat bite fever *As the name implies, it is a condition exhibited by fever, nausea and skin erythema after one is bitten by a rat.*	Rattenbißkrankheit;
reaction *A response to an action.*	Reaktion
reactive *A response to a stimulus.*	reaktiv
rebound *A term used to describe a type of tenderness found with peritonitis.*	Nachreflex; Rückprall
receptor *A cell or organ that accepts stimuli and transmits data to a sensory nerve.*	Rezeptor
recessive *This refers to genetic controlled traits that are only inherited when code from both parents is the same.*	rezessiv
recollection *Memory.*	Erinnerung
recovery room *The immediate post-operative room where patients are stabilized prior to going to a general ward.*	Aufwachraum
rectal digital examination *Use of a gloved finger to assess the rectal vault.*	rektale Untersuchung
rectal *Referring to the rectum.*	rektale
rectocele *A herniation of the wall between the rectum and vagina.*	Rektozele
rectoscopy *Visualization of the rectum with a scope.*	Rektoskopie
rectosigmoidectomy *Surgical resection of the rectum and sigmoid colon.*	Rektosigmoidektomie
rectovesical septum *The wall between the rectum and the urinary bladder.*	rektovesikal Scheidewand
rectus abdominis muscle *The pair of long, flat muscles that connect the sternum with the pubis.*	gerader Bauchmuskel
recumbent *Lying down.*	zurückgelehnt
red nucleus *A collection of gray matter near the subthalamus that receives data from the superior cerebellar peduncle.*	Nukleus ruber
reduction *Return of a dislocated joint or fractured bone to its proper position.*	Reduktion
referred pain *Pain felt in an area distinct from the original source.*	fortgeleiteter Schmerz

138

English	German
regardless of *Without consideration of.*	unangesehen
regurgitation *1. Backflow of blood in the heart. 2. Movement of gastric contents into the mouth.*	Regurgitation
relapse *The return to a prior state of ill health.*	Rückfall
relapsing fever *A recurrent bacterial infection, with fever, caused by Spirochetes.*	Rückfallfieber
related to *Causally connected.*	bezogen auf
relation *1. A person who has a blood or marriage connection.*	Beziehung
relaxant *Term generally used to refer to a muscle relaxant.*	Entspannungsmittel
relaxin *A hormone secreted by the placenta which dilates the cervix.*	Relaxin
releasing hormone *Hormones that come from one gland such as the thalamus that cause release of hormones from another gland such as the pituitary.*	Releasing-Hormon
reliable *Trustworthy.*	zuverlässig
relief *Alleviation from pain or discomfort.*	Entlastung
relieve, to (pain) *To make less severe.*	lindern; ausgleichen
REM (rapid eye movement) sleep *This period of sleep is associated with irregular respirations and heart rate, involuntary movements and dreaming.*	schnelle Augenbewegung-Schlaf
remission *A decrease in severity or a temporary resolution.*	Remission
removal *The act of removing something.*	Herausnahme
renal *Referring to the kidney.*	renal; nieren-
renal colic *Pain caused by passage of a calculus through the ureter.*	Nierenkolik
renal failure *Diminution of kidney function.*	Nierenversagen
renal pelvis *The kidney collecting system.*	Nierenbecken
renin *A renal enzyme that facilitates the production of angiotensin.*	Renin
resection *The removal of tissue.*	Resektion
residual urine *The amount of urine remaining in the bladder after a person voids.*	Restharn
residual volume (RV) *The amount of air left in the lung after a maximal exhalation.*	Residualvolumen
resin *An organic substance that is insoluble in water. There are many types. Cholestyramine resin is used for hypercholesterolemia.*	Harz
resorbable suture (chromic) *Suture that is not intended to be permanent as it is dissolved by normal body processes.*	Chromkatgutnaht
respirator *A device used to artificially ventilate a patient.*	Beatmungsgerät
respiratory *Referring to respiration or the organs of respiration.*	respiratorisch
respiratory distress syndrome *A disease in infants that is caused by a surfactant deficiency.*	Atemnotsyndrom
respiratory rate *The number of breaths per minute.*	Atemfrequenz
rest *Relaxation or respite.*	Ruhe; Rast
restless legs *Associated with a syndrome exhibited by continuous movement of the legs from uncertain etiology.*	unruhige Beine (Wittmaak-Ekbon Syndrom)
retching *Spasm of the stomach without presence of gastric material.*	Brechreiz
reticular *Referring to a matrix of membranous tubules inside the cytoplasm of a eukaryotic cells.*	reitikulär
reticulo-endothelial *Referring to the system of phagocytes involved in the immune system.*	retikuloendotheliales
reticulocyte *A red blood cell without a nucleus.*	Retikulozyt

English	German
reticulocytosis *An abnormal increase in circulating reticulocytes.*	Retikulozytose
retina *The innermost of three layers of the eyeball; it surrounds the vitreous body and is continuous with the optic nerve.*	Netzhaut; Retina
retinal detachment *A tear or hole in the retina caused by vitreous traction.*	Netzhautablösung
retinitis *Inflammation of the retina.*	Renititis
retinoblastoma *A tumor consisting of retinal germ cells.*	Retinoblastom
retinopathy *Any one of a number of retinal inflammatory conditions.*	Retinopathie
retraction *Being drawn back.*	Retraktion
retractor *A device for pulling back tissue during surgery.*	Retraktor; Wundhaken
retrobulbar optic neuritis *An inflammatory, demyelinating condition in the retrobulbar region.*	Retrobulbärneuritis
retroflexed uterus *Bending back of the uterus so that the top portion pushes against the rectum.*	retroflektiert Uterus
retrograde *Referring to backward movement.*	retrograd
retroperitoneal *Situated or referring to the area posterior to the peritoneum.*	retroperitoneal
retropharyngeal abscess *A collection of purulent material posterior to the pharynx.*	retropharyngealer Abszeß
retropharyngeal *Referring to the area posterior to the pharynx.*	retropharyngeal
Rett syndrome. *A rare inherited disorder causing developmental delays and is seen mostly in girls.*	Rett Syndrom
rhabdomyolysis *A acute destruction of muscle documented by myoglobinemia and myoglobinuria.*	Rhabdomyolyse
rhagade *Fissures in the skin, particularly adjacent to body orifices.*	Rhagade
rheumatic *Referring to rheumatism.*	rheumatisch
rheumatic fever *A febrile streptococcal disease causing pain and joint swelling.*	Febris rheumatica
rheumatic heart disease *A manifestation of rheumatic fever, frequently causing valvular dysfunction.*	rheumatisch Herzkrankheit
rheumatism *Any condition exhibited by inflammation and pain in the joints and muscles.*	Rheumatismus
rheumatoid arthritis *A symmetric peripheral polyarthritis.*	rheumatoide Arthritis
rhinitis *A viral infection or allergic reaction exhibited by nasal mucosal inflammation.*	Rhinitis
rhinoplasty *Plastic surgery performed on the nose.*	Nasenplastik
rhinorrhea *Abundant nasal mucosal drainage.*	Rhinorrhöe
rhinoscopy *Examination of the nasal passages.*	Rhinoskopie
rhizotomy *Interruption of the spinal nerve roots within the spinal canal.*	Rhizotomie
rhodopsin *A reddish purple light sensitive pigment in the human retina.*	Rhodopsin
rhomboid *A back muscle that elevates, retracts and adducts the scapula.*	Raute
rhonchus *A coarse, dry sound heard on auscultation of the lungs.*	Giemen
rhythm *The pattern or cadence.*	Rhythmus
rib *A series of curved paired boney articulations protecting the thorax.*	Rippe
riboflavin *Also called vitamin B2, this essential vitamin is present in food such as eggs and is synthesized in the small bowel.*	Riboflavin

English	German
ribonucleic acid *An acid present in all living cells, it is a messenger for DNA.*	Ribonukleinsäure
ribosomal RNA *Four chains designated by their appropriate coefficients.*	ribosomale Ribonukleinsäure
rice-field fever *An infection cause by a species of Leptospira, affecting rice workers in Italy and Sumatra.*	Bativiafieber
rickets *A condition exhibited by softening and bowing of the long bones; caused by Vitamin D deficiency.*	Rachitis
rickettsia *A disease transmitted by ticks or fleas, caused by a bacterium from the genus Rickettsieae. Rocky Mountain Spotted fever is one of many diseases caused by this bacterium.*	Rickettsie
Rift valley fever *A human febrile illness that is an endemic disease in sheep, transmitted by mosquitos and direct contact and caused by a virus of the family Bunyaviridae.*	Rifttalfieber
right *Opposite of left.*	rechts
right-handed *Having a preference to use the right hand.*	rechtshändig
rigor mortis *The normal stiffening of the muscles and joints that occurs a few hours after death.*	Rigor mortis
ring *A small circular band.*	Ring
ringing in the ears *Common term for tinnitus.*	Ohrensausen
ringworm *A fungal skin infection exhibited by pruritic well circumscribed patches on the scalp or feet.*	Dermatophytose
risus sardonicus *A spasm of the facial muscles causing what appears to be a smile on one's face.*	Risus sardonicus
Ritgen's maneuver *A procedure that controls the rate of delivery of the infant's head during childbirth.*	Ritgen Handgriff
rodent *A gnawing mammal that includes rats and mice.*	Nagetier
Roentgen *One unit of ionizing radiation named after the German physicist Wilhelm Conrad Röntgen.*	Röntgen
room *A division in a building surrounded by walls.*	Zimmer
root *An embedded part of an organ or structure.*	Wurzel
rosacea *Erythema of the cheeks and nose caused by chronic vascular and follicular dilation.*	Rosazea
Rossolimo reflex *Flexion of the toes when the tips of the toes are flicked. This abnormal resonse is present in pyramidal tract lesions.*	Rossolimoreflex
rotation *Movement around an axis.*	Drehung
rotator cuff *The structure around the capsule of the shoulder joint formed by the infraspinatus, supraspinatus, teres minor and subscapularis muscles.*	Rotatorenmanschette
round ligament of the uterus *The supporting structure of the uterus.*	Ligamentum teres uteri
rub *A sound heard at times with pericarditis called more specifically a pericardial friction sound.*	Reibegeräusch
rubefacient *A substance that reddens the skin.*	Rubefaciens
rubella *Also called German measles, it is characterized by a rash, fever, headache.*	Röteln
Rubeola *Another term for measles, an acute exanthematous disease.*	Masern
rude *Ill-mannered.*	unhöflich
rugine *A surgical instrument that resembles a rasp.*	Schaber
rule out, to *To perform a test or exam to exclude an illness or disease.*	ausschließen

English	German
running suture *A method of sewing a wound in which there is a knot at each end and continuous otherwise.*	fortlaufend Sutur
rupia *A sign of tertiary syphilis in which there are bullae or vesicles formed on the skin that erupt and form crusts.*	Rupia
rupture *An instance of bursting suddenly.*	Ruptur
sacral *Referring to the sacrum.*	sakral
sacral canal *The portion of the vertebral canal that progresses into the sacrum.*	Sakralkanal
sacralization *The fusion of the fifth lumbar vertebra to the sacrum.*	Sakralisation
sacrum *The bone formed by five fused vertebrae that is situated between the two hip bones.*	Sakrum; Kreuzbein
saddle joint *A joint that exhibits two saddle type surfaces at a 90 degree angle to each other, such as the carpometacarpal joint.*	Sattelgelenk
sadness *The state of being sad.*	Trauer
sagittal suture *The line where the two parietal bones meet.*	Scheitelsutur
Saint Ignatius' itch *Pruritis noted with a cluster of symptoms related to niacin deficiency. Generally referred to as pellagra.*	Pellagra
Saint Vitus' dance *Historic name for chorea minor characterized by hypotonia and emotional lability months after a streptococcal infection.*	Veitstanz; Chorea minor
saline *A solution of sodium chloride.*	salzig; Saline
saliva *The watery liquid secreted by the salivary glands.*	Speichel
salivary gland *The parotid, submandibular and sublingual glands that secrete saliva.*	Speicheldrüse
salivation *The process of secreting saliva.*	Speichelfluß
salpingectomy *Surgical resection of the fallopian tubes.*	Salpingektomie
salpingitis *Inflammation of the fallopian tubes.*	Salpingitis
salpingography *Roentgenography of the fallopian tubes after administration of contrast media.*	Salpingographie
salpingostomy *A surgical procedure involving cutting the fallopian tube.*	Salpingostomie
salt *Typically referring to sodium chloride.*	Salz
saluretic *An agent that promotes excretion of sodium and chloride in the urine.*	saluretisch
sampling *The taking of samples.*	Probensammeln
sandfly fever *A febrile illness transmitted by a sandfly, from the genus Phlebotomus, and found in the Mediterranean.*	Pappatacifieber
sanitary napkin *Cloth or synthetic material used to absorb menstrual blood.*	Monatsbinde
saphena *Referring to either of the two superficial saphenous veins.*	Vena saphena
saponify,to *The creation of soap from oil using an alkali.*	verseifen
saprophyte *Any organism living on dead organic material.*	Saprophyt
sarcoid *Referring to sarcoidosis.*	sarkoid
sarcoidosis *A chronic disease characterized by lymphadenopathy and widespread granulomas.*	Sarkoidose
sarcolemme *The sheath that covers skeletal muscle fibers.*	Sarkolemm
sarcoma *A non-epithelial malignant tumor.*	Sarkom
sartorius muscle *The thigh muscle that runs from the pelvis to the proximal, medial aspect of the tibia.*	sartorius Muskel

English	German
saturation *An amount, expressed in a percentage, that expresses the degree something is absorbed versus the maximal absorption possible.*	Sättigung
saw *A hand or power-driven tool used for cutting.*	Säge
scabies *A skin condition exhibited by intense pruritis and a macular rash commonly in the perineal and interdigital spaces.*	Skabies; Krätze
scald *A burn injury from extremely hot water.*	Verbrühung
scale *A device to check a person's weight.*	Waage
scalp *The skin covering the head except for the face.*	Kopfhaut
scalp avulsion *An injury causing the skin along with some subcutaneous tissue to be pulled from the skull.*	Skalpierung
scalpel *A knife used during surgery for incision of skin and tissue.*	Skalpell
scaphocephaly *A condition exhibited by a long narrow skull because of early closure of the sagittal sutures.*	Skaphocephalie
scaphoid bone *The most lateral of the carpal bones; it articulates with the radius.*	Kahnbein; Navikulare
scapula *Medical term for the shoulder blade.*	Schulterblatt
scarification *Multiple small scratches of the skin, as is sometimes used for vaccine administration.*	Skarifikation
scarlet fever *A condition caused by streptococci that is exhibited by fever and a bright red (scarlet) rash.*	Scharlach
scatter *The degree to which repeated measurements differ.*	Streuung
scheme *A program or plan.*	Programm
schistocyte *Part of a red blood cell seen in hemolytic anemia.*	Schistozyt
schistosomiasis *A condition, sometimes known as bilharzia, which involves infestation with flukes of the genus Schistosoma.*	Schistosomiasis; Bilharziose
schizophrenia *A chronic mental condition exhibited by delusions, hallucinations, and faulty perception.*	Schizophrenie
schmorl's nodule *Protrusion of the nucleus pulposus through the vertebral body endplast into the adjacent vertebra.*	Schmorlsches Knötchen
sciatica *Pain radiating from the buttock down the back of the leg; it is caused by a compressed spinal nerve root.*	Ischiassyndrom
scimitar sign *An abnormal radiologic finding associated with anomalous pulmonary venous drainage.*	Scimitar-Syndrom
scirrhus *A cancer that is hard to palpation.*	Szirrhus
scissors *A cutting instrument with two blades, joined at the middle.*	Schere
sclera *The white outer covering of the eyeball.*	Sklera
scleritis *Inflammation of the eyeball.*	Skleritis
sclerodactylia *Scleroderma of the digits.*	Sklerodaktylie
scleroderma *A systemic disease of the connective tissues.*	Skleröderm
sclerotomy *Surgical incision of the sclera.*	Sclerotomie
scolex *The front end of a tapeworm.*	Skolex
scoliosis *A lateral curvature of the spine.*	Skoliose
scopophilia *Sexual please attained by viewing sexual organs.*	Skopophilie
scotoma *A blind spot within an otherwise normal visual field.*	Skotom
scrape *An injury caused by having a body part rubbed against a rough surface.*	Kratzer
scratch *A long, narrow superficial wound.*	Kratzen; Schramme
screening *An evaluation as part of a methodical study.*	Reihenuntersuchung

143

English	German
scrofula *Cervical tuberculous lymphadenitis.*	Skrofulose
scrotal *Referring to the scrotum.*	skrotal
scrotal hydrocele *A benign collection of fluid in the scrotum.*	Hydrozele testis
scrotum *The sac which contains the testes.*	Skrotum; Hodensack
scurvy *A disease of vitamin C deficiency exhibited by bleeding gums.*	Skorbut
scutulum *A crust of tinea capitis.*	Skutulum
scybalum *A hard, dry formation of stool in the bowel.*	Skybala
seal *A device or substance used to bind two things together.*	Robbe; Siegel
sebaceous *Referring to a sebaceous gland or what it secretes.*	talgig
sebaceous gland *A gland in the skin that secretes sebum.*	Talgdrüse
seborrhea *Abnormal amount of sebum production.*	Seborrhöe
secretin *A hormone that increases secretion from the pancreas and liver.*	Sekretin
secretion *The discharge of substances from cells or glands.*	Sekretion; Absonderung
sedative *A medication used to facilitate sleep or calm a person.*	Sedativum
seizure *An episode of tonic/clonic movement noted in epilepsy.*	Anfall; Krampf
semen analysis *Evaluation of semen used as part of a fertility workup.*	Spermauntersuchung
semicircular canal *The anterior, posterior and lateral canals in the inner ear that assist in balance control.*	Bogengang
seminiferous tubules *Used for transport of semen.*	Samenkanälchen
seminoma *A malignant tumor of the testis.*	Seminom
senescence *The normal process of deterioration with age.*	Seneszenz
senile *Generally referring to mental deterioration associated with aging.*	senil
senility *The process of being senile.*	Senilität
sensation *A perception when one is touched.*	Sinneseindruck
sensibility *Ability to feel or perceive.*	Sensibilität
sensible *When referring to a choice, chosen with wisdom.*	fühlbar
sensitization *The change in an organ by a hormone so it will respond to another stimulus.*	Sensibilisierung
sensitized *Being abnormally sensitive to a substance.*	sensibilisiert
sensory nerve *A nerve that receives input from various receptors.*	sensorisches nerven
sepsis *A condition exhibited by overwhelming inflammation due to infection.*	Sepsis
septic *Referring to a state of sepsis.*	septisch
septicemia *A systemic disease in which microorganisms or their toxins are in the blood stream.*	Septikämie
septum *A wall separating two chambers, the nasal septum for example.*	Septum; Scheidewand
sequela *A medical problem related to an initial injury or disease.(late sequelae)*	Folgekrankheit (Spätkomplikation)
sequestrum *Necrotic bone present in an injured or diseased bone.*	Sequesterbildung
serial *In a series.*	reihenmäßig
serotonin *A neurotransmitter that constricts blood vessels.*	Serotonin
serous *Referring to serum or similar to serum.*	serös
serpiginous *A skin lesion having wavy margin.*	serpiginös
serum *The fluid that isolates out when blood coagulates.*	Serum
sessile *Having a broad base with no stalk.*	sessil

144

English	German
severe *Intense or very great.*	ernst
sex *Gender.*	Geschlecht
sexual intercourse *The act of copulation.*	Geschlechtsverkehr
sexually transmitted disease (STD) *A condition one obtains from another during sexual relations.*	Geschlechtskrankheit
Sézary syndrome *Symptoms are exfoliative dermatitis with intense itching caused by cutaneous infiltration by mononuclear cells,*	Sézary-Syndrom
shake, to *To tremble uncontrollably.*	schütteln
sharp (pain) *When describing pain, a piercing sensation.*	stechend
sheath *A covering.*	Scheide; Hülle
sheet (bed) *A rectangular fabric covering a bed.*	Bettlaken
shellfish *An aquatic shelled crustacean or mollusk.*	Schalentier
shield *A protective device, as in face shield.*	Schild; Hülse
shin *Refers to the anterior tibial region.*	Schienbein
shingles *A reactivation of herpes zoster.*	Zoster
shiver *A trembling.*	Schauer
shock *A condition characterized by systemic hypoperfusion.*	Schock
shoe *Article of clothing worn on each foot.*	Schuh
shortening *Notable for having a shorter length.*	Verkürzung
shoulder *The joint were the scapula joins the clavicle and humerus.*	Schulter
shunt *An alternate path for blood or fluid.*	Ablenkung
sialadenitis *Inflammation of a salivary gland.*	Sialadenitis
sialogogue *A substance that increase salivary flow.*	Sialagogum
sialolith *A calculus in a salivary duct.*	Sialolith
siblings *Brothers or sisters.*	Geschwister
sickle-cell anemia *A hereditary type of anemia characterized by crescent shaped red blood cells.*	Sichelzellenanämie
sickness *Illness or a state of disease.*	Krankheit; Unwohlsein
side *A position medial or lateral to center.*	Seite
side effect *An expected but unwanted effect of a medication.*	Nebenwirkung
siderosis *Discoloration of a part due to iron deposition.*	Siderose
sigh, to *A long deep exhalation that expresses an emotion, as in relief.*	seufzen
sigmoid flexure *The S shaped curve located between the descending colon and rectum.*	Sigmoidflexur
sigmoid *Referring to the portion of the colon that leads into the rectum.*	Colon sigmoideum; Sigmoid
sigmoidoscopy *Visualization of the sigmoid colon with a scope.*	Sigmoidoskopie
sigmoidostomy *Formation of an opening in the sigmoid colon that communicates with the outside of the body.*	Sigmoidostomie
silent *Absence of noise or no indication of something.*	still
silicosis *Grinders's disease; fibrotic lung disease caused by inhalation of silica.*	Silikose
silver *A precious metal with atomic number 47.*	Silber
silver nitrate stick *A medical device used to treat hypergranulation tissue.*	silbernitrat Stock
simultaneous *Occurring at the same time.*	gleichzeitig
single *Only one.*	einzig
single *Not married.*	ledig

145

English	German
sinistrocardia *Location of the heart toward the left (more than normally seen).*	Sinistrokardie
sinistrotorsion *Distorsion toward the left; in reference to the eye generally.*	Sinistrotorsion
sinoatrial *Referring to the cardiac node of the same name.*	sinuatrial
sinoatrial node *A mass of cardiac tissue that acts as the pacemaker.*	Sinusknoten; Keith-Flack Knoten
sinus arrhythmia *Cardiac dysrhythmias related to sinoatrial nodal dysfunction.*	Sinusarrhythmie
sinusitis *Inflammation of the sinuses.*	Sinusitis
sinusoid *An irregular vessel having almost no adventitia that is found in the liver, heart, parathyroid, spleen and pancreas.*	Sinusoid
sip, to *To slowly take small drinks of a fluid.*	nippen
Sister Mary Joseph nodule *A nodule at the umbilicus associated with metastatic abdominal cancer.*	metastatisch Umbilikalknöten
site *Location.*	Site
size *The dimensions of something.*	Umfang; Größe
Sjogren's syndrome. *Characterized by dryness of the mouth and eyes, it is sometimes linked to rheumatoid arthritis.*	Sjögren Syndrom
skeletal traction *Use of a pulley system to reduce a fracture.*	Skelattartigtraction
skeleton *Internal bony framework.*	Skelett
skin *Flesch.*	Haut
skin fold *An overlapping of skin formed by subcutaneous tissue.*	Hautfalte
skin lesion *An abnormal but not necessarily cancerous lesion.*	Hautläsion
skin rash *Dermal exanthema.*	Hautausschlag
sleep *A nap or a snooze.*	Schlaf
sleep apnea *Episodic apnea during sleep that is exhibited by daytime symptoms of fatigue, difficulty concentrating and sleepiness.*	Schlafapnoesyndrom
sleeping sickness *Also called Trypanosomiasis, this disease is caused by a parasitic protozoa and transmitted by the tsetse fly.*	Schlafkrankheit
slice *A sliver or shaving.*	Scheibe
slide *A thin, rectangular piece of glass used for viewing specimen under a microscope.*	Objektträger
slight *Minor or small.*	gering
sling *A device used to give support to an injured extremity.*	Schlinge
slow *Unhurried.*	langsam
sludge *A viscous fluid.*	Schlamm
slurring *Indistinct yet comprehensible speech.*	beschimpfend
smallpox *Variola.*	Pocken
smear *Used to refer to a specimen smeared on a slide.*	Schmiere
smegma *A thick curdled secretion found around the clitoris and the prepuce.*	Smegma
smoke, to *To inhale on a cigarette.*	rauchen
sneeze, to *To suddenly expel air from the nose and mouth because of nasal irritation.*	niesen
sniffing *Short, rapid nasal inhalation.*	Schnüffeln
snore, to *To snore or grunt while breathing during sleep.*	schnarchen

146

English	German
soap *A compound made with fats/oils and an alkali; it is used for washing.*	Seife
sob, to *To cry uncontrollably.*	schluchzen
socket *An anatomical hollow that is part of an articulation. (eyeball socket)*	Aussparung (Augenhöhle)
socks *Worn on the feet before one puts on shoes.*	Socken
sodium chloride *A colorless, crystalline compound; also table salt.*	Natriumchlorid
soft *Easy to mold or compress.*	weich
solar plexus *A cluster of ganglia and nerves, located at the base of the sternum, that surround the celiac trunk.*	Plexus solaris
sole of foot *Common term for plantar aspect of the foot.*	Fußsohle
soleus muscle *Assists with ankle plantar flexion.*	Soleus
solvent *Able to dissolve with other chemicals.*	Lösungsmittel
somatic *Referring to the body.*	somatisch
somnambulism *Sleepwalking.*	Somnambulismus
somnolence *Drowsiness.*	Somnolenz
soporific *Promoting drowsiness or sleep.*	Schlafmittel
sore throat *Common term for pharyngitis.*	Halsschmerzen
sorrow *A feeling of deep despair.*	Sorge
sound *Vibrations that travel through air and are heard when reaching the ears.*	Schall; Ton
sour *An acid or bitter taste.*	sauer
span *A distance between two objects.*	Spannweite
sparing *Economical.*	sparsam
spasm *An involuntary contraction of muscles.*	Spasmus
spasmolytic *A substance that diminishes spasms.*	spasmolytisch
spastic *Stiff, awkward movement of the muscles.*	Spastiker
spasticity *Refers to continuous spastic movement.*	Spastizität
specific *Clearly defined.*	spezifisch
specimen *A sample for medical testing.*	Probe
spectrometry *The use of a device to measure spectra.*	Spektrometrie
spectroscope *A device for producing and recording spectra.*	Spektroskop
speculum *A device used to open a canal for inspection. (vaginal speculum)*	Spekulum (Scheidenspekulum)
speech *Oral articulation.*	Sprache
speech therapist *A person trained to assist people with speech and language disorders.*	Sprachtherapie
sperm *Short term for spermatozoon.*	Sperma
spermatic cord *The structure containing the ductus deferens, testicular artery, and nerves that goes from the inguinal ring to the testis.*	Samenstrang
spermatocele *A cyst in the epididymis containing spermatozoa.*	Spermatozele
spermatogenesis *The production of spermatozoa.*	Spermatogenese
spermatozoon *A mature male germ cell that is capable of fertilizing an ovum.*	Spermatozoon
spermicide *A substance capable of killing sperm.*	Spermizid
sphenoidal sinus *Part of the sphenoid bone; it communicates with the most superior aspect of the nasal meatus.*	Sinus sphenoidalis

147

English	German
spherocyte *An erythrocyte without the usual central pallor; it is noted in spherocytosis and some hemolytic anemias.*	Spherozyt
spherocytosis *The presence of spherocytes in the blood.*	Spherozytose
sphincter *A muscle the surrounds an orifice or duct so it closes when the muscle contracts.*	Sphinkter; Schließmuskel
sphincterotomy *Surgical incision of the anal sphincter.*	Sphinkterotomie
sphygmomanometer *Device for measuring blood pressure.*	Sphygmomanometer; Blutdruckapparat
spica *A figure of eight bandage.*	Spica
spicule *A sharp, slender part.*	Spitz
spider nevus *A papule with telangiectases radiating from the center.*	Spider-Nävus
spinal *Referring to the spine.*	spinal
spinal cord abscess *A localized collection of purulent material in or adjacent to the spinal cord.*	Rückenmarkabszeß
spinal cord *The bundle of nerves that with the brain comprise the central nervous system.*	Rückenmark
spinal ganglion *The ganglion located on the dorsal root of each spinal nerve.*	Spinalganglion
spinal nerve *The term for each of the thirty pairs of nerves that originate in the spine and traverse between the vertebrae. There are eight cervical, twelve thoracic, five lumbar, five sacral and one coccygeal nerve pairs.*	Spinalnerv
spinal reflex *A reflex that has an arc passing through the spine.*	spinaler Reflex
spinal shock *Hypotension related to injury or intervention of the spine.*	spinaler Shock
spine *The spinal column or a thorny protrusion.*	Wirbelsäule; Rückgrat
spirograph *A device used to record respiratory movements.*	Spirograph
spirometer *A device used to measure pulmonary capacity.*	Spirometer
spit *A term used to describe saliva that is ejected from the mouth.*	Auswurf
splanchnic nerves *The nerves supplying the abdominal viscera and blood vessels.*	Nervus splanchnicus
spleen *The visceral organ that is involved with production and removal of blood cells.*	Milz
splenectomy *Surgical excision of the spleen.*	Splenektomie; Milzexstirpation
splenic flexure of the colon *The portion of the colon that turns from the transverse to the descending colon.*	Versammlung der transversal Kolon und abstammen Kolon
splenic *Referring to the spleen.*	splenisch
splenomegaly *An abnormally enlarged spleen.*	Splenomegalie; Milzvergröberung
splint *A rigid support used to immobilize and extremity.*	Schiene
splinter *A small, thin object; usually refers to the object being imbedded in the body.*	Splitter
spondylitis *Inflammation of the vertebrae.*	Spondylitis
spondylolisthesis *The overlapping of one vertebra over another.*	Spondylothisthese
spondylolysis *Dissolution of the vertebra.*	Spondylolyse
sponge *Sterile fabric used to soak up fluid during surgery.*	Schwamm
spongiosis *Edema of the spongy layer of the skin.*	Spongiose
spontaneous *Occurring without provocation.*	spontan
spoon nail *Also referred to as koilonychia, the nail is concave and is generally associated with anemia.*	Löffeffel

148

English	German
spoonful *A measurement that does not specify teaspoon or tablespoon.*	Löffel
sporotrichosis *A Sporotrichum schenckii infection manifested by formation of lymphatic and subcutaneous nodules.*	Sporotrichose
sprain *A joint injury without fracture.*	Verstauchung
spray *Liquid blown through the air in the form of fine droplets.*	Spray; Zerstäuber
sputum *A mixture of respiratory tract secretions and saliva.*	Sputum
squama *A scale or platelike body.*	Schuppe; Squama
squamous *Scaly.*	squamös
square root *The result noted when a number is multiplied by itself.*	Quadratwurzel
squeeze, to *To apply pressure.*	quetschen
squint, to *To look at something with the eyes partially closed.*	schielen
squirt, to *To eject a liquid from a small opening.*	spritzen
stab wound *An injury occurring with a sharp object.*	Stichwunde
stabbing pain *A sharp piercing quality to pain.*	stechender Schmerz
stagger, to *To walk in an unsteady fashion.*	schwanken
staging *Refers to a stratification of cancer for example.*	Stadieneinteilung; Feststellung
stamina *Ability to maintain physical or mental exertion for a long period.*	Ausdauer
stammering *The impulse to repeat the first letter of words and involuntary pauses while speaking.*	Stammeln
standing *Position or status.*	stehend
stapedectomy *Surgical excision of the stapes.*	Stapedektomie
stapedius muscle *Located in the tympanic interior, it reduces stapedial movement.*	stapedius Muskel
stapes *This auditory ossicle is the innermost of three ossicles and is shaped like a stirrup.*	Steigbügel
staphyloma *Protrusion of the cornea due to inflammation.*	Staphylom
staphylorrhaphy *Surgical repair of a defect between the soft palate and uvula.*	Staphylorrhaphie
starvation *Death related to starvation.*	Hungerustand; Hahrungsentzug
stasis *Lack of movement.*	Stase
state *Status.*	Zustand
statement *A written or oral commentary.*	Aussage
static *Not changing.*	statisch
status *Position or condition*	Status
steady state *In equilibrium.*	Fließgleichgewicht
steatoma *A sebaceous cyst or lipoma.*	Steatom
steatorrhea *Excrement with an abnormally high fat content.*	Steatorrhöe
steatosis *Fatty degeneration; when referring to the liver it involves invasion of fat into hepatocytes.*	Steatose
stellate ganglion *Formed by the seventh cervical, eighth cervical and first thoracic ganglia.*	Ganglion stellatum
stenosis *Narrowing of an orifice.*	Stenose
stercobilin *A substance created by the reduction of bilirubin and gives excrement the brown hue.*	Sterkobilin
stereognosis *The ability to identify an object by touch.*	Astereognosie
sterile *1. Infertile 2. Refers to equipment that is free of contamination.*	steril
sterilization *A procedure done to prevent production of offspring.*	Sterilisierung

English	German
sternal *Referring to the sternum.*	sternal
sternocleidomastoid *The pair of muscles that connect the sternum, clavicle and mastoid process.*	Sternocleidomastoideus
sternum *Commonly called the breast bone, it consists of the corpus, manubrium and xiphoid process.*	Sternum; Brustbein
sterol *Unsaturated steroid alcohols such as cholesterol.*	Sterin
stethoscope *Device used to auscultate the heart, lungs and over arteries to assess for abnormalities.*	Stehoskop; Hörrohr
stiff *Not easily bent.*	steif
stiff-neck *Cervical sprain with reduced range of motion.*	einen steifen Nacken
stillborn *Refers to a newborn that died in utero.*	totgeboren
sting *A small puncture as in a bee sting.*	Stich
stippling *Having numerous small specks or spots.*	Tüpfelung
stirrup *An attachment to an exam table where a woman puts her legs to assist examination of the genitalia.*	Steigbügel
stomach *Organ of digestion between the esophagus and small bowel.*	Magen
stomach cramps *Sensation of muscle contraction in the epigastric area.*	Magenkrämpfe
stomach pain *Discomfort in the abdomen in the epigastric area.*	Magenschmerz
strabismus *An anomaly of ocular movement.*	Strabismus
strain *As in a muscle strain.*	Anstrengung
strait-jacket *A device used to temporarily restrain the arms of patients who are psychotic and violent.*	Zwangjacke
strange *Unusual in an unsettling way.*	außergewöhnlich
straw itch *Pruritis associated with exposure to straw that is infested with the mite Pyemotes ventricosus. Also referred to as dermatitis pediculoides ventricosus.*	Pediculoides ventricosus
strawberry tongue *A characteristic discoloration of the tongue seen in an early phase of scarlet fever.*	Erdbeerzunge
stream *The flow of a liquid.*	Strom
strength *Force, might or vigor.*	Stärke
stress *Strain or pressure.*	Stress; Druck; Belastung
stress fracture *A long bone fracture caused by repetitive mechanical stress.*	Streßfraktur
stretcher *A device used to carry a patient in the supine position.*	Tragbahre; Strecker
stria *A narrow bandlike body.*	Stria; Streifen
stricture *A narrowing of a canal or duct.*	Striktur
stride *Walk with long definitive steps.*	Schritt
stridor *An abnormal, high-pitched, musical sound caused by an obstruction in the largynx or stenosis of the vocal cords.*	Stridor
stroke *Common term for cerebrovascular accident.*	zerebrale Durchblutungsstörung
stroke volume *The amount of blood ejected from the ventricle with each contraction.*	Schlagvolumen
stroma *A term used to describe the framework of an organ.*	Stroma
strong *Having the power to move heavy objects.*	kräftig
stump *Term used to designate what remains of an amputated extremity.*	Stumpf
Strümpell's disease *Also known as spondylitis deformans, it is characterized by arthritis and osteitis deformans of the spinal cord with a rounded kyphosis and rigidity.*	Strümpellsche Krankheit

English	German
Strümpell reflex *Flexion of the leg and adduction of the foot elicited by stroking of the thigh or abdomen.*	Strümpellreflex
stupor *A reduced level of consciousness.*	Stupor
stuttering *Involuntary repetition of the first consonant.*	Stottern
sty *Also called hordeolum externum, it is inflammation of the sebaceous gland of an eyelash.*	Liddrüsentzündung
stylet *A thin wire within a catheter that is removed after the catheter is in place.*	Stilett; Mandrin
subacute *A stage between acute and chronic.*	subakut
subarachnoid *The layer of the brain covering between the arachnoid and pia mater.*	subarachnoidal
subareolar abscess *A purulent fluid collection in the areolar gland.*	Subareolärabszeß
subclavian *Refers to the area under the clavicle; the subclavian vein runs below the clavicle.*	subklavikulär
subclavian steal syndrome *Retrograde vertebral artery flow due to ipsilateral subclavian artery stenosis.*	Anzapfsyndrom der Arteria subclavia
subdural *The area between the dura mater and the arachnoid membrane.*	subdural
subdural hematoma *Formation of a blood clot between the dura mater and the arachnoid membrane.*	Subduralhämatom
suberosis *A type of hypersensitivity pneumonitis related to inhalation of moldy cork dust.*	Suberose; Korkarbeiterkrankheit
sublingual *Situated under the tongue.*	sublingual
submaxillary *Situated below the maxilla.*	submaxillär
subphrenic *Referring to below the diaphragm.*	subphrenisch
succussion *The presence of a splashing sound when a body cavity is moved indicating presence of both air and fluid.*	Succussio Hippocratis
suck, to *As in, to suction fluid.*	saugen
suckle, to *An infant taking to his mother's nipple.*	säugen
sudamina *White vesicles noted because of retained sweat in the layers of the epidermis.*	Schweißbläschen
sudden infant death syndrome *A leading cause of death of infants from one month to one year; the etiology is unknown.*	plötzlicher Kindstod
suffer, to *To be affected by an illness or sickness.*	leiden; klagen
suffocation *To die from a lack of air or inability to breathe.*	Erstickung
sugar *A sweet crystalline substance made from a plant such as sugar cane.*	Zucker
suicide *To kill oneself intentionally.*	Suizid; Selbsttötung
sulcus *A groove, like in the brain.*	Sulkus
sulfonamide *A class of drugs derived from sulfanilamide that are antibacterial.*	Sulfonamid
sulfur *A chemical element with atomic number of 16.*	Schwefel
summer itch *Pruritis noted upon exposure to hot weather, also known as pruritis aestivalis.*	Pruritis aestivalis
superciliary arch *The area superior to the upper border of each orbit.*	Augenbrauenarcus
superfecundation *The fertilization of two different ova by spermatozoa of two different males.*	Superfekundation
superficial inguinal ring *The opening of the aponeurosis of the external oblique muscle for the round ligament or spermatic cord.*	Oberflächenleistenring

English	German
superior *In a position above something else.*	oberer
supination *Turning the sole of the foot or the palm of the hand upward..*	Supination
supine *Flat on one's back.*	Rückenlage
supplies *Stock or reserves.*	liefert
suppository *A delivery system for medication placed in an orifice.*	Suppositorium; Zäpfchen
suppuration *Formation of purulent material.*	Eiterung
supranuclear ophthalmoplegia *A disorder that effects the extraocular movements especially limiting the upward movement of the eyes.*	supranukleär Ophthalmoplegie
supraorbital *Situated above the orbit.*	supraorbital
suprapubic *Situated above the pubis.*	suprapubisch
sural *Referring to the calf of the leg.*	waden
surfactant *A substance that reduces surface tension in the lungs.*	Oberflächenaktive Substanz
surgeon *A physician who performs surgery.*	Chirurgin
surgery *The incision of a body part using sterile technique in order to treat disease or injury.*	Chirurgie
surgical *Referring to surgery.*	chirurgisch
surname *One's given "last" name that generally changes for women upon marriage to that of the man's surname.*	Nachname
sustain, to *To keep or maintain.*	aufrechterhalten
sustained release tablet *Describes a medicine that is slowly dispersed so it has a lasting effect.*	Retardtablette
suture *Thread used for sewing together a wound.*	Sutur
swab *An absorbant material used for cleaning wounds or applying ointment.*	Tupfur; Abstrich
swallow, to *To cause something to pass down the esophagus.*	schlucken
sweat *Moisture exuded through the pores of the skin.*	Schweiß
sweat, to *The action of releasing moisture through pores of the skin.*	schwitzen
swelling *An abnormal enlarged from fluid collection.*	Schwellung; Geschwulst
swimmer's itch *Pruritis caused by exposure to schistosomes.*	Badedermatitis; Schwimmerkrätze
swollen (distended) abdomen	geschwollen Bauch
sycosis *A bacterial infection affecting the hair follicles on a person's face.*	Sycose
Sydenham chorea *Historically known as Saint Vitus' dance, it is a childhood chorea associated with rheumatic fever.*	Chorea Sydenham
symbiosis *The living together of two organisms.*	Symbiose
symmetry *Being equally bilaterally.*	Symmetrie
sympathectomy *The surgical resection of a sympathetic nerve to reduce undesired effects.*	Sympathektomie
sympathetic nervous system *The nerves responsible for the flight or fight response.*	sympathisches Nervensystem
symptom *A physical feature that is characteristic of disease.*	Symptom; Krankheitszeichen
synapse *The intersection of two nerve cells.*	Synapse
synarthrosis *Adjacent bones connected by a joint but the joint is fixed.*	Synarthrose
synchondrosis *A joint with little motion that uses cartilage such as the vertebral bodies.*	Synchondrose
syncope *Sudden loss of consciousness.*	Synkope; Ohnmachtsanfall

English	German
syncytial knot *Aggregation of syncytiotrophoblastic nuclei in the villi of the placenta during early pregnancy.*	Synzytienbildung
synechia *The adhesion of two body parts, such as synechia vulvae in which the labia minora are congenitally adherent.*	Synechie
synovectomy *Surgical resection of a synovial membrane.*	Synvektomie
synovial fluid *The fluid that surrounds, for example, the knee within a capsule.*	Synovia
synovitis *Inflammation of the synovium.*	Synovitis
syphilis *A infectious disease caused by Treponema pallidum that causes a painless penile ulcer in the primary stage but can lead to irreversible brain damage in the untreated tertiary stage.*	Syphilis; Lues
syringe *A device used for administering medication through various routes.*	Spritze
syringomelia *A condition exhibited by fluid-filled cavities in the spinal cord.*	Syringomyelie
syrup *A thick sweet liquid.*	Sirup
systole *The phase of the cardiac cycle in which the ventricles contract.*	Systole
systolic *Referring to systole or that which occurs during systole.*	systolisch
tablespoon *An eating utensil that holds 15milliliters of fluid.*	Esslöffel; Eßlöffel
tablet *A small disk of a compressed solid substance.*	Tablette
tachycardia *Heart rate higher than physiologic normal.*	Tachykardie
tachypnea *Breathing faster than normal.*	Tachypnoe
tactile *Able to be felt.*	taktil
talipes calcaneus *A foot deformity exhibited by abnormal dorsiflexion.*	Hackenfuß
talipes equinovaro *Medical term for what is commonly known as club foot.*	Spitz-Klumpfuß
talipes equinus *A foot deformity exhibited by abnormal plantar flexion.*	Spitzfuß
talon *The ball of the ankle joint.*	Kralle; Klaue
talus *The most superior tarsal bone that articulates with the tibia.*	Talus
tampon *Disposible intravaginal product used to collect blood from menstruation.*	Tampon
tamponade *1. Stopping bleeding during surgery with a cotton pledget. 2. When referring to cardiac tamponade, it is the limitation of cardiac contraction because of blood or fluid accumulation in the pericardial sac.*	tamponade
tap *A puncture with the intent of draining fluid as in spinal tap.*	Punktion; Klopfen
tape measure *A long length of tape, marked at intervals for measuring.*	Bandmaß
tapeworm *A parasitic, intestinal flatworm.*	Bandwurm
tarantula *A large hairy spider found mainly in the tropics.*	Tarantel
target *An objective towards which efforts are directed.*	Bremskoltz; Ziel
target cell *An abnormal cell that is present in liver disease and certain hemoglobinopathies.*	Zielzelle
tarsal *Referring to any bone in the tarsus.*	tarsal
tarsal tunnel syndrome *Characterized by impingement of various nerves of the ankle.*	Tarsaltunnelsyndrom
tarsalgia *Pain in any of the tarsal bones.*	Tarsalgie
tarsectomy *Surgical excision of all or part of the tarsus.*	Tarsektomie; Tarsusresektion
tarsorrhaphy *Suturing the eyelids in order to tighten the palpebral fissure.*	Tarsorrhaphie

English	German
tarsus *The group of seven bones of the ankle or foot (three cuneiform bones, talus, calcaneus, navicular, cuboid bones).*	Fußwurzel; Lidknorpel; Lidplatte
taste *Sensation of flavor percieved in one's mouth.*	Geschmack
tattoo *A design made by inserting indelible ink into the skin.*	Tätowierung
taurocholic acid *A bile acid composed of cholic acid and taurine.*	Taurocholsäure
tear *As in, to shed a tear.*	Träne
tear *Referring to a vaginal tear after childbirth.*	Aufbruch
teaspoon *A measure instrument that holds 5 milliliters of fluid.*	Teelöffel
tectum *A roof-like body.*	Tectum
tectum mesencephali *The posterior portion of the mesencephalon including the sup. and inf. colliculi and tectal lamina.*	Tectum mesencephali
telangiectasis *A condition exhibited by red, dilated capillaries on the skin.*	Teleangiektasie
telemetry *Use of radio signals to transmit patient data. The most common form is for electrocardiography in a patient who is ambulatory.*	Fernmessung; Telemetrie
temperature *The degree of internal heat in a person's body.*	Temperatur
temporomandibular joint *The hinged joint of the temporal bone and mandible.*	Unterkiefergelenk
tendinitis *Inflammation of a tendon.*	Tendinitis
tendon *Fibrous tissue that connects muscle to bone.*	Sehne
tendon reflex *A deep reflex elicited by gently tapping the tendon.*	Sehnenreflex
tenesmus *The attempt to defecate but attempts elicit pain and are ineffective.*	Tenesmus
tennis elbow *Inflammation at the lateral aspect of the epicondyle where the muscle and tendon join; lateral epicondylitis.*	Epikondylitis
tenoplasty *Surgical repair of a tendon.*	Tendoplastik
tenorrhaphy *The surgical repair with suture of a separated tendon.*	Tenorrhaphie
tenosynovitis *Inflammation and swelling of an articulation.*	Tendovaginitis; Sehnenscheidenentzündung
tenotomy *Incision of a tendon as is done for strabismus.*	Tenotomie
tepid *Lukewarm.*	lauwarm
teratogen *A substance that induces fetal anomalies.*	Teratogen
teratoma *A tumor made up of tissue not usually at the location (a mass of hair, teeth and gingival tissue in a leg tumor for instance).*	Teratom
terebrant *Having a piercing quality.*	stechend; bohrend
terminal illness *A disease with no viable treatment with death being inevitable.*	terminale Krankheit
tertian fever *A febrile syndrome caused by Plasmodium vivax which produces a fever spike every 48 hours.*	Tertiana
tertiary *Third in order or designating medical care at a specialized hospital.*	tertiär
test tube *A glass or plastic tube used to hold a medical specimen.*	Reagenzglas
testicle *One of a pair of organs in the male scrotum that produces sperm.*	Hoden
testicular torsion *Rotation of the spermatic cord resulting in testicular ischemia.*	Hodentorsion
testosterone *This steroid hormone produces secondary male sexual characteristics.*	Testosteron

154

English	German
tetanus *A condition caused by Clostridium tetani which produces spasm and rigidity of voluntary muscles.*	Wundstarrkrampf
tetany *A condition caused by the hypocalcemic effect of hypoparathyroidism, exhibited by periodic muscle spasms, convulsions, and peri-oral numbness.*	Tetanie
tetracycline *An antibiotic used for gram positive and gram negative infections.*	Tetracyclin
tetradactylous *Referring to a condition of having only four digits on a hand or foot.*	Tetradaktylie
thalamic syndrome *Caused by an infarct of the posteriorinferior thalamus, there is transient hemiparesis, severe sensory loss with preserved crude pain in the hypalgic limbs.*	Thalamussyndrom; Déjerine-Roussy Syndrom
thalamus *A paired structure located adjacent to the third ventricle.*	Thalmus
thalassemia *A hereditary hemolytic anemia first observed in people from the Mediterranean area.*	Thalassämie
thalidomide *A drug used originally as a sedative, after it was found to cause congenital anomalies, its use was restricted. Now it is used for a few conditions such as multiple myeloma.*	Thalidomid
theca *A tendon or ovarian follicle sheath.*	Hülle; Kapsel
thecoma *A tumor composed of theca cells.*	Thekazelltumor
thenar eminence *Formed by the bellies of the abductor pollicis brevis, flexor pollicis brevis and opponens pollicis.*	Daumenballen
therapeutic range *The highest to lowest value that will produce a desired effect.*	therapeutische Breite
thermometer *A device used to measure temperature.*	Thermometer
thiamine *Also called vitamin B1; a deficiency causes beriberi.*	Thiamin
thigh *The body region between the inguinal crease and knee.*	Oberschenkel
thin *Lean or slender.*	dünn; mager
thirst *The desire to drink.*	Durst
thoracentesis *Insertion of a needle into the pleural space to drain and or obtain a specimen for analysis.*	Thorakozentese
thoracic *Referring to the thorax.*	thorakal
thoracoplasty *Surgical removal of ribs.*	Thorakoplastik
thoracoscopy *Visualization of the thoracic cavity with a scope.*	Thorakoskopie
thoracotomy *Surgical incision of the thorax.*	Thorakotomie
thorax *The part of the body between the neck and abdomen.*	Brustkorb
three way foley *A urinary tube used for irrigation of the bladder.*	Dreiwegsonde
threonine *An amino acid needed for the growth in infants.*	Threonin
throat *The anterior aspect of the neck.*	Rachen; Schlund
throb, to *The beat with strong regular rhythm.*	pochen
thrombectomy *Excision of a thrombus from a vein or artery.*	Thrombektomie
thrombin *An enzyme that is a catalyst for the conversion of fibrinogen to fibrin in the formation of a clot.*	Thrombin
thromboangiitis *Inflammation and thrombosis in a blood vessel.*	Thrombangitis
thromboarteritis *Thrombosis of an inflamed artery.*	Thromboarteriitis
thrombocytopenia *Abnormal decrease in the number of blood platelets.*	Thrombozytopenie
thrombophlebitis *Inflammation of a venous wall associated with a thrombus.*	Thrombophlebitis

English	German
thrombosis *Formation of a clot in a vein or artery.*	Thrombose
thrush *Candida albicans*	Mundsoor
thumb *The first digit of each hand.*	Daumen
thymectomy *Surgical excision of the thymus.*	Thymektomie
thymine *A chemical with a pyrimidine base found in DNA.*	Thymin
thymocyte *A lymphocyte located in the thymus.*	Thymozyt
thymoma *A tumor composed of thymic tissue and is sometimes associated with myasthenia gravis.*	Thymom
thymus *A body organ located in the neck and it produces T cells to improve immune function.*	Thymusdrüse
thyroglossal cyst *A common congenital growth in the thyroglossal duct.*	Thyreoglossuszyste
thyroid *A gland in the neck that secretes hormones regulating metabolism.*	Schilddrüse
thyroid stimulating hormone (TSH) *A thyroid secreted by the pituitary that regulates the thyroid.*	Thyreotropin
thyroidectomy *Surgical resection of all or part of the thyroid.*	Thyreoidektomie
thyrotoxicosis *Abnormal increase in thyroid activity exhibited by thinning hair, hypertension, tachycardia and at times atrial fibrillation.*	Thyreotoxikose
thyroxine *An iodine containing hormone, referred to T4.*	Thyroxin
tibia *The larger of two long bones in the lower leg.*	Schienbein
tic *Periodic spasmodic facial muscle contractions.*	Tic
tic douloureux *Also referred to as trigeminal neuralgia.*	Tic douloureux
tick bite	Zeckenbiß
tick-borne fever *A relapsing fever caused by a spirochete of the genus Borrelia.*	Zeckenfieber
tickle, to *To lightly touch a person to cause one to laugh.*	kitzeln
tidal volume *The amount of air inspired with each breath. One can set a ventilator to deliver a preset number of milliliters of oxygenated air with each breath.*	Atemzugvolumen
tight junction *An intercellular junction with an impermeable membrane.*	Zonula occludens
tincture *1. A very small amount of something. 2. A medicine dissolved in alcohol.*	Tinktur
tinea barbae *Ringworm on the face in the region a man shaves.*	Tinea barbae
tinea capitis *Ringworm of the scalp, a fungal infection.*	Tinea capitis
tinea corporis *Ringworm of the body, a fungal infection.*	Tinea corporis
tinea cruris *Ringworm in the inguinal region, a fungal infection.*	Tinea cruris; Eczema marginatum
tinea *Medical term for ringworm.*	Dermatophytose; Tinea
tinea pedis *Ringworm of the feet, a fungal infection.*	Tinea pedis; Fußpilz
tingling *Prickling or stinging sensation.*	kribbelnd
tinnitus *Medical term for ringing in the ears. It is associated with Meniere's syndrome among other conditions.*	Ohrensausen
tired *Fatigued.*	müde
tissue *Any of the distinct materials people are made of.*	Gewebe
tocopherol *Vitamin E.*	Tokopherol
toe *Any of the digits of of the feet.*	Zehe

English	German
toenail *The nail at the tip/dorsal aspect of each toe.*	Zehennagel
tongs *A medical device used for holding or grasping.*	Zange
tongue *The fleshy muscular organ of the mouth.*	Zunge
tongue depressor; tongue blade *As the name implies, the stick pushes the tongue down so the posterior aspect of the mouth can be viewed more readily.*	Zungendrücker
tonometer *A device used to measure ocular pressure in glaucoma.*	tonometrisch
tonsil *A rounded mass of lymphoid tissue, most commonly referring to the pharyngeal tonsil.*	Tonsille; Mandel
tonsillectomy *Excision of the tonsils.*	Tonsillektomie
tonsillitis *Inflammation of the tonsils.*	Tonsillitis
tooth *One of a set of hard, bony enamel coated structure in the jaw.*	Zahn
toothache *Dental pain.*	Zahnschmerzen; Zahnweh
toothless *Edentulous.*	zahnlos
torpor *Unresponsiveness to normal stimuli.*	Torpidität
torsade de pointe *Ventricular cardiac rhythm disturbance.*	torsade de pointes
torsion *Refers to twisting. Testicular torsion is the twisting of the spermatic cord that can lead to ischemia and gangrene of the testicle.*	torsion
torsion spasm *Also called dystonia musculorum deformans, a genetic condition exhibited by twisting contortions sideways and forward while walking.*	Torsionsdystonie
torso *The trunk of the body.*	Rumpf
torticollis *A condition exhibited by the head being turned to one side continuously.*	Tortikollis; Schiefhals
touch *Tactile stimulation.*	Berührung
tourniquet *A device tied tightly around an extremity to diminish blood flow or blood loss.*	Stauschlauch; Tourniquet
toxemia *The release of toxic substances into the blood stream from a local infection. Toxemia of pregnancy is a synonym for preeclampsia.*	Toxämie
toxic *Relating to or caused by poison.*	toxisch
toxicology *The study of the nature, effects and detection of poisons.*	Toxikologie
toxin *A poison of plant or animal origin.*	Toxin
toxoid *A chemically modified toxin that can be used as a vaccine.*	Toxoid
toxoplasmosis *A disease caused by an organism from the genus Toxoplasma. One can have simple malaise to central nervous system involvement.*	Toxoplasmose
trabecule *A connective tissue strand that goes from a capsule to the enclosed organ.*	Trabekel
trabeculotomy *A surgery for open angle glaucoma.*	Trabekulotomie
trachea *The ringed canal between the pharynx and bronchi.*	Luftröhre
tracheitis *Inflammation of the trachea.*	Tracheitis
trachelorrhaphy *Surgical repair of a lacerated cervix.*	Emmet Operation
tracheobronchitis *Inflammation of the trachea and bronchi.*	Tracheobronchitis
tracheostomy *Creation of a surgical opening in the trachea so a tube could be placed in the trachea.*	Tracheostomie
tracheotomy *Surgical incision of the trachea.*	Tracheotomie
trachoma *An infection of the cornea and conjunctiva caused by Chlamydia.*	Trachom
tract *A large bundle of fibers or a major passage in the body.*	Strang; Kanal

English	German
traction *Sustained pull on a muscle or bone to correct alignment.*	Zug; Ziehen
tragus *The fleshy prominence anterior to the opening of the ear.*	Tragus
tranquilizer *A medication used to diminish anxiety.*	Tranquilizer
transabdominal *Through the abdominal wall.*	transabdominal
transaminase *An enzyme that facilitates the transfer of an amino group to an amino acid.*	Transaminase
transdermal *Through the skin.*	transdermal
transfusion *Administration of blood products intravenously.*	Transfusion
transient ischemic attack *Cerebral ischemic changes resulting from transitory hypoperfusion.*	transitorische ischämische Attacke
transpire, to *To release vapor from the skin or respiratory mucosa.*	schwitzen
transplant, to *To move a body part from one location to another.*	transplantieren
transplantation *The grafting of tissues.*	Transplantation
transrectal ultrasound *Insertion of an ultrasound probe into the rectum to view adjacent structures.*	transrektal Ultraschall
transudation *The movement of body tissue through a membrane that is usually the result of inflammation.*	Transsudation
transvaginal ultrasound *Insertion of an ultrasound probe in the vagina to view adjacent structures.*	transvaginal Ultraschall
trapezium *The lateral bone in the distal row of carpal bones.*	großes Vieleckbein
trapezius muscle *The muscle with an origin of occipital bone and seventh cervical vertebra, insertion of clavicle and scapula, and it draws the scapula backward.*	Trapezius
trapezoid bone *A bone that articulates with the second metacarpal, trapezium, capitate and scaphoid.*	kleines Vieleckbein
trauma *A physical injury or emotional shock.*	Trauma
treadmill *An exercise machine on a continuous belt used for walking.*	Laufband
treatment *Medical care one receives for illness or injury.*	Behandlung
trematoda *A parasitic fluke such as Schistosoma.*	Trematode
tremor *Involuntary contraction and relaxation of small muscle groups.*	Tremor
trench mouth *Inflammation and ulceration of the gingivae.*	Zahnfleischentzündung; Mundfäule
trephination *Cutting away a circular disc of bone or the cornea.*	Trepanation
triceps *Referring to something having three heads like the triceps muscle.*	Trizeps
triceps reflex *A tendon reflex causing extension of the arm when the triceps tendon is gently tapped.*	Trizepsreflex
trichiasis *Inversion of the eyelashes.*	Trichiasis
trichinosis *A disease caused by meat infected by Trichinella spiralis causing fever and gastrointestinal effects.*	Trichinose
trichomoniasis vaginitis *Infection related to a species of Trichomonas.*	Trichomonas vaginitis
trichophytosis *A skin or nail fungal infection caused by Trichophyton.*	Trichophytose
tricuspid valve *The cardiac valve located between the right atrium and right ventricle.*	Trikuspidalklappe
trigeminal *Generally refers to the fifth cranial nerve.*	trigeminal
trigeminal nerve *The fifth cranial nerve which supplies the motor function of mastication and has three sensory branches, the ophthalmic, maxillary and mandibular.*	Trigeminus

158

English	German
trigeminal neuralgia *Pain in the region of one or more branches of the fifth cranial nerve sensory branches.*	Trigeminusneuralgie
trigger finger *A condition in which one's finger gets stuck in the flexed position and when extended it snaps like a trigger. Also called stenosing tenosynovitis.*	schnellender Finger
trigone of bladder *Refers to the area at the base of the bladder between the openings of the ureters and the urethra.*	Dreieck
triplegia *Paralysis of three extremities.*	Triplegie
triplets *Three infants born during one birth.*	Drillinge
triploid *Referring to a cell with three homologous sets of chromosomes.*	triploid
trismus *Commonly called lockjaw, it is a spasm of the muscles supplied by the trigeminal nerve and is an early symptom of tetanus.*	Trismus; Kieferklemme
trisomy 21 *A congenital anomaly in which chromosome 21 is effected and results in Down's syndrome.*	trisomie 21
trisomy *A general category of congenital anomalies in which there is an extra set of chromosomes in the cell nucleus.*	Trisomie
trivial *Of little importance or value.*	trivial
trocar *A device enclosed in a catheter that is used to withdraw fluid from a body cavity.*	Trokar
trochanter *Refers to the greater or lesser trochanter; the prominences on the femoral neck.*	Trochanter
trochlea *A pulley-shaped structure such as the groove at the distal humerus.*	Rolle
trochlear *Referring to a trochlea.*	trochleär
trochlear nerve *The fourth cranial nerve that supplies the superior oblique muscle of the eyeball.*	Trochlearis
trophoblast *A layer of endodermal tissue that helps attach an ovum to the uterine wall.*	Trophoblast
truncal *Referring to the trunk of a body or a nerve.*	trunkulär
truss *A synthetic device for containing a hernia within the abdomen.*	binden
trypanosomiasis *A disease caused by a protozoa of the genus Trypanosoma that can cause sleeping sickness and Chagas' disease.*	Trypanosomiasis
trypsin *An enzyme whose precursor is secreted by the pancreas that breaks down proteins in the intestine.*	Trypsin
trypsinogen *The precursor to trypsin that is secreted by the pancreas.*	Trypsinogen
tryptophan *An amino acid that is a precursor of serotonin. If present in the body in appropriate levels it can prevent pellegra even if niacin levels are low.*	Tryptophan
tsetse fly *An insect that transmits the protozoa trypanosoma and can cause sleeping sickness.*	Tsetsefleige
tsutsugamushi disease *An acute febrile infectious disease caused by Rickettsia tsutsugamushi. It is characterized by fever, pain lymphadenopathy, small black lesions on the genitals, neck or axilla.*	Tsutsugamushifiebrer
tubal *Referring to a tube, as in fallopian tube.*	tublar
tubercle *1. A granulomatous nodule produced by Mycobacterium tuberculosis. 2. A small prominence on a bone.*	Tuberkel
tuberculin *A solution containing M. tuberculosis or M. bovis that is used to test for tuberculosis by injecting the solution intradermally and looking for a reaction.*	Tuberkulin

English	German
tuberculoma *1. A tuberculous growth in the brain. 2. A mass that is produced from enlargement of a caseous tubercle.*	Tuberkulom
tuberculosis *Any infectious disease caused by Mycobacterium.*	Tuberkulose
tuberculous *Referring to tuberculosis.*	tuberkuös
tuberosity *A protuberance. For instance the iliac tuberosity is a prominence on the surface of the ilium.*	Tuberosität
tuberous sclerosis *An inherited neurocutaneous disorder exhibited by benign hamartomas of the brain, lung, kidney, skin and other organs.*	Tuberös Hirnskerlose; Bourneville-Pringle-Syndrom
tubo-ovarian *Referring to the fallopian tube or ovary.*	tuboovarial
tubular *Referring to a hollow, round-shaped organ.*	tubulär
tularemia *An infectious disease caused by Francisella tularensis. The symptoms range from mild constitutional complaints to septic shock.*	Tularämie; Hasenfieber
tumefaction *An area of swelling.*	Schwellung
tumor *A benign or malignant overgrowth of tissue.*	Tumor
tunica *Generally a covering of a body part or organ. The tunica mucosa nasi is the mucous membrane lining the nasal cavity.*	Tunica
tuning fork *A device used to distinguish between perceptive and conductive hearing loss.*	Stimmgabel
tunnel vision *Constiction in the visual field as though looking through a tube or hollow cylinder. Also called tubular vision.*	Tunnelblick; Röhrensehen
turbinate bones *The three curved shelves in the nasal cavity.*	Nasenmuschel
turbinectomy *Surgical excision of a turbinate bone.*	Turbinektomie; Konchektomie
turgid *Congested and swollen.*	aufgetrieben; schwülstig
turgor *Referring to the elasticity of skin. If one pinches skin and it remains in place the patient is dehydrated.*	turgor
twins *Two infants born at the same birthing.*	Zwillinge
twitch *A sudden jerking movement.*	Zuckung
two times *One action being done on two occasions.*	zweimalig
tympanic *Referring to the tympanic membrane or having a resonant quality to percussion.*	tympanisch
tympanic cavity *The air chamber medial to the tympanic membrane in the temporal bone, between the external acoustic meatus and the inner ear.*	Paukenhöhle
tympanic membrane *The membrane between the external and middle ear.*	Trommelfell
tympanoplasty *Restoration of the tympanic membrane's continuity.*	Tympanoplastik
typhoid fever *A condition caused by ingestion of food or water containing salmonella typhi that is exhibited by fever and abdominal signs and symptoms.*	Typhus abdominalis; Salmonellenenteritis
typhus fever *A rickettsiae infection exhibited by rash, fever, headache and myalgia.*	Fleckfieber
tyrosine *An amino acid important in the synthesis of hormones.*	Tyrosin
ulcer *A concave wound caused by a break in the integrity of skin or mucous membrane. (duodenal ulcer)*	Geschwür; Ulkus (Zwölffingerdarmgeschwür)
ulcerative *Referring to ulceration.*	ulzerativ
ulcerative colitis *Recurrent episode of inflammation of the membranous layer of the colon.*	Colitis ulcerosa

160

English	German
ulnar nerve *Arises from the C8-T1 nerves and supplies the hand. (Injury to the ulnar nerve causes loss of flexion of the metacarpophalangeal joints and extension at the interphalangeal joints, thus the common term, claw hand.)*	Nervus ulnaris
ultrasonography *Visualization of body structures with the echoes of ultrasound pulses.*	Ultrasonographie
ultrasound *A sound or vibration of ultrasonic frequency.*	Ultraschall
ultraviolet rays *Electromagnetic radiation with wavelength longer than x rays.*	Ultraviolettstrahlen
umbilical cord *The stalk between the placenta and the unborn infant.*	Nabelschnur
umbilicated *Referring to depressed areas that resemble the umbilicus.*	genabelt
umbilicus *The scar that denotes the end of the umbilical cord.*	Nabel; Umbilicus
unciform *Another term for hamate bone in the wrist.*	hakenförmig
uncinariasis *Hookworm infestation of genus Uncinaria.*	Unzinariasis
unciforme bone *Hamate bone. The bone on the ulnar side of the distal row of the carpus. It articulates withe the 4th and 5th metacarpal, triquetral, lunate and capitate.*	Hamatum
unconsciousness *Unable to respond to sensory stimuli.*	Bewusstlosigkeit
under; infra *Sometimes used when indicating a patient is "under treatment" for a condition (active treatment).*	unter; unterhalb
underlying *Causative, unexposed, or fundamental.*	zugrundeliegend
undulant fever *Wave-like variations in the fever, going from very high to normal and back again, as seen in Brucellosis.*	undulierendes Fieber
unexpected *Unforeseen.*	unerwartet
unicellular *A term describing organisms like protozoans that only have cell.*	einzellig
unigravida *Term used to describe a woman's first pregnacy.*	Unigravida
unilateral *One side only.*	einseitig; unilateral
uniovolar *Referring to one fertilized ovum.*	eineiig
uniparous *Refers to a single birth.*	Uniparose
unknown *Uncertain or undisclosed.*	unbekannt
unstable knee *A condition with giving way of the knee due to ligamentous or cartilaginous dysfunction.*	instabil Knie
unsteady *Unstable or wobbly.*	unstetig
upper limb *Referring to either arm.*	Oberglied
upper respiratory tract *Generally considered the part of the respiratory tract superior to the vocal cords.*	Oberrespirationstrakt
upright *Vertical or standing.*	aufrecht
urachus *A connection between the bladder and the allantois in the fetus.*	Urachus
urate *The salt of uric acid.*	Urat
urea *A nitrogenous product of protein metabolism; excreted in urine.*	Harnstoff
uremia *An excess of urea and creatinine in the blood.*	Urämie
ureter *The conduit between each kidney and the urinary bladder.*	Ureter; Harnleiter
ureteral *Referring to one of two tubes from the kidneys to the bladder that carry urine.*	Harnleiter-; Ureter-
ureterectomy *Surgical resection of one or both ureters.*	Ureterektomie
ureteritis *Inflammation of the ureter.*	Harnleiterentzündung

English	German
ureterocele *Protrusion of the distal portion of the ureter into the bladder.*	Ureterozele
ureterolith *Presence of a stone in the ureter.*	Ureterolith
ureterolithotomy *Removal of a ureteral stone.*	Ureterolithotomie
ureterovaginal *Referring to the ureter and vagina.*	ureterovaginal
ureterovesical *Referring to the ureter and urinary bladder.*	ureterovesikal
urethra *The canal connecting the urinary bladder with the outside of the body.*	Urethra; Harnhöhre
urethral *Referring to the urethra.*	urethral
urethritis *Inflammation of the urethra.*	Urethritis
urethrocele *A prolapse of the urethra through the meatus.*	Urethrozele
urethrography *Imaging of the urethra after instillation of contrast media.*	Urethrographie
urethroplasty *Surgical repair of the urethra.*	Urethroplastik
urethroscope *A scope used to visualize the inside of the urethra.*	Urethroskop
urethrotomy *A surgical opening of the urethra.*	Urethrotomie
urgency *Emvergency or priority.*	Dringlichkeit
uric acid *Uric acid is a purine-derived product of nitrogen metabolism that can increase the risk of gout and calculi.*	Harnsäure
urinalysis *Chemical and microscopic examination of the urine.*	Harnanalyse; Urinstatus
urinary *Referring to the urine.*	urinär
urinary bladder *The organ collecting urine from the ureters prior to discharge via the urethra.*	Harnblase
urinary casts *A protein precipitated from renal tubules and excreted in the urine.*	Harnzylinder
urinary sediments *The debris that settles in a urine sample when left undisturbed.*	Harnsediment
urinary tract *The organs and canals associated with urine secretion including the kidneys, ureters, bladder and urethra.*	Harntrakt
urine *The fluid concentrated by the kidneys and expelled via the urethra.*	Urin; Harn
urinometer *A device for measuring urine specific gravity.*	Urometer
urobilin *A brownish pigment that is an oxidized form of urobilinogen.*	Urobilin
urobilinogen *A colorless substance produced in the intestines when bilirubin is reduced.*	Urobilingen
urochrome *A yellow pigment in the urine that gives urine its color.*	Urochrom
urodynamics *A study done to determine whether a person has the contractile capacity in the bladder to void spontaneously.*	Urodynamik
urogenital *Referring to the urinary and genital systems.*	urogential
urography *Roentgenography of the urinary tract after administration of contrast media.*	Urographie
urolith *Urinary calculi.*	Harnstein
urology *Surgical specialty involving medical and surgical treatment of the urogenital system.*	Urologie
urticaria *A diffuse pruritic macular rash, caused by an allergy.*	Urtikaria
usual *Typical or normal.*	üblich
uterine *Referring to the uterus.*	uterin
uterine bleeding *Bleeding that eminates from the uterus.*	Uterusblutung

English	German
uterine fibroids *Benign tumors made up of muscular and fibrous tissue in the uterus. This is an older term for what is now known as leiomyoma.*	Uterinleiomyom
uterine prolapse *Protrusion of the uterus out the vagina.*	Gebärmuttersenkung
uterovesical *Referring to the uterus and urinary bladder.*	uterovesikal
uterus *The hollow organ in the female pelvis where a fertilized ovum embeds and grows.*	Uterus; Gebärmutter
utricle *A small sac. It can refer to a division of the membranous labyrinth.*	Utriculus
uveitis *Inflammation of the uvea.*	Uveitis
uvula *A fleshy pendent at the back of the soft palate.*	Zäpfchen
uvulectomy *Excision of the uvula.*	Uvulektomie
uvulitis *Inflammation of the uvula.*	Uvulitis
vaccination *The act of receiving a vaccine.*	Vakzination; Impfung
vaccine *A solution of attenuated microorganisms given to prevent or treat a disease.*	Vakzine
vaccine certificate *A document that denotes what vaccines have been received by the holder.*	Impfnachweis
vacuole *A cavity that develops in a cell.*	Vakuole
vagal *Referring to the vagus nerve.*	vagal
vagina *The canal in a female that extends from the vulva to the cervix.*	Vagina; Scheide
vaginal *Referring to the vagina.*	vaginal
vaginismus *Involuntary contraction of the vagina muscles that causes a painful spasm.*	Vaginsmus
vagitus *An infant cry that can be further defined as vagitus vaginalis in which the infant cries while its head is in the vaginal canal.*	Vagitus vaginalis
vagotomy *Incision of the vagus nerve.*	Vagotomie
vagus nerve *The tenth cranial nerve that supplies the heart, lungs visceral organs; its function is tested by assessment of elevation of the uvula.*	Nervus vagus
valgus *Refers to a joint being abnormally angulated away from the midline of the body.*	valgus
valine *An essential amino acid that assists with nitrogen equilibrium.*	Valin
Valsalva's maneuver *A technique in which one attempts to exhale with the mouth and nose closed; this equalizes pressure in the ears.*	Valsalva Versuch
valvulotomy *Surgical incision of a valve.*	Valvulotomie
varicella *A virus that causes chickenpox and shingles. Also called herpes zoster.*	Varizellen; Windpocken
varicocele *A cluster of varicose veins in the scrotum.*	Varikozele
varicose *Referring to an abnormally distended, irregular vein.*	varikös
varix *A twisted, distended vein, artery or lymph vessel.*	Varize
varus position *Refers to a joint being abnormally angulated toward the midline of the body.*	Varusstellung
vascular *Referring to a blood vessel.*	vaskulär
vasculitis *Inflammation of a blood vessel.*	Vaskulitis
vasectomy *The surgical separation of each vas deferens with the intent of producing a sterile person.*	Vasektomie
vasoconstriction *The process of making the blood vessels smaller which increases blood pressure.*	Vasokonstriktion

163

English	German
vasodilatation *The process of making the blood vessels larger which decreases blood pressure.*	Vasodilatation
vasomotor *Referring to the constriction or dilation of vessels.*	Vasomotor
vasopressin *A hormone secreted by the pituitary that facilitates the retention of sodium and water and also increases blood pressure.*	Vasopressin; antidiuretisches Hormon (ADH)
vasospasm *The abrupt constriction of a blood vessel.*	Vasospasmus; Angiospasmus
vasovagal *Referring to overstimulation of the vagus nerve, exhibited by hypotension, pallor, nausea and diaphoresis.*	vasovagal
vector *An organism that transmits disease.*	Vektor; Träger
vegetation *Abnormal growth, such as cardiac valve vegetations as found in endocarditis.*	Vegetation
vein *A vessel carrying blood back toward the heart.*	Vene; Vena
velum *A veil-like part or covering of the palate; soft palate; Velum palatinum.*	Gaumensegel
vena cava *The large vein that carries deoxygenated blood to the right atrium.*	Vena cava
vena cava filter *A screen placed in the inferior vena cava to prevent blood clots from causing a pulmonary embolism.*	Kavaschirm
venereal disease *A condition transmitted via sexual intercourse.*	Geschlechtskrankheit
venereal wart *Common term for condyloma acuminatum.*	Condyloma acuminatum
venography *Roentgenography of a vein after administration of contrast media.*	Venographie
venom *A term used to describe the toxin injected via a bite or sting.*	Gift
venous *Referring to the veins.*	venös
ventilation *The movement of air into the lungs; generally meant to suggest by an artificial process.*	Ventilation; Lüftung
ventral *Referring to the underside but in humans, a ventral hernia, for example, refers to an abdominal hernia.*	ventral
ventricle *1. One of two chambers of the heart. 2. The four inter-connected cavities in the center of the brain.*	Ventrikel
ventricular septal defect *An abnormal communication between the right and left ventricles via a hole in the septum.*	Ventrikelseptumdefekt
ventriculography *Roentgenography of the ventricles after administration of contrast media.*	Ventrikulographie
ventriculostomy *A tube placed into the third ventricle to relieve increased intracranial pressure.*	Ventrikulostomie
venula *The vessels that connect the capillary plexuses to veins.*	Venole
verminous *Referring to presence of worms.*	niederträchtig
verminous ileus *Obstruction due to masses of intestinal parasites.*	Wurmileus
verruca *A hyperplastic epidermal lesion, sometimes referred to as plantar wart.*	Warze; Verruca
vertebra *A term for each bone surrounding the spine.*	Wirbel
vertebral column *The cervical, thoracic and lumbar vertebrae.*	Wirbelsäule; Rückgrat
vertebrobasilar insufficiency *Diminished flow to the vertebral and basilar arteries causing posterior fossa symptoms.*	Vertebrobasilärinsuffizienz
vertex *The crown of the head.*	Scheitel
vertigo *A sensation of imbalance with many possible causes.*	Vertigo; Schwindel
vesical *Referring to the urinary bladder.*	vesikal
vesicovaginal *Referring to the urinary bladder and vagina.*	vesikovaginal

English	German
vesiculitis *Inflammation of the urinary bladder.*	Vesikulitis
vestibular *Referring to a vestibule.*	vestibulär
vestigial *Rudimentary.*	rudimentär
viable *Referring to a fetus that can survive childbirth.*	lebensfähig
vial *A small cylindrical container typically used to hold liquid medicine.*	Fläschchen
vibration *An instance of oscillation of parts.*	Vibration
villous *Covered with many villi.*	villös
villus *A small vascular prominence from a membrane surface.*	Zotte
virilization *The result of androgen; a process of development of masculine characteristics.*	Virilisierung
virology *The study of viruses.*	Virologie
virulence *The potential severity of a disease or poison.*	Virulenz
visceral *Referring to the organs in the abdominal or thoracic cavity.*	viszeral
viscometer *A device used to measure viscosity.*	Viskosimeter
viscous *Having a thick, sticky consistency.*	viskös
vision *State of being able to see.*	Vision; Sehvermögen
vision, blurred *Haziness of the visual field.*	Seheintrübung; verschwommenes Sehen
visual field *The complete area a person can see with their eyes in a fixed position.*	Sehefeld; Gesichtsfeld
vital capacity (VC) *The maximal amount of air exhaled after a maximal inhalation.*	Vitalkapazität
vital signs *The designation for blood pressure, pulse, respirations and temperature.*	Lebenszeichen
vitamin B12 neuropathy *Abnormal sensation related to a chronic deficiency of cyanocobalamin;also called subacute combined degeneration of the spinal cord or Putnam-Dana syndrome.*	Putnam-Dana Syndrom
vitelline *Referring to the yolk of an egg or ovum.*	Vitellin
vitreous *Glass appearance; used to describe the vitreous body of the eye.*	glasig
vivisection *Animal surgery done for purposes of research.*	Vivisektion
vocal *Referring to that which eminates from the vocal cords.*	vokal
vocal cords *Paired folds of mucous membranes stretched across the larynx.*	Stimmband
voice *The sound produced through the larygnx and out the mouth.*	Stimme
voiding *The act of urinating.*	Wasserlassen
voiding cystography *Roentgenography of the bladder and urethra after administration of contrast media.*	Miktionsurographie
volunteer *A person who performs work without expecting compensation.*	Freiwillige
volvulus *Twisting of the bowel leading to obstruction and sometimes perforation.*	Volvulus; Darmverschlingung
vomit *The gastric contents that are expelled through the mouth.*	Erbrechen
vomit, to *To expel gastric contents out the mouth.*	erbrechen
vulval cleft *The area between the labia majora where the vagina and urethra rest.*	Fissura pupendi
vulvectomy *Surgical resection of the vulva.*	Vulvektomie
vulvitis *Inflammation of the vulva.*	Vulvitis

English	German
vulvovaginitis *Inflammation of the vulva and vagina.*	Vulvovaginitis
waddling gait *Walking in short steps in a swaying fashion.*	Watschelgang
walker *A metal frame used to facilitate walking.*	Gehgestell
walking cast *A cast used for simple fractures of the lower leg.*	Gehverband
ward *A section of a hospital where patients reside.*	Station
wart *A flesh colored growth that is also called verruca.*	Verruca; Warze
wasp *Any one of a winged hymenopterous insects.*	Wespen
water *A colorless, odorless liquid.*	Wasser; Aqua
wax *Cerumen.*	Cerumen; Zerumen
weak *Feeble or deconditioned.*	kraftlos
weakness *Feebleness.*	Schwäche
weekly *That which occurs every seven days.*	wöchentlich
weep, to *To ooze fluid, such as from a wound.*	nässen
weep, to *To shed tears.*	weinen
wet *Covered in moisture.*	feucht
wheal *A circumscribed urticarial lesion.*	Quaddel
wheelchair *A wheeled device used for propulsion.*	Rollstuhl
wheeze *A whistling or musical sound made by air passing through a narrowed airway.*	Keuchen
whiplash *Common term for cervical strain following a sudden deceleration.*	Schleudertrauma
whipworm *A parasitic, intestinal nematode worm of the genus Trichuris.*	Peitschenwurm; Trichuris trichiura
whisper *Speech in a volume that is barely discernible.*	Geflüster
whispered pectoriloquy *The sound heard through the stethoscope when listening to a person's lungs. The sound resonates as it would when listening over a bronchus if there is an area of consolidation.*	geflüstert Pektoriloquie
whisper test *The examiner whispers into one ear while blocking the other ear to see if the patient can hear in the ear whispered into.*	Flüsterprobe
whisper, to *To speak in a volume that is barely discernible.*	zuflüstern
whistle, to *To make a high pitch noise by forcing air through the lips.*	pfeifen
white *Of the color of snow.*	weiß
white matter *The brain tissue consisting of myelin sheaths and nerve fibers.*	Kleinhirnmark
whitlow *An abscess occurring on the palmar surface of the fingertips.*	Panaritium
whooping cough *Pertussis*	Pertussis; Keuchhusten
wick *A drain using a thin piece of cloth or tubing.*	Dochtdrainage
widespread *Encompassing or spanning.*	umfassend
width *Side to side measurement.*	Breite
wisdom tooth *Third molar.*	Weisheitszahn
wise *Possessing much knowledge.*	weise
withdrawal *The action of being without drugs or alcohol.*	Entzug
withhold, to *To refuse to give something.*	vorenthalten
World Health Organization (WHO)	Weltgesundheitsorganisation
worm *Any of long, slender, legless, soft-bodied invertebrates.*	Wurm
worry, to *To fret or have unease.*	sorgen
worsen, to *To deteriorate.*	verschlechtern

English	German
wound *A tissue injury of varying severity.*	Wunde
wound care *The treatment applied to a tissue injury.*	Wundversogung
wrist *The articulation of the hand and radius/ulna.*	Handgelenk
wrist drop *The inability to hyperextend the wrist due to radial nerve injury.*	Fallhand; Kusshand
xanthine *A purine derivative that is found in the blood and urine after the metabolism of nucleic acids to uric acid.*	Xanthin
xanthochromia *A yellow tone to the skin or spinal fluid.*	Xanthochromie
xanthoma *A lipid deposition on the skin exhibited by an irregular yellow patch.*	Xanthom
xerodermia *A mild form of ichthyosis.*	Xerodermie
xerophthalmia *A manifestation of Vitamin A deficiency exhibited by dryness of the cornea and conjunctiva.*	Xerophthalmie
xeroradiography *A form of radiography using photoelectric cells.*	Xeroradiolgrapie
xerosis *Pathological dryness of the skin or mucous membranes.*	Xerose
xerostomia *A dry mouth from salivary gland hypofunction.*	Xerostomie
xiphoid process *The inferior segment of the sternum.*	Schwertfortsatz
yawn *Opening one's mouth and inhaling deeply due to sleepiness/ boredom*	Gähnen
yaws *A tropical disease characterized by ulcers on the extremities, caused by Treponema pertenue.*	Frambösie
year *A time period that covers 365 days.*	Jahr
yearly *Occurring once each year.*	jährlich
yeast *A unicellular fungus.*	Hefe
yell, to *To speak in a loud tone.*	schreien
yellow *A color between green and orange in the spectrum*	gelb
yellow fever *A viral, hemorrhagic fever transmitted by mosquitos.*	Gelbfieber
young *Having lived for a short period.*	jung
youth *The time between childhood and being an adult.*	Jugend
zero *No quantity.*	null
Ziehl-Neelsen carbolfuchsin stain *A stain used to detect acid-fast bacilli that appear red on the methylene blue background.*	Ziehl-Neelsen Färbung
zinc *A chemical with atomic number 30.*	Zink; Zincum
zonula *A small zone or junction.*	Zonula
zoology *The study of animals.*	Zoologie
zoonosis *An animal-born disease that can be transmitted to humans, such as rabies.*	Zoonose
zygomatic bone *The triangular cheek bone.*	Jochbein; Wangenbein
zygote *A fertilized ovum.*	Zogote
zymogen *An inactive compound that is metabolized to an active state.*	Zymogen

Abasie	**abasia** *Inability to walk due to impaired coordination.*
Abdomen, Bausch	**abdomen** *The portion of the body bordered by the diaphragm and the pelvis.*
Abductor pollicis brevis	**abductor pollicis brevis** *Abducts the thumb.*
Abductor pollicis longus	**abductor pollicis longus** *Abducts and flexes the thumb.*
abduzierend	**abducent** *Abducting or to separate.*
aberrierend	**aberrant** *Different than normal.*
abflachen	**flatten, to** *To make even.*
Abführmittel; Kathartikum	**cathartic** *To be cleansed or evacuated, referring to thought or the cleansing of the bowels.*
Abgleichung;Zuordnung	**matching** *Corresponding in pattern or style.*
Ablatio	**ablation** *Surgical removal or amputation.*
Ablaufdatum	**expiration date** *The date when a medication should no longer be used.*
Ablenkung	**shunt** *An alternate path for blood or fluid.*
Abmachung	**agreement** *Accordance in opinion or feeling.*
Abnahme	**decrease** *Becoming smaller or fewer.*
abnorm	**abnormal**
ABO-blutgruppensystem	**ABO system** *The system using human blood antigens to determine blood type.*
Abortus	**abortion** *Premature expulsion of the fetus from the uterus.*
Abortus artificialis	**induced abortion** *Surgical or medical evacuation of the fetus.*
Abrißfraktur	**fracture, avulsion** *A broken bone associated with a ligament or tendon pulling a piece of the bone away.*
absagen	**cancel, to** *To stop or revoke.*
Absatz; Ferse	**heel** *Proximal portion of the plantar aspect of the foot.*
Abschnürung; Konstriktion; Einschnürung	**constriction** *Circumferential tightening*
Abschuppung; Desquamation	**desquamation** *The shedding of skin in flakes or sheets.*
Abschuppung; Exfoliation	**exfoliation** *The shedding of scales.*
absesenheit von	**absence of**
absteigend	**descending** *Moving toward the inferior portion.*
Abszess	**abscess** *A localized collection of pus.*
abwarten	**expect, to** *To suppose or presume.*
abwesend Verlaufsuntersuchung	**lost to follow-up** *This describes a situation in which a patient has a chronic medical problem but has not been seen regularly.*
acanthosis nigricans	**acanthosis nigricans** *A skin disorder characterized by dark, thick, velvety skin in the body folds and creases.*
Acaridose	**acariasis** *Mite infestation.*
accretio	**accretion** *The expected growth of tissue from the intake of nutrients.*
Acetabulum, Hüftpfanne	**acetabulum** *The cup-shaped cavity with which the head of the femur articulates.*
Acetonämie	**acetonemia** *The presence of acetone in the blood.*
Acetonurie	**acetonuria** *The presence of acetone in the urine.*
Acetylcholin	**acetylcholine** *A reversible acetic acid ester of choline.*
Acetylsalicylsäure	**acetylsalicylic acid** *The chemical name for common aspirin.*

Achalasie	**achalasia** *Inability to relax the smooth muscle fibers of the gastrointestinal tract. In the case of esophageal achalasia one has dilatation and hypertrophy of the esophagus.*
Achillessehnen-reflex	**Achilles tendon reflex** *The normal response to tapping the achilles tendon with a reflex hammer is the plantar flexion of the foot.*
Achilliodynie	**achilliodynia** *Pain around the calcaneal tendon.*
Achillobursitis	**achillobursitis** *Inflammation around the calcaneal tendon.*
Achlorhydrie	**achlorhydria** *The absence of hydrochloric acid in gastric secretions.*
Acholie	**acholia** *The lack of bile.*
Achondrodysplasie	**achondroplasia** *A congenital inadequacy of enchondral bone formation resulting in a type of dwarfism.*
achromatischspindel	**achromatic spindle** *The threads between the poles of the spindle in karyokinesis.*
Achromatopsie	**achromatopsia** *Inability to differentiate yellow, blue, red or their intermediates.*
Achselnerv	**circumflex nerve** *The axillary nerve that has an origin in the posterior branch of the brachial plexus.*
Achylie	**achylia** *The absence of chyle.*
acne rosacea	**acne rosacea** *A chronic disease characterized by the presence of flushing of the skin of the nose, forehead and cheeks.*
acne vulgaris	**acne vulgaris** *Chronic acne occurring on the face, chest and back of youth.*
Actin, Aktin	**actin** *A protein in the muscle that, along with myosin, facilitates muscle contraction and relaxation.*
Adaktylie	**adactylia** *A congenital condition exhibited by the absence of toes and fingers.*
Adams-Stokes Syndrom	**Adams-Stokes Syndrome** *Characterized by bradycardia, syncope and convulsions.*
Adamsapfel	**Adam's apple** *A prominence on the anterior neck caused by the thyroid cartilage of the larynx.*
Addison Krankheit	**Addison's disease** *A disease of the adrenal gland exhibited by anemia, hypotension and a bronze tone to the skin.*
Adduktion	**adduction** *To bring toward the midline.*
Adduktor	**adductor** *A muscle that brings a part to the midline.*
adenal	**adrenal** *Referring to being near the kidney.*
Adenektomie	**adenectomy** *The removal of a gland.*
Adenitis	**adenitis** *The inflammation of a gland.*
Adenofibrom	**adenofibroma** *Connective tissue with glands that form a tumor.*
Adenohypophyse	**adenohypophysis** *The anterior portion of the pituitary gland.*
adenoid	**adenoid** *Referring to a gland.*
Adenoidektomie	**adenoidectomy** *Removal of the adenoids.*
Adenokanthom	**adenocanthoma** *Malignant tumor comprised of glandular tissue.*
Adenokarzinom	**adenocarcinoma** *Cancer from glandular tissue.*
Adenolymphom	**adenolymphoma** *A salivary gland tumor, also called Warthin's tumor.*
Adenomyom	**adenomyoma** *A tumor characterized by the overgrowth of endometrial and uterine muscle tissue.*
Adenomyose	**adenomyosis** *A condition characterized by the overgrowth of endometrial and uterine muscle tissue.*

Adenopathie	**adenopathy** *Generally referring to a condition of the lymphatic glands.*
Adenosindiphosphorsäure	**adenosine diphosphate** *A product of hydrolysis of ATP.*
Adenosinmonophosphat	**adenosine monophosphate** *A nucleotide, it is produced when ATP is converted to ADP.*
Adenosintriphosphat	**adenosine triphosphate (ATP)** *A chemical that represents the energy reserve of the muscle.*
Adenovirus	**adenovirus** *A type of a virus that can cause upper respiratory tract infections.*
Aderhaut	**choroid** *Similar to the chorion (fertilized ovum or zygote)*
Adhäsion	**adhesion** *The abnormal adherence of tissue exposed to inflammation or after surgery.*
adhäsive Kapselentzündung	**adhesive capsulitis** *Also known as frozen shoulder.*
Adiadochokinese	**adiadochokinesia** *The inability to perform rapid alternating movements.*
Adie Pupille	**Adie's pupil** *Characterized by a weak light reaction and a strong but slow near response.*
adipös (Fettgewebe)	**adipose** *Referring to fat. (adipose tissue)*
Adipsie	**adipsia** *Absence of thirst which can be caused by SIADH, hydrocephalus or injury/tumor to/of the hypothalamus.*
Aditus	**aditus** *The entrance to an organ or part.*
Adiuretin	**antidiuretic hormone** *Vasopressin.*
Adjuvans	**adjuvant** *Term used to describe the medical treatment after initial therapy, as in adjuvant radiation therapy after initial chemotherapy.*
Adnexa	**adnexa** *The appendages, for example, of the uterus are the ovaries, fallopian tubes and the ligaments of the uterus.*
Adnexitis	**pelvic inflammatory disease** *Generally a bacterial infection affecting a woman with potential invovlement of the uterus, fallopian tubes, ovaries and cervix.*
Adrenalin	**adrenaline (epinephrine)** *A hormone secreted by the adrenal glands and a synthetic medication used for treatment of allergic reactions and cardiac arrest.*
adrenergisch	**adrenergic** *That which is activated or transmitted by epinephrine.*
adrenokortikotropes Hormon	**adrenocorticotrophic hormone (ACTH)** *A hormone that influences the cortex of the adrenal glands.*
Adson Handgriff	**Adson maneuver** *A test used to screen for thoracic outlet syndrome.*
Adventitia	**adventitia** *Outermost.*
Aerobier	**aerobe** *An organism that grows in the presence of oxygen.*
Aerodontalgie, Höhenzahnschmerzen	**aerodontalgia** *The dental pain that occurs with low atmospheric pressure, like during airflight.*
Aerophagie, Luftschlucken	**aerophagy or aerophagia** *A condition associated with hysteria in which one swallow repeatedly swallows air and then belches.*
afebril	**afebrile** *Absence of fever.*
Affekt	**affect** *The expression of emotions or feelings.*
Affenhand	**monkey-paw** *An appearance due to median nerve palsy causing atrophy of the thenar eminence with adduction and elevation of the thumb, resembling that of a simian.*
Affenpocken	**monkeypox** *A viral disease that is similar to smallpox which occurs primarily in monkeys and rarely in humans.*
Affinität	**affinity** *To have a natural liking for.*

170

affiziert	**affected**
Afibrinogenämie	**afibrinogenemia** *Marked deficiency of fibrinogen in the blood.*
Aflatoxin	**aflatoxin** *A toxin produced by Aspergillus flavus.*
Afterfurche	**gluteal fold** *The horizontal crease between the buttock and upper thigh.*
Agar	**agar** *Media used for bacterial cultures.*
Agenesis (Kleinhirnagenesie)	**agenesis** *The absence of an organ. (cerebellar agenesis)*
Agglutination	**agglutination** *The process of adherence of a mass.*
Aggression	**aggression** *Violent or hostile behavior.*
Agitiertheit	**agitation** *A state of extreme emotional disturbance.*
Agnathie	**agnathia** *Congenital abnormality characterized by the absence of the mandible.*
Agnosie	**agnosia** *A condition exhibited by the loss of sensory stimuli.*
Agonie	**agony** *Anguish or torment.*
Agonist	**agonist** *A synthetic compound that activates cells normally activated by natural chemicals.*
Agoraphobie; Platzangst	**agoraphobia** *The fear of being in a large open space.*
Agranulozytose	**agranulocytosis** *A condition characterized by leukopenia and neutropenia.*
Agraphie	**agraphia** *The inability to express one's thoughts in writing.*
Ahornsirupkrankheit	**maple syrup urine disease** *A condition characterized by an enzyme defect causing an increase in leucine in the urine.*
Aicardi Syndrom	**Aicardi syndrome** *A rare genetic anomily in which the corpus collosum is absent or insufficient. It is characterized by seizures, microphthalmos, coloboma and developmental delays.*
Akalkulie	**acalculia** *The inability to perform mathematical calculations.*
Akanthom	**acanthoma** *An adult cornyfying squamous carcinoma.*
Akanthose	**acanthosis** *Hypertrophy of the prickle cell layer of the skin.*
Akapnie	**acapnia** *A condition of lower than normal carbon dioxide level in the blood.*
Akarizid	**acaricide** *A treatment for mite infestation.*
Akatalasie	**acatalasia** *A condition characterized by the congenital absence of the enzyme catalase.*
Akinästhesie	**akinesthesia** *Lack of perception of movement.*
Akinesie	**akinesia** *An absence of movement or sparsity of movement.*
Akinomykose	**actinomycosis** *A chronic bacterial infection that effects the face and neck and is caused by Actinomyces israelii. In rare cases it can cause a pulmonary infection.*
Akklimatisierng	**acclimatization** *The process of becoming adapted to a new environment.*
Akkommodation	**accommodation** *A term used to describe the ability of the eye to adjust to various distances.*
Akne	**acne** *Inflamed or infected sebaceous glands.*
Akorie	**acorea** *The absence of the pupil of the eye.*
Akrodermatitis	**acrodermatitis** *Inflammation of the skin of the hands and/or feet.*
Akrodynie	**acrodynia** *An infantile condition exhibited by swollen bluish-red extremities and later polyarthritis..*
Akromegalie	**acromegaly** *Hyperplasia of the nose, jaw, fingers and toes.*

171

Akromioklavikulargelek	**acromioclavicular joint** *Referring to the junction of the acromion and clavicle.*
Akromion	**acromion** *The flattened process extending laterally from the spine of the scapula which forms the most prominent point of the shoulder.*
Akrozephalie	**acrocephaly** *A condition characterized by a pointed head.*
Akrozyanose	**acrocyanosis, Raynaud's disease** *A benign condition in which the feet and hands are cyanotic, cold and sweating.*
Aktathisie	**akathisia** *A condition exhibited by motor restlessness and inability to sit quietly.*
Akte	**file** *Patient record or folder.*
aktinisch Dermatose	**actinic dermatosis** *A skin disease caused by exposure to radiation from the sun, ultraviolet waves or gamma radiation.*
Aktinon	**actinon** *A radioactive element, radon-219; short lived isotope of radon.*
Aktionpotential	**action potential** *The alteration in electrical potential associated with the movement along a nerve cell.*
Aktivitär	**activity**
Aktomyosin	**actomyosin** *Myosin and actin complex present in muscles.*
Akupunktur	**acupuncture** *Traditionally an aspect of Chinese medicine involving insertion of needles into the skin.*
Akustikusneurinom	**acoustic neuroma** *A nonmalignant tumor that can cause deafness, tinnitus and vertigo.*
akustisch	**acoustic** *Referring to the auditory system.*
akut	**acute** *Abrupt onset.*
akute Konjunktivitis	**pink eye** *Common term for acute contagious conjunctivitis.*
akutkranke Person	**acutely ill person** *Patient who has a sudden and severe illness.*
Albinismus	**albinism** *Congenital absence of pigment in the eyes, skin and hair.*
Albino	**albino** *A person who lacks pigment in the eyes, skin and hair.*
Albright-McCune-Sternberg Syndrom	**Mucune-Albright syndrome** *Polyostotic fibrous dysplasia with cutaneous brown patches, endocrine dysfunction that exhibits in females as precocious puberty.*
Albumin	**albumin** *A protein that is soluble in water and coagulates if heated.*
Albuminurie	**albuminuria** *The presence of albumin in the urine.*
Aldehyd	**aldehyde** *A substance derived by oxidizing and containing a CHO group from alcohol.*
Aldosteron	**aldosterone** *A steroid secreted by the adrenal cortex that regulates electrolytes.*
Aldosteronismus	**aldosteronism** *A condition characterized by the excessive secretion of aldosterone.*
Alexie; Buchstabenblindheit	**alexia** *Inability to read due to a central brain lesion.*
Algen	**algae** *Nonflowering plants containing chlorophyll but without stems, roots, or leaves.*
Algolagnie	**algophilia** *Sexual perversion; getting pleasure in giving or receiving pain.*
alimentär	**alimentary** *Referring to the gastrointestinal tract.*
Alkali	**alkali** *A class of compounds that form soluble carbonates.*
Alkaliruie	**alkalinuria** *The urine in an alkaline state.*
alkalisch; basisch	**alkaline** *Referring to something with properties of an alkali.*
Alkaloid	**alkaloid** *Plant derived nitrogenous organic compound.*

172

Alkalose	**alkalosis** *A condition in which the pH is increased.*
Alkaptonurie	**alkaptonuria** *A condition exhibited by the urine turning dark upon standing because of the presence of alkapton bodies in it.*
Alkohol	**alcohol** *Ethanol or ethyl alcohol.*
Alkoholabhängigkeit	**alcoholism** *An addiction to alcohol.*
Alkoholembryopathie	**fetal alcohol syndrome** *A condition caused by acohol use by the mother during pregnancy and exhibited by poor intrauterine growth, decreased muscle tone, delayed development and widened palpebral fissures.*
Alkoholisch	**alcoholic** *A person with alcohol dependence.*
Allantois	**allantois** *A posterior portion of the hind-gut of an embryo.*
Allel	**allele** *A type of a gene; in humans there are two alleles per chromosome pair.*
Allergene	**allergens** *Compounds that cause an allergic reaction.*
Allergie	**allergy** *An immune response by the body to a compound it is hypersensitive to.*
Allgemeinbefinden	**general appearance** *The overall look of a patient.*
Allopathie	**allopathy** *Treatment of disease with minute amounts of natural substances.*
Allotransplantat	**allograft** *A tissue transplant of from someone of the same species but different genotype.*
Alopezie; Haarausfall	**alopecia** *The absence of hair in areas where it normally exists.*
Alphafetoprotein	**alpha-fetoprotein** *A glycoprotein that has a high serum level in hepatocellular and nonseminomatous germ cell tumors.*
Alphawelle	**alpha wave** *Electroencephalographic waves with a frequency of 8-13 per second.*
Alptraum	**nightmare** *An unpleasant or frightening dream.*
Alter	**age** *Length of life.*
alternd	**aging** *Becoming older.*
alveolär	**alveolar** *Referring to the alveolus.*
Alveolus	**alveolus** *A small sac like structure commonly used for the pulmonary alveolus.*
Alzheimer krankheit	**Alzheimer's disease** *A dementia of unknown cause or pathogenesis.*
am ganzen Körper	**all over the body**
am Tage vorkommend; diurnus	**diurnal** *Occurring during the day.*
Amagdala	**amygdala** *Any almond shaped structure such as the tonsil*
Amalgam	**amalgam** *An alloy that includes mercury as one ingredient.*
Amastie	**amastia** *A development condition exhibited by the absence of breasts.*
Amaurose	**amaurosis** *Blindness that occurs without an ocular lesion but may include the optic nerve.*
Amaurosis-fugax-Attacke	**amaurosis fugax** *This transient monocular blindness is considered a sign of an impending stroke.*
amaurotisch Pupille	**amaurotic pupil** *A pupil that will not respond to light when directly exposed but will respond when the other eye is exposed to light.*
Amblyopsie; Schwachsichtigkeit	**amblyopia** *Decreased vision without an ocular lesion.*
Amboß	**incus** *The middle ear bone between the stapes and malleus.*
ambulante	**ambulatory** *Referring to one's ability to walk.*

173

ambulante Messung elektrokardiografisch	**ambulatory electrocardiographic monitoring** *A continuous recording of the electrocardiogram used to detect occult dysrhythmias.*
Amelie	**amelia** *A congenital anomaly exhibited by the absence of limbs.*
Amenorrhö	**amenorrhea** *The absence of menses.*
Amentia	**amentia** *The absence of mental ability.*
Ametropie; Fehlsichtigkeit	**ametropia** *Abnormal refractive ability of the eyes resulting in hypermetropia, myopia or astigmatism.*
Aminosäure	**amino acid** *A compound containing a carboxyl and an amino group.*
Ammoniak	**ammonia** *A colorless alkaline gas.*
Ammonshorn	**hippocampus** *The area at the base of the cerebral ventricles thought to be the center of memory and emotion.*
Amnesie	**amnesia** *The inability to remember past events.*
amnestische Schlaganfall	**amnesic stroke** *Cerebral infarct exhibited by loss of memory.*
Amniographie	**amniography** *X-ray of the gravid uterus after insertion of opaque dye.*
Amnion	**amnion** *The membrane lining the placenta which produces the amniotic fluid.*
Amniozentese	**amniocentesis** *Transabdominal aspiration of amniotic fluid.*
amorph	**amorphous** *A fetus with no heart and no definitive shape.*
Amöbe	**ameba** *A one-celled protozoan.*
Amöbenabszess der Leber	**amebic liver abscess** *A pus filled fluid collection within the liver caused by amoebe.*
Amöbiasis	**amebiasis** *A condition in which one is infected with amebae, mostly commonly Entamoeba histolytica.*
amöbizid	**amebicide** *A compound used to treat amebiasis.*
Amöbom	**ameboma** *A mass caused by inflammation as seen in amebiasis.*
Ampulla	**ampulla** *The dilated end of a duct.*
ampullaris Leiste	**acoustic crest** *A prominence on ampulla of the semicircular ducts.*
Amyelhämie	**aplastic anemia** *Bone marrow failure causing a decrease in all types of blood cells.*
Amylase	**amylase** *An enzyme involved in the hydrolysis of starch.*
Amyloidose	**amyloidosis** *The accumulation of amyloid in body tissues.*
Amyotonie	**amyotonia** *A condition associated with the lack of muscle tone.*
Amytrophie	**amyotrophy** *Atrophy of muscle tissue.*
amytrophische Lateralsklerose	**amyotrophic lateral sclerosis** *A progressive neurodegenerative disorder.*
Anabolismus	**anabolism** *The formation of molecules in organisms from simpler molecules.*
Anaerobier	**anaerobe** *An organism that lives in the absence of oxygen.*
anakrot	**anacrotic** *Referring to a prominent bulge on the ascending portion of a pulse recording.*
anal	**anal** *Near or referring to the anus.*
Analeptikum	**analeptic** *A medication used as a stimulant to the central nervous system.*
Analfistel	**anal fistula** *An opening in the skin that tracts to the anal canal thus causing some fecal material to leak from the opening in the skin.*
Analgesie	**analgesia** *The absence of pain.*
Analgetikum; Schmerzmittel	**analgesic** *A medication used to remove pain.*

174

analog	**analogous** *To resemble or be similar to.*
Anaphase	**anaphase** *A stage in mitosis following metaphase.*
Anaphorese	**anaphoresis** *Reduced activity of the sweat glands.*
anaphylaktoide Purpura	**Henoch purpura** *Exhibited by vomiting, diarrhea, abdominal pain and hematuria; a non-thrombocytopenic purpura.*
Anaphylaxie	**anaphylaxis** *An exaggerated response to a foreign substance.*
Anaplasie	**anaplasia** *The loss of normal differentiation of tumor cells.*
Anastomose	**anastomosis** *Surgical formation of a connection between two previously separate parts.*
anatomicum	**anatomical** *Referring to the anatomy.*
anatomicum Totraum	**anatomical dead space** *The area between the mouth and pulmonary alveoli.*
Anatomie	**anatomy** *The study of body structure.*
anatomische Tabelle	**anatomical chart** *A pictorial diagram of part of the anatomy.*
Anämie; Blutarmut	**anemia** *Lower than normal red blood cell count.*
Anästhesie	**anesthesia** *Loss of sensation.*
Anästhesist	**anesthetist** *A person who administers anesthesia.*
Anästhetikum	**anesthetic** *A chemical that produces anesthesia.*
Ancylostomiasis	**ancylostomiasis** *A type of nematode parasite, also called hookworm.*
Androgen	**androgen** *A compound that produces masculinizing characteristics.*
androgyn	**androgynous** *Referring to a female pseudohermaphroditism (a genetic female with masculine characteristics).*
androides Becken	**android pelvis** *A pelvis shaped like a man's.*
Androsteron	**androsterone** *A hormone excreted in the urine of men and women.*
Anencephalie	**anencephaly** *The congenital absence of the cranial vault and cerebral hemispheres.*
Aneroid	**aneroid** *The absence of liquid.*
Aneurysma	**aneurysm** *A condition exhibited by the dilatation of the walls of an artery or vein to form a blood-filled sac.*
Anfall	**attack** *A fit or paroxysm.*
Anfall; Einsetzen	**onset** *The beginning of an event.*
Anfall; Krampf	**seizure** *An episode of tonic/clonic movement noted in epilepsy.*
angeblich	**ostensibly** *Synonym of apparently and seemingly.*
angeborene Syphilis	**congenital syphilis** *Passed to the child in utero, the child may have failure to thrive, fever and a flattened bridge of the nose.*
angeborener Herzfehler	**congenital heart disease** *A cardiac disorder present prior to birth.*
Angehöriger	**paramedical** *Hospital support staff excluding physicians.*
angemessen	**adequate** *Sufficient.*
Angiektasie	**angiectasia** *Dilation of a blood or lymph vessel.*
Angiitis	**angitis or angiitis** *The inflammation of a lymph or blood vessel.*
Angina pectoris	**angina pectoris** *Exercise induced myocardial ischemia.*
Angiogramm	**angiogram** *Radiologic imaging of blood vessels.*
Angiographie	**angiography** *Roentgenographic imaging of blood vessels.*
Angiom	**angioma** *A tumor comprised of blood or lymph vessels.*
angioneurotisch	**angioneurotic** *Caused by a neurosis affecting the blood vessels, like vasospasm.*

175

angioneurotisches Ödem	**angioedema** *Also called angioneurotic edema, it is caused by a histamine reaction. It can produce welts in mild cases but in severe cases can cause swelling of the lips and tongue.*
angioneurotisches Ödem	**angioneurotic edema** *A condition exhibited by sudden edema of skin and mucous membranes.*
Angioplastie	**angioplasty** *Surgical alteration of blood vessels.*
Angiosarkom	**angiosarcoma** *A sarcoma comprised of blood vessels.*
Angiospasmus; Gefäßkrampf	**angiospasm** *A spasm of a blood vessel.*
Angiotensin	**angiotensin** *A blood protein that increases aldosterone secretion.*
Angiotensin Konversionsenzym Hemmer	**angiotensin converting enzyme inhibitors (ACEI)** *A class of medicines that prevent conversion of angiotension I to angiotensin II, a potent vasoconstrictor.*
Angst	**anxiety** *Nervousness or unease.*
Angstneurose	**anxiety neurosis** *Abnormal presence of anxiety.*
Anhidrose	**anhidrosis** *A condition exhibited by reduced quantity of sweat.*
Aniseikonie	**aniseikonia** *A condition in which the ocular image of an object is viewed differently by each eye.*
Anisokorie	**anisocoria** *Pupillary diameter inequality.*
Anisomelie	**anisomelia** *Unequal size of arms or legs.*
Anisometropie	**anisometropia** *Refractive power inequality between the two eyes.*
Anisozytose	**anisocytosis** *Variation in size of erythrocytes.*
Ankyloglossie	**ankyloglossia** *Limitation of tongue motion because of a short frenulum.*
Ankylose; Gelenksteife	**ankylosis** *Abnormal immobility of a joint.*
Anonychie	**anonychia** *Congenital absence of fingernails or toenails.*
anoperineal	**anoperineal** *Referring to the anus and perineum.*
Anorchie	**anorchous** *The absence of testicles.*
Anordnung zum Verzicht auf Wiederbelebung	**DNR Do not resuscitate.** *The term used to indicate a person should not have life sustaining measures taken if they were to have cardiopulmonary arrest.*
anorektal	**anorectal** *Referring to the anus and rectum.*
anorektalabszess	**anorrectal abscess** *A localized collection of pus in the anorrectal region.*
Anorexie	**anorexia** *The loss of appetite.*
Anorexie nervosa	**anorexia nervosa** *A mental disorder characterized by the desire to avoid eating and to lose weight.*
anorganisch	**inorganic** *Not coming from natural growth.*
Anosmie	**anosmia** *Lack of the sense of smell.*
anovulatorisch	**anovulatory** *Lack of ovulation.*
anovulatorischzyklus	**anovulatory cycle** *A menstrual cycle in which no ovum is released.*
Anoxämie	**anoxemia** *Reduction in blood oxygen concentration.*
Anoxie	**anoxia** *Reduced oxygen levels in body tissues.*
Anpassung	**adjustment** *A modification of a plan.*
anspruchsvoll	**demanding** *Requiring a lot of skill or requiring a lot of others.*
ansteckend; kontagiös	**contagious** *Description of a disease that can be spread by direct or indirect contact.*
Anstrengung	**effort** *Attempt or endeavor.*
Anstrengung	**strain** *As in a muscle strain.*

	English
Antacidum	**antacid** *A medication, usually with a calcium or magnesium base that binds with acid in the stomach.*
Antagonist	**antagonist** *A muscle or agent that acts in counteract to effects of another muscle or agent.*
anterograd	**anterograde** *Moving forward.*
anterograde Amnesie	**amnesia, antegrade** *The inability to remember events which occurred after the insult that caused the condition.*
anteroinferior	**anteroinferior** *Toward the front and lower part.*
anterolateral	**anterolateral** *Toward the front and away from the midline.*
anteromedian	**anteromedian** *Toward the front and toward the midline.*
anteroposterior	**anteroposterior** *From front to the back. (An AP x-ray has the beam directed from the front to the back.)*
anterosuperior	**anterosuperior** *Toward the front and the upper part.*
Anteversio	**anteversion** *The forward leaning of an organ.*
Anthelmintikum	**anthelmintic** *An agent used to destroy worms.*
Anthracosis	**anthracosis** *Pneumoconiosis caused by coal dust.*
Anthrax; Milzbrand	**anthrax** *An infectious disease caused by Bacillus anthracis; there are cutaneous, inhalation and gastrointestinal syndromes.*
Antibiotikum	**antibiotic** *A medication that inhibits or kills microorganisms.*
Anticholinergikum	**anticholinergic** *Parasympathetic blocker.*
Anticholinesterase	**anticholinesterase** *Cholinesterase blocker.*
Antidepressivum	**antidepressant** *Medication used to treat depression.*
Antidot; Gegengift	**antidote** *A medication that neutralizes a toxin.*
Antiemetikum	**antiemetic** *A medication used to control nausea.*
Antigen	**antigen** *A foreign substance, like bacteria, that induces an immune response.*
Antiglobulin Konsumptionstest	**antiglobulin test (Coombs' test)** *Test used to detect erythroblastosis fetalis.*
antihemolitisch Faktor	**antihemophilic factor** *Also called factor VIII. A deficiency of the factor causes hemophilia.*
Antihist-aminikum	**antihistamine** *Medication used to treat conditions exhibited by a histamine response*
Antikoagulans	**anticoagulant** *Medication used to inhibit coagulation.*
AntiKodon	**anticodon** *A series of three nucleotides that form a unit of genetic code for transfer RNA.*
Antikonvulsivum	**anticonvulsant** *Medication used to treat seizures.*
Antikörper	**antibody** *A protein that combines with and counteracts foreign substances.*
antilymogizytär Globulin	**antilymphocyte globulin** *The gamma globulin portion of antilymphocyte serum.*
Antilymphozyten	**antilymphocyte** *A serum globulin that has antibodies to lymphocytes.*
Antimetabolit	**antimetabolite** *A substance that impedes metabolism.*
Antimitotikum	**antimitotic** *Impeding mitosis.*
Antimykotikum	**antimycotic** *Inhibition of fungal growth.*
antinukleärer Antikörper (ANA)	**antinuclear factor** *Also called antinucleic antibody (ANA); it is found in conditions such as lupus and rheumatoid arthritis.*
antiperistaltisch	**antiperistaltic** *An agent that impedes normal peristalsis.*
Antipruriginosum	**antipruritic** *Medication used to treat pruritus.*

177

Antipyretikum; Fiebermittel	**antipyretic** *Medication used to treat fever.*
Antiseptikum	**antiseptic** *A substance that inhibits microorganism growth.*
Antiserum	**antiserum** *A substance that contains antibodies to specific antigens.*
Antispasmodikum; krampflösend	**antispasmodic** *Medication used to treat muscle spasm.*
Antithrombin	**antithrombin** *A substance that inhibits thrombin, thus decreasing the body's ability to coagulate.*
Antitoxin	**antitoxin** *A substance that inhibits the effect of a toxin.*
Antitussivum; Hustenmittel	**antitussive** *Medication used to diminish a cough.*
Antivenin; Schlangenserum	**antivenin** *An antitoxin formulated for various types of snake bites.*
Antrotomie	**antrotomy** *To cut open the antrum.*
Antrum	**antrum** *Referring to a cavity or chamber.*
anular	**annular** *Referring to a ring.*
Anurie	**anuria** *The lack of urine excretion.*
Anus; After	**anus** *The body opening distal to the rectum.*
Anzapfsyndrom der Arteria subclavia	**subclavian steal syndrome** *Retrograde vertebral artery flow due to ipsilateral subclavian artery stenosis.*
Aorta	**aorta** *The large artery originating at the left ventricle and going to the pelvis where it bifurcates.*
aortal	**aortic** *Referring to the aorta.*
Aortenisthmusstenose	**coarctation of the aorta** *A stricture, as in narrowing of the aorta.*
Aortenklappen	**aortic valve** *The valve situated between the left ventricle and the aorta.*
Aortenklappeninsuffizienz	**aortic insufficiency** *A dysfunction of the aortic valve allowing backflow of blood into the heart.*
Aortenklappenstenose	**aortic stenosis** *Narrowing of the aortic orifice.*
Apathie	**apathy** *Lack of interest in one's environment or indifference.*
Apektomie	**apicectomy** *Removal of the apex of the petrous portion of the temporal bone.*
Aperistaltik	**aperistalsis** *Lack of intestinal peristalsis.*
Apex	**apex** *The highest point of something.*
Apgar-Score	**Apgar score** *A scoring system for newborns that utilizes heart rate, respiratory effort, muscle tone, responsiveness and skin color.*
Aphagie	**aphagia** *The lack of eating.*
Aphakie	**aphakia** *The congenital absence of the lens of the eye.*
Aphasie	**aphasia** *Diminished ability to communicate via speech or writing.*
Aphonie	**aphonia** *The loss of voice.*
Aphthe	**canker sore** *An ulceration, usually of the mouth or lips.*
Aphthen	**aphthous stomatitis** *Grouped small lesions that occur on the tongue or in the mouth.*
Apiphobie	**melissophobia** *Also called apiphobia, a fear of bees.*
Apnoe	**apnea** *Absence of respiration.*
Aponeurose	**aponeurosis** *A tendinous expansion that connects with muscle to move a part.*
Apophyse	**apophysis** *Generally a bony outgrowth that forms a process or tubercle.*
Apoplexie	**apoplexy** *Extravasation of blood within an organ.*
Appendektomie	**appendectomy** *Surgical excision of the appendix.*
Appendix; Blinddarm	**appendix** *An appendage of the cecum.*

Appendizitis	**appendicitis** *Inflammation of the appendix.*
Apperzeption	**apperception** *The ability to interpret sensory impressions.*
Applikator	**applicator** *A device used to apply a topical medication.*
Apraxie	**apraxia** *The inability to carry out intentional movements when paralysis is not present.*
Aptyalismus	**aptyalism** *Diminished or absence of saliva.*
Aquilibrium; Gleichgewicht	**equilibrium** *When opposing forces are in balance.*
Arachnodaktylie	**arachnodactyly** *A condition exhibited by abnormally long and slender fingers.*
Arachnoid	**arachnoid** *Refers to that which resembles a spider web.*
Arboviren	**arbovirus** *Virus that is transmitted by arthropods; responsible for diseases such as Yellow fever and dengue fever.*
Arcuatusnukleus	**arcuate nucleus** *Small masses of gray matter found on the medulla oblongata.*
Arcus	**arcus** *Narrow opaque band.*
Argininosukzinurie	**argininosuccinicaciduria** *Presence of arginosuccinic acid in the urine; associated with mental retardation.*
Argyll Robertson Phänomen	**Argyll Robertson symptom** *Presence of small pupils that do not react to light but will constrict when the person focuses on a near object.*
Argyrie	**argyria** *The greyish discoloration of the skin and conjunctiva.*
Arm	**arm** *One of two upper extremities.*
Armbruch	**broken (arm)** *Fracture of the arm.*
Armplexuslähmung	**brachial plexus neuropathy** *Characterized by acute arm or shoulder pain followed by focal muscle weakness.*
Arrhenoblastom	**arrhenoblastoma** *An ovarian tumor that results in masculine secondary sex characteristics.*
Arrhythmie	**arrhythmia** *An abnormal heart rhythm.*
Artefakt	**artifact** *An aberration from the normal.*
Arterie	**artery** *Vessel that carries oxygenated blood from the heart to the periphery.*
Arteriectomie	**arteriectomy** *Surgical excision of an artery.*
arteriell	**arterial** *Referring to an artery.*
Arteriitis	**arteritis** *Inflammation of an artery.*
Arteriographie	**arteriography** *Roentgenography of an artery after infusion of contrast media.*
Arterioplastie	**arterioplasty** *Surgical repair of an artery.*
Arteriosklerose	**arteriosclerosis** *Hardening and thickening of arterial walls.*
Arteriotomie	**arteriotomy** *Creation of an opening in an artery.*
arteriovenöse Missbildung	**arteriovenous malformation** *A sac like structure created by the abnormal communication of an adjacent artery and vein.*
Arthritis gonorrhoica	**gonorrheal arthritis** *A type of arthritis caused by the gram negative diplococcus Neisseria gonorrhoeae.*
Arthritis; Gelenkentzündung	**arthritis** *Joint inflammation.*
Arthrodese	**arthrodesis** *Surgical fusion of a joint.*
Arthrodynie	**arthrodynia** *Joint pain.*
Arthrographie	**arthrography** *Joint roentgenography.*
Arthrosis deformans	**osteoarthrosis** *Arthritis without inflammation.*

179

Arthroskopie	**arthroscopy** *Viewing of the inside of a joint with a specially designed scope.*
Arthrotomie	**arthrotomy** *Surgical opening of a joint.*
articularis	**articular** *Referring to a joint.*
artifiziell; künstlich	**artificial** *Not natural produced.*
Artz	**physician** *Medical practitioner.*
arytenoideus	**arytenoid** *Referring to the cartilage in the posterior larynx.*
Arzneimittelexanthem	**drug eruption** *A diffuse rash caused by a medication.*
Arzneimittelreaktion	**drug reaction** *Typically refers to an adverse effect of medication.*
Arzneimittelträgersubstanz	**excipient** *An inactive substance used to deliver an active substance.*
Asbest	**asbestos** *A heat resistant silicate material.*
Asbestosis pulmonum	**asbestosis** *Lung disease caused by the inhalation of asbestos.*
Ascaris lumbricoides	**ascaris** *A nematode from genus intestinal lumbricoid parasite, also called round worm.*
Asepsis	**asepsis** *Lack of infection.*
aseptisch	**aseptic** *Being free of septic matter.*
asexuell; geschlechtslos	**asexual** *Without sex or sex organs.*
Askorbinsäure	**ascorbic acid** *Commonly known as vitamin C; a deficiency of this vitamin causes scurvy.*
Asperger-Syndrom	**Asperger's syndrome** *A condition characterized by disturbed social interaction; if was named after the Austrian scientist who first described it.*
Aspermie	**aspermia** *Absence of sperm.*
Asphyxie	**asphyxia** *A condition exhibited by a lack of oxygen and subsequent loss of consciousness or death.*
Aspirationsbiopsie	**aspiration biopsy** *Removal of fluid from a cavity for pathologic analysis.*
Aspirationspneumonie.	**aspiration pneumonia** *Taking air or matter into the lungs.*
Aspirator	**aspirator** *A device used to remove fluid from a cavity.*
Assay	**assay** *A procedure for measuring the activity of a biological sample.*
Asteatosis	**asteatosis** *A condition exhibited by diminished sebaceous secretion.*
Astereognosie	**astereognosis** *Lack of ability to recognize objects by touching them.*
Astereognosie	**stereognosis** *The ability to identify an object by touch.*
Asterixis; Flattertremor	**asterixis** *Commonly known as a flapping tremor, it is characterized by involuntary jerking movements of the hands and is seen commonly in hepatic encephalopathy.*
Asthenie	**asthenia** *Diminished strength and energy.*
Asthenopie	**asthenopia** *Visual fatigue accompanied by ocular pain.*
Astroglia	**astroglia** *The neurologic tissue which is composed of astrocytes.*
Astrozytom	**astrocytoma** *A tumor comprised of astrocytes.*
Asymmetrie	**asymmetry** *Lack of symmetry.*
Asymptomatisch	**asymptomatic** *The absence of symptoms.*
Asynklitismus; Scheitelbeineinstellung	**asynclitism** *Oblique presentation of the head during delivery.*
Aszites	**ascites** *Serous fluid in the abdominal cavity.*
Atavismus	**atavism** *The inheritance of characteristics from remote rather than immediate ancestors.*
Ataxie	**ataxia** *Lack of muscular coordination.*

	English
Atelektase	**atelectasis** *Incomplete expansion or collapse of a lung.*
Atem	**breath** *One respiration.*
Atemalkoholtest	**breath test (for alcohol)** *A check of alcohol level by testing exhaled air.*
Atemflussrate	**peak flow** *A measurement of lung function used in asthma.*
Atemfrequenz	**respiratory rate** *The number of breaths per minute.*
Atemgeräusche	**breath sounds** *The noise heard upon auscultation with a stethoscope.*
Atemnotsyndrom	**respiratory distress syndrome** *A disease in infants that is caused by a surfactant deficiency.*
Atemzugvolumen	**tidal volume** *The amount of air inspired with each breath. One can set a ventilator to deliver a preset number of milliliters of oxygenated air with each breath.*
atherogen	**atherogenic** *Something that causes atheromatous lesions in arterial walls.*
Atherom	**atheroma** *Degenerative arteriosclerosis.*
Athetose	**athetosis** *An involuntary symptom exhibited by continuous slow, writhing movements, mostly in the hands.*
Atlas; erster Halswirbel	**atlas** *The first cervical vertebra.*
Atonie	**atony** *Absence of normal muscle tone.*
Atresie	**atresia** *Closure of a body orifice as in atresia ani in which there is a congenital imperforate anus.*
atrial	**atrial** *Referring to the atrium.*
atriales natriuretisches Hormon	**atrial natriuretic factor** *A chemical secreted by the right atrium that promotes sodium excretion in the urine.*
Atrioventrikularblock	**atrio-ventricular block** *An interruption of the electrical conduction at the atrio-ventricular node.*
atrioventrikulär	**atrioventricular** *Referring to the atrium and ventricle.*
Atrophie	**atrophy** *A diminution in the size of a part.*
atrophisch	**atrophic** *Referring to atrophy.*
Atropin	**atropine** *A parasympathetic agent derived from Atropa belladonna.*
atypisch	**atypical** *Not usual.*
Audiogramm; Hörkurve	**audiogram** *The recording of a one's hearing in decibels.*
Audiologe	**audiologist** *A specialist in the field of hearing.*
Audiometer	**audiometer** *A device used to measure hearing.*
auditorisch	**auditory** *Referring to hearing.*
auditorische agnosie; Seelentaubheit	**auditory agnosia** *Caused by a temporal lobe lesion, it is characterized by inability to recognize sounds as words.*
auf Geratewohl	**at random** *Occurring by chance alone.*
Aufblähung	**distension** *Swollen.*
Aufbruch	**tear** *Referring to a vaginal tear after childbirth.*
Aufflackern	**flare-up** *A sudden worsening one's condition.*
aufgedunsen	**bloated** *Sensation of having an abnormally large amount of air in the viscera.*
Aufgedunsensein	**puffiness** *Having a soft, swollen area.*
aufgetrieben	**gross** *Distended; not well defined.*
aufgetrieben; schwülstig	**turgid** *Congested and swollen.*
aufgrund	**owing to** *On account of.*
Aufguß; Infusion	**infusion** *The injection of fluid into tissue or a vein.*

Auflösung	**dissolution** *Disintegration.*
aufmerksham	**alert** *Being in a watchful, ready state.*
Aufnahme	**intake** *An amount of food taken into the body.*
aufplatzen	**burst, to** *To rupture.*
aufrecht	**upright** *Vertical or standing.*
aufrechterhalten	**sustain, to** *To keep or maintain.*
Aufsaugen	**absorption (intestinal absorption)**
Auftragen	**application** *The forms one fills out to obtain a grant.*
Auftreten	**emergence** *Coming into prominence.*
Auftreten; Erscheinungsbild	**appearance** *The way someone looks or presents.*
Aufwachraum	**recovery room** *The immediate post-operative room where patients are stabilized prior to going to a general ward.*
Augenabziehnerv	**abducens nerve** *A motor nerve (6th cranial nerve) that controls the lateral rectus muscle of the eye.)*
Augenbrau	**eyebrow** *Supercilium.*
Augenbrauenarcus	**superciliary arch** *The area superior to the upper border of each orbit.*
Augengläser	**eyeglasses** *Eye wear used for cosmetic or prescription purposes.*
Augenheilkunde	**ophthalmology** *The study of diseases of the eye.*
Augenhintergrund	**eyeground** *The fundus that is visualized with an ophthalmoscope.*
Augenhintergrund	**fundus oculi** *Portion of the interior eyeball in the posterior aspect which can be viewed by an ophthalmoscope.*
Augenlid, Augenlider	**palpebra, palpebrae** *Eyelid, eyelids.*
Augenlid.	**eyelid** *Palpebra.*
Augenmuskellähmung	**ocular paralysis.** *Paralysis of intraocular and extraocular muscles.*
Augentropfen	**eye drops** *Liquid applied to eyes for various medical problems.*
Augenwimper.	**eyelash** *Each of the short hairs on the eyelid.*
Auricula;Ohrmuschel	**auricle** *The external portion of the ear.*
Aurikular	**auricular** *Referring to the auricle.*
aurikulotemporal	**auriculotemporal** *The area of the ear and temple.*
Ausbruch	**outbreak (of a disease)** *A sudden start of a disease in a population.*
Ausdauer	**stamina** *Ability to maintain physical or mental exertion for a long period.*
auseinander	**apart** *Separated by a distance.*
Auskultation	**auscultation** *The act of listening to sounds emanating from the body.*
ausrotten	**extirpate, to** *To totally destroy.*
Aussage	**statement** *A written or oral commentary.*
Aussatz	**Hansen's disease** *Leprosy*
ausschließen	**rule out, to** *To perform a test or exam to exclude an illness or disease.*
außergewöhnlich	**strange** *Unusual in an unsettling way.*
Aussparung (Augenhöhle)	**socket** *An anatomical hollow that is part of an articulation. (eyeball socket)*
ausstatten	**endow, to** *To supply or provide for.*
Austauschtransfusion	**exchange transfusion** *Treatment of hyperbilirubinemia in neonates.*
Austrocknung	**desiccation** *The act of drying up.*
Auswertung	**evaluation** *Assessment or evaluation.*
Auswurf	**spit** *A term used to describe saliva that is ejected from the mouth.*
Auszehrung	**emaciation** *Abnormally thin and weak.*

ausziehen	**disrobe, to** *To remove clothing.*
Autismus	**autism** *A mental condition exhibited by difficulty in forming relationships, communicating and uses abstract thought.*
autistisch	**autistic** *Referring to autism.*
Autoantigen	**autoantigen** *A normal tissue constituent that prompts a cell-mediated response.*
Autoantikörper	**autoantibody** *An antibody that acts against the organism's own tissue.*
autogen	**autogenous** *Self-generated.*
Autohypnose	**autohypnosis** *Self-hypnosis.*
Autoimmunisierung	**autoimmunization** *The body's ability to promote an immune response without external resources.*
Autoklav; Hochdrucksterilisator	**autoclave** *A device used for sterilization with the use of steam under pressure.*
Autolyse	**autolysis** *A state of self destruction of cells within a body.*
autonomes Nervensystem	**autonomic nervous system** *Responsible for regulation of cardiac muscle, smooth muscle and glandular activity.*
Autoplastik	**autograft** *Grafting tissue from one part of person to another part of the same person.*
Autopsie; Leichenschau	**autopsy** *Examination of a body post-mortem in an attempt to determine cause of death.*
Autopsie; Leichenschau	**necropsy** *Synonym of autopsy.*
autosomal	**autosomal** *Referring to an autosome.*
Autotransfusion	**autotransfusion** *The reinfusion of one's own blood.*
avaskulär	**avascular** *An area with no blood supply.*
avaskulär Nekrose	**avascular necrosis** *Bone death caused by poor blood supply.*
aviär	**avian** *Referring to birds.*
Avitaminose	**avitaminosis** *A state of vitamin deficiency.*
Axilla	**axilla** *The hollow beneath the arm.*
axillar	**axillary** *Referring to the axilla.*
Axis; zweiter Halswirbel	**axis** *The second cervical vertebra.*
Axon	**axon** *The structure along which nerve impulses are transmitted from the cell body to other cells.*
azephalisch	**acephalous** *A absence of a head.*
azetäbular	**acetabular** *Referring to the acetabulum.*
Azidämie	**acidemia** *A lower than normal pH in the blood.*
Azidität	**acidity** *Referring to an acid state.*
azinös Drüse	**acinous gland** *The exocrine part of the pancreas.*
Azinus	**acinus** *A very small grape shaped portion of an acinous gland.*
azobezogen Jucken	**azo itch** *A pruritis noted in people who use azo dyes.*
Azoospermie	**azoospermia** *The absence of spermatozoa in the semen.*
Azorean Krankheit	**Azorean disease** *A form of hereditary ataxia found in peoples of Azorean descent. Also called Machado-Joseph disease or Portuguese-Azorean disease.*
Azotämie	**azotemia** *Prerenal disease.*
Azoturie	**azoturia** *An excess of urea in the urine.*
älter	**elderly** *Advanced in years.*
älter	**older** *Being around more than compared with another.*
Änderung	**alteration** *The process of change or modification.*

	English
Ärztezentrum	**health center** *A physical location where patients are treated.*
Ätiologie	**etiology** *The underlying cause of a problem.*
äußerer Gehörgang	**external ear canal** *Auditory canal.*
äußerlich	**external** *Outside of the body.*
Babinski-Zeichen	**Babinski's sign** *A reflex that occurs when the plantar surface of the foot is stimulated. The great toe turns upward- normal in infancy but when it turns upward in an adult it means there is central nervous system injury.*
Babinskisches Zeichen	**extensor plantar response** *Great toe extension indicating a positive Babinski sign.*
Baby	**baby** *A newborn.*
Baby-Waage	**baby-scale** *A device used to weigh an infant.*
Backenmuskel	**buccinator muscle** *Pulls the mouth posteriorly.*
Backenzahn	**molar tooth** *Any of the most posterior teeth bilaterally which includes 8 deciduous and usually 12 permanent teeth.*
Badedermatitis; Schwimmerkrätze	**swimmer's itch** *Pruritis caused by exposure to schistosomes.*
Bagassose	**bagassosis** *A pulmonary disorder contracted from inhalation of the waste of sugar cane (bagasse dust).*
Bainbridgereflex	**Bainbridge reflex** *Increase in heart rate due to increased pressure in teh right atrium.*
Baker-Zyste; Poplitealzyste	**Baker cyst** *A synovial fluid collection in the popliteal fossa.*
Bakteriämie	**bacteremia** *The presence of bacteria in the blood.*
bakteriell	**bacterial** *Referring to bacteria.*
Bakterien	**bacteria** *Plural for any organism of the order Eubacteriales.*
bakteriostatisch	**bacteriostatic** *An agent that impedes bacterial growth.*
Bakteriurie	**bacteriuria** *The presence of bacteria in the urine.*
bakterizid	**bactericidal** *An agent that destroys bacteria.*
Balanitis	**balanitis** *Inflammation of the glans of the penis.*
Ballenzeh	**bunion** *Swelling of the bursa of the metatarsal head of the first metatarsal.*
Ballottement	**ballottement** *Presence of movement of a floating object by palpation.*
Balsum	**balm** *A topical medical preparation.*
Bandmaß	**tape measure** *A long length of tape, marked at intervals for measuring.*
Bandscheibenvorfall	**herniated disc** *Prolapse of the nucleus pulposus into the spinal cord.*
Bandwurm	**tapeworm** *A parasitic, intestinal flatworm.*
Bandwurmglied	**proglottis** *Any segment of a tapeworm.*
Bartfinne; Bartflechte	**barber's itch** *Ringworm that is transmitted by contaminated shaving equipment.*
Bartholinitis	**Bartholin's cyst or abscess** *This is a purulent fluid collection in the Bartholin cysts which are located in the perivaginal area.*
Bartter-Syndrom	**Bartter's syndrome** *An autosomal recessive renal disorder with a defect in chloride reabsorption and secondary hyperaldosteronism.*
basal	**basal** *Referring to the base.*
Basalganglien	**basal ganglia** *Structures adjacent to the thalamus that are involved with coordination of movement.*
Basedowsche Krankheit	**Graves' disease** *A form of hyperthyroidism exhibited by a goiter and exophthalmos.*

basilär	**basilar** *Referring to the base or lower segment.*
Basophil	**basophil** *A polymorphonuclear granulocyte.*
Bativiafieber	**rice-field fever** *An infection cause by a species of Leptospira, affecting rice workers in Italy and Sumatra.*
Bauchfell	**peritoneum** *The serous membrane covering the abdominal organs and lining the abdominal walls.*
Bauchhautreflex	**abdominal reflex** *Elicited by stroking the abdomen lightly from mid-axillary line to umbilicus. A normal response is contraction of the umbilicus toward the stimulated side.*
Bauchpunktion	**abdominocentesis** *Puncturing of the abdominal wall for drainage purposes.*
Bauchumfang	**abdominal girth** *Waist circumference.*
bazillär	**bacillary** *Referring to bacilli.*
Bazillus	**bacillus** *A rod-shaped bacterium.*
Bändelung	**banding** *The process of encircling with a thin piece of material.*
Beatmung	**assisted ventilation** *The act of helping one breathe through artificial means.*
Beatmungsgerät	**respirator** *A device used to artificially ventilate a patient.*
Becherzelle	**goblet cell** *Aids in the secretion of respiratory and intestinal mucous.*
Bechterewreflex	**Bechterew-Mendel reflex** *Plantar flexion of the toes when the examiner percusses the dorsum of the foot; seen with pyramidal lesion.*
Becken	**pelvis** *The bony structure at the base of the spine.*
Beckenausgang	**inferior pelvis strait** *The pelvic outlet.*
Beckenausgangsdurchmesser	**conjugate diameter** *A pelvic inlet measurement used to determine whether a woman is capable of delivering a fetus vaginally.*
Beckenendlage	**breech presentation** *Position of the feet or buttocks near the cervix.*
Bedarf	**need** *A want or obligation.*
bedeutungslos	**meaningless** *Having no significance.*
beeinträchtigt	**impaired** *Having a disability.*
Beeinträchtigung	**impairment** *A specific disability.*
Befruchtung	**fertilization** *The melding of male and female gametes to form a zygote.*
Begabund	**aptitude** *A natural talent for something.*
beginnend	**incipient** *Starting to happen.*
Behandlung	**treatment** *Medical care one receives for illness or injury.*
Behçet-Syndrom	**Behçet syndrome** *Characterized by recurrent oral and genital ulcers, uveitis, iridocyclitis and frequently arthritis.*
Beidhändig	**ambidextrous** *Ability to use both hands equal ability.*
Bein	**leg** *One of two lower extremities.*
bekannt	**known** *Recognized or familiar.*
belanglos	**irrelevant** *Not pertinent.*
Belastungsangina	**exercised induce angina** *Chest pain noted during exertion related to coronary artery disease.*
Belastungsdyspnöe	**exercise-induced dyspnea**
Beleibtheit	**corpulence** *Fatness.*
Bemerkung	**comment** *A remark providing an opinion.*
benebelt	**hazy** *Cloudy.*
benigne	**benign** *Not harmful.*
Benommenheit; Schwindel	**dizziness** *Sensation of losing one's balance.*

	English
Beobachten	**monitoring** *A person that observes a process or a monitoring device.*
berechtigen	**qualify** *To become eligible by fullfilling a necessary standard.*
Berührung	**touch** *Tactile stimulation.*
Berylliosis	**berylliosis** *A lung exhibited by granulomas and caused by inhalation of beryllium.*
Beschäftigungstherapie	**occupational therapy** *Rehabilitation focusing on activities of daily living.*
beschimpfend	**slurring** *Indistinct yet comprehensible speech.*
beschleunigen	**accelerate** *(To accelerate the healing process).*
Besorgnis	**apprehension** *A fear that something unpleasant will happen.*
besorgt	**anxious** *Experiencing nervousness or unease.*
besser als die Norm	**greater than normal** *Above normal.*
bessergehen	**feel better, to** *To have improved health symptomatically.*
bester; beste	**best** *Optimal or ideal.*
Bestrahlung; Irradiation	**irradiation** *The process of being irradiated.*
Betablocker	**betablocker** *A substance that inhibits adrenergic stimulation. It is used to reduce pulse, blood pressure and to treat angina.*
beteiligt	**involved** *Difficult to comprehend.*
Betrieb; Bedienung	**operation** *A surgical procedure.*
Bett	**bed** *A mattress resting on a frame.*
Bettlaken	**sheet (bed)** *A rectangular fabric covering a bed.*
bettlägerig	**bedridden** *Term used to indicate one is so ill they cannot get out of bed.*
Bettlägerigkeit	**confinement** *Confined to bed.*
Bettpfanne	**bedpan** *A metal or plastic vestibule one sits on while in bed to defecate.*
Bettruhe	**bed rest** *A medical order requiring one to stay in bed.*
Beulenpest	**bubonic plague** *A form of plague exhibited by the formation of buboes.*
Beurteilung	**assessment** *An medical evaluation.*
bewusst	**conscious** *Being award and being able to respond to one's surroundings.*
Bewusstlosigkeit	**unconsciousness** *Unable to respond to sensory stimuli.*
Bewusstseinsverlust	**loss of consciousness** *Unresponsive to verbal and tactile stimuli.*
Beziehung	**relation** *1. A person who has a blood or marriage connection.*
Bezoar	**bezoar** *A concretion composed of either hair, vegetable/fruit fibers or hair and vegetable/fruit fibers that is found in the stomach.*
bezogen auf	**related to** *Causally connected.*
Bezold-Jarisch-Reflex	**Bezold-Jarisch reflex** *A reflex in the vagus, originating in the heart, resulting in sinus bradycardia, hypotension and periperal vasodilation.*
Bibliothek	**library**
Bienenstich	**bee sting** *A piercing from a bee.*
bikuspid	**bicuspid** *Having two points as in bicuspid valve or a premolar tooth.*
Bilharzia	**Bilharzia** *Historical name of a genus of flukes or nematodes now known as Schistosoma.*
Bilirubin	**bilirubin** *A pigment found in bile that is responsible for the yellow color seen in patients with elevated serum levels of bilirubin.*
Bilirubinurie	**biliuria** *The presence of bile in the urine.*

	English
Biliverdin	**biliverdin** *A green pigment formed by oxidation of bilirubin.*
Bill Handgriff	**Bill maneuver** *During childbirth, use of forceps at midpelvis to help extract the head.*
billiär	**biliary** *Referring to bile, bile ducts or gallbladder.*
bimanuell; zweihändig	**bimanual** *Use of two hands, as in bimanual pelvic examination in which the right hand touches the cervix uteri and the left hand presses above the mons pubis.*
binaural	**binaural** *Referring to both ears.*
Bindehautentzündung	**conjunctivitis** *Inflammation of the conjunctiva.*
Bindehautfarbe	**color of conjunctiva** *A point of assessment to check for pallor.*
binden	**truss** *A synthetic device for containing a hernia within the abdomen.*
binokular; beidäugig	**binocular** *Referring to both eyes.*
Bioassay	**bioassay** *A laboratory test determination as compared to normal.*
Biochemie	**biochemistry** *The study of chemistry and physiochemical processes in living organisms.*
Biologie	**biology** *The study of living organisms.*
Biopsie	**biopsy** *The removal and examination of bodily tissues or fluids.*
Biotin	**biotin** *A vitamin involved in the synthesis of fatty acids and glucose.*
Bioverfügbarkeit	**bioavailability** *The portion of a drug that is able to be utilized by the body after it is introduced to the body.*
bipolare affektive Psychose	**manic-depressive psychosis** *A mental disorder exhibited by alternating periods of depression and mania.*
bisexuell	**ambisexual** *Referring to both sexes.*
bitemporale Hemianopsie	**bitemporal hemianopsia** *A visual defect seen commonly in pituitary tumors in which the visual defect is in the temporal portion of each eye.*
bitterer Geschmack	**bitter (taste)** *Having a harsh, unpleasant taste.*
Bizeps	**biceps** *A muscle with two heads usually referring to the biceps brachii which is used for forearm flexion.*
Bizeps(sehnen)reflex (BSR); Bizeps-femoris-Reflex	**biceps reflex** *The biceps brachii tendon is hit with a reflex hammer and results in flexion of the forearm as a normal response. This assesses the C5-C6 region.*
Blase	**blister** *Common term for bulla.*
blast Verletzung	**blast injury** *Trauma from a wave of air pressure.*
Blastomykose	**blastomycosis** Infection caused by organisms of genus Blastomyces.
Blattlaus	**aphid** *A minute insect that feeds on plants.*
blau	**blue** *A color between green and violet.*
Blässe	**pallor** *Unusually pale appearance.*
Blei	**lead** *An element with an atomic number of 82.*
bleibende Zähne	**permanent teeth** *Dentition that comes in after the primary teeth.*
Bleichmittel	**bleach** *A solution that includes sodium hypochlorite.*
Bleivergiftung	**lead poisoning** *The ingestion of lead, exhibited in severe cases by paralysis, encephalopathy, purple gingiva, and colic.*
Blendung	**glare** *An angry stare.*
Blennorrhö	**blennorrhea** *Discharge from the mucous membranes, usually referring to gonorrhea.*
Blepharitis; Lidrandentzündung	**blepharitis** *Inflammation of the eyelids.*
Blepharospasmus	**blepharospasm** *A spasm of the orbicularis oculi muscle that causes closure of the eyelid.*

Blick	**gaze** *Steady, intent look.*
Blick	**glance** *A brief look at something.*
blind	**blind** *Absence of sight.*
blinder Fleck	**blind spot** *An area of insensitivity to light located at the point of entry of the optic nerve on the retina.*
Blindheit	**blindness** *Absence of visual perception.*
Blindsack-Syndrom	**blind loop syndrome** *A condition in which there is a non-functional section of the bowel that is thought to be responsible for malabsorption and Vitamin B12 deficiency.*
blinzelnd	**blinking** *The rapid opening and closing of the eyelid.*
Blut	**blood** *Plasma containing erythrocytes, leukocytes and platelets.*
blut Schlauch	**blood tubing** *(used for infusion of blood)*
Blut-Hirn-Schranke	**blood brain barrier** *A matrix of capillaries that move blood between the blood and brain, as well as, limiting some substances from passing.*
Blutalkoholkonzentration	**blood alcohol level** *A quantitative measurement of the amount of alcohol in the blood.*
Blutaustritt	**extravasation** *Referring to a situation in which blood or fluid goes out of a vessel it is normally flowing into.*
Blutbank	**blood bank** *An area where blood products are stored for later use.*
Blutdruck	**blood pressure** *Written as the measurement in mmHg at the time of systole of the left ventricle over the time of diastole.*
Blutegel	**leech** *An annelid used in some tropical regions for drawing out blood; they have an anticoagulant effect locally and have been attached to digits of persons with acute peripheral ischemia.*
Bluter; Hämophilier	**hemophiliac** *A person with hemophilia.*
Blutgasanalyse (BGA)	**arterial blood gas** *Measurement of the arterial concentration of carbon dioxide and oxygen.*
Blutgerinnsel	**blood clot** *A mass of coagulated blood.*
Blutgruppen	**blood type** *Determined and listed in the ABO system.*
Blutgruppenserologie	**blood grouping** *Testing blood to determine which type should be used for transfusion.*
Bluthochcholesterinspiegel	**high cholesterol** *Elevated serum cholesterol.*
Bluthochdruck	**high blood pressure** *Elevated arterial blood pressure.*
Blutprobenauskreuzung	**cross-matching (blood)** *Evaluation of blood to determine compatibility between the donor and recipient prior to transfusion.*
Blutsenkunsgeschwindigkeit	**blood sedimentation rate (ESR)** *The settling time of erythrocytes in a prepared sample. This is a measure of the abnormal concentration of substances that are associated with pathological states.*
Blutstatus	**complete blood count** *An assay that includes white blood cell, red blood cell, platelet count, hemoglobin, hematocrit and white blood cell differential.*
Blutstrom	**blood stream** *Common term or the arterial or venous systems.*
Blutsverwandtschaft	**consanguinity** *The relationship by blood.*
Blutung	**bleeding** *Loss of blood.*
Blutungszeit	**bleeding time** *The time of bleeding after a controlled standardized puncture of the earlobe.*
Blutvolumen	**blood volume** *The amount of blood cells/plasma in the circulatory system.*
Blutzellen	**blood cells** *A common term that does not differentiate between erythrocyte or leukocyte.*

Bodenkrätze	**ground itch** *Marked pruritis caused by a hookworm larvae, known otherwise as cutaneous larva migrans.*
Boerhaave-Syndrom	**Boerhaave Syndrome** *Rupture of the esophagus from vigorous vomiting, with resultant mediastinitis.*
Bogengang	**semicircular canal** *The anterior, posterior and lateral canals in the inner ear that assist in balance control.*
Bohrer	**drill** *Cylindrical metal tool uses for creating a hole in bone in surgery.*
Bougierung	**bougienage** *Passage of a bougie through a body orifice with the goal of increasing the diameter of the orifice.*
bovine spongiforme Enzephalopathie	**mad cow disease** *Bovine spongiform encephalopathy, a disease that cause cerebral degeneration exhibited by ataxia.*
brachial	**brachial** *Referring to the arm.*
Bracht Handgriff	**Bracht maneuver** *Delivery of a fetus in a breech position.*
Brachyzephalie	**brachycephaly** *The presence of a short broad skull.*
Bradykardie	**bradycardia** *Lower than normal cardiac rate measured in beats per minute.*
Bradykinin	**bradykinin** *A peptide that causes contraction of smooth muscle and dilation of blood vessels.*
branchialis; kiemenförmig	**branchial** *Referring to or resembling the gills of a fish.*
Brandwunde	**burn** *An injury caused by exposure to heat.*
braun	**brown** *Coffee-colored.*
Brechmittel	**emetic** *An agent that induces vomiting.*
Brechreiz	**retching** *Spasm of the stomach without presence of gastric material.*
Brechschale	**emesis basin** *A small bowl used to catch vomitus.*
Bregma	**bregma** *Located at the convergence of the coronal and sagittal sutures.*
Breite	**width** *Side to side measurement.*
Bremskoltz; Ziel	**target** *An objective towards which efforts are directed.*
Brille	**goggles** *Close fitting, protective eyeglasses.*
bringen	**bring, to** *To carry or transport something.*
Bromidrosis	**bromidrosis** *Foul smelling perspiration.*
Bromismus	**bromism** *Poisoning caused by excessive intake of bromine.*
bronchial	**bronchial** *Referring to the bronchus.*
Bronchialkarzinom	**bronchial carcinoma** *A general term for a malignancy of the bronchi.*
Bronchiektasie	**bronchiectasis** *The presence of abnormally wide bronchi or branches.*
Bronchiolitis	**bronchiolitis** *Inflammation of the pulmonary bronchioles.*
Bronchiolus	**bronchiole** *A small branch that a bronchus divides into.*
Bronchitis	**bronchitis** *Inflammation of the mucous membranes of the bronchioles that causes bronchospasm and cough.*
bronchogen	**bronchogenic** *Referring to the bronchi.*
Bronchographie	**bronchography** *Roentgenography of the bronchi after administration of contrast media.*
Bronchopneumonie	**bronchopneumonia** *Pneumonia that starts in the distal bronchioles.*
Bronchoskopie	**bronchoscopy** *Use of a scope to visualize the bronchi.*
Bronchospasmus	**bronchospasm** *Bronchial smooth muscle spasm.*
Bronchus	**bronchus** *The major air channels that bifurcate from the distal trachea.*

189

Brown-Séquard-Syndrom	**Brown-Séquard syndrome** *Unilateral spinal cord lesions, proprioception loss and weakness occur ipsilateral to the lesion, while pain and temperature loss occur contralateral.*
Brucellose	**brucellosis** *A gram-negative bacteria in cattle that causes persistent fever in humans.*
Bruch	**break** *A common term for a fracture in a bone.*
Brudzinskireflex	**Brudzinski sign** *Involuntary flexion of the knees and hips after flexion of the neck while supine; seen in meningitis.*
Brust	**breast** *Mammary tissue including the areola.*
Brustdrüse	**mammary gland** *The mass of tissue posterior to the nipples which has the essential task of milk production.*
Brustfell; Pleura	**pleura** *The serous membrane lining each lung.*
Brustkorb	**thorax** *The part of the body between the neck and abdomen.*
Brustwand	**chest wall** *Thoracic wall.*
Brustwandableitung	**chest leads** *Leads going from the skin to an electrocardiographic device.*
Brustwarzenhof	**areola** *The pigmented skin surrounding a nipple.*
Brutkasten; Inkubator	**incubator** *A warming device for infants.*
Brücke	**pons** *The part of the brainstem that connects the medulla oblongata with the thalamus.*
Bubo	**bubo** *An inflamed, swollen lymph node in the axilla or inguinal region.*
Buccinator	**buccinator** *A thin, flat muscle in the cheek wall.*
Budd-Chiari-Syndrom	**Budd-Chiari syndrome** *Hepatomegaly, severe portal hypertension and ascites related to thrombosis of the hepatic vein.*
bukkal; buccalis	**buccal** *Referring to the cheek.*
Bulbär-paralyse	**bulbar palsy** *Paralysis due to changes in the motor center of the medulla oblongata.*
Bulbokavernosus-Reflex	**bulbocavernosus reflex** *Brisk contraction of the ischiocavernosus and bulbocavernosus muscles when the glans penis is compressed.*
bulbomimischer Reflex; Mondonesi-Reflex	**facial reflex or bulbomimic reflex** *Pressure on the eyeballs causes contraction of facial muscles on the side contralateral to the side of the lesion in the patient in a coma. In coma from a metabolic problem the reflex is present bilaterally.*
Bulimie	**bulimia** *Pathologic increase in hunger.*
Bulimie	**hyperphagia** *Excessive food ingestion.*
Bumke Pupillenzeichen	**Bumke's pupil** *Dilation of the pupil in response to anxiety.*
Bursitis	**bursitis** *Inflammation of the bursa.*
Buzzard Handgriff	**Buzzard maneuver** *Testing of the patellar reflex while the client firmly touches the floor with their toes in a sitting position.*
Bürste; Pinsel	**brush** *Implement used for cleaning or for taking a tissue sample.*
Bürstenabstrich	**brush biopsy** *The process of tissue sampling using a brush.*
Bypass; Umweg	**bypass** *An alternate route, typically referring to an arterial bypass.*
Byssinose; Baumwollfieber	**byssinosis** *A disease caused by inhalation of cotton dust; a type of pneumoconiosis.*
Byssus	**pubic hair** *Hair present in the perineal area.*
Caissonkrankheit	**caisson disease** *Decompression sickness.*
Calcaneus; Kalkaneus	**calcaneus** *Commonly called the heel bone.*
Calciferol	**calciferol** *It is formed when egesterol is exposed to ultraviolet light; a D vitamin.*

	English
Calcitonin	**calcitonin** *A thyroid hormone that lowers serum calcium levels.*
Calcium; Kalzium	**calcium** *A chemical element that is an essential component in teeth and bone.*
Calculus; Stein	**calculus** *A stone of minerals that can lead to the blockage of the bile duct or ureters.*
Calvaria	**calvaria** *The portion of the skull that is composed of the superior aspects of the occipital, parietal and frontal bones.*
Canaliculus; Kanälchen	**canaliculus** *A term for various small channels.*
Caplan-Syndrom	**Caplan nodules** *These are pulmonary nodules noted in people with rheumatoid arthritis who were exposed to coal dust.*
Caput succedaneum	**caput succedaneum** *Edema that occurs in the scalp of an infant during child-birth.*
Caput; Kopf	**caput** *The head.*
Carotin	**carotene** *A hydrocarbon that can be converted to vitamin A.*
Casoni Intrakutantest	**Casoni's test** *Hydatid fluid is injected intradermally; subsequent formation of a larger papule indicates hydatid disease.*
caudatus	**caudate** *Referring to the caudate nucleus.*
Celsius-Skala	**centigrade** *A scale with 100 gradations, usually referring to a temperature scale.*
Cerumen; Zerumen	**wax** *Cerumen.*
Cestoda; Bandwurm	**cestode** *A class of parasitic flatworms.*
Cheilitis; Lippenentzüdung	**cheilitis** *Inflammation of the lip.*
Chelatbildner	**chelating agent** *A compound used to bind with metal typically used in the treatment of poisoning.*
Chemorezeptor	**chemoreceptor** *A sense organ that responds to stimuli.*
Chemosis	**chemosis** *Swelling of conjunctival tissue adjacent to the cornea.*
Chemotaxis	**chemotaxis** *The response of an organism to chemical agents.*
Chemotherapie	**chemotherapy** *Use of medication (chemical agents) in the treatment of disease. This term is commonly used to refer to the treatment of cancer patients with medication.*
Cheyne-Stokes-Atmung	**Cheyne-Stokes respirations** *A breathing pattern characterized by alternating apnea with hyperpnea.*
Chiasma	**chiasma** *The optic chiasma is the area inferior to the hypothalamus where the optic nerves cross.*
Chimäre	**chimera** *A mixture of genetically distinct tissues.*
Chininvergiftung	**cinchonism** *The toxic effects induced by ingestion of cinchona bark; it is exhibited by tinnitus, deafness and cognitive changes.*
Chiropraktik	**chiropractic** *Referring to the medical practice of adjusting malaligned joints.*
Chiropraktiker	**chiropractor** *A medical practitioner who is involved with the treatment of disease by manipulating malaligned joints.*
Chirurgie	**surgery** *The incision of a body part using sterile technique in order to treat disease or injury.*
Chirurgin	**surgeon** *A physician who performs surgery.*
chirurgisch	**surgical** *Referring to surgery.*
Chlamydieninfektion	**chlamydiosis** *A disease caused by the species Chlamydia.*
Chloasma	**chloasma** *Brown or black macula that occur on the face during pregnancy or when there is ovarian dysfunction.*

191

	English
Chloroform	**chloroform** *A colorless, sweet smelling liquid formerly used as a general anesthetic.*
Chlorom	**chloroma** *A malignant tumor associated with myelogenous leukemia.*
Choanalatresie	**choanal atresia** *A congenital condition characterized by blockage of the nasal passages by tissue.*
Choane	**choanae** *The two openings between the nasal cavity and the nasopharynx.*
Cholagogum	**cholagogue** *A compound used to stimulate flow of bile from the liver.*
Cholangiogramm	**cholangiogram** *Radiologic imaging of the gallbladder and bile ducts.*
Cholangitis	**cholangitis** *Inflammation of the bile ducts.*
Cholämie	**cholemia** *Bile or bile products in the blood.*
Choledocholithotomie	**choledocholithotomy** *Creation of an incision in the bile duct for the purpose of removing a stone.*
Cholelithiasis	**cholelithiasis** *Presence or creation of gallstones.*
Cholera	**cholera** *An infectious disease exhibited by vomiting and diarrhea and caused by Vibrio cholerae.*
cholestatische Hepatitis	**cholestatis hepatitis** *Liver inflammation caused by obstruction of bile flow from the liver to the duodenum.*
Cholesteatom	**cholesteatoma** *A cystic mass that has a lining made of keratinizing material and cholesterol.*
Cholesterin	**cholesterol** *A compound or its derivatives are found in cell membranes and precursors to hormones but high levels can cause atherosclerosis.*
Cholezystektomie	**cholecystectomy** *Surgical excision of the gallbladder.*
Cholezystenterostomie	**cholecystenterostomy** *Creation of a surgical anastomosis between the intestine and the gallbladder.*
Cholezystitis	**cholecystitis** *Inflammation of the gallbladder.*
Cholezystolithiasis	**cholecystolithiasis** *The presence of gallstones in the gallbladder.*
cholinerg	**cholinergic** *Referring to the stimulation, activation or transmission of acetylcholine.*
Cholinesterase	**cholinesterase** *An esterase used to cleave acetylcholine into choline and acetic acid.*
Cholurie	**choluria** *Term indicating the presence of bile in the urine.*
Chondralgie	**chondralgia** *Cartilaginous pain.*
Chondritis	**chondritis** *Cartilaginous inflammation.*
Chondrom	**chondroma** *Cartilaginous hyperplastic growth.*
Chondromalazie	**chondromalacia** *Excessive softening of the cartilages.*
Chondrosarkom	**chondrosarcoma** *Cartilaginous tumor which exhibits rapid growth.*
Chorda	**chorda** *A cord or sinew.*
Chorditis	**chorditis** *Inflammation of a vocal or spermatic cord.*
Chorditis; Stimmbandentzündung	**choroiditis** *Inflammation of the choroid.*
Chorea	**chorea** *Involuntary, continuous rapid, jerking movements.*
Chorea Sydenham	**Sydenham chorea** *Historically known as Saint Vitus' dance, it is a childhood chorea associated with rheumatic fever.*
Choreomanie; Springend Krankheit	**miryachit** *A disease of Siberia characterized by an exaggerated startle response; also referred to as jumping disease.*
Chorionzotte	**chorionic villus** *Cord-like projections of a fertilized ovum.*
choroidozyklitis	**choroidocyclitis** *Inflammation of the ciliary processes and choroid.*
Chromatin	**chromatin** *A desocyribose nucleic acid that carries the genes of inheritance.*

	English
Chromkatgutnaht	**resorbable suture (chromic)** *Suture that is not intended to be permanent as it is dissolved by normal body processes.*
Chromosom	**chromosome** *A structure in the nucleus of living cells that carries genetic information.*
chronisch	**chronic** *When referring to an illness, it means recurring or persistent.*
Chylomikron	**chylomicron** *A one micron particle of emulsified fat.*
chylos	**chylous** *Referring to chyle.*
Chylus; Milchsaft	**chyle** *A combination of lymph fluid and fat that enters the blood via the thoracic duct.*
Chymus	**chyme** *The gruel produced by gastric digestion.*
Cilia; Zilien	**cilia** *The hairs growing on the eyelid or a motile extension of a cell surface.*
Cisterna chyli	**ampulla chyli** *Also called cisterna chyli; it is a dilated area of the thoracic duct that collects lymph from several areas.*
Claudicatio; Hinken	**claudication** *Intermittent claudication is a phrase used to describe pain experienced in the leg from arterial insufficiency.*
Click	**click** *A sound heard by the sudden closure of a heart valve.*
Clusterkopfschmerz	**cluster headache** *A unilateral, severe, recurrent headache.*
Coccus; Kokke	**coccus** *A spherical shaped bacterium.*
Cochlea; Schnecke	**cochlea** *The essential organ of hearing which is in a spiral form.*
Codein	**codeine** *A morphine derived analgesic.*
Colitis ulcerosa	**ulcerative colitis** *Recurrent episode of inflammation of the membranous layer of the colon.*
Colon ascendens	**ascending colon** *The portion of the colon between the cecum and the right colic flexure.*
Colon sigmoideum; Sigmoid	**sigmoid** *Referring to the portion of the colon that leads into the rectum.*
Computertomographie	**CT scan** *Computerized axial tomography.*
Condyloma acuminatum	**venereal wart** *Common term for condyloma acuminatum.*
contre-coup Kopfverletzung	**injury, contrecoup of brain** *An injury to the brain on the side opposite of that which was struck.*
Cotton-Wool-Herde	**cotton wool spots** *Condition characterized by blue or white discoloration on the retina related to nerve ischemia.*
Credé Handgriff	**Credé's maneuver** *Manual pressure over the bladder to assist in expression of urine in an atonic bladder.*
Crohn Krankheit	**Crohn's disease** *An inflammatory bowel disease.*
Crush-Syndrom	**crush syndrome** *Rhabdomyolysis occurring as a result of muscle injury from mechanical stress.*
Curare	**curare** *A toxic botanical substance used at one time in poison darts in South America. Curare derivatives have been used in general anesthesia.*
Cushing-Syndrom	**Cushing's syndrome** *Characterized by trunkal obesity, moon face, acne, abdominal striae, hypertension, decreased carbohydrate tolerance, protein catabolism, psychiatric disturbances, and osteoporosis.*
Cyanocobalamin	**cyanocobalamin** *Also called B12; used to treat pernicious and other macrocytic anemias.*
Cystinose	**cystinosis** *A congenital disorder of increased cystine that leads to renal insufficiency, rickets and dwarfism.*
daher	**hence** *Thus.*

193

Dakryoadenitis	**dacryoadenitis** *Inflammation of the lacrimal gland.*
Dakryolith	**dacryolith** *A stone in the lacrimal sac or duct.*
Dakryozystitis	**dacryocystitis** *Inflammation of a lacrimal sac.*
Dakryozystorhinostomie	**dacryocystorhinostomy** *Surgical reaction of a communication between the lacrimal sac and nasal cavity.*
Darm	**intestine** *A general term used for the section of bowel from the stomach to the anus.*
Darmbeinkamm	**iliac crest** *The upper border of the ilium.*
Darmstein	**enterolith** *A calculus of the intestine.*
Darmverschluß	**intestinal obstruction** *Blockage of the intestine by mass or volvulus.*
das heißt	**i.e.** *A latin derived abbreviation for "that is to say"(In latin: id est)*
das Krankenhaus verlassen	**hospital discharge** *To leave the hospital.*
Dauerkatheter	**indwelling foley** *A catheter inserted into the urinary bladder with an inflatable ballon on the tip.*
Daumen	**thumb** *The first digit of each hand.*
Daumenballen	**thenar eminence** *Formed by the bellies of the abductor pollicis brevis, flexor pollicis brevis and opponens pollicis.*
Debilität	**debility** *Physical weakness.*
decidua	**decidua** *The mucous membrane lining the uterus during pregnancy.*
Defäkation	**defecation** *The discharge of feces from the rectum.*
Defekt	**defect** *A shortcoming or imperfection.*
Defibrillator	**defibrillator** *A device used to convert an abnormal cardiac rhythm (ventricular fibrillation) into a normal rhythm with use of electrical stimulation.*
Defizienz	**deficiency** *Insufficiency or deficit.*
Deformität	**deformity** *A malformation or imperfection.*
Deglutition; Schluckakt	**deglutition** *The process of swallowing.*
dehnen	**extend, to** *To expand or stretch out.*
Dehydratation	**dehydration** *The status of having a decrease in total body water.*
dekapitieren	**decapitate, to** *The physical separation of the head from the body.*
Dekompensation	**decompensation** *The inability of an organ to respond to functional overload.*
Dekompression	**decompression** *The surgical procedure relieving pressure on a part.*
Delirium	**delirium** *An acute mental state exhibited by altered thought processes and restlessness.*
delirium tremens	**delirium tremens** *A condition seen when alcohol is withdrawn which is exhibited by restlessness, hallucinations and tremors.*
dellenbildendes Ödem	**pitting edema** *Edema of the lower extremities characterized by an indentation being left when the examiner applies pressure with their thumb.*
Deltoideus	**deltoid** *A term referring to "three". The deltoid muscle has its origin at three areas: clavicle, acromion, and spine of the scapula.*
Demarkation	**demarcation** *Having a fixed boundary.*
Demenz	**dementia** *A chronic brain disorder exhibited by memory loss, personality changes and faulty reasoning.*
Demographie	**demography** *The study of the structure of human populations.*
Dendrit	**dendrite** *Impulses are transmitted along a dendrite to a nerve cell body.*

Denguefieber	**dengue** *A mosquito-borne viral disease exhibited by fever and joint pain.*
dental	**dental** *Referring to teeth.*
Dentatusnukleus	**dentatum** *Also referred to as dentate nucleus of cerebellem.*
Depression	**depression** *A medical condition exhibited by profound despondency.*
deprimiert	**depressed** *Melancholy.*
Deprivation	**deprivation** *The lack of a necessity.*
Dermatitis	**dermatitis** *Non-specific inflammation of the skin.*
Dermatologe	**dermatologist** *A physician specializing in dermatology.*
Dermatologie	**dermatology** *The medical profession involving the treatment of skin conditions.*
Dermatom	**dermatome** *The area of sensation of the skin supplied by a single posterior spinal root.*
Dermatomykose	**dermatomycosis** *An infection of the skin by Trichophyton, Microsporum or Epidermophyton fungi.*
Dermatomyositis	**dermatomyositis** *Inflammation of the skin, subcutaneous tissue and adjacent muscle.*
Dermatophyt; Haupilz	**dermatophyte** *A fungal parasite living on the skin.*
Dermatophytose	**ringworm** *A fungal skin infection exhibited by pruritic well circumscribed patches on the scalp or feet.*
Dermatophytose; Tinea	**tinea** *Medical term for ringworm.*
Dermatose	**dermatosis** *Any skin disease.*
Dermis; Haut	**dermis** *The "true skin" that lies beneath the epidermis.*
Dermographie	**dermatography** *A description of the skin.*
Dermographie	**dermographia** *A raised, pale line with hyperemic borders is elicited upon scratching the skin with a dull instrument, in this condition.*
Dermoidzyste	**dermoid cyst** *An abnormal growth containing hair follicles, skin and sebaceous glands.*
desensibilisieren	**desensitize, to** *To gradually expose a person to an offending agent to prevent an abnormal response upon a secondary exposure.*
Desinfektion	**disinfectant** *A substance that kills bacteria.*
Desmoid; Fibromatose	**desmoid** *A tumor typically found in the abdomen which contains. muscle and connective tissue.*
Desorientierung	**disorientation** *Mental confusion.*
Desoxyribonukleinsäure	**deoxyribonucleic acid (DNA)** *The carrier of genetic information.*
Desoxyribonukleinsäure	**DNA Deoxyribonucleic acid.** *The hereditary material in humans and almost all other organisms.*
Detritus	**detritus** *Particulate matter produced by the decomposition of an organic substance.*
Detrusor urinae	**detrusor urinae** *Smooth muscle fibers that extend from the urinary bladder to the pubis.*
Deuteranomalie	**deuteranomaly** *Abnormal color vision sometimes called "green weakness".*
Deviation; Abweichung	**deviation** *Away from the norm.*
Dextran	**dextran** *A high glucose polymer used as a plasma substitute.*
Dextrokardie	**dextrocardia** *Location of the heart in the right hemithorax.*
Dezerebrationsstarre; Enthirnungsstarre	**decerebrate rigidity** *Rigid extension of the arms which is an abnormal posture associated with increased intracranial pressure.*
Dezibel	**decibel** *A unit used in the measurement of sound.*

195

	English
Diabetes insipidus	**diabetes insipidus** *Caused by a deficiency in vasopressin, it is exhibited by great thirst and large volume urine output (and normal blood sugar).*
Diabetes mellitus	**diabetes mellitus** *A disease exhibited by a deficiency of the pancreatic hormone insulin.*
Diabetiker	**diabetic** *A person who has diabetes mellitus.*
diabetische Neuropathie	**diabetic neuropathy** *Pain and burning initially in the feet, associated with diabetes mellitus.*
diagnostisch	**diagnostic** *A specific symptom or characteristic.*
Diapedese	**diapedesis** *The outward passage of blood elements through an intact vessel wall.*
Diaphoretikum	**diaphoretic** *Exhibited by profuse perspiration.*
Diaphragma; Zwerchfell	**diaphragm** *The muscular separation between the thoracic and abdominal cavities.*
Diaphyse	**diaphysis** *The central part of a long bone.*
Diarrhö; Durchfall	**diarrhea** *Increase in frequency and a loose consistency of the stools.*
Diarthrose	**diarthrosis** *An articulation allowing free movement.*
Diastase	**diastase** *Amylase.*
Diastole	**diastole** *The period of dilatation of the heart; between the first and second heart sounds.*
Diathermie	**diathermy** *The use of heat produced from high-frequency electric currents to medically or surgically treat someone.*
Diathese	**diathesis** *A medical tendency to develop a specific condition.*
Diät	**diet** *The kinds of food a person eats.*
Diätetiker	**dietitian** *A professional who works with diet and nutrition.*
Dichte	**density** *The denseness of an object.*
Dickdarmafter; Kolostomie	**colostomy** *Surgically creating an opening in the colon that is extended to outside the abdominal wall.*
Differential	**differential** *A term used to refer to the various options for diagnoses.*
Differentialdiagnose	**differential diagnosis** *A list of possible alternative diagnoses for a patient who is ill.*
differentiell Leukozytenzählung	**differential leukocyte count** *The percentage of different types of leukocytes.*
Digitalis	**digitalis** *Cardiac medication derived from the leaf of Digitalis purpurea.*
Dilatator; Dehner	**dilator** *An instrument that dilates.*
Dimercaprol	**dimercaprol** *A medication used as a binding agent for heavy metal poisoning.*
Dioptrie	**dioptre** *Referring to refraction or transmitted and refracted light.*
Dioxid	**dioxide** *A compound containing two oxygen atoms.*
Diphtherie	**diphtheria** *A contagious bacterial disease characterized by a grey membrane on the pharynx along with respiratory or cutaneous symptoms; caused by Corynebacterium diphtheriae.*
Diplegie	**diplegia** *The paralysis of both arms or both legs.*
diploid	**diploid** *A nucleus containing two complete sets of chromosomes.*
Diplokokkus	**diplococcus** *A bacterium that occurs in pairs including pneumococcus and Neisseria gonorrhoeae and Neisseria meningitidis.*
Diplopie	**diplopia** *Double vision.*
Dipsomanie	**dipsomania** *Twins that are joined at some part of their bodies.*

	English
Disaccahrid	**disaccharide** *A type of sugar that yields two monosaccharides upon hydrolysis.*
Dislokation	**dislocation** *The displacement of a bone when referring to an articulation.*
Dissemination	**dissemination** *To be spread or dispersed widely.*
dissezierendes Aneurysma	**dissecting aneurysm** *A condition in which blood is present between the layers of an artery.*
distal	**distal** *Situated away from the center of the body.*
Distichiasis	**distichiasis** *Presence of two rows of eyelashes on one eyelid which are turned inward toward the globe.*
Diurese	**diuresis** *Increased excretion of urine.*
Diuretikum	**diuretic** *Medication which causes an increased excretion of urine.*
Divertikel	**diverticulum** *A sac or pouch created by herniation of a mucous membrane in the alimentary canal.*
Divertikulitis	**diverticulitis** *Inflammation of the diverticulum.*
Divertikulose	**diverticulosis** *Presence of diverticulum.*
Dochtdrainage	**wick** *A drain using a thin piece of cloth or tubing.*
Dopamin	**dopamine** *An intermediate product in the creation of norepinephrine.*
Dopareaktion	**dopa reaction** *A dopa-oxidase reaction, changing dopa into melanin.*
doppelseitig; bilateral	**bilateral** *Referring to both sides.*
doppelt	**double** *Twice the size, quantity or strength.*
Dornwarze	**plantar wart** *A viral epidermal growth on the bottom of the foot.*
dorsal	**dorsal** *Referring to the back or back surface.*
Dorsalflexion	**dorsiflexion** *Backward bending of the foot or hand.*
Dosierung	**dosage** *The amount and frequency a medication is given.*
Dosis	**dose** *The quantity of a medication.*
Dosisintervall	**dosing interval** *The number of times per unit a medication is given.*
Douglasscher Raum	**Douglas' pouch** *A recess in the peritoneum between the rectum and the uterus. Also called the rectouterine pouch.*
Drakunkulose	**guinea worm infection** *Caused by a parasitic nematode worm that lives under the skin, formally called Dracunculus medinensis.*
drastisch	**drastic** *Having significant effect.*
Drehung	**rotation** *Movement around an axis.*
Dreieck	**trigone of bladder** *Refers to the area at the base of the bladder between the openings of the ureters and the urethra.*
Dreiwegsonde	**three way foley** *A urinary tube used for irrigation of the bladder.*
Drillinge	**triplets** *Three infants born during one birth.*
Dringlichkeit	**urgency** *Emvergency or priority.*
Drogenabhängigkeit	**drug dependence** *Addiction to a substance.*
Drosselgrube	**jugular notch** *The notch on the upper border of the sternum.*
Drosselvene	**jugular vein (s)** *Includes the internal, external and anterior jugular veins.*
Druckgeschwür; Dekubitus	**pressure ulcer** *Loss in skin integrity due to a portion of the body being in the same position for too long and possibly other factors.*
Druckverband	**pressure dressing** *A dressing used for compression to reduce bleeding.*
Dualdiagnose	**dual diagnosis** *Term used to describe the presence of alcohol/drug addiciton associated with a psychiatric diagnosis such as depression.*

197

Ductus arteriosus	**ductus arteriosus** *A fetal artery that communicates between the pulmonary artery and the descending aorta.*
Ductus cysticus	**cystic duct** *The duct connecting the gallbladder to the common bile duct.*
Dumpingsyndrom	**dumping syndrome** *Characterized by rapid bowel evacuation after eating in patients with prior gastric surgery.*
Dunkeladaptation	**dark adaptation** *Adjustment to low light by reflex dilation of the pupil.*
duodenal	**duodenal** *Referring to the duodenum.*
Duodenektomie	**duodenectomy** *Excision of the duodenum.*
Duodenitis	**duodenitis** *Inflammation of the duodenum.*
Duplikation	**duplication** *The process of duplicating something.*
Dupuytrensche Kontraktur	**Dupuytren's contracture** *A disease of the palmar fascia causing a flexion contracture of the fourth and fifth fingers.*
Dura mater	**dura mater** *The outermost covering of the brain and spinal cord.*
Durchleuchtung	**fluoroscopy** *The continuous viewing of roentgenographic images with a fluorescent screen.*
durchsichtig	**clear** *Transparent.*
Durst	**thirst** *The desire to drink.*
Dusche	**douche** *Cleansing of a canal; unless otherwise specified it refers to cleansing of the vaginal canal.*
dünn; mager	**thin** *Lean or slender.*
Dysaphie	**dysaphia** *Altered sense of touch.*
Dysarthie	**dysarthria** *Difficulty in articulation of speech.*
Dysästhesie; Mißempfindung	**dysesthesia** *1. Impairment of the sense of touch. 2. The presence of persistent pain upon receiving a light touch.*
Dysbarismus	**dysbarism** *Condition caused by a change in pressure, noted most commonly among scuba divers.*
Dyschezie	**dyschezia** *Pain experienced during defecation.*
Dyschondroplasie	**dyschondroplasia** *The formation of cartilaginous and bony tumors near the epiphyses.*
Dysdiadochokinesie	**dysdiadocokinesia** *The inability to arrest one motor response and substitute its opposite.*
Dysenterie; Ruhr	**dysentery** *A severe form of diarrhea with blood and mucous in the stool.*
Dysfunktion	**dysfunction** *Abnormal function in a gland or body organ.*
Dyshidrose	**dyshidrosis** *Disregulation of sweating*
Dyskinesie	**dyskinesia** *Abnormal movement.*
Dyskorie	**dyscoria** *A discordance in pupillary reaction.*
Dyskrasie	**dyscrasia** *An abnormal condition, mostly referring to the blood.*
Dyslalie	**dyslalia** *The absence of comprehensible speech articulation.*
Dyslexie	**dyslexia** *Difficulty in learning or reading written language with no effect on intelligence.*
Dysmenorrhöe	**dysmenorrhea** *Pain during menstruation.*
Dyspareunie	**dyspareunia** *Pain during sexual intercourse.*
Dyspepsie	**dyspepsia** *Indigestion.*
Dysphagie; Schluckstörung	**dysphagia** *Difficulty in swallowing.*
Dysphagie; Sprachstörung	**dysphasia** *Difficulty in speaking caused by cerebral dysfunction.*

Dysplasie	**dysplasia** *The increase in organ size due to an increase in the number of abnormal cell types.*
Dyspnöe	**dyspnea** *Difficult breathing.*
Dystokie	**dystocia** *Difficult birth caused by fetal position, narrow pelvis or lack of opening of the cervix.*
Dysurie	**dysuria** *Difficulty or pain upon urination.*
Echinokokkus	**Echinococcus** *A tapeworm of the family Taeniidae that can cause hydatid cysts.*
Echokardiographie	**echocardiography** *The use of ultrasound waves to visualize the heart and its structures.*
Echolalie	**echolalia** *The meaningless repetition of the words spoken by another person.*
Eckzähne	**canine teeth** *Located between the incisors and premolars.*
Eczema marginatum	**jock itch** *Pruritis caused by tinea cruris.*
Effektor	**effector** *An organ that responds to a stimulus.*
egozentrisch	**egocentric** *Thinking of self without considering the feelings or thoughts of others.*
Ehelichberatung	**marital counseling** *Therapy aimed at marriage reconciliation.*
ehernalig	**former** *Prior.*
Ehestand	**marital status** *Single verus married status.*
Ehrlichiose	**ehrlichiosis** *A tickborne infectious disease.*
Ei	**egg**
Ei	**ovule** *An immature ovum.*
Eichel	**glans penis** *The distal aspect of the penis.*
eichen	**calibrate, to** *To adjust an instrument using a standard.*
Eichung	**calibration** *The process of calibrating an instrument.*
Eierstock	**oophoron** *Synonym for ovary.*
Eierstockentzündung	**ovaritis** *Synonym for oophoritis.*
Eifeiter	**oviduct** *The channel which an ovum passes from the ovary.*
Eileiter; Tuba uterina	**fallopian tubes** *Either of a pair of long narrow ducts located in a female's abdominal cavity that transport the male sperm cells to the egg.*
ein Problem entschärfen	**alleviate a problem, to**
Eindringen	**penetration** *The process of making a way through something.*
eineiig	**uniovolar** *Referring to one fertilized ovum.*
eineiige Zwillinge	**identical twins** *Twins from the same zygote.*
einen steifen Nacken	**stiff-neck** *Cervical sprain with reduced range of motion.*
einer Lage gewachsen sein	**cope with a situation, to**
Einfühlungsvermögen	**empathy** *To be concerned for and share the feelings of another.*
Einführung	**insertion** *The act of inserting something.*
eingewachsener Nagel	**ingrown nail** *Also referred to as onychocryptosis.*
Eingeweidewurm; Helminthe	**helminth** *A fluke, tapeworm or nematode.*
Einkapselung	**loculated** *Divided into small cavities.*
Einlieferung	**admission (to hospital)**
Einrebung	**inunction** *The application of lotion with friction.*
Einrichter	**bonesetter** *A person who sets bones without being a physician.*
Einschlußkörperchen	**inclusion body** *Variably shaped bodies in the nuclei of cells found in infections such as rabies and herpes.*

einseitig; unilateral	**unilateral** *One side only.*
Eintagsfieber	**ephemeral fever** *A fever lasting no more than 24-48 hours.*
einwilligen	**comply, to** *Adhere to.*
einzellig	**unicellular** *A term describing organisms like protozoans that only have cell.*
einzeln	**discrete** *Separate and distinct.*
einzig	**single** *Only one.*
Eisen; Fe	**iron** *An element found in hemoglobin.*
Eisenmangelanämie	**iron-deficiency anemia** *A microcytic anemia.*
Eiter	**pus** *Thick yellow or green opaque liquid as seen with infection.*
eiterbildend	**pyogenic** *Referring to the formation of pus.*
eiterbildend Leberabszeß	**pyogenic liver abscess** *A pus filled fluid collection in the liver.*
eiterig	**purulent** *Referring to pus.*
eitern	**fester, to** *To become infected.*
Eiterung	**suppuration** *Formation of purulent material.*
Ejakulation	**ejaculation** *The emission of semen at the moment of sexual climax in a male.*
Ekchondrom	**ecchondroma** *Hyperplastic growth of cartilage on the surface of other cartilage.*
Ekchymose	**ecchymosis** *Skin discoloration caused by bleeding beneath the epidermis.*
Eklampsie	**eclampsia** *A maternal condition characterized by convulsions and hypertension that can lead to maternal and fetal death.*
Ekmnesie	**ecmnesia** *Memory loss for recent events but retained memory of remote events.*
Ektasie	**ectasia** *Expansion or distension.*
Ektoderm	**ectoderm** *The outermost layer of the three layers of the embryo.*
ektopisch	**ectopic** *Abnormal position.*
Ektrodaktylie	**ectrodactylia** *A congenital anomaly exhibited by absence of one digit or part of a digit.*
Ektropion	**ectropion** *Eversion of the eyelid, usually the lower lid.*
Ekzem	**eczema** *A medical condition exhibited by pruritic, red, scaly patches on the scalp, cheeks and extensor surfaces.*
Elastin	**elastin** *A connective tissue-based glycoprotein.*
elastische Binde	**elastic bandage** *A stretch gauze used for compression of an extremity.*
elektiv	**elective** *Non-urgent and not life-saving.*
Elektrode	**electrode** *A device used to facilitate conduction of electricity to or from a body.*
Elektroenzephalogramm	**electroencephalogram (EEG)** *A display of brain waves used in the diagnosis of brain disorders, especially epilepsy.*
Elektrokardiogramm	**electrocardiogram** *Display of a person's heart beat that can be used in the diagnosis of cardiac disorders.*
Elektrokrampftherapie	**electroconvulsive therapy (ECT)** *The electrical stimulation of the brain to treat mental disorders.*
Elektrolyt	**electrolyte** *The ionized constituents including potassium, sodium, chloride and others.*
Elektromyographie	**electromyography** *The display of the electrical activity of muscle.*
Elektronenmikroskop	**electron microscope** *A device that uses electron beams and lenses to give high magnification.*

Elektrophorese	**electrophoresis** *The movement of charged particles in a fluid that is under the influence of an electric field. This is used in testing for various maladies in the form of serum protein electrophoresis.*
Elephantiasis	**elephantiasis** *A condition caused by nematode parasites leading to lymphatic obstruction and limb or scrotal swelling.*
Elixir	**elixir** *A medical solution.*
Ellenbogen	**elbow** *The joint between the humerus and radius/ulna.*
Ellenbogengrube	**cubital fossa** *The bend at the elbow.*
Embolektomie	**embolectomy** *The removal of an embolus.*
Embolus	**embolus** *A blood clot, air bubble or fatty deposit that cause obstruction of a vessel.*
Embryo	**embryo** *The term used to describe a fertilized ovum in the first 8 weeks of development.*
Embryologie	**embryology** *The study of the embryo.*
Emmet Operation	**trachelorrhaphy** *Surgical repair of a lacerated cervix.*
Emmetropie	**emmetropia** *The normal correlation between eye refraction and the axial length of the eyeball.*
Emolliens	**emollient** *Having softening or soothing qualities.*
Emphysem	**emphysema** *Abnormal enlargement of the airspaces distal to the terminal bronchioles.*
Empyem	**empyema** *A collection of purulent material in a body cavity, usually referring to a thoracic empyema.*
Emulsion	**emulsion** *The dispersion of one liquid into another, but it is not dissolved.*
Enarthrose	**enarthrosis** *The type of joint in which a spherical bone is set into the socket of another bone.*
Enchondrom	**enchondroma** *An abnormal increase in cartilage growth on the inside of bone or of other cartilage.*
Endarteriitis	**endarteritis** *Tunica intima inflammation.*
Endemie; endemisch	**endemic** *When a disease is commonly found in a location or in a people group.*
Endobrachyöso-phagus	**Barretts's esophagus** *A condition characterized by varying degrees of esophageal injury from gastric acid.*
Endoderm	**endoderm** *The innermost layer of the embryonic germ cell layers.*
endogen	**endogenous** *Originating from within.*
Endokarditis	**endocarditis** *Inflammation of the endocardium.*
endokrin	**endocrine** *Referring to glands that secrete hormones and other chemicals into the blood.*
endokrine Drüse	**endocrine gland** *A gland that secrete hormones and other substances into the blood.*
Endokrinologie	**endocrinology** *The study of endocrine glands and hormones.*
Endolymphe	**endolymph** *The fluid collection the labyrinth of the ear.*
Endometritis	**endometritis** *Inflammation of the endometrium.*
Endometritis cervicis	**endocervicitis** *Inflammation of the mucosal lining of the cervix.*
Endometrium	**endometrium** *The mucous membrane lining of the uterus.*
Endomitriom	**endometrioma** *An isolated benign mass containing endometrial tissue.*
Endomitriose	**endometriosis** *Presence of uterine mucosal tissue in the pelvis in abnormal locations.*

Endoneurium	**endoneurium** *The tissue in a peripheral nerve that separates the individual nerve fibers.*
endoplasmatisches Retikulum	**endoplasmic reticulum** *A framework of tubules within the cytoplasm of eukaryotic cells.*
Endorgan	**end organ** *The encapsulated end of a sensory nerve.*
Endorphin	**endorphin** *Hormone secreted that activates the body's opiate receptors and acts as an analgesic.*
Endoskop	**endoscope** *A device used to view the interior of a hollow organ (sigmoidoscope, gastroscope)*
Endotheliom	**endothelioma** *A mass that propagates from the endothelium of blood vessels, lymphatics or serous cavities.*
endotracheal	**endotracheal** *Within the trachea.*
Endzeitpuntk	**end point** *The last stage of a process.*
Enkephalin	**enkephalin** *Peptide found in the brain that has similar effects as the endorphins.*
Enophthalmus	**enophthalmos** *Posterior displacement of the eyeball in the orbit.*
Enostose	**enostosis** *The abnormal bony growth inside a bone or on the cortex.*
Entasslungdatum	**discharge date** *The day a patient is released from the hospital.*
entbinden	**deliver, to** *To give birth.*
enteral	**enteric** *Referring to the intestines.*
enterale Ernährung	**enteral feeding** *Nutrition supplied via the alimentary canal.*
Enterektomie	**enterectomy** *Surgical resection of part of the intestine.*
Enteritis	**enteritis** *Inflammation of the intestines.*
Enterobiasis	**enterobiasis** *An infection caused by worms from the genus Enterobius.*
Enterokokke	**enterococcus** *A gram positive cocci that occurs naturally in the intestine but is pathogenic elsewhere in the body.*
Enteroptose	**enteroptosis** *Inferior displacement of the intestines in the abdomen.*
Enterotomie	**enterotomy** *A surgical opening of the intestines.*
Entfaltungsknisterm	**crackles or rales** *A crackling noised noted while auscultating the lungs.*
Entgiftung	**detoxification** *The process of removing toxins from the body.*
Enthaarungsmittel	**depilatory** *An agent used to remove hair.*
Entlastung	**relief** *Alleviation from pain or discomfort.*
Entmakungskrankheit	**demyelinating disease** *A condition characterized by the loss of myelin.*
entnerven	**denervate, to** *To remove nerve supply.*
Entspannungsmittel	**relaxant** *Term generally used to refer to a muscle relaxant.*
entsprechend	**according to**
Entzug	**withdrawal** *The action of being without drugs or alcohol.*
Entzündung	**inflammation** *Localized redness, excessive warmth and swelling.*
Entzündungshemmer	**anti-inflammatory agents** *Medications used to reduce inflammation.*
Enukleation	**enucleation** *Surgical removal of a globe.*
Enurese; Einnässen	**enuresis** *Involuntary urination.*
Enzephalitis	**encephalitis** *Inflammation of the brain.*
Enzephalocele	**encephalocele** *The protrusion of the brain through a defect in the skull.*
Enzephalographie	**encephalography** *Roentgenography of the brain.*
Enzephalomazie	**encephalomacia** *Abnormal softness of the brain.*
Enzephalomylitis	**encephalomyelitis** *Inflammation of the brain and spinal cord.*

Enzephalon	**encephalic** *Referring to the brain.*
Enzephalopathie	**encephalopathy** *Degeneration of cerebral function.*
Enzym; Ferment	**enzyme** *A compound that acts as a catalyst for reactions within cells as assists with digestion outside of cells.*
Eosinophiler	**eosinophil** *A cell with eosin stain used to designate a type of leukocyte that is elevated during allergic reactions.*
Eosinophilie	**eosinophilia** *An increased number of eosinophils in the blood.*
Ependym	**ependyma** *The glial lined covering of the cerebral ventricles and the central portion of the spinal cord.*
Ependymom	**ependymoma** *A tumor composed of cells that line the ventricles of the brain.*
Ephedrin	**ephedrine** *A chemical used to treat asthma because it expands bronchial passages and used to control spinal anesthesia associated shock because it constricts blood vessels.*
Epiblepharon	**epiblepharon** *A condition exhibited by the eyelashes pressing against the eyeball.*
Epidemie	**epidemic** *Ubiquitous development of an infectious disease.*
Epidemiologie	**epidemiology** *The study of the incidence, development and control of disease.*
Epidermis	**epidermis** *The skin cells overlying the dermis.*
Epidermophytie	**epidermophytosis** *A fungal skin infection caused by an organism from the genus Epidermophyton.*
Epididymitis	**epididymitis** *Inflammation of the duct that moves sperm from the testis to the vas deferens.*
Epididymoorchitis	**epididymo-orchitis** *Inflammation of the epididymis and the testis.*
epidural	**epidural** *The space around the dura of the spinal cord.*
Epiduralanästhesie	**epidural anesthesia** *Medication into this space produces analgesia for surgical procedures.*
Epiduralhämatom	**epidural hematoma** *Formation of a collection of blood outside the dural layer of the brain; usually caused by trauma.*
Epigastrium	**epigastrium** *The section of the abdomen that overlies the stomach.*
Epiglottis; Kehldeckel	**epiglottis** *Tissue at the base of the tongue that covers the trachea when one swallows.*
Epikard	**epicardium** *The serous membranous, innermost lining of the pericardium.*
Epikondylitis	**epicondylitis** *Inflammation of the epicondyle.*
Epikondylitis	**tennis elbow** *Inflammation at the lateral aspect of the epicondyle where the muscle and tendon join; lateral epicondylitis.*
Epikondylus	**epicondyle** *A protrusion at the distal end of the humerus.*
Epikranium	**epicranium** *The skin, fibrous layer (aponeurosis), and muscles lining the scalp.*
Epilation	**epilation** *Removal of hair and the roots.*
Epilepsie	**epilepsy** *A condition associated with abnormal brain activity and exhibited by sudden, recurrent convulsions, sensory disturbances and loss of consciousness.*
epileptiform	**epileptiform** *Being similar to epilepsy.*
Epileptischer Anfall	**epileptic seizure** *A convulsion related to abnormal brain activity (as opposed to being precipitated by hypoglycemia.)*
epileptogen	**epileptogenic** *That which induces seizures.*
Epinephrin	**epinephrine** *A hormone secreted by the adrenal gland.*

Epiphyse cerebri	**epiphysis cerebri** *A small structure situated on the mesencephalon between the two sections of the thalamus.*
Epiphysitis	**epiphysitis** *Inflammation of the end of a long bone that is separated from the shaft by a cartilaginous disc.*
Episiotomie; Dammschnitt	**episiotomy** *A surgical incision of the vagina used to aid childbirth.*
Episkleritis	**episcleritis** *Inflammation of the tissue lying above the sclera.*
Epispadie	**epispadias** *A congenital condition characterized by the urethral meatus being at the superior aspect of the penis*
Epistaxis; Nasenbluten	**epistaxis** *Bleeding emanating from the nose.*
Epithel	**epithelium** *The tissue lining the skin and the gastrointestinal tract that is derived from the embryonic ectoderm and endoderm..*
epithelial	**epithelial** *Referring to the epithelium.*
Epitheliom	**epithelioma** *A malignant tumor composed of epithelial cells.*
Epithelzylinder	**epithelial cast** *Debris found in the urine composed of columnar renal epithelium.*
Epitrochlea	**epitrochlea** *The medial condyle of the humerus.*
Erbrechen	**emesis** *Vomiting.*
Erbrechen	**vomit** *The gastric contents that are expelled through the mouth.*
erbrechen	**vomit, to** *To expel gastric contents out the mouth.*
Erdbeerzunge	**strawberry tongue** *A characteristic discoloration of the tongue seen in an early phase of scarlet fever.*
Erfrierung; Frostbeule	**frostbite** *Local tissue destruction after exposure to cold.*
Ergebniskrankheit	**disease outcome** *The response obtained from treatment.*
Ergometer	**ergometer** *A device that measures energy expenditure.*
Ergonomie	**ergonomics** *The study of workplace design that focuses on reducing work-related injuries.*
Ergosterin	**ergosterol** *A compound converted to vitamin D2 upon exposure to ultraviolet light.*
Erguss	**effusion** *The accumulation of fluid in a body cavity.*
Erhaltungsdosis	**dose, maintenance** *The chronic dose given after the initial bolus.*
Erhaltungtherapie	**maintenance therapy** *Continuing a form of treatment long-term.*
erhältlich	**available** *Attainable, obtainable.*
Erhältlichkeit	**availability** *A person or thing that is available.*
erhöhen	**raise, to** *To lift or bring up.*
Erinnerung	**recollection** *Memory.*
Erkältung	**cold** *Viral upper respiratory tract infection.*
erleiden; ertragen	**bear, to** *To endure or resist.*
Ermüdung	**fatigue** *Tiredness and exhaustion.*
Ernährung	**nutrition** *The process of supplying food needed for growth.*
Ernährungszustand	**nutritional status** *The relative state of one's nutrition.*
Ernährungverhalten	**feeding behavior** *How a child is tolerating breast or cup feeding.*
ernst	**severe** *Intense or very great.*
Erosion	**erosion** *The gradual destruction of surface tissue.*
erreichen	**achieve, to** *To complete something one was striving for.*
Ersatz; Prothese (Oberschenkelprothese) [Unterschenkelprothese]	**prosthesis** *An artificial body part. (above the knee) [below the knee]*
Erste Hilfe	**first aid** *The intial treatment after an injury.*

ersticken	**choke, to** *To retch, cough or fight for breath.*
Erstickung	**suffocation** *To die from a lack of air or inability to breathe.*
Ertrinken	**drowning** *The process of dying from submerging in and inhaling water.*
Eruktation	**eructation** *Belch or burp.*
Erwachen	**awakening** *The state of being conscious.*
erwähnen	**mention, to** *Refer to or allude to.*
Erweiterung	**dilatation** *The process of becoming wider or larger.*
erworbenes Immunmangelsyndrom (AIDS)	**Acquired Immunodeficiency Syndrome (AIDS)** *Presence of an AIDS defining illness or having a CD4 of less than 200/mm3.*
erworbenes Immunmangelsyndrom (AIDS)	**AIDS** *Acquired Immunodeficiency Syndrome*
Erysipel	**erysipelas** *An acute infection caused by Streptococcus pyogenes that causes fever along with swelling and inflammation. The infection frequently effects the face or one leg.*
Erythema exsudativum multiforme	**erythema mutliforme** *A skin condition exhibited by purpuric lesions and bullae usually on the distal parts of extremities but can affect the face and trunk.*
Erythema nodosum	**erythema nodosum** *The presence of red or purple nodules on the pretibial area.*
Erythroblast	**erythroblast** *A nucleus containing immature erythrocyte.*
Erythroblastose fetalis	**erythroblastosis fetalis** *A hemolytic disease of the newborn.*
Erythropoese	**erythropoiesis** *The production of red blood cells.*
Erythrozyanose	**erythrocyanosis** *A condition exhibited by purple patches with asymmetric swelling, pruritis and burning.*
Erythrozyt	**erythrocyte** *Called a red blood cell, it transports oxygen and carbon dioxide to and from the tissues.*
Erythrozytopenie	**erythrocytopenia** *Low level of erythrocytes in the blood stream.*
Erythrozytose	**erythrocytosis** *A higher than normal level of erythrocytes in the blood stream.*
Erziehung	**education** *Instruction or guidance.*
Eserin; Physostigmin	**eserine** *Physostigmine.*
Esotropie; Strabismus convergens; Einwärtsschielen	**esotropia** *Medial deviation of the eyes at primary gaze.*
Ess-Sucht	**adephagia** *Insatiable hunger.*
essen	**eat, to** *To consume food.*
Esslöffel; Eßlöffel	**tablespoon** *An eating utensil that holds 15milliliters of fluid.*
Eßstörung	**eating disorder** *General term for pathologic eating habits.*
Estrogen; Östrogen	**estrogen** *A hormone involved with developing and maintaining female sexual characteristics.*
ethanol	**ethanol** *Synonym for ethyl alcohol.*
Eunuch	**eunuch** *A man who has been castrated.*
Eustachio Röhre	**pharyngotympanic tube** *Synonym for eustachian tube.*
Euthanasie	**euthanasia** *Killing someone painlessly who is thought to have a terminal condition.*
Evakuierung	**evacuation** *The emptying of an organ of fluids or gas.*
Eventration	**eventration** *Protrusion of the intestines from the abdomen.*
Eversion	**eversion** *To turn outward.*
Eviszeration	**evisceration** *The removal of bowels from the body.*

evoziertes Potential	**evoked potential** *Electrical impulses that can be noted after stimulation of sensory organs.*
Evulsion	**evulsion** *Forcible extraction.*
Exanthem	**exanthema** *A rash that accompanies a disease or fever.*
Exartikulation	**disarticulation** *The separation or amputation of a joint.*
Exazerbation	**exacerbation** *Worsening of an existing problem.*
Exenteration	**exenteration** *Complete surgical removal of an organ.*
Exhumierung	**exhumation** *The process of removing a dead body from a grave.*
Exkoriation; Abschürfung	**excoriation** *Superficial loss of skin.*
Exkrement	**excrement** *Feces.*
Exkrete	**excreta** *Fecal material.*
exogen	**exogenous** *Referring to external factors.*
Exomphalos; Nabelschnurvorfall	**exomphalos** *Umbilical hernia.*
Exostose	**exostosis** *A bony prominence growing from the surface of a bone.*
Exotoxin	**exotoxin** *A toxin released from a living cell.*
Exotropie Strabismus externus; Auswärtsschielen	**exotropia** *A type of strabismus that is characterized by the eyes turned outward.*
Expansion	**expansion** *Enlargement or increase in size.*
Expektorans	**expectorant** *A substance that promotes the secretion of sputum.*
Expektoration	**expectoration** *The presence of sputum that has been coughed out.*
expiratorische	**expiratory** *Referring to exhalation of air from the lungs.*
expiratorisches Reservevolumen	**expiratory reserve volume** *Amount of air left in the lung after a maximal exhalation, in liters.*
Expulsion; Austreibung	**expulsion** *Evacuation or elimination.*
Exstirpationsbiopsie	**excisional biopsy** *Surgical removal of tissue for pathologic examination.*
Extensor; Streckmuskel	**extensor** *Referring to the extension of an extremity or part of an extremity.*
extrakapsulär	**extracapsular** *Situated outside a capsule.*
Extrakt	**extract** *A substance in a concentrated form.*
extrapyramidales System	**extrapyramidal tract** *Motor nerves that are not part of the pyramidal tract.*
Extrasystole	**extrasystole** *Either a premature atrial or ventricular contraction.*
extrazellulär	**extracellular** *Outside the cell.*
Extremität	**extremity** *Refers to one arm or one leg.*
Extremität	**limb** *An extremity or branch.*
extrinsisch	**extrinsic** *Coming from outside or external sources.*
Extubation; Extubieren	**extubation** *The removal of a tube that was in a body orifice.*
Exudat	**exudate** *The fluid, cells, and debris found in the tissues or a cavity (like pleural space) during inflammation.*
Exzeß	**excess** *Surplus or overabundance.*
Facette	**facet** *A small flat surface of a bone.*
Facies	**facies** *A facial expression that is typical for a particular disease.*
falciform	**falciform** *Referring to something that is curved. The falciform ligament attaches the liver to the diaphragm.*
falciparum Malaria	**cerebral malaria** *A severe form of malaria manifested by seizures and a decreased level of consciousness.*

Fallfuß	**drop foot** *The symptom in a person with a nerve injury causing impaired ankle dorsiflexion.*
Fallfuß	**foot drop** *Caused by palsy of the nerve controlling foot dorsiflexion.*
Fallhand; Kusshand	**wrist drop** *The inability to hyperextend the wrist due to radial nerve injury.*
Fallotsche Tetralogie	**Fallot, tetrology of** *Congenital cardiac defects including ventricular septal defect, pulmonic valve stenosis or infundibular stenosis, and dextroposition of the aorta.*
Falte; Plica	**plica** *A fold, as in a fold in the peritoneum.*
familiär	**familial** *Referring to the family*
Familie	**family**
Familienanamnese	**family history** *A review of past medical history of related persons.*
Familienplanung	**family planning** *Birth control.*
Fanconi-Syndrom	**Fanconi's syndrome** *An idiopathic refractory anemia exhibited by pancytopenia, bone marrow hypoplasia and congenital anomalies.*
Farardisation	**faradism** *The gradual increasing and decreasing of the amplitude of electricity.*
Farbenblindheit	**color blindness** *The inability to distinguish colors.*
Farmerlunge	**farmer's lung** *Coined because farmers are susceptible to this disease by inhaling fungi from hay; also called Aspergillosis.*
Fasciitis	**fasciitis** *Inflammation of a fascia.*
Faserknorpelentzündung	**fibrochondritis** *The inflammation of a structure composed of cartilage and fibrous tissue.*
Faszie	**fascia** *The fibrous sheath enclosing a muscle or organ.*
Faszikel	**fascicle** *A bundle of nerve or muscle fibers.*
Faszikulation; faszikuläre Zuckung	**fasciculation** *Involuntary contraction of muscle fibers.*
Fasziotomie	**fasciotomy** *Incision into a fascia.*
Faust	**fist** *When a person has their fingers clenched tightly to the palm.*
Favus	**favus** *Tinea capitis caused by Trichopyton schoenleini.*
Fazialislähmung	**facial paralysis** *Lack of movement or sensation in the distribution of the facial nerve.*
Färbeindex	**color chart** *A card used to check for color blindness.*
Fäzes	**feces** *Excrement.*
febril	**febrile** *Presence of an supraphysiologic temperature.*
Febris rheumatica	**rheumatic fever** *A febrile streptococcal disease causing pain and joint swelling.*
Fehlbehandlung	**malpractice** *Negligent professional activity.*
Fehleistung	**parapraxis** *1. Unable to perform purposeful movements. 1. Irrational behavior.*
Fehler	**error** *Mistake or inaccuracy.*
Fehlernährung; Mangelernährung; Malnutrition	**malnutrition** *Lack of appropriate nutrition.*
Fehlgebrut; Spontanabort	**miscarriage** *Spontaneous abortion.*
Fehlstellung	**malunion** *The union of a fracture in a faulty position.*
Feigwarze	**genital wart** *The common term for Condylomata acuminata.*
Felty-Syndrom	**Felty syndrome** *Rheumatoid arthritis with leukopenia and splenomegaly.*

207

femoral Dreieck	**femoral triangle** *An area that is bordered by the sartorius muscle, the adductor longus muscle and the inguinal ligament.*
Fensterung	**fenestration** *Usually referring to a surgical window.*
fernab von	**away from** *Separated from.*
Fernmessung; Telemetrie	**telemetry** *Use of radio signals to transmit patient data. The most common form is for electrocardiography in a patient who is ambulatory.*
Fersensporn	**calcaneal spur** *A bony protrusion on the calcaneus.*
fest	**firm** *Hard or unyielding.*
festhalten	**adherence** *To stick to something figuratively or literally.*
feststellen	**ascertain, to** *Synonym of "to determine".*
fetal	**fetal** *Referring to the fetus.*
Fetal distress	**fetal distress** *Term used to describe an abnormal heart rate or rhythm in a fetus indicating the need for urgent childbirth.*
Fetischismus	**fetichism** *The glorification of an inanimate object.*
Fett	**fat** *A greasy or oiling substance naturally occurring in the body.*
Fettembolie	**fat embolism** *A deposit of fat that obstructs a vessel.*
fettig	**fatty** *Greasy or oily.*
Fettleibigkeit	**obesity** *Having a body mass index over 30kilograms/meters squared.*
fettreduzierte Lebensmittel	**low-fat foods** *Nutrients with lower than normal fat content.*
Fettsäure	**fatty acid** *A carboxylic acid occurring as a an ester in fats and oils.*
feucht	**moist** *Damp or humid.*
feucht	**wet** *Covered in moisture.*
Feuermal	**port-wine mark** *Also called nevus flammeus, it is a vascular anomaly characterized by purplish skin discoloration.*
Fibrin	**fibrin** *An insoluble protein formed when fibrinogen is acted upon by thrombin.*
Fibroadenom	**fibroadenoma** *A benign breast mass composed of fibrous and glandular tissue.*
Fibroblast	**fibroblast** *A collagen producing cell in connective tissue.*
Fibroelastose	**fibroelastosis** *The abnormal increase in growth of fibrous and elastic tissue.*
Fibroid	**fibroid** *A benign mass, typically uterine, composed of fibrous and muscle tissue.*
Fibromyom	**fibromyoma** *A mass containing fibrous and muscle tissue.*
Fibrosarkom	**fibrosarcoma** *A sarcoma composed primarily of malignant fibroblasts.*
Fibrose	**fibrosis** *Connective tissue that is scarred and thickened after injury.*
Fibrositis	**fibrositis** *Fibrous connective tissue that is inflamed.*
Fibula; Wadenbein	**fibula** *The smaller of two bones in the lower leg.*
Fieber	**fever** *A temperature above the normal range.*
Fieber	**pyrexia** *Fever.*
Filarie	**filaria** *A parasitic nematode worm that is transmitted by flies and mosquitos causing filariasis.*
filiform; fadenförmig	**filiform** *Threadlike.*
Filum terminale	**filum terminale** *The thin structure at the end of the conus medullaris which connects the spinal cord with the coccyx.*

208

Filzlaus	**crab louse** *Phthirus pubis is formal name for a louse that infests pubic hair and causes intense itching.*
Fimbrie	**fimbria** *A slender projection at the end of the fallopian tube near the ovary.*
Finger	**finger** *Any of the five digits on the hand.*
Finger-Nasenversuch	**finger nose test** *A test for dysmetria in which a person reaches out to touch their own nose with an extended finger with their eyes closed.*
Finger; Zahl	**digit** *Finger.*
fingeragnosie	**finger agnosia** *The inability to distinguish which finger is being touched.*
Fingerknacken	**crack one's knuckles** *Moving the fingers side to side or with flexion in such a manner to cause a popping or crackling sound.*
Fingerknöchel	**knuckle** *A metacarpophalagngeal joint or a finger joint when the fist is closed.*
Fingernagel	**fingernail** *Thin horny plate over the dorsal aspect of the end of finger.*
Fingernägelbeißen; Nägelkauen; Onychophagie	**nail biting** *A habit of chewing on one's fingernails.*
Fingerspitze	**fingertip** *Distal aspect of a finger.*
Fingerstichverrichtung	**fingerstick device** *A device used to project a lancet into the skin so a drop of blood can be obtained for analysis.*
Finkelstein-Reaktion	**Finkelstein test** *Pain elicited with thumb flexion and wrist flexion is indicitive of De Quervain tenosynovitis.*
Fisch	**fish** *A cold-blooded vertebrate with gills and fins.*
Fissur; Spalt	**fissure** *A general term for a cleft or deep groove. An anal fissure, for example, is a small ulcer adjacent to the anus.*
Fissura pupendi	**vulval cleft** *The area between the labia majora where the vagina and urethra rest.*
Fistel	**fistula** *An abnormal communication between two organs or an organ and the skin, as in rectovaginal fistula.*
Fixierung; Bindung	**fixation** *1. An obsessive interest. 2. The securing of a body part.*
flach Nasenrücken	**low nasal bridge** *A flattening of the top part of the nose.*
flache; eben	**flat** *Level or even; without bulges.*
Flagellation	**flagellation** *1. The protrusion found on flagella. 2. Massage administered by tapping a body part with fingers.*
Flammenphotometer	**flame photometer** *A device used to measure the intensity of light.*
Flasche	**bottle** *A container used for the storage of liquids.*
Flatterbrust	**flail chest** *The term used when one has multiple rib fractures causing a segment of the chest wall to move incongruently with the rest of the chest wall.*
Flattern	**flutter** *Used to describe a cardiac rhythm disturbance, as in atrial flutter.*
Flatulenz; Blähung	**flatulence** *The gas expulsed from the anus.*
Flatulenz; Blähung	**flatus** *Term for air that is expelled from the anus.*
Fläschchen	**vial** *A small cylindrical container typically used to hold liquid medicine.*
Fleck	**macula** *1. The area of the eye of greatest visual acuity that surrounds the fovea. 2. A small flat discoloration of the skin (synonym for macule).*
Fleckfieber	**mite fever** *Synonym of typhus fever.*

	English
Fleckfieber	**typhus fever** *A rickettsiae infection exhibited by rash, fever, headache and myalgia.*
Fleisch	**flesh** *The tissue between the skin and bones.*
fleischig	**carneous** *Synonym of fleshy.*
Flexor; Beuger	**flexor** *A muscle that bends an extremity or part of an extremity.*
Flexur; Biegung	**flexure** *The action of bending.*
Fließgleichgewicht	**steady state** *In equilibrium.*
Flimmern	**fibrillation** *Uncoordinated, ineffective contraction as in atrial fibrillation.*
Floh	**flea** *A small wingless insect that feeds on blood of mammals.*
flott	**brisk** *Rapid or fast.*
fluktuierend	**floating** *Bouyant or suspended.*
Fluor	**fluorine** *A chemical that causes severe burns if exposed to the skin.*
Fluoreszein	**fluoresceine** *A fluorane dye used to check for corneal ulcers.*
Fluoreszenz-Treponema-pallidum-Antikörper-Absorptions-Test	**FTA test** *Fluorescent treponemal antibody test for syphilis.*
Fluoreszenztest	**fluorescent antibody test (FTA test)**
Fluorierung	**fluoridation** *The addition of fluorine to something.*
Fluß; Strom	**flow** *Movment in a continuous stream.*
Flüssigkeitslunge	**fluid intake** *The amount of oral consumption plus the amount of intravenous fluids administered.*
Flüsterprobe	**whisper test** *The examiner whispers into one ear while blocking the other ear to see if the patient can hear in the ear whispered into.*
Foetor	**fetor** *A foul odor.*
Folat; Folsäure	**folic acid** *Also called pteroylglutamic acid; a deficiency can cause megaloblastic anemia.*
Foley Urethralsonde	**Foley catheter** *A drainage tube placed in the urinary bladder via the urethra.*
Folgekrankheit (Spätkomplikation)	**sequela** *A medical problem related to an initial injury or disease.(late sequelae)*
Follikelreifungshormon	**follicle stimulating hormone (FSH)** *An anterior pituitary gland hormone responsible for production of sperm or ova.*
follikulär	**follicular** *Referring to a small secretory gland.*
Fontanelle	**fontanelle or fontanel** *The space between the bones in the skull that are separate at birth.*
Foramen magnum	**foramen magnum** *The hole in the skull that the spinal cord passes through.*
Foramen nutricium	**nutrient foramen** *A conduit for passage of nutrient vessels in the marrow of bone.*
Foramen ovale	**foramen ovale** *A hole in the atrial septal wall in a fetus.*
Foramen; Loch	**foramen** *An opening in a bone.*
forciertes Vitalkapazität	**forced vital capacity** *Vital capacity measured as the patient is exhaling as rapidly as possible.*
forensisch	**forensic** *Referring to the scientific method of studying crime.*
fortgeleiteter Schmerz	**referred pain** *Pain felt in an area distinct from the original source.*
fortgeschrittenem Stadium	**advanced stage** *A late period of a disease.*
fortlaufend Sutur	**running suture** *A method of sewing a wound in which there is a knot at each end and continuous otherwise.*

210

fortschreitend	**progressive** *Developing gradually.*
Fovea	**fovea** *The area on the retina where the visual acuity is optimal.*
Foville-Syndrom	**Foville's syndrome** *Caused by a lesion within the pons, there is ipsilateral facial and abducens nerve paralysis and contralateral hemiplegia.*
Fötus	**fetus** *Medical term for the infant prior to birth.*
Frakturfehlstellung	**malalignment (dental)** *Displacement of the teeth from their normal position.*
Frambösie	**framboesia; yaws** *An endemic tropical disease caused by Treponema pertenue.*
Frambösie	**yaws** *A tropical disease characterized by ulcers on the extremities, caused by Treponema pertenue.*
frei	**free** *Lacking or absent.*
frei von	**free from** *Without or clear of.*
Freiwillige	**volunteer** *A person who performs work without expecting compensation.*
Fremitus	**fremitus** *A vibration that is appreciated with palpation.*
Fremkörper	**foreign bodies** *Term used to describe objects found in a body orifice that are not part of the body.*
Frequenz; Häufigkeit	**frequency** *Rate of occurrence.*
Freßreflex	**fress reflex** *Chewing and sucking movements elicted by stimulation of the face and lips.*
Friesel	**prickly heat** *A rash with small vesicles that is pruritic and associated with a warm moist environment.*
frontal	**frontal** *Referring to the anterior aspect, as in frontal lobe.*
Fruchtbarkeit	**fecundity** *The capability of producing offspring quickly and frequently.*
Fruchtbarkeit	**fertility** *The ability of a person to contribute to contraception.*
Fruchtwasser	**amniotic fluid** *The fluid surrounding the fetus.*
Fruktosurie	**fructosuria** *Presence of fructose in the urine.*
Frühgeborenes	**infant, pre-term** *A neonate born prior to normal gestation.*
frühreif; vorzeitig	**premature** *Occurring earlier than expected.*
fulminante	**fulminant** *Sudden and severe.*
Fundus gastrikus	**fundus of the stomach** *Referring to the part of the stomach above the cardiac notch.*
Fungizid	**fungicide** *An agent that destroys fungus.*
Funiculus; kleiner Strang	**funiculus of the spinal cord** *The white matter of the spinal cord that is further defined by location.*
Funikulitis	**funiculitis** *Inflammation of the funiculi.*
Funktion	**function** *An activity natural to a person or thing.*
Funktionsverlust	**loss of function** *Inability to complete routine activities.*
Furcht	**fear** *Fright or trepidation.*
Furunkel	**furuncle** *A painful erythematous nodule with a central core.*
Furunkulose	**furunculosis** *The presence of multiple furuncles.*
furzen	**fart, to** *Slang term for releasing flatus.*
fusionieren	**amalgamate,to** *To make an amalgam by dissolving a metal in mercury.*
fühlbar	**sensible** *When referring to a choice, chosen with wisdom.*

211

fühlbare Kindsbewegung	**quickening** *Signs of life noted by a mother as the fetus moves.*
Fünfte Krankheit; Ringelrötein	**Fifth disease** *Erythema infectiosum is a viral disease caused by parovirus B19.*
Fuß	**foot** *The lower extremity distal to the ankle.*
Fußklonus	**ankle clonus** *An abnormal response exhibited by alternating plantar- and dorsiflexion noted after the examiner rapidly dorsiflexes the foot.*
Fußpfleger	**chiropodist** *A doctor trained in the treatment of feet.*
Fußpilz	**athlete's foot** *Common term for tinea pedis.*
Fußsohle	**sole of foot** *Common term for plantar aspect of the foot.*
Fußwurzel; Lidknorpel; Lidplatte	**tarsus** *The group of seven bones of the ankle or foot (three cuneiform bones, talus, calcaneus, navicular, cuboid bones).*
Galaktorrhö	**galactorrhea** *Excessive production of milk.*
Galaktosämie	**galactosemie** *1. Galactose in the blood. 2. A congenital condition exhibited by impaired carbohydrate metabolism.*
Galaktose	**galactose** *A sugar that is a constituent of lactose.*
Galaktozele	**galactocele** *A milk-filled cyst in the mammary gland.*
Galle	**bile** *An alkaline fluid secreted by the liver to aid digestion.*
Gallenblase	**gallbladder** *The organ adjacent to the liver that stores bile and secretes it into the duodenum.*
Gallenfarbstoff	**bile pigments** *The golden brown or green-yellow color associated with bile.*
Gallensäuren	**bile salts** *Normally occurring salts of bile acids.*
Gallenstein	**gallstone** *Calculus produced in the bile duct or gallbladder.*
Gallenwege	**bile ducts** *The structures that are conduits for passage of bile from the liver and gallbladder to the duodenum.*
gallig; biliös	**bilious** *Something that contains bile.*
Galopprhythmus	**cantering rhythm** *Gallop rhythm.*
Galopprhythmus	**gallop** *An abnormal heart sound.*
Galvanismus	**galvanism** *The use of electric currents for medical treatment.*
Galvanmeter	**galvanometer** *A device used to measure small electric currents.*
Gamet	**gamete** *A germ cell that is able to unite with another germ cell of the opposite gender to form a zygote.*
Gamma-Strahl	**gamma ray** *A type of electromagnetic radiation.*
Gammaglobulin	**gamma globulin** *A blood serum protein with little electrophoretic mobility.*
Gamstorp Syndrom	**hypokalemic periodic paralysis** *An inherited disorder that leads to muscle weakness related to a low serum potassium level.*
Gang	**meatus** *Opening to the body, such as urethral meatus.*
Gang; Durchgang	**duct** *Hollow tubular tissue used to carry fluid from a secretory organ.*
Ganglion stellatum	**stellate ganglion** *Formed by the seventh cervical, eighth cervical and first thoracic ganglia.*
Ganglionektomie	**ganglionectomy** *The removal of a benign swelling on a tendon sheath.*
Gangrän	**gangrene** *Tissue death from either impaired blood flow or an infection.*
gangränöse Stomatitis	**cancrum oris** *Gangrenous stomatitis.*
Gasbrand	**gas gangrene** *A life and limb threatening disorder caused associated with tissue death and caused by an anaerobic bacterium in the genus of Clostridium.*
Gastrektomie	**gastrectomy** *Complete or partial surgical resection of the stomach.*

Gastrin	**gastrin** *Hormones that stimulates gastric secretions.*
gastrisch	**gastric** *Referring to the stomach.*
gastroduodenales Ulkus	**gastroduodenal ulcer** *A lesion in the mucosal lining of the stomach or duodenum.*
Gastroenteritis	**gastroenteritis** *A bacterial or viral infection that leads to vomiting and diarrhea.*
Gastroenterostomie	**gastroenterostomy** *A surgical opening in the stomach or intestine.*
Gastrointestinaltrakt	**gastrointestinal tract** *The alimentary canal from the distal esophagus to the cecum.*
Gastrojejunostomie	**gastrojejunostomy** *A surgical procedure that directly connects the stomach to the jejunum.*
Gastrokolischreflex	**gastrocolic reflex** *Peristalsis of the colon produced by food entering the stomach.*
gastroösophagealer Reflux	**GERD gastroesophageal reflux disease** *A condition characterized by gastric contents being regurgitated into the esophagus or mouth.*
Gastropexie	**gastropexy** *Securing the stomach to the abdominal wall.*
Gastroskopie; Magenspiegelung	**gastroscopy** *Use of an endoscope to directly visualize the stomach.*
Gastrostomie	**gastrostomy** *A surgical creation of an opening in the stomach.*
Gaumen	**palate** *The roof of the mouth.*
Gaumensegel	**velum** *A veil-like part or covering of the palate; soft palate; Velum palatinum.*
Gaze; Verbandmull	**gauze** *A fabric used for dressing changes.*
Gähnen	**yawn** *Opening one's mouth and inhaling deeply due to sleepiness/ boredom*
Gänsehaut	**goose bumps** *Cutis anserina.*
gebären	**bear, to** *To give birth to a child.*
Gebärmutterhals	**cervix uteri** *The narrow end of the uterus.*
Gebärmuttersenkung	**prolapse of the uterus** *Eversion of the uterus through the vagina.*
Gebärmuttersenkung	**uterine prolapse** *Protrusion of the uterus out the vagina.*
gebläht Harnblase	**distended bladder** *Urinary bladder filled beyond the normal capacity.*
gebogen Fingernagel	**parrot-beak nail** *A curved fingernail.*
geboren werden	**born** *Being present as a result of birth.*
Geburt	**birth** *The process of bearing offspring from the uterus.*
Geburt	**childbirth** *Parturition; the process of labor and delivery of an infant.*
Geburt; Partus	**parturition** *The process of giving birth.*
Geburtenhäufigkeit	**birth rate** *The number of live births per 1000 of a given population per year.*
Geburtenkontrolle; Schwangerschaftsverhütung	**birth control** *Any method of limiting contraception.*
Geburtsdatum	**date of birth**
Geburtsfehler	**birth defect** *A congenital anomaly.*
Geburtshelfer	**obstetrician** *A physician who specializes in the management of pregnancy, labor and the peuperium.*
Geburtshilfe	**midwifery** *The occupation of assisting in childbirth.*
geburtshilflich	**obstetric** *Referring to The management of pregnancy, labor and the peuperium.*
Geburtsname	**maiden name** *The surname a woman uses prior to being married.*
Geburtswehen	**labor pains** *The intermittent pain associated with uterine contractions.*

Gedankenflucht	**flight of ideas** *Streams of unrelated ideas noted in a manic phase.*
Gedächtnis	**memory** *Ability to remember.*
geeignet	**convenient** *Opportune or well-timed.*
Geflüster	**whisper** *Speech in a volume that is barely discernible.*
geflüstert Pektoriloquie	**whispered pectoriloquy** *The sound heard through the stethescope when listening to a person's lungs. The sound resonates as it would when listening over a bronchus if there is an area of consolidation.*
gefroren	**frozen** *Past participle of to freeze. Freeze: turn a liquid into a solid.*
gefühllos	**insensible** *Unable to perceive a stimulus.*
Gefühlloskinn-Syndrom	**numb chin syndrome.** *Generally associated with metastatic breast or prostate cancer, it is characterized by unilateral sensory loss of the chin and lower lip.*
Gegenanzeige	**contraindication** *A situation in which two elements are inconsistent.*
gegensätlich	**contradictory** *Two elements that are inconsistent.*
Gegrunze	**grunting** *A low guttural sound used to describe a person with profound respiratory difficulty.*
gehemmt	**obstructed** *To be blocked or halted.*
Gehen	**ambulation** *A walk.*
Gehgestell	**walker** *A metal frame used to facilitate walking.*
Gehirn; Hirn	**brain** *A common term for cerebrum.*
Gehirnprolaps	**brainstem herniation** *Movement of the brainstem into the incisura because of increased intracranial pressure.*
Gehör; Hören	**hearing** *Auditory perception.*
Gehörschärfe 2. Schärfe	**acuity** *1. Relating to accuracy of hearing, as in hearing acuity. 2. Severity of illness as in, "What is the patient's acuity?"*
Gehverband	**walking cast** *A cast used for simple fractures of the lower leg.*
Geißel; Flimmer	**flagellum** *A slender appendage that allows protozoa to swim.*
geisteskrank	**insane** *A term not used in formal medical evaluations that when used by a layperson means a serious mental illness.*
Geisteskrankheit	**insanity** *Referring to a serious mental illness.*
Geisteskrankheit; Wahnsinn	**madness** *Common term for insanity.*
Gel	**gel** *A jellylike substance.*
gelb	**yellow** *A color between green and orange in the spectrum*
Gelbfieber	**yellow fever** *A viral, hemorrhagic fever transmitted by mosquitos.*
Gelbkörper des Eierstocks	**corpus luteum** *A structure that is discharged from an ovary; it degenerates if it is not impregnated.*
Gelbkörperphase; Progesteron	**progesterone** *A steroid hormone that prepares the uterus for pregnancy.*
Geldrollenbildung	**nummulation** *Formed as round, flat discs.*
Gelenk; Articulatio	**joint** *Articulation of two adjacent bones.*
Gelenkschmerz	**arthralgia** *Joint pain.*
Gelenplastik	**arthroplasty** *Plastic surgery involving a joint.*
Gemeindeschwester	**nurse practitioner** *A person with advanced training capable of acting as a patient's primary care provider.*
gemeinsam	**common** *That which is usual.*
Gemütsbewegung	**emotion** *An intense feeling.*
Gemütskrankheit	**affective disorders** *Manic-depressive psychosis.*
Gen	**gene** *A unit of heredity that is passed on from parent to child.*

214

genabelt	**umbilicated** *Referring to depressed areas that resemble the umbilicus.*
generell; allgemein	**general** *Common or expected.*
genetische	**genetic** *Referring to genes or heredity.*
genetische Beratend	**genetic counseling** *A discussion of the concerns related to genetic testing.*
Genikulatumneuralgie	**geniculate neuralgia** *Severe intermittent pain in the external ear and deep in the ear.*
genital Unklarheit	**genital ambiguity** *A disorder of sexual development in which the genitalia are not sufficiently developed to tell clearly if the person is male or female.*
Genom	**genome** *A full set of genetic information for an organism.*
Gentianaviolett	**gentian violet** *An antiseptic derived from rosaniline.*
Genu valgum	**knock knees** *Common term for genu valgum.*
Genu valgum; X-Bein	**genu valgum** *A condition exhibited by the knees turning inward, commonly referred to as knock-knee.*
Genu varum; O-Bein	**genu varum** *A condition exhibited by the knees turning outward, commonly referred to as bowleg.*
gerader Bauchmuskel	**rectus abdominis muscle** *The pair of long, flat muscles that connect the sternum with the pubis.*
Gerät; Ausstattung	**equipment** *Apparatus or instrument.*
Geräusch	**murmur** *An abnormal heart sound heard with a stethoscope.*
Geräusch carotis	**carotid bruit** *An abnormal noise heard over the carotid artery that may be a sign of stenosis or aortic valvular disease.*
Gerhirn entfernen	**decerebrate** *The removal of the brain.*
Geriatrie	**geriatrics** *The study of the health of old people.*
gering	**slight** *Minor or small.*
Gerontologie	**gerontology** *The study of old persons.*
Gerstenkorn	**hordeolum** *Inflammation of the sebaceous gland of the eye.*
Gerstmannsyndrom	**Gerstmann syndrome** *Finger agnosia, agraphia and acalculia caused by a lesion between the occipital region and angular gyrus.*
Geruch; Duft	**odor** *A smell that is given off someone or something.*
Gerücht	**bruit** *An abnormal sound heard through a stethoscope indicating turbulent blood flow.*
Gesäß	**buttocks** *The bilateral region covering the gluteal muscles.*
Gesäßmuskel; Glutealmuskel	**gluteal or gluteus muscle** *A paired set of three muscles, the gluteus maximus, medius and minimus, that all have origins in the ilium and insertions in the femur. (buttocks)*
Geschlecht	**sex** *Gender.*
Geschlechtskrankheit	**sexually transmitted disease (STD)** *A condition one obtains from another during sexual relations.*
Geschlechtskrankheit	**venereal disease** *A condition transmitted via sexual intercourse.*
Geschlechtsorgane; Genitalien	**genitalia** *Genitals.*
Geschlechtsverkehr	**sexual intercourse** *The act of copulation.*
geschlossene	**closed**
geschlossene Fraktur	**fracture, closed** *A broken bone where there is no break in the skin.*
geschlossene Reposition	**closed reduction** *The realignment of a fracture without use of surgery.*
Geschmack	**taste** *Sensation of flavor percieved in one's mouth.*
geschmacklich	**gustatory** *Referring to sense of taste.*

geschmacklich Agnosie	**gustatory agnosia** *The loss of the sense of taste.*
Geschwister	**siblings** *Brothers or sisters.*
geschwollen Bauch	**swollen (distended) abdomen**
Geschwür; Ulkus (Zwölffingerdarmgeschwür)	**ulcer** *A concave wound caused by a break in the integrity of skin or mucous membrane. (duodenal ulcer)*
Gesicht	**face** *Anterior aspect of the head from the forehead to the chin.*
Gesichtslage	**face presentation** *Referring to the part of the body coming out of the cervix first during childbirth.*
Gesichtslähmung	**Bell's palsy** *Unilateral facial paralysis related to dysfunction of the seventh cranial nerve.*
Gesichtsrötung	**flushing** *Transient erythema due to heat, stress or disease.*
gesprenkelt	**mottled** *An irregular arrangement of patches of color.*
gestielt	**pediculate** *Referring to pedicle.*
gesund	**healthy** *In good health.*
Gesundheit	**health** *The state of being free of illness.*
gewährleisten	**ensure, to** *To make certain of.*
Gewebe	**tissue** *Any of the distinct materials people are made of.*
Gewinn; Zunahme	**gait** *The way one walks.*
Gewohnheit; Angewohnheit	**habit** *A custom or inclination.*
Gewölbe	**fornix** *A vaulted structure.*
Giardiasis	**giardiasis** *A flagellate protozoa, Giardia lamblia, that causes diarrhea.*
Gibbus	**hunchback** *Synonym of kyphosis.*
Gicht	**gout** *Monosodium urate crystal deposition disease.*
Giemen	**rhonchus** *A coarse, dry sound heard on auscultation of the lungs.*
Gift	**poison** *A substance that causes illness or death.*
Gift	**venom** *A term used to describe the toxin injected via a bite or sting.*
gingival	**gingival** *Referring to the gums.*
Gingivitis; Zahnfleischentzündung	**gingivitis** *Inflammation of the gums.*
Ginglymus;Scharniergelenk	**ginglymus** *A joint that allows movement in one direction only.*
Gips; Abdruck	**cast; plaster cast** *Use of plaster of paris to immobilize an extremity.*
Gipsabdruck; Gispverband	**plaster cast** *Use of gypsum impregnated gauze to immobilize fractured extremities.*
Glasgow-Komaskala	**Glasgow coma scale** *A scale used to grade one's level of consciousness with a score of 3 being totally unresponsive and a score of 15 being normal.*
glasig	**vitreous** *Glass appearance; used to describe the vitreous body of the eye.*
Glaskörper	**humor, vitreous** *The fluid circulating between the lens and retina.*
Glatze; Glabella	**glabella** *The area of the forehead above and between the eyebrows.*
Glaukom; grüner Star	**glaucoma** *A condition characterized by increased intraocular pressure.*
gleich	**equal** *The same or uniform.*
Gleichgewichtsstörung	**disequilibrium** *The absence of stability.*
gleichzeitig	**simultaneous** *Occurring at the same time.*
glenoidal	**glenoid** *Referring to the fossa that is a shallow depression, such as the hollow of the scapula where the humeral head sets.*

Glied	**member** *Referring to an extremity (arm or leg).*
Gliom	**glioma** *A neural malignant tumor of glial cells.*
Gliomyom	**gliomyoma** *A mass with gliomatous and myomatous characteristics.*
Glomerulonephritis	**glomerulonephritis** *Inflammation of the renal glomeruli, usually from hemolytic streptococcus.*
Glomerulum	**glomerulus** *A grouping of capillaries where waste is filtered from the blood.*
Glomustumor	**glomus tumor** *A reddish-blue painful papule that occurs on the distal aspects of the digits.*
Glossektomie	**glossectomy** *Surgical resection of the whole or part of the tongue.*
Glossitis; Zungenentzündung	**glossitis** *Inflammation of the tongue.*
Glossodynie	**glossodynia** *Tongue pain.*
glossopharyngeal	**glossopharyngeal** *The name for cranial nerve IX that supplies the tongue and pharynx.*
Glossotrichie; Haarzunge	**hairy tongue** *Lingua villosa, a benign condition associated with antibiotic used caused by candida albicans infection.*
Glukagon	**glucagon** *A pancreatic enzyme responsible for breakdown of glycogen to glucose.*
Glukosetoleranztest	**glucose tolerance test** *The oral administration of a carbohydrate load and then evaluation of the blood sugar at timed intervals.*
gluteal; glutäal	**gluteal** *Referring to the gluteus.*
Glutealreflex	**gluteal reflex** *After the skin of the buttocks are stimulated the gluteal muscles contract.*
Glycerin	**glycerin** *A byproduct in the manufacture of soap that is used as a laxative.*
Glykämie	**glycemia** *The amount of glucose in the blood.*
Glykogen	**glycogen** *A compound that stores glucose and when it undergoes hydrolysis forms glucose.*
Glykogenese	**glycogenesis** *The production of glycogen from glucose.*
Glykolyse	**glycolysis** *The production of energy and pyruvic acid when glucose is broken down by enzymes.*
Glykoprotein	**glycoprotein** *A protein that has a carbohydrate attached to its polypeptide chain.*
Glykosurie	**glycosuria** *Presence of glucose in the urine.*
Gnosie	**gnosia** *Ability to recognize things and people.*
Gold	**gold** *Precious metal with atomic number of 79.*
Gonadendysgenesie	**gonadal dysgenesis** *The lack of complete development of the gonads.*
Gonadotropin	**gonadotrophin** *Pituitary hormone that promotes gonadal activity.*
Gonoblennorhö	**gonorrheal ophthalmia** *An acute purulent conjunctivitis that can occur in neonates within 2-5 days of birth.*
Gonokokke	**gonococcus** *A diploccocal bacteria that is the causative agent in gonorrhea, formally Neisseria gonorrhoeae.*
Gonorrhö; Tripper	**gonorrhea** *A sexually transmitted disease that is exhibited by purulent discharge from the vagina or penis.*
Goodpasture-Syndrom	**Goodpasture' syndrome** *Glomerulonephritis, preceded by hemoptysis. The nephritis can quickly progress to death from renal failure.*
Graefesches Zeichen	**Graefe's sign** *Also called lid lag, a sign characterized by the upper eyelid not closing over the globe. This is seen commonly in exophthalmic goiter.*

Gramm	**gram** *A unit of mass, 1/1000th of a kilogram.*
Granulationsgewebe	**granulation tissue** *Vascular connective tissue forming granular protrustions on the surface of a healing wound.*
Granulom	**granuloma** *A mass of granulation tissue.*
Granulozyt	**granulocyte** *A white blood cell with cytoplasmic secretory granules.*
graue Substanz	**gray matter** *The section of the brain and spinal cord composed of branching dendrites and nerve cell bodies.*
Gravidität extrauterine	**ectopic pregnancy** *A pregnancy that is not intrauterine.*
Greifkraft	**grip strength** *Quantitative measurement of the force of a hand grip.*
Greifreflex	**grasp reflex** *Flexion of the fingers or toes when stimulated.*
Griff	**clasp** *Holding onto something with one's hand.*
Grippe; Influenza	**influenza** *Viral infection causing fever, muscle aches and catarrh.*
großes Vieleckbein	**trapezium** *The lateral bone in the distal row of carpal bones.*
Großhirnbalken	**corpus callosum** *A point of connection between the two cerebral hemispheres.*
Großwuchs	**macrostomia** *Abnormal increase in the width of the mouth.*
Grube	**fossa** *A shallow depression.*
Grünholzfraktur	**fracture, greenstick** *A spiral fracture.*
Gryposis pensi	**chordee** *Downward bending of the penis.*
Guajak-Harz	**guaiac** *A substance derived from guaiacum trees used to test for trace amounts of blood, in stool for instance.*
Guillain-Barré-Syndrom	**Guillain-Barré syndrome** *An acute autoimmune disorder that causes nerve inflammation subsequently muscle weakness.*
Gumma	**gumma** *A soft granulomatous tumor of the skin or cardiovascular system seen in tertiary syphilis.*
gurgeln	**gargle, to** *To rinse one's mouth out and exhale through the liquid.*
gutteral	**guttural** *Having a harsh quality; coming from the back of the throat.*
Gürtel	**belt** *A strap used to hold clothing up.*
Gürtelrose	**herpes zoster; shingles** *A unilateral vesicular rash along one dermatome and caused by inflammation of a posterior nerve root by "the chicken pox virus".*
Gynäklogie	**gynecology** *The branch of medicine associated with the reproductive system of women.*
Gynäkomastie	**gynecomastia** *Enlargement of the breasts.*
Gyrus; Windung	**gyrus** *Convolutions of the brain where there is infolding.*
Haarfollikel	**hair follicle** *Tubelike invagination of the epidermis that the hair shaft develops from.*
Haarig	**hairy** *A profuse amount of hair.*
Haarzelle	**hair cell** *Epithelial cells with hairlike projections.*
Hackenfuß	**talipes calcaneus** *A foot deformity exhibited by abnormal dorsiflexion.*
hakenförmig	**unciform** *Another term for hamate bone in the wrist.*
Hakenwurm	**hookworm** *A parasitic infection of the family Strongylidae that can cause anemia.*
halb	**half** *Divided in two.*
Halbwertszeit	**half-life** *The time a drug decreases its effect in half over time.*
Hallux valgus	**hallux valgus** *Also called bunion, it is the lateral deviation of the great toe.*
Hallux varus	**hallux varus** *Medial deviation of the great toe.*

Halluzination	**hallucination** *A perception that is not based on reality.*
Halluzinogen	**hallucinogen** *A substance that elicits hallucinations.*
Hals-, Nasen-, Ohren- (HNO)	**ENT** *Abbreviation for ears, nose and throat.*
Hals-Nasen-Ohrenarzt	**otolaryngologist** *Surgical specialist concerned with organs of the ears, nose and throat.*
Hals; Nacken	**neck** *The part of the body that connects the body to the head.*
Halsentzündung	**quinsy** *Peritonsillar inflammation or abscess.*
Halsschmerzen	**sore throat** *Common term for pharyngitis.*
haltungsmäßig	**postural** *Referring to position or posture.*
Hamarton	**hamartoma** *A nodule of superfluous tissue.*
Hamatum	**hamate bone; uncinate bone** *The medial bone in the distal row of carpal bones adjacent to the fifth metacarpal.*
Hamatum	**unciforme bone** *Hamate bone. The bone on the ulnar side of the distal row of the carpus. It articulates withe the 4th and 5th metacarpal, triquetral, lunate and capitate.*
Hamman-Rich-Syndrom	**Hamman-Rich syndrome** *Idiopathic pulmonary fibrosis.*
Hammerfinger	**mallet finger** *Flexion contracture of the distal phalanx.*
Hammerzehe	**hammer toe** *A condition characterized by extension of the proximal phalanx and flexion of the second and distal phalanges.*
Hampton Handgriff	**Hampton maneuver** *Rolling a patient during gastrointestinal fluoroscopy in order to obtain an air contrast of the antrum and duodenum.*
Hand	**hand** *The upper extremity distal to the wrist.*
Handbuch	**compendium** *A concise summary about a subject.*
Handgelenk	**wrist** *The articulation of the hand and radius/ulna.*
Handgelenkschoner	**cock-up splint** *A splint used to maintain the wrist in dorsiflexion; used for carpal tunnel syndrome.*
Handschuh	**glove** *A covering for hand protection.*
Handschuhanästhesie	**glove anesthesia** *Absence of sensation of the hand and wrist.*
Handteller; Handfläche; Palma	**palm** *The anterior aspect of the hand.*
Handwurzel; Karpus	**carpus** *The joint between the hand and wrist.*
Hanhart-Syndrom	**Hanhart's syndrome** *Also referred to as micrognathia with peromelia. There is hypoplasia of the mandible, malformed or missing teeth, birdlike face and severe upper extremity deformities.*
Haploid	**haploid** *Either a single set of chromosomes or a set of nonhomologous chromosomes.*
Hapten	**hapten** *The molecular component that determines immunologic specificity.*
Harnanalyse; Urinstatus	**urinalysis** *Chemical and microscopic examination of the urine.*
Harnblase	**bladder, urinary** *Vestibule for urine prior to being expelled via the urethra.*
Harnblase	**urinary bladder** *The organ collecting urine from the ureters prior to discharge via the urethra.*
Harnleiter-; Ureter-	**ureteral** *Referring to one of two tubes from the kidneys to the bladder that carry urine.*
Harnleiterentzündung	**ureteritis** *Inflammation of the ureter.*
Harnsäure	**uric acid** *Uric acid is a purine-derived product of nitrogen metabolism that can increase the risk of gout and calculi.*

	English
Harnsediment	**urinary sediments** *The debris that settles in a urine sample when left undisturbed.*
Harnstein	**urolith** *Urinary calculi.*
Harnstoff	**urea** *A nitrogenous product of protein metabolism; excreted in urine.*
Harntrakt	**urinary tract** *The organs and canals associated with urine secretion including the kidneys, ureters, bladder and urethra.*
Harnzylinder	**urinary casts** *A protein precipitated from renal tubules and excreted in the urine.*
Harz	**resin** *An organic substance that is insoluble in water. There are many types. Cholestyramine resin is used for hypercholesterolemia.*
hastig	**abrupt** *Suddenly or hastily.*
Haustier	**pet** *An animal kept for companionship.*
Hauswanze	**bedbug Cimex lectularius.** *A small insect that is parasitic and hides in clothing or bedding.*
Haut	**integument** *Outer protective layer.*
Haut	**skin** *Flesch.*
hautablederung Verletzung	**injury, degloving** *Trauma that involves the ripping of skin and subcutaneous tissue from the underlying tissue.*
Hautausschlag	**pox** *A general term for fluid filled papules that upon rupturing leave pockmarks.*
Hautausschlag	**rash** *Exanthema or urticaria.*
Hautausschlag	**skin rash** *Dermal exanthema.*
Hautfalte	**skin fold** *An overlapping of skin formed by subcutaneous tissue.*
Hautläsion	**skin lesion** *An abnormal but not necessarily cancerous lesion.*
Häm	**heme** *A constituent of hemoglobin that is an insoluble iron protoporphyrin.*
Hämagglutinin	**hemagglutinin** *An antibody that facilitates the agglutination of blood.*
Hämangiom; Blutschwamm	**hemangioma** *A benign tumor composed of blood vessels.*
Hämarthrose	**hemarthrosis** *Presence of intra-articular blood.*
Hämatemesis	**hematemesis** *Vomiting blood.*
Hämatin	**hematin** *The insoluble iron protoporphyrin component of hemoglobin.*
Hämatochezie	**hematochezia** *Presence of blood in the excrement.*
Hämatokrit	**hematocrit** *The measurement of the volume of red blood cells compared to the total volume of blood; recorded in percent.*
Hämatom	**hematoma** *A mass containing blood.*
Hämatometra	**hematometra** *The accretion of blood in the uterus.*
Hämatomyelie	**hematomyelia** *Accumulation of blood in the spinal cord.*
Hämatoperitoneum	**hemoperitoneum** *Abnormal presence of blood in the peritoneum.*
Hämatoporphyrin	**hematoporphyrin** *A derivative of heme that does not contain iron.*
Hämatosalpinx	**hematosalpinx** *Presence of blood in the fallopian tube.*
Hämatozele	**hematocele** *A mass or area of swelling caused by the accumulation of blood.*
Hämaturie	**hematuria** *The presence of blood in the urine.*
Hämochromatose	**hemochromatosis** *A hereditary condition exhibited by iron deposition in the tissue and leading to liver disease, bronze discoloration of the skin and diabetes.*
Hämodialyse	**hemodialysis** *The process of filtering blood outside the body to remove toxins normally excreted by functioning kidneys.*

Hämoglobin	**hemoglobin** *An iron containing protein used for the transport of oxygen in blood.*
Hämoglobinurie	**hemoglobinuria** *Presence of free hemoglobin in the urine.*
Hämokonzentration	**hemoconcentration** *Decrease in the total fluid content of the blood, leading at times to a falsely elevated hematocrit.*
Hämolyse	**hemolysis** *Breakdown of hemoglobin.*
hämolytisch	**hemolytic** *Something that causes hemolysis.*
hämolytisch Anämie	**hemolytic anemia** *Reduced number of erythrocytes due to shortened survival and inability of the bone marrow to compensate.*
Hämoperikard	**hemopericardium** *Abnormal presence of blood in the pericardium.*
Hämophilie	**hemophilia** *A hereditary bleeding disorder characterized by hemarthroses and deep tissue bleeding as a result of absence of a coagulation factor such as factor VIII.*
hämophilie Arthropathie	**hemophilic arthropathy** *The permanent joint disease caused by recurrent bleeding into the joint.*
Hämophthalmus	**hemophthalmia** *Bleeding within the eye.*
Hämopoese	**hemopoiesis** *The production of blood cells from stem cells.*
hämopoetisch	**hemopoietic** *Referring to a hormone secreted by the kidneys that stimulates the bone marrow to produce erythrocytes.*
Hämoptyse	**hemoptysis** *Expectoration of blood.*
Hämorrhagie; Blutung	**hemorrhage** *Bleeding from a damaged blood vessel.*
Hämorrhoidektomie	**hemorrhoidectomy** *Surgical excision of a hemorrhoid.*
Hämorrhoiden	**hemorrhoids** *Engorgement of the veins in the anus or rectum.*
Hämostase	**hemostasis** *The control of bleeding.*
Hämothorax	**hemothrorax** *The abnormal presence of blood in the pleural cavity.*
Hämotopneumothorax	**hemopneumothorax** *Accumulation of blood and air in the pleural space.*
Hämozytometer	**hemocytometer** *A device used for counting cells from a blood sample.*
Hebamme; Entbindungspfeger	**midwife** *A person trained to assist in childbirth.*
heben	**lift, to** *Raise to a higher level.*
Hebephrenie	**hebephrenia** *A type of schizophrenia exhibited by hallucinations and inappropriate laughter.*
Heberden-Knötchen	**Heberden's node** *Hard nodules formed at the distal interphalangeal joints in osteoarthritis.*
Hedonismus	**hedonism** *Devoting oneself to being happy.*
Hefe	**yeast** *A unicellular fungus.*
Heilmittel	**curative** *A remedy capable of healing completely.*
Heilung	**healing** *The process of becoming healthy again.*
Heilung; Kur	**cure** *A remedy for a medical illness.*
Heimlich Handgriff	**Heimlich maneuver** *A forceful upward thrust to the diaphragm to dislodge an airway obstruction.*
heimtückisch	**insidious** *A slow, gradual and harmful advancement.*
heiser	**hoarse** *A rough, harsh sounding voice.*
Heiserkeit	**frog in the throat, to have** *An expression describing hoarseness.*
heiß	**hot** *Very warm.*
Heliotherapie	**heliotherapy** *Treatment of disease with sunlight.*
Helium	**helium** *An inert gas that is the lightest of the noble gases.*
hell	**light** *Illumination, bright.*

Helminthiasis	**helminthiasis** *Being infected by a helminth.*
Hemianopsie	**hemianopsia** *Blindness over half the field of vision.*
Hemiballismus	**hemiballismus** *Severe motor restlessness unilaterally, usually from a subthalamic lesion.*
Hemikolektomie	**hemicolectomy** *Surgical removal of part of the colon.*
Hemikranie	**hemicrania** *1. Pain on one side of the head. 2. Incomplete anencephaly.*
Hemiparese	**hemiparesis** *Unilateral muscle weakness (half the body).*
Hemiplegie; Halbseitenlähmung	**hemiplegia** *Paralysis of one side of the body.*
Hemisphäre	**hemisphere** *Referring to either the right or left portion of the cerebrum.*
hemizygot	**hemizygote** *A cell with only one set of genes.*
Henri Syndrom	**Henri, syndrome of** *Congenital anomaly exhibited by different sized external orifices of the nostrils.*
Heparin	**heparin** *A polysaccharide that occurs naturally in the liver and is used as a medication to induce a hypocoagulable state.*
Hepatektomie; Leberresktion	**hepatectomy** *Partial or complete surgical resection of the liver.*
hepatisch	**hepatic** *Referring to the liver.*
Hepatitis	**hepatitis** *Inflammation of the liver.*
hepatojugulärer Reflux	**hepatojugular reflex** *The presence of jugular venous distension with compression of the abdomen for at least 10 seconds.*
Hepatom	**hepatoma** *A tumor of the liver.*
Hepatomegalie; Lebervergrößerung	**hepatomegaly** *Enlargement of the liver.*
Hepatosplenomegalie	**hepatosplenomegaly** *Enlargement of the spleen and the liver.*
Hepatozyt	**hepatocyte** *A liver cell.*
heranführen	**acquaint, to** *To make someone familiar with something.*
Herausnahme	**removal** *The act of removing something.*
herausplatzen mit	**blurt out, to** *To speak without considering the repercussions.*
Hermeralopie	**hemeralopia** *Night blindness.*
Hermesstab	**caduceus** *An ancient herald's wand with two serpents twined around that is a symbol of the medical arts.*
Herniorrhaphie	**herniorrhaphy** *The surgical repair of a hernia.*
Heroin	**heroin** *A morphine derivative that is highly addictive.*
Herpangina	**herpangina** *An infectious disease caused by Coxsackie virus exhibited by vesicular lesion on the soft palate.*
Herpes	**herpes** *A skin condition exhibited by formation of clustered vesicular lesions; herpes simplex is at times referred to, albeit incompletely, as herpes.*
Herpes genitalis	**genital herpes** *A sexually transmitted infection caused by herpes simplex.*
Herpes-simplex-Virus	**cold sore** *A perioral blister caused by herpes simplex.*
herpetiform	**herpetiform** *Something that is characteristic of herpes.*
herpetisch	**herpetic** *Referring to herpes.*
herum	**around** *On every side of.*
Herz	**heart** *Muscular organ that pumps blood thru the circulatory system.*
Herz-Lungemaschine	**heart lung machine** *Device used during cardiac surgery to replace the function of the heart and lungs while surgery is performed.*

Herzblock	**heart block** *An alteration in the cardiac electrical conduction system.*
Herzfrequenz	**heart rate** *Number or cardiac contactions per minute.*
Herzfrequenzsteuerung	**cardiac pacing** *Electromechanical stimulation of the heart.*
Herzgeräusch	**heart murmur** *An abnormal heart sound usually related to valvular disease.*
Herzkranzgefäß	**coronary vessel** *Referring to a coronary artery.*
Herzminutenvolumen	**cardiac output** *Amount of blood pumped by the heart in liters per minute.*
Herzmittel	**cardiac** *Referring to the heart.*
Herzmuskelentzündung	**myocarditis** *An inflammation of the heart.*
Herzschlagen	**heart beat** *A single contraction of the heart.*
Herzspitze	**apex of heart** *Normally found 8cm to the left of the midsternal line in the 5th intercostal space.*
Herzstillstand	**cardiac arrest** *Cessation of function of the heart.*
Herzversagen	**cardiac failure** *Decreased cardiac output of the heart.*
heterochromie Iridis	**heterochromia iridis or syndrome of Eric** *Congenital anomaly in which the iris of each eye is of a different color.*
heterogen	**heterogenous** *That which originates outside the organism.*
Heterotropie; Strabismus	**heterotropia** *Synonym of strabismus.*
heterozygot	**heterozygous** *Having different alleles concerning a certain trait.*
Heufieber	**hay fever** *An allergy exhibited by pruritis of the eyes and nose, rhinorrhea and excessive lacrimal secretion.*
Hiatushernie	**hiatus hernia** *Protrusion of part of the stomach through the esophageal hiatus of the diaphragm.*
Hidradenitis; Schweißdrüsenentzündung	**hidradenitis** *Inflammation of a sweat gland. When there is purulent discharge it is called hidradenitis suppurativa.*
Hiemalisdermatitis	**frost itch** *A pruritis noted when exposed to cold weather.*
hilär	**hilar** *Referring to a hilus.*
Hilfe	**assistance** *The act of helping.*
Hillis-Müller Handgriff	**Hillis-Müller maneuver** *A procedure to determine the descent of the head during active labor.*
Hilus	**hilum or hilus** *A depression where blood vessels and nerve fibers enter an organ.*
hintere Augenkammer	**posterior chamber of the eye** *An aqueous filled space between the cornea and the lens.*
hinterer; posterior	**posterior** *Further back in position; opposite of anterior.*
Hinterstrang	**posterior columns** *The dorsal portion of the gray matter of the spinal cord.*
Hinterwurzel	**dorsal root** *A description of the site of ganglion found on the dorsal root of each spinal nerve.*
hinunter	**down** *In a lower position.*
hinzufügen	**add, to** *To count.*
Hiobsyndrom	**Job syndrome** *Also known as hyperimmunoglobulin E syndrome, there are high levels if IgE, a leukocyte chemotactic defect, recurrent staph infections and cold abscess formation in the skin.*
hippkratischer Eid	**Hippocratic oath** *An vow taken by doctors, indicating they will treat people properly.*
Hirnanhangdrüse	**pituitary gland** *A gland at the base of the hypothalamus.*

223

	English
Hirnsichel	**falx cerebri** *A fold in the dura that separates the two cerebral hemispheres.*
Hirnstamm	**brain stem** *An organ that consists of the medulla oblongata, pons and midbrain.*
Hirntätigkeit	**cerebration** *Operating activity of the cerebrum.*
Hirntod	**brain death** *Cessation of cerebral functioning.*
Hirschzecke	**deer tick** *Ixodes scapularis.*
Hirsutismus	**hirsutism** *Abnormal growth on hair on a person's face and body.*
His-bündel	**bundle of His** *The atrial contraction rhythm is facilitated by this bundle to the ventricles.*
His-bündle	**atrioventricular bundle** *Also called bundle of His.*
Histidin	**histidine** *An amino acid precursor to histamine.*
Histimin	**histamine** *A chemical responsible for the reaction exhibited when a person has an allergic reaction.*
Histiozyt	**histiocyte** *A phagocytic cell found in connective tissue.*
Histochemie	**histochemistry** *Study of intracellular distribution of chemicals, reaction sites and enzymes.*
Histologie; Gewebelehre	**histology** *The study of the structure and composition of minute structures.*
Histoplasmose	**histoplasmosis** *A fungal pulmonary infection from bat and bird excrement.*
Hitzekollaps; Wärmeschaden	**heat exhaustion** *A condition that occurs secondary to prolonged exposure to high ambient temperature; it is exhibited by subnormal temperature, dizziness and nausea.*
Hitzewallung	**hot flash** *A symptom of menopause manifested as a sudden sensation of fever.*
Hitzschlag	**heat stroke** *A condition caused by excessive exposure to high ambient temperature; it is exhibited by dry skin, thirst, vertigo, muscle cramps and nausea. The three forms are heat exhaustion, heat cramps and sunstroke.*
hoch; hohe	**high** *Elevated.*
Hoden	**testicle** *One of a pair of organs in the male scrotum that produces sperm.*
Hodentorsion	**testicular torsion** *Rotation of the spermatic cord resulting in testicular ischemia.*
hohes Alter	**old age** *A relative term for the period of advanced years.*
Hohlfuß	**pes cavus** *Excessive height of the longitudinal arch of the foot.*
Hohlmeißel	**gouge** *A chisel with a concave blade used in surgery.*
homolateral	**homolateral** *Ipsilateral.*
homolog	**homologous** *Referring to something derived from the same species but different genotype.*
homosexuelle Person	**homosexual** *A person sexually attracted to someone of the same gender.*
Homozygot	**homozygous** *Having identical alleles for a particular trait.*
Homöopathie	**homeopathy** *A treatment of disease by use of minute doses of toxic substances that would normally be harmful.*
Homöostase	**homeostasis** *The tendency of an organism to maintain a stable and uniform state.*
Homöotransplantat	**homograft** *A graft of tissue from the same species as the recipient.*

224

Hormon	**hormone** *A substance produced in the body that effects a specific organ.*
Horn	**horn** *A keratinized outgrowth.*
Horner-Syndrom	**Horner syndrome** *A lesion of the cervical sympathetic chain causes ipsilateral myosis, ptosis and facial anhydrosis.*
Hornhautreflex	**corneal reflex** *Closure of the eyelids when the cornea is touched lightly with a soft material. Also called the lid reflex.*
Hornhauttransplantation	**corneal transplant** *Surgical replacement of a cornea with a donor cornea.*
Höhe	**height** *Distance between the bottom of the foot and top of the head.*
Höhenangst	**acrophobia** *The morbid fear of heights.*
Höhenkrankheit	**altitude sickness** *A general term used for an illness that occurs at high altitude.*
Höhle	**cavity** *Pouch or chamber.*
Hörgerät	**hearing aid** *A device that fits in the ear used to amplify sound.*
Hueter Handgriff	**Hueter's maneuver** *The application of downward and forward pressure on the tongue while passing an gastric tube.*
Hufeisenniere	**horseshoe kidney** *Anomalous renal development.*
humanes Immundefektvirus	**HIV** *Abbreviation for human immunodeficiency virus.*
Humerus; Oberarm	**humerus** *The long bone in the upper arm.*
Hunger	**hunger** *A sense of discomfort caused by a lack of food.*
Hungerustand; Hahrungsentzug	**starvation** *Death related to starvation.*
Huntingtonische Chorea	**Huntington's chorea** *A neurodegenerative disease characterized initially by behavioral changes and later by a movement disorder. Called Huntington's disease now.*
Husten	**cough** *Forceful expulsion of air from the lungs.*
Hustenanfall	**coughing fit** *An episode of prolonged, forceful coughing.*
Hutchinson Maske	**Hutchington's mask** *The sensation the face is covered in cobwebs, associated with tabes dorsalis.*
Hutchinson Pupille	**Hutchinson's pupil** *Dilation of a pupil related to third nerve palsy on the side of the lesion as seen in herniation.*
Hüfte; Haggebutte	**hip** *The lateral eminence of the pelvis from the waist to the thigh; it is formed by the iliac crest and greater trochanter.*
Hüftendoprothese	**hip replacement** *Both joint surfaces are replaced by high density material such as plastic or metal.*
Hüftgelenk	**hip joint** *The lateral eminence of the pelvis from the waist to the thigh; it is formed by the iliac crest and greater trochanter.*
Hülle; Kapsel	**theca** *A tendon or ovarian follicle sheath.*
hyalin	**hyaline** *Having a glassy, transparent appearance.*
Hyalin	**hyaloid** *Transparent.*
Hybride	**hybrid** *An animal or plant produced from two different species.*
Hydarthrose	**hydrarthrosis** *An accumulation of water-like fluid in a joint cavity.*
hydatidiform	**hydatiform** *Referring to a hydatid cyst.*
Hydatidzyst; Echinokokkuszyste	**hydatid cyst** *A cyst produced by and containing tapeworm larvae.*
Hydratation	**hydration** *Used to describe fluid balance.*
Hydrochlorid	**hydrochloride**
Hydrocortison	**hydrocortisone** *A natural steroid hormone secreted by the adrenal cortex and used in a synthetic formulation for treatment of various medical conditions.*

	English
Hydrolyse	**hydrolysis** *A reaction with water causing a compound to breakdown.*
Hydronephrose; Wassersackniere	**hydronephrosis** *Enlargement of a kidney due to interruption of outflow of urine from that kidney.*
Hydrophobie	**hydrophobia** *Abnormal fear of water.*
Hydropneumothorax	**hydropneumothorax** *Abnormal accumulation of fluid and air in the pleural space.*
Hydrops	**hydrops** *The abnormal collection of fluid in a cavity.*
Hydrops fetalis	**hydrops fetalis** *The total body accumulation of fluid in a fetus; the result of a hemolytic reaction in a Rh neg mother.*
Hydrosalpinx	**hydrosalpinx** *Collection of fluid in a fallopian tube.*
Hydrothorax	**hydrothorax** *Accumulation of fluid within the thoracic cavity.*
Hydrozele	**hydrocele** *The accumulation of fluid in a body sac.*
Hydrozele testis	**scrotal hydrocele** *A benign collection of fluid in the scrotum.*
Hydrozephalus; Wasserkopf	**hydrocephalus** *The excessive accumulation of cerebral spinal fluid in the brain causing enlargement of the head.*
Hygrom	**hygroma** *A cyst or bursa filled with fluid.*
hygroskopisch	**hygroscopic** *The tendency to absorb moisture from the air.*
Hymen	**hymen** *A membrane in the vagina.*
Hymenektomie	**hymenotomy** *Surgically creating an opening in the hymen.*
Hypästhesie	**hypoesthesia** *Abnormally decreased skin sensitivity.*
Hyperaktivität	**hyperactivity** *Abnormal increase in activity.*
Hyperalgesie	**hyperalgesia** *Greater than normal sensitivity to pain.*
Hyperazidität; Übersäuerung	**hyperacidity** *An abnormally high acid level.*
Hyperämie	**hyperemia** *An increase in blood for the area of concern.*
Hyperästhesie	**hyperesthesia** *Higher than normal skin sensitivity.*
hyperbare	**hyperbaric** *Use of gas at a higher than normal pressure.*
Hyperbilirubinämie	**hyperbilirubinemia** *Higher than normal level of bilirubin in the blood.*
Hypercholesterinämie	**hypercholesterolemia** *Higher than normal level of cholesterol in the blood.*
Hyperchromasie	**hyperchromia** *An excessive level of hemoglobin in erythrocytes.*
Hyperextension	**hyperextension** *Extension of an articulation beyond the normal range.*
hyperextension-hyperflexion Verletzung	**injury, hyperextension-hyperflexion** *An injury, usually to the cervical spine, that involves rapid deceleration, causing pronounced extension and flexion.*
Hyperflexion	**hyperflexion** *Flexion of an articulation beyond the normal range.*
Hyperglykämie	**hyperglycemia** *Higher than normal level of glucose in the blood.*
Hypergonadismus	**hypergonadism** *A condition of excessive gonadal activity and subsequently precocious sexual development.*
Hyperhidrose	**hyperhidrosis** *Excessive perspiration.*
Hyperkaliämie	**hyperkalemia** *Higher than normal level of potassium in the blood stream.*
Hyperkalzämie	**hypercalcemia** *Higher than normal level of calcium in the blood.*
Hyperkapnie	**hypercapnia** *Higher than normal level of carbon dioxide in the blood stream.*
Hyperkeratose	**hyperkeratosis** *Excessive thickening of the outer layer of skin.*
Hyperkinese	**hyperkinesis** *Excessive activity and inability to concentrate.*
Hyperlipidämie	**hyperlipidemia** *Higher than normal level of lipids in the blood stream.*

Hypermetropie; Übersichtigkeit	**hypermetropia** *Farsightedness.*
Hypermnesie	**hypermnesia** *Unusually good memory.*
Hypernatriämie	**hypernatremia** *Elevated level of sodium in the blood.*
Hypernephrom	**hypernephroma** *A renal tumor that mimic adrenal cortical tissue.*
Hyperonychie	**hyperonychia** *Hypertrophic nails.*
Hyperopie; Übersichtigkeit	**hyperopia** *Farsightedness.*
Hyperosmie	**hyperosmia** *Increased sense of smell.*
Hyperparathyreoidismus	**hyperparathyroidism** *Excessive level of parathyroid hormones in the blood stream causing weak bones and hypocalcemia.*
Hyperphorie	**hyperphoria** *Upward deviation of the visual axis of the eye.*
Hyperpituitarismus	**hyperpituitarism** *Excessive eosinophilic hormone resulting in acromegaly or excessive basophilic hormone resulting in pituitary compression and ultimately hypopituitarism.*
Hyperplasie	**hyperplasia** *Excessive growth of normal cells.*
Hyperpnoe	**hyperpnea** *Abnormal increase in rate and depth of respiration.*
Hyperpyrexie	**hyperpyrexia** *Fever.*
Hyperreflexie	**hyperreflexia** *Abnormally brisk and vigorous reflex.*
Hypersalivation	**polysialia** *Abnormal increase in saliva.*
Hypersensitivität; Überempfindlichkeit	**hypersensitivity** *Abnormal increase in sensitivity.*
Hypersplenie	**hypersplenism** *Excessive splenic activity resulting in decreased peripheral blood elements and sometimes splenomegaly.*
Hypertension; Bluthochdruck	**hypertension** *Higher than normal blood pressure.*
Hyperthermie	**hyperthermia** *Fever.*
Hyperthyreose	**hyperthyroidism** *Increased thyroid activity resulting in exophthalmos and increased metabolic rate.*
Hypertonie	**hypertonia** *Excessive tone or tension.*
hypertonie	**hypertonic** *Increased osmotic pressure.*
Hypertrichose	**hypertrichosis** *Excessive hair growth.*
Hypertrophie	**hypertrophy** *Pathologic organ enlargement.*
hypertrophisch Synovitis	**Brodie's knee** *Also referred to as chronic hypertrophic synovitis of the knee.*
Hyperurikämie	**hyperuricemia** *Elevated level of uric acid in the blood.*
Hyperventilation	**hyperventilation** *Rapid and deep respirations.*
Hypervolämie	**hypervolemia** *Abnormally large amount of fluid in the blood stream.*
Hyphäma	**hyphema** *A blood collection in the front of the eye.*
hypnotisch	**hypnotic** *Sleep inducing agent.*
Hypochlorhydrie	**hypochlorhydria** *A state of decreased secretion of hydrochloric acid in the stomach.*
Hypochonder	**hypochondriac** *A person suffering from hypochondriasis.*
Hypochondrie	**hypochondriasis** *Abnormal increase in concern about one's own health.*
Hypochondrium	**hypochondrium** *The upper abdomen lateral to the epigastrium.*
hypochrom	**hypochromic** *Referring to the abnormal decrease in hemoglobin content of erythrocytes.*
Hypofibrinogenämie	**hypofibrinogenemia** *Diminished blood fibrinogen level.*
hypogastrisch	**hypogastric** *Referring to the hypogastrium.*

227

Hypogastrium	**hypogastrium** *The area of the central abdomen located below the stomach.*
Hypoglossus	**hypoglossal nerve** *Twelfth cranial nerve pair.*
Hypoglykämie	**hypoglycemia** *Abnormally low blood sugar.*
Hypogonadismus	**hypogonadism** *Abnormal decrease in gonadal function with associated diminished growth and sexual development.*
Hypokaliämie	**hypokalemia** *Diminished level of potassium in the blood stream.*
Hypokalzämie	**hypocalcemia** *Lower than normal level of calcium in the blood.*
Hypokapnie	**hypocapnia** *A decreased level of carbon dioxide in the blood.*
Hypomanie	**hypomania** *A moderate form of mania.*
Hyponatriämie	**hyponatremia** *Diminished level of sodium in the blood stream.*
Hypoparathyreoidismus	**hypoparathyroidism** *Abnormal decrease in parathyroid function.*
Hypophorie	**hypophoria** *Downward deviation of the visual axis of the eye.*
Hypophosphatasie	**hypophosphatasia** *A genetic defect of diminished alkaline phosphatase in the cells leading to bone demineralization.*
Hypophyse; Hirnanhangdrüse	**hypophysis** *Pituitary gland.*
Hypophysektomie	**hypophysectomy** *Surgical removal of the pituitary gland.*
Hypopituitarismus	**hypopituitarism** *Diminished pituitary activity exhibited by obesity and persistence of adolescent characteristics.*
Hypoplasie; Unterentwicklung	**hypoplasia** *Incomplete development.*
Hypopyon	**hypopyon** *The presence of purulent fluid in the anterior chamber of the eye.*
Hyposalivation	**hyposalivation** *Secretion of saliva below the normal rate.*
Hypospadie	**hypospadias** *Congenital condition exhibited by development of the urethral meatus on the inferior aspect of the penis.*
Hypostase	**hypostasis** *The formation of a deposit.*
Hypotension	**hypotension** *Abnormally low blood pressure.*
Hypothalamus	**hypothalamus** *Located inferior to the thalamus it controls visceral activities, water balance, temperature and sleep.*
Hypothermie	**hypothermia** *Lower than normal temperature.*
Hypothyreose	**hypothyroidism** *Reduced functioning of the thyroid.*
Hypoxie; Sauerstoffmangel	**hypoxia** *Diminished oxygen content.*
Hysterektomie	**hysterectomy** *Surgical removal of the uterus.*
Hysterie	**hysteria** *A psychological condition exhibited by uncontrolled emotion or exaggerated manifestations.*
Hysterographie	**hysterography** *1. Recording of uterine contractions. 2. Roentgenography of the uterus after administration of contrast media.*
Hysteromyomektomie	**hysteromyomectomy** *Surgical removal of a uterine myoma.*
Hysteropexie	**hysteropexy** *Surgical fixation of the uterus by shortening of the round ligaments or by other means.*
Hysterosalpingographie	**hysterosalpingography** *Roentgenography of the uterus and fallopian tubes after instillation of contrast media.*
Hysterotomie	**hysterotomy** *Surgical opening of the uterus.*
iatrogen	**iatrogenic** *A problem caused by medical treatment.*
Ichthyose	**ichthyosis** *A congenital anomaly exhibited by excessively dry, thick skin.*
idiopathisch	**idiopathic** *Relating to a disease with an unknown cause.*
Ikterus; Gelbsucht	**icterus** *Yellowing of the skin and sclerae because of excess bilirubin.*

Ikterus; Gelbsucht	**jaundice** *Yellowing of the sclerae and skin because of excessive bilirubin in the blood.*
Ileitis	**ileitis** *Inflammation of the ileum.*
Ileokolitis	**ileocolitis** *Inflammation of the ileum and cecum.*
Ileokolotomie	**ileocolostomy** *Creating a surgical opening between the ileum and colon.*
Ileoproktostomie	**ileoproctostomy** *Creating a surgical opening between the ileum and the rectum.*
Ileostomie	**ileostomy** *Surgical creation of an opening in the ileum that is placed at the skin surface.*
Ileozäkalklappe	**ileocecal valve** *The membranous folds between the ileum and cecum.*
Ileum	**ileum** *The portion of the small bowel from the jejunum to the cecum.*
Ileus; Darmverschluss	**ileus** *A temporary obstruction in the intestine.*
iliokokzygeal	**iliococcygeal** *Referring to the ilium and coccyx.*
Ilium	**ilium** *The large bone at the superior aspect of the pelvis which is present bilaterally.*
im Voraus	**beforehand** *In advance or previously.*
immun	**immune** *Being resistant to an infection.*
Immunchemie	**immunochemistry** *The study of immune response and biochemistry.*
Immundefizienz	**immunodeficiency** *An inadequate immune response.*
Immunelektrophorese	**immunoelectrophoresis** *A means of differentiating proteins and other compounds by comparing their mobility and antigenic specificities.*
Immunglobulin	**immunoglobulin** *Serum and cellular proteins of the immune system.*
Immunisierung	**immunization** *A medication given to provide immunity.*
Immunreaktion	**immune response** *The body's reaction to what is perceived as a foreign substance.*
Immunsuppression	**immunosuppression** *The inhibition of the immune response.*
impaktierter Zahn	**impacted tooth** *A tooth that does not erupt because adjacent teeth prevent it.*
Impfnachweis	**vaccine certificate** *A document that denotes what vaccines have been received by the holder.*
Implantat	**implant** *A device or prosthesis implanted in a person.*
Impotenz; Zeugungsunfähigkeit	**impotence** *Inability to act or inability to achieve a penile erection.*
Impressionsfraktur	**fracture, depressed** *The presence of concavity associated with a fracture as in a depressed skull fracture.*
in Bauchlage	**prone** *Lying with the abdomen and face downward.*
Inanition	**inanition** *Generalized weakness from lack of nutrition.*
Incisura	**incisura** *A notch or indentation usually on the edge of a bone.*
Indolent	**indolent** *1. Causing little pain. 2. Slow healing ulcer.*
Induratio penis plastica	**Peyronie's disease** *Curvature of the penis during an erection to to plaque.*
Induration	**induration** *An area that is abnormally hard.*
induzieren	**induce, to** *Facilitated. When referring to labor, it means medication was given to assist in delivery of the fetus.*
Inertie	**inertia** *The tendency to remain unchanged.*
infantil	**infantile** *Referring to babies or young children.*
Infarkt	**infarct** *Referring to dead tissue.*
Infarzierung	**infarction** *Dead tissue, for example, myocardial infarction.*

infektiös	**infectious** *Contagious.*
infraspinal	**infraspinous** *Below the scapular spine.*
Infundibulum	**infundibulum** *The connection between the hypothalamus and the posterior pituitary gland.*
Ingelligenzquotient	**intelligence quotient (IQ)** *A number representing a person's ability to problem solve compared to a matched-control.*
Ingestion; Aufnahme	**ingestion** *The intake of food or liquid orally.*
inguinal	**inguinal** *Referring to the groin.*
Inhalation	**inhalation** *The act of breathing in.*
Inhalt; Gehalt	**content** *What something is made up of.*
Injektion	**injection** *The act of a needle being inserted into a body.*
inkarzerierte Hernie	**hernia, incarcerated** *An irreducible hernia.*
inkohärent	**incoherent** *Absence of intelligible speech.*
Inkontinenz	**incontinence** *Inability to control urination.*
Inkoordination	**incoordination** *Absence of smooth, efficient body movement.*
Inkrement	**increment** *An increase on a fixed scale.*
innen	**inside** *Inner part, center.*
Innenohr	**inner ear** *Made up of the cochlea and semicircular canals.*
innerlich	**internal** *Situated on the inside.*
Innervation	**innervation** *The presence of a nerve supply.*
Inokulation	**inoculation** *Injection with a vaccine to provide immunity.*
Insel	**islet** *Tissue that is structurally separate from adjacent tissues.*
Inspiration; Atemzug	**inspiration** *Drawing in a breath.*
inspiratorisches Reservevolumen	**inspiratory reserve volume** *The amount of air that can be inhaled after a normal inhalation.*
instabil Knie	**unstable knee** *A condition with giving way of the knee due to ligamentous or cartilaginous dysfunction.*
Insulin	**insulin** *A hormone produced by the pancreas and synthetically to control blood glucose levels.*
Insulin	**inulin** *A polysaccharide used in the testing of renal function.*
Insulinom	**insulinoma** *An islet cell tumor that causes abnormally high insulin secretion and thus hypoglycemia.*
Intensionstremor	**intention tremor** *The tremulous movement noted when a person is beginning to perform a task but not seen at rest.*
intensiv	**intensive** *Very thorough or vigorous.*
Intensivpflege	**intensive care** *Vigorous treatment of the acutely ill.*
interartikulär	**interarticular** *Between the articular surfaces of a joint.*
intermittierend	**intermittent** *Occurring at irregular intervals.*
interossär	**interosseous** *Referring to something between bones, like the interosseous muscles of the hand.*
interstitiell	**interstitial** *Referring to the interstices of tissue.*
Intertrigo	**intertrigo** *Irritation present because adjacent surfaces rub together.*
intertrochantär	**intertrochanteric** *Referring to the space within the trochanter.*
Intervall	**interval** *An intervening time.*
interventrikulär	**interventricular** *Between the ventricles.*
interzellular	**intercellular** *Between cells.*
intestinal	**intestinal** *Referring to the intestines.*

intra-abdominal	**intraabdominal** *Within the abdominal cavity.*
intra-abdominal Abszeß	**intraabdominal abscess** *A collection of pus in the abdomen.*
intraartikulär	**intraarticular** *Within a joint space.*
intradermal	**intradermal** *Within the dermis.*
intradural	**intradural** *Within the dural space.*
intrakraniell	**intracranial** *Within the cranial vault.*
intramedullär	**intramedullary** *1. Within the medulla oblongata. 2. Within the bone marrow.*
intramuskulär	**intramuscular** *Within a muscle.*
intraokular Flüssigkeit	**intraocular fluid** *Fluid within the globe.*
intraossär	**intraosseous** *Within a bone.*
intraperitoneal	**intraperitoneal** *Within the peritoneal cavity.*
intrathekal	**intrathecal** *Technically means within a sheath but this term is used when medication is instilled in the dura mater spinalis.*
intrauterin	**intrauterine** *Within the uterus.*
Intrauterinspiral	**intrauterine contraceptive device (IUD)** *A device used to physically prevent the implantation of a fertilized ovum.*
intravenöse	**intravenous** *Within a vein.*
intravenöse Anwendung	**intravenous infusion** *Administration of fluid into a vein.*
Intravenöseschlauch	**intravenous tubing** *The tubing used to administer fluids.*
intrazellulär	**intracellular** *Within a cell.*
intrazerebral	**intracerebral** *Within the cerebrum.*
Intubation	**intubation** *Placement of a tube; commonly used to refer to endotracheal intubation.*
intumescentia Ganglioformis	**geniculate ganglion** *The sensory ganglion of the facial nerve.*
Intussuszeption; Invagination	**intussusception** *The inversion of one portion of the bowel into another.*
Involucrum	**involucrum** *A wrap or covering (referring to a sequestrum).*
involutiv	**involutional** *The shrinkage of an organ when it is not in use, as in the uterus after childbirth.*
Inzest	**incest** *Sexual relations between related people.*
Inzision; Schnitt	**incision** *An intentional surgical cut in the skin.*
Inzisur; Einschnitt	**incisure** *A notch or incision.*
Iod	**iodine** *A chemical used as an antiseptic and a deficiency of it can lead to goiter.*
Ionenkanal	**ion channel** *A selectively permeable cell membrane to certain ions.*
ionisierende Strahlung	**ionizing radiation** *High energy radiation that produces ion pairs in matter.*
ipsilateral	**ipsilateral** *On the same side.*
iridektomie	**iridectomy** *Surgical removal of part of the iris.*
Iridoplegie	**iridoplegia** *Paralysis of part of the iris with subsequent lack of contraction or dilation of the pupil.*
Iridotomie	**iridotomy** *A surgical opening of the iris.*
Iridozyklitis	**iridocyclitis** *Inflammation of the ciliary body and the iris.*
Iris; Regenbogenhaut	**iris** *The colored membrane posterior to the cornea.*
Ischämie	**ischemia** *Inadequate blood supply to a part of the body.*
ischämisch Herzkrankheit	**ischemic heart disease** *Inadequate blood supply to the heart.*

ischämisch Kontraktur	**ischemic contracture** *A muscle's resistance to passive stretch that is related to a decrease in arterial flow from any reason.*
ischämisch Optikoneuropathie	**ischemic optic neuropathy** *A general category of a cause of blindness with several subcategories.*
Ischiassyndrom	**sciatica** *Pain radiating from the buttock down the back of the leg; it is caused by a compressed spinal nerve root.*
Ischium	**ischium** *The inferoposterior portion of the pelvis.*
Isoantikörper	**isoantibody** *A situation in which an antibody of person A reacts with an antigen of person B.*
Isolation; Absonderung; Isolierung	**isolation** *To be kept separate or apart.*
Isolierstation	**isolation ward** *A ward where patients with infectious disease are housed.*
Isthmus	**isthmus** *A narrow piece of tissue connecting two larger body parts.*
Itai-Itai Krankheit.	**ouch-ouch disease** *Common term for Itai-Itai disease that is derived from "it hurts, it hurts" said by patients suffering from cadmium poisoning.*
ja sogar	**indeed** *As a matter of fact.*
Jahr	**year** *A time period that covers 365 days.*
jahrelang	**long-standing** *Having existed for a long time.*
Jahrzehnt	**decade** *Ten years.*
janseits	**beyond** *On the farther side.*
jährlich	**yearly** *Occurring once each year.*
jede	**every** *Each or all possible.*
jeden Tag	**every day** *Each day.*
jeden zweiten Tag	**every other day** *On alternate days.*
Jejunektomie	**jejunectomy** *Surgical removal of the jejunum.*
Jejunostomie	**jejunostomy** *Surgical creation of an opening in the jejunum.*
Jendrassikscher Handgriff	**Jendrassik's maneuver** *A method of distracting a patient while checking the patellar reflex.*
Jochbein; Wangenbein	**zygomatic bone** *The triangular cheek bone.*
Jodismus	**iodism** *A condition caused by excessive iodine intake resulting in diarrhea , weakness, and convulsions.*
Jucken; Krätze;	**itch** *A sensation that makes one want to scratch.*
Jugend	**adolescence**
Jugend	**youth** *The time between childhood and being an adult.*
jugendlich Angiofibrom	**juvenile angiofibroma** *A noncancerous growth in the nose or pharyngeal region.*
jugulär	**jugular** *Referring to the neck, as in jugular vein.*
jung	**young** *Having lived for a short period.*
juxtaartikulär	**juxta-articular** *Positioned near a joint.*
juxtaglomerulärer Apparat	**juxtaglomerular apparatus** *Cells located in the tunica media of the afferent glomerular arterioles.*
Kabeljau	**cod** *A large marine fish, also called codfish.*
Kachexie	**cachexia** *Generalized weakness and severe wasting.*
Kadaver	**cadaver** *A dead body.*
Kaffeesatzartiges Erbrechen	**coffee-ground emesis** *Black vomitus with appearance of ground coffee.*

	English
Kahnbein; Navikulare	**navicular bone** *The most lateral bone in the proximal row of carpal bones.*
Kahnbein; Navikulare	**scaphoid bone** *The most lateral of the carpal bones; it articulates with the radius.*
Kaiserschnitt	**cesarian section** *Incision of the abdominal and uterine walls in order to deliver a fetus when natural delivery is not possible.*
Kala-Azar; viszerale Leishmaniase	**kala-azar** *A disease caused by Leishmania donovani that is exhibited by weight loss, fever, anemia and hepatosplenomegaly.*
Kalium	**potassium** *A chemical of the alkali metal group.*
kalkig	**calcareous** *Referring to something containing lime or calcium.*
Kallus; Hornschwiele	**callus** *Thickened hardened skin.*
Kalorie	**calorie** *A unit of heat.*
kalt	**algid** *cold*
kalt	**cold** *Having a sense of being cold.*
kalt; kühlen	**cool** *Chilly or cold.*
Kalzifikation; Verkalkung	**calcification** *Deposition of calcium salts causing hardening of an organic tissue.*
Kalzium-antagonisten	**calcium channel blocker** *A medication used to treat angina, supraventricular arrhythmias and hypertension; it works by blocking calcium influx into myocytes and vascular smooth muscle cells.*
Kamm	**comb**
Kammerwasser	**aqueous humor** *The fluid between the cornea and lens, anterior to the globe.*
Kammerwasser	**humor, aqueous** *The gelatinous fluid circulating between the cornea and lens.*
Kankroid	**cancroid** *A tumor occurring in the stomach, small or large bowel.*
Kannabis	**cannabis** *A plant from the Cannibidaceae family that is known for its psychotropic effects.*
Kanüle	**cannula** *A tube inserted into the body.*
Kapillare	**capillary** *A vessel that connects arterioles to venules.*
Kapillarfragilitätsprobe	**capillary fragility test** *Application of a blood pressure cuff high enough to restrict venous return and after five minutes count the number or petechiae produced.*
kapilläres Hämangiom	**capillary nevus** *A growth of skin that involves the capillaries.*
Kapitatum	**capitate bone** *The bone at the base of the palm that articulates with the third metacarpal.*
Kaposi Sarkom; Sarcoma idiopathicum mutiplex haemorrhagicum	**Kaposi sarcoma** *Typically seen in AIDS patients, it is characterized by cutaneous reddish-purple macules and plaques.Also called multiple idiopathic hemorrhagic sarcoma.*
Kapsel	**capsule** *A membranous sheath that covers an organ or structure.*
Kapselentzündung	**capsulitis** *Inflammation of a capsule.*
Kapseleröffnung	**capsulotomy** *Incision of a capsule as in with eye surgery.*
Kararakt	**cataract** *An opacity of an eye lens or the capsule.*
Kardia	**cardia** *The superior aspect of the stomach at the opening of the esophagus.*
Kardiologie	**cardiology** *A specialty of medical practice involve treatment and prevention of heart disease.*
Kardiomyopathie	**cardiomyopathy** *Chronic cardiac muscle disease.*

kardiopulmonale Reanimation	**cardiorespiratory assistance** *Use of artificial means to support respiration and circulation.*
kardiovaskulär	**cardiovascular** *Referring to the heart or circulatory system.*
Karditis	**carditis** *Inflammation of the heart.*
Karies	**caries** *Referring to decay or death of a tooth.*
Karina	**carina** *The protrusion of the lowest tracheal cartilage.*
Karotis	**carotid** *Referring to the large artery on each side of the neck.*
Karotiskörper	**carotid body** *Carotid artery receptors that are sensitive to blood chemistry changes.*
Karotissinusreflex	**carotid sinus reflex** *Bradycardia as a result of pressure on the carotid sinus.*
Karotissinussyndrom	**carotid sinus syncope** *Dizziness and syncope that results from hyperactivity of the carotid sinus reflex.*
Karpaltunnelsyndrom	**carpal tunnel syndrome** *Paresthesia that results from compression of the median nerve.*
karpometakarpal	**carpometacarpal** *Referring to the carpus and metacarpus.*
Karpopedalspasmus	**carpopedal spasm** *A spasm of the carpus and the foot.*
Karunkel	**caruncle** *A small fleshy protuberance.*
Karyokinese	**karyokinesis** *A part of mitosis involving the cell nucleus division.*
Karyotyp	**karyotype** *The arrangement of chromosomes in a single cell.*
karzinogen	**carcinogenic** *That which causes cancer.*
Karzinoid	**carcinoid** *A tumor occurring in the stomach, intestine and colon.*
Karzinom	**carcinoma** *A malignant growth.*
Karzinomatose	**carcinomatosis** *Dissemination of cancer throughout the body.*
Kasein	**casein** *The principal protein in milk, a phospholipid.*
Kastration	**castration** *Excision of the gonads.*
Katabolismus	**catabolism** *The reduction of complex molecules to more simple ones in living organisms.*
Katalepsie	**catalepsy** *A condition exhibited by rigidity and the person maintains the same position if he is moved by another.*
Kataphorese	**cataphoresis** *The use of an electric field to move charged particles in fluid.*
Kataplexie	**cataplexy** *A condition exhibited by rigidity and immobility.*
Katatonie	**catatonia** *Seen in schizophrenia, it is a state of stupor or excitability and abnormal movements.*
Katharsis	**catharsis** *The act of cleansing or purging, usually referring to thought.*
Katheter	**catheter** *A flexible tube inserted into the body.*
Katrrah	**catarrh** *Inflammation of a mucous membrane.*
Katzenauge	**cat's eye pupil** *A pupil in the shape of an oval.*
Katzenkratzkrankheit	**cat scratch fever** *An infectious disease characterized by local inflammation a the site of the scratch, local lymph adenopathy and fever.*
Katzenschrei-Syndrom	**cat cry syndrome** *A hereditary congenital disorder exhibited by microcephaly, hypertelorism, and cognitive deficits.*
Kauda syndrom	**cauda equina syndrome** *Neurologic condition manifested by pain, paresthesia and weakness but no bowel/bladder dysfunction.*
kaudal	**caudal** *Referring to a cauda.*
kauen	**chew, to** *Masticate.*

	English
Kaugummi	**gum (chewing gum)**
Kaustikum	**caustic** *Abrasive or corrosive.*
Kauterisation	**cautery** *Application of an electric current to cut something.*
Kavaschirm	**vena cava filter** *A screen placed in the inferior vena cava to prevent blood clots from causing a pulmonary embolism.*
kavernöse Blutleiter	**cavernous sinus** *Large venous sinus located adjacent to the sphenoid bone and posterior to the petrosal sinuses.*
kavernöse Sinusthrombose	**cavernous sinus thrombosis** *A blood clot in the base of the brain.*
kavernöses Hämagiom	**cavernous hemangioma** *A tumor composed of connective tissue with blood filled areas.*
Kawasaki-Syndrom	**Kawasaki syndrome** *Begins with fever for 5 days, skin rashes, strawberry tongue, lymphadenopathy and swollen hands and feet. It is known to cause coronary artery aneurysms. Also called mucocutaneous lymph node syndrome.*
Kälteempfindung; Kryäasthesia	**cryesthesia** *Abnormal sensitivity to cold.*
Kältegefühl	**chill** *Sensation of coldness.*
Kehlkopfstenose	**laryngostenosis** *Abnormal narrowing of the larynx.*
Keifer-Gaumen-Spalte	**cleft palate** *A congenital abnormal opening in the palate.*
keilförmig	**cuneiform** *The three bones between the navicular bone and the metatarsals.*
Keim	**germ** *Microorganism.*
Keimdrüse; Gonade	**gonad** *A testis or an ovary.*
Kekubitus	**decubitus ulcer** *A wound caused by laying in one position for too long; also referred to as a pressure ulcer.*
Keloid	**keloid** *Hypertrophic scar tissue that forms after a minor cut or surgical procedure.*
kephalisch	**cephalic** *Towards the head.*
Keratektasie	**keratectasia** *Obtrusion of the cornea.*
Keratektomie	**keratectomy** *Excision of a portion of the cornea.*
Keratin	**keratin** *A protein found in the skin, hair, nails and enamel of the teeth.*
keratisch	**keratic** *Referring to the cornea.*
Keratom	**keratoma** *A protuberance of horny tissue.*
Keratomalazia	**keratomalacia** *Softening of the cornea.*
Keratose	**keratosis** *A growth of keratin such as a wart or callosity.*
Kerbe	**nick** *A small groove or notch.*
Kern	**core** *Central part of a structure.*
Kernikterus	**kernicterus** *A condition associated with high bilirubin levels that causes yellow staining of cerebral tissues and subsequent neurologic dysfunction.*
Kernspinresonanz (NMR)	**nuclear magnetic resonance (NMR)** *A type a diagnostic body imaging utilizing electromagnetic radiation in a magnetic field.*
Kerze	**candle** *A cylindrical piece of wax with a central wick.*
Ketoazidose	**ketoacidosis** *Usually referring to diabetic ketoacidosis in which ketones are broken down, causing a decrease in blood pH.*
Ketonämie	**ketonemia** *Presence of ketone in the blood.*
Ketonkörper	**ketone body** *One ketone with a decarboxylation product of acetone.*
Ketonurie	**ketonuria** *Presence of ketone in the urine.*
Ketose	**ketosis** *The presence of an abnormally high level of ketones in the blood and body tissues.*

235

Keuchen	**wheeze** *A whistling or musical sound made by air passing through a narrowed airway.*
Keuchhusten; Pertussis	**pertussis** *Synonym for whooping cough.*
Kiefer	**gnathic** *Referring to the jaws.*
Kiefer	**jaw** *Mandible.*
Kinase	**kinase** *An enzyme that facilitates movement of phosphate from ATP to another molecule.*
Kind	**child** *A person aged 1 to 8 years old.*
Kind mit Normal Schwangerschaftsdauer	**infant, term** *A neonate born at expected date.*
Kindbett; Wochenbett	**puerperium** *The six week period after childbirth.*
Kindheit	**childhood** *The time between infancy and puberty.*
kindliche Herztöne	**fetal heart tone** *Refers to the cardiac rate and pattern of the fetus.*
Kinds-Lage	**fetal position** *Refers to how the fetus lies within the uterus.*
Kindsbewegungen	**fetal movements** *Sensations by the mother of fetal activity.*
Kineplastie	**kineplasty** *An amputation done in a fashion to facilitate ambulation.*
Kinesis	**kinesis** *Movement of a part in response to a stimulus.*
Kinn	**chin** *Mentum; the anterior projection of the lower jaw.*
Kissen	**cushion** *A pillow or stuffed pad used to sit on.*
Kissen	**pillow** *An encased fabric covering soft material used for a cushion.*
kitzeln	**tickle, to** *To lightly touch a person to cause one to laugh.*
klaffend	**gaping** *Wide open.*
Klage	**complaint** *Grievance.*
Klappensegel	**leaflet** *Cusp.*
klar	**clear** *Lucid.*
Klauehand; Krallenhand	**clawhand** *A hand deformity caused by ulnar nerve palsy exhibited by the hyperextension of the metacarpophalangeal joints and flexion of the interphalangeal articulations.*
Klaustrophobie	**claustrophobia** *An unreasonable fear of being in an enclosed environment.*
Klavikula; Schlüsselbein	**clavicle** *A bone that articulates with the sternum and scapula.*
Klavus; Hühnerauge	**clavus** *A corn or horny protrusion.*
Klärung	**clearance** *The process of removing something.*
Klebestreifen	**adhesive tape** *Tape used to secure dressings or intravenous lines to the body.*
kleidokraniale Dysostose	**cleidocranial dysostosis** *A congenital condition exhibited by abnormal ossification of the cranial bones and absence of clavicles.*
Kleidotomie	**cleidotomy** *A procedure used in difficult deliveries in which the clavicle is broken to facilitate childbirth.*
kleine Kompresse	**pledget** *A small plug of cotton or other synthetic material inserted into a wound.*
kleine schamlippe Frenulum	**fourchette** *The fork shaped fold of skin where the labia minora meet superior to the perineum.*
kleiner Riss	**crevice** *A narrow opening.*
kleines Vieleckbein	**trapezoid bone** *A bone that articulates with the second metacarpal, trapezium, capitate and scaphoid.*
Kleinfingerballen	**hypothenar eminence** *The prominence on the palm at the base of the fingers adjacent to the ulna.*

Kleinhirn	**cerebellum** *The part of the brain in the posterior portion of the skull that controls muscle coordination and movement.*
Kleinhirnbindearm	**brachium cerebelli** *Synonym of pedunculus cerebellaris superior (upper portion the cerebellum).*
Kleinhirnmark	**white matter** *The brain tissue consisting of myelin sheaths and nerve fibers.*
Klette	**burr or bur** *A rotary cutting instrument.*
Klinefelter-Syndrom	**Klinefelter's syndrome** *Presence of an extra X chromosome, it is exhibited by longer legs, narrow shoulders, small testicles and gynecomastia.*
Klinik	**clinic** *A building where patients are evaluated.*
klinische Untersuchung	**clinical examination** *Physical assessment data.*
Klistier	**enema** *A procedure involving insertion of fluid into the rectum.*
Klitoris	**clitoris** *A small erectile body in the anterosuperior aspect of the vulva.*
klonisch	**clonic** *Referring to a spasm that alternates in rigidity and relaxation.*
Kneihöcker	**geniculate body** *Protrusions on the thalamus that relay visual and auditory signals to the brain.*
Knickfuß	**pes valgus** *Abnormal longitudinal arch- it is flat.*
Knie-Ellenbogen Lage	**knee elbow position** *Knees and elbows are on the table and the chest is in the air.*
Knie-Hacken-Versuch	**heel-shin test (heel to knee to toe test)** *A test of position sense and coordination; one moves the heel of one foot from the knee on the other foot down to the foot.*
Knie; Genu	**knee** *The joint at the distal femur and proximal tibia.*
knieförmig	**geniculate** *Bent at a sharp angle.*
Kniekehle	**popliteal fossa** *The hollow in the posterior aspect of the knee joint.*
kniend	**kneeling** *Being on one's knees as in the prayer position.*
Kniescheibe	**kneecap** *Common term for patella.*
Kniescheibenknorpelerweichung	**chondromalacia of the patella** *Softening of the articular cartilage of the patella.*
Kniesehne	**hamstrings** *Tendons of the posterior thigh.*
Knochen	**bone** *Skeletal tissue formed by osteoblasts.*
Knochenmark	**bone marrow** *The soft material filling the cavity of bones.*
Knochenmarkpunktion	**bone marrow puncture** *The aspiration of marrow to look for pressure of disease.*
Knochenmarkstift	**pin, intramedullary** *Hardware used for fracture management or during joing replacement.*
Knochenscan	**bone scan** *Bone imaging using technetium 99m (99mTc) diphosphate.*
Knochenspan	**bone graft** *The transfer of bone to aid in the healing of a complex fracture.*
Knoten	**knot** *A fastening made by tying a suture, for instance.*
Knoten	**lump** *A protuberance.*
Knoten	**node** *A swelling or prominence.*
Knöchel	**ankle** *The area of the ankle joint.*
Knöchelchen (Gehörknöchelchen)	**ossicle** *A small bone. (auditory ossicle)*
Knöchelödem	**ankle edema or dependent edema** *Extracellular fluid volume noted by swelling or pitting.*

237

Knöchelschwellung	**ankle swelling** *Enlargement of the ankle region with or without pitting.*
Knöchelstütze	**ankle support** *A mechanical device or banding to support the ankle.*
knöchern	**osseous** *Possessing the quality of bone.*
Knötchen	**nodule** *A small node in the skin of up to 1cm and in the lung up to 3cm.*
Koagulation; Gerinnung	**coagulation** *The formation of a clot.*
Kobalt	**cobalt** *A metal that with causes polycythemia with increased ingestion.*
Kodon	**codon** *A series of three nucleotides that form a unit of genetic code.*
Kognition	**cognition** *The process of acquiring thought or understanding.*
Kognitionsdefizite	**cognitive disorders** *Any disease process that involves altered cognition.*
Kohlendioxid	**carbon dioxide gas** *A gas expelled during exhalation.*
Kohlenhydrat	**carbohydrate** *A group of organic compounds including sugar and starch.*
Kohlenmonoxidhämoglobin	**carboxyhemoglobin** *A compound formed from hemoglobin when it is exposed to carbon monoxide.*
Kohlenmonoxidvergiftung	**carbon monoxide poisoning** *This tasteless, odorless gas causes constitutional symptoms but can lead to death upon inhalation.*
Koilonychie	**koilonychia** *Thin and concave fingernails.*
Koitus	**coitus** *Sexual intercourse between members of the opposite sex.*
Kokain	**cocaine** *A highly addictive opiate derivative.*
Kokainabhängigkeit	**cocaine addiction** *Physical habituation to cocaine.*
Kokzygodynie	**coccydynia** *Coccygeal pain.*
Kolben; Flasche	**flask** *A narrow-necked container.*
Kolektomie	**colectomy** *Surgical removal of part of the colon.*
Kolik	**colic** *Acute abdominal pain.*
Kolitis	**colitis** *Inflammation of the colon.*
Kollagen	**collagen** *The principal supportive protein bone, skin, tendon and cartilage.*
Kollaps	**collapse** *A physical or mental breakdown.*
Kollodium	**collodion** *A product of the breakdown of colloid.*
Kolloid	**colloid** *A solution used for infusion, such as albumin or hetastarch, that are more likely to remain in the intravascular space than crystalloids.*
Kolobom	**coloboma** *A congenital defect that involves a fissure of the eye.*
Kolon; Colon	**colon** *The portion of the large intestine that goes from the cecum to the rectum.*
Kolonoskopie; Dickdarmspiegelung	**colonoscopy** *Inspection the color, ideally to the cecum, with a lighted scope.*
Kolostomiebeutel	**colostomy bag** *A pouch attached to the skin with a mild adhesive that collects stool emitted from a colostomy.*
Kolostrum	**colostrum** *The fluid secreted by the mammary glands a few days around parturition.*
Kolpitis; Scheidenentzündung	**colpitis;** *vaginitis Inflammation of the vagina.*
Kolporrhaphie	**colporrhaphy** *A surgical procedure that involves suturing the vagina.*
Kolposkop	**colposcope** *A scope used to visualize the vagina.*
Kolposkopie	**colposcopy** *Use of a scope to visualize the vagina and cervix.*

238

Kolpozele	**colpocele** *A hernia into the vagina.*
Koma	**coma** *A state of unconsciousness.*
komatös	**comatose** *Referring to a coma.*
kommensal	**commensal** *Living in or on another organism without being a detriment.*
Komplementbindungsreaktion	**complement fixation test** *A laboratory test for the presence of an antibody in the serum that involves inactivation of the complement in the serum.*
Kompression	**compression** *Squeezing together.*
Kondom	**condom** *A covering for the penis or the vagina (female condom) used during sexual intercourse that is meant to reduce the chance of pregnancy or infection.*
Kondylom	**condyloma** *A warty papule near the anus or vulva.*
Kondylus	**condyle** *A rounded protrusion of a bone.*
Konfabulation	**confabulation** *The fabrication of experiences to compensate for memory loss.*
Konflikt	**conflict** *Dispute or disagreement.*
kongenital	**congenital** *A disease or anomaly present from birth.*
kongestive	**congestive**
Konjunktiva; Bindehaut	**conjunctiva** *The membrane that lines the eyelid.*
Konjunktivaireflex	**conjunctival reflex** *Closure of the eyes in response to irritation of the conjunctiva.*
Konkrement	**concretion** *A hard solid mass.*
Konkussion; Erschütterung	**concussion** *Head trauma resulting in temporary loss of consciousness.*
konsensueller Lichtreflex	**consensual light reflex** *Constriction of the pupil of one eye in sync with the other pupil upon exposure to light.*
konservativ	**conservative** *Control rather than elimination of a disease.*
konsistent	**consistent** *Compatible with something or congruous with.*
Konsolidierung	**consolidation** *An area of fixed secretions in the lung.*
Kontakt; Berührung	**contact** *The touching of two bodies or a person who has been exposed to a contagious disease.*
Kontaktlinse	**contact lens** *A lens that fits over the cornea to correct refractive errors.*
Kontrasteinlauf	**barium enema** *Administration of barium into the rectum followed by roentgenography to check for rectal or colon abnormalities.*
Kontrazeptivum	**contraceptive** *A device or medication used to prevent pregnancy.*
Kontusion	**contusion** *An area of broken capillaries in the skin causing discoloration; commonly called a bruise.*
Konus	**cone** *A light sensitive cell in the retina.*
Konversionsneurose	**conversion reaction** *When referring to a psychiatric condition it is the exhibition of physical symptoms as a manifestation of mental disease.*
konvex	**convex** *Having an exterior curved the outside of a sphere.*
Konvulsion	**convulsion** *An involuntary series of tonic and clonic movements.*
Konzentration	**concentration** *The quantity of a substance per unit volume.*
konzentrisch	**concentric** *Referring to circles or arcs that share the same center.*
Konzeption; Empfängnis	**conception** *The act of an egg being fertilized by sperm.*
Kopf; Haupt	**head**
Kopfgrind; Kopfschuppen	**dandruff** *Dead skin found in the hair.*

Kopfhaar	**hair (of head)**
Kopfhaut	**scalp** *The skin covering the head except for the face.*
Kopfschmerzen	**headache** *Cephalgia.*
Kopfverletzung	**head trauma** *Any injury to the brain.*
Kopfverletzung	**injury, closed head** *Brain trauma not associated with damage to the dura or skull.*
Koplik-Flecken	**Koplik's spots** *Red buccal macules with a blue center; seen in measles.*
Kopophobie	**kopophobia** *A morbid fear of fatigue.*
Kopulation	**copulation** *Sexual relations.*
Korakoidfortsatz	**coracoid** *A prominence on the scapula to which the biceps is attached.*
Kornea	**cornea** *The transparent segment located at the anterior part of the eye.*
korneal	**corneal** *Referring to the cornea.*
Koronar	**coronal suture** *The line of intersection of the frontal bone and the two parietal bones.*
Koronarangiographie	**coronary angiography** *Roentgenographic visualization of the coronary vessels after injection of dye.*
Koronarverschluss	**coronary occlusion** *A blockage in a coronary artery.*
koronoid	**coronoid** *Crown-shaped.*
Korpuskel	**corpuscle** *A red or white blood cell.*
Kortex; Rinde	**cortex** *An external layer.*
kortikal	**cortical** *Referring to the cortex.*
Kortikosteroid	**corticosteroid** *A hormone developed in the adrenal cortex.*
Kortikotropin	**corticotropin** *A hormone of the adrenal cortex.*
Kortisol	**cortisol** *An adrenal cortical hormone, also called hydrocortisone.*
Kortison	**cortisone** *An adrenal cortical hormone responsible for carbohydrate regulation.*
Kotstein	**fecal impaction** *The presence of hard excrement in the rectum that requires manual removal.*
Koxalgie	**coxalgia** *Pain in the hip.*
Köhler Krankheit	**Köhler's disease** *A genetic disease characterized by osteonecrosis and subsequent collapse of the tarsal navicular bone.*
Körpergewicht	**body weight** *Relative mass as measured in kilograms or pounds.*
Körperhaar	**hair (of body)**
körperlisch Untersuchung	**physical exam** *Examination of a client to assess their medical status.*
Körperoberfläche	**body surface area** *Dubois formula is: (weight in kilograms)to the 0.425th power x (height in centimeters) to the 0.725th power x 0.007184.*
kraftlos	**weak** *Feeble or deconditioned.*
Kraktur; Bruch	**fracture** *A broken bone.*
Kralle; Klaue	**talon** *The ball of the ankle joint.*
Krampf	**cramp** *A painful contraction of muscles.*
Kranial	**cranial** *Referring to the skull.*
Kranial Mononeuropathie III	**cranial mononeuropathy III** *Dysfunction of the third cranial nerve causes double vision and eyelid drooping.*
Kranial Mononeuropathie VI	**cranial mononeuropathy VI** *A disorder of the sixth cranial nerve causes double vision.*
Kranioklast	**cranioclast** *An instrument used to crush a fetal skull.*

Kraniopharyngiom; Erdheim-Tumor	**craniopharyngioma** *A tumor that originates in the hypophyseal stalk.*
Kraniosynostose	**craniosynostosis** *Closure of the sutures of the skull that occurs prematurely.*
Kraniotabes	**craniotabes** *Softening of the skull bones causing widened sutures; this occurs in rickets.*
Kraniotomie	**craniotomy** *Surgical creation of a hole in the skull.*
Krankenakte	**clinical record** *The ongoing medical summary.*
Krankenbericht	**medical record** *The electronic or paper report on a patient.*
Krankenhaus	**hospital** *Acute care medical/surgical facility.*
Krankenpflege	**nursing care** *The assessment and treatment provided by nurses.*
Krankenschwester; Pflegeperson	**nurse** *A person trained to care for the sick.*
Krankheit; Morbus; Erkrankung	**disease** *Malady or disorder.*
Krankheit; Unwohlsein	**sickness** *Illness or a state of disease.*
Kratzen; Schramme	**scratch** *A long, narrow superficial wound.*
Kratzer	**scrape** *An injury caused by having a body part rubbed against a rough surface.*
Kraurosis Vulvae	**kraurosis vulvae** *Dryness and shrinkage of the vulva.*
kräftig	**strong** *Having the power to move heavy objects.*
Krämerkrätze	**copra itch** *A pruritis noted in people working with copra (dried kernel from a coconut).*
Kreatin	**creatine** *A compound involved with muscle contraction.*
Kreatinin	**creatinine** *A compound excreted in the urine that is produced by the metabolism of creatine.*
Krebs; Karzinom	**cancer; carcinoma** *A disease of uncontrolled abnormal cell growth.*
Kreißsaal	**labor room** *The hospital room used while a woman is in labor.*
Kremasterreflex	**cremasteric reflex** *Retraction of the testicle and scrotum upon stroking of the ipsilateral inner thigh.*
Krenotherapie	**crenotherapy** *A form of treatment from mineral springs.*
Krepitation; Knochenreiben	**crepitus** *A noise heard when one auscultates the lungs that is similar to the sound of rubbing hair between one's fingers. It is also considered the sound of two broken bones rubbing together.*
Kretinismus	**cretinism** *A chronic condition caused by diminished thyroid hormone secretion.*
kreuzförmig	**cruciform** *Shaped like a cross.*
Kreuzschmerz	**low back pain** *Pain in the lumbar region.*
Kreuzschmerzen	**back pain** *Discomfort on the dorsal surface of the torso.*
Kreuzung	**decussation** *An area of intersection.*
kribbelnd	**tingling** *Prickling or stinging sensation.*
kribrifrom	**cribriform** *Like a sieve; the olfactory nerves pass through the cribriform plate of the ethmoid bone.*
Kriebelmücken	**black fly** *From the family Simuliidae, a gnat that can cause disease in humans; also called buffalo fly.*
Krise	**crisis** *A turning point in the treatment of a disease.*
Kristalloid	**crystalloid** *A substance that can pass through a semipermeable membrane; not a colloid.*
Kristallurie	**crystalluria** *The presence of crystals in the urine.*
Kropf; Struma	**goiter** *Swelling of the thyroid gland.*

241

Krupp	**croup** *An acute laryngeal condition that is accompanied by a hoarse, barking cough.*
krural	**crural; femoral** *Referring to the femur or leg.*
Kruste; Borke	**crust** *Dried serous exudate covering a wound.*
Krücke	**crutch** *Long metal or wooden stick used for support while walking.*
Krüppel	**cripple** *A person with a physical disability; not used in polite society.*
Kryochirurgie	**cryosurgery** *The application of extreme cold to destroy tissue.*
Kryotherapie	**cryotherapy** *The use of cold for therapeutic purposes.*
Kryptokokkenmeningitis	**cryptococcal meningitis** *A meningeal infection associated with AIDS.*
Kryptorchismus	**cryptorchism** *A condition characterized by the failure of the testes to descend into the scrotum.*
Kryptosporidose	**cryptosporidiosis** *A parasitic related diarrhea seen in AIDS.*
Kuhmilch	**cow's milk**
Kuhpocken	**cowpox; vaccinia** *A viral disease of cows that was used for an original smallpox vaccine.*
Kuldoskopie	**culdoscopy** *Examination of the female pelvic viscera with a scope inserted through the posterior vaginal fornix.*
Kultur	**culture** *The growth of bacteria in artificial medium.*
Kulturmedium; Nährboden	**culture broth** *A medium used to grow bacteria.*
Kummer	**grief** *Deep sorrow.*
kumulative Wirkung	**cumulative effect** *A consequence of successive additions.*
Kupfer	**copper** *A chemical element with atomic number of 29.*
Kussmaul Atmung	**Kussmaul respiration** *The slow, deep breathing noted in patients with acidosis.*
kutan	**cutaneous** *Referring to the skin.*
Küchenschabe	**cockroach** *A bettlelike insect with long legs and antennae.*
künstliches Gebiß	**denture** *A frame that holds artificial teeth.*
Kürettage	**curettage** *Removal of tissues from a cavity.*
Kürette	**curette** *The instrument used during a curettage.*
Kwashiorkor	**kwashiorkor** *A form of malnutrition from inadequate protein intake.*
Kyasnur-Wald-Krankheit	**Kyasanur Forest disease** *A viral fever noted in Mysore, India transmitted by Haemaphysalis spinigera. It is characterized by fever, headach, generalized pains, diarrhea, and intestinal bleeding.*
Kyphose	**kyphosis** *Abnormal outward curvature of the spine.*
Kyphoskoliose	**kyphoscoliosis** *An abnormal outward and lateral curvature of the spine.*
Kystadenom	**cystadenoma** *Adenoma associated with cysts of neoplastic origin.*
labial	**labial** *Referring to the lip.*
labil	**labile** *Easily altered; emotionally unstable.*
Labium	**labium** *Referring to any lip shaped structure.*
Labium majus	**labium majus (plural= labia majora)** *The folds of skin forming the lateral borders of the pudendal cleft.*
Labium minus	**labium minus (plural=labia minora)** *The folds of skin posterior to the labia majora.*
Labor	**laboratory** *A room equiped to run blood, tissue and fluid samples.*
Laborergebnis; Laborbefunde	**lab result** *The data obtained from a laboratory test.*
Labrum	**labrum** *An edge or lip. The labrum acetabular is the fibrocartilagous rim attached to the acetabulum.*

Labyrinth	**labyrinth** *Inner ear structure concerned with balance.*
Labyrinthitis	**labyrinthitis** *Inflammation of the labyrinth.*
lachen	**laugh, to**
Lackmus	**litmus** *A dye that turns red with low pH and blue with high pH.*
Lagehypotonie	**postural hypotension** *A significant drop in blood pressure when going from the supine or sitting position to standing.*
Lagophthalmus	**lagophthalmos** *Characterized by the inability to close the eyelid completely over the eye.*
Lakrimal	**lacrimal** *Referring to the secretion of tears.*
Laktalbumin	**lactalbumin** *Proteins found in milk.*
Laktase	**lactase** *An enzyme that facilitates the breakdown of lactose to glucose and galactose.*
Laktation	**lactation** *The secretion of milk from mammary glands.*
Laktose	**lactose** *A disaccharide present in milk.*
Laktoseintoleranz	**lactose intolerance** *The inability of the small bowel to digest lactose.*
lakunärer Infarkt	**lacunar infarction** *Small non-cortical cerebral infarcts.*
Lakune	**lacuna** *A small cavity or depression.*
Lalochezie	**lalochezia** *Relief of stress by uttering obsenities.*
Lalophobie	**laliophobia** *Abnormal fear of speaking or stuttering.*
lambdaförmig	**lambdoid** *The suture connecting the parietal bones with the occipital bone.*
Lamelle	**lamella** *A thin layer of bone.*
Laminektomie	**laminectomy** *The surgical removal of part of a vertebrae.*
lang wirkend	**long-acting** *Referring to a drug with long lasting effects.*
langsam	**slow** *Unhurried.*
Langzeitbetreuung	**long-term care** *Generally referring to nursing home care.*
Lanzette	**lancet** *A small sharp instrument used to obtain a drop of blood for testing.*
Laparoskop	**laparoscope** *A fiber-optic instrument used to visualize the peritoneal contents.*
Laparoskopie	**laparoscopy** *A procedure utilizing a laparoscope.*
Laparotomie	**laparotomy** *A surgical incision of the abdomen.*
Lappen	**flap** *A term used to describe a piece of tissue partially excised and placed over an adjacent surface.*
Lappen	**lobe** *A body part divided by a fissure.*
laryngeal	**laryngeal** *Referring to the larynx.*
Laryngektomie	**laryngectomy** *Surgical removal of the larynx.*
Laryngitis	**laryngitis** *Inflammation of the larynx.*
Laryngologie	**laryngology** *The study of the larynx and related diseases.*
Laryngopharynx	**laryngopharynx** *The pharyngeal space between the superior aspect of the glottis and the opening of the larynx.*
Laryngospasmus	**laryngospasm** *Sudden, involuntary muscle contraction of the larynx.*
Laryngotomie	**laryngotomy** *Surgical creation of an opening in the larynx.*
Larynx	**larynx** *A hollow muscular structure that contains the vocal cords.*
lateral	**lateral** *Referring to the side of the body.*
Lathyrismus	**lathyrism** *A disease characterized by tremors, spastic paralysis and paresthesias caused by Lathyrus sativus.*
Latwerge; Electuarium	**lincture** *A medicine mixed with a sweet substance.*

243

	English
Laufband	**treadmill** *An exercise machine on a continuous belt used for walking.*
lauwarm	**tepid** *Lukewarm.*
Lähmung	**palsy** *Paralysis that is usually associated with tremors.*
Länge	**length** *The end to end measurement.*
Läppchen	**lobule** *A small lobe.*
Läppchenprobe; Epikutantest	**patch test** *A test used to determine which substances provoke an allergic response in a patient.*
Läuse	**lice** *Plural for louse, a small parasite that lives on the skin. Pediculus humanus capitis is a head louse.*
Lävulose; Fruktose	**levulose** *Synonym for fructose.*
lebensbedrohlich	**life-threatening** *Potentially fatal.*
Lebensdauer	**longevitiy** *Long life.*
Lebenserwartung	**life expectancy** *The length of time a person is anticipated to live.*
lebensfähig	**viable** *Referring to a fetus that can survive childbirth.*
Lebensmittelvergiftung	**food poisoning** *Poisoning where the active agent is in the food.*
Lebenszeichen	**vital signs** *The designation for blood pressure, pulse, respirations and temperature.*
Lebenszeit	**lifetime** *Duration of a person's life.*
Leber	**liver** *A large glandular organ in the right upper quadrant that functions in digestive processes, as well as, neutralizing toxins.*
Leberabszeß	**liver abscess** *A localized collection of pus in the liver.*
Leberwege	**hepatic duct** *The right and left hepatic ducts join the cystic duct to form the common bile duct.*
Leckage	**leakage** *Unintentional escape of gas or fluid.*
ledig	**single** *Not married.*
leer	**empty** *Containing nothing.*
Legionärskrankheit	**legionnaires' disease** *The name was derived after an outbreak at a convention of the American Legion; it is manifested by fever, chills, dyspnea, and cough.*
Leichenbeschauer	**coroner** *A person who investigates sudden or suspicious deaths.*
Leichenfleck	**post-mortem lividity** *The purplish discoloration occurring 30-120 minutes after death in dependent body parts.*
Leichenschaushaus	**morgue** *A room where deceased patients are housed until sent to a funeral home.*
Leichensektion	**dissection** *Autopsy or postmortem exam.*
leicht	**light** *Not heavy.*
leiden; klagen	**suffer, to** *To be affected by an illness or sickness.*
Leim	**glue** *Plastic cements*
Leishmaniase	**leishmaniasis** *A condition caused by a flagellate protozoan parasite that is exhibited by visceral or dermatologic manifestations.*
Leistengegend	**groin** *The genital region.*
Leistenhernie	**hernia, inguinal** *Protrusion of abdominal-cavity contents through the inguinal canal.*
Leistenring	**inguinal ring (deep)** *Indirect inguinal hernias exit the abdominal cavity via the deep inguinal ring.*
Leistenverletzung	**groin pull** *A muscle strain in the inguinal region.*
Leitungsanästhesie	**nerve block anesthesia** *Locally administered anesthesia.*

Lendenbruch	**hernia, lumbar** *Defect in the lumbar muscles or the posterior fascia, below the 12th rib and above the iliac crest.*
Lentigo	**lentigo** *A benign condition exhibited by flat brown patches on the skin.*
lentikulär; linsenförmig	**lenticular** *Referring to the lens of the eye.*
Leontiasis	**leontiasis ossea** *Bilateral hypertrophy of the bones of the face and cranium.*
Leopold Handgriff	**Leopold's maneuver** *Used to determine fetal position.*
Lepra	**leprosy** *A contagious disease caused by Mycobacterium leprae that causes insensate papules and disfiguration.*
Leprom	**leproma** *A superficial granulatomous papule that is seen in leprosy.*
Leptomeningitis	**leptomeningitis** *A general term used to describe meningitis of the pia and arachnoid of the brain.*
Leptospirose	**leptospirosis** *A zoonosis caused by the spirochete Leptospira interrogans transmitted by rats and contaminated water.*
Lernen	**learning** *The intentional aquisition of knowledge.*
Lesbe	**lesbian** *A woman with same gender preference.*
letal	**lethal** *Deadly.*
letale Dosis	**lethal dose** *The amount of a drug required to cause death.*
Letalität	**lethargy** *Absence of energy.*
letzte	**last** *Final.*
leuchtend	**bright** *Giving out a lot of light.*
Leukämie	**leukemia** *A malignant disease causing an increase in the number of abnormal and immature leukocytes.*
Leukin	**leukine (or leucine)** *An amino acid obtained from hydrolysis of some proteins.*
Leukoderm	**leukodermia** *A localized loss of skin pigment.*
Leukonychie	**leukonychia** *A whitish discoloration of the fingernails and toenails.*
Leukopenie	**leukopenia** *A decreased number of leukocytes in the blood.*
Leukopoese	**leukopoiesis** *Production of white blood cells.*
Leukorrhö	**leukorrhea** *Thick white vaginal discharge.*
Leukozyt	**leukocyte** *A white blood cell.*
Leukozythemie	**leukocythemia** *Synonym of leukemia.*
Leukozytolysis	**leukocytolysis** *Destruction of white blood cells.*
Leukozytose	**leukocytosis** *An increase in the number of leukocytes.*
Leuzinose; Ahornsirupkrankheit	**leucinosis; maple syrup urine disease** *A condition characterized by an enzyme defect causing an increase in leucine in the urine.*
Levator	**levator** *A muscle that raises part of the body; the levator labii superioris raised the upper lip.*
Lezithin	**lecithin** *A compound widely used by tissues, derived from egg yolks and it consists of phospholipids linked to choline.*
Libido	**libido** *Sexual desire.*
Libman-Sachs-Syndrom	**Libman-Sachs syndrome** *A verrucous endocarditis associated with disseminated lupus erythematosus; also called nonbacterial verrucous endocarditis.*
Lichen	**lichen** *A term used to describe a variety of papular skin diseases. Lichen planus is a shiny, flat, violaceous eruption of the mucous membranes, skin and genitalia.*
Lichtanpassung	**light adaptation** *The pupillary adjustment after going from a dark environment to one of bright light.*

Liddrüsentzündung	**sty** *Also called hordeolum externum, it is inflammation of the sebaceous gland of an eyelash.*
liefert	**supplies** *Stock or reserves.*
Ligament; Band	**ligament** *A band of fibrous connective tissue that connects two bones or cartilage.*
ligamentum bifurcatum	**bifurcate ligament** *A ligament on the dorsum of the foot that includes the calcaneonavicular and calcaneocuboid ligaments.*
ligamentum latum uteri	**broad ligament of uterus** *Supports the uterus on both sides.*
Ligamentum teres uteri	**round ligament of the uterus** *The supporting structure of the uterus.*
Ligatur; Unterbindung	**ligature** *A thread used to tie a vessel.*
Limbus	**limbus** *The margin of a structure, for example, of the cornea and sclera.*
lindern; ausgleichen	**relieve, to (pain)** *To make less severe.*
Linderungsmittel	**demulcent** *Something that relieves irritation or inflammation.*
Linea alba	**linea alba** *The tendinous portion of the anterior abdomen between the two rectus muscles.*
Lingua pilosa nigra	**lingua nigra** *A condition characterized by a dark fur-like covering on the dorsum of the tongue.*
links	**left**
linkshändig	**left-handed** *The preference of using the left hand for common tasks.*
Linse	**lens** *The transparent chamber between the posterior chamber and the vitreous body.*
Lipase	**lipase** *A pancreatic enzyme that facilitates the breakdown of fats.*
Lipämie	**lipemia** *Abnormally high fat content in the blood.*
Lipid	**lipid** *A compound that is a fatty acid which is insoluble in water but soluble in organic solvents.*
lipidsenkend Medikation	**lipid-lowering agent** *A medication used to treat hyperlipidemia.*
Lipoatrophie	**lipoatrophy** *Fatty tissue atrophy.*
Lipochondrodystrophie; Pfaundler-Hurler-Syndrom	**lipochondrodystrophy** *A congenital condition exhibited by short stature, kyphosis, mental deficiency and short fingers.*
Lipodystrophie	**lipodystrophy** *Abnormal fat metabolism.*
Lipoid; fettähnlich	**lipoid** *Referring to fat.*
Lipoidose	**lipoidosis** *Abnormal lipid metabolism.*
Lipom	**lipoma** *A benign tumor consisting of fat cells.*
Lipoprotein	**lipoprotein** *A soluble protein used to transport fat or lipids.*
lipotrop Substanz	**lipotrophic substance** *A compound which causes an increase in body fat.*
Lipozyt	**lipocyte** *A fat cell.*
Lippenspalte	**cleft lip** *A congenital abnormal opening of the lip.*
Liquor cerebrospinalis	**cerebrospinal fluid (CSF)** *The fluid between the pia mater and arachnoid membrane.*
Liquor cerebrospinalis	**CSF** *Abbreviation for cerebrospinal fluid.*
Lispeln; Sigmatismus	**lisping** *A speech problem in which "s" and "z" are pronounced "th".*
Listeriose	**listeriosis** *A disease caused by Listeria monocytogenes that occurs in the pregnant and immunocompromised.*
Lithagogum	**lithagogue** *A treatment of a calculus.*
Litholapaxie	**litholapaxy** *The crushing and then removal of a calculus.*
Lithotomie; Steinschnitt	**lithotomy** *Surgical removal of a calculus.*

246

Lithotriptor	**lithotriptor** *An instrument used to crush a calculus.*
lobär	**lobar** *Referring to a lobe.*
Lobektomie	**lobectomy** *Surgical removal of a lobe (generally lung or liver).*
Lobo Krankheit; Blasttomycosis queloidana	**Lobo's disease** *A condition exhibited by small, red, hard papules in the sacral region caused by Lacazia loboi.*
Lobotomie	**lobotomy** *Surgical incision into the prefrontal lobe; historically a treatment of mental illness.*
Lochien	**discharge, postpartum vaginal** *The secretions noted after delivery.*
Lochien; Wochenfluss	**lochia** *Vaginal secretions noted within two weeks of childbirth.*
Locked-in-Syndrom; Eingeschlossensein-Syndrom	**locked-in syndrome** *A neurologic condition characterized by a person being conscious of their surroundings but being unable to verbally communicate that understanding.*
locker; frei	**loose** *Not tight.*
Loiasis; Loa-loa-Filariose	**loiasis** *A disease caused by the filarial nematode Loa loa.*
lokaliseirt	**localized** *Toward one point or area.*
Lokalisierung	**localization** *Establishment of a site of a disease process.*
Lordose	**lordosis** *An abnormal depth of the inward curvature of the spine.*
Löffeffel	**spoon nail** *Also referred to as koilonychia, the nail is concave and is generally associated with anemia.*
Löffel	**spoonful** *A measurement that does not specify teaspoon or tablespoon.*
Lösungsmittel	**solvent** *Able to dissolve with other chemicals.*
Luft	**air**
Luftembolie	**air embolism** *The blockage of an artery or vein by an air bubble.*
Lufthunger	**air hunger** *The sensation of shortness of breath.*
Luftröhre	**trachea** *The ringed canal between the pharynx and bronchi.*
Luftstrom	**air flow** *The rate of air movement.*
Lumbago	**lumbago** *Pain in the region of the lumbar spine.*
lumbal	**lumbar** *Referring to the spinal region inferior to the thoracic spine.*
Lumbalpunktion	**lumbar puncture** *Insertion of a needle into the spinal canal in the region of L3-4 to obtain a sample of CSF.*
Lumbalpunktionsnadel	**needle for lumbar puncture**
Lumen	**lumen** *A hollow cavity.*
Lunge	**lung** *One of a pair of respiratory organs.*
Lungenembolie	**pulmonary embolism** *A sudden blockage of a lung artery frequently eminating from a blood clot in one's leg.*
Lungenkapazität	**lung capacity** *The amount of air in the lungs after a maximal inhalation.*
Lungenödem	**pulmonary edema** *Characterized by abnormal fluid buildup in the lungs.*
Lunula	**lunula** *The pale area at the base of a fingernail.*
Lupus erythrematodes	**lupus erythematosous** *An autoimmune inflammatory disease exhibited by a butterfly shaped rash on the face along with visceral and connective tissue abnormalities.*
luteinisierendes Hormon	**luteinizing hormone (LH)** *A pituitary hormone that stimulates ovulation in females and androgen in males.*
luteotrop	**luteotropic** *Synonym of prolactin.*

	English
Lyell-Syndrom	**Lyell's syndrome** *Also called toxic epidermal necrolysis, there are large portions of the skin that become erythematous with epidermal necrosis as seen with 2nd degree burns. This reaction can be seen with use of nevirapine or Bactrim.*
Lymphadenitis	**lymphadenitis** *Inflammation of a lymph node.*
Lymphangiektasie	**lymphangiectasis** *Distention of the lymph channels.*
Lymphangiom	**lymphangioma** *A mass composed of newly formed lymph tissue.*
Lymphangitis	**lymphangitis** *Inflammation of the lymph vessels.*
lymphatisch	**lymphatic** *Referring to the lymph system.*
lymphatische Leukämie	**lymphocytic leukemia** *Chronic accumulation of functionally incompetent lymphocytes.*
Lymphe	**lymph** *A transparent and sometimes opalescent fluid that flows in the lymph channels.*
Lymphknoten	**lymph node** *An area of organized lymphatic tissue.*
Lymphogranulomatose	**Hodgkin's disease** *Also called Hodgkin's lymphoma, it is a cancer that begins in the lymphocytes.*
lymphoid	**lymphoid** *Similar to lymph.*
Lymphom	**lymphoma** *A malignant disease of the lymph system, Hodgkin's lymphoma for example.*
Lymphosarkom	**lymphosarcoma** *A malignant disease of the lymph system that does not include Hodgkin's lymphoma.*
Lymphozyt	**lymphocyte** *A white blood cell produced by the lymph tissue.*
Lymphozytopenie	**lymphocytopenia** *Decrease in the usual number of lymphocytes in the blood.*
Lymphozytose	**lymphocythemia** *Abnormally high number of lymphocytes in the blood.*
Lymphozytose	**lymphocytosis** *The organization of cysts containing lymph.*
Lyse	**lysis** *The rupture of a cell wall or membrane.*
Lysin	**lysine** *An amino acid found in most proteins.*
Lysosom	**lysosome** *An organelle contained in the cytoplasm of eukaryotic cells.*
Lysozym	**lysozyme** *An enzyme in tears that facilitates destruction of certain bacterial cell walls.*
lytisch	**lytic** *Referring to lysis.*
Macula solaris	**macula solaris** *Formal medical term describing a freckle.*
Madenwurm; Enterobius vermicularis	**pinworm** *Common term for Enterobius vermincularis; a nematode worm that is a parasite.*
Madurafuß	**mycetoma** *Persistent inflammation of the tissues caused by an infection.*
Magen	**stomach** *Organ of digestion between the esophagus and small bowel.*
Magenhernie	**gastrocele** *Protrusion of part of the stomach in the form of a hernia.*
Magenkrämpfe	**stomach cramps** *Sensation of muscle contraction in the epigastric area.*
Magensaft	**gastric secretions** *Fluids secreted from gastric mucosa.*
Magenschleimhautentzündung	**gastritis** *Inflammation of the stomach.*
Magenschmerz	**stomach pain** *Discomfort in the abdomen in the epigastric area.*
Magenspülung	**gastric lavage** *Instillation and removal of large quantities of saline into the stomach in order to treat poisoning.*
Magnet	**magnet** *A piece of iron with atoms ordered to make it magnetic.*
magnetisch	**magnetic** *Having the properties of a magnet.*

Magnetresonanztomographie (MRT)	**magnetic resonance imaging (MRI)** *Images are produced by evaluating the response of body tissue. nuclei to radio waves in a magnetic field.*
Makel	**blemish** *A small mark on one's skin.*
Makrocheilie	**macrocheilia** *Abnormally large lips.*
Makrodaktylie	**macrodactyly** *Abnormally large digits.*
Makroencephalie	**macroencephaly** *Having an abnormally large head.*
Makroglobulinämie	**macroglobulinemia** *A condition exhibited by an increase number of macroglobulins in the blood.*
Makroglossie	**macroglossia** *Abnormally large tongue.*
Makromastie	**macromastia** *Abnormally large breasts.*
Makromelie	**macromelia** *Abnormally large head or extremity.*
Makrophage	**macrophage** *A phagocytic cell that originates in the tissues.*
Makrozephalie	**megacephaly** *Having a larger than normal cranial capacity.*
Makrozyt	**macrocyte** *A large red blood cell.*
Makrozytose	**macrocytosis** *Referring to the status of an increased number of large erythrocytes as seen in Vitamin B12 deficiency.*
makuopapulös	**maculopapular** *A skin lesion that is similar to both a macule and a papule.*
Malaria	**malaria** *A condition caused by a protozoan of the genus Plasmodium. It is transmitted by mosquitos and is exhibited by fever, chills, headache. In the severe form it can lead to convulsions, increased ICP and death.*
Malariamittel	**antimalarial** *Medication used to treat malaria.*
Malazie	**malacia** *The abnormal softening of a body part or tissue.*
maligne	**malignant** *Tendency of a tumor to invade normal tissue.*
maligner Hypotonus	**malignant hypertension** *Sudden, severe hypertension associated with neuroretinitis.*
Malleolus lateralis	**malleolus, lateral** *The lateral aspect of the distal fibula.*
Malleolus medialis	**malleolus, medial** *The medial aspect of the distal portion of the tibia.*
Malleolus; Fußnöchel	**malleolus** *A bony protrusion on medial and lateral aspect of each ankle.*
Malleus	**malleus** *Small bone in the inner ear that articulates with the incus.*
Mallory-Weiss-Syndrom	**Mallory-Weiss syndrome** *Upper GI bleeding related to a laceration at the gastroesophageal junction caused by vigorous vomiting.*
Maltose; Malzzucker	**maltose** *A disaccharide hydrolyzed by amylase.*
mamillär	**mammillary** *Referring to a nipple.*
Mamille; Brustwarze	**nipple** *The small projection on the breast thru which milk is secreted.*
Mammaplastik	**mammaplasty** *Plastic surgery of the breast.*
mammär	**mammary** *Referring to the breast.*
Mammographie	**mammography** *Roentgenography of the breasts, used as a screening test for cancer.*
Manie; Tobsucht	**mania** *A mental disorder exhibited by hyperexcitability, delusions and euphoria.*
manifest	**overt** *Not hidden.*
Mann	**man** *Male human.*
Manometer	**manometer** *Device used for pressure monitoring.*
Manschettentubus	**cuffed endotracheal tube** *A cannula that has an balloon on the tip that can be inflated with air and placed into the trachea.*

Manteltablette	**coated tablet** *A pill covered with a substance to slow absorption or reduce gastric irritation.*
Manubrium sterni	**manubrium sterni** *The superior segment of the sternum which articulates with the clavicle and first rib.*
Mapping; Kartierung	**mapping** *A collection of data points showing spatial distribution.*
Marasmus	**marasmus** *Progressive weight loss and emaciation.*
Marfan Syndrom	**Marfan syndrome** *A connective tissue disease exhibited by long limbs, joint laxity and cardiovascular defects.*
Marihuana	**marijuana** *Cannabis.*
Marsupialisation	**marsupialization** *Creation of a surgical pouch.*
Masern	**measles** *A childhood viral, infectious disease exhibited by rash and fever.*
Masern	**Rubeola** *Another term for measles, an acute exanthematous disease.*
Maß	**gauge** *The size or thickness of something. An 18gauge needle.*
Masse	**mass** *Tumor.*
Mastektomie	**mastectomy** *Surgical resection of one or both breasts.*
Mastikation; Kaubewegung	**mastication** *Chewing.*
Mastitis	**mastitis** *Inflammation of the breast.*
Mastodynie	**mastodynia** *Breast pain.*
Mastoidektomie	**mastoidectomy** *Surgical removal of the mastoid.*
Mastoiditis	**mastoiditis** *Inflammation of the mastoid process.*
Mastzelle	**mast cell** *A cell containing basophilic granules that releases histamine and other substances during allergic reactions.*
Matratze	**mattress** *A fabric case filled with material, used for sleeping.*
Matratzennaht	**mattress suture** *A double stitch that forms a loop and there is eversion of the edges when tied.*
Maul- und Klauenseuche	**foot and mouth disease** *A contagious viral disease exhibited by oral and digital vesicles.*
maxillofazial	**maxillofacial** *Referring to the maxilla and the face.*
Mayerscher Grundreflex	**finger-thumb reflex** *Opposition and adduction of the thumb with flexion at the MCP joint and extension at the interphalangeal joint when there is flexion of the 3rd, 4th, and 5th finger. This is present normally and absent with with pyramidal lesions.*
Mazamorra	**mazamorra** *Dermatitis caused by hookworm larvae indigenous to Peurto Rico.*
Mcdonald Manöver	**Mcdonald's maneuver** *A measurement of the uterus in centimeters that corresponds to gestational age in weeks.*
medial	**medial** *Situated toward the midline.*
Mediastinoskopie	**medianstinoscopy** *Visual inspection of the mediastinum with a scope.*
Mediastinum	**mediastinum** *The thoracic area between the lungs.*
Medikament; Droge	**drug** *A medication, sometimes with negative connotation.*
Medikament gegen Ascaris	**ascaricide** *Agent that destroys ascaris.*
Medikamentenverzeichnis	**formulary** *A list of medicines that are permissible to prescribe.*
medikamentöse Behandlung der Migräne	**antimigraine** *Medication used to treat headaches.*
Medikation	**medication** *A substance used for medical treatment.*
medikochirurgisch	**medicosurgical** *Referring to medicine and surgery.*
Medizin; Heilkunde	**medicine** *A substance used for medical treatment or the art and science of healing patients.*

Medulla oblongata	**medulla oblongata** *The inferior portion of the brainstem.*
medullär	**medullary** *1. The inner part of an organ. 2. Referring to the medulla oblongata.*
Medulloblastom	**medulloblastoma** *A malignant tumor of the cerebellum found mostly in children.*
Megakaryozyt	**megakaryocyte** *A cell found in the bone marrow that is a source of platelet production.*
Megakolon	**megacolon** *Abnormal enlargement and dilatation of the colon.*
Megaloblast	**megaloblast** *A large red blood cell noted primarily in pernicious anemia.*
Megalomanie; Größenwahn	**megalomania** *A mental disorder characterized by abnormal feelings of self-importance.*
Mehrfachverletzung	**polytrauma** *A condition exhibited by multiple injuries from blunt or penetrating trauma.*
mehrkammerig	**multilocular** *The presence of more than one cell within a cavity.*
Meibom-Zyste	**meibomian cyst** *An enclosed fluid collection along a sebaceous gland of the eyelid.*
Meilenstein	**milestone** *An event indicative of a certain stage of development.*
Meiose	**meiosis** *Cell division creating two daughter cells each with half the number of cells as the parent cell.*
Mekonium; Kindspech	**meconium** *The first newborn feces which are green.*
Mekoniumaspirationssyndrom	**meconium aspiration** *Presence of meconium on the newborn indicating there was fetal distress in-utero.*
Melaena	**black stools** *Common term for melena.*
Melaena	**melena** *The passage of black, tarry stools indicative of upper gastrointestinal bleeding.*
Melancholie	**melancholia** *Profound sadness.*
Melanom	**melanoma** *Malignant cancer, typically found in the skin.*
Melitis	**melitis** *Inflammation of the cheek.*
Menarche	**menarche** *The time of the initial menstrual period.*
Menge	**amount** *The total or the aggregate.*
meningeal	**meningeal** *Referring to the dura mater, arachnoid and the pia mater.*
Meningeom	**meningioma** *A tumor of the meningeal tissue; generally benign.*
Meningismus	**meningism** *Signs and symptoms of meningitis without infection of the meninges.*
Meningitis	**meningitis** *Inflammation of the meninges exhibited by fever, photophobia, nuchal rigidity and in severe cases coma and convulsions.*
Meningokokkemie	**meningococcemia** *Presence of N. meningitidis in the blood.*
Meningozele	**meningocele** *A congenital defect exhibited by protrusion of the meninges through a defect in the spinal column.*
Meniskektomie	**meniscectomy** *Surgical excision of a meniscus.*
Meniskus	**meniscus** *A thin cartilage between joint surfaces.*
Menkes-Syndrom; Trichopoliodystrophie	**kinky-hair syndrome** *Inborn error of copper metabolism, noted in the first few weeks of life. Exhibited by sparse kinky hair, failure to thrive and seizures. Also called Menke's syndrome or trichopoliodystrophy.*
Menlanin	**melanin** *A dark pigment found on the skin, hair or iris.*
Menopause	**menopause** *The time when menstruation ceases.*
Menorrhagie	**menorrhagia** *Abnormally large amount of menstrual blood.*

menschlich	**human** *Homo sapien.*
Menstruation	**menstruation** *Synonym of menses.*
Menstruationsbinde	**feminine pad** *Gauze specially designed to absorb menstrual flow.*
mental; geistig	**mental** *Cognitive or psychological.*
Mesarteriitis	**mesarteritis** *Inflammation of the middle layer of an artery.*
Mesenchym	**mesenchyme** *Organized mesodermal cells that produce connective tissue, lymphatics and bone.*
Mesenterium	**mesentery** *The fold of peritoneum that connects the small bowel, pancrease and spleen to the posterior portion of the abdominal wall.*
Mesoappendix	**mesoappendix** *The portion of the mesentery vermiform appendix.*
Mesoderm	**mesoderm** *The middle germ layer in an embryo that is the source of bone, muscle and skin.*
Mesokolon	**mesocolon** *The mesentery connecting the colon to the posterior abdominal wall.*
Mesonephrom	**mesonephroma** *Usually a tumor of the female genital tract that is thought to stem from the mesonephros.*
Mesosalpinx	**mesosalpinx** *A portion of the broad ligament supporting the fallopian tubes.*
Mesotheliom	**mesothelioma** *A tumor that stems from mesothelial tissue; a known cause is asbestos exposure.*
Mesovarium	**mesovarium** *The portion of the mesentery connecting the ovary with the abdominal wall.*
metabolisch	**metabolic** *Referring to the physical and chemical reactions involved with keeping an organism functioning.*
metakarophalangeal	**metacarpophalangeal** *Referring to the metacarpus and the phalanges.*
metakarpal	**metacarpal** *The name for any of the five hand bones.*
Metaphyse	**metaphysis** *The region between the diaphysis and the epiphysis.*
Metaplasie	**metaplasia** *Abnormal change in the nature or character of tissue.*
metastatisch Umbilikalknöten	**Sister Mary Joseph nodule** *A nodule at the umbilicus associated with metastatic abdominal cancer.*
metatarsal	**metatarsal** *Any of the bones of the foot.*
Metatarsalgie	**metatarsalgia** *Foot pain.*
Meter (Meßgerät)	**meter** *Unit if measurement. (instrument for measurement)*
Methämoglobin	**methemoglobin** *A substance formed with the oxidation of hemoglobin.*
Methionin	**methionine** *A sulfur-containing amino acid used in the biosynthesis of cysteine.*
Metorrhagie	**metrorrhagia** *Uterine bleeding in normal amounts but at irregular intervals.*
metrisches Maßsystem	**metric system**
Migräne	**migraine** *An episodic, unilateral headache accompanied by nausea.*
Mikrobe	**microbe** *A microorganism.*
Mikrobiologie	**microbiology** *The study of microorganisms.*
Mikrognathie	**micrognathia** *Abnormally small maxilla or mandible.*
Mikrogramm	**microgram** *One millionth of one gram.*
Mikrometer	**micrometer** *One millionth of one meter.*
Mikroophthalmus	**microphthalmos** *A congenital condition characterized by smallness of the eyes.*
Mikroorganismus	**microorganism** *An organism only seen with a microscope.*

Mikroskop	**microscope** *A instrument used to magnify and view small objects.*
mikrozephal	**microcephalic** *A congenital deformity exhibited by an abnormally small head.*
Mikrozyt	**microcyte** *An unusually small erythrocyte associated with anemias, such as iron deficiency anemia.*
Miktion	**micturition** *Synonym of urination.*
Miktionsurographie	**voiding cystography** *Roentgenography of the bladder and urethra after administration of contrast media.*
Milbe	**acarus** *A mite.*
Milch	**lactic** *Referring to milk.*
Milchführendgang	**lactiferous duct** *A canal that carries milk.*
Milchgebiß	**deciduous teeth** *The first teeth.*
mild, leicht	**mild** *Slight, nominal.*
miliar	**miliary** *Referring to a disease that is exhibited by small seed-like lesions (millet), such as miliary tuberculosis.*
Milkmansyndrom	**Milkman syndrome** *Osteomalacia with multiple pseudofractures.*
Milligramm	**milligram** *A unit of weight, 1/1000 of a gram.*
Milliliter	**milliliter** *A unit of volume, 1/1000 of a liter.*
Millimeter	**millimeter** *A unit of measurement, 1/1000 of a meter.*
Milz	**spleen** *The visceral organ that is involved with production and removal of blood cells.*
Minute	**minute** *A unit of time.*
Misanthropie	**misanthropy** *A severe dislike of homo sapiens.*
Mischinfektion	**cross-infection** *Transfer of infection between individuals, each with a different organism.*
Missbrauch (sexueller Missbrauch)	**abuse (sexual abuse)**
Mitesser	**comedones** *The medical term for blackheads.*
Mitochondrien	**mitochondria** *Organelle found in cells responsible for energy production.*
Mitose	**mitosis** *Cell division in which two daughter cells are formed that have the same number of chromosomes as the parent cell.*
mitral	**mitral** *Referring to the mitral valve.*
Mitralinsuffizienz	**mitral regurgitation** *Backflow of blood from the left ventricle to the left atrium because of dysfunctional valve.*
Mitralklappe	**mitral valve** *The valve with two cusps between the left atrium and ventricle.*
Mitralstenose	**mitral stenosis** *Narrowing of the left atrioventricular orifice.*
Mittelhirn	**mesencephalon** *Midbrain.*
Mittelhirn	**midbrain** *The portion of the brainstem superior to the pons.*
Mittellinie	**midline** *A median line of bilateral separation.*
Mittelohr	**ear, middle** *Auris media.*
Mittelohr	**middle ear** *The portion of the ear containing the stapes, incus and malleus.*
Mittelstrahlurin	**clean catch urine specimen** *A urine specimen obtained by having a patient cleanse the perineal area prior to voiding in a collection device.*
Mittelstrahlurin	**midstream urine** *A specimen of urine that is collected after the initial stream of urine is initiated and before one finishes urinating.*

Modiolus	**modiolus** *A column located in the cochlea.*
Molalität	**molality** *The number of moles of a solution per kilogram of pure solvent.*
Molokül	**molecule** *A combination of at least two atoms.*
Monatsbinde	**sanitary napkin** *Cloth or synthetic material used to absorb menstrual blood.*
Monatsblutung	**menses** *The blood and other material expelled from the uterus during menstruation.*
Mondbein; Os lunatum	**lunate bone** *A carpal bone that articulates with the wrist.*
Monoaminoxidasehemmer	**monoamine oxidase inhibitor (MAOI)** *A drug used to treat depression that allows accumulation of serotonin and norepinephrine.*
Monodiplopie	**monodiplopia** *Double vision in only one eye.*
monoklonal	**monoclonal** *Asexual formation of a clone from a single cell.*
Monomanie	**monomania** *A psychotic obsession about a single subject.*
Mononeuritis	**mononeuritis** *Inflammation of a single nerve.*
mononukleär	**mononuclear** *A cell having only one nucleus.*
Mononukleose; Pfeiffer-Drüsenfieber	**mononucleosis** *An infectious disease exhibited by malaise and lymphadenopathy.*
Monoplegie	**monoplegia** *Paralysis of a single limb.*
Monozyt	**monocyte** *A leukocyte with an oval nucleus and grey cytoplasm.*
Monozytose	**monocytosis** *An abnormal increase in the number of monocytes in the blood.*
moosfasern	**mossy fiber** *Nerve fibers that surround the nerve cells of the cerebellar cortex.*
morbid	**morbid** *Indicative of disease.*
Morbidität	**morbidity** *The state of disease.*
Mord	**homicide** *When one person kills another.*
Morgagnisyndrom	**Morgagni's syndrome** *Also called metabolic craniopathy and Stewart-Morel syndrome, it is exhibited by hyperostosis frontalis interna, obesity and neuropsychiatric disorders.*
moribund	**moribund** *Near death.*
Morphin	**morphine** *An opioid analgesic.*
Morphologie	**morphology** *The study of living organisms and the correlation between their structure.*
Morula	**morula** *A solid mass created by the splitting of an ovum.*
Moskitonetz	**mosquito net** *A fine mesh fabric hung over a bed as a mosquito repellent.*
motorisch	**motor** *Referring to muscles.*
motorisch Einheit	**motor unit** *The complex of one motor cell and its attached muscle fibers.*
motorisch Endplatte	**motor end plate** *The expansions on a motor nerve where the branches terminate on muscle fiber.*
Mucosa; Schleimhaut	**mucosa** *A mucous membrane like the buccal mucosa.*
mukoid	**mucoid** *Referring to mucous.*
mukolytisch	**mucolytic** *A substance that breaks down mucous.*
Mukopolysacchaaridose Typ 1	**mucopolysaccharidosis type I** *Also referred to as Hurler syndrome, persons cannot make lysosomal alpha-L-iduronidase which breaks down glycosaminoglycans.*

254

Mukopolysacchaaridose Typ 1s	**mucopolysaccharidosis type Is** *Also referred to as Scheie syndrome, persons cannot produce lysosomal alpha-L-iduronidase. Symptoms include cloudy cornea, hirsutism, prognathism and stiff joints.*
Mukopolysacchaaridose Typ 1V	**mucopolysaccharidosis type IV** *Also referred to as Morquio syndrome, persons do not produce galactosamine-6-sulfatase or in some cases beta-galactosidase. Symptoms include hypermobile joints, macrocephaly, short stature and wide spaced teeth.*
Mukopolysacchaaridose Typ 2	**mucopolysaccharidosis type II** *Also referred to as Hunter syndrome, persons with this inherited condition cannot produce iduronate sulfatase. There are mild to severe forms but all forms have deafness, coarse facial features, hypertrichosis and macrocephaly.*
Mukopolysacchaaridose Typ 3	**mucopolysaccharidosis type III** *Also referred to as Sanfilippo syndrome, persons cannot catabolize the heparan sulfate sugar chain. Symptoms include stiff joints, thick eyebrows, coarse facial features and developmental delays.*
Mukopolysacchaaridose Typ V1	**mucopolysaccharidosis type VI** *Also referred to as Maroteaux-Lamy syndrome. It is characterized by hydrocephalus, macroglossia and coarse facial features but normal intelligence.*
mukopurulent; schleimig-eitrig	**mucopurulent** *That which contains both mucous and pus.*
Mukozele	**mucocele** *An accumulation of mucous in a dilated cavity.*
Mukus; Schleim	**mucus** *A substance secreted by mucous membranes.*
Mulde	**hollow** *An indendation.*
Multigravida	**multigravida** *A woman who has been pregnant more than once.*
Multipara; Mehrgebärende	**multipara** *A woman with more than one live births.*
multiple Sklerose	**multiple sclerosis** *A chronic neurologic disease exhibited by numbness, vision and speech problems, and motor incoordination.*
Mumps; Parotitis epidemica	**mumps** *A contagious viral disease that is exhibited by parotid swelling and puts males at risk for sterility.*
Mund	**mouth** *The orifice on the lower part of the face.*
Mund-zu-Mund	**mouth to mouth** *A manner of artificial respiration.*
Mund-zu-Mund Beatmung	**mouth to mouth resuscitation** *A form of emergency management of respiratory failure.*
Mundgeruch	**halitosis** *Foul odor eminating from the mouth.*
Mundhygiene	**oral hygiene** *Cleansing of the mouth and associated structures.*
Mundsoor	**thrush** *Candida albicans*
Mundvol	**mouthful** *A large quantity of something in one's mouth.*
Muschel	**concha** *A part of the body that is spiral shaped. Nasal concha are the small bones in the sides of the nasal cavity.*
Muskel	**muscle** *A band if fibrous tissue that can contract.*
Muskeldystrophie; Dystrophie musculorum	**muscular dystrophy** *A hereditary condition exhibited by progressive muscular weakness and muscle atrophy.*
Muskelhypertonie	**hypermyotonia** *Excessive muscle tone.*
Muskelschwäche	**muscle weakness** *Decreased muscular function.*
muskulär	**muscular** *Refering to muscles.*
muskuläre Abwehrspannung	**guarding** *A symptom used to describe a patient resisting an examination because of severe pain; often seen in patients with peritonitis.*
mussitierend	**mumble, to** *To speak quietly and indistinctly.*
Mutation	**mutation** *A gene alteration that can be passed to the next generation.*
Mutismus	**mutism** *Inability to speak.*

Muzin	**mucin** *A glycoprotein that is the primary constituent in mucous.*
müde	**tired** *Fatigued.*
mündlich	**orally** *By mouth.*
Myalgie	**myalgia** *Muscle pain.*
Myasthenie gravis pseudoparalytica; Hoppe-Goldflam Syndrom	**myasthenia gravis** *An autoimmune disease characterized by fluctuating weakness of the ocular, limb and respiratory muscles.*
Mydriasis	**mydriasis** *Pupillary dilation.*
Myelin	**myelin** *The substance that forms a sheath around some nerve fibers.*
Myelitis	**myelitis** *Inflammation of the spinal cord.*
Myelogramm	**myelogram** *CT scan or roentgenography of the spinal canal after injection of contrast media.*
myeloid	**myeloid** *Referring to the bone marrow or spinal cord.*
Myelom; Plasmozytom	**myeloma** *Malignant tumor of the bone marrow.*
Myelomatose	**myelomatosis** *A leukemic disease in which there is an abnormally high amount of myeloblasts in the blood.*
Myelomeningozele	**myelomeningocele** *A protrusion of the spinal cord and its meninges through a defect in the vertebral canal.*
Myelopathie	**myelopathy** *A condition of the spinal cord.*
Myelozele	**myelocele** *Protrusion of the spinal cord through a defect in the bony structure.*
Mykose	**mycosis** *A disease caused by a fungal infection.*
Mykotoxin	**mycotoxin** *A substance toxic to fungus.*
Myoglobin	**myoglobin** *A protein within muscle that carries and stores oxygen.*
Myokard	**myocardium** *The middle layer of the heart wall.*
myokardial	**myocardial** *Referring to the muscular tissue of the heart.*
Myokardinfarkt; Herzinfarkt	**myocardial infarction** *The death of myocardial tissue as a result of an interruption in flow to the region supplied by a coronary vessel.*
Myoklonus	**myoclonus** *Contraction or spasm of a group of muscles.*
Myom	**myoma** *A benign neoplasm of muscular tissue.*
Myomektomie	**myomectomy** *Surgical resection of a myoma.*
Myometrium	**myometrium** *The smooth muscle layer of the uterus.*
Myopathie	**myopathy** *Muscle disease.*
myope Person	**myope** *A person who is nearsighted.*
Myopie	**myopia** *Nearsightedness.*
Myosarkom	**myosarcoma** *A mass with myoma and sarcoma characteristics.*
Myosin	**myosin** *A protein that when coupled with actin form the contractile complex of a muscle cells.*
Myositis ossificans	**myositis ossificans** *Inflammation of muscle tissue with presence of bony deposits.*
Myositis; Muskelentzündung	**myositis** *Inflammation of muscle tissue.*
Myotomie	**myotomy** *The surgical removal of muscle tissue.*
Myotonie dystrophica	**myotonia dystrophica; Steinert's disease** *A condition exhibited initially by hypertonic muscles followed by atrophy of the facial and neck muscles.*
Myringitis; Trommelfellentzündung	**myringitis** *Inflammation of the tympanic membrane.*
Myringoplastik	**myringoplasty** *Surgical repair of tympanic membrane defects.*

Myringotomie	**myringotomy** *Surgical opening of the tympanic membrane.*
Mysophobie	**mysophobia** *Severe fear of dirt or contamination from common objects.*
Myxom	**myxoma** *A tumor composed of mucous tissue.*
Myxosarkom	**myxosarcoma** *A sarcoma that also has mucous tissue.*
Myxödem	**myxedema** *Diffuse edema with a wax-like appearance of the skin; this condition is associated with hypothyroidism.*
Nabel	**navel** *Umbilicus.*
Nabel; Umbilicus	**umbilicus** *The scar that denotes the end of the umbilical cord.*
Nabelentzündung	**omphalitis** *Inflammation of the umbilicus.*
Nabelhernie	**hernia, umbilical** *Protrusion of abdominal contents at the umbilicus.*
Nabelschnur	**umbilical cord** *The stalk between the placenta and the unborn infant.*
Nabelschnurvorfall	**cord presentation** *The presence of the umbilical cord at the cervix during active labor.*
Nabelschnurvorfall	**prolapse of the umbilical cord** *Refers to the umbilical cord protruding from the cervix during active labor.*
Nachgeburt; Plazenta	**afterbirth** *The tissue expelled after the birth of a child that includes the placenta and allied membranes.*
Nachgeschmack	**after-taste** *The sensation of a prolonged savor following eating/ drinking.*
Nachkommenschaft	**offspring** *One's children.*
Nachlast	**after-load** *Referring to the amount of pressure the heart needs to pump against. If one has left heart failure it is beneficial to reduce after-load.*
Nachname	**surname** *One's given "last" name that generally changes for women upon marriage to that of the man's surname.*
Nachreflex; Rückprall	**rebound** *A term used to describe a type of tenderness found with peritonitis.*
Nachtarbeit	**night shift** *The late shift, typically beginning at 19:00 or 23:00 hours.*
Nachtblindheit	**night blindness** *Common term for nyctalopia, it refers to low vision with reduced illumination, often seen with Vitamin A deficiency.*
nachteilig	**detrimental** *Harmful.*
Nachträufeln des Urins	**dribbling of urine** *Slow, drip-by-drip urine flow.*
Nachtschweiß	**night sweats** *Profuse sweating at night occurring with tuberculosis among other conditions.*
Nachwehen	**after-pains** *The pain experienced after childbirth caused by uterine contractions.*
Nadel	**needle** *The slender cylindrical device attached to a syringe.*
Nadelbiopsie	**needle biopsy** *Use of a needle to aspirate body contents for microscopic or pathologic examination.*
Nadelhalter	**needle holder** *A surgical instrument used to grasp a needle during suturing.*
Nadelstichverletzung	**needle-stick injury** *The inadvertent self-puncture with a needle that had been used previously to inject a patient.*
Naevus	**nevus** *A benign, well-circumscribed growth of tissue of congenital origin.*
Nagel	**nail** *The hard surface on the dorsal surface of the toes or fingers.*
Nagelbett	**nailbed** *The area just beneath a finger or toenail.*
Nagelbettentzündung	**onychia** *Inflammation of the toenail or fingernail matrix.*

Nagelung	**nailing** *Referring to placement of an intramedullary rod in a long bone in order to treat a fracture.*
Nagetier	**rodent** *A gnawing mammal that includes rats and mice.*
nah	**near** *In close proximity.*
Nahrung	**food** *Nutrition.*
Nahrungsbrei	**bolus** *A fluid bolus is a phrase used for rapid infusion of fluid.*
Nahrungsmittelaufnahme	**food intake** *Quantitative record of nutritional intake.*
Name; Bezeichnung	**name** *A word by which a person is known.*
namelos	**innominate** *Referring to the innominate artery.*
Namelosarterie	**innominate artery** *The first branch off the aortic arch that branches into the right common carotid and right subclavian arteries.*
Narbe	**cicatrix (scar)** *New tissue in a healed wound.*
narbig	**cicatricial** *Referring to cicatrix.*
Narkolepsie; Gélineau Syndrom	**narcolepsy** *A condition exhibited by a strong desire to sleep and by sudden onset of sleep at increased intervals.*
Narkose; Betäubung	**narcosis** *A reversible medication-induced condition of excessive drowsiness or unconsciousness.*
Narzissmus	**narcissism** *Abnormally excessive self-interest.*
nasal	**nasal** *Referring to the nose.*
Nase	**nose** *The midface protuberance used for smelling and breathing.*
Nasenbluten; Epistaxis	**nosebleed** *Common term for epistaxis.*
Nasenloch	**nostril** *One of two openings in the nose used for air passage.*
Nasenmuschel	**turbinate bones** *The three curved shelves in the nasal cavity.*
nasenneben	**paranasal** *Situated adjacent to the nose.*
Nasennebenhöhle	**paranasal sinuses** *Any of the sinuses (ethmoidal, frontal, maxillary or sphenoidal) that communicate with the nasal cavity.*
Nasenplastik	**rhinoplasty** *Plastic surgery performed on the nose.*
Nasenscheidewandverkrümmung	**deviated septum** *Characterized by deviation of the nasal septum.*
Nasensekret	**discharge, nasal** *Nasal secretions.*
nasolakrimal	**nasolacrimal** *Referring to the nose and tear apparatus.*
Nasomagensonde	**nasogastric tube** *A tube that is inserted into the nose with the distal tip in the stomach; it is used for irrigation or drainage of gastric contents.*
Nasomagensonde einbringen	**nasogastric tube placement** *Insertion of a tube that is placed in the stomach via the nostril; it is used for administration of fluid or to suction gastric contents.*
nasopharyngeal	**nasopharyngeal** *Referring to the nose and pharynx.*
Nasopharynx; Nasenrachenraum	**nasopharynx** *The part of the pharynx which lies superior to the soft palate.*
nativ	**indigenous** *Naturally occurring.*
Natriumchlorid	**sodium chloride** *A colorless, crystalline compound; also table salt.*
Nausea; Übelkeit; Brechreiz	**nausea** *A feeling that one wants to vomit.*
navikulär	**navicular** *1. boat shaped 2. Referring to the navicular bone of the hand or foot.*
nächste	**next** *The following or upcoming.*
nächtlich	**nocturnal** *Referring to events that happen at night.*
Nährstoff; Nahrungsstoff	**nutrient** *A substance that provides essential nourishment.*
nässen	**weep, to** *To ooze fluid, such as from a wound.*
Nebelfleck	**nebula** *An opaque spot on the cornea causing impaired vision.*

	English
Nebenniere	**adrenal gland** *A gland located on the superior aspect of both kidneys.*
Nebennierenextrirpation	**adrenalectomy** *Excision of the adrenal gland.*
Nebennierenmark	**adrenal medulla** *The innermost part of the adrenal gland.*
Nebennierenrinde	**adrenal cortex** *The outer layer of the adrenal gland.*
Nebenwirkung	**adverse effect** *In reference to medication use, it is an undesirable consequence of the drug.*
Nebenwirkung	**side effect** *An expected but unwanted effect of a medication.*
negativ	**negative** *Contrary or opposing.*
Nekrose	**necrosis** *The death of most of the cells of the affected part.*
nekrotisch	**necrotic** *Referring to necrosis.*
Nematode	**nematode** *An endoparasite belonging to the class of the Nemathelminthes including roundworms and threadworms.*
neonatal	**neonatal** *Referring to the first four weeks after birth.*
Neoplasma	**neoplasm** *A new and abnormal growth.*
Nephrektomie	**nephrectomy** *Surgical removal of a kidney.*
Nephritis; Nierenentzündung	**nephritis** *A general term meaning inflammation of a kidney that is further categorized depending on the associated pathology.*
Nephroblastom; Wilms-Tumor	**nephroblastoma** *Congenital tumor of the kidney, also called Wilms' tumor.*
Nephrokalzinose	**nephrocalcinosis** *A condition exhibited by calcium phosphate deposition in the renal tubules; a cause of renal insufficiency.*
Nephrolithiasis	**nephrolithiasis** *A calculus in the kidney.*
Nephrolithotomie	**nephrolithotomy** *Surgical removal of a renal calculus.*
Nephrom; Nierentumor	**nephroma** *A renal tumor.*
Nephron	**nephron** *A functional unit of the kidney that consists of the glomerulus, the proximal and distal convoluted tubules, the loop of Henle and the collecting tubule.*
Nephropathie	**nephropathy** *Renal disease.*
Nephropexie	**nephropexy** *The surgical fixation of a kidney that was previously floating.*
Nephroptose	**nephroptosis** *Inferior displacement of the kidney.*
Nephrose	**nephrosis** *A kidney disease exhibited by edema and proteinuria; also called nephrotic syndrome.*
Nephrosklerose	**nephrosclerosis** *Hardening of the kidney.*
Nephrostomie	**nephrostomy** *Surgical creation of an opening between the renal pelvis and an opening in the skin.*
nephrotisch	**nephrotic** *Referring to nephrosis.*
Nephrotomie	**nephrotomy** *Surgical incision of the kidney.*
Nerv	**nerve** *A fibrous band made up of axons and dendrites that connects the nervous systems with other organs.*
Nervenimpuls	**nerve impulse** *A signal transmitted along a nerve fiber.*
Nervenkompressionssyndrom	**entrapment neuropathy** *Weakness or numbness caused by compression of a peripheral nerve.*
Nervus accessorius	**accessory nerve (XI)** *Supplies motor innervation to the sternocleidomastoid and trapezius.*
Nervus facialis	**facial nerve** *Cranial nerve VII that supplies the face and tongue.*
Nervus okulomotorisch	**oculomotor nerve** *Referring to cranial nerve III which is one of the nerves responsible for extraocular movements.*

Nervus splanchnicus	**splanchnic nerves** *The nerves supplying the abdominal viscera and blood vessels.*
Nervus ulnaris	**ulnar nerve** *Arises from the C8-T1 nerves and supplies the hand. (Injury to the ulnar nerve causes loss of flexion of the metacarpophalangeal joints and extension at the interphalangeal joints, thus the common term, claw hand.)*
Nervus vagus	**vagus nerve** *The tenth cranial nerve that supplies the heart, lungs visceral organs; its function is tested by assessment of elevation of the uvula.*
Netzhaut; Retina	**retina** *The innermost of three layers of the eyeball; it surrounds the vitreous body and is continuous with the optic nerve.*
Netzhautablösung	**retinal detachment** *A tear or hole in the retina caused by vitreous traction.*
Neugeborenenikterus	**jaundice of the newborn** *A form of jaundice seen in newborns in the first two weeks of life; also called icterus neonatorum.*
Neugeborenes	**neonate** *The term for a newborn infant for the first four weeks.*
Neugrad	**grade** *A level of rank or quality.*
neural	**neural** *Referring to a nerve or nerve impulse.*
Neuralgie	**neuralgia** *Severe pain along the course of a nerve.*
Neurapraxie	**neurapraxia** *Paralysis from nerve injury but no degeneration of the nerve.*
Neurasthenie	**neurasthenia** *A psychoneurosis exhibited by severe fatigue.*
Neurektomie	**neurectomy** *Excision of a section of a nerve.*
Neurilemm	**neurilemma** *The membrane covering a myelinated nerve fiber or the axon of an unmyelinated nerve fiber.*
Neuritis; Nervenentzündung	**neuritis** *Inflammation of a nerve.*
Neuroblastom	**neuroblastoma** *A nervous system malignant tumor composed of neuroblasts.*
Neurochirurgie	**neurosurgery** *Surgery of the brain or spinal cord.*
Neurodermatitis; atopisches Ekzem	**neurodermatitis** *A pruritic, thickened eruption in the axillary and inguinal thought to be exacerbated by emotions.*
Neuroepithel	**neuroepithelium** *Cells specialized to serve as sensory cells such as cells of the cochlea and tongue.*
Neurofibrom	**neurofibroma** *A tumor formed by excessive growth of perineurium and endoneurium.*
Neurofibromatose; Reckinghausen-Krankheit	**neurofibromatosis** *A hereditary condition exhibited by formation of multiple soft tumors scattered throughout the skin surface. Also known as von Recklinghausen disease.*
Neuroglia	**neuroglia** *A type of connective tissue of the nervous system.*
Neuroleptikasyndrom	**neuroleptic malignant syndrome** *A severe reaction to neuroleptic medications characterized by hyperthermia with autonomic and extrapyramidal symptoms.*
Neuroleptikum	**neuroleptic** *A drug that causes neurologic symptoms.*
Neurologe	**neurologist** *A physician who specializes in the study of the nervous system.*
Neurologie	**neurology** *The study of the nervous system.*
Neurom	**neuroma** *A mass composed of nerve cells and fibers.*
Neuron	**neuron** *A nerve cell.*
Neuropathie	**neuropathy** *Structural of pathologic changes of the peripheral nervous system.*

neuropathisch	**neuropathic** *Referring to neuropathy.*
Neurose	**neurosis** *A mental disorder.*
Neurosyphilis	**neurosyphilis** *Infection of the central nervous system with Treponema pallidum.*
Neurotmesis	**neurotmesis** *The severing of a nerve.*
Neurotomie	**neurotomy** *Surgical incision into a nerve.*
Neurotransmitter	**neurotransmitter** *A substance released at the end of a nerve fiber that facilitates transmission of an impulse.*
Neurtropenie	**neutropenia** *Diminished number of neutrophils in the blood.*
Neutrophile	**neutrophil** *A polymorphonuclear leukocyte.*
nicht perforiert	**imperforate** *Lack of an opening. An infant with an imperforate anus has a congenital defect with no anal opening.*
Nichtrückatmungsmaske	**non-rebreather mask** *A type of oxygen mask used to deliver a higher oxygen concentration.*
Nickbewegung	**nutation** *Referring to nodding of the head.*
Nickerchen	**nap** *A brief sleep or catnap.*
Nicotinsäure	**nicotinic acid** *A deficiency of this substance results in pellagra.*
Nidation	**implementation** *The process of putting a plan into effect.*
niederträchtig	**verminous** *Referring to presence of worms.*
Niednagel	**hangnail** *A loose piece of skin attached near the medial or lateral nail fold.*
Niere	**kidney** *One of two glandular organs that form urine.*
Nierenbecken	**renal pelvis** *The kidney collecting system.*
Nierenkelch (renalis)	**calyx** *A cup shaped organ or cavity.*
Nierenkolik	**renal colic** *Pain caused by passage of a calculus through the ureter.*
Nierenversagen	**renal failure** *Diminution of kidney function.*
niesen	**sneeze, to** *To suddenly expel air from the nose and mouth because of nasal irritation.*
nippen	**sip, to** *To slowly take small drinks of a fluid.*
Nonne-Milroy-Krankheit; Lymphödem	**Milroy's disease** *Hereditary disease exhibited by leg edema.*
Noradrenalin	**norepinephrine** *A hormone secreted by the adrenal medulla and a synthetic drug used as a pressor agent.*
Normoblast	**normoblast** *A precursor cell for erythrocytes.*
Normozyt	**normocyte** *A normal erythrocyte.*
Nosologie	**nosology** *The medical science of disease classification.*
Nosophobie	**nosophobia** *Unwarranted, excessive fear of any disease.*
Notfall	**emergency** *An urgent, life-threatening situation.*
Notfallstation	**emergency room** *A ward used for initial treatment of critical patients.*
nsokomiale infektion	**nosocomial infection** *An infection occurring after admission to a hospital.*
Nuklearmedizin	**nuclear medicine** *The branch of medicine associated with the use of radioactive material in the evaluation and treatment of disease.*
nukleär	**nuclear** *Referring to a nucleus.*
Nukleinsäure	**nucleic acid** *An organic compound found in living cells; its molecules contain nucleotides linked in long chains.*
Nukleoprotein	**nucleoprotein** *A substance composed of a nucleic acid and a protein.*

Nukleus ruber	**red nucleus** *A collection of gray matter near the subthalamus that receives data from the superior cerebellar peduncle.*
null	**zero** *No quantity.*
Nulligravida	**nulligravida** *A woman who has never been pregnant.*
Nullipara	**nullipara** *A woman who has never given birth.*
nüchtern; Fasten	**fasting** *Absence of caloric intake for a specified period.*
Nykturie; nächtliches Wasserlassen	**nocturia** *Urination at night.*
Nylon-Sutur	**non-resorbable suture (nylon)** *Suture used to be permanent as it is not removed by normal body processes.*
Nystagmus	**nystagmus** *Rapid involuntary movement of the eyes; it can be horizontal, vertical or rotary.*
obdachlos	**homeless** *Having nowhere to live.*
oben, über	**above**
Oberarmarterie	**brachial artery** *A continuation of the axillary artery and branches into the radial and ulnar among others.*
oberer	**superior** *In a position above something else.*
Oberflächenaktive Substanz	**surfactant** *A substance that reduces surface tension in the lungs.*
Oberflächenleistenring	**superficial inguinal ring** *The opening of the aponeurosis of the external oblique muscle for the round ligament or spermatic cord.*
Oberglied	**upper limb** *Referring to either arm.*
Oberhaut	**cuticle** *The dead skin at the base of the toenail or fingernail, also called the eponychium.*
Oberkiefer	**maxilla** *The upper jaw that also forms the inferior portion of the orbit and part of the nose.*
Oberlippe	**lip, upper** *Labium superius oris.*
Oberrespirationstrakt	**upper respiratory tract** *Generally considered the part of the respiratory tract superior to the vocal cords.*
Oberschenkel	**thigh** *The body region between the inguinal crease and knee.*
Oberschenkelarterie	**femoral artery** *Continuation of the external iliac to the popliteal artery.*
Oberschenkelhals	**neck of the femur** *The portion of the femur between the shaft and head.*
Oberschenkelknochen	**femur** *The long bone in the thigh.*
Oberschenkelnerv	**femoral nerve** *Supplies the motor function of the quadriceps and the sensation over the anterior and medial thigh.*
Objektträger	**slide** *A thin, rectangular piece of glass used for viewing specimen under a microscope.*
obligatorisch	**mandatory** *Obligatory.*
obsolet	**obsolete** *No longer in use; antiquated.*
Obstipation; Darmträgheit; Verstopfung	**constipation** *A condition exhibited by difficulty in having a bowel movement due to hard stools.*
Obturator	**obturator** *A device used to close an artificial or natural opening.*
Odontalgie; Zahnschmerz	**odontalgia** *Tooth pain.*
odontoid	**odontoid** *A prominence on the second cervical vertebra on which the first cervical vertebra pivots.*
Odontologie	**odontology** *Synonym of dentistry.*
offene Fraktur	**fracture, open** *A fracture in which there is a break in the skin and bone is exposed.*

offene Reposition	**open reduction (of fractures)** *The realignment of a fractured bone using a surgical approach.*
offener Fraktur	**compound fracture** *Open fracture.*
offensichtlich	**evident** *Obvious.*
Offnung	**aperture** *An opening or hole, as in the hole the light passes through in a camera.*
Ohnmacht; kurze Gedächtnisstörung	**blackout** *Common term for loss of consciousness.*
Ohr	**ear** *The organ of hearing and balance.*
Ohr äußeres; Außenohr	**ear, external** *Auris externa.*
Ohr inneres	**ear, inner** *Auris interna.*
Ohrenfluß	**discharge, ear** *Otic secretions.*
Ohrensausen	**ringing in the ears** *Common term for tinnitus.*
Ohrensausen	**tinnitus** *Medical term for ringing in the ears. It is associated with Meniere's syndrome among other conditions.*
Ohrenschmerz	**earache** *Pain associated with the ear.*
Ohrläppchen	**earlobe** *The soft, fleshy inferior portion of the pinna.*
Ohrsignal	**aural** *Referring to the ear.*
Okklusion; Verschluß	**occlusion** *A pathway that is blocked or obstructed.*
Okklusivverband	**occlusive dressing** *A synthetic covering for a wound that has a semipermeable membrane.*
okkultes Blut	**occult blood** *Presence of blood from an unknown source.*
Okular; okulär	**ocular** *Referring to the eye.*
okulogyre	**oculogyric** *Referring to movement of the eye around the anteroposterior axis.*
okzipital	**occipital** *Referring to the back part of the head.*
okzipitofrontal Muskel	**occipitofrontal muscle** *Raises the eyebrows.*
Olekranon	**olecranon** *The bony protrusion at the proximal ulna at the elbow.*
olfaktorisch	**olfactory** *Referring to the sense of smell.*
Oligodaktylie	**oligodactyly** *Presence of fewer than 5 digits on a hand or foot.*
Oligodendroglia	**oligodendroglia** *The ectodermal cells forming part of the central nervous system.*
Oligohydramnie	**oligohydramnios** *Inadequate amount of amniotic fluid.*
Oligomenorrhö	**oligomenorrhea** *Infrequent menstruation or low volume menstrual flow.*
Oligosialie	**oligoptyalism** *Insufficient secretion of saliva; also oligosialia.*
Oligospermie	**oligospermia** *Abnormally low sperm count.*
Oligotrichie	**oligotrophia or hypotrichosis** *Less than normal amount of head/body hair.*
Oligurie	**oliguria** *Abnormally low urine output.*
Ombrophobie	**ombrophobia** *An abnormal fear of rain.*
Omentopexie	**omentopexy** *Surgically fastening the omentum to an adjacent tissue it was not previously attached to.*
Omentozele	**omentocele** *A herniated protrusion of omentum.*
Omentum; Netz	**omentum** *A fold of peritoneum fastening the stomach to other organs in the viscera.*
Omphalozele	**omphalocele** *A large congenital, umbilical hernia with only a thin membranous covering.*

263

Onchozerkose	**craw-craw** *A pruritic papular skin eruption sometimes caused by Onchocerca.*
Onkologe	**oncologist** *A phyisician specializing in the treatment of cancer.*
Onkologie	**oncology** *The study of cancer.*
Onychocryptose	**onychocryptosis** *Ingrown toenail.*
Onychogryphose	**onychogryphosis** *A deformed nail that is incurved or hooked.*
Onychomykose	**onychomycosis** *Fungal disease of the toenails or fingernails.*
Onychophagie	**onychophagia** *Habitually chewing on one's fingernails.*
Oogenese	**oogenesis** *The initiation and development of an ovum.*
Oophorektomie	**oophorectomy** *Surgical removal of an ovary.*
Oophoritis; Eierstockentzündung	**oophoritis** *Inflammation of an ovary.*
Oophorosalpingektomie	**oophorosalpingectomy** *Surgical removal of an ovary and fallopian tube.*
Oozyt	**oocyte** *An ovarian cell that needs to undergo meiotic division to become an ovum.*
Operationsabdecktuch	**drape** *The fabric used as a sterile covering in the OR.*
Operationsbericht	**operative note** *A detailed description of a surgical procedure performed on a specific patient.*
Operationskittel	**gown** *A sterile gown used during surgical procedures.*
Ophthalmie	**ophthalmia** *Profound inflammation of the eye or its structures.*
ophthalmisch	**ophthalmic** *Referring to the eye.*
Ophthalmologe	**ophthalmologist** *A physician specializing in diseases of the eye.*
Ophthalmoplegie	**ophthalmoplegia** *Paralysis of the eye muscles.*
Ophthalmoskop; Augenspiegel	**ophthalmoscope** *A device used to visually inspect the interior eye.*
Opiat	**opiate** *Referring to opium.*
Opiat; Betäubungsmittel	**narcotic** *A medication that produces narcosis.*
opioid	**opioid** *A substance similar to opium that binds to at least one of the opium receptors in the body.*
Opisthotonus	**opisthotonos** *A profound spasm in which the head/neck is hyperextended, the feet are touching the bed and with the patient supine the body arched upward.*
Opium	**opium** *An addictive drug derived from opium poppy; synthetic versions are used as analgesics.*
Oppenheimreflex	**Oppenheim reflex** *Extension of the toes elicited by scratching of the medial leg; present when the patient has cerebral irritation.*
Opponens	**opponens** *Synonym for opponent muscle.*
Opsonin	**opsonin** *An antibody used to facilitate phagocytosis of a bacterium.*
Optiker	**optician** *A person who makes eyeglasses.*
optisch	**optic** *Referring to the eye.*
Optometrie	**optometry** *The profession of examination of the eyes for disease (not a medical doctor).*
Optometrist	**optometrist** *A person who pratices optometry.*
oral	**oral** *Relating to the mouth.*
orales Kontrazeptivum	**oral contraceptive** *Tablet taken by mouth to prevent pregnancy.*
orbikulär	**orbicular** *Rounded or circular.*
Orbita	**orbit** *The bony structure enclosing the eyeball.*
Orchialgie	**orchialgia** *Testicular pain.*
Orchidopexie	**orchidopexy** *Surgical repair of an undescended testis.*

Orchiektomie; Hodenentfernung	**orchidectomy** *Synonym of orchiectomy; removal of one or both testes.*
Orchiepididymitis	**orchiepididymitis** *Inflammation of the testis and epididymis.*
Orchitis	**orchitis** *Inflammation of one or both testes.*
Organ	**organ** *A part of the body that is self contained and serves a vital function.*
Organomegalie	**organomegaly** *Enlargement of an organ,typically referring to an intraabdominal organ.*
Orientbeule; Nilbeule	**oriental sore** *A stigmata of cutaneous leishmaniasis caused by a bite from a sand fly.*
Ornithose	**ornithosis** *A viral infection transmitted by birds that is manifested by chills, headache, photophobia, fever, nausea and vomiting.*
Orohypopharynx	**oropharynx** *The portion of the pharynx between the soft palate and the superior aspect of the epiglottis.*
Orthese	**orthosis** *Straightening of a malaligned part with the use of braces and other supportive devices.*
Orthodontie	**orthodontics** *A subspecialty of dentistry concerned with treatment of dental irregularities and malocclusion, including the use of braces.*
Orthopädie	**orthopedics** *A surgical specialty concerned with treatment of skeletal problems.*
Orthopnoe	**orthopnea** *The inability to breath comfortably except in the upright position.*
orthostatisch	**orthostatic** *Referring to the standing position. Orthostatic hypotension is low blood pressure in the standing position.*
ortibal	**orbital** *Referring to the orbit.*
Osmol	**osmole** *The recognized unit of osmotic pressure.*
Osmolalität	**osmolality** *The concentration expressed in total number of solute particles per kilogram.*
Osmose	**osmosis** *The movement of a solvent from a solution of greater concentration to one of lower concentration through a semi-permeable membrane until the two solutions have equal concentration.*
osmotisch	**osmotic** *Referring to osmosis.*
Ossifikation	**ossification** *The formation of bone.*
Osteoarthritis	**osteoarthritis** *A long term, progressive degenerative joint disease.*
Osteoblast	**osteoblast** *A cell that matures from a fibroblast and produces bone.*
osteochondral	**osteochondral** *Referring to bone and cartilage.*
Osteochondritis	**osteochondritis** *Inflammation of bone and cartilage.*
Osteochondrom	**osteochondroma** *A tumor with bony and cartilaginous characteristics.*
Osteodystrophie	**osteodystrophy** *Abnormal bone formation.*
Osteogenese	**osteogenesis** *Development of new bones.*
Osteogenesis imperfecta	**fragilitas ossium** *A condition exhibited by excessively brittle bones. Also called osteogenesis imperfecta.*
Osteogenesis imperfecta	**ostogenesis imperfecta** *A connective tissue disorder characterized by bone fragility, skeletal deformity, blue sclerae, ligament laxity, and hearing loss.*
Osteoklasie	**osteoclasis** *The surgical fracture of a bone usually in order to restore proper alignment.*
Osteoklast	**osteoclast** *A large bone cell that is associated with bone reabsorption and removal.*
Osteoklastom	**osteoclastoma** *A tumor composed of giant cells or osteoclasts.*

osteolytisch	**osteolytic** *Referring to the removal or loss of calcium from the bone.*
Osteomalazie	**osteomalacia** *Softening of the bones because of a deficiency of vitamin D, calcium or phosphorus.*
Osteopathie	**osteopathy** *1. Any disease of the bone. 2. Medical practice concerning treatment of disease by manipulation and massage of bones, joints, and muscles.*
Osteopetrose	**osteopetrosis** *Increased bone density with no change in modeling.*
Osteophonie	**osteophony** *The sound conduction of bone.*
Osteophyt	**osteophyte** *Abnormal growth of a bone protuberance.*
Osteoporose	**osteoporosis** *Loss of bone substance because the osteoblasts fail to produce bone matrix.*
Osteosarkom	**osteosarcoma** *A tumor composed of a sarcoma and osseous material.*
Osteosklerose	**osteosclerosis** *Abnormal hardening of bone.*
Osteotomie	**osteotomy** *Creation of a surgical opening in bone.*
Osteozyt	**osteocyte** *An osteoblast within the bone matrix.*
Ostitis	**osteitis** *Inflammation of the bone.*
Ostium; Mündung	**ostium** *A vessel or body cavity opening.*
Ostomyelitis	**osteomyelitis** *Inflammation of the bone or bone marrow because of a microorganism.*
Otalgie	**otalgia** *Ear pain.*
Otitis; Ohrenentzündung	**ear infection** *General term referring to otitis media or otitis externa.*
Otitis; Ohrenentzündung	**otitis** *Inflammation of the ear. (otitis media or otitis externa)*
Otolith	**otolith** *A calcium based calculus in the inner ear.*
Otologie	**otology** *Study of conditions and anatomy of the ear.*
Otomykose	**otomycosis** *Fungal infection of the ear.*
Otosklerose	**otosclerosis** *A hereditary condition exhibited by progressive hearing loss because of bone overgrowth in the inner ear.*
Otoskop	**otoscope** *A device used for inspection of the tympanic membrane.*
ototoxisch	**ototoxic** *A substance harmful to the ear or its nerve supply.*
Ovarialzyst	**ovarian cysts** *Generally used to describe benign tumors.*
Ovulation	**ovulation** *The release of an ova from the ovary.*
Oxalurie	**oxaluria** *Existence of oxalates in the urine.*
Oxidation	**oxidation** *The process of a chemical combining with oxygen.*
Oximeter	**oximeter** *A medical device used to measure the percent of oxygen that is saturated in the blood (oxygen saturation).*
Oxyhämoglobin	**oxyhemoglobin** *The combination of oxygen and hemoglobin using a covalent bond.*
Oxytocicum	**oxytocic** *Referring to rapid parturition.*
Oxytocin	**oxytocin** *A natural hormone released by the pituitary or a synthetic hormone that facilitates uterine contraction.*
Ozäna	**ozena** *Various nasal conditions, all of which include fetid discharge.*
Ozon	**ozone** *A toxic chemical that has profound oxidizing properties. It has three atoms in its molecule compared with oxygen which has two.*
Ödem	**edema** *Extravascular fluid accumulation.*
ödematös	**edematous** *Referring to the presence of edema.*
ödematös Beine	**lower extremity edema** *Interstitial edema of the legs.*
Öffnung; Mündung	**orifice** *Synonym of foramen.*
ösophageal	**esophageal** *Referring to the esophagus.*

Ösophagektomie	**esophagectomy** *Surgical removal of the esophagus.*
Ösophagitis	**esophagitis** *Inflammation of the esophagus.*
Ösophagoskopie	**esophagoscopy** *Visual inspection the esophagus utilizing a scope.*
Ösophagus; Speiseröhre	**esophagus** *The muscular tube that connects the throat to the stomach.*
Pachydermie	**pachydermia** *An abnormally thick skin.*
Pachymeningitis	**pachymeningitis** *Inflammation of the dura mater.*
Pagophagie	**pagophagia** *Compulsive need to eat ice which is usually associated with iron deficiency anemia.*
palatinal Myoklonus	**palatal myoclonus** *An involuntary, persistent, rapid regular tremor of the soft palate and face.*
Palatoplegie	**palatoplegia** *Paralysis of the palate.*
palliativ	**palliative** *A treatment used to reduce pain when cure is not possible.*
Pallidektomie	**pallidectomy** *Surgical resection of all or part of the palate.*
Pallidum	**globus pallidus** *A portion of the lentiform nucleus in the brain.*
palmar	**palmar** *Referring to the palm.*
Palpation	**palpation** *The assessment of the body with the use of one's hands.*
Palpitation; Herzklopfen	**palpitation** *Sensation of a forceful, rapid, irregular heartbeat present after exercise or with anxiety.*
Panaritium	**whitlow** *An abscess occurring on the palmar surface of the fingertips.*
Panarthritis	**panarthritis** *Inflammation of the joints.*
Pandemie	**pandemic** *When a disease is present over an entire region.*
Panhypopituitarismus	**panhypopituitarism** *Insufficiency of the anterior pituitary.*
Panikattacke	**panic attack** *Sudden, profound anxiety.*
Pankarditis	**pancarditis** *Inflammation of pericardium, myocardium and endocardium.*
Pankreas; Bauchspeicheldrüse	**pancreas** *A gland that secretes digestive enzymes into the duodenum and insulin and glucagon into the blood.*
Pankreatektomie	**pancreatectomy** *Surgical excision of part or all of the pancreas.*
Pankreatitis	**pancreatitis** *Inflammation of the pancreas.*
Pankreozymin	**pancreozymin** *A duodenal mucosal enzyme that facilitates the secretion of amylase and other enzymes from the pancreas.*
Pannikulitis	**panniculitis** *Inflammation of a section of subcutaneous tissue containing large amounts of fat.*
Pannusoperation	**peritomy** *Surgically creating an opening of the periosteum.*
Panophthalmitis	**panophthalmia** *Inflammation of the eye and all its structures.*
Panotitis	**panotitis** *Inflammation of each part of a bone.*
Papel	**papule** *A small, well-circumscribed elevation of the skin.*
Papillenödem	**papilledema** *Swelling of the optic disc.*
Papillitis	**papillitis** *Swelling of a papilla.*
Papillom	**papilloma** *A benign, lobulated tumor coming from epithelium.*
Papilloma-Virus	**HPV human papillomavirus** *The virus that causes genital warts.*
Pappatacifieber	**sandfly fever** *A febrile illness transmitted by a sandfly, from the genus Phlebotomus, and found in the Mediterranean.*
Para-Aminobenzoesäure	**para-aminobenzoic acid** *A natural product (not FDA approved) reportedly beneficial for Peyronie's disease and scleroderma. It is a component of folic acid.*
Para-Aminohippusäure	**para-aminohippuric acid (PAH)** *A chemical used for calculation of renal plasma flow.*

	English
Paracetamol	**acetaminophen** *Mild analgesic drug used for pain relief.*
paradoxe Pupillenreaktion	**paradoxical pupil** *Constriction of the pupil when exposed to darkness.*
Parakusis	**paracusia** *Any abnormality in the sense of hearing.*
Paralyse agitans	**paralysis agitans** *Synonym of Parkinson's disease.*
paralytisch ; Gelähmter	**paralytic** *1. Referring to paralysis. 2. A person who is paralyzed.*
paramedian	**paramedian** *Situated toward the middle of the body.*
Parametritis	**parametritis** *Inflammation of the parametrium.*
Parametrium	**parametrium** *The connective tissue and smooth muscle between the broad ligament serous layers.*
Paramnesie	**paramnesia** *A condition exhibited by a person's belief they have memory for an event that never happened.*
Paranoia	**paranoia** *A mental condition exhibited by delusions of persecution.*
paranoid	**paranoid** *Having the symptom of paranoia.*
Paraphimose	**paraphimosis** *A condition in which the foreskin is retracted but cannot be replace because of a restricted foreskin.*
Paraplegie	**paraplegia** *Paralysis of the lower extremities.*
pararektal	**pararectal** *Adjacent to the rectum.*
Parasit	**parasite** *An organism that lives on or within another organism without benefit to the latter.*
Parasitenbefall	**infestation** *The presence of large numbers, as in lice infestation.*
Parasomie; Riechstörung	**parosmia** *An alteration in the sense of smell.*
parasympathisch	**parasympathetic** *Part of the autonomic nervous system that opposes sympathetic stimulation.*
Parathormon	**parathormone** *Synonym for parathyroid hormone.*
Parathyreoidea; Nebenschilddrüse	**parathyroid** *Positioned adjacent to the thyroid.*
paravertebral	**paravertebral** *Positioned adjacent to the vertebra.*
Parazentese	**nyxis** *Paracentesis or a puncture.*
Parazentese	**paracentesis** *A procedure involving aspiration of fluid from the abdominal cavity.*
Paräthesie; Missempfindung	**paresthesia** *An abnormal sensation usually described as pins and needles.*
parenchymatös	**parenchyma** *The functional elements of an organ.*
parenteral	**parenteral** *Other than the alimentary canal.*
Parese	**paresis** *Incomplete paralysis.*
parietal	**parietal** *Referring to the wall of a part or cavity.*
Parietalzelle	**parietal cell** *Acid secreting cells of the stomach.*
Parkinson-Syndrom; Parkinsonismus	**Parkinson's disease** *A progressive neuromuscular disease exhibited by masklike facial expression, resting tremor, cogwheel rigidity and abnormal gait.*
parodontal Krankheit	**periodontal disease** *Present around to a tooth.*
Paronychie; Nagelgeschwür; Umlauf	**paronychia** *Inflammation of the tissue bordering a fingernail*
Parotis; Ohrspeicheldrüse	**parotid** *A gland near the ear.*
Parotitis	**parotiditis** *Inflammation of the parotid gland.*
paroxysmal; anfallsweise	**paroxysmal** *Occurring in sudden attacks.*
Parulis	**gumboil** *Swelling noted on the gingiva over a dental abscess.*
passend	**apt** *Suitable in the circumstances.*

passiv	**passive** *Not achieved through active effort.*
Paste; Salbe	**paste** *A thick, soft moist substance usually with medicine mixed in.*
Patella; Kniescheibe	**patella** *The bone situated in the anterior portion of the knee.*
Patellarsehnenreflex	**knee jerk reflex** *Contraction of the quadriceps, yielding leg extension when the quadriceps tendon is tapped.*
Patellektomie; Patellaentfernung	**patellectomy** *Surgical excision of the patella.*
Patellofemoral Syndrom	**patellofemoral stress syndrome** *Overuse syndrome causing anterior knee pain from excessive lateral motion.*
pathogen	**pathogenic** *Referring to an organism that can cause disease.*
Pathogenese	**parthenogenesis** *Reproduction that occurs without an egg being fertilized by sperm.*
Pathogenese	**pathogenesis** *The course of a disease.*
pathognomonisch	**pathognomonic** *Characteristic of something.*
Pathologie	**pathology** *1. The branch of medicine dealing with the study of tissues and the forensic application. 2. Referring to a condition that is abnormal.*
pathologisch	**pathological** *Referring to pathology.*
Patient; Patientin	**patient** *The client being treated for a medical or surgical condition.*
Patientenkartei	**patient chart** *The file containing the client's medical record.*
Paukenhöhle	**tympanic cavity** *The air chamber medial to the tympanic membrane in the temporal bone, between the external acoustic meatus and the inner ear.*
Pavor nocturnus; Nachtangst	**night terror** *Sensation of profound fear upon wakening.*
Pädiater	**pediatrician** *Physician who is a specialist in pediatrics.*
Pädiatrie	**pediatrics** *Medical specialty concerned with the treatment and prevention of childhood disease.*
Pecten ossis pubis	**pectineal ligament** *A continuation of the lacunar ligament along the pectineal line in the pubis.*
Pediculoides ventricosus	**straw itch** *Pruritis associated with exposure to straw that is infested with the mite Pyemotes ventricosus. Also referred to as dermatitis pediculoides ventricosus.*
Pediculose	**pediculosis** *Lice infestation.*
Peitschenwurm; Trichuris trichiura	**whipworm** *A parasitic, intestinal nematode worm of the genus Trichuris.*
pektoral	**pectoral** *Referring to the pectoral muscle.*
Pektoriloquie	**pectoriloquy** *The examiner's voice is clearly audible when the patient speaks as when the examiner listens to an area of consolidation in the lungs of the speaker.*
Pellagra	**pellagra** *A deficiency in nicotinic acid exhibited by diarrhea and dermatitis.*
Pellagra	**Saint Ignatius' itch** *Pruritis noted with a cluster of symptoms related to niacin deficiency. Generally referred to as pellagra.*
Pelvimetrie; Beckenmessung	**pelvimetry** *Measurement of the dimensions of the pelvis to determine whether a patient is capable of natural childbirth.*
pelvin	**pelvic** *Referring to the pelvis.*
Pemphigoid bullöses	**bullous pemphigoid** *A benign disease of the aged characterized by large bullae forming on the torso and extremities.*
Pemphigus	**pemphigus** *A skin disorder with large bullous lesions.*
Pendelnystagmus	**oscillating nystagmus** *Abnormal movement of the eyes in a wave-like pattern.*

Penicillin	**penicillin** *A synthetic antibiotic originally produced from blue mold.*
Penis	**penis** *Male genital organ used for the transfer of sperm and elimination of urine.*
Pentosurie	**pentosuria** *The presence of pentose in the urine (a monosaccharide with five carbon atoms in the molecule).*
Pepsin	**pepsin** *A proteolytic gastric enzyme.*
Peptid	**peptide** *A compound with low molecular weight and containing two or more amino acids.*
peptisch	**peptic** *Referring to pepsin or concerning digestion.*
Perforation	**perforation** *Presence of a hole.*
periaquäduktial graue Substanz	**periaqueductal gray matter** *Refers to the brain gray matter adjacent to the periaqueductal.*
Periarteriitis nodosa	**polyarteritis nodosa** *A systemic necrotizing vasculitis that effects medium sized arteries.*
Periarthritis	**periarthritis** *Inflammation of the tissues around a joint.*
Perichondritis	**perichondritis** *Inflammation of the perichondrium.*
Perichondrium	**perichondrium** *The membrane that encloses a cartilage.*
Perikard	**pericardium** *The structure enclosing the heart which contains a fibrous outer layer and serous inner layer.*
Perikardial	**pericardial** *Referring to around the heart.*
Perikarditis	**pericarditis** *Inflammation of the pericardium.*
Perikolitis	**pericolitis** *Inflammation of the membrane covering the colon.*
perikorneal Anulus	**pericorneal ring** *Also known as Kayser-Fleischer rings exhibited by presence of brown or grey-green rings on the cornea. This is from the deposition of copper and seen in Wilson's disease.*
Perilymphe	**perilymph** *The fluid separating the membranous and osseous labyrinth.*
Perinatologie	**perinatology** *The study of disease in the period just before and right after birth.*
perineal	**perineal** *Referring to the perineum.*
Perinealriß; Dammriß	**perineal laceration** *Tearing of the tissue adjacent to the vaginal that can occur during childbirth.*
Perineorrhaphie	**perineorrhaphy** *Surgical repair of the perineum.*
perinephritisch; perirenal	**perinephric** *Around the kidney.*
Perineum; Damm	**perineum** *The area between the anus and scrotum or anus and vulva.*
periodische Atmung; Adynamia episodica hereditaria	**periodic paralysis** *A familial muscle disorder exhibited by recurrent episodes flaccid paralysis without change in level of consciousness.*
Periositis	**periostitis** *Inflammation of the periosteum.*
Periost	**periosteum** *A layer of connective tissue covering the bones.*
peripher	**peripheral** *Referring to an outward part or surface.*
Periproktitis	**periproctitis** *Inflammation of the tissue encircling the anus and rectum.*
perisotal	**periosteal** *Referring to the periosteum.*
Peristaltik	**peristalsis** *The contraction of the longitudinal and circular muscle fibers of the alimentary canal so food is propelled.*
peritoneal	**peritoneal** *Referring to the peritoneum.*
Peritonitis	**peritonitis** *Inflammation of the peritoneum.*
peritonsillär	**peritonsillar** *Surrounding the tonsils.*
peritonsillär Abszeß	**peritonsillar abscess**

270

periurethral	**periurethral** *Surrounding the urethra.*
Perkussion	**percussion** *A manual procedure involving tapping a body part to determine the size or density (liquid or air) of a part.*
perniziös	**pernicious** *1. Having a detrimental effect. 2. Pernicious anemia is a reduced red blood cell count due to Vitamin B12 deficiency.*
peroneal Atrophie	**peroneal atrophy** *Progressive muscle atrophy in the peroneal region.*
peroneal; fibular	**peroneal** *Referring to the fibula or the outer part of the leg.*
persistierender Ductus arteriosus	**patent ductus arteriosus** *A condition exhibited by failure of the ductus arteriosus (communication between the aorta the the pulmonary artery normally noted in a fetus) to close.*
persistierendes Foramen ovale	**patent foramen ovale** *A congenital anomaly in which there is a defect in the wall between the right and left atria; this can be a benign condition or result in cryptogenic strokes.*
Persönlichkeit; Charakter	**personality** *Qualities that form a person's unique character.*
Perspiration; Schwitzen	**perspiration** *The process of sweating.*
Pertussis; Keuchhusten	**whooping cough** *Pertussis*
Pessar	**pessary** *A supportive device placed in the rectum or vagina.*
Petechie	**petechia** *A small red or purple macule on the skin caused by bleeding.*
Pétrissage; Knetmassage	**petrissage** *Massage using a kneading action.*
Pfaundler-Hurlersche Krankheit	**gargoylism** *A congenital defect, also known as Hurler syndrome, it is characterized by skeletal anomalies, mental retardation and gargoylelike facial features.*
pfeifen	**whistle, to** *To make a high pitch noise by forcing air through the lips.*
Pflaster	**plaster** *Dehydrated gypsum that has water added to it in order to immobilize fractured extremities.*
Pflegekraft	**caregiver** *A person who provides care to another.*
Pfortaderhochdruck	**portal hypertension** *Hypertension in the portal system of the liver as seen in conditions causing obstruction to the portal vein.*
Phagozyt	**phagocyte** *A cell capable of surrounding and digesting microorganisms.*
Phagozytose	**phagocytosis** *The action of a phagocyte.*
Phalanx	**phalanx** *One of the long bones of the fingers or toes.*
Phantomgliedschmerz	**phantom limb pain** *Pain sensed in an area where one has had an amputation as though the limb is still present.*
Pharmakokinetik	**pharmacokinetics** *The study of the distribution, absorption and excretion of drugs within the body.*
Pharmakologie	**pharmacology** *The study of all aspects of medicines.*
Pharmazeut; Apotheker	**pharmacist** *A professional who prepares and sells medicine through various systems, including governmental organizations like the Veterans Administration.*
Pharmazie; Apotheke	**pharmacy** *A business that sells prescription medication.*
pharyngeal	**pharyngeal** *Referring to the pharynx.*
Pharyngektomie	**pharyngectomy** *Surgical excision of part of the pharynx.*
Pharyngitis	**pharyngitis** *Inflammation of the pharynx.*
Pharyngolaryngektomie	**pharyngolaryngectomy** *Surgical removal of part of the pharynx and larynx.*
Phänotyp	**phenotype** *The visual expression exhibited by a person from the association of the genotype with the environment.*
Phegmasie	**phlegmasia** *Inflammation or fever.*

271

	English
Phenylketonurie	**phenylketonuria** *A hereditary condition in which a person cannot excrete phenylalanine; untreated it causes brain and spinal cord dysfunction.*
Phimose	**phimosis** *Stricture of the prepuce preventing it from being pulled back over the glans penis.*
Phlebektomie	**phlebectomy** *Surgical excision of a vein.*
Phlebitis	**phlebitis** *Inflammation of a vein.*
Phlebothrombose	**phlebothrombosis** *Presence of a clot in a vein, without associated inflammation.*
Phlegmasia alba dolens	**phlegmasia alba dolens** *Phlebitis of the femoral vein that can occur after pregnancy or typhoid fever.*
Phlykänulär	**phlyctenular** *Related to the formation of small vesicles on the cornea or conjunctiva.*
Phobie	**phobia** *An profound fear of something.*
Phonation	**phonation** *The vocalization of sounds.*
Phoniatrie	**phoniatrics** *The treatment of speech abnormalities.*
Phophornekrose	**phosphonecrosis** *The breakdown of the mandible caused by excessive exposure to phosphorus.*
Phosphaturie	**phosphaturia** *Presence of phosphates in the urine.*
Phospholipid	**phospholipid** *A substance, such as lecithin, that when hydrolyzed produces fatty acids, glycerin, and a nitrogen compound.*
Photophobie	**photophobia** *Abnormal sensitivity to light.*
Photosensibilisierung	**photosensitization** *The process of reacting to sunlight by developing edema and dermatitis.*
Phrenikektomie	**phrenicectomy** *Surgical excision of the phrenic nerve.*
phrenisch	**phrenic** *Referring to the diaphragm.*
Phrenoplegie	**phrenoplegia** *Paralysis of the diaphragm.*
physikalische Therapie	**physical therapy** *Treatment of disease by heat, massage and exercise as opposed to medications.*
physikalische Therapie	**physiotherapy** *Physical therapy.*
Physiologie	**physiology** *A subspecialty of biology that studies the normal functioning of the body.*
physiologisch Totraum	**physiologic dead space** *The combination of anatomic and alveolar dead space.*
physiologische Kochsalzlösung	**physiological saline** *0.9% normal saline.*
Pia mater	**pia mater** *The first layer of three covering the brain and spinal cord.*
Pica	**pica** *A desire for unusual substances as occurs in pregnancy and some psychological conditions.*
Pille	**pill** *A medicated tablet or capsule.*
Pilonidalsinus	**pilonidal cyst** *A small cone-shaped cluster of tissue situated posterior to the third ventricle of the brain.*
Pilz	**fungus** *A spore-producing organism that feeds on organic matter.*
Pinguecula	**pinguecula** *The yellow tissue on the bulbar conjunctiva adjacent to the sclerocorneal junction.*
Pinozytose	**pinocytosis** *The absorption of fluid into a cell by the formation of vesicles on the cell membrane.*
Pipette	**dropper** *A device used to administer medicines one drop at a time.*
Pipette	**pipet** *A slender tube with a bulb used for transferring liquids.*

272

Pityriasis rosea	**pityriasis rosea** *A skin disease characterized by dry pink oval papulosquamous eruptions.*
placebo-kontrollierte Studie	**placebo controlled study** *When a study is placebo controlled it means part of the group received an inactive treatment while the other group received active therapy.*
Placenta praevia	**placenta praevia** *A condition in which the placenta covers the cervical os.*
Placenta; Mutterkuchen	**placenta** *The vascular tissue that nourishes a fetus through an umbilical cord.*
plantar	**plantar** *Referring to the bottom of the foot.*
Plantarfibromatose	**plantar fibromatosis** *Deep fascia nodules on the plantar aspect of the feet.*
Plasmapherese	**plasmapheresis** *A method of removing blood and reinfusing it after the elimination of antibodies.*
Plasmazellenvermehrung	**plasmacytosis** *The existence of plasma cells in the blood.*
Plathelminthe; Plattwurm	**flatworm** *A class of worms that includes parasitic flukes and tapeworms.*
Plattfuß; Senkfuß	**flatfoot** *Common term for pes planus.*
Plazentaaustreibung	**expulsion of placenta** *Passage of the placenta out the cervix after childbirth.*
Plazentalösung	**abruptio placentae** *The premature detachment of a normally implanted placenta resulting in maternal decompensation.*
plazentar	**placental** *Referring to the placenta.*
Plaziozephalie	**plagiocephaly** *A condition characterized by an asymmetric skull because the cranial sutures do not close normally.*
Plättchen	**platelet** *An oval cell without a nucleus used in coagulation; also called a thrombocyte.*
Pleomorphie	**pleomorphism** *The ability of an organism or substance to attain distinct forms.*
Plethora	**plethora** *An excess of something.*
Plethysmograph	**plethysmograph** *A device used to measure the amount of blood flowing through a body part; impedance plethysmography is used to check for deep venous thrombosis.*
Pleuraerguss; Pleuraerguß	**pleural effusion** *An abnormal collection of fluid between the internal chest wall and the pleura.*
Pleurakuppel	**cervical pleura** *The dome-like cap of the pleura.*
Pleurareizung	**pleurisy** *Inflammation of the pleura.*
Plexus brachialis	**brachial plexus** *A cluster of nerves coming off the last four cervical and first thoracic spinal nerves form the nerve supply the the chest and arms.*
Plexus solaris	**solar plexus** *A cluster of ganglia and nerves, located at the base of the sternum, that surround the celiac trunk.*
plötzlicher Kindstod	**sudden infant death syndrome** *A leading cause of death of infants from one month to one year; the etiology is unknown.*
Plummer-Vinson-Syndrom	**Plummer-Vinson syndrome** *Also called sideropenic dysphagia. Exhibited by iron deficiency anemia, dysphagia, esophageal stenosis and atrophic glossitis. The cause is not known.*
Pneumatozele	**pneumatocele** *1. A hernia-like protrusion of lung tissue. 2. A collection of gas in a sac such as the scrotum.*
Pneumaturie	**pneumaturia** *Presence of air or gas in the urine.*

Pneumocystis-jirovecii Pneumonie	**pneumocystis jiroveci pneumonia**. *A pulmonary infection associated with AIDS. Formerly called pneumocystis carinii pneumonia*
Pneumokokkus	**pneumococcus** *A bacterium causing pneumonia and meningitis. A common type is Streptococcus pneumoniae.*
Pneumokoniose	**pneumoconiosis** *Fibrosis of the lung due to dust inhalation.*
Pneumonektomie	**pneumonectomy** *Surgical excision of all or part of a lung.*
Pneumonie	**pneumonia** *Inflammation of the lung due to an infection caused by a virus or bacterium.*
Pneumoperitoneum	**pneumoperitoneum** *Abnormal or induced presence of air or gas in the peritoneum.*
Pneumothorax	**pneumothorax** *Abnormal presence of air between the lung and chest wall.*
pochen	**throb, to** *The beat with strong regular rhythm.*
Pocken	**smallpox** *Variola.*
Poikilothermie	**poikilothermy** *A condition of cold-blooded animals in which their temperature varies based on the ambient temperature.*
Poikilozytose	**poikilocytosis** *The presence of abnormally shaped erythrocytes.*
Polioenzephalitis	**polioencephalitis** *Polio infection of the brain.*
Poliomyelitis	**poliomyelitis** *An infectious viral disease exhibited by constitutional symptoms that can lead to quadriplegia.*
Pollutio	**nocturnal emission** *Involuntary emission of semen at night.*
Polster; Kissen	**pad** *A thick piece of soft clothing.*
Polychondritis	**polychondritis** *Inflammation of the cartilage at more than one site.*
Polydaktylie	**polydactyly** *Congenital anomaly exhibited by more than 5 digits on the hands and/or feet.*
Polydipsie	**polydipsia** *Profound thirst.*
Polymenorrhöe	**polymenorrhea** *Increase in the frequency of menstruation.*
Polymyositis	**polymyositis** *Inflammation of several muscle groups at once.*
polyneuritis	**polyneuritis** *Inflammation of more than one nerve.*
Polyneuropathie	**polyneuropathy** *A condition involving more than one nerve.*
Polyopsie	**polyopia** *A condition in which one object is seen abnormally as two or more.*
Polyp	**polypus** *Synonym of polyp (a prominent growth from a mucous membrane).*
Polypose	**polyposis** *The formation of multiple polyps.*
Polysaccharid	**polysaccharide** *A carbohydrate that upon hydrolysis forms more than ten monosaccharides.*
Polyurie	**polyuria** *Abnormal increase in volume of urine excreted.*
polyzystisch	**polycystic** *Possessing more than one cyst.*
Polyzythämie	**polycythemia** *Excess in the number of erythrocytes in the blood.*
Polyzythämie vera	**polycythemia vera** *Condition characterized by increase in erythrocytes, thrombocytes and leukocytes, as well as, splenomegaly.*
Pompholyx	**dyshidrotic eczema** *A dermatitis characterized by vescicobullous lesions.*
Pompholyx	**pompholyx** *A condition exhibited by interdigital vesicles of the hands and feet.*
pontin	**pontine** *Referring to the pons.*
popliteal	**popliteal** *Referring to the posterior aspect of the knee.*
porös	**cancellous** *A bony mesh-like structure with many pores.*

274

Porphyrie	**porphyria** *A hereditary condition currently classified based on the specific enzyme deficiency. The most common form is porphyria cutanea tarda that causes blistering lesions.*
Porphyrin	**porphyrin** *A class of pigments that contain a flat ring of four heterocyclic groups.*
portal	**portal** *Referring to an entrance such as porta hepatis.*
positiv	**positive** *Indicating the presence of something.*
Positronenemissionstomographie	**PET scan Positron emission tomography.** *Production of tomographic images revealing biochemical tissue properties by analyzing positrons emitted when radioactively tagged substances are taken in tissues.*
postiktal	**postictal** *The period of time after a seizure.*
Postnasensekret	**post-nasal drip** *The descent of sinus drainage.*
Potenz; Leistungsfähigkeit	**potency** *Strength or power.*
Potter-Syndrom	**Potter's syndrome** *A group of findings associated with oligohydramnios. Renal failure is the primary problem but the infant has abnormal limbs, broad nasal bridge, low set ears and receding chin. Death usually ensues due to renal and respiratory failure.*
Praecordium	**precordium** *The area occupying the epigastrum and lower sternum.*
präaurikulär	**preauricular** *Anterior to the ear.*
Präeklampsie	**preeclampsia** *Hypertension with proteinuria and/or edema in the setting of pregnancy.*
präkanzerös	**precancerous** *Referring to an early stage in cancer development.*
Präkordialschmerz	**precordialgia** *Pain in the precordium.*
prämenstruell	**premenstrual** *Occurring prior to the onset of menstruation.*
prämenstruelles Syndrom	**premenstrual syndrome** *A cluster of emotional, behavioral, and physical symptoms that occur in the premenstrual phase of the menstrual cycle and resolve with the onset of menstruation.*
Prämolar	**premolar** *The teeth anterior to the molars.*
pränatal	**antenatal** *Refers to events before birth.*
pränatal	**prenatal** *Referring to the time prior to birth.*
präsystolisch	**presystolic** *The time just before systole.*
Präzipitin	**precipitin** *An antibody-antigen reaction producing a precipitate.*
Presbyakusis	**presbyacusia** *An age related, progressive hearing loss.*
Presbyopie; Alterssichtigkeit	**presbyopia** *Farsightedness associated with aging.*
pressen	**bearing down** *As in during labor.*
Priapismus	**priapism** *A painful and abnormally prolonged erection.*
Primipara	**primipara** *A woman giving birth for the first time.*
Probe	**specimen** *A sample for medical testing.*
Probelaparotomie	**exploratory laparotomy** *Abdominal surgery with the intent of examining the abdominal contents.*
Probensammeln	**sampling** *The taking of samples.*
Problem	**problem** *Difficulty or complaint.*
Procktoskopie	**proctoscopy** *Inspection of the rectum with a scope.*
Progerie	**progeria** *A childhood disorder exhibited by signs of aging including gray hair, wrinkled skin and short height.*
Prognathie	**prognathism** *Protrusion of the mandible which can cause malocclusion.*
Prognose	**prognosis** *The likely course of a disease.*

Programm	**scheme** *A program or plan.*
Proktalgie	**proctalgia** *A chronic high, dull rectal pain worse with sitting position.*
Proktektomie	**proctectomy** *Surgical excision of the rectum.*
Proktitis	**proctitis** *Inflammation of the rectum.*
Proktozele	**proctocele** *A hernia-type protrusion of the rectum into the vagina.*
Prolaktin	**prolactin** *A pituitary hormone that facilitates milk production.*
Prolaps; Vorfall	**prolapse** *The slipping downward of a body part, such as rectal prolapse.*
Promonozyt	**promonocyte** *An intermediate cell stage between monocyte and monoblast.*
Promontorium	**promontory** *A protruding eminence.*
Pronation	**pronation** *Turning posteriorly. When the hand is pronated, it is turned medially until the palm is facing posteriorly (when the body was initially in the anatomic position).*
Prophylaxe	**prophylaxis** *That which is done to prevent disease.*
Propriorezeptor	**proprioceptor** *A receptor that responds to sensory input including position sense.*
Prostaglandin	**prostaglandin** *A compound first found in semen (thus "prosta" in the name from prostate) with many effects including uterine contraction.*
Prostatektomie	**prostatectomy** *Surgical excision of the prostate.*
Prostazyklin	**prostacyclin** *A prostaglandin that functions as an anticoagulant and vasodilator.*
Prostration	**prostration** *Profound exhaustion.*
Protein; Eiweiß	**protein** *A class of nitrogenous organic compound.*
Proteinurie	**proteinuria** *The presence of protein in the urine.*
Proteolyse	**proteolysis** *Enzyme action on proteins to form amino acids.*
Prothromin	**prothrombin** *A compound converted to thrombin during coagulation of blood.*
Protoplasma	**protoplasm** *The cytoplasm, organelles and nucleus of a living cell.*
Protozoon	**protozoa** *A single celled microscopic organism including amoebas among others.*
provozieren	**provoke, to** *To evoke or elicit.*
proximal	**proximal** *Situated closer to the center of the body (opposed to that which is farther away, as in distal).*
Prurigo	**prurigo** *A chronic, pruritic papular skin eruption.*
Pruritis aestivalis	**summer itch** *Pruritis noted upon exposure to hot weather, also known as pruritis aestivalis.*
Pruritis; Hautjucken	**pruritis** *A general term for conditions exhibited by itching.*
Pseudoarthrose	**pseudarthrosis** *Deossification of weight bearing long bones.*
Pseudobulbärparalyse	**pseudobulbar palsy** *Sudden outbursts of laughter or tearfulness sometimes seen in amyotrophic lateral sclerosis.*
Pseudomnsesie	**pseudomnesia** *Sensing the memory of an event that has never happened.*
Psittakose	**psittacosis** *A chlamydial pneumonia that is transmitted by birds.*
Psoriasis	**psoriasis** *A chronic papulosquamous dermatosis characterized by silver plaques.*
Psychasthenie	**psychasthenia** *Essentially any non-hysterical neuroses.*
Psychiatrie	**psychiatry** *A branch of medicine specializing in the treatment of mental disorders.*

Psychologe	**psychologist** *A professional specializing in psychology.*
Psychologie	**psychology** *The study of the human mind and emotions.*
Psychoneurose	**psychoneurosis** *A mental disorder that could include depression or anxiety but does not include hallucinations.*
Psychopathologie	**psychopathology** *Scientific examination of mental disease.*
Psychose	**psychosis** *A profound mental disorder that can include delusions and hallucinations.*
psychosomatisch	**psychosomatic** *Physical ailments arising from mental disease.*
Psychotherapie	**psychotherapy** *Treatment of mental disease with cognitive-behavioral approaches.*
Pterygium; Flügelfell	**pterygium** *A membrane in the interpalpebral fissure present from the conjunctiva to the cornea.*
Ptose	**ptosis** *Drooping of the upper eyelid usually due to paralysis of the third cranial nerve.*
Pubertät	**puberty** *The time when adolescents become capable of sexual reproduction.*
pubisch	**pubis** *The anterior inferior part of the hip bone on each side that articulates at the pubic symphysis.*
pudendal	**pudendal** *Referring to the female genitalia*
Pudendum femininum; Vulva	**pudendum** *The mons, pubis, labia majora, labia minora and the vagina.*
Puder	**powder** *Fine dry particles.*
Puerpera	**puerpera** *A woman who just gave birth.*
pulmonal	**pulmonary** *Referring to the lungs.*
Pulmonalstenose	**pulmonary stenosis** *A stricture between the pulmonary artery and the right ventricle.*
Pulpa	**pulp** *The tissue filling the root canals of a tooth.*
Pulpitis	**pulpitis** *Dental pulp inflammation.*
Puls	**pulse** *The rhythmic throbbing of arteries felt at major vessels.*
Pulsation	**pulsation** *The action of expanding and contracting.*
pulsieren	**pulsatile** *Relating to pulsation.*
Pulsus alternans	**pulsus alternans** *A regular alternation of weak and strong beats of the pulse.*
Punktion; Klopfen	**tap** *A puncture with the intent of draining fluid as in spinal tap.*
Pupille	**pupil** *The opening at the center of the iris.*
Purpura	**purpura** *The presence of patches of ecchymosis or petechiae.*
Putnam-Dana Syndrom	**vitamin B12 neuropathy** *Abnormal sensation related to a chronic deficiency of cyanocobalamin; also called subacute combined degeneration of the spinal cord or Putnam-Dana syndrome.*
Putzfrauenknie	**housemaid's knee** *Also referred to as prepatellar bursitis.*
Pyämie	**pyemia** *Sepsis characterized by the presence of secondary abscesses.*
Pyelitis	**pyelitis** *Renal pelvis inflammation.*
Pyelographie	**pyelography** *Use of a contrast agent to radiologically study the kidney, ureters and bladder.*
Pyelolithotomie	**pyelolithotomy** *Surgical excision of a calculus from the renal pelvis.*
Pyelonephritis	**pyelonephritis** *Inflammation of the renal parenchyma usually due to bacterial infection.*
Pyelonephrose	**pyelonephrosis** *Term, rarely used anymore, used to describe disease of the renal pelvis.*

pyknisch	**pyknic** *Possessing a short, stocky physique.*
Pyknose	**pyknosis** *The degeneration of a cell with the nucleus shrinking.*
pylorisch	**pyloric** *Referring to the pylorus.*
Pylorus	**pylorus** *The opening at the distal stomach that opens into the duodenum.*
Pylorusplastik	**pyloroplasty** *Surgical enlargement of a pylorus that previously was stenotic.*
Pyodermie	**pyoderma** *A purulent skin infection.*
Pyonephrose	**pyonephrosis** *Injury to the renal parenchyma due to pus.*
Pyorrhöe	**pyorrhea** *Emission of pus.*
Pyosalpinx	**pyosalpinx** *Purulent material in the oviduct.*
pyramidal	**pyramidal** *A term that is used to describe various spinal tracts that originate in the cerebral cortex.*
Pyridoxin	**pyridoxine** *Synonym for vitamin B6.*
Pyrogen	**pyrogen** *A fever producing substance released by bacteria.*
Pytalin	**ptyalin** *An enzyme found in saliva.*
Pyurie	**pyuria** *Presence of purulent material in the urine.*
Q-Fieber	**Q fever** *A disease caused by rickettsiae from the ingestion of unpasteurized milk.*
Quaddel	**wheal** *A circumscribed urticarial lesion.*
Quadrantenanopsie	**quadranic hemianopia** *Loss of a quarter of the visual field in one or both eyes. If bilateral, it may be further described as homonymous, heteronymous, binasal, bitemporal, or crossed.*
Quadratwurzel	**square root** *The result noted when a number is multiplied by itself.*
Quadriplegie	**quadriplegia** *Paralysis of all four extremities.*
Quadrizeps	**quadriceps** *The anterior thigh muscle composed of four muscles.*
Quadrizepssehnenreflex; Patellarsehnenreflex	**quadriceps jerk (reflex)** *Also referred to as the patellar reflex.*
Qual	**anguish** *Significant mental or physical pain.*
Quarantäne	**quarantine** *A place of isolation for infectious persons until it can be certain it is safe to let them mingle.*
Querschnitt	**cross-section** *A transverse section through a specimen or structure.*
querulatorisch	**querulousness** *Whining or complaining.*
quetschen	**squeeze, to** *To apply pressure.*
Quetschung	**bruise** *Common term for ecchymosis.*
Rachen; Pharynx	**pharynx** *The membranous cavity from the mouth to esophagus.*
Rachen; Schlund	**throat** *The anterior aspect of the neck.*
Rachenmandelentzündung	**adenoiditis** *Inflammation of the adenoids.*
Rachenmandelwucherungen	**adenoids** *Pharyngeal tonsils.*
Rachenreflex; Würgreflex	**gag reflex** *Contraction of the pharynx muscles when the back of the pharynx is stimulated by touch.*
Rachitis	**rickets** *A condition exhibited by softening and bowing of the long bones; caused by Vitamin D deficiency.*
radial	**radial** *Referring to the radius.*
Radikulitis	**radiculitis** *Inflammation of a spinal nerve root.*
radioaktiv	**radioactive** *Referring to the emission of ionizing particles or radiation.*
Radiobiologie	**radiobiology** *The study of the effects of radiation on organisms.*

Radiographie; Röentgenograpie	**radiography** *The department where images are produced on sensitive film by x-rays.*
Radioisotop	**radioactive isotope** *An isotope with an unstable nucleus that is used in diagnostic imaging.*
Radiologe	**radiologist** *A physician specializing in radiology.*
Radiologie	**radiology** *The branch of medicine concerned with roentgenography and other high-energy radiation.*
Radionuklid	**radionuclide** *A radioactive nuclide.*
Ramus; Zweig	**ramus** *A branch; a term used to describe a smaller vessel branching off from a larger one.*
Rand	**border** *Margin.*
Ranula; Froschgeschwulst	**ranula** *A retention cyst formed because of obstruction of a salivary gland in the floor of the mouth.*
Raserei	**rage** *Uncontrollable anger.*
Rasselgeräusch	**rale** *An abnormal lung sound noted during auscultation.*
raten	**advise, to** *To give counsel.*
Rattenbißkrankheit;	**rat bite fever** *As the name implies, it is a condition exhibited by fever, nausea and skin erythema after one is bitten by a rat.*
rauchen	**smoke, to** *To inhale on a cigarette.*
Raute	**rhomboid** *A back muscle that elevates, retracts and adducts the scapula.*
Rautenhirn	**hindbrain** *The brainstem which includes the pons, medulla oblongata and cerebellum.*
razemös	**racemose** *A gland having the form of a cluster.*
Reagenzglas	**test tube** *A glass or plastic tube used to hold a medical specimen.*
Reaktion	**reaction** *A response to an action.*
reaktiv	**reactive** *A response to a stimulus.*
Rechnung	**bill** *A financial statement that indicates how much one owes.*
Rechtherzhypertrophie (bezogen auf Lungenkrankheit)	**cor pulmonale** *Heart disease that is secondary to lung disease.*
rechts	**right** *Opposite of left.*
rechts; dexter	**dexter;** *right; straight; erect*
Rechtschreibfehler	**misspelling** *Incorrect spelling of a word.*
rechtshändig	**right-handed** *Having a preference to use the right hand.*
Rechtskolon Flexur	**hepatic flexure of the colon** *The junction of the ascending and transverse portion of the colon.*
Reduktion	**reduction** *Return of a dislocated joint or fractured bone to its proper position.*
Regurgitation	**regurgitation** *1. Backflow of blood in the heart. 2. Movement of gastric contents into the mouth.*
Reibegeräusch	**rub** *A sound heard at times with pericarditis called more specifically a pericardial friction sound.*
Reibegeräusch	**friction rub** *A noise heard during cardiac auscultation in patients with pericarditis, for example.*
Reibung	**friction** *Grating or rasping.*
Reifgeborenes	**full-term** *A normal length pregnancy.*
reihenmäßig	**serial** *In a series.*
Reihenuntersuchung	**screening** *An evaluation as part of a methodical study.*
Reisekrankheit	**motion sickness** *Nausea associated with travel.*

reitende Sutur	**overriding suture** *The overlapping of cranial sutures noted on vaginal exam when the head is descended.*
reitikulär	**reticular** *Referring to a matrix of membranous tubules inside the cytoplasm of a eukaryotic cells.*
reizen	**flush, to** *Term used to describe an irrigation procedure, as in flushing an NG tube.*
Reizhusten	**dry cough** *A cough without sputum production.*
Reizkolon	**irritable bowel syndrome** *A condition exhibited by chronic diarrhea or constipation and abdominal pain; it is sometimes associated with a labile emotional state.*
rektale	**rectal** *Referring to the rectum.*
rektale Untersuchung	**rectal digital examination** *Use of a gloved finger to assess the rectal vault.*
Rektosigmoidektomie	**rectosigmoidectomy** *Surgical resection of the rectum and sigmoid colon.*
Rektoskopie	**rectoscopy** *Visualization of the rectum with a scope.*
rektovesikal Scheidewand	**rectovesical septum** *The wall between the rectum and the urinary bladder.*
Rektozele	**rectocele** *A herniation of the wall between the rectum and vagina.*
Relaxin	**relaxin** *A hormone secreted by the placenta which dilates the cervix.*
Releasing-Hormon	**releasing hormone** *Hormones that come from one gland such as the thalamus that cause release of hormones from another gland such as the pituitary.*
Remission	**remission** *A decrease in severity or a temporary resolution.*
renal; nieren-	**renal** *Referring to the kidney.*
Renin	**renin** *A renal enzyme that facilitates the production of angiotensin.*
Renititis	**retinitis** *Inflammation of the retina.*
Resektion	**resection** *The removal of tissue.*
Residualvolumen	**residual volume (RV)** *The amount of air left in the lung after a maximal exhalation.*
respiratorisch	**respiratory** *Referring to respiration or the organs of respiration.*
Restharn	**residual urine** *The amount of urine remaining in the bladder after a person voids.*
Retardtablette	**sustained release tablet** *Describes a medicine that is slowly dispersed so it has a lasting effect.*
retikuloendotheliales	**reticulo-endothelial** *Referring to the system of phagocytes involved in the immune system.*
Retikulozyt	**reticulocyte** *A red blood cell without a nucleus.*
Retikulozytose	**reticulocytosis** *An abnormal increase in circulating reticulocytes.*
Retinoblastom	**retinoblastoma** *A tumor consisting of retinal germ cells.*
Retinopathie	**retinopathy** *Any one of a number of retinal inflammatory conditions.*
Retraktion	**retraction** *Being drawn back.*
Retraktor; Wundhaken	**retractor** *A device for pulling back tissue during surgery.*
Retrobulbärneuritis	**retrobulbar optic neuritis** *An inflammatory, demyelinating condition in the retrobulbar region.*
retroflektiert Uterus	**retroflexed uterus** *Bending back of the uterus so that the top portion pushes against the rectum.*
retrograd	**retrograde** *Referring to backward movement.*

retroperitoneal	**retroperitoneal** *Situated or referring to the area posterior to the peritoneum.*
retropharyngeal	**retropharyngeal** *Referring to the area posterior to the pharynx.*
retropharyngealer Abszeß	**retropharyngeal abscess** *A collection of purulent material posterior to the pharynx.*
Rett Syndrom	**Rett syndrome.** *A rare inherited disorder causing developmental delays and is seen mostly in girls.*
Rezeptor	**receptor** *A cell or organ that accepts stimuli and transmits data to a sensory nerve.*
rezessiv	**recessive** *This refers to genetic controlled traits that are only inherited when code from both parents is the same.*
Rhabdomyolyse	**rhabdomyolysis** *A acute destruction of muscle documented by myoglobinemia and myoglobinuria.*
Rhagade	**rhagade** *Fissures in the skin, particularly adjacent to body orifices.*
rheumatisch	**rheumatic** *Referring to rheumatism.*
rheumatisch Herzkrankheit	**rheumatic heart disease** *A manifestation of rheumatic fever, frequently causing valvular dysfunction.*
Rheumatismus	**rheumatism** *Any condition exhibited by inflammation and pain in the joints and muscles.*
rheumatoide Arthritis	**rheumatoid arthritis** *A symmetric peripheral polyarthritis.*
Rhinitis	**rhinitis** *A viral infection or allergic reaction exhibited by nasal mucosal inflammation.*
Rhinorrhöe	**rhinorrhea** *Abundant nasal mucosal drainage.*
Rhinoskopie	**rhinoscopy** *Examination of the nasal passages.*
Rhizotomie	**rhizotomy** *Interruption of the spinal nerve roots within the spinal canal.*
Rhodopsin	**rhodopsin** *A reddish purple light sensitive pigment in the human retina.*
Rhythmus	**rhythm** *The pattern or cadence.*
Riboflavin	**riboflavin** *Also called vitamin B2, this essential vitamin is present in food such as eggs and is synthesized in the small bowel.*
Ribonukleinsäure	**ribonucleic acid** *An acid present in all living cells, it is a messenger for DNA.*
ribosomale Ribonukleinsäure	**ribosomal RNA** *Four chains designated by their appropriate coefficients.*
Ricinus communis Bohne	**castor bean** *A bean that can yield the poisonous compound ricin.*
Rickettsie	**rickettsia** *A disease transmitted by ticks or fleas, caused by a bacterium from the genus Rickettsieae. Rocky Mountain Spotted fever is one of many diseases caused by this bacterium.*
riechend	**odiferous** *Having an unpleasant or distinctive smell.*
riesig	**enormous** *Very large.*
riesig	**giant** *Huge or massive.*
Rifttalfieber	**Rift valley fever** *A human febrile illness that is an endemic disease in sheep, transmitted by mosquitos and direct contact and caused by a virus of the family Bunyaviridae.*
Rigor mortis	**rigor mortis** *The normal stiffening of the muscles and joints that occurs a few hours after death.*
Ring	**ring** *A small circular band.*
Ringknorpel; Ringförmig	**cricoid cartilage** *The ring-shaped cartilage of the larynx.*

Rippe	**rib** *A series of curved paired boney articulations protecting the thorax.*
Rippe; Kosten	**cost** *The fee or penalty.*
Rippenknorpelentzündung	**costochondritis** *Inflammation of the rib and or its cartilage.*
Rist	**instep** *The medial aspect of the foot between the ankle and the ball of the foot.*
Risus sardonicus	**risus sardonicus** *A spasm of the facial muscles causing what appears to be a smile on one's face.*
Ritgen Handgriff	**Ritgen's maneuver** *A procedure that controls the rate of delivery of the infant's head during childbirth.*
Robbe; Siegel	**seal** *A device or substance used to bind two things together.*
Rolle	**trochlea** *A pulley-shaped structure such as the groove at the distal humerus.*
Rollstuhl	**wheelchair** *A wheeled device used for propulsion.*
Rosazea	**rosacea** *Erythema of the cheeks and nose caused by chronic vascular and follicular dilation.*
Rossolimoreflex	**Rossolimo reflex** *Flexion of the toes when the tips of the toes are flicked. This abnormal resonse is present in pyramidal tract lesions.*
rot werden	**blush, to** *To have an increased volume of blood flow to one's face causing a red tint to the skin.*
Rotatorenmanschette	**rotator cuff** *The structure around the capsule of the shoulder joint formed by the infraspinatus, supraspinatus, teres minor and subscapularis muscles.*
Röntgen	**Roentgen** *One unit of ionizing radiation named after the German physicist Wilhelm Conrad Röntgen.*
Röntgenschirm	**fluorescent screen** *A screen used to view x-rays.*
Röntgenthoraxaufnahme	**chest x-ray** *Roentography of the thorax.*
Röteln	**rubella** *Also called German measles, it is characterized by a rash, fever, headache.*
Röteln; Rubella	**German measles** *(rubella) A contagious viral infection.*
Rubefaciens	**rubefacient** *A substance that reddens the skin.*
rudimentär	**vestigial** *Rudimentary.*
Ruhe; Rast	**rest** *Relaxation or respite.*
ruhend	**quiescent** *A time of inactivity.*
ruhig	**quiet** *Making little or no noise.*
Rumpf	**torso** *The trunk of the body.*
Rupia	**rupia** *A sign of tertiary syphilis in which there are bullae or vesicles formed on the skin that erupt and form crusts.*
Ruptur	**rupture** *An instance of bursting suddenly.*
Rücken	**dorsum** *The back part.*
Rückenlage	**supine** *Flat on one's back.*
Rückenmark	**spinal cord** *The bundle of nerves that with the brain comprise the central nervous system.*
Rückenmarkabszeß	**spinal cord abscess** *A localized collection of purulent material in or adjacent to the spinal cord.*
Rückenmarkkompression	**cord compression** *Pressure being applied to the spinal cord.*
Rückfall	**relapse** *The return to a prior state of ill health.*
Rückfallfieber	**relapsing fever** *A recurrent bacterial infection, with fever, caused by Spirochetes.*

sakral	**sacral** *Referring to the sacrum.*
Sakralisation	**sacralization** *The fusion of the fifth lumbar vertebra to the sacrum.*
Sakralkanal	**sacral canal** *The portion of the vertebral canal that progresses into the sacrum.*
Sakrum; Kreuzbein	**sacrum** *The bone formed by five fused vertebrae that is situated between the two hip bones.*
Salbe; Unguentum	**ointment** *A petroleum jelly based topical medication.*
Salpingektomie	**salpingectomy** *Surgical resection of the fallopian tubes.*
Salpingitis	**salpingitis** *Inflammation of the fallopian tubes.*
Salpingographie	**salpingography** *Roentgenography of the fallopian tubes after administration of contrast media.*
Salpingostomie	**salpingostomy** *A surgical procedure involving cutting the fallopian tube.*
saluretisch	**saluretic** *An agent that promotes excretion of sodium and chloride in the urine.*
Salz	**salt** *Typically referring to sodium chloride.*
salzig; Saline	**saline** *A solution of sodium chloride.*
Salzsäure	**hydrochloric acid** *A solution with a low pH formed by dissolving hydrogen chloride in water.*
Samenkanälchen	**seminiferous tubules** *Used for transport of semen.*
Samenstrang	**spermatic cord** *The structure containing the ductus deferens, testicular artery, and nerves that goes from the inguinal ring to the testis.*
Saprophyt	**saprophyte** *Any organism living on dead organic material.*
sarkoid	**sarcoid** *Referring to sarcoidosis.*
Sarkoidose	**sarcoidosis** *A chronic disease characterized by lymphadenopathy and widespread granulomas.*
Sarkolemm	**sarcolemme** *The sheath that covers skeletal muscle fibers.*
Sarkom	**sarcoma** *A non-epithelial malignant tumor.*
sartorius Muskel	**sartorius muscle** *The thigh muscle that runs from the pelvis to the proximal, medial aspect of the tibia.*
Sattelgelenk	**saddle joint** *A joint that exhibits two saddle type surfaces at a 90 degree angle to each other, such as the carpometacarpal joint.*
sauer	**sour** *An acid or bitter taste.*
Sauerstoff	**oxygen** *A colorless, odorless gas with atomic number 8.*
Sauerstoffbehandlung	**oxygen therapy** *Utilization of supplemental oxygen.*
Sauerstoffsättigung	**oxygenation** *Saturated with oxygen.*
Sauerstoffverbrauch	**oxygen consumption** *The body's utilization of oxygen per unit of time.*
Sauerstoffzelt	**oxygen tent** *A manner of giving supplement oxygen to a neonate.*
saugen	**suck, to** *As in, to suction fluid.*
saure Phosphatase	**acid phosphatase** *A phosphate derived chemical that is optimally active in an acidic environment.*
Säge	**saw** *A hand or power-driven tool used for cutting.*
Sättigung	**saturation** *An amount, expressed in a percentage, that expresses the degree something is absorbed versus the maximal absorption possible.*
Säuer	**acid** *Substance with a pH less than 7.*
säugen	**suckle, to** *An infant taking to his mother's nipple.*
Säugling; Kleinkind	**infant** *Newborn.*

Säuglingsalter	**infancy** *Early childhood.*
Säure-Basen-Gleichgewicht	**acid-base balance** *The equilibrium of the electrolytes in the body.*
Scabies norvegica; Boeck-Skabies	**Norway itch** *A severe pruritis caused by scabies and is associated with immune disorders such as AIDS.*
Schaber	**rugine** *A surgical instrument that resembles a rasp.*
schaffen	**accomplish, to** *Achieve.*
Schalentier	**shellfish** *An aquatic shelled crustacean or mollusk.*
Schalg	**beat** *As in heart beat.*
Schall; Ton	**sound** *Vibrations that travel through air and are heard when reaching the ears.*
Schamhügel; Mons pubis	**mons pubis** *The fleshy protuberance over the symphysis pubis.*
Schanker	**chancre** *The initial ulcer that is the source of entry for a pathogen.*
Schankroid	**chancroid** *A sexually transmitted disease caused by Haemophilus ducreyi that is exhibited by ulcers without indurated margins.*
Scharlach	**scarlet fever** *A condition caused by streptococci that is exhibited by fever and a bright red (scarlet) rash.*
Schauer	**shiver** *A trembling.*
Schaum	**foam** *A mass of small bubbles in a liquid.*
Schaum vor dern Mund haben	**froth at the mouth, to** *To have a mass of saliva with small bubbles in it coming out of the mouth.*
Schädel	**cranium** *The skeleton of the head.*
Schädelmpressionsfraktur	**depressed skull fracture** *Concave fracture deformity of the skull.*
schädigen	**injure, to** *To hurt or to wound.*
Schädigung; Verletzung	**injury** *A wound, abrasion or contusion.*
schädlich	**noxious** *Harmful or poisonous.*
schäumend	**froth** *Covered with a mass of small bubbles.*
Scheibe	**slice** *A sliver or shaving.*
Scheide; Hülle	**sheath** *A covering.*
Scheidenausfluß	**discharge, vaginal** *Vaginal secretions.*
scheidend	**parting** *Separating.*
Scheitel	**vertex** *The crown of the head.*
Scheitelsutur	**sagittal suture** *The line where the two parietal bones meet.*
Schenkelblock	**bundle branch block** *A cardiac dysrhythmia produced by a blockage of a branch of the bundle of His.*
Schenkelhernie	**hernia, femoral** *A bulge in the upper thigh/groin region because of bowel protruding through the muscle.Also called crural hernia.*
Schere	**scissors** *A cutting instrument with two blades, joined at the middle.*
Schicht; Lage	**layer** *A stratum or thickness.*
schielen	**squint, to** *To look at something with the eyes partially closed.*
Schienbein	**shin** *Refers to the anterior tibial region.*
Schienbein	**tibia** *The larger of two long bones in the lower leg.*
Schiene	**splint** *A rigid support used to immobilize and extremity.*
Schild; Hülse	**shield** *A protective device, as in face shield.*
Schilddrüse	**thyroid** *A gland in the neck that secretes hormones regulating metabolism.*
Schistosomiasis; Bilharziose	**schistosomiasis** *A condition, sometimes known as bilharzia, which involves infestation with flukes of the genus Schistosoma.*
Schistozyt	**schistocyte** *Part of a red blood cell seen in hemolytic anemia.*

Schizophrenie	**schizophrenia** *A chronic mental condition exhibited by delusions, hallucinations, and faulty perception.*
Schlaf	**sleep** *A nap or a snooze.*
Schlafapnoesyndrom	**sleep apnea** *Episodic apnea during sleep that is exhibited by daytime symptoms of fatigue, difficulty concentrating and sleepiness.*
schlafen	**asleep** *To be in a dormant or inactive state.*
schlaff	**flaccid** *Limp. A term applied to an extremity one cannot move actively.*
Schlaffheit	**laxity** *A description of a joint that is loose.*
Schlaffheit; Lockerung	**looseness** *Possessing a quality of not being tight.*
Schlafkrankheit	**sleeping sickness** *Also called Trypanosomiasis, this disease is caused by a parasitic protozoa and transmitted by the tsetse fly.*
Schlaflosigkeit	**insomnia** *Sleeplessness.*
Schlafmittel	**soporific** *Promoting drowsiness or sleep.*
Schlaganfall	**cerebrovascular accident (stroke)** *A decrease in level of consciousness and paralysis caused by a cerebrovascular thrombosis, hemorrhage or vasospasm.*
Schlagvolumen	**stroke volume** *The amount of blood ejected from the ventricle with each contraction.*
Schlamm	**sludge** *A viscous fluid.*
Schlauchdrainage	**drainage tube** *A cannula used to allow outflow of fluids.*
Schläfrigkeit	**drowsiness** *Sleepiness.*
schlechte Anpassung	**maladjustment** *Having the trait of being unable to cope normally.*
Schleim	**mucilage** *1. A viscous bodily fluid. 2. A polysaccharide used in medicines and glue.*
Schleudertrauma	**whiplash** *Common term for cervical strain following a sudden deceleration.*
Schlinge	**sling** *A device used to give support to an injured extremity.*
schluchzen	**sob, to** *To cry uncontrollably.*
Schluckauf	**hiccup** *Involuntary spasm of the diaphragm with sudden closure of the glottis; this causes a characteristic cough.*
Schluckähmung	**aglutition** *The inability to swallow.*
schlucken	**swallow, to** *To cause something to pass down the esophagus.*
Schluckschmerz	**odynophagia** *Pain associated with swallowing.*
Schlundtasche	**pharyngeal pouch** *A lateral diverticulum of the pharynx.*
schlurfender Gang; Trippelgang	**festinating gait** *Walking with increased speed involuntarily; often seen in Parkinson's disease.*
Schlüsselbein	**collarbone** *Common term for the clavicle.*
Schmerz	**pain** *Physical suffering or discomfort.*
schmerzhaft	**painful** *Affected with pain.*
Schmerztablette	**aspirin** *Common name for acetylsalicylic acid.*
Schmiere	**smear** *Used to refer to a specimen smeared on a slide.*
Schmiermittel	**lubricant** *Emollient.*
Schmorlsches Knötchen	**schmorl's nodule** *Protrusion of the nucleus pulposus through the vertebral body endplast into the adjacent vertebra.*
schmutzig	**dirty** *Unclean.*
schnarchen	**snore, to** *To snore or grunt while breathing during sleep.*
Schneidezahn	**incisor** *Sharp-edged tooth; humans have four incisors.*

285

schnelle Augenbewegung	**Rapid Eye Movement** *The movement of a person's eyes during this period of sleep.*
schnelle Augenbewegung-Schlaf	**REM (rapid eye movement) sleep** *This period of sleep is associated with irregular respirations and heart rate, involuntary movements and dreaming.*
schnellender Finger	**trigger finger** *A condition in which one's finger gets stuck in the flexed position and when extended it snaps like a trigger. Also called stenosing tenosynovitis.*
Schnitt	**cut** *An incision.*
Schnupfen	**coryza** *An acute condition exhibited by copious nasal discharge.*
Schnüffeln	**sniffing** *Short, rapid nasal inhalation.*
Schnüffelnsucht	**glue sniffing addiction** *Habituation of plastic cement fumes inhalation which includes toluene, xylene and benzene.*
Schock	**shock** *A condition characterized by systemic hypoperfusion.*
Schorf	**eschar** *Dry, hard, dead tissue commonly seen with a chronic pressure ulcer or anthrax.*
schreien	**yell, to** *To speak in a loud tone.*
Schritt	**stride** *Walk with long definitive steps.*
Schritt; Gang	**pace** *Consistent and continuous movement.*
Schrittmacher	**pacemaker** *An electrical device used to stimulate the heart used for bradyarrhythmias.*
Schuh	**shoe** *Article of clothing worn on each foot.*
Schulteersteife	**frozen shoulder** *Common term for adhesive capsulitis.*
Schulter	**shoulder** *The joint were the scapula joins the clavicle and humerus.*
Schulterblatt	**scapula** *Medical term for the shoulder blade.*
Schuppe; Squama	**squama** *A scale or platelike body.*
Schußwunde	**gunshot wound** *An penetrating injury sustained from a bullet.*
Schüttelfrost	**ague** *A term used to describe recurrent fever and shivering typically associated with malaria.*
schütteln	**shake, to** *To tremble uncontrollably.*
schwach	**faint** *Weak and dizzy.*
schwachpulsig	**acrotic** *Referring to great weakness or absence of a pulse.*
schwachsinnig	**feeble-minded** *Antiquated term used to describe a person unable to make seemingly simple decisions because of a cognitive impairment.*
Schwamm	**sponge** *Sterile fabric used to soak up fluid during surgery.*
Schwangere	**gravida** *Pregnant.*
Schwangerenbetreuung	**prenatal care** *Medical care received while one is pregnant.*
Schwangerschaft	**gestation** *The development of a fetus from conception until birth.*
Schwangerschaft; Gravidität	**pregnancy** *The period of being pregnant.*
Schwangerschaftserbrechen	**morning sickness** *Nausea associated with pregnancy.*
schwanken	**stagger, to** *To walk in an unsteady fashion.*
schwarz	**black** *Referring to the color, as in the color of coal.*
Schwarzwasserfieber	**blackwater fever** *A term used to describe the fever associated with malaria when the urine is reddish-black.*
Schwäche	**weakness** *Feebleness.*
Schwefel	**sulfur** *A chemical element with atomic number of 16.*
Schweiß	**sweat** *Moisture exuded through the pores of the skin.*

	English
Schweißbläschen	**sudamina** *White vesicles noted because of retained sweat in the layers of the epidermis.*
Schweißdrüse	**apocrine gland** *A gland that releases some of its cytoplasm in secretions; an example is axillary sweat glands.*
schweißhemmend	**anhidrotic** *Something the reduces the quantity of sweat.*
Schweißsekretion	**hidrosis** *The production and secretion of sweat.*
Schwellenreiz	**liminal stimulus** *Referring to a stimulus of threshold strength.*
Schwellung	**tumefaction** *An area of swelling.*
Schwellung; Geschwulst	**swelling** *An abnormal enlarged from fluid collection.*
schwer	**hard** *Rigid or very firm.*
schwer	**heavy** *Possessing great weight.*
schwerhörig	**hard of hearing** *Decreased sense of hearing.*
Schwertfortsatz	**xiphoid process** *The inferior segment of the sternum.*
Schwindel	**giddiness** *A tendency to fall or dizziness.*
schwitzen	**sweat, to** *The action of releasing moisture through pores of the skin.*
schwitzen	**transpire, to** *To release vapor from the skin or respiratory mucosa.*
Scimitar-Syndrom	**scimitar sign** *An abnormal radiologic finding associated with anomalous pulmonary venous drainage.*
Sclerotomie	**sclerotomy** *Surgical incision of the sclera.*
Seborrhöe	**seborrhea** *Abnormal amount of sebum production.*
Sedativum	**sedative** *A medication used to facilitate sleep or calm a person.*
Sehefeld; Gesichtsfeld	**visual field** *The complete area a person can see with their eyes in a fixed position.*
Seheintrübung	**blurred vision** *Low visual acuity.*
Seheintrübung; verschwommenes Sehen	**vision, blurred** *Haziness of the visual field.*
Sehkraft	**eyesight** *A person's ability to see.*
Sehne	**tendon** *Fibrous tissue that connects muscle to bone.*
Sehnenreflex	**tendon reflex** *A deep reflex elicited by gently tapping the tendon.*
Sehnervpapille	**optic disk** *The area of the retina where the optic nerve enters.*
Seife	**soap** *A compound made with fats/oils and an alkali; it is used for washing.*
Seite	**side** *A position medial or lateral to center.*
Seitenstrang	**funiculus, lateral** *The lateral white colum of the spinal cord between the anterior and posterior nerve roots.*
Seitverbiegung	**laterodeviation** *Pushed to the lateral aspect.*
Sekretin	**secretin** *A hormone that increases secretion from the pancreas and liver.*
Sekretion; Absonderung	**secretion** *The discharge of substances from cells or glands.*
Sekundenkapazität	**forced expiratory volume per second (FEV1)** *The amount of air exhaled with maximal effort, measured in liters, over one second.*
Seminom	**seminoma** *A malignant tumor of the testis.*
Seneszenz	**senescence** *The normal process of deterioration with age.*
senil	**senile** *Generally referring to mental deterioration associated with aging.*
Senilität	**senility** *The process of being senile.*
Senkfuß	**pes planus** *Medical term for flat foot.*
sensibilisiert	**sensitized** *Being abnormally sensitive to a substance.*

287

Sensibilisierung	**sensitization** *The change in an organ by a hormone so it will respond to another stimulus.*
Sensibilität	**sensibility** *Ability to feel or perceive.*
sensorimotorisch Polyneuropathie	**onion bulb neuropathy** *Also known as hypertrophic interstitial neuropathy which is a sensorimotor polyneuropathy.*
sensorisches nerven	**sensory nerve** *A nerve that receives input from various receptors.*
Sepsis	**sepsis** *A condition exhibited by overwhelming inflammation due to infection.*
Septikämie	**septicemia** *A systemic disease in which microorganisms or their toxins are in the blood stream.*
septisch	**septic** *Referring to a state of sepsis.*
Septum; Scheidewand	**septum** *A wall separating two chambers, the nasal septum for example.*
Sequesterbildung	**sequestrum** *Necrotic bone present in an injured or diseased bone.*
Serotonin	**serotonin** *A neurotransmitter that constricts blood vessels.*
serös	**serous** *Referring to serum or similar to serum.*
serpiginös	**serpiginous** *A skin lesion having wavy margin.*
Serum	**serum** *The fluid that isolates out when blood coagulates.*
sessil	**sessile** *Having a broad base with no stalk.*
seufzen	**sigh, to** *A long deep exhalation that expresses an emotion, as in relief.*
Sézary-Syndrom	**Sézary syndrome** *Symptoms are exfoliative dermatitis with intense itching caused by cutaneous infiltration by mononuclear cells,*
Sialadenitis	**sialadenitis** *Inflammation of a salivary gland.*
Sialagogum	**sialogogue** *A substance that increase salivary flow.*
Sialolith	**sialolith** *A calculus in a salivary duct.*
sich erkälten	**catch a cold** *To come down with a viral upper respiratory tract infection.*
sich fühlen	**feel, to** *To perceive or discern.*
sich räuspern	**clear one's throat, to** *To cough lightly in attempt to speak more clearly.*
Sichelzellenanämie	**sickle-cell anemia** *A hereditary type of anemia characterized by crescent shaped red blood cells.*
sickern	**ooze, to** *To slowly leak.*
Siderose	**siderosis** *Discoloration of a part due to iron deposition.*
Siebbein	**ethmoid bone** *A bone at the root of the nose which has perforations for the olfactory nerves to transit.*
Sigmoidflexur	**sigmoid flexure** *The S shaped curve located between the descending colon and rectum.*
Sigmoidoskopie	**sigmoidoscopy** *Visualization of the sigmoid colon with a scope.*
Sigmoidostomie	**sigmoidostomy** *Formation of an opening in the sigmoid colon that communicates with the outside of the body.*
Silber	**silver** *A precious metal with atomic number 47.*
silbernitrat Stock	**silver nitrate stick** *A medical device used to treat hypergranulation tissue.*
Silikose	**silicosis** *Grinders's disease; fibrotic lung disease caused by inhalation of silica.*
Simulant	**malingerer** *A person who feigns illness.*
Sinistrokardie	**sinistrocardia** *Location of the heart toward the left (more than normally seen).*

Sinistrotorsion	**sinistrotorsion** *Distorsion toward the left; in reference to the eye generally.*
Sinneseindruck	**sensation** *A perception when one is touched.*
sinuatrial	**sinoatrial** *Referring to the cardiac node of the same name.*
Sinus frontalis; Stirnhöhle	**frontal sinus** *A paranasal sinus on both sides of the lower part of the frontal bone.*
Sinus sphenoidalis	**sphenoidal sinus** *Part of the sphenoid bone; it communicates with the most superior aspect of the nasal meatus.*
Sinusarrhythmie	**sinus arrhythmia** *Cardiac dysrhythmias related to sinoatrial nodal dysfunction.*
Sinusitis	**sinusitis** *Inflammation of the sinuses.*
Sinusknoten; Keith-Flack Knoten	**sinoatrial node** *A mass of cardiac tissue that acts as the pacemaker.*
Sinusoid	**sinusoid** *An irregular vessel having almost no adventitia that is found in the liver, heart, parathyroid, spleen and pancreas.*
Sirup	**syrup** *A thick sweet liquid.*
Site	**site** *Location.*
Sjögren Syndrom	**Sjogren's syndrome.** *Characterized by dryness of the mouth and eyes, it is sometimes linked to rheumatoid arthritis.*
Skabies; Krätze	**scabies** *A skin condition exhibited by intense pruritis and a macular rash commonly in the perineal and interdigital spaces.*
Skalpell	**scalpel** *A knife used during surgery for incision of skin and tissue.*
Skalpell; Seziermesser	**bistoury; scalpel** *A surgical knife.*
Skalpierung	**scalp avulsion** *An injury causing the skin along with some subcutaneous tissue to be pulled from the skull.*
Skaphocephalie	**scaphocephaly** *A condition exhibited by a long narrow skull because of early closure of the sagittal sutures.*
Skarifikation	**scarification** *Multiple small scratches of the skin, as is sometimes used for vaccine administration.*
Skelattartigtraction	**skeletal traction** *Use of a pulley system to reduce a fracture.*
Skelett	**skeleton** *Internal bony framework.*
Sklera	**sclera** *The white outer covering of the eyeball.*
Skleritis	**scleritis** *Inflammation of the eyeball.*
Sklerodaktylie	**sclerodactylia** *Scleroderma of the digits.*
Skleröderm	**scleroderma** *A systemic disease of the connective tissues.*
Skolex	**scolex** *The front end of a tapeworm.*
Skoliose	**scoliosis** *A lateral curvature of the spine.*
Skopophilie	**scopophilia** *Sexual please attained by viewing sexual organs.*
Skorbut	**scurvy** *A disease of vitamin C deficiency exhibited by bleeding gums.*
Skotom	**scotoma** *A blind spot within an otherwise normal visual field.*
Skrofulose	**scrofula** *Cervical tuberculous lymphadenitis.*
skrotal	**scrotal** *Referring to the scrotum.*
Skrotum; Hodensack	**scrotum** *The sac which contains the testes.*
Skutulum	**scutulum** *A crust of tinea capitis.*
Skybala	**scybalum** *A hard, dry formation of stool in the bowel.*
Smegma	**smegma** *A thick curdled secretion found around the clitoris and the prepuce.*
Socken	**socks** *Worn on the feet before one puts on shoes.*
Sodbrennen	**heartburn** *Synonym of pyrosis.*

Sodbrennen	**pyrosis** *Synonym for heartburn.*
Soleus	**soleus muscle** *Assists with ankle plantar flexion.*
somatisch	**somatic** *Referring to the body.*
Somnambulismus	**somnambulism** *Sleepwalking.*
Somnolenz	**somnolence** *Drowsiness.*
Sonde	**probe** *A device used for exploration.*
Sondenernährung	**gavage** *The instillation of food into the stomach with use of a tube.*
Sondenernährungsonde	**gavage tube** *A tube used for instillation of liquids into the stomach.*
Sondenernährungspritze	**gavage syringe** *A syringe used for irrigation.*
Sorge	**sorrow** *A feeling of deep despair.*
sorgen	**worry, to** *To fret or have unease.*
Spaltung; Furchung	**cleavage** *A sharp division or demarcation.*
Spannungsblase	**bulla** *A large cutaneous serous filled vesicle.*
Spannweite	**span** *A distance between two objects.*
sparsam	**sparing** *Economical.*
spasmolytisch	**spasmolytic** *A substance that diminishes spasms.*
Spasmus	**spasm** *An involuntary contraction of muscles.*
Spastiker	**spastic** *Stiff, awkward movement of the muscles.*
Spastizität	**spasticity** *Refers to continuous spastic movement.*
spät	**late** *A time later than expected.*
Spätgeburt	**infant, post-term** *A neonate born after the normal gestation.*
Spätgeburt	**post-term birth** *An infant born after the normal length of pregnancy.*
Spätphase; terminale	**end stage** *Terminal stage. End stage cancer means there is no cure possible and death is imminent.*
Speichel	**saliva** *The watery liquid secreted by the salivary glands.*
Speicheldrüse	**salivary gland** *The parotid, submandibular and sublingual glands that secrete saliva.*
Speichelfluß	**salivation** *The process of secreting saliva.*
Speigel	**mirror** *A device used for reflecting an image.*
Spektrometrie	**spectrometry** *The use of a device to measure spectra.*
Spektroskop	**spectroscope** *A device for producing and recording spectra.*
Spekulum (Scheidenspekulum)	**speculum** *A device used to open a canal for inspection. (vaginal speculum)*
Spender	**donor** *Referring to a person who donates tissue or an organ.*
Sperma	**sperm** *Short term for spermatozoon.*
Spermatogenese	**spermatogenesis** *The production of spermatozoa.*
Spermatozele	**spermatocele** *A cyst in the epididymis containing spermatozoa.*
Spermatozoon	**spermatozoon** *A mature male germ cell that is capable of fertilizing an ovum.*
Spermauntersuchung	**semen analysis** *Evaluation of semen used as part of a fertility workup.*
Spermizid	**spermicide** *A substance capable of killing sperm.*
sperrig	**bulky** *Voluminous or substantial.*
spezifisch	**specific** *Clearly defined.*
Spherozyt	**spherocyte** *An erythrocyte without the usual central pallor; it is noted in spherocytosis and some hemolytic anemias.*
Spherozytose	**spherocytosis** *The presence of spherocytes in the blood.*

Sphinkter; Schließmuskel	**sphincter** *A muscle the surrounds an orifice or duct so it closes when the muscle contracts.*
Sphinkterotomie	**sphincterotomy** *Surgical incision of the anal sphincter.*
Sphygmomanometer; Blutdruckapparat	**sphygmomanometer** *Device for measuring blood pressure.*
Spica	**spica** *A figure of eight bandage.*
Spider-Nävus	**spider nevus** *A papule with telangiectases radiating from the center.*
spinal	**spinal** *Referring to the spine.*
spinaler Reflex	**spinal reflex** *A reflex that has an arc passing through the spine.*
spinaler Shock	**spinal shock** *Hypotension related to injury or intervention of the spine.*
Spinalganglion	**spinal ganglion** *The ganglion located on the dorsal root of each spinal nerve.*
Spinalnerv	**spinal nerve** *The term for each of the thirty pairs of nerves that originate in the spine and traverse between the vertebrae. There are eight cervical, twelve thoracic, five lumbar, five sacral and one coccygeal nerve pairs.*
spindelförmig	**fusiform** *Spindle-shaped.*
Spirograph	**spirograph** *A device used to record respiratory movements.*
Spirometer	**spirometer** *A device used to measure pulmonary capacity.*
Spitz	**spicule** *A sharp, slender part.*
Spitz-Klumpfuß	**talipes equinovaro** *Medical term for what is commonly known as club foot.*
Spitzfuß	**talipes equinus** *A foot deformity exhibited by abnormal plantar flexion.*
Spitzschädel	**oxycephaly** *The deformation of the skull so that it appears pointed.*
Splenektomie; Milzexstirpation	**splenectomy** *Surgical excision of the spleen.*
splenisch	**splenic** *Referring to the spleen.*
Splenomegalie; Milzvergröberung	**splenomegaly** *An abnormally enlarged spleen.*
Splitter	**splinter** *A small, thin object; usually refers to the object being imbedded in the body.*
Splitterfraktur	**fracture, comminuted** *A broken bone where one segment overrides the other.*
Spondylarthritis ankylopoetica	**ankylosing spondylitis** *A type of arthritis found in the spine that is exhibited by bony fusion.*
Spondylitis	**spondylitis** *Inflammation of the vertebrae.*
Spondylolyse	**spondylolysis** *Dissolution of the vertebra.*
Spondylothisthese	**spondylolisthesis** *The overlapping of one vertebra over another.*
Spongiose	**spongiosis** *Edema of the spongy layer of the skin.*
spongiöser Konchen	**cancellous bone** *Describing the cancellous interior of bone.*
spontan	**spontaneous** *Occurring without provocation.*
Spontanfraktur	**fracture, pathologic** *A fracture due at least in part to another condition, such as a fracture at a location where there is bone cancer.*
Sporotrichose	**sporotrichosis** *A Sporotrichum schenckii infection manifested by formation of lymphatic and subcutaneous nodules.*
Sprache	**speech** *Oral articulation.*
Sprachtherapie	**speech therapist** *A person trained to assist people with speech and language disorders.*
Spray; Zerstäuber	**spray** *Liquid blown through the air in the form of fine droplets.*

Sprechschmerz	**odynophonia** *Pain associated with speaking.*
Spritze	**syringe** *A device used for administering medication through various routes.*
spritzen	**squirt, to** *To eject a liquid from a small opening.*
Sprunggelenk	**ankle joint** *The articulation of the tibia/fibula and talus.*
Sputum	**sputum** *A mixture of respiratory tract secretions and saliva.*
squamös	**squamous** *Scaly.*
Stadieneinteilung; Feststellung	**staging** *Refers to a stratification of cancer for example.*
Stahlung; Bestrahlung	**radiation** *1. The emission of energy in the form of electromagnetic waves. 2. Divergence from a common point.*
Stammeln	**stammering** *The impulse to repeat the first letter of words and involuntary pauses while speaking.*
Stapedektomie	**stapedectomy** *Surgical excision of the stapes.*
stapedius Muskel	**stapedius muscle** *Located in the tympanic interior, it reduces stapedial movement.*
Staphylom	**staphyloma** *Protrusion of the cornea due to inflammation.*
Staphylorrhaphie	**staphylorrhaphy** *Surgical repair of a defect between the soft palate and uvula.*
Stase	**stasis** *Lack of movement.*
Station	**ward** *A section of a hospital where patients reside.*
statisch	**static** *Not changing.*
Status	**status** *Position or condition*
Stauschlauch; Tourniquet	**tourniquet** *A device tied tightly around an extremity to diminish blood flow or blood loss.*
Stauungsinsuffizienz	**congestive heart failure** *A diminished cardiac output leading to passive engorgement.*
Stärke	**strength** *Force, might or vigor.*
Steatom	**steatoma** *A sebaceous cyst or lipoma.*
Steatorrhöe	**steatorrhea** *Excrement with an abnormally high fat content.*
Steatose	**steatosis** *Fatty degeneration; when referring to the liver it involves invasion of fat into hepatocytes.*
stechend	**sharp (pain)** *When describing pain, a piercing sensation.*
stechend; bohrend	**terebrant** *Having a piercing quality.*
stechender Schmerz	**stabbing pain** *A sharp piercing quality to pain.*
stehend	**standing** *Position or status.*
Stehoskop; Hörrohr	**stethoscope** *Device used to auscultate the heart, lungs and over arteries to assess for abnormalities.*
steif	**stiff** *Not easily bent.*
Steigbügel	**stapes** *This auditory ossicle is the innermost of three ossicles and is shaped like a stirrup.*
Steigbügel	**stirrup** *An attachment to an exam table where a woman puts her legs to assist examination of the genitalia.*
steinartig	**petrous** *Possessing a density of a stone.*
Steinschnittlage	**lithotomy position** *Buttocks positioned at the end of the OR table, the hips and knees flexed and the feet strapped in. Dorsosacral position.*
Steißbein	**coccyx** *The small bone formed by the natural fusion of rudimentary vertebrae.*
Steißgeburt	**breech birth** *Delivery with the feet or buttocks coming first.*

Stenose	**stenosis** *Narrowing of an orifice.*
Steppergang	**drop foot gait** *A gait characterized by dragging the foot, as there is no ankle dorsiflexion; usually associated with steppage gait.*
sterben	**die, to** *To stop living, to expire.*
steril	**sterile** *1. Infertile 2. Refers to equipment that is free of contamination.*
Sterilisierung	**sterilization** *A procedure done to prevent production of offspring.*
Sterin	**sterol** *Unsaturated steroid alcohols such as cholesterol.*
Sterkobilin	**stercobilin** *A substance created by the reduction of bilirubin and gives excrement the brown hue.*
sternal	**sternal** *Referring to the sternum.*
Sternocleidomastoideus	**sternocleidomastoid** *The pair of muscles that connect the sternum, clavicle and mastoid process.*
Sternum; Brustbein	**sternum** *Commonly called the breast bone, it consists of the corpus, manubrium and xiphoid process.*
Stich	**sting** *A small puncture as in a bee sting.*
Stichwunde	**stab wound** *An injury occurring with a sharp object.*
Stickoxidul	**nitrous oxide** *An inhalant gas used as an anesthetic agent.*
Stickstoff	**nitrogen** *A colorless, odorless gas used as a coolant in the liquid form.*
Stiel	**pedicle** *Part of a skin/tissue graft temporarily left connected to the original site.*
Stiel	**peduncle** *1. A stalk-like protrusion. 2. A bundle of nerve fibers connecting two parts of the brain.*
Stift	**pin** *Hardware used in surgery.*
Stilett; Mandrin	**stylet** *A thin wire within a catheter that is removed after the catheter is in place.*
still	**silent** *Absence of noise or no indication of something.*
Stillen	**breast feeding** *The process of giving milk to a baby via the nipple.*
Stimmband	**vocal cords** *Paired folds of mucous membranes stretched across the larynx.*
Stimme	**voice** *The sound produced through the larygnx and out the mouth.*
Stimmgabel	**tuning fork** *A device used to distinguish between perceptive and conductive hearing loss.*
Stimmritz	**glottis** *Essentially the vocal structure, including the true vocal cords and the opening between them.*
Stimmung; Laune	**mood** *A temporarty state of mind or feeling.*
Stirnlage	**brow presentation** *The term used to describe which part of the body (forehead) is being delivered first in childbirth.*
Stottern	**stuttering** *Involuntary repetition of the first consonant.*
Stöhnen	**groan** *A deep inarticulate sound made due to pain or despair.*
Strabismus	**strabismus** *An anomaly of ocular movement.*
Strahl	**frog** *A tailless amphibian that is short with long hind legs for jumping.*
Strahlenempfindlichkeit	**radiosensitivity** *The susceptibility of the skin to radiation.*
Strahlenhautschaden	**radioepithelitis** *The injury to epithelial cells due to effects of radiation.*
Strahlentherapie	**radiotherapy** *Treatment of cancer with radiation.*
Strang; Kanal	**tract** *A large bundle of fibers or a major passage in the body.*
Stratum granulosum	**granular layer** *A deep layer of the cerebellum.*
Streckung	**extension** *Going from a bent to straight position.*

	English
streiten (sich streiten)	**argue, to** *To debate or reason. (quarrel)*
Stress; Druck; Belastung	**stress** *Strain or pressure.*
Streßfraktur	**fracture, stress** *A fracture associated with overuse.*
Streßfraktur	**stress fracture** *A long bone fracture caused by repetitive mechanical stress.*
Streuung	**scatter** *The degree to which repeated measurements differ.*
Stria; Streifen	**stria** *A narrow bandlike body.*
Stridor	**stridor** *An abnormal, high-pitched, musical sound caused by an obstruction in the largynx or stenosis of the vocal cords.*
Stridor laryngealis	**laryngismus stridulus** *Sudden, severe laryngeal spasm.*
Striktur	**stricture** *A narrowing of a canal or duct.*
Strom	**stream** *The flow of a liquid.*
Strom; Fluss	**current** *Flow or stream.*
Stroma	**stroma** *A term used to describe the framework of an organ.*
Strümpellreflex	**Strümpell reflex** *Flexion of the leg and adduction of the foot elicited by stroking of the thigh or abdomen.*
Strümpellsche Krankheit	**Strümpell's disease** *Also known as spondylitis deformans, it is characterized by arthritis and osteitis deformans of the spinal cord with a rounded kyphosis and rigidity.*
Stuab	**dust** *Dry earthen particles found on the ground and surfaces.*
Stuhlinkontinenz; Enkopresis	**encopresis** *Involuntary defecation.*
stumm	**mute** *Refraining from or being speechless.*
stumpf	**blunt** *Having a flat or rounded end.*
stumpf	**obtuse** *Rather insensitive or hard to understand.*
Stumpf	**stump** *Term used to designate what remains of an amputated extremity.*
Stupor	**stupor** *A reduced level of consciousness.*
Stützapparat	**brace** *A splint.*
stützen	**brace, to** *Application of a splint.*
subakut	**subacute** *A stage between acute and chronic.*
subarachnoidal	**subarachnoid** *The layer of the brain covering between the arachnoid and pia mater.*
Subareolärabszeß	**subareolar abscess** *A purulent fluid collection in the areolar gland.*
subdural	**subdural** *The area between the dura mater and the arachnoid membrane.*
Subduralhämatom	**subdural hematoma** *Formation of a blood clot between the dura mater and the arachnoid membrane.*
Suberose; Korkarbeiterkrankheit	**suberosis** *A type of hypersensitivity pneumonitis related to inhalation of moldy cork dust.*
subjektives Hauptsymptom	**presenting symptom** *The initial subjective complaint that initiated a visit.*
subklavikulär	**subclavian** *Refers to the area under the clavicle; the subclavian vein runs below the clavicle.*
subkutane injektion	**hypodermic injection** *Subcutaneous injection.*
sublingual	**sublingual** *Situated under the tongue.*
submaxillär	**submaxillary** *Situated below the maxilla.*
subphrenisch	**subphrenic** *Referring to below the diaphragm.*

Succussio Hippocratis	**succussion** *The presence of a splashing sound when a body cavity is moved indicating presence of both air and fluid.*
Suizid; Selbsttötung	**suicide** *To kill oneself intentionally.*
Sulfonamid	**sulfonamide** *A class of drugs derived from sulfanilamide that are antibacterial.*
Sulkus	**sulcus** *A groove, like in the brain.*
Sumpffieber	**paludism** *Synonym of malaria.*
Superfekundation	**superfecundation** *The fertilization of two different ova by spermatozoa of two different males.*
Supination	**supination** *Turning the sole of the foot or the palm of the hand upward..*
Suppositorium; Zäpfchen	**suppository** *A delivery system for medication placed in an orifice.*
supranukleär Ophthalmoplegie	**supranuclear ophthalmoplegia** *A disorder that effects the extraocular movements especially limiting the upward movement of the eyes.*
supraorbital	**supraorbital** *Situated above the orbit.*
suprapubisch	**suprapubic** *Situated above the pubis.*
Sutur	**suture** *Thread used for sewing together a wound.*
Süchtigkeit	**addiction** *An abnormal dependency.*
Sycose	**sycosis** *A bacterial infection affecting the hair follicles on a person's face.*
Symbiose	**symbiosis** *The living together of two organisms.*
Symmetrie	**symmetry** *Being equally bilaterally.*
Sympathektomie	**sympathectomy** *The surgical resection of a sympathetic nerve to reduce undesired effects.*
sympathisches Nervensystem	**sympathetic nervous system** *The nerves responsible for the flight or fight response.*
Symptom; Krankheitszeichen	**symptom** *A physical feature that is characteristic of disease.*
Synapse	**synapse** *The intersection of two nerve cells.*
Synarthrose	**synarthrosis** *Adjacent bones connected by a joint but the joint is fixed.*
Synchondrose	**synchondrosis** *A joint with little motion that uses cartilage such as the vertebral bodies.*
Syndrom der leeren Sella	**empty sella syndrome** *Compressed or flattened pituitary related to herniating arachnoid, surgery or radiotherapy.*
Synechie	**synechia** *The adhesion of two body parts, such as synechia vulvae in which the labia minora are congenitally adherent.*
Synkope; Ohnmachtsanfall	**syncope** *Sudden loss of consciousness.*
Synovia	**synovial fluid** *The fluid that surrounds, for example, the knee within a capsule.*
Synovitis	**synovitis** *Inflammation of the synovium.*
Synvektomie	**synovectomy** *Surgical resection of a synovial membrane.*
Synzytienbildung	**syncytial knot** *Aggregation of syncytiotrophoblastic nuclei in the villi of the placenta during early pregnancy.*
Syphilis; Lues	**syphilis** *A infectious disease caused by Treponema pallidum that causes a painless penile ulcer in the primary stage but can lead to irreversible brain damage in the untreated tertiary stage.*
Syringomyelie	**syringomelia** *A condition exhibited by fluid-filled cavities in the spinal cord.*
Systole	**systole** *The phase of the cardiac cycle in which the ventricles contract.*
systolisch	**systolic** *Referring to systole or that which occurs during systole.*

Szirrhus	**scirrhus** *A cancer that is hard to palpation.*
Tabatière Anatomique	**anatomical snuff-box** *The area on the back of the hand near the base of the thumb that is between the extensor pollicus longus and extensor pollicus brevis.*
Tablette	**tablet** *A small disk of a compressed solid substance.*
Tachykardie	**tachycardia** *Heart rate higher than physiologic normal.*
Tachypnoe	**tachypnea** *Breathing faster than normal.*
taktil	**tactile** *Able to be felt.*
Talgdrüse	**sebaceous gland** *A gland in the skin that secretes sebum.*
talgig	**sebaceous** *Referring to a sebaceous gland or what it secretes.*
Talus	**astragalus** *Synonym of talus.*
Talus	**talus** *The most superior tarsal bone that articulates with the tibia.*
Tampon	**tampon** *Disposible intravaginal product used to collect blood from menstruation.*
tamponade	**tamponade** *1. Stopping bleeding during surgery with a cotton pledget. 2. When referring to cardiac tamponade, it is the limitation of cardiac contraction because of blood or fluid accumulation in the pericardial sac.*
Tarantel	**tarantula** *A large hairy spider found mainly in the tropics.*
tarsal	**tarsal** *Referring to any bone in the tarsus.*
Tarsalgie	**tarsalgia** *Pain in any of the tarsal bones.*
Tarsaltunnelsyndrom	**tarsal tunnel syndrome** *Characterized by impingement of various nerves of the ankle.*
Tarsektomie; Tarsusresektion	**tarsectomy** *Surgical excision of all or part of the tarsus.*
Tarsorrhaphie	**tarsorrhaphy** *Suturing the eyelids in order to tighten the palpebral fissure.*
Taschenmesserphänomen	**clasp knife reflex** *The lengthening of the extensor muscles resulting in flexion.*
taub	**deaf** *Absence of the sense of hearing.*
Taubenmilbekrätze	**poultryman's itch** *Pruritis associated with the mite Dermanyssus gallinae.*
Taubheit	**deafness** *Having impaired hearing.*
Taubheit	**numbness** *Decreased sensation to tactile stimuli.*
taubstumm	**deaf-mute** *Inability to hear or speak.*
Taucher	**diver** *A person who swims in deep water.*
Taurocholsäure	**taurocholic acid** *A bile acid composed of cholic acid and taurine.*
Tätowierung	**tattoo** *A design made by inserting indelible ink into the skin.*
Tectum	**tectum** *A roof-like body.*
Tectum mesencephali	**tectum mesencephali** *The posterior portion of the mesencephalon including the sup. and inf. colliculi and tectal lamina.*
Teelöffel	**teaspoon** *A measure instrument that holds 5 milliliters of fluid.*
Teleangiektasie	**telangiectasis** *A condition exhibited by red, dilated capillaries on the skin.*
Temperatur	**temperature** *The degree of internal heat in a person's body.*
Tendinitis	**tendinitis** *Inflammation of a tendon.*
Tendoplastik	**tenoplasty** *Surgical repair of a tendon.*
Tendovaginitis de Quervain	**De Quervain tenosynovitis** *Inflammation of the tendons of the wrist including the abductor pollicis longus and extensor pollicis brevis.*

Tendovaginitis; Sehnenscheidenentzündung	**tenosynovitis** *Inflammation and swelling of an articulation.*
Tenesmus	**tenesmus** *The attempt to defecate but attempts elicit pain and are ineffective.*
Tenorrhaphie	**tenorrhaphy** *The surgical repair with suture of a separated tendon.*
Tenotomie	**tenotomy** *Incision of a tendon as is done for strabismus.*
Teratogen	**teratogen** *A substance that induces fetal anomalies.*
Teratom	**teratoma** *A tumor made up of tissue not usually at the location (a mass of hair, teeth and gingival tissue in a leg tumor for instance).*
Termin	**appointment** *A previously scheduled time to see a person.*
Termin	**deadline** *Cutoff date.*
terminale Krankheit	**terminal illness** *A disease with no viable treatment with death being inevitable.*
Tertiana	**tertian fever** *A febrile syndrome caused by Plasmodium vivax which produces a fever spike every 48 hours.*
tertiär	**tertiary** *Third in order or designating medical care at a specialized hospital.*
Testosteron	**testosterone** *This steroid hormone produces secondary male sexual characteristics.*
Tetanie	**tetany** *A condition caused by the hypocalcemic effect of hypoparathyroidism, exhibited by periodic muscle spasms, convulsions, and peri-oral numbness.*
Tetracyclin	**tetracycline** *An antibiotic used for gram positive and gram negative infections.*
Tetradaktylie	**tetradactylous** *Referring to a condition of having only four digits on a hand or foot.*
Thalamussyndrom; Déjerine-Roussy Syndrom	**thalamic syndrome** *Caused by an infarct of the posteriorinferior thalamus, there is transient hemiparesis, severe sensory loss with preserved crude pain in the hypalgic limbs.*
Thalassämie	**thalassemia** *A hereditary hemolytic anemia first observed in people from the Mediterranean area.*
Thalidomid	**thalidomide** *A drug used originally as a sedative, after it was found to cause congenital anomalies, its use was restricted. Now it is used for a few conditions such as multiple myeloma.*
Thalmus	**thalamus** *A paired structure located adjacent to the third ventricle.*
Thekazelltumor	**thecoma** *A tumor composed of theca cells.*
therapeutische Breite	**therapeutic range** *The highest to lowest value that will produce a desired effect.*
Thermometer	**thermometer** *A device used to measure temperature.*
Thiamin	**thiamine** *Also called vitamin B1; a deficiency causes beriberi.*
thorakal	**thoracic** *Referring to the thorax.*
Thorakoplastik	**thoracoplasty** *Surgical removal of ribs.*
Thorakoskopie	**thoracoscopy** *Visualization of the thoracic cavity with a scope.*
Thorakotomie	**thoracotomy** *Surgical incision of the thorax.*
Thorakozentese	**thoracentesis** *Insertion of a needle into the pleural space to drain and or obtain a specimen for analysis.*
Thorax; Brustkorb	**chest** *Thorax.*
Threonin	**threonine** *An amino acid needed for the growth in infants.*
Thrombangitis	**thromboangiitis** *Inflammation and thrombosis in a blood vessel.*

Thrombektomie	**thrombectomy** *Excision of a thrombus from a vein or artery.*
Thrombin	**thrombin** *An enzyme that is a catalyst for the conversion of fibrinogen to fibrin in the formation of a clot.*
Thromboarteriitis	**thromboarteritis** *Thrombosis of an inflammed artery.*
Thrombophlebitis	**thrombophlebitis** *Inflammation of a venous wall associated with a thrombus.*
Thrombose	**thrombosis** *Formation of a clot in a vein or artery.*
Thrombozytopenie	**thrombocytopenia** *Abnormal decrease in the number of blood platelets.*
Thrombus	**clot** *A thrombus or embolus.*
Thymektomie	**thymectomy** *Surgical excision of the thymus.*
Thymin	**thymine** *A chemical with a pyrimidine base found in DNA.*
Thymom	**thymoma** *A tumor composed of thymic tissue and is sometimes associated with myasthenia gravis.*
Thymozyt	**thymocyte** *A lymphocyte located in the thymus.*
Thymusdrüse	**thymus** *A body organ located in the neck and it produces T cells to improve immune function.*
Thyreoglossuszyste	**thyroglossal cyst** *A common congenital growth in the thyroglossal duct.*
Thyreoidektomie	**thyroidectomy** *Surgical resection of all or part of the thyroid.*
Thyreostatikum	**antithyroid** *A substance inhibiting the effect of the thyroid.*
Thyreotoxikose	**thyrotoxicosis** *Abnormal increase in thyroid activity exhibited by thinning hair, hypertension, tachycardia and at times atrial fibrillation.*
Thyreotropin	**thyroid stimulating hormone (TSH)** *A thyroid secreted by the pituitary that regulates the thyroid.*
Thyroxin	**thyroxine** *An iodine containing hormone, referred to T4.*
tibial	**cnemial** *Referring to the shin.*
Tic	**tic** *Periodic spasmodic facial muscle contractions.*
Tic douloureux	**tic douloureux** *Also referred to as trigeminal neuralgia.*
tief	**deep** *Having significant depth.*
tief Venenthrombose	**deep vein thrombosis (DVT)** *A blood clot that forms within a vein, typically in the lower extremities.*
Tiefenreflex	**deep tendon reflex** *Reflexes exhibited by the stretching of a tendon.*
Tinea barbae	**tinea barbae** *Ringworm on the face in the region a man shaves.*
Tinea capitis	**tinea capitis** *Ringworm of the scalp, a fungal infection.*
Tinea corporis	**tinea corporis** *Ringworm of the body, a fungal infection.*
Tinea cruris; Eczema marginatum	**tinea cruris** *Ringworm in the inguinal region, a fungal infection.*
Tinea pedis; Fußpilz	**tinea pedis** *Ringworm of the feet, a fungal infection.*
Tinktur	**tincture** *1. A very small amount of something. 2. A medicine dissolved in alcohol.*
Tochter	**daughter**
Tod	**death** *The action of dying.*
Tokopherol	**tocopherol** *Vitamin E.*
Tollwut	**rabies** *An infectious viral disease transmitted through the bite of a mammal. Symptoms include hydrophobia, pharyngeal spasms and hyperactivity.*
tonometrisch	**tonometer** *A device used to measure ocular pressure in glaucoma.*

Tonsille; Mandel	**tonsil** *A rounded mass of lymphoid tissue, most commonly referring to the pharyngeal tonsil.*
Tonsillektomie	**tonsillectomy** *Excision of the tonsils.*
Tonsillitis	**tonsillitis** *Inflammation of the tonsils.*
Tonuserniedrigung; Hypotonus	**hypotonia** *Reduced tone or activity.*
Torpidität	**torpor** *Unresponsiveness to normal stimuli.*
torsade de pointes	**torsade de pointe** *Ventricular cardiac rhythm disturbance.*
torsion	**torsion** *Refers to twisting. Testicular torsion is the twisting of the spermatic cord that can lead to ischemia and gangrene of the testicle.*
Torsionsdystonie	**torsion spasm** *Also called dystonia musculorum deformans, a genetic condition exhibited by twisting contortions sideways and forward while walking.*
Tortikollis; Schiefhals	**torticollis** *A condition exhibited by the head being turned to one side continuously.*
tot	**dead** *Deceased.*
totgeboren	**stillborn** *Refers to a newborn that died in utero.*
Totraum	**dead space** *The area in the respiratory tract where air is not exchanged.*
Toxämie	**toxemia** *The release of toxic substances into the blood stream from a local infection. Toxemia of pregnancy is a synonym for preeclampsia.*
Toxikologie	**toxicology** *The study of the nature, effects and detection of poisons.*
Toxin	**toxin** *A poison of plant or animal origin.*
toxisch	**toxic** *Relating to or caused by poison.*
Toxoid	**toxoid** *A chemically modified toxin that can be used as a vaccine.*
Toxoplasmose	**toxoplasmosis** *A disease caused by an organism from the genus Toxoplasma. One can have simple malaise to central nervous system involvement.*
Trabekel	**trabecule** *A connective tissue strand that goes from a capsule to the enclosed organ.*
Trabekulotomie	**trabeculotomy** *A surgery for open angle glaucoma.*
Tracheitis	**tracheitis** *Inflammation of the trachea.*
Tracheobronchitis	**tracheobronchitis** *Inflammation of the trachea and bronchi.*
Tracheostomie	**tracheostomy** *Creation of a surgical opening in the trachea so a tube could be placed in the trachea.*
Tracheotomie	**tracheotomy** *Surgical incision of the trachea.*
Trachom	**trachoma** *An infection of the cornea and conjunctiva caused by Chlamydia.*
Tragbahre; Strecker	**stretcher** *A device used to carry a patient in the supine position.*
Tragus	**tragus** *The fleshy prominence anterior to the opening of the ear.*
Tranquilizer	**tranquilizer** *A medication used to diminish anxiety.*
transabdominal	**transabdominal** *Through the abdominal wall.*
Transaminase	**transaminase** *An enzyme that facilitates the transfer of an amino group to an amino acid.*
transdermal	**transdermal** *Through the skin.*
Transfusion	**transfusion** *Administration of blood products intravenously.*
transitorische ischämische Attacke	**transient ischemic attack** *Cerebral ischemic changes resulting from transitory hypoperfusion.*
Transplantat; Implantat	**graft** *A piece of tissue surgically transplanted.*
Transplantation	**transplantation** *The grafting of tissues.*

	English
transplantieren	**transplant,to** *To move a body part from one location to another.*
transrektal Ultraschall	**transrectal ultrasound** *Insertion of an ultrasound probe into the rectum to view adjacent structures.*
Transsudation	**transudation** *The movement of body tissue through a membrane that is usually the result of inflammation.*
transvaginal Ultraschall	**transvaginal ultrasound** *Insertion of an ultrasound probe in the vagina to view adjacent structures.*
Trapezius	**trapezius muscle** *The muscle with an origin of occipital bone and seventh cervical vertebra, insertion of clavicle and scapula, and it draws the scapula backward.*
traubenartig	**cirsoid** *Similar to a tortuous vein, artery or lymph vessel.*
Trauer	**mourning** *A period of grieving.*
Trauer	**sadness** *The state of being sad.*
Trauerfall	**bereavement** *The sorrow one feels with the loss of a loved one.*
Traum	**dream** *The thoughts or images occurring during sleep.*
Trauma	**trauma** *A physical injury or emotional shock.*
Träne	**tear** *As in, to shed a tear.*
Tränen	**lacrimation** *The secretion of tears.*
Tränenflüssigkeit	**lacrimal fluid** *Fluid secreted by the lacrimal gland.*
Trematode	**fluke** *Parasitic nematode worm; an example is Schistosoma.*
Trematode	**trematoda** *A parasitic fluke such as Schistosoma.*
Tremor	**tremor** *Involuntary contraction and relaxation of small muscle groups.*
Trepanation	**trephination** *Cutting away a circular disc of bone or the cornea.*
Trepanationsloch	**burr hole** *A treatment of subdural hematoma that involves drilling a hole into the cranium to release the hematoma.*
treten	**kick, to** *To strike an object with one's foot.*
Trichiasis	**trichiasis** *Inversion of the eyelashes.*
Trichinose	**trichinosis** *A disease caused by meat infected by Trichinella spiralis causing fever and gastrointestinal effects.*
Trichomonas vaginitis	**trichomoniasis vaginitis** *Infection related to a species of Trichomonas.*
Trichophytose	**trichophytosis** *A skin or nail fungal infection caused by Trichophyton.*
Trichterbrust	**funnel chest** *Anterior thorax funnel shaped depression, also called pectus excavatum.*
trigeminal	**trigeminal** *Generally refers to the fifth cranial nerve.*
Trigeminus	**trigeminal nerve** *The fifth cranial nerve which supplies the motor function of mastication and has three sensory branches, the ophthalmic, maxillary and mandibular.*
Trigeminusneuralgie	**trigeminal neuralgia** *Pain in the region of one or more branches of the fifth cranial nerve sensory branches.*
Trikuspidalklappe	**tricuspid valve** *The cardiac valve located between the right atrium and right ventricle.*
trinken	**drink, to** *To imbibe.*
trinkfauler Säugling	**lazy feeder** *An infant slow to take to the breast or to the bottle.*
Trinkwasser	**drinking water** *Water clean enough to ingest orally.*
Triplegie	**triplegia** *Paralysis of three extremities.*
triploid	**triploid** *Referring to a cell with three homologous sets of chromosomes.*

300

Trismus; Kieferklemme	**trismus** *Commonly called lockjaw, it is a spasm of the muscles supplied by the trigeminal nerve and is an early symptom of tetanus.*
Trisomie	**trisomy** *A general category of congenital anomalies in which there is an extra set of chromosomes in the cell nucleus.*
trisomie 21	**trisomy 21** *A congenital anomaly in which chromosome 21 is effected and results in Down's syndrome.*
Trisomie-21-Syndrom; Down Syndrom	**Down's syndrome** *A congenital chromosomal defect (trisomy 21) that causes diminished intellectual function, short stature and a broad face.*
trivial	**trivial** *Of little importance or value.*
Trizeps	**triceps** *Referring to something having three heads like the triceps muscle.*
Trizepsreflex	**triceps reflex** *A tendon reflex causing extension of the arm when the triceps tendon is gently tapped.*
Trochanter	**trochanter** *Refers to the greater or lesser trochanter; the prominences on the femoral neck.*
Trochlearis	**trochlear nerve** *The fourth cranial nerve that supplies the superior oblique muscle of the eyeball.*
trochleär	**trochlear** *Referring to a trochlea.*
trocken	**dry** *Absence of moisture.*
Trokar	**trocar** *A device enclosed in a catheter that is used to withdraw fluid from a body cavity.*
Trombiculalarve	**chigger** *A parasitic mite of the genus Trombicula.*
Trommelfell	**ear-drum** *Common term for tympanic membrane.*
Trommelfell	**tympanic membrane** *The membrane between the external and middle ear.*
Trommelschlägelfinger	**clubbing** *Increase in the mass of the soft tissue of the terminal phalanges.*
Tropenringwurm	**Malabar itch.** *Pruritis associated with tinea imbricata which is characterized by overlapping rings of papulosquamous patches. It is also known as oriental ringworm.*
Tropfen	**drop** *A single bit of fluid as in a drop seen while giving IV fluids.*
Tropfen je Minute	**drops per minute** *Refers to iv fluid rate.*
tropfenweise	**drop by drop** *Expression meaning little by little.*
Trophoblast	**trophoblast** *A layer of endodermal tissue that helps attach an ovum to the uterine wall.*
trotz	**despite** *Notwithstanding.*
Trunkenheit	**drunk** *Inebriated.*
Trunkenheit; Rausch	**inebriation** *Intoxication with drugs or alcohol.*
trunkulär	**truncal** *Referring to the trunk of a body or a nerve.*
Trypanosomiasis	**trypanosomiasis** *A disease caused by a protozoa of the genus Trypanosoma that can cause sleeping sickness and Chagas' disease.*
Trypsin	**trypsin** *An enzyme whose precursor is secreted by the pancreas that breaks down proteins in the intestine.*
Trypsinogen	**trypsinogen** *The precursor to trypsin that is secreted by the pancreas.*
Tryptophan	**tryptophan** *An amino acid that is a precursor of serotonin. If present in the body in appropriate levels it can prevent pellegra even if niacin levels are low.*
Tryptophanmalabsorptions Syndrom	**blue diaper syndrome** *A disorder of tryptophan absorption. Excess tryptophan is metabolized to indicans in the bowel, excreted in the urine and oxidized in the diaper to indigo, thus the blue diaper.*

	English
Tsetsefleige	**tsetse fly** *An insect that transmits the protozoa trypanosoma and can cause sleeping sickness.*
Tsutsugamushifiebrer	**tsutsugamushi disease** *An acute febrile infectious disease caused by Rickettsia tsutsugamushi. It is characterized by fever, pain lymphadenopathy, small black lesions on the genitals, neck or axilla.*
Tuberkel	**tubercle** *1. A granulomatous nodule produced by Mycobacterium tuberculosis. 2. A small prominence on a bone.*
Tuberkulin	**tuberculin** *A solution containing M. tuberculosis or M. bovis that is used to test for tuberculosis by injecting the solution intradermally and looking for a reaction.*
Tuberkulom	**tuberculoma** *1. A tuberculous growth in the brain. 2. A mass that is produced from enlargement of a caseous tubercle.*
Tuberkulose	**tuberculosis** *Any infectious disease caused by Mycobacterium.*
tuberkuös	**tuberculous** *Referring to tuberculosis.*
Tuberosität	**tuberosity** *A protuberance. For instance the iliac tuberosity is a prominence on the surface of the ilium.*
Tuberös Hirnsklerose; Bourneville-Pringle-Syndrom	**tuberous sclerosis** *An inherited neurocutaneous disorder exhibited by benign hamartomas of the brain, lung, kidney, skin and other organs.*
tublar	**tubal** *Referring to a tube, as in fallopian tube.*
tuboovarial	**tubo-ovarian** *Referring to the fallopian tube or ovary.*
tubulär	**tubular** *Referring to a hollow, round-shaped organ.*
Tularämie; Hasenfieber	**tularemia** *An infectious disease caused by Francisella tularensis. The symptoms range from mild constitutional complaints to septic shock.*
Tumor	**tumor** *A benign or malignant overgrowth of tissue.*
Tunica	**tunica** *Generally a covering of a body part or organ. The tunica mucosa nasi is the mucous membrane lining the nasal cavity.*
Tunnelblick; Röhrensehen	**tunnel vision** *Constiction in the visual field as though looking through a tube or hollow cylinder. Also called tubular vision.*
Tupfur; Abstrich	**swab** *An absorbant material used for cleaning wounds or applying ointment.*
Turbinektomie; Konchektomie	**turbinectomy** *Surgical excision of a turbinate bone.*
turgor	**turgor** *Referring to the elasticity of skin. If one pinches skin and it remains in place the patient is dehydrated.*
Tüpfelung	**stippling** *Having numerous small specks or spots.*
tympanisch	**tympanic** *Referring to the tympanic membrane or having a resonant quality to percussion.*
Tympanoplastik	**tympanoplasty** *Restoration of the tympanic membrane's continuity.*
Typhus abdominalis; Salmonellenenteritis	**typhoid fever** *A condition caused by ingestion of food or water containing salmonella typhi that is exhibited by fever and abdominal signs and symptoms.*
Tyrosin	**tyrosine** *An amino acid important in the synthesis of hormones.*
Uhrzeigersinn	**clockwise** *Movement in the same direction as a normal clock.*
Ulcus duodeni	**duodenal ulcer** *A defect in the lining of the first portion of the small bowel, typically caused by H. pylori.*
Ultraschall	**ultrasound** *A sound or vibration of ultrasonic frequency.*
Ultrasonographie	**ultrasonography** *Visualization of body structures with the echoes of ultrasound pulses.*
Ultraviolettstrahlen	**ultraviolet rays** *Electromagnetic radiation with wavelength longer than x rays.*
ulzerativ	**ulcerative** *Referring to ulceration.*

Umfang	**circumference** *The distance around an object or part.*
Umfang; Größe	**size** *The dimensions of something.*
umfassend	**widespread** *Encompassing or spanning.*
umschriebene Sklerodermie	**morphea** *A condition exhibited by an elevated or depressed patch of pink skin with a purple border.*
unangesehen	**regardless of** *Without consideration of.*
unartikuliert	**inarticulate** *Indistinct speech.*
unbedenklich	**harmless** *Safe or benign.*
unbedingt	**absolute**
unbekannt	**unknown** *Uncertain or undisclosed.*
undulierendes Fieber	**undulant fever** *Wave-like variations in the fever, going from very high to normal and back again, as seen in Brucellosis.*
undurchdringlich	**impervious** *Not affected by.*
unerwartet	**unexpected** *Unforeseen.*
Unfall	**accident**
Unfähigkeit	**disability** *Decreased or impaired mental or physical ability.*
ungebildet	**illiterate** *Unable to read or write.*
ungefähr	**approximate** *Nearly but not totally accurate.*
ungefähr	**approximately** *Nearly but not completely.*
unhöflich	**rude** *Ill-mannered.*
Unigravida	**unigravida** *Term used to describe a woman's first pregnacy.*
Uniparose	**uniparous** *Refers to a single birth.*
Unordnung; Störung	**disorder** *Impairment.*
unparteiisch	**fair** *Equitable.*
Unpässlichkeit	**malaise** *A vague feeling of discomfort or unease.*
unruhige Beine (Wittmaak-Ekbon Syndrom)	**restless legs** *Associated with a syndrome exhibited by continuous movement of the legs from uncertain etiology.*
unschrieben; zirkumskript	**circumscribed** *To have well defined borders.*
unstetig	**unsteady** *Unstable or wobbly.*
unter	**below** *Under.*
unter Null	**freezing (as in ambient temperature)** *Below 0 Celsius.*
unter; unterhalb	**under; infra** *Sometimes used when indicating a patient is "under treatment" for a condition (active treatment).*
Unterarm	**forearm** *Segment of the arm from the elbow to wrist.*
Unterarmkrücke	**forearm crutch** *A long stick with a place for a hand-grip to aid in ambulation when there is lower extremity weakness.*
unterer; inferior	**inferior** *The lower aspect.*
Unterkiefer	**mandible** *The lower jaw.*
Unterkiefergelenk	**temporomandibular joint** *The hinged joint of the temporal bone and mandible.*
Unterkieferreflex	**jaw reflex** *Contraction of the temporal muscles when a relaxed mandible is given a downward tap. Also, masseter reflex or jaw jerk.*
Unterleib	**abdomen, lower**
Unterlippe	**lip, lower** *Labium inferius oris.*
Untersuchung	**examination** *Assessment or evaluation.*
unvermeidlich	**inevitable** *Not preventable.*
Unvermögen ruhig zu sitzen	**acathisia** *The inability to sit quietly or to have motor restlessness.*

Unwhohlsein	**discomfort** *A feeling of physical or mental unease.*
Unzinariasis	**uncinariasis** *Hookworm infestation of genus Uncinaria.*
Urachus	**urachus** *A connection between the bladder and the allantois in the fetus.*
Urat	**urate** *The salt of uric acid.*
Urämie	**uremia** *An excess of urea and creatinine in the blood.*
Ureter; Harnleiter	**ureter** *The conduit between each kidney and the urinary bladder.*
Ureterektomie	**ureterectomy** *Surgical resection of one or both ureters.*
Ureterolith	**ureterolith** *Presence of a stone in the ureter.*
Ureterolithotomie	**ureterolithotomy** *Removal of a ureteral stone.*
ureterovaginal	**ureterovaginal** *Referring to the ureter and vagina.*
ureterovesikal	**ureterovesical** *Referring to the ureter and urinary bladder.*
Ureterozele	**ureterocele** *Protrusion of the distal portion of the ureter into the bladder.*
Urethra; Harnhöhre	**urethra** *The canal connecting the urinary bladder with the outside of the body.*
urethral	**urethral** *Referring to the urethra.*
Urethritis	**urethritis** *Inflammation of the urethra.*
Urethrographie	**urethrography** *Imaging of the urethra after instillation of contrast media.*
Urethroplastik	**urethroplasty** *Surgical repair of the urethra.*
Urethroskop	**urethroscope** *A scope used to visualize the inside of the urethra.*
Urethrotomie	**urethrotomy** *A surgical opening of the urethra.*
Urethrozele	**urethrocele** *A prolapse of the urethra through the meatus.*
Urin; Harn	**urine** *The fluid concentrated by the kidneys and expelled via the urethra.*
urinär	**urinary** *Referring to the urine.*
Urobilin	**urobilin** *A brownish pigment that is an oxidized form of urobilinogen.*
Urobilingen	**urobilinogen** *A colorless substance produced in the intestines when bilirubin is reduced.*
Urochrom	**urochrome** *A yellow pigment in the urine that gives urine its color.*
Urodynamik	**urodynamics** *A study done to determine whether a person has the contractile capacity in the bladder to void spontaneously.*
urogenital	**genitourinary** *Referring to the urinary system through the organs or urine excretion.*
urogential	**urogenital** *Referring to the urinary and genital systems.*
Urographie	**urography** *Roentgenography of the urinary tract after administration of contrast media.*
Urologie	**urology** *Surgical specialty involving medical and surgical treatment of the urogenital system.*
Urometer	**urinometer** *A device for measuring urine specific gravity.*
ursächlich	**causative** *Something that induces an effect.*
Urtikaria	**urticaria** *A diffuse pruritic macular rash, caused by an allergy.*
uterin	**uterine** *Referring to the uterus.*
uterinagenesie	**ametria** *Obsolete term for congenital uterine agenesis.*
Uterinleiomyom	**uterine fibroids** *Benign tumors made up of muscular and fibrous tissue in the uterus. This is an older term for what is now known as leiomyoma.*

uterovesikal	**uterovesical** *Referring to the uterus and urinary bladder.*
Uterus; Gebärmutter	**uterus** *The hollow organ in the female pelvis where a fertilized ovum embeds and grows.*
Uterusblutung	**uterine bleeding** *Bleeding that eminates from the uterus.*
Utriculus	**utricle** *A small sac. It can refer to a division of the membranous labyrinth.*
Uveitis	**uveitis** *Inflammation of the uvea.*
Uvulektomie	**uvulectomy** *Excision of the uvula.*
Uvulitis	**uvulitis** *Inflammation of the uvula.*
Überdosis	**overdose** *An above normal dose of a medication.*
Überdruckkammer	**hyperbaric chamber** *A device used to treat decompression illness.*
Übergewicht	**overweight** *Defined as BMI over 25kilograms per meters squared.*
überholt	**outdated** *Something that has passed the expiration date.*
überprüfen	**check for, to**
Überreife	**postmaturity** *Generally referring to a pregnancy that goes beyond the due date.*
üblich	**usual** *Typical or normal.*
vagal	**vagal** *Referring to the vagus nerve.*
Vagina; Scheide	**vagina** *The canal in a female that extends from the vulva to the cervix.*
vaginal	**vaginal** *Referring to the vagina.*
Vaginsmus	**vaginismus** *Involuntary contraction of the vagina muscles that causes a painful spasm.*
Vagitus vaginalis	**vagitus** *An infant cry that can be further defined as vagitus vaginalis in which the infant cries while its head is in the vaginal canal.*
Vagotomie	**vagotomy** *Incision of the vagus nerve.*
Vakuole	**vacuole** *A cavity that develops in a cell.*
Vakzination; Impfung	**vaccination** *The act of receiving a vaccine.*
Vakzine	**vaccine** *A solution of attenuated microorganisms given to prevent or treat a disease.*
valgus	**valgus** *Refers to a joint being abnormally angulated away from the midline of the body.*
Valin	**valine** *An essential amino acid that assists with nitrogen equilibrium.*
Valsalva Versuch	**Valsalva's maneuver** *A technique in which one attempts to exhale with the mouth and nose closed; this equalizes pressure in the ears.*
Valvulotomie	**valvulotomy** *Surgical incision of a valve.*
Varikozele	**varicocele** *A cluster of varicose veins in the scrotum.*
varikös	**varicose** *Referring to an abnormally distended, irregular vein.*
Varize	**varix** *A twisted, distended vein, artery or lymph vessel.*
Varizellen; Windpocken	**varicella** *A virus that causes chickenpox and shingles. Also called herpes zoster.*
Varusstellung	**varus position** *Refers to a joint being abnormally angulated toward the midline of the body.*
Vasektomie	**vasectomy** *The surgical separation of each vas deferens with the intent of producing a sterile person.*
vaskulär	**vascular** *Referring to a blood vessel.*
Vaskulitis	**vasculitis** *Inflammation of a blood vessel.*
Vasodilatation	**vasodilatation** *The process of making the blood vessels larger which decreases blood pressure.*

	English
Vasokonstriktion	**vasoconstriction** *The process of making the blood vessels smaller which increases blood pressure.*
Vasomotor	**vasomotor** *Referring to the constriction or dilation of vessels.*
Vasopressin; antidiuretisches Hormon (ADH)	**vasopressin** *A hormone secreted by the pituitary that facilitates the retention of sodium and water and also increases blood pressure.*
Vasospasmus; Angiospasmus	**vasospasm** *The abrupt constriction of a blood vessel.*
vasovagal	**vasovagal** *Referring to overstimulation of the vagus nerve, exhibited by hypotension, pallor, nausea and diaphoresis.*
Vegetation	**vegetation** *Abnormal growth, such as cardiac valve vegetations as found in endocarditis.*
Veitstanz; Chorea minor	**Saint Vitus' dance** *Historic name for chorea minor characterized by hypotonia and emotional lability months after a streptococcal infection.*
Vektor; Träger	**vector** *An organism that transmits disease.*
vena basilica	**basilic vein** *A vein in the hand that joins the brachial veins to form the axillary vein.*
Vena cava	**vena cava** *The large vein that carries deoxygenated blood to the right atrium.*
Vena saphena	**saphena** *Referring to either of the two superficial saphenous veins.*
Vene; Vena	**vein** *A vessel carrying blood back toward the heart.*
Venographie	**venography** *Roentgenography of a vein after administration of contrast media.*
Venole	**venula** *The vessels that connect the capillary plexuses to veins.*
venös	**venous** *Referring to the veins.*
Ventilation; Lüftung	**ventilation** *The movement of air into the lungs; generally meant to suggest by an artificial process.*
ventral	**ventral** *Referring to the underside but in humans, a ventral hernia, for example, refers to an abdominal hernia.*
Ventrikel	**ventricle** *1. One of two chambers of the heart. 2. The four interconnected cavities in the center of the brain.*
Ventrikelseptumdefekt	**ventricular septal defect** *An abnormal communication between the right and left ventricles via a hole in the septum.*
Ventrikulographie	**ventriculography** *Roentgenography of the ventricles after administration of contrast media.*
Ventrikulostomie	**ventriculostomy** *A tube placed into the third ventricle to relieve increased intracranial pressure.*
Verband	**bandage** *A strip of gauze used to immobilize or support.*
Verband	**dressing** *The gauze applied to a wound.*
verbessern	**ameliorate** *To make better or improve.*
Verbrühung	**scald** *A burn injury from extremely hot water.*
Verdauung	**digestion** *The process of enzymatic breakdown of food in the alimentary canal.*
Verdauungsstörungen	**indigestion** *Inadequate digestion for various reasons.*
verdicken	**inspissate, to** *To thicken or congeal.*
Verdünnung	**dilution** *The process of making a weaker solution.*
vererbung Sphärozytose	**hereditary spherocytosis** *A familial hemolytic disease exhibited by abnormally thick erythrocytes.*
vererbung; Erblichkeit	**hereditary** *That which is transmitted genetically*

306

Verfahren	**algorhithm** *Any procedure designed to solve a problem in a step-by-step or mechanical fashion.*
Verfall	**decline** *A decrease in status or health.*
Vergewaltigung	**rape** *Forced sexual relations.*
Vergrößerung; Erweiterung	**enlargement** *Becoming bigger.*
Verhaltensstörung	**behavior disorder** *An abnormal mental state.*
verhängnisvoll	**fatal** *Lethal.*
verhätscheln	**pamper, to** *Indulge with comfort and kindness.*
Verkürzung	**shortening** *Notable for having a shorter length.*
Verlagerung	**displacement** *Movement from normal position.*
Verlangen	**craving** *An unusually strong urge for something.*
Verlängerung	**lengthening** *Becoming longer.*
Verletzter	**casualty** *A person who is killed or seriously injured.*
vermeidbar	**avoidable** *That which can be stopped or inhibited.*
Vernebler	**atomizer** *A device for propelling a fine mist.*
Vernebler	**nebulizer** *A device used for transforming a liquid into a fine mist for inhalation as in nebulized albuterol for an acute exacerbation of asthma.*
vernebler Verfahren	**nebulizer treatment** *Administration of medication such as albuterol via a fine mist using a nebulizer.*
Verruca; Warze	**wart** *A flesh colored growth that is also called verruca.*
Versammlung der transversal Kolon und abstammen Kolon	**splenic flexure of the colon** *The portion of the colon that turns from the transverse to the descending colon.*
verschieben	**postpone, to** *To delay.*
verschlechtern	**worsen, to** *To deteriorate.*
Verschlechterung	**deterioration** *Worsening in one's medical condition.*
Verschwartung; Callositas	**callosity** *Callus; thickened hardened skin.*
Verschwinden	**disappearance** *An instance of something/someone gone missing.*
verseifen	**saponify,to** *The creation of soap from oil using an alkali.*
Versogung	**management** *The process of dealing with things or people.*
verspäteter Blasensprung	**prolonged rupture of the membranes** *Rupture of the membranes more than 24 hours before delivery.*
Verstauchung	**sprain** *A joint injury without fracture.*
Verständnis	**comprehension** *Understanding.*
verstellen	**adjust, to** *To modify a plan.*
Vertebrobasilärinsuffizienz	**vertebrobasilar insufficiency** *Diminished flow to the vertebral and basilar arteries causing posterior fossa symptoms.*
Verteilung	**distribution** *The manner in which something is shared or spread out.*
Vertigo; Schwindel	**vertigo** *A sensation of imbalance with many possible causes.*
Vertrauen	**confidence** *Self-assurance.*
verträglich	**compatible** *To coexist without problems.*
verunreinigen	**contaminate, to** *To make impure by exposing to an polluted agent.*
Verwechslung	**confusion** *Disorientation.*
verweigern	**deny, to** *To reject or repudiate.*
Verweilkatheter	**indwelling catheter** *Continuous use tube usually referring to a tube in the urinary bladder.*
Verwesung; Fäulnis	**putrefaction** *The rotting or decaying of organic matter.*

	English
vesikal	**vesical** *Referring to the urinary bladder.*
vesikovaginal	**vesicovaginal** *Referring to the urinary bladder and vagina.*
Vesikulitis	**vesiculitis** *Inflammation of the urinary bladder.*
vestibulär	**vestibular** *Referring to a vestibule.*
vestibulär Neuronitis	**kubisagari** *Vestibular neuronitis.*
Vibration	**vibration** *An instance of oscillation of parts.*
viel	**lots of** *An abundance of.*
Vierhügel	**quadrigeminal bodies** *The cranial and caudal colliculi.*
Vigilitätsreaktion	**arousal reaction** *The change in brain wave patterns upone awakening.*
villös	**villous** *Covered with many villi.*
Virilisierung	**virilization** *The result of androgen; a process of development of masculine characteristics.*
Virologie	**virology** *The study of viruses.*
Virulenz	**virulence** *The potential severity of a disease or poison.*
Vision; Sehvermögen	**vision** *State of being able to see.*
Viskosimeter	**viscometer** *A device used to measure viscosity.*
viskös	**viscous** *Having a thick, sticky consistency.*
viszeral	**visceral** *Referring to the organs in the abdominal or thoracic cavity.*
Vitalkapazität	**vital capacity (VC)** *The maximal amount of air exhaled after a maximal inhalation.*
Vitellin	**vitelline** *Referring to the yolk of an egg or ovum.*
Vivisektion	**vivisection** *Animal surgery done for purposes of research.*
Vogelgrippe	**avian flu** *A viral disease found in birds and fowl that can be transmitted to humans; it is exhibited by respiratory and gastrointestinal symptoms but can lead to encephalitis.*
vokal	**vocal** *Referring to that which eminates from the vocal cords.*
Volumendehnbarkeit	**compliance** *The act of going along with a plan.*
Volvulus; Darmverschlingung	**volvulus** *Twisting of the bowel leading to obstruction and sometimes perforation.*
vor dem Tod	**antemortem** *Refers to: before death.*
vorbeugen	**prevent, to** *To stave off or hinder.*
Vorder-	**anterior** *Toward the front.*
Vorderhaupt; Stirn	**forehead** *Section of the face from the hairline to the eyebrows.*
Vorderhirn	**forebrain** *The part of the brain that includes the thalamus, hypothalamus and cerebral hemispheres.*
Vorderwurzel	**anterior root** *A motor nerve root that is in the anterior part of the spinal cord between the anterior and lateral funiculi.*
voreingenommen	**biased** *Prejudiced.*
vorenthalten	**withhold, to** *To refuse to give something.*
Vorgeschichte	**past history** *Prior medical problems experienced by a patient.*
Vorhaut	**foreskin** *Also called prepuce, the skin that naturally covers the glans but can be rolled back.*
Vorherigzustand	**prior status** *Referring to a person's previous state of health.*
Vorhof; Atrium	**atrium** *Referring to a chamber used as an entrance, as in the entrance to the heart.*
Vorhofflattern	**atrial flutter** *Sawtooth waves on an electrocardiogram with atrial rate of 250-330 per minute.*

Vorhofseptumdefekt (VSD)	**atrial septal defect** *An abnormal communication between the atria of the heart.*
Vorschrift	**prescription** *The action of prescribing a medication or treatment.*
Vorsteherdrüse; Prostate	**prostate** *A gland found in men that surrounds the neck of the urethra and bladder.*
vorwärts	**forwards** *Towards the front.*
Vorwärtsverlagerung	**proptosis oculi** *Synonym of exophthalmos; bulging of the eye.*
Vulvektomie	**vulvectomy** *Surgical resection of the vulva.*
Vulvitis	**vulvitis** *Inflammation of the vulva.*
Vulvovaginitis	**vulvovaginitis** *Inflammation of the vulva and vagina.*
Waage	**scale** *A device to check a person's weight.*
Wachstum	**growth** *The increase in physical size.*
wachstumshormon Releasing-Faktor	**growth hormone-releasing factor** *Released by the hypothalamus, it induces the release of somatotropin.*
wackelig	**groggy** *Drowsy.*
Wade	**calf** *Muscles of the posterior portion of the lower leg.*
waden	**sural** *Referring to the calf of the leg.*
Wahn; Täuschung	**delusion** *A belief that is contradictory to rational thought.*
wahnhaft	**delusional** *Referring to a delusion.*
Wahrscheinlichkeit	**likelihood** *The probability or feasibility.*
Wandthrombus	**mural thrombus** *A thrombus attached to a diseased portion of endocardium.*
Wange; Backe	**cheek** *Lateral facial tissue.*
Wanze	**bug** *Insect.*
Warze; Verruca	**verruca** *A hyperplastic epidermal lesion, sometimes referred to as plantar wart.*
Warzenfortsatz	**mastoid** *Referring to the mastoid process.*
Warzenfortsatz	**mastoid process** *The posterior part of the temporal bone bordered by the parietal bone superiorly and the occipital bone posteriorly.*
Waschbecken	**basin** *A small bowl used for washing.*
Wasser; Aqua	**water** *A colorless, odorless liquid.*
wasserfrei	**anhydrous** *Lacking water.*
Wasserlassen	**voiding** *The act of urinating.*
Watschelgang	**waddling gait** *Walking in short steps in a swaying fashion.*
Watte	**cotton wool** *Raw cotton.*
Wärme; Hitze	**heat** *The quality of being hot.*
Wäscherkrätz	**dhobie itch** *So called because the contact dermatitis is caused by the soap used by laundry workers in India who are called "dhobie".*
wässerig	**aqueous** *Use of water as a solvent or medium.*
wegdrückbares Ödem	**nonpitting edema** *Subcutaneous swelling that cannot be indented with compression.*
Wehenbeginn	**labor onset** *The time when a pregnant woman begins uterine contractions in the process of childbirth.*
Wehenschreiber	**fetal monitor** *Device used to monitor fetal heart rate and rhythm.*
weiblich	**female** *Feminine.*
weich	**soft** *Easy to mold or compress.*
weinen	**weep, to** *To shed tears.*
weise	**wise** *Possessing much knowledge.*

Weisheitszahn	**wisdom tooth** *Third molar.*
weiß	**white** *Of the color of snow.*
weitergehend	**on going** *Continuing,*
Weitsichtigkeit; Hyperopie	**longsighted** *Synonym of hyperopia.*
Weltgesundheitsorganisation	**World Health Organization (WHO)**
weniger	**less** *A smaller amount.*
wesentlich	**essential** *Crucial or necessary.*
Wespen	**wasp** *Any one of a winged hymenopterous insects.*
Whal	**choice** *Selection or decision.*
Wiege	**cradle** *A bed for an infant.*
Windel	**diaper** *Undergarment worn to absorb urine in incontinent persons.*
Windelerythem	**diaper rash** *Macular rash in the inguinal/perineal region related to exposure to urine.*
Windpocken; Varizellen	**chicken pox, varicella** *A viral disease characterized by extremely pruritis blisters over the entire body.*
winzig	**minute** *Something very small.*
Wirbel	**vertebra** *A term for each bone surrounding the spine.*
Wirbelsäule; Rückgrat	**spine** *The spinal column or a thorny protrusion.*
Wirbelsäule; Rückgrat	**vertebral column** *The cervical, thoracic and lumbar vertebrae.*
Wirbeltuberkulose	**Pott's disease** *Also referred to as tuberculous spnodylitis it is caused by a spinal deformity caused by a tuberculosis infection of the spine.*
wirkungslos	**ineffective** *Unsuccessful or inefficient.*
wirkungsvoll	**efficacious** *Effective.*
Wochenbettpsychose	**postpartum psychosis** *A episode of abnormal thought or hallucinations following delivery.*
Wolhynisches Fieber; Quintana; Fünftagefieber	**quintan fever** *Also known as trench fever as it was first noted during trench warfare in WW I. It is a rickettsial fever caused by Bartonella quintana and transmitted by a louse; signs and symptoms are myalgia, headache, malaise, fever and chills.*
Wortfindungsstörung	**anomia** *Inability to name or recognize familiar objects.*
wöchentlich	**weekly** *That which occurs every seven days.*
Wölbung	**bulge** *A proturberance on a flat surface.*
Wölbung	**concavity** *The state of being concave.*
Wundausschneidung	**debridement** *Trimming the dead tissue adjacent to a wound.*
Wunde	**wound** *A tissue injury of varying severity.*
Wundstarrkrampf	**tetanus** *A condition caused by Clostridium tetani which produces spasm and rigidity of voluntary muscles.*
Wundversogung	**wound care** *The treatment applied to a tissue injury.*
Wurm	**worm** *Any of long, slender, legless, soft-bodied invertebrates.*
Wurmileus	**verminous ileus** *Obstruction due to masses of intestinal parasites.*
Wurzel	**root** *An embedded part of an organ or structure.*
Xanthin	**xanthine** *A purine derivative that is found in the blood and urine after the metabolism of nucleic acids to uric acid.*
Xanthochromie	**xanthochromia** *A yellow tone to the skin or spinal fluid.*
Xanthom	**xanthoma** *A lipid deposition on the skin exhibited by an irregular yellow patch.*
Xerodermie	**xerodermia** *A mild form of ichthyosis.*

310

Xerophthalmie	**xerophthalmia** *A manifestation of Vitamin A deficiency exhibited by dryness of the cornea and conjunctiva.*
Xeroradiolgrapie	**xeroradiography** *A form of radiography using photoelectric cells.*
Xerose	**xerosis** *Pathological dryness of the skin or mucous membranes.*
Xerostomie	**xerostomia** *A dry mouth from salivary gland hypofunction.*
Zahn	**tooth** *One of a set of hard, bony enamel coated structure in the jaw.*
Zahnarst	**dentist** *A professional capable of treating diseases of the teeth and gums.*
Zahnen	**dentition** *The natural teeth.*
Zahnfleisch	**gum** *Gingiva.*
Zahnfleischentzündung; Mundfäule	**trench mouth** *Inflammation and ulceration of the gingivae.*
Zahnkaries	**dental caries** *Decay of teeth.*
zahnlos	**toothless** *Edentulous.*
Zahnradphänomen	**cog wheel** *As in cogwheel rigidity which is a jerky passive movement after there was increased tone.*
Zahnschmerzen; Zahnweh	**toothache** *Dental pain.*
Zahnstein	**dental calculus** *Calcium phosphate and carbonate adhered to the teeth.*
Zange	**tongs** *A medical device used for holding or grasping.*
Zange; Pinzette	**forceps** *A surgical instrument, commonly called tweezers.*
zählen	**count, to** *To determine a number.*
Zäkum	**cecum** *The portion of the bowel between the ileum and and the ascending colon.*
Zäpfchen	**uvula** *A fleshy pendent at the back of the soft palate.*
Zeckenbiß	**tick bite**
Zeckenfieber	**tick-borne fever** *A relapsing fever caused by a spirochete of the genus Borrelia.*
Zehe	**toe** *Any of the digits of of the feet.*
Zehennagel	**toenail** *The nail at the tip/dorsal aspect of each toe.*
Zelle	**cell** *The smallest functional unit of an organism.*
Zellgift	**cytotoxin** *That which is harmful to cells.*
Zellkörper	**cell body** *The portion of the cell containing the nucleus.*
Zellmembran	**cell membrane** *The semipermeable structure surrounding the cytoplasm of a cell.*
Zellplasma	**plasma cell** *A cell that produces only one type of antibody.*
Zellstoff	**cellulose** *A polysaccharide that occurs naturally in fibrous products.*
Zellulitis	**cellulitis** *Infection characterized by diffuse, subcutaneous inflammation.*
Zellwand	**cell wall** *The peripheral border of the cell.*
Zentimeter	**centimeter** *One hundredth of a meter.*
Zentralnervensystem	**central nervous system (CNS)** *The brain and spinal cord.*
Zentrifuge	**centrifuge** *Machine used to separate substances of different weights.*
zentripetal	**centripetal** *The movement toward the center.*
Zentrum	**center** *A point equidistant from all sides.*
zerbrechlich Nagelbettentzündung	**onychia sicca** *Brittle fingernails or toenails.*
zerebral	**cerebral** *Referring to the cerebrum.*

311

	English
zerebrale Durchblutungsstörung	**stroke** *Common term for cerebrovascular accident.*
zerebrale Lähmung	**cerebral palsy** *A condition exhibited by motor incoordination and speech changes that is the result of brain injury occurring ante-, intra- or post- partum.*
Zerkarie	**cercaria** *Larval trematode worm that live in a molluscan.*
Zerreißung; Rißwunde; Einriss	**laceration** *An injury that produced a cut in the skin or tissue such as a tear during childbirth.*
Zerumen	**cerumen** *Waxy substance found normally in the external ear canals.*
Zeruminalpfropf	**cerumen impaction** *External ear canal full of wax resulting in hearing loss until the impaction is removed.*
zervikal	**cervical** *Referring to the neck or the cervix.*
Zervixinsuffizienz	**Cervical insufficiency (formerly incompetent cervix)** *Painless changes in the cervix that result in recurrent second semester pregnancy loss.*
Zervixresektion	**cervicectomy** *Excision of the cervix uteri.*
Zervizitis	**cervicitis** *Inflammation of the cervix.*
Ziehl-Neelsen Färbung	**Ziehl-Neelsen carbolfuchsin stain** *A stain used to detect acid-fast bacilli that appear red on the methylene blue background.*
ziehst	**pull, to** *To exert force on something.*
Zielzelle	**target cell** *An abnormal cell that is present in liver disease and certain hemoglobinopathies.*
Ziliarkörper	**ciliary body** *The connection between the iris and the choroid.*
Zimmer	**room** *A division in a building surrounded by walls.*
Zink; Zincum	**zinc** *A chemical with atomic number 30.*
Zirbeldrüse	**pineal gland** *A small body posterior to the third ventricle of the brain.*
zirkadian	**circadian** *Referring to a 24 hour period.*
zirkadianer Rhythmus	**circadian rhythm** *Naturally recurring fluctuations in a 24 hour period.*
Zirkumzision; Beschneidung	**circumcision** *Surgical excision of the foreskin.*
Zirrhose	**cirrhosis** *A liver disease characterized by destruction of liver cells and increased connective tissue.*
Zisternenpunktion	**cisternal puncture** *A trans-occipitoatlantoid ligament puncture of the cisterna magna so CSF can be obtained.*
Zitrat-zyklus; Krebs-Zyklus	**Krebs cycle** *The process of aerobic respiration by which living cells generate energy.*
Zogote	**zygote** *A fertilized ovum.*
Zonula	**zonula** *A small zone or junction.*
Zonula occludens	**tight junction** *An intercellular junction with an impermeable membrane.*
Zoologie	**zoology** *The study of animals.*
Zoonose	**zoonosis** *An animal-born disease that can be transmitted to humans, such as rabies.*
Zoster	**shingles** *A reactivation of herpes zoster.*
Zotte	**villus** *A small vascular prominence from a membrane surface.*
zöliakal	**celiac** *Referring to the abdominal cavity.*
Zucker	**sugar** *A sweet crystalline substance made from a plant such as sugar cane.*
Zuckung	**twitch** *A sudden jerking movement.*
zuflüstern	**whisper, to** *To speak in a volume that is barely discernible.*

Zuführend, Afferent	**afferent** *Moving toward the center.*
zuführende Schlinge Syndrom	**afferent loop syndrome** *The obstruction of the duodenum or jejunum after gastrojejunostomy, resulting in duodenal distention.*
Zug; Ziehen	**traction** *Sustained pull on a muscle or bone to correct alignment.*
Zugang	**access** *Means of entry.*
zugrundeliegend	**underlying** *Causative, unexposed, or fundamental.*
Zullasungdatum	**date of admission** *Beginning date of hospitalization.*
Zunge	**tongue** *The fleshy muscular organ of the mouth.*
Zungen	**glossal** *Referring to the tongue.*
Zungenbändchen	**frenulum** *The tissue that connects the inferior portion of the tongue to the base of the mouth.*
Zungenbein	**hyoid bone** *A horseshoe shaped bone located between the chin and thyroid cartilage.*
Zungendrücker	**tongue depressor; tongue blade** *As the name implies, the stick pushes the tongue down so the posterior aspect of the mouth can be viewed more readily.*
zur Zeit	**currently** *Presently.*
zurückgelehnt	**recumbent** *Lying down.*
zusammengesetzt	**compound** *A substance formed by covalent union of two or more atoms.*
zusammenzählen	**approximate, to** *To bring together, as in wound margins.*
zusammenziehend	**astringent** *An agent causing contraction of the skin.*
zusätzlich	**accessory** *Complimentary or concomitant.*
Zustand	**state** *Status.*
Zustimmung	**approval** *Accepting something as satisfactory.*
zuverlässig	**reliable** *Trustworthy.*
Zwangjacke	**strait-jacket** *A device used to temporarily restrain the arms of patients who are psychotic and violent.*
Zwangsvorstelung	**obsession** *A pathologic preoccupation.*
zweieiig	**binovular** *Derived from two different ova.*
zweieiige Zwillinge	**dizygotic twins** *Twins from two separate zygotes (non-identicle twins).*
zweiköpfiger Wadenmuskel	**gastrocnemius** *A large muscle in the lower leg, responsible for ankle plantar flexion, that is attached to the distal femur and achilles tendon.*
zweimalig	**two times** *One action being done on two occasions.*
zweitleilig	**bifid** *Presence of two branches.*
zweizackig	**bifurcate** *When one branch divides into two branches.*
Zwerchfellhernie	**diaphragmatic hernia** *Protrusion of visceral contents through the diaphragm.*
Zwerg	**dwarf** *Abnormally small person.*
Zwillinge	**twins** *Two infants born at the same birthing.*
Zwitter	**hermaphrodite** *A person possessing gonadal characteristics of both sexes.*
zwölf Uhr mittags	**noon** *The 12 o'clock mid-day hour.*
Zwölffingerdarm	**duodenum** *The portion of the small bowel between the stomach and jejunum.*
Zyanose	**cyanosis** *Bluish discoloration of the skin and mucous membranes.*

313

zyklisch Erbrechen	**cyclical vomiting** *Periods of recurrent vomiting with no apparent pathologic cause and the person has a normal state of health between the episodes.*
Zyklitis; Ziliarkörperentzndung	**cyclitis** *Inflammation of the ciliary body.*
Zyklodialyse	**cyclodialysis** *The surgical creation of a communication between the anterior chamber of the eye and the suprachorodial space for the purpose of treating glaucoma.*
Zykloplegie	**cycloplegia** *Paralysis of the ciliary muscle.*
Zyklothymie	**cyclothymia** *Manic-depressive tendencies.*
Zyklotomie	**cyclotomy** *Surgically creating an opening in the ciliary body.*
Zymogen	**zymogen** *An inactive compound that is metabolized to an active state.*
Zystecktomie	**cystectomy** *Surgical removal of a cyst or the bladder.*
Zystinurie	**cystinuria** *The presence of cystine in the urine.*
Zystirzerkose	**cysticercosis** *The state of being infected with a type of tapeworm.*
zystisch	**cystic** *Referring to a cyst.*
zystische Fibrose; Mukoviszidose	**cystic fibrosis** *A congenital disorder exhibited by abnormal thick mucous which leads to problems in the intestines, pancreas and lungs.*
Zystitis; Blasenentzündung	**cystitis** *Inflammation of the urinary bladder.*
Zystographie	**cystography** *Roentgenographic visualization of the urinary bladder after insertion of contrast media.*
Zystolithiasis	**cystolithiasis** *Presence of a calculus in the urinary bladder.*
Zystolzele; Blasenhernie	**cystocele** *Protrusion of the urinary bladder through the vaginal wall.*
Zystoskop	**cystoscope** *A device used to visualized the urinary bladder.*
Zystoskopie	**cystoscopy** *Direct visualization of the urinary bladder with a cystoscope.*
Zytologie	**cytology** *The study of cells, their function and structure.*
Zytoplasma	**cytoplasm** *The protoplasm of the cell except for the nucleus.*
zytotoxisch	**cytotoxic** *Referring to being harmful to cells.*

314

Other books by A.H. Zemback

English-Kinyarwanda-French Dictionary

English-Kinyarwanda Dictionary

English-Kirundi-French Dictionary

English-Kirundi Dictionary

English-Swahili-French Dictionary

English-Swahili Dictionary

English-French Medical Dictionary and Phrasebook

English-Spanish Medical Dictionary and Phrasebook

www.ingramcontent.com/pod-product-compliance
Lightning Source LLC
Chambersburg PA
CBHW070628290526
45790CB00001B/43